Sports Illustrated For Kids

YEAR IN SPORTS 2005

from the Editors of Sports Illustrated For Kids

SCHOLASTIC REFERENCE
AN IMPRINT OF
SCHOLASTIC

Cover photography credits
LeBron James: David Sherman/NBAE/Getty Images
Priest Holmes: Brian Bahr/Getty Images
Mia Hamm: Howard C. Smith/Icon SMI
Ilya Kovalchuk: Jeffrey A. Salter/SPORTS ILLUSTRATED
Pedro Martinez: Lou Capozzola
Diana Taurasi: David Bergman/SPORTS ILLUSTRATED
Chellsie Memmel: Stephen Dunn/Getty Images

Back-cover photography credits
Jason White: John W. McDonough/SPORTS ILLUSTRATED
Ruth Riley: Allen Einstein/WNBAE/Getty Images
Shaun White: Robert Beck

SPORTS ILLUSTRATED FOR KIDS Year in Sports 2005 is a production of SPORTS ILLUSTRATED FOR KIDS and SPORTS ILLUSTRATED FOR KIDS Books: Erin Egan, Senior Editor/Editorial Projects; Beth Bugler, Art Director; Ed Duarte, Designer; Andrew Erbelding, Photo Editor; Nick Friedman, Ellen Labrecque, Senior Editors; Justin Tejada, Andrea Whittaker, Associate Editors; Sachin Shenolikar, Chief of Reporters; André Carter, Ted Keith, Shawn Nicholls, Solange Reyner, Reporters; Timothy E. Pitt, Director of Editorial Operations; Howard Gotfryd (Manager), Steve Chanin (Deputy), Page Makeup

Scholastic Reference staff: Kenneth Wright, Editorial Director; Mary Varilla Jones, Editor; Danielle Denega, Assistant Editor; Karyn Browne, Managing Editor; Melinda Weigel, Production Editor; Nancy Sabato, Art Director; Kirk Howle, Manufacturing Coordinator

0-439-65082-8

10 9 8 7 6 5 4 3 2 1 04 05 06 07 08

Printed in the U.S.A. 23
First printing, December 2004

CONTENTS

4 FOOTBALL

64 BASEBALL

112 BASKETBALL

176 HOCKEY

206 SOCCER

232 ACTION SPORTS

250 GOLF

260 MOTOR SPORTS

268 TENNIS

278 SWIMMING

288 TRACK AND FIELD

298 SUMMER OLYMPICS

310 WINTER OLYMPICS

314 SPORTS DIRECTORY

FOOTBALL

The New England Patriots took a giant step toward becoming a dynasty in 2003. The Pats earned the Vince Lombardi Trophy for the second time in three years by defeating the Carolina Panthers, 32–29, in Super Bowl XXXVIII.

The game was one of the most exciting in Super Bowl history. It began as a defensive struggle. The first points were scored with three minutes and ten seconds left in the second quarter. Both teams put up a flurry of points in the second half until the game was tied, 29–29, with nine seconds to play. Adam Vinatieri of the Patriots nailed the game-winning 41-yard field goal. His 26-year-old teammate, quarterback Tom Brady, was awarded the Super Bowl MVP trophy for the second time in his young career.

The 2003 season saw a revival of strong running backs. An NFL-record six running backs gained at least 1,500 yards on the ground, including the Baltimore Ravens' Jamal Lewis, who became just the fifth player to rush for at least 2,000 yards in a season (2,066). He also set the single-game rushing record (295 yards), against the Cleveland Browns on September 14.

The playoffs will be remembered for last-minute heroics and heart-stopping finishes. Seven games were decided by seven points or less, and two overtime games ended with dramatic plays. The Green Bay Packers defeated the Seattle Seahawks on cornerback Al Harris's 52-yard interception return for a touchdown, and the Carolina Panthers defeated the St. Louis Rams on quarterback Jake Delhomme's 69-yard pass in double overtime.

AFC TEAM

- Baltimore Ravens
- Buffalo Bills
- Cincinnati Bengals
- Cleveland Browns
- Denver Broncos
- Houston Texans
- Indianapolis Colts
- Jacksonville Jaguars
- Kansas City Chiefs
- Miami Dolphins
- New England Patric
- New York Jets
- Oakland Raiders
- Pittsburgh Steelers
- San Diego Chargers
- Tennessee Titans

With four seconds left in Super Bowl XXXVIII, Adam Vinatieri booted a 41-yard field goal to give the New England Patriots a 32–29 victory.

BILL FRAKES/SPORTS ILLUSTRATED

But the biggest news of the season came four days after the Super Bowl. District Court Judge Shira Scheindlin ruled the NFL policy that forbids players to enter the draft until three years after graduating from high school violated U.S. antitrust laws. Ohio State running back Maurice Clarett had challenged the league's policy so that he could enter the 2004 NFL Draft. The NFL appealed the ruling, and on May 24 an appeals court said that federal labor policy allows the NFL to set rules for when players can enter the league, keeping Clarett and wide receiver Mike Williams of USC out of the NFL in 2004.

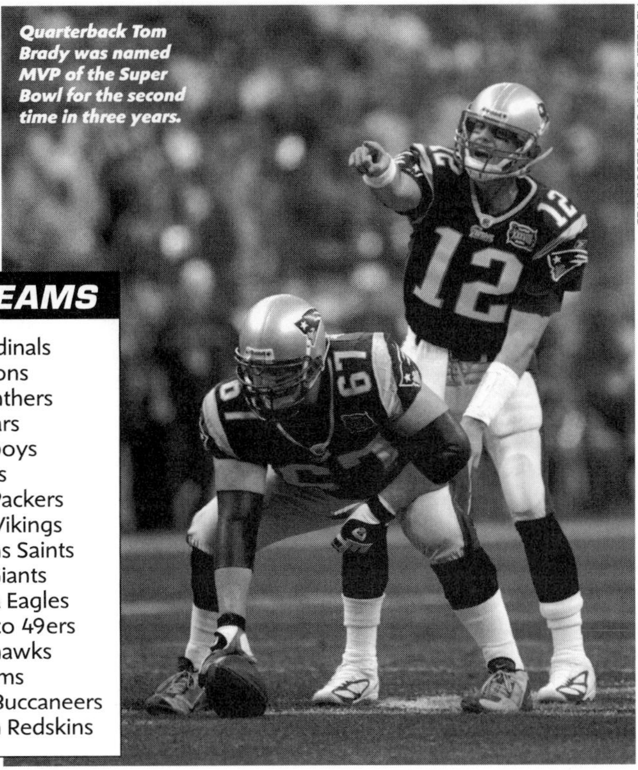

Quarterback Tom Brady was named MVP of the Super Bowl for the second time in three years.

AL TIELEMANS/SPORTS ILLUSTRATED

NFC TEAMS

Arizona Cardinals
Atlanta Falcons
Carolina Panthers
Chicago Bears
Dallas Cowboys
Detroit Lions
Green Bay Packers
Minnesota Vikings
New Orleans Saints
New York Giants
Philadelphia Eagles
San Francisco 49ers
Seattle Seahawks
St. Louis Rams
Tampa Bay Buccaneers
Washington Redskins

2003 NFL Final Standings

AFC East

Team	W	L	T	PCT	PF	PA
*yz-Patriots	14	2	0	.875	348	238
Dolphins	10	6	0	.625	311	261
Bills	6	10	0	.375	243	279
Jets	6	10	0	.375	283	299

AFC North

Team	W	L	T	PCT	PF	PA
y-Ravens	10	6	0	.625	391	281
Bengals	8	8	0	.500	346	384
Steelers	6	10	0	.375	300	327
Browns	5	11	0	.312	254	322

AFC South

Team	W	L	T	PCT	PF	PA
y-Colts	12	4	0	.750	447	336
x-Titans	12	4	0	.750	435	324
Jaguars	5	11	0	.312	276	331
Texans	5	11	0	.312	255	380

AFC West

Team	W	L	T	PCT	PF	PA
yz-Chiefs	13	3	0	.812	484	332
x-Broncos	10	6	0	.625	381	301
Raiders	4	12	0	.250	270	379
Chargers	4	12	0	.250	313	441

NFC East

Team	W	L	T	PCT	PF	PA
*yz-Eagles	12	4	0	.750	374	287
x-Cowboys	10	6	0	.625	289	260
Redskins	5	11	0	.312	287	372
Giants	4	12	0	.250	243	387

NFC North

Team	W	L	T	PCT	PF	PA
y-Packers	10	6	0	.625	442	307
Vikings	9	7	0	.562	416	353
Bears	7	9	0	.438	283	346
Lions	5	11	0	.312	270	379

NFC South

Team	W	L	T	PCT	PF	PA
y-Panthers	11	5	0	.688	325	304
Saints	8	8	0	.500	340	326
Buccaneers	7	9	0	.438	301	264
Falcons	5	11	0	.312	299	422

NFC West

Team	W	L	T	PCT	PF	PA
yz-Rams	12	4	0	.750	447	328
x-Seahawks	10	6	0	.625	404	327
49ers	7	9	0	.438	384	337
Cardinals	4	12	0	.250	225	452

x-clinched playoff berth y-clinched division title z-clinched first-round bye *clinched home-field advantage

KEY W=win; L=loss; T=tie; PCT=winning percentage; PF=points for; PA=points against

2003 NFL Playoffs

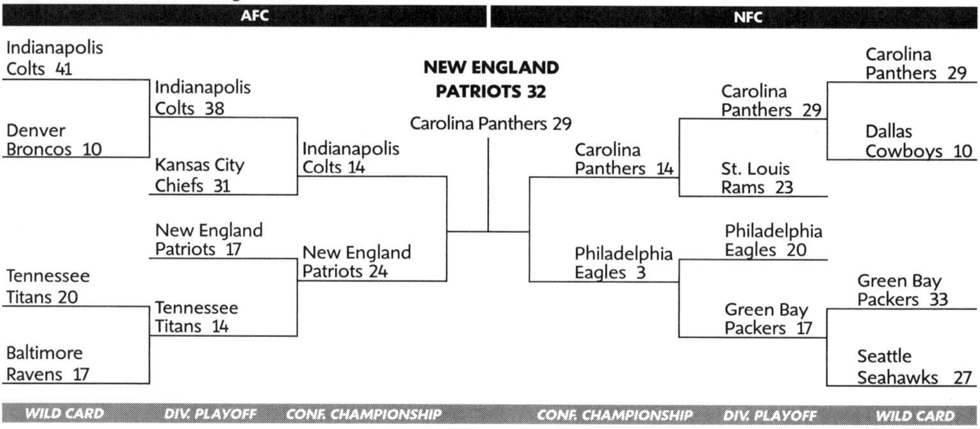

AFC Wild-Card Games

Indianapolis Colts 41
Denver Broncos 10

SCORING SUMMARY

	1Q	2Q	3Q	4Q	OT	T
BRONCOS	3	0	0	7	—	10
COLTS	14	17	10	0	—	41

1ST QUARTER
TD Brandon Stokley, 31-yard pass from Peyton Manning (Mike Vanderjagt, extra point), 11:55. Drive: 6 plays, 70 yards in 3:05.
FG Jason Elam, 49 yards, 3:41. Drive: 12 plays, 47 yards in 8:14.
TD Marvin Harrison, 46-yard pass from Peyton Manning (Mike Vanderjagt, extra point), 0:24. Drive: 8 plays, 81 yards in 3:17.

2ND QUARTER
TD Marvin Harrison, 23-yard pass from Peyton Manning (Mike Vanderjagt, extra point), 7:28. Drive: 8 plays, 80 yards in 3:49.
TD Brandon Stokley, 87-yard pass from Peyton Manning (Mike Vanderjagt, extra point), 1:51. Drive: 1 play, 87 yards in 0:10.
FG Mike Vanderjagt, 27 yards, 0:00. Drive: 6 plays, 49 yards in 0:55.

3RD QUARTER
TD Reggie Wayne, 7-yard pass from Peyton Manning (Mike Vanderjagt, extra point), 5:19. Drive: 12 plays, 64 yards in 5:45.
FG Mike Vanderjagt, 20 yards, 0:55. Drive: 6 plays, 17 yards in 3:38.

4TH QUARTER
TD Rod Smith, 7-yard pass from Jake Plummer (Jason Elam, extra point), 7:04. Drive: 12 plays, 62 yards in 6:18.

Tennessee Titans 20
Baltimore Ravens 17

SCORING SUMMARY

	1Q	2Q	3Q	4Q	OT	T
TITANS	7	0	7	6	—	20
RAVENS	7	3	0	7	—	17

1ST QUARTER
TD Chris Brown, 6-yard run (Gary Anderson, extra point), 8:54. Drive: 10 plays, 67 yards in 5:03.
TD Will Demps, 56-yard interception return (Matt Stover, extra point), 6:12.

2ND QUARTER
FG Matt Stover, 43 yards, 1:55. Drive: 9 plays, 55 yards in 4:23.

3RD QUARTER
TD Justin McCareins, 49-yard pass from Steve McNair (Gary Anderson, extra point), 7:59. Drive: 6 plays, 79 yards in 3:16.

4TH QUARTER
FG Gary Anderson, 45 yards, 9:13. Drive: 4 plays, 3 yards in 2:20.
TD Todd Heap, 35-yard pass from Anthony Wright (Matt Stover, extra point), 4:30. Drive: 9 plays, 71 yards in 4:43.
FG Gary Anderson, 46 yards, 0:29. Drive: 8 plays, 35 yards in 2:15.

NFC Wild-Card Games

Carolina Panthers 29
Dallas Cowboys 10

SCORING SUMMARY

	1Q	2Q	3Q	4Q	OT	T
COWBOYS	0	3	0	7	—	10
PANTHERS	6	10	7	6	—	29

1ST QUARTER
FG John Kasay, 18 yards, 8:40. Drive: 7 plays, 77 yards in 3:47.
FG John Kasay, 38 yards, 1:02. Drive: 7 plays, 21 yards in 1:57.

NFC Wild-Card Games (cont.)

2ND QUARTER
TD Stephen Davis, 23-yard run (John Kasay, extra point), 6:10. Drive: 8 plays, 51 yards in 3:49.
FG Billy Cundiff, 37 yards, 1:12. Drive: 10 plays, 59 yards in 4:58.
FG John Kasay, 19 yards, 0:01. Drive: 6 plays, 71 yards in 1:11.

3RD QUARTER
TD Steve Smith, 32-yard pass from Jake Delhomme (John Kasay, extra point), 9:44. Drive: 4 plays, 63 yards in 1:28.

4TH QUARTER
FG John Kasay, 32 yards, 12:45. Drive: 10 plays, 46 yards in 5:43.
TD Quincy Carter, 9-yard run (Billy Cundiff, extra point), 7:36. Drive: 9 plays, 47 yards in 5:09.
FG John Kasay, 34 yards, 3:12. Drive: 4 plays, -5 yards in 1:47.

Green Bay Packers 33
Seattle Seahawks 27

SCORING SUMMARY

	1Q	2Q	3Q	4Q	OT	T
SEAHAWKS	3	3	14	7	—	27
PACKERS	0	13	0	14	6	33

1ST QUARTER
FG Josh Brown, 30 yards, 7:01. Drive: 10 plays, 57 yards in 4:53.

2ND QUARTER
FG Ryan Longwell, 31 yards, 9:13. Drive: 5 plays, 37 yards in 2:01.
FG Josh Brown, 35 yards, 6:50. Drive: 8 plays, 51 yards in 2:23.
TD Bubba Franks, 23-yard pass from Brett Favre (Ryan Longwell, extra point), 4:37. Drive: 5 plays, 80 yards in 2:13.
FG Ryan Longwell, 27 yards, 0:46. Drive: 6 plays, 30 yards in 1:32.

3RD QUARTER
TD Shaun Alexander, 1-yard run (Josh Brown, extra point), 9:28. Drive: 10 plays, 74 yards in 5:32.
TD Shaun Alexander, 1-yard run (Josh Brown, extra point), 1:57. Drive: 11 plays, 77 yards in 4:57.

4TH QUARTER
TD Ahman Green, 1-yard run (Ryan Longwell, extra point), 10:01. Drive: 12 plays, 60 yards in 6:56.
TD Ahman Green, 1-yard run (Ryan Longwell, extra point), 2:44. Drive: 12 plays, 51 yards in 6:46.
TD Shaun Alexander, 1-yard run (Josh Brown, extra point), 0:51. Drive: 7 plays, 67 yards in 1:53.

OVERTIME
TD Al Harris, 52-yard interception return, 10:35.

AFC Divisional Games

Indianapolis Colts 38
Kansas City Chiefs 31

SCORING SUMMARY

	1Q	2Q	3Q	4Q	OT	T
COLTS	14	7	10	7	—	38
CHIEFS	3	7	14	7	—	31

1ST QUARTER
TD Brandon Stokley, 29-yard pass from Peyton Manning (Mike Vanderjagt, extra point), 9:20. Drive: 10 plays, 70 yards in 5:40.
FG Morten Andersen, 22 yards, 3:38. Drive: 11 plays, 73 yards in 5:42.
TD Edgerrin James, 11-yard run (Mike Vanderjagt, extra point), 0:37. Drive: 6 plays, 76 yards in 3:01.

2ND QUARTER
TD Dante Hall, 9-yard pass from Trent Green (Morten Andersen, extra point), 8:35. Drive: 12 plays, 77 yards in 7:02.
TD Tom Lopienski, 2-yard pass from Peyton Manning (Mike Vanderjagt, extra point), 4:29. Drive: 9 plays, 71 yards in 4:06.

3RD QUARTER
FG Mike Vanderjagt, 45 yards, 9:24. Drive: 11 plays, 51 yards in 5:08.
TD Priest Holmes, 1-yard run (Morten Andersen, extra point), 5:26. Drive: 8 plays, 55 yards in 3:58.
TD Reggie Wayne, 19-yard pass from Peyton Manning (Mike Vanderjagt, extra point), 1:48. Drive: 7 plays, 64 yards in 3:38.
TD Dante Hall, 92-yard kick return (Morten Andersen, extra point), 1:35.

4TH QUARTER
TD Edgerrin James, 1-yard run (Mike Vanderjagt, extra point), 11:14. Drive: 10 plays, 81 yards in 5:21.
TD Priest Holmes, 1-yard run (Morten Andersen, extra point), 4:22. Drive: 17 plays, 76 yards in 6:52.

New England Patriots 17
Tennessee Titans 14

SCORING SUMMARY

	1Q	2Q	3Q	4Q	OT	T
TITANS	7	0	7	0	—	14
PATRIOTS	7	7	0	3	—	17

1ST QUARTER
TD Bethel Johnson, 41-yard pass from Tom Brady (Adam Vinatieri, extra point), 10:59. Drive: 6 plays, 69 yards in 2:52.
TD Chris Brown, 5-yard run (Gary Anderson, extra point), 7:31. Drive: 6 plays, 61 yards in 3:28.

2ND QUARTER
TD Antowain Smith, 1-yard run (Adam Vinatieri, extra point), 13:46. Drive: 11 plays, 57 yards in 5:02.

3RD QUARTER
TD Derrick Mason, 11-yard pass from Steve McNair (Gary Anderson, extra point), 4:14. Drive: 11 plays, 70 yards in 7:47.

4TH QUARTER
FG Adam Vinatieri, 46 yards, 4:06. Drive: 8 plays, 13 yards in 2:34.

NFC Divisional Games

Carolina Panthers 29
St. Louis Rams 23

SCORING SUMMARY

	1Q	2Q	3Q	4Q	OT	2OT	T
PANTHERS	0	10	6	7	—	6	29
RAMS	3	6	3	11	—	—	23

1ST QUARTER
FG Jeff Wilkins, 20 yards, 5:34. Drive: 11 plays, 81 yards in 6:37.

2ND QUARTER
FG Jeff Wilkins, 26 yards, 13:26. Drive: 6 plays, 17 yards in 2:15.
TD Muhsin Muhammad, 0-yard fumble return (John Kasay, extra point), 11:22.
FG Jeff Wilkins, 24 yards, 6:58. Drive: 8 plays, 48 yards

NFC Divisional Games (cont.)

in 4:24.
FG John Kasay, 45 yards, 1:07. Drive: 9 plays, 32 yards in 5:51.

3RD QUARTER
FG Jeff Wilkins, 51 yards, 11:25. Drive: 8 plays, 42 yards in 3:35.
FG John Kasay, 52 yards, 7:45. Drive: 7 plays, 49 yards in 3:40.
FG John Kasay, 34 yards, 0:43. Drive: 13 plays, 64 yards in 6:29.

4TH QUARTER
TD Brad Hoover, 7-yard run (John Kasay, extra point), 8:50. Drive: 7 plays, 73 yards in 4:18.
TD Marshall Faulk, 1-yard run (Marc Bulger pass to Dane Looker for 2-point conversion), 2:39. Drive: 15 plays, 57 yards in 3:50.
FG Jeff Wilkins, 33 yards, 0:00. Drive: 5 plays, 43 yards in 2:39

OVERTIME
None

SECOND OVERTIME
TD Steve Smith, 69-yard pass from Jake Delhomme, 14:50. Drive: 3 plays, 65 yards in 1:11.

Philadelphia Eagles 20
Green Bay Packers 17

SCORING SUMMARY

	1Q	2Q	3Q	4Q	OT	T
PACKERS	14	0	0	3	—	17
EAGLES	0	7	0	10	3	20

1ST QUARTER
TD Robert Ferguson, 40-yard pass from Brett Favre (Ryan Longwell, extra point), 7:37. Drive: 1 play, 40 yards in 0:04.
TD Robert Ferguson, 17-yard pass from Brett Favre (Ryan Longwell, extra point), 1:22. Drive: 8 plays, 77 yards in 4:19.

2ND QUARTER
TD Duce Staley, 7-yard pass from Donovan McNabb (David Akers, extra point), 6:29. Drive: 6 plays, 77 yards in 3:03.

3RD QUARTER
None

4TH QUARTER
TD Todd Pinkston, 12-yard pass from Donovan McNabb (David Akers, extra point), 14:48. Drive: 8 plays, 89 yards in 4:59.
FG Ryan Longwell, 21 yards, 10:22. Drive: 5 plays, 48 yards in 2:00.
FG David Akers, 37 yards, 0:05. Drive: 12 plays, 61 yards in 2:16.

OVERTIME
FG David Akers, 31 yards, 10:12. Drive: 6 plays, 21 yards in 2:45.

Trivia Challenge

Which city has hosted the Super Bowl the most times?

New Orleans, Louisiana, which has hosted the championship game nine times.

AFC Conference Championship

New England Patriots 24
Indianapolis Colts 14

SCORING SUMMARY

	1Q	2Q	3Q	4Q	OT	T
COLTS	0	0	7	7	—	14
PATRIOTS	7	8	6	3	—	24

1ST QUARTER
TD David Givens, 7-yard pass from Tom Brady (Adam Vinatieri, extra point), 8:16. Drive: 13 plays, 65 yards in 6:44.

2ND QUARTER
FG Adam Vinatieri, 31 yards, 12:44. Drive: 13 plays, 67 yards in 5:42.
FG Adam Vinatieri, 25 yards, 8:06. Drive: 11 plays, 52 yards in 4:22.
SAFETY Justin Snow, fumble out-of-bounds in end zone, 4:08.

3RD QUARTER
TD Edgerrin James, 2-yard run (Mike Vanderjagt, extra point), 9:44. Drive: 12 plays, 52 yards in 5:16.
FG Adam Vinatieri, 27 yards, 7:20. Drive: 6 plays, 48 yards in 2:24.
FG Adam Vinatieri, 21 yards, 1:32. Drive: 8 plays, 66 yards in 4:45.

4TH QUARTER
TD Marcus Pollard, 7-yard pass from Peyton Manning (Mike Vanderjagt, extra point), 2:27. Drive: 13 plays, 67 yards in 3:43.
FG Adam Vinatieri, 34 yards, 0:50. Drive: 4 plays, 4 yards in 0:51.

NFC Conference Championship

Carolina Panthers 14
Philadelphia Eagles 3

SCORING SUMMARY

	1Q	2Q	3Q	4Q	OT	T
PANTHERS	0	7	7	0	—	14
EAGLES	0	3	0	0	—	3

1ST QUARTER
None

2ND QUARTER
TD Muhsin Muhammad, 24-yard pass from Jake Delhomme (John Kasay, extra point), 10:12. Drive: 8 plays, 79 yards in 4:48.
FG David Akers, 41 yards, 2:56. Drive: 14 plays, 44 yards in 7:16.

3RD QUARTER
TD DeShaun Foster, 1-yard run (John Kasay, extra point), 4:11. Drive: 4 plays, 37 yards in 2:07.

4TH QUARTER
None

SUPER BOWL XXXVIII

New England Patriots 32
Carolina Panthers 29

FEBRUARY 1, 2004
RELIANT STADIUM, HOUSTON, TEXAS

SCORING SUMMARY

	1Q	2Q	3Q	4Q	OT	T
PANTHERS	0	10	0	19	—	29
PATRIOTS	0	14	0	18	—	32

1ST QUARTER
None

2ND QUARTER
TD Deion Branch, 5-yard pass from Tom Brady (Adam Vinatieri, extra point), 3:05. Drive: 4 plays, 20 yards in 2:10.
TD Steve Smith, 39-yard pass from Jake Delhomme (John Kasay, extra point), 1:07. Drive: 8 plays, 95 yards in 1:58.
TD David Givens, 5-yard pass from Tom Brady (Adam Vinatieri, extra point), 0:18. Drive: 6 plays, 78 yards in 0:49.
FG John Kasay, 50 yards, 0:00. Drive: 2 plays, 21 yards in 0:18.

3RD QUARTER
None

4TH QUARTER
TD Antowain Smith, 2-yard run (Adam Vinatieri, extra point), 14:49. Drive: 8 plays, 71 yards in 4:08.
TD DeShaun Foster, 33-yard run (Jake Delhomme 2-point conversion pass failed), 12:39. Drive: 6 plays, 81 yards in 2:10.
TD Muhsin Muhammad, 85-yard pass from Jake Delhomme (Jake Delhomme 2-point conversion pass failed), 6:53. Drive: 3 plays, 90 yards in 0:45.
TD Mike Vrabel, 1-yard pass from Tom Brady (Kevin Faulk run for 2-point conversion), 2:51. Drive: 11 plays, 68 yards in 4:02.
TD Ricky Proehl, 12-yard pass from Jake Delhomme (John Kasay, extra point), 1:08. Drive: 7 plays, 80 yards in 1:43.
FG Adam Vinatieri, 41 yards, 0:04. Drive: 6 plays, 37 yards in 1:04.

Legends

Jim Brown played in the NFL for nine seasons and led the league in rushing in eight of them.

JAMES DRAKE

Jim Brown, running back, b. February 17, 1936, St. Simons Island, Georgia. The Hall of Famer and Cleveland Browns legend is considered the greatest running back in NFL history, if not the greatest player. Brown is sixth on the NFL's career rushing list (12,312 yards). He holds the all-time record for most seasons as the league's rushing leader (8) and most consecutive seasons as its rushing leader (5). Brown was the second-youngest player inducted into the Pro Football Hall of Fame (age 35). Running back Gayle Sayers of the Chicago Bears was the youngest (34).

John Elway, quarterback, b. June 28, 1960, Port Angeles, Washington. Elway walked away from football the way every athlete would like to — as a champion. He cemented his legacy by winning the Super Bowl in each of his last two seasons (1998, 1999), with the Denver Broncos. Elway was named MVP in the last game of his career, 1999's Super Bowl XXXIII. He is one of only two quarterbacks to throw for at least 50,000 yards in a career. He ranks second all-time for most career passing yards (51,475), most seasons with at least 3,000 passing yards (12), and most career completions (4,123).

Dick Butkus, linebacker, b. December 9, 1942, Chicago, Illinois. Butkus was the NFL's most feared linebacker. The seven-time All-NFL and eight-time Pro Bowler ranks fifth in NFL history in fumble recoveries (27). He played his nine-season career with the Chicago Bears and was elected to the Pro Football Hall of Fame in 1979.

SUPER BOWL XXXVIII (cont.)

Team Stats

	PANTHERS	PATRIOTS
First Downs	17	29
Rushing	3	7
Passing	12	19
Penalty	2	3
3rd-Down Conversions	4-12	8-17
4th-Down Conversions	0-0	1-1
Total Net Yards	387	481
Total Plays	53	83
Average Gain	7.3	5.8
Net Yards Rushing	92	127
Rushes	16	35
Avg. Per Rush	5.8	3.6

	PANTHERS	PATRIOTS
Net Yards Passing	295	354
Comp.-Att.	16-33	32-48
Yards Per Pass	8.0	7.4
Sacked-Yards Lost	4-28	0-0
Had Intercepted	0	1
Punts-Average	7-44.3	5-34.6
Return Yards	130	120
Punts-Returns	1-2	5-42
Kickoffs-Returns	6-116	4-78
Int.-Returns	1-12	0-0
Penalties-Yards	12-73	8-60
Fumbles-Lost	1-1	1-0
Time of Pos.	21:02	38:58

Player Statistics: Panthers

OFFENSE

PASSING	COMP-ATT	YDS	TD	INT
J. Delhomme	16-33	323	3	0

RUSHING	ATT	YDS	TD	LG
S. Davis	13	49	0	21
D. Foster	3	43	1	33

RECEIVING	REC	YDS	TD	LG
M. Muhammad	4	140	1	85
S. Smith	4	80	1	39
R. Proehl	4	71	1	31
J. Wiggins	2	21	0	15
D. Foster	1	9	0	9
K. Mangum	1	2	0	2

DEFENSE	T-A	SCK	INT	FF
D. Morgan	11-7	0	0	0
M. Minter	9-5	0	0	0
W. Witherspoon	7-6	0	0	0
R. Howard	6-0	0	1	0
R. Manning	4-2	0	0	0
S. Burton	3-2	0	0	0
T. Cousin	3-4	0	0	0
G. Favors	3-0	0	0	0
D. Grant	3-2	0	0	0
K. Jenkins	3-0	0	0	0
A. Wallace	3-3	0	0	0
J. Peppers	2-0	0	0	0
B. Allen	1-0	0	0	0
C. Branch	1-0	0	0	0
B. Buckner	1-2	0	0	0
J. Cooper	1-2	0	0	0
K. Hankton	1-0	0	0	0
B. Hoover	1-0	0	0	0
K. Rasmussen	1-0	0	0	0
M. Rucker	1-1	0	0	0
T. Sauerbrun	1-0	0	0	0
R. Smart	1-0	0	0	0
T. Steussie	1-0	0	0	0

Player Statistics: Patriots

OFFENSE

PASSING	COMP-ATT	YDS	TD	INT
T. Brady	32-48	354	3	1

RUSHING	ATT	YDS	TD	LG
A. Smith	26	83	1	9
K. Faulk	6	42	0	23
T. Brady	2	12	0	12
T. Brown	1	-10	0	-10

RECEIVING	REC	YDS	TD	LG
D. Branch	10	143	1	52
T. Brown	8	76	0	13
D. Givens	5	69	1	25
D. Graham	4	46	0	33
K. Faulk	4	19	0	7
M. Vrabel	1	1	1	1

DEFENSE	T-A	SCK	INT	FF
R. Harrison	8-1	1	0	0
T. Law	5-0	0	0	0
R. Phifer	5-0	0	0	0
M. Vrabel	4-2	2	0	1
B. Hamilton	3-1	0	0	0
T. Bruschi	2-2	0	0	0
M. Chatham	2-0	0	0	0
R. Seymour	2-0	0	0	0
C. Akins	1-0	0	0	0
J. Cherry	1-0	0	0	0
L. Izzo	1-0	0	0	0
B. Johnson	1-0	0	0	0
D. Koppen	1-0	0	0	0
S. Mayer	1-0	0	0	0
W. McGinest	1-3	1	0	0
T. Poole	1-2	0	0	0
A. Vinatieri	1-0	0	0	0

KEY COMP-ATT=completions-attempts; YDS=yards; TD=touchdowns; INT=interceptions; ATT=attempts; LG=long; REC=receptions; T-A=tackles-assists; SCK=sacks; FF=forced fumbles

Fast Fact: The Indianapolis Colts and Kansas City Chiefs set the AFC record for most touchdowns in one post-season game when they combined for nine in an AFC Divisional game in 2004. The Colts won, 38–31.

2003 A.P. All-Pro Team

DAVID E. KLUTHO/SPORTS ILLUSTRATED

Tony Gonzalez, Kansas City Chiefs

Offense

QUARTERBACK
Peyton Manning, Indianapolis Colts

RUNNING BACKS
Jamal Lewis, Baltimore Ravens
Priest Holmes, Kansas City Chiefs

TIGHT END
Tony Gonzalez, Kansas City Chiefs

WIDE RECEIVERS
Torry Holt, St. Louis Rams
Randy Moss, Minnesota Vikings

TACKLES
Jon Ogden, Baltimore Ravens
William Roaf, Kansas City Chiefs
Orlando Pace, St. Louis Rams

GUARDS
Steve Hutchinson, Seattle Seahawks
Will Shields, Kansas City Chiefs

CENTER
Tom Nalen, Denver Broncos

KICKER
Mike Vanderjagt, Indianapolis Colts

KICK RETURNER
Dante Hall, Kansas City Chiefs

Defense

ENDS
Michael Strahan, New York Giants
Leonard Little, St. Louis Rams

TACKLES
Kris Jenkins, Carolina Panthers
Richard Seymour, New England Patriots

OUTSIDE LINEBACKERS
Keith Bulluck, Tennessee Titans
Julian Peterson, San Francisco 49ers

INSIDE LINEBACKERS
Zach Thomas, Miami Dolphins
Ray Lewis, Baltimore Ravens

CORNERBACKS
Ty Law, New England Patriots
Chris McAlister, Baltimore Ravens

SAFETIES
Roy Williams, Dallas Cowboys
Rodney Harrison, New England Patriots

PUNTER
Shane Lechler, Oakland Raiders

2003 Regular-Season Results—AFC

Baltimore Ravens

Week	Opponent	Score	W/L/T
1	at Steelers	15–34	L
2	BROWNS	33–13	W
3	at Chargers	24–10	W
4	CHIEFS	10–17	L
5	BYE WEEK	—	—
6	at Cardinals	26–18	W
7	at Bengals	26–34	L
8	BRONCOS	26–6	W
9	JAGUARS	24–17	W
10	at Rams	22–33	L
11	at Dolphins	6–9	L
12	SEAHAWKS	44–41	W
13	49ERS	44–6	W
14	BENGALS	31–13	W
15	at Raiders	12–20	L
16	at Browns	35–0	W
17	STEELERS	13–10	W

Buffalo Bills

Week	Opponent	Score	W/L/T
1	PATRIOTS	31–0	W
2	at Jaguars	38–17	W
3	at Dolphins	7–17	L
4	EAGLES	13–23	L
5	BENGALS	22–16	W
6	at Jets	3–30	L
7	REDSKINS	24–7	W
8	at Chiefs	5–38	L
9	BYE WEEK	—	—
10	at Cowboys	6–10	L
11	TEXANS	10–12	L
12	COLTS	14–17	L
13	at Giants	24–7	W
14	JETS	17–6	W
15	at Titans	26–28	L
16	DOLPHINS	3–20	L
17	at Patriots	0–31	L

Cincinnati Bengals

Week	Opponent	Score	W/L/T
1	BRONCOS	10–30	L
2	at Raiders	20–23	L
3	STEELERS	10–17	L
4	at Browns	21–14	W
5	at Bills	16–22	L
6	BYE WEEK	—	—
7	RAVENS	34–26	W
8	SEAHAWKS	27–24	W
9	at Cardinals	14–17	L
10	TEXANS	34–27	W
11	CHIEFS	24–19	W
12	at Chargers	34–27	W
13	at Steelers	24–20	W
14	at Ravens	13–31	L
15	49ERS	41–38	W
16	at Rams	10–27	L
17	BROWNS	14–22	L

Cleveland Browns

Week	Opponent	Score	W/L/T
1	COLTS	6–9	L
2	at Ravens	13–33	L
3	at 49ers	13–12	W
4	BENGALS	14–21	L
5	at Steelers	33–13	W
6	RAIDERS	13–7	W
7	CHARGERS	20–26	L
8	at Patriots	3–9	L
9	BYE WEEK	—	—
10	at Chiefs	20–41	L
11	CARDINALS	44–6	W
12	STEELERS	6–13	L
13	at Seahawks	7–34	L
14	RAMS	20–26	L
15	at Broncos	20–23	L
16	RAVENS	0–35	L
17	at Bengals	22–14	W

Note: Home games are capitalized.

2003 Regular-Season Results—AFC (cont.)

Denver Broncos

Week	Opponent	Score	W/L/T
1	at Bengals	30–10	W
2	at Chargers	37–13	W
3	RAIDERS	31–10	W
4	LIONS	20–16	W
5	at Chiefs	23–24	L
6	STEELERS	17–14	W
7	at Vikings	20–28	L
8	at Ravens	6–26	L
9	PATRIOTS	26–30	L
10	BYE WEEK	—	—
11	CHARGERS	37–8	W
12	BEARS	10–19	L
13	at Raiders	22–8	W
14	CHIEFS	45–27	W
15	BROWNS	23–20	W
16	at Colts	31–17	W
17	at Packers	3–31	L

Houston Texans

Week	Opponent	Score	W/L/T
1	at Miami	21–20	W
2	at Saints	10–31	L
3	CHIEFS	14–42	L
4	JAGUARS	24–20	W
5	BYE WEEK	—	—
6	at Titans	17–38	L
7	JETS	14–19	L
8	at Colts	21–30	L
9	PANTHERS	14–10	W
10	at Bengals	27–34	L
11	at Bills	12–10	W
12	PATRIOTS	20–23	L
13	FALCONS	17–13	W
14	at Jaguars	0–27	L
15	at Buccaneers	3–16	L
16	TITANS	24–27	L
17	COLTS	17–20	L

Indianapolis Colts

Week	Opponent	Score	W/L/T
1	at Browns	9–6	W
2	TITANS	33–7	W
3	JAGUARS	23–13	W
4	at Saints	55–21	W
5	at Buccaneers	38–35	W
6	PANTHERS	20–23	L
7	BYE WEEK	—	—
8	TEXANS	30–21	W
9	at Dolphins	23–17	W
10	at Jaguars	23–28	L
11	JETS	38–31	W
12	at Bills	17–14	W
13	PATRIOTS	34–38	L
14	at Titans	29–27	W
15	FALCONS	38–7	W
16	BRONCOS	17–31	L
17	at Texans	20–17	W

Jacksonville Jaguars

Week	Opponent	Score	W/L/T
1	at Panthers	23–24	L
2	BILLS	17–38	L
3	at Colts	13–23	L
4	at Texans	20–24	L
5	CHARGERS	27–21	W
6	DOLPHINS	10–24	L
7	BYE WEEK	—	—
8	TITANS	17–30	L
9	at Ravens	17–24	L
10	COLTS	28–23	W
11	at Titans	3–10	L
12	at Jets	10–13	L
13	BUCCANEERS	17–10	W
14	TEXANS	27–0	W
15	at Patriots	13–27	L
16	SAINTS	20–19	W
17	at Falcons	14–21	L

Kansas City Chiefs

Week	Opponent	Score	W/L/T
1	CHARGERS	27–14	W
2	STEELERS	41–20	W
3	at Texans	42–14	W
4	at Ravens	17–10	W
5	BRONCOS	24–23	W
6	at Packers	40–34	W
7	at Raiders	17–10	W
8	BILLS	38–5	W
9	BYE WEEK	—	—
10	BROWNS	41–20	W
11	at Bengals	19–24	L
12	RAIDERS	27–24	W
13	at Chargers	28–24	W
14	at Broncos	27–45	L
15	LIONS	45–17	W
16	at Vikings	20–45	L
17	BEARS	31–3	W

Miami Dolphins

Week	Opponent	Score	W/L/T
1	TEXANS	20–21	L
2	at Jets	21–10	W
3	BILLS	17–7	W
4	BYE WEEK	—	—
5	at Giants	23–10	W
6	at Jaguars	24–10	W
7	PATRIOTS	13–19	L
8	at Chargers	26–10	W
9	COLTS	17–23	L
10	at Titans	7–31	L
11	RAVENS	9–6	W
12	REDSKINS	24–23	W
13	at Cowboys	40–21	W
14	at Patriots	0–12	L
15	EAGLES	27–34	L
16	at Bills	20–3	W
17	JETS	23–21	W

2003 Regular-Season Results—AFC (cont.)

New England Patriots

Week	Opponent	Score	W/L/T
1	at Bills	0–31	L
2	at Eagles	31–10	W
3	JETS	23–16	W
4	at Redskins	17–20	L
5	TITANS	38–30	W
6	GIANTS	17–6	W
7	at Dolphins	19–13	W
8	BROWNS	9–3	W
9	at Broncos	30–26	W
10	BYE WEEK	—	—
11	COWBOYS	12–0	W
12	at Texans	23–20	W
13	at Colts	38–34	W
14	DOLPHINS	12–0	W
15	JAGUARS	27–13	W
16	at Jets	21–16	W
17	BILLS	31–0	W

New York Jets

Week	Opponent	Score	W/L/T
1	at Redskins	13–16	L
2	DOLPHINS	10–21	L
3	at Patriots	16–23	L
4	COWBOYS	6–17	L
5	BYE WEEK	—	—
6	BILLS	30–3	W
7	at Texans	19–14	W
8	at Eagles	17–24	L
9	GIANTS	28–31	L
10	at Raiders	27–24	W
11	at Colts	31–38	L
12	JAGUARS	13–10	W
13	TITANS	24–17	W
14	at Bills	6–17	L
15	STEELERS	6–0	W
16	PATRIOTS	16–21	L
17	at Dolphins	21–23	L

Oakland Raiders

Week	Opponent	Score	W/L/T
1	at Titans	20–25	L
2	BENGALS	23–20	W
3	at Broncos	10–31	L
4	CHARGERS	34–31	W
5	at Bears	21–24	L
6	at Browns	7–13	L
7	CHIEFS	10–17	L
8	BYE WEEK	—	—
9	at Lions	13–23	L
10	JETS	24–27	L
11	VIKINGS	28–18	W
12	at Chiefs	24–27	L
13	BRONCOS	8–22	L
14	at Steelers	7–27	L
15	RAVENS	20–12	W
16	PACKERS	7–41	L
17	at Chargers	14–21	L

Pittsburgh Steelers

Week	Opponent	Score	W/L/T
1	RAVENS	34–15	W
2	at Chiefs	20–41	L
3	at Bengals	17–10	W
4	TITANS	13–30	L
5	BROWNS	13–33	L
6	at Broncos	14–17	L
7	BYE WEEK	—	—
8	RAMS	21–33	L
9	at Seahawks	16–23	L
10	CARDINALS	28–15	W
11	at 49ers	14–30	L
12	at Browns	13–6	W
13	BENGALS	20–24	L
14	RAIDERS	27–7	W
15	at Jets	0–6	L
16	CHARGERS	40–24	W
17	at Ravens	10–13	L

San Diego Chargers

Week	Opponent	Score	W/L/T
1	at Chiefs	14–27	L
2	BRONCOS	13–37	L
3	RAVENS	10–24	L
4	at Raiders	31–34	L
5	at Jaguars	21–27	L
6	BYE WEEK	—	—
7	at Browns	26–20	W
8	DOLPHINS	10–26	L
9	at Bears	7–20	L
10	VIKINGS	42–28	W
11	at Broncos	8–37	L
12	BENGALS	27–34	L
13	CHIEFS	24–28	L
14	at Lions	14–7	W
15	PACKERS	21–38	L
16	at Steelers	24–40	L
17	RAIDERS	21–14	W

Tennessee Titans

Week	Opponent	Score	W/L/T
1	RAIDERS	25–20	W
2	at Colts	7–33	L
3	SAINTS	27–12	W
4	at Steelers	30–13	W
5	at Patriots	30–38	L
6	TEXANS	38–17	W
7	at Panthers	37–17	W
8	at Jaguars	30–17	W
9	BYE WEEK	—	—
10	DOLPHINS	31–7	W
11	JAGUARS	10–3	W
12	at Falcons	38–31	W
13	at Jets	17–24	L
14	COLTS	27–29	L
15	BILLS	28–26	W
16	at Texans	27–24	W
17	BUCCANEERS	33–13	W

2003 Regular-Season Results—NFC

Arizona Cardinals

Week	Opponent	Score	W/L/T
1	at Lions	24–42	L
2	SEAHAWKS	0–38	L
3	PACKERS	20–13	W
4	at Rams	13–37	L
5	at Cowboys	7–24	L
6	RAVENS	18–26	L
7	BYE WEEK	—	—
8	49ERS	16–13	W
9	BENGALS	17–14	W
10	at Steelers	15–28	L
11	at Browns	6–44	L
12	RAMS	27–30	L
13	at Bears	3–28	L
14	at 49ers	14–50	L
15	PANTHERS	17–20	L
16	at Seahawks	10–28	L
17	VIKINGS	18–17	W

Did You Know?

At the University of Tennessee, Peyton Manning spent part of the 1994 season as backup quarterback to Todd Helton. Helton is now an All-Star first baseman for the Colorado Rockies.

Fast Fact: Only one Super Bowl MVP has been a member of the losing team. Linebacker Chuck Howley of the Dallas Cowboys was the MVP of Super Bowl V. The Cowboys lost to the Baltimore Colts, 16–13.

Today's Stars

Randy Moss of the Vikings led the NFL in touchdown receptions (17) in 2003.

Randy Moss, wide receiver, b. February 13, 1977, Rand, West Virginia. Moss's combination of size and speed makes him the ultimate threat at wide receiver. In 2003, the Minnesota Viking led the NFL in touchdown receptions (17) and finished second in receiving yards (1,632) and receptions (111). It was the sixth-straight season in which he gained at least 1,000 receiving yards. His performance broke the NFL record of five straight 1,000-yard seasons to start a career, which he had set the year before.

Priest Holmes, running back, b. October 7, 1973, Fort Smith, Arkansas. Holmes spent most of his first four NFL seasons as a backup for the Baltimore Ravens. Since joining the Kansas City Chiefs in 2001, he has turned into the NFL's most versatile running back. In 2003, he set the league's single-season records for rushing touchdowns and total touchdowns (27). He had a league-leading 51 touchdowns in the past two seasons. He was named the NFL's Offensive Player of the Year in 2002.

Peyton Manning, quarterback, b. March 24, 1976, New Orleans, Louisiana. In many ways, 2003 was a breakout season for Manning. He won the first two playoff games of his six-year pro career and was named the NFL's co-MVP. Manning led the NFL in passing yards (4,267) and was second in touchdown passes (29). He was the first player in NFL history with at least 3,000 passing yards in each of his first six pro seasons, the second-longest active streak in the league.

2003 Regular-Season Results—NFC (cont.)

Atlanta Falcons

Week	Opponent	Score	W/L/T
1	at Cowboys	27–13	W
2	REDSKINS	31–33	L
3	BUCCANEERS	10–31	L
4	at Panthers	3–23	L
5	VIKINGS	26–39	L
6	at Rams	0–36	L
7	SAINTS	17–45	L
8	BYE WEEK	—	—
9	EAGLES	16–23	L
10	at Giants	27–7	W
11	at Saints	20–23	L
12	TITANS	31–38	L
13	at Texans	13–17	L
14	PANTHERS	20–14	W
15	at Colts	7–38	L
16	at Buccaneers	30–28	W
17	JAGUARS	21–14	W

Carolina Panthers

Week	Opponent	Score	W/L/T
1	JAGUARS	24–23	W
2	at Buccaneers	12–9	W
3	BYE WEEK	—	—
4	FALCONS	23–3	W
5	SAINTS	19–13	W
6	at Colts	23–20	W
7	TITANS	17–37	L
8	at Saints	23–20	W
9	at Texans	10–14	L
10	BUCCANEERS	27–24	W
11	REDSKINS	20–17	W
12	at Cowboys	20–24	L
13	EAGLES	16–25	L
14	at Falcons	14–20	L
15	at Cardinals	20–17	W
16	LIONS	20–14	W
17	at Giants	37–24	W

Chicago Bears

Week	Opponent	Score	W/L/T
1	at 49ers	7–49	L
2	at Vikings	13–24	L
3	BYE WEEK	—	—
4	PACKERS	23–38	L
5	RAIDERS	24–21	W
6	at Saints	13–20	L
7	at Seahawks	17–24	L
8	LIONS	24–16	W
9	CHARGERS	20–7	W
10	at Lions	10–12	L
11	RAMS	21–23	L
12	at Broncos	19–10	W
13	CARDINALS	28–3	W
14	at Packers	21–34	L
15	VIKINGS	13–10	W
16	REDSKINS	27–24	W
17	at Chiefs	3–31	L

Dallas Cowboys

Week	Opponent	Score	W/L/T
1	FALCONS	13–27	L
2	at Giants	35–32	W
3	BYE WEEK	—	—
4	at Jets	17–6	W
5	CARDINALS	24–7	W
6	EAGLES	23–21	W
7	at Lions	38–7	W
8	at Buccaneers	0–16	L
9	REDSKINS	21–14	W
10	BILLS	10–6	W
11	at Patriots	0–12	L
12	PANTHERS	24–20	W
13	DOLPHINS	21–40	L
14	at Eagles	10–36	L
15	at Redskins	27–0	W
16	GIANTS	19–3	W
17	at Saints	7–13	L

Detroit Lions

Week	Opponent	Score	W/L/T
1	CARDINALS	42–24	W
2	at Packers	6–31	L
3	VIKINGS	13–23	L
4	at Broncos	16–20	L
5	at 49ers	17–24	L
6	BYE WEEK	—	—
7	COWBOYS	7–38	L
8	at Bears	16–24	L
9	RAIDERS	23–13	W
10	BEARS	12–10	W
11	at Seahawks	14–35	L
12	at Vikings	14–24	L
13	PACKERS	22–14	W
14	CHARGERS	7–14	L
15	at Chiefs	17–45	L
16	at Panthers	14–20	L
17	CARDINALS	30–20	W

Green Bay Packers

Week	Opponent	Score	W/L/T
1	VIKINGS	25–30	L
2	LIONS	31–6	W
3	at Cardinals	13–20	L
4	at Bears	38–23	W
5	SEAHAWKS	35–13	W
6	CHIEFS	34–40	L
7	at Rams	24–34	L
8	BYE WEEK	—	—
9	at Vikings	30–27	W
10	EAGLES	14–17	L
11	at Buccaneers	20–13	W
12	49ERS	20–10	W
13	at Lions	14–22	L
14	BEARS	34–21	W
15	at Chargers	38–21	W
16	at Raiders	41–7	W
17	BRONCOS	31–3	W

Note: Home teams are capitalized.

2003 Regular-Season Results—NFC (cont.)

Minnesota Vikings

Week	Opponent	Score	W/L/T
1	at Packers	30-25	W
2	BEARS	24-13	W
3	at Lions	23-13	W
4	49ERS	35-7	W
5	at Falcons	39-26	W
6	BYE WEEK	—	—
7	BRONCOS	28-20	W
8	GIANTS	17-29	L
9	PACKERS	27-30	L
10	at Chargers	28-42	L
11	at Raiders	18-28	L
12	LIONS	24-14	W
13	at Rams	17-48	L
14	SEAHAWKS	34-7	W
15	at Bears	10-13	L
16	CHIEFS	45-20	W
17	at Cardinals	17-18	L

New Orleans Saints

Week	Opponent	Score	W/L/T
1	at Seahawks	10-27	L
2	TEXANS	31-10	W
3	at Titans	12-27	L
4	COLTS	21-55	L
5	at Panthers	13-19	L
6	BEARS	20-13	W
7	at Falcons	45-17	W
8	PANTHERS	20-23	L
9	at Buccaneers	17-14	W
10	BYE WEEK	—	—
11	FALCONS	23-20	W
12	at Eagles	20-33	L
13	at Redskins	24-20	W
14	BUCCANEERS	7-14	L
15	GIANTS	45-7	W
16	at Jaguars	19-20	L
17	COWBOYS	13-7	W

New York Giants

Week	Opponent	Score	W/L/T
1	CARDINALS	23-13	W
2	COWBOYS	32-35	L
3	at Redskins	24-21	W
4	BYE WEEK	—	—
5	DOLPHINS	10-23	L
6	at Patriots	6-17	L
7	EAGLES	10-14	L
8	at Vikings	29-17	W
9	at JETS	31-28	W
10	FALCONS	7-27	L
11	at Eagles	10-28	L
12	at Buccaneers	13-19	L
13	BILLS	7-24	L
14	REDSKINS	7-20	L
15	at Saints	7-45	L
16	at Cowboys	3-19	L
17	PANTHERS	24-37	L

Philadelphia Eagles

Week	Opponent	Score	W/L/T
1	BUCCANEERS	0-17	L
2	PATRIOTS	10-31	L
3	BYE WEEK	—	—
4	at Bills	23-13	W
5	REDSKINS	27-25	W
6	at Cowboys	21-23	L
7	at Giants	14-10	W
8	JETS	24-17	W
9	at Falcons	23-16	W
10	at Packers	17-14	W
11	GIANTS	28-10	W
12	SAINTS	33-20	W
13	at Panthers	25-16	W
14	COWBOYS	36-10	W
15	at Dolphins	34-27	W
16	49ERS	28-31	L
17	at Redskins	31-7	W

San Francisco 49ers

Week	Opponent	Score	W/L/T
1	BEARS	49-7	W
2	at Cardinals	24-27	L
3	BROWNS	12-13	L
4	at Vikings	7-35	L
5	LIONS	24-17	W
6	at Seahawks	19-20	L
7	BUCCANEERS	24-7	W
8	at Cardinals	13-16	L
9	RAMS	30-10	W
10	BYE WEEK	—	—
11	STEELERS	30-14	W
12	at Packers	10-20	L
13	at Ravens	6-44	L
14	CARDINALS	50-14	W
15	at Bengals	38-41	L
16	at Eagles	31-28	W
17	SEAHAWKS	17-24	L

Seattle Seahawks

Week	Opponent	Score	W/L/T
1	SAINTS	27-10	W
2	at Cardinals	38-0	W
3	RAMS	24-23	W
4	BYE WEEK	—	—
5	at Packers	13-35	L
6	49ERS	20-19	W
7	BEARS	24-17	W
8	at Bengals	24-27	L
9	STEELERS	23-16	W
10	at Redskins	20-27	L
11	LIONS	35-14	W
12	at Ravens	41-44	L
13	BROWNS	34-7	W
14	at Vikings	7-34	L
15	at Rams	22-27	L
16	CARDINALS	28-10	W
17	at 49ers	24-17	W

2003 Regular-Season Results—NFC (cont.)

St. Louis Rams

Week	Opponent	Score	W/L/T
1	at Giants	13–23	L
2	49ERS	27–24	W
3	at Seahawks	23–24	L
4	CARDINALS	37–13	W
5	BYE WEEK	—	—
6	FALCONS	36–0	W
7	PACKERS	34–24	W
8	at Steelers	33–21	W
9	at 49ers	10–30	L
10	RAVENS	33–22	W
11	at Bears	23–21	W
12	at Cardinals	30–27	W
13	VIKINGS	48–17	W
14	BROWNS	26–20	W
15	SEAHAWKS	27–22	W
16	BENGALS	27–10	W
17	LIONS	20–30	L

Tampa Bay Buccaneers

Week	Opponent	Score	W/L/T
1	at Eagles	17–0	W
2	PANTHERS	9–12	L
3	at Falcons	31–10	W
4	BYE WEEK	—	—
5	COLTS	35–38	L
6	at Redskins	35–13	W
7	at 49ers	7–24	L
8	COWBOYS	16–0	W
9	SAINTS	14–17	L
10	at Panthers	24–27	L
11	PACKERS	13–20	L
12	GIANTS	19–13	W
13	at Jaguars	10–17	L
14	at Saints	14–7	W
15	TEXANS	16–3	W
16	FALCONS	28–30	L
17	at Titans	13–33	L

Washington Redskins

Week	Opponent	Score	W/L/T
1	JETS	16–13	W
2	at Falcons	33–31	W
3	GIANTS	21–24	L
4	PATRIOTS	20–17	W
5	at Eagles	25–27	L
6	BUCCANEERS	13–35	L
7	at Bills	7–24	L
8	BYE WEEK	—	—
9	at Cowboys	14–21	L
10	SEAHAWKS	27–20	W
11	at Panthers	17–20	L
12	at Dolphins	23–24	L
13	SAINTS	20–24	L
14	at Giants	20–7	W
15	COWBOYS	0–27	L
16	at Bears	24–27	L
17	EAGLES	7–31	L

Did You Know?

In 2003, the Tampa Bay Buccaneers became the 11th Super Bowl champion to miss the playoffs the season after winning the title.

2003 Individual Leaders—AFC

TOUCHDOWNS	TEAM	TD	RSH	REC	RET	PTS
Priest Holmes	KC	27	27	0	0	162
LaDainian Tomlinson	SD	17	13	4	0	102
Jamal Lewis	BAL	14	14	0	0	84
Clinton Portis	DEN	14	14	0	0	84
Travis Henry	BUF	11	10	1	0	66
Edgerrin James	IND	11	11	0	0	66
Chris Chambers	MIA	11	0	11	0	66
Marvin Harrison	IND	10	0	10	0	60
Ricky Williams	MIA	10	9	1	0	60
Santana Moss	NYJ	10	0	10	0	60
Chad Johnson	CIN	10	0	10	0	60
Hines Ward	PIT	10	0	10	0	60
Tony Gonzalez	KC	10	0	10	0	60

KEY TD=touchdowns; RSH=rushing touchdowns; REC=receiving touchdowns; RET=returns; PTS=points

2003 Individual Leaders—AFC (cont.)

KICKING	TEAM	FGM	FGA	LONG	XPM	XPA	PTS
Mike Vanderjagt	IND	37	37	50	46	46	157
Matt Stover	BAL	33	38	49	35	35	134
Gary Anderson	TEN	27	31	43	42	42	123
Jason Elam	DEN	27	31	51	39	39	120
Adam Vinatieri	NE	25	34	48	37	38	112
Shayne Graham	CIN	22	25	48	40	40	106
Morten Andersen	KC	16	20	49	59	58	106
Doug Brien	NYJ	27	32	48	24	24	105
Jeff Reed	PIT	23	32	51	31	32	100
Olindo Mare	MIA	22	29	52	33	34	99

PASSER RATING	TEAM	YDS	ATT	COMP	TD	INT	LONG	RATING
Steve McNair	TEN	3,215	400	250	24	7	73	100.4
Peyton Manning	IND	4,267	566	379	29	10	79	99.0
Trent Green	KC	4,039	523	330	24	12	67	92.6
Jake Plummer	DEN	2,182	302	189	15	7	60	91.2
Jon Kitna	CIN	3,591	520	324	26	15	82	87.4
Tom Brady	NE	3,620	527	317	23	12	82	85.9
Chad Pennington	NYJ	2,139	297	189	13	12	65	82.9
Tommy Maddox	PIT	3,414	519	298	18	17	53	75.3
Kelly Holcomb	CLE	1,797	302	193	10	12	68	74.6
Rich Gannon	OAK	1,274	225	125	6	4	46	73.5

BOB ROSATO/SPORTS ILLUSTRATED

Steve McNair, Tennessee Titans

RECEPTIONS	TEAM	REC	YDS	AVG	TD	LONG
LaDainian Tomlinson	SD	100	725	7.3	4	73
Hines Ward	PIT	95	1,163	12.2	10	50
Derrick Mason	TEN	95	1,303	13.7	8	50
Marvin Harrison	IND	94	1,272	13.5	10	79
Chad Johnson	CIN	90	1,355	15.1	10	82
Peter Warrick	CIN	79	819	10.4	7	77
Santana Moss	NYJ	74	1,105	14.9	10	65
Rod Smith	DEN	74	845	11.4	3	38
Priest Holmes	KC	74	690	9.3	0	36
Tony Gonzalez	KC	71	916	12.9	10	67

RECEIVING YARDS	TEAM	REC	YDS	AVG	TD	LONG
Chad Johnson	CIN	90	1,355	15.1	10	82
Derrick Mason	TEN	95	1,303	13.7	8	50
Marvin Harrison	IND	94	1,272	13.5	10	79
Hines Ward	PIT	95	1,163	12.2	10	50
Santana Moss	NYJ	74	1,105	14.9	10	65
Andre Johnson	HOU	66	976	14.8	4	46
Chris Chambers	MIA	64	963	15.0	11	57
Tony Gonzalez	KC	71	916	12.9	10	67
David Boston	SD	70	880	12.6	7	46
Jerry Rice	OAK	63	869	13.8	2	47

KEY FGM=field goals made; FGA=field goals attempted; XPA=extra points attempted; XPM=extra points made; PTS=points; YDS=yards; ATT=attempts; COMP=completions; TD=touchdowns; INT=interceptions; REC=receptions; AVG=average

2003 Individual Leaders—AFC (cont.)

RUSHING	TEAM	YDS	ATT	AVG	TD	LONG
Jamal Lewis	BAL	2,066	387	5.3	14	82
LaDainian Tomlinson	SD	1,645	313	5.3	13	73
Clinton Portis	DEN	1,591	290	5.5	14	65
Fred Taylor	JAC	1,572	345	4.6	6	62
Priest Holmes	KC	1,420	320	4.4	27	31
Ricky Williams	MIA	1,372	392	3.5	9	45
Travis Henry	BUF	1,356	331	4.1	10	64
Curtis Martin	NYJ	1,308	323	4.0	2	56
Edgerrin James	IND	1,259	310	4.1	11	43
Eddie George	TEN	1,031	312	3.3	5	27
Domanick Davis	HOU	1,031	238	4.3	8	51

Jamal Lewis, Baltimore Ravens

INTERCEPTIONS	TEAM	INT	YDS	TD	LONG
Patrick Surtain	MIA	7	59	0	32
Ed Reed	BAL	7	132	1	54
Marcus Coleman	HOU	7	95	0	41
Ty Law	NE	6	112	1	65
Tyrone Poole	NE	6	81	0	44
Ray Lewis	BAL	6	99	1	37
Earl Little	CLE	6	41	0	21
Samari Rolle	TEN	6	141	0	52
Dexter McCleon	KC	6	-3	0	0
Greg Wesley	KC	6	63	0	27
Phillip Buchanon	OAK	6	176	2	83

SACKS	TEAM	SACKS	TACKLES
Adewale Ogunleye	MIA	15.0	62
Jason Taylor	MIA	13.0	57
Shaun Ellis	NYJ	12.5	69
Terrell Suggs	BAL	12.0	27
Aaron Schobel	BUF	11.5	60
Bertrand Berry	DEN	11.5	36
Dwight Freeney	IND	11.0	31
Mike Vrabel	NE	9.5	52
Jevon Kearse	TEN	9.5	41

Three tied with 8.5 sacks.

PUNTING	TEAM	NO.	YDS	AVG	NAVG	LG	TB	BLK	IN 20	RET	RET AVG	RET TD
Shane Lechler	OAK	96	4,503	46.9	37.2	73	13	0	27	52	12.9	0
Brian Moorman	BUF	85	3,788	44.6	37.1	71	3	0	20	52	11.1	0
Craig Hentrich	TEN	71	3,117	43.9	37.8	58	8	0	26	30	9.2	1
Micah Knorr	DEN	68	2,937	43.2	32.2	62	6	0	14	46	12.2	1
Hunter Smith	IND	62	2,617	42.2	35.5	55	3	0	20	32	10.0	0
Chris Gardocki	CLE	72	3,019	41.9	34.8	60	10	0	18	33	9.6	0
Josh Miller	PIT	84	3,521	41.9	36.0	72	8	0	27	47	6.4	0
Darren Bennett	SD	82	3,436	41.9	36.2	56	3	0	28	38	10.8	2
Chad Stanley	HOU	97	4,028	41.5	36.7	58	3	0	36	43	9.5	1
Mark Royals	JAC	45	1,852	41.2	34.8	51	5	0	9	24	7.7	0

2003 Individual Leaders—NFC

TOUCHDOWNS	TEAM	TD	RSH	REC	RET	PTS
Ahman Green	GB	20	15	5	0	120
Randy Moss	MIN	17	0	17	0	102
Shaun Alexander	SEA	16	14	2	0	96
Brian Westbrook	PHI	13	7	4	2	78
Torry Holt	STL	12	0	12	0	72
T.J. Duckett	ATL	11	11	0	0	66
Marshall Faulk	STL	11	10	1	0	66
Joe Horn	NO	10	0	10	0	60

Five tied with 9 touchdowns.

KEY NO.=number; NAVG=net average; LG=long; TB=touchback; BLK=blocked; IN 20=inside 20-yard line; RET=returned; RET AVG=return average; RET TD=returned for a touchdown

2003 Individual Leaders—NFC (cont.)

KICKING	TEAM	FGM	FGA	LONG	XPA	XPM	PTS
Jeff Wilkins	STL	39	42	53	46	46	163
John Kasay	CAR	32	38	53	30	29	125
Ryan Longwell	GB	23	26	50	51	51	120
Josh Brown	SEA	22	30	58	48	48	114
David Akers	PHI	24	29	57	42	42	114
Paul Edinger	CHI	26	36	54	27	27	105
John Carney	NO	22	30	50	37	36	102
Aaron Elling	MIN	18	25	51	48	48	102
John Hall	WAS	25	33	54	27	26	101
Billy Cundiff	DAL	23	29	52	31	30	99

PASSER RATING	TEAM	YDS	ATT	COMP	TD	INT	LONG	RATING
Daunte Culpepper	MIN	3,479	454	295	25	11	59	96.4
Brett Favre	GB	3,361	471	308	32	21	66	90.4
Matt Hasselbeck	SEA	3,841	513	313	26	15	80	88.8
Aaron Brooks	NO	3,546	518	306	24	8	76	88.8
Brad Johnson	TB	3,811	570	354	26	21	76	81.5
Marc Bulger	STL	3,845	532	336	22	22	48	81.4
Jake Delhomme	CAR	3,219	449	266	19	16	67	80.6
Jeff Garcia	SF	2,704	392	225	18	13	75	80.1
Donovan McNabb	PHI	3,216	478	275	16	11	59	79.6
Patrick Ramsey	WAS	2,166	337	179	14	9	64	75.8

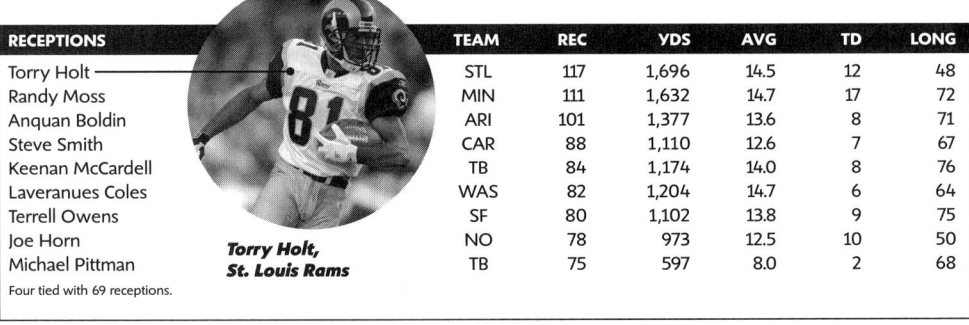

MITCHELL LAYTON/NEWSPORT

Torry Holt, St. Louis Rams

RECEPTIONS	TEAM	REC	YDS	AVG	TD	LONG
Torry Holt	STL	117	1,696	14.5	12	48
Randy Moss	MIN	111	1,632	14.7	17	72
Anquan Boldin	ARI	101	1,377	13.6	8	71
Steve Smith	CAR	88	1,110	12.6	7	67
Keenan McCardell	TB	84	1,174	14.0	8	76
Laveranues Coles	WAS	82	1,204	14.7	6	64
Terrell Owens	SF	80	1,102	13.8	9	75
Joe Horn	NO	78	973	12.5	10	50
Michael Pittman	TB	75	597	8.0	2	68

Four tied with 69 receptions.

RECEIVING YARDS	TEAM	REC	YDS	AVG	TD	LONG
Torry Holt	STL	117	1,696	14.5	12	48
Randy Moss	MIN	111	1,632	14.7	17	72
Anquan Boldin	ARI	101	1,377	13.6	8	71
Laveranues Coles	WAS	82	1,204	14.7	6	64
Keenan McCardell	TB	84	1,174	14.0	8	76
Darrell Jackson	SEA	68	1,137	16.7	9	80
Steve Smith	CAR	88	1,110	12.6	7	67
Terrell Owens	SF	80	1,102	13.8	9	75
Amani Toomer	NYG	63	1,057	16.8	5	77
Isaac Bruce	STL	69	981	14.2	5	41

2003 Individual Leaders—NFC (cont.)

RUSHING	TEAM	YDS	ATT	AVG	TD	LONG
Ahman Green	GB	1,883	355	5.3	15	98
Deuce McAllister	NO	1,641	351	4.7	8	76
Stephen Davis	CAR	1,444	318	4.5	8	40
Shaun Alexander	SEA	1,435	326	4.4	14	55
Tiki Barber	NYG	1,216	278	4.4	2	27
Anthony Thomas	CHI	1,024	244	4.2	6	67
Kevan Barlow	SF	1,024	201	5.1	6	78
Troy Hambrick	DAL	972	275	3.5	5	42
Marcel Shipp	ARI	830	228	3.6	0	36
Marshall Faulk	STL	818	209	3.9	10	52

INTERCEPTIONS	TEAM	INT	YDS	TD	LONG
Brian Russell	MIN	9	185	0	50
Tony Parrish	SF	9	202	0	49
Corey Chavous	MIN	8	143	1	39
Dexter Jackson	ARI	6	122	0	30
Dre' Bly	DET	6	89	1	48
Renaldo Hill	ARI	5	119	1	70
Darren Sharper	GB	5	78	0	50
Dwight Smith	TB	5	3	0	3
Brian Williams	MIN	5	205	1	77

Trivia Challenge

Placekicker Gary Anderson of the Tennessee Titans retired after the 2003 season as the NFL's all-time career points leader (2,346). How many placekickers are in the Pro Football Hall of Fame?

One. Jan Stenerud played for the Kansas City Chiefs, Green Bay Packers, and Minnesota Vikings from 1967 through 1985. He was inducted into the Hall in 1991.

SACKS	TEAM	SACKS	TACKLES
Michael Strahan	NYG	18.5	76
Simeon Rice	TB	15.0	50
Leonard Little	STL	12.5	47
Mike Rucker	CAR	12.0	58
Kevin Williams	MIN	10.5	51
Kabeer Gbaja-Biamila	GB	10.0	45
Lance Johnstone	MIN	10.0	28
Charles Grant	NO	10.0	57
Chike Okeafor	SEA	8.0	47
Greg Ellis	DAL	8.0	48
Ellis Johnson	ATL	8.0	41

Michael Strahan, New York Giants

PUNTING	TEAM	NO.	YDS	AVG	NAVG	LG	TB	BLK	IN 20	RET	RET AVG	RET TD
Todd Sauerbrun	CAR	77	3,433	44.6	35.6	64	9	0	22	35	11.5	1
Mitch Berger	NO	71	3,144	44.3	38.2	59	5	0	28	36	8.2	0
Tom Tupa	TB	83	3,590	43.3	35.9	60	6	0	26	39	12.5	0
Scott Player	ARI	82	3,511	42.8	34.4	64	9	0	19	41	11.5	2
Sean Landeta	STL	59	2,525	42.8	32.9	57	5	0	14	32	15.1	2
Josh Bidwell	GB	69	2,875	41.7	35.1	60	7	0	16	32	9.9	0
Tom Rouen	SEA	67	2,762	41.2	37.1	61	3	0	29	29	4.8	0
Brad Maynard	CHI	79	3,258	41.2	34.6	53	9	0	23	36	7.7	0
Dirk Johnson	PHI	79	3,207	40.6	34.6	60	10	0	27	35	7.8	0
Jeff Feagles	NYG	90	3,641	40.5	33.9	59	6	0	31	40	10.8	2

TEAM-BY-TEAM STATS—AFC

BALTIMORE RAVENS

Passing

Player	ATT	COMP	YDS	PCT COMP	YDS/ATT	TD	INT	Rating
Kyle Boller	224	116	1,260	51.8	5.6	7	9	62.4
Anthony Wright	178	94	1,199	52.8	6.7	9	8	72.3

Rushing

Player	NO.	YDS	AVG	LG	TD
Jamal Lewis	387	2,066	5.3	82	14
Chester Taylor	63	276	4.4	32	2
Alan Ricard	19	79	4.2	30	0
Anthony Wright	28	73	2.6	17	0
Kyle Boller	30	62	2.1	15	0
Travis Taylor	11	62	5.6	16	0
Musa Smith	9	31	3.4	11	2

Receiving

Player	NO.	YDS	AVG	LG	TD
Todd Heap	57	693	12.2	33	3
Travis Taylor	39	632	16.2	73	3
Marcus Robinson	31	451	14.5	50	6
Jamal Lewis	26	205	7.9	26	0
Frank Sanders	14	170	12.1	44	0
Terry Jones	19	159	8.4	25	3
Chester Taylor	20	132	6.6	23	0

Kicking

Player	FGM	FGA	PCT COMP	XPM	XPA
Matt Stover	34	39	87.2	37	37

Punting

Player	NO.	AVG	NET AVG	TB	IN 20	LG	BLK
Dave Zastudil	89	41.0	35.2	8	21	67	0

Interceptions Ed Reed, 7

Sacks Terrell Suggs, 12

BUFFALO BILLS

Passing

Player	ATT	COMP	YDS	PCT COMP	YDS/ATT	TD	INT	Rating
Drew Bledsoe	471	274	2,860	58.2	6.1	11	12	73.0

Rushing

Player	NO.	YDS	AVG	LG	TD
Travis Henry	331	1,356	4.1	64	10
Joe Burns	39	113	2.9	12	0
Sammy Morris	19	70	3.7	12	1
Josh Reed	3	38	12.7	16	0
Drew Bledsoe	24	29	1.2	11	2

Receiving

Player	NO.	YDS	AVG	LG	TD
Eric Moulds	64	780	12.2	49	1
Bobby Shaw	56	732	13.1	54	4
Josh Reed	58	588	10.1	26	2
Mark Campbell	34	339	10.0	31	1
Travis Henry	28	158	5.6	18	1
Sammy Morris	14	100	7.1	24	0
Sam Gash	11	83	7.5	18	0
Dave Moore	7	82	11.7	28	2

Kicking

Player	FGM	FGA	PCT COMP	XPM	XPA
Rian Lindell	17	24	71.0	24	24

Punting

Player	NO.	AVG	NET AVG	TB	IN 20	LG	BLK
Brian Moorman	85	44.6	37.1	3	20	71	0

Interceptions Nate Clements, 3

Sacks Aaron Schobel, 11.5

KEY ATT=attempts; COMP=completions; YDS=yards; PCT COMP=completion percentage; YDS/ATT=yards per attempt; TD=touchdowns; INT=interceptions; NO.=number; AVG=average; LG=long; FGM=field goals made; FGA-field goals attempted; XPM=extra points made; XPA=extra points attempted; NET AVG=net average; TB=touchbacks; IN 20=inside 20-yard line; BLK=blocked

CINCINNATI BENGALS

Passing

Player	ATT	COMP	YDS	PCT COMP	YDS/ATT	TD	INT	Rating
Jon Kitna	520	324	3,591	62.3	6.9	26	15	87.4

Rushing

Player	NO.	YDS	AVG	LG	TD
Rudi Johnson	215	957	4.5	54	9
Corey Dillon	138	541	3.9	39	2
Brandon Bennett	56	173	3.1	19	0
Peter Warrick	18	157	8.7	50	0
Jon Kitna	38	113	3.0	15	0
Jeremi Johnson	15	41	2.7	12	1

Receiving

Player	NO.	YDS	AVG	LG	TD
Chad Johnson	90	1,355	15.1	82	10
Peter Warrick	79	819	10.4	77	7
Matt Schobel	24	332	13.8	45	2
Kelley Washington	22	299	13.6	51	4
Tony Stewart	21	212	10.1	21	0
Brandon Bennett	25	176	7.0	16	1
Rudi Johnson	21	146	7.0	17	0

Kicking

Player	FGM	FGA	PCT COMP	XPM	XPA
Shayne Graham	22	25	88.0	40	40

Punting

Player	NO.	AVG	NET AVG	TB	IN 20	LG	BLK
Kyle Richardson	49	40.0	33.5	5	9	58	0
Nick Harris	28	38.7	30.0	3	5	53	0

Interceptions Tory James, 4

Sacks Duane Clemons, John Thornton, 6

CLEVELAND BROWNS

Passing

Player	ATT	COMP	YDS	PCT COMP	YDS/ATT	TD	INT	Rating
Kelly Holcomb	302	193	1,797	63.9	6.0	10	12	74.6
Tim Couch	203	120	1,319	59.1	6.5	7	6	77.6

Rushing

Player	NO.	YDS	AVG	LG	TD
William Green	142	559	3.9	26	1
James Jackson	102	382	3.7	18	3
Lee Suggs	56	289	5.2	78	2
Jamel White	70	266	3.8	23	1
Dennis Northcutt	12	83	6.9	23	0
Tim Couch	11	39	3.5	17	1

Receiving

Player	NO.	YDS	AVG	LG	TD
Dennis Northcutt	62	729	11.8	44	2
Andre Davis	40	576	14.4	49	5
Quincy Morgan	38	516	13.6	71	3
Kevin Johnson	41	381	9.3	41	2
Jamel White	46	303	6.6	22	1
Steve Heiden	18	134	7.4	17	0
James Jackson	14	114	8.1	18	0
Darnell Sanders	15	95	6.3	12	1

Kicking

Player	FGM	FGA	PCT COMP	XPM	XPA
Phil Dawson	18	21	86.0	20	21

Punting

Player	NO.	AVG	NET AVG	TB	IN 20	LG	BLK
Chris Gardocki	72	41.9	34.8	10	18	60	0

Interceptions Earl Little, 6

Sacks Kenard Lang, 8

DENVER BRONCOS

Passing

Player	ATT	COMP	YDS	PCT COMP	YDS/ATT	TD	INT	Rating
Jake Plummer	302	189	2,182	62.6	7.2	15	7	91.2
Danny Kanell	103	53	442	51.5	4.3	2	5	49.1

Rushing

Player	NO.	YDS	AVG	LG	TD
Clinton Portis	290	1,591	5.5	65	14
Quentin Griffin	94	345	3.7	23	0
Mike Anderson	70	257	3.7	44	3
Jake Plummer	37	205	5.5	40	3
Rod Smith	10	98	9.8	26	0

Receiving

Player	NO.	YDS	AVG	LG	TD
Rod Smith	74	845	11.4	38	3
Shannon Sharpe	62	770	12.4	28	8
Ashley Lelie	37	628	17.0	60	2
Clinton Portis	38	314	8.3	72	0
Ed McCaffrey	19	195	10.3	23	0
Reuben Droughns	9	87	9.7	15	2
Quentin Griffin	8	61	7.6	24	0
Mike Anderson	12	53	4.4	18	2
Dwayne Carswell	6	53	8.8	19	1

Kicking

Player	FGM	FGA	PCT COMP	XPM	XPA
Jason Elam	27	31	87.1	39	39

Punting

Player	NO.	AVG	NET AVG	TB	IN 20	LG	BLK
Micah Knorr	68	43.2	32.2	6	14	62	0

Interceptions Kelly Herndon, 3

Sacks Bertrand Berry, 11.5

HOUSTON TEXANS

Passing

Player	ATT	COMP	YDS	PCT COMP	YDS/ATT	TD	INT	Rating
David Carr	295	167	2,013	56.6	6.8	9	13	69.5
Tony Banks	102	61	693	59.8	6.8	5	3	84.3

Rushing

Player	NO.	YDS	AVG	LG	TD
Domanick Davis	238	1,031	4.3	51	8
Stacey Mack	93	253	2.7	13	4
David Carr	27	151	5.6	36	2
Tony Hollings	38	102	2.7	17	0

Receiving

Player	NO.	YDS	AVG	LG	TD
Andre Johnson	66	976	14.8	46	4
Corey Bradford	24	460	19.2	78	4
Jabar Gaffney	34	402	11.8	33	2
Billy Miller	40	355	8.9	25	3
Domanick Davis	47	351	7.5	17	0

Kicking

Player	FGM	FGA	PCT COMP	XPM	XPA
Kris Brown	18	22	81.8	27	27

Punting

Player	NO.	AVG	NET AVG	TB	IN 20	LG	BLK
Chad Stanley	97	41.5	36.7	3	36	58	0

Interceptions Marcus Coleman, 7

Sacks Jamie Sharper, 4

INDIANAPOLIS COLTS

Passing

Player	ATT	COMP	YDS	PCT COMP	YDS/ATT	TD	INT	Rating
Peyton Manning	566	379	4,267	67.0	7.5	29	10	99.0

Rushing

Player	NO.	YDS	AVG	LG	TD
Edgerrin James	310	1,259	4.1	43	11
Dominic Rhodes	37	157	4.2	25	0
Ricky Williams	48	155	3.2	19	2
James Mungro	24	60	2.5	9	2

Receiving

Player	NO.	YDS	AVG	LG	TD
Marvin Harrison	94	1,272	13.5	79	10
Reggie Wayne	68	838	12.3	57	7
Marcus Pollard	40	541	13.5	70	3
Troy Walters	36	456	12.7	46	3
Dallas Clark	29	340	11.7	42	1
Edgerrin James	51	292	5.7	17	0
Brandon Stokley	22	211	9.6	37	3
Ricky Williams	22	157	7.1	17	1

Kicking

Player	FGM	FGA	PCT COMP	XPM	XPA
Mike Vanderjagt	37	37	100.0	46	46

Punting

Player	NO.	AVG	NET AVG	TB	IN 20	LG	BLK
Hunter Smith	62	42.2	35.5	3	20	55	0

Interceptions Nicholas Harper, 4

Sacks Dwight Freeney, 11

JACKSONVILLE JAGUARS

Passing

Player	ATT	COMP	YDS	PCT COMP	YDS/ATT	TD	INT	Rating
Byron Leftwich	418	239	2,819	57.2	6.7	14	16	73.0
Mark Brunell	82	54	484	65.9	5.9	2	0	89.7

Rushing

Player	NO.	YDS	AVG	LG	TD
Fred Taylor	345	1,572	4.6	62	6
LaBrandon Toefield	53	212	4.0	30	2
Chris Fuamatu-Ma'afala	35	144	4.1	18	1
Byron Leftwich	25	108	4.3	18	2
Mark Brunell	8	19	2.4	12	1
Marc Edwards	7	13	1.9	3	1

Receiving

Player	NO.	YDS	AVG	LG	TD
Jimmy Smith	54	805	14.9	67	4
Troy Edwards	35	487	13.9	84	3
Fred Taylor	48	370	7.7	60	1
Kyle Brady	29	281	9.7	26	1
Kevin Johnson	17	253	14.9	28	1
Marc Edwards	31	226	7.3	32	0
Matthew Hatchette	15	203	13.5	45	2

Kicking

Player	FGM	FGA	PCT COMP	XPM	XPA
Seth Marler	20	33	60.6	30	30

Punting

Player	NO.	AVG	NET AVG	TB	IN 20	LG	BLK
Mark Royals	45	41.2	34.8	5	9	51	0

Interceptions Mike Peterson, 3

Sacks Tony Brackens, 6

KANSAS CITY CHIEFS

Passing

Player	ATT	COMP	YDS	PCT COMP	YDS/ATT	TD	INT	Rating
Trent Green	523	330	4,039	63.1	7.7	24	12	92.6

Rushing

Player	NO.	YDS	AVG	LG	TD
Priest Holmes	320	1,420	4.4	31	27
Derrick Blaylock	22	112	5.1	25	2
Johnnie Morton	8	94	11.8	39	0
Larry Johnson	20	85	4.3	15	1
Trent Green	26	83	3.2	14	2

Receiving

Player	NO.	YDS	AVG	LG	TD
Tony Gonzalez	71	916	12.9	67	10
Eddie Kennison	56	853	15.2	51	5
Johnnie Morton	50	740	14.8	50	4
Priest Holmes	74	690	9.3	36	0
Dante Hall	40	423	10.6	67	1
Derrick Blaylock	15	181	12.1	63	1

Kicking

Player	FGM	FGA	PCT COMP	XPM	XPA
Morten Andersen	16	20	80.0	58	59

Punting

Player	NO.	AVG	NET AVG	TB	IN 20	LG	BLK
Jason Baker	80	39.5	33.2	7	21	68	0

Interceptions Greg Wesley, Dexter McCleon, 6

Sacks Vonnie Holliday, 5.5

MIAMI DOLPHINS

Passing

Player	ATT	COMP	YDS	PCT COMP	YDS/ATT	TD	INT	Rating
Jay Fiedler	314	179	2,138	57.0	6.8	11	13	72.4
Brian Griese	130	74	813	56.9	6.3	5	6	69.2

Rushing

Player	NO.	YDS	AVG	LG	TD
Ricky Williams	392	1,372	3.5	45	9
Travis Minor	41	193	4.7	26	1
Jay Fiedler	34	88	2.6	14	3
James McKnight	2	75	37.5	68	1

Receiving

Player	NO.	YDS	AVG	LG	TD
Chris Chambers	64	963	15.0	57	11
Randy McMichael	49	598	12.2	46	2
Derrius Thompson	26	359	13.8	31	0
Ricky Williams	50	351	7.0	59	1
James McKnight	23	285	12.4	80	2

Kicking

Player	FGM	FGA	PCT COMP	XPM	XPA
Olindo Mare	22	29	75.8	33	34

Punting

Player	NO.	AVG	NET AVG	TB	IN 20	LG	BLK
Matt Turk	68	38.7	34.5	7	23	57	0

Interceptions Patrick Surtain, 7

Sacks Adewale Ogunleye, 15

NEW ENGLAND PATRIOTS

Passing

Player	ATT	COMP	YDS	PCT COMP	YDS/ATT	TD	INT	Rating
Tom Brady	527	317	3,620	60.2	6.9	23	12	85.9

Rushing

Player	NO.	YDS	AVG	LG	TD
Antowain Smith	182	642	3.5	30	3
Kevin Faulk	178	638	3.6	23	0
Mike Cloud	27	118	4.4	42	5
Larry Centers	21	82	3.9	13	0
Tom Brady	42	63	1.5	11	1

Receiving

Player	NO.	YDS	AVG	LG	TD
Deion Branch	57	803	14.1	66	3
David Givens	34	510	15.0	57	6
Troy Brown	40	472	11.8	82	4
Kevin Faulk	48	440	9.2	27	0
Daniel Graham	38	409	10.8	38	4
Christian Fauria	28	285	10.2	28	2
Bethel Johnson	16	209	13.1	45	2
Larry Centers	19	106	5.6	14	1

Kicking

Player	FGM	FGA	PCT COMP	XPM	XPA
Adam Vinatieri	25	34	73.5	37	38

Punting

Player	NO.	AVG	NET AVG	TB	IN 20	LG	BLK
Ken Walter	76	37.7	33.6	3	25	52	0

Interceptions Ty Law, Tyrone Poole, 6

Sacks Mike Vrabel, 9.5

NEW YORK JETS

Passing

Player	ATT	COMP	YDS	PCT COMP	YDS/ATT	TD	INT	Rating
Chad Pennington	297	189	2,139	63.6	7.2	13	12	82.9
Vinny Testaverde	198	123	1,385	62.1	7.0	7	2	90.6

Rushing

Player	NO.	YDS	AVG	LG	TD
Curtis Martin	323	1,308	4.0	56	2
LaMont Jordan	46	190	4.1	39	4
Santana Moss	10	67	6.7	25	0
Chad Pennington	21	42	2.0	10	2

Receiving

Player	NO.	YDS	AVG	LG	TD
Santana Moss	74	1,105	14.9	65	10
Curtis Conway	46	640	13.9	45	2
Jerald Sowell	47	436	9.3	44	1
Anthony Becht	40	356	8.9	29	4
Wayne Chrebet	27	289	10.7	29	1
Curtis Martin	42	262	6.2	29	0

Kicking

Player	FGM	FGA	PCT COMP	XPM	XPA
Doug Brien	27	32	84.3	24	24

Punting

Player	NO.	AVG	NET AVG	TB	IN 20	LG	BLK
Dan Stryzinski	71	37.4	31.3	4	22	55	0

Interceptions Aaron Beasley, 3

Sacks Shaun Ellis, 12.5

OAKLAND RAIDERS

Passing

Player	ATT	COMP	YDS	PCT COMP	YDS/ATT	TD	INT	Rating
Rich Gannon	225	125	1,274	55.6	5.7	6	4	73.5
Rick Mirer	221	116	1,267	52.5	5.7	3	5	64.8

Rushing

Player	NO.	YDS	AVG	LG	TD
Tyrone Wheatley	159	678	4.3	41	4
Charlie Garner	120	553	4.6	33	3
Justin Fargas	40	203	5.1	53	0
Zack Crockett	48	145	3.0	44	7
Rick Mirer	20	83	4.2	20	1

Receiving

Player	NO.	YDS	AVG	LG	TD
Jerry Rice	63	869	13.8	47	2
Tim Brown	52	567	10.9	36	2
Charlie Garner	48	386	8.0	46	1
Jerry Porter	28	361	12.9	35	1
Doug Jolley	31	250	8.1	26	1
Teyo Johnson	14	128	9.1	21	1
Tyrone Wheatley	12	120	10.0	25	0

Kicking

Player	FGM	FGA	PCT COMP	XPM	XPA
Sebastian Janikowski	22	25	88.0	28	29

Punting

Player	NO.	AVG	NET AVG	TB	IN 20	LG	BLK
Shane Lechler	96	46.9	37.2	13	27	73	0

Interceptions Phillip Buchanon, 6

Sacks Rod Coleman, 5.5

PITTSBURGH STEELERS

Passing

Player	ATT	COMP	YDS	PCT COMP	YDS/ATT	TD	INT	Rating
Tommy Maddox	519	298	3,414	57.4	6.6	18	17	75.3

Rushing

Player	NO.	YDS	AVG	LG	TD
Jerome Bettis	246	811	3.3	21	7
Amos Zereoue	132	433	3.3	22	2

Receiving

Player	NO.	YDS	AVG	LG	TD
Hines Ward	95	1,163	12.2	50	10
Plaxico Burress	60	860	14.3	47	4
Antwaan Randle El	37	364	9.8	32	1
Amos Zereoue	40	310	7.8	29	0
Chris Doering	18	240	13.3	53	1
Jay Riemersma	10	138	13.8	24	1
Jerame Tuman	12	113	9.4	23	0

Kicking

Player	FGM	FGA	PCT COMP	XPM	XPA
Jeff Reed	23	32	71.8	31	32

Punting

Player	NO.	AVG	NET AVG	TB	IN 20	LG	BLK
Josh Miller	84	41.9	36.0	8	27	72	0

Interceptions Brent Alexander, 4

Sacks Kimo von Oelhoffen, 8

SAN DIEGO CHARGERS

Passing

Player	ATT	COMP	YDS	PCT COMP	YDS/ATT	TD	INT	Rating
Drew Brees	356	205	2,108	57.6	5.9	11	15	67.5
Doug Flutie	167	91	1,097	54.5	6.6	9	4	82.8

Rushing

Player	NO.	YDS	AVG	LG	TD
LaDainian Tomlinson	313	1,645	5.3	73	13
Doug Flutie	33	168	5.1	17	2
Tim Dwight	9	88	9.8	20	0
Drew Brees	21	84	4.0	18	0
Lorenzo Neal	18	40	2.2	7	1

Receiving

Player	NO.	YDS	AVG	LG	TD
David Boston	70	880	12.6	46	7
LaDainian Tomlinson	100	725	7.3	73	4
Antonio Gates	24	389	16.2	48	2
Kassim Osgood	13	278	21.4	57	2
Eric Parker	18	244	13.6	33	3
Tim Dwight	14	193	13.8	32	0
Justin Peelle	16	133	8.3	24	1

Kicking

Player	FGM	FGA	PCT COMP	XPM	XPA
Steve Christie	15	20	75.0	36	36

Punting

Player	NO.	AVG	NET AVG	TB	IN 20	LG	BLK
Darren Bennett	82	41.9	36.2	3	28	56	0

Interceptions Quentin Jammer, 4

Sacks DeQuincy Scott, 6.5

TENNESSEE TITANS

Passing

Player	ATT	COMP	YDS	PCT COMP	YDS/ATT	TD	INT	Rating
Steve McNair	400	250	3,215	62.5	8.0	24	7	100.4
Billy Bolek	69	44	545	63.8	7.9	4	1	101.4

Rushing

Player	NO.	YDS	AVG	LG	TD
Eddie George	312	1,031	3.3	27	5
Chris Brown	56	221	3.9	28	0
Robert Holcombe	63	201	3.2	21	1
Steve McNair	38	138	3.6	23	4

Receiving

Player	NO.	YDS	AVG	LG	TD
Derrick Mason	95	1,303	13.7	50	8
Justin McCareins	47	813	17.3	73	7
Drew Bennett	32	504	15.8	48	4
Erron Kinney	41	381	9.3	28	3
Tyrone Calico	18	297	16.5	45	4
Frank Wycheck	17	165	9.7	25	2
Eddie George	22	163	7.4	22	0

Kicking

Player	FGM	FGA	PCT COMP	XPM	XPA
Gary Anderson	27	31	87.0	42	42
Craig Hentrich	4	5	80.0	1	1

Punting

Player	NO.	AVG	NET AVG	TB	IN 20	LG	BLK
Craig Hentrich	71	43.9	37.8	8	26	58	0

Interceptions Samari Rolle, 6

Sacks Jevon Kearse, 9.5

TEAM-BY-TEAM STATS—NFC

ARIZONA CARDINALS

Passing

Player	ATT	COMP	YDS	PCT COMP	YDS/ATT	TD	INT	Rating
Jeff Blake	367	208	2,247	56.7	6.1	13	15	69.6
Josh McCown	166	95	1,018	57.2	6.1	5	6	70.3

Rushing

Player	NO.	YDS	AVG	LG	TD
Marcel Shipp	228	830	3.6	36	0
Emmitt Smith	90	256	2.8	22	2
Jeff Blake	30	177	5.9	19	2
Josh McCown	28	158	5.6	16	1

Receiving

Player	NO.	YDS	AVG	LG	TD
Anquan Boldin	101	1,377	13.6	71	8
Freddie Jones	55	517	9.4	34	3
Bryant Johnson	35	438	12.5	54	1
Bryan Gilmore	17	208	12.2	32	2
Marcel Shipp	30	184	6.1	34	0
Nate Poole	13	177	13.6	37	1
Emmitt Smith	14	107	7.6	36	0

Kicking

Player	FGM	FGA	PCT COMP	XPM	XPA
Neil Rackers	9	12	75.0	8	8
Tim Duncan	6	10	60.0	5	6
Bill Gramatica	3	4	75.0	6	6

Punting

Player	NO.	AVG	NET AVG	TB	IN 20	LG	BLK
Scott Player	82	42.8	34.4	9	19	64	0

Interceptions Dexter Jackson, 6

Sacks Raynoch Thompson, Dennis Johnson, 3

ATLANTA FALCONS

Passing

Player	ATT	COMP	YDS	PCT COMP	YDS/ATT	TD	INT	Rating
Doug Johnson	243	136	1,655	56.0	6.8	8	12	67.5
Michael Vick	100	50	585	50.0	5.8	4	3	69.0
Kurt Kittner	114	44	391	38.6	3.4	2	6	32.5

Rushing

Player	NO.	YDS	AVG	LG	TD
T.J. Duckett	197	779	4.0	55	11
Warrick Dunn	125	672	5.4	69	3
Michael Vick	40	255	6.4	43	1
Justin Griffith	38	168	4.4	15	0

Receiving

Player	NO.	YDS	AVG	LG	TD
Peerless Price	64	838	13.1	49	3
Alge Crumpler	44	552	12.5	63	3
Brian Finneran	26	368	14.2	38	2
Warrick Dunn	37	336	9.1	86	2
Justin Griffith	21	122	5.8	24	2

Kicking

Player	FGM	FGA	PCT COMP	XPM	XPA
Jay Feely	19	27	70.3	32	33

Punting

Player	NO.	AVG	NET AVG	TB	IN 20	LG	BLK
Chris Mohr	87	39.9	36.0	2	19	54	0

Interceptions Juran Bolden, Keion Carpenter, Tod McBride, 3 **Sacks** Ellis Johnson, 8

CAROLINA PANTHERS

Passing

Player	ATT	COMP	YDS	PCT COMP	YDS/ATT	TD	INT	Rating
Jake Delhomme	449	266	3,219	59.2	7.2	19	16	80.6

Rushing

Player	NO.	YDS	AVG	LG	TD
Stephen Davis	318	1,444	4.5	40	8
DeShaun Foster	113	429	3.8	21	0

Receiving

Player	NO.	YDS	AVG	LG	TD
Steve Smith	88	1,110	12.6	67	7
Muhsin Muhammad	54	837	15.5	60	3
Ricky Proehl	27	389	14.4	66	4
DeShaun Foster	26	207	8.0	47	2
Kris Mangum	17	199	11.7	34	0
Stephen Davis	14	159	11.4	25	0

Kicking

Player	FGM	FGA	PCT COMP	XPM	XPA
John Kasay	32	38	84.2	29	30

Punting

Player	NO.	AVG	NET AVG	TB	IN 20	LG	BLK
Todd Sauerbrun	77	44.6	35.6	9	22	64	0

Interceptions Deon Grant, Ricky Manning, Mike Minter, 3 **Sacks** Mike Rucker, 12

CHICAGO BEARS

Passing

Player	ATT	COMP	YDS	PCT COMP	YDS/ATT	TD	INT	Rating
Kordell Stewart	251	126	1,418	50.2	5.6	7	12	56.8
Chris Chandler	192	107	1,050	55.7	5.5	3	7	61.3

Rushing

Player	NO.	YDS	AVG	LG	TD
Anthony Thomas	244	1,024	4.2	67	6
Kordell Stewart	59	290	4.9	25	3
Brock Forsey	50	191	3.8	17	2
Stanley Pritchett	21	93	4.4	18	2

Receiving

Player	NO.	YDS	AVG	LG	TD
Marty Booker	52	715	13.8	61	4
Dez White	49	583	11.9	49	3
Desmond Clark	44	433	9.8	31	2
David Terrell	43	361	8.4	35	1
Justin Gage	17	338	19.9	57	2
Bobby Wade	12	137	11.4	24	0
Stanley Pritchett	18	83	4.6	20	0

Kicking

Player	FGM	FGA	PCT COMP	XPM	XPA
Paul Edinger	26	36	72.2	27	27

Punting

Player	NO.	AVG	NET AVG	TB	IN 20	LG	BLK
Brad Maynard	79	41.2	34.6	9	23	53	0

Interceptions Charles Tillman, Jerry Azumah, 4 **Sacks** Alex Brown, 5.5

DALLAS COWBOYS

Passing

Player	ATT	COMP	YDS	PCT COMP	YDS/ATT	TD	INT	Rating
Quincy Carter	505	292	3,302	57.8	6.5	17	21	71.4

Rushing

Player	NO.	YDS	AVG	LG	TD
Troy Hambrick	275	972	3.5	42	5
Richie Anderson	70	306	4.4	19	1
Quincy Carter	68	257	3.8	19	2
Aveion Cason	40	220	5.5	63	2
Adrian Murrell	28	107	3.8	17	0

Receiving

Player	NO.	YDS	AVG	LG	TD
Terry Glenn	52	754	14.5	51	5
Joey Galloway	34	672	19.8	64	2
Antonio Bryant	39	550	14.1	54	2
Richie Anderson	69	493	7.1	37	4
Jason Witten	35	347	9.9	36	1
Dan Campbell	20	195	9.8	23	1

Kicking

Player	FGM	FGA	PCT COMP	XPM	XPA
Billy Cundiff	23	29	79.3	30	31

Punting

Player	NO.	AVG	NET AVG	TB	IN 20	LG	BLK
Toby Gowin	94	39.0	34.9	8	25	59	0

Interceptions Terence Newman, 4

Sacks Greg Ellis, 8

DETROIT LIONS

Passing

Player	ATT	COMP	YDS	PCT COMP	YDS/ATT	TD	INT	Rating
Joey Harrington	554	309	2,880	55.8	5.2	17	22	63.9

Rushing

Player	NO.	YDS	AVG	LG	TD
Shawn Bryson	158	606	3.8	39	3
Olandis Gary	113	384	3.4	27	2

Receiving

Player	NO.	YDS	AVG	LG	TD
Az-Zahir Hakim	49	449	9.2	28	4
Mikhael Ricks	37	434	11.7	38	2
Bill Schroeder	36	397	11.0	26	2
Shawn Bryson	54	340	6.3	26	0
Scotty Anderson	17	325	19.1	72	2
Cory Schlesinger	34	247	7.3	33	2
Charles Rogers	22	243	11.0	33	3
Casey Fitzsimmons	23	160	7.0	22	2

Kicking

Player	FGM	FGA	PCT COMP	XPM	XPA
John Hanson	22	23	95.6	26	27

Punting

Player	NO.	AVG	NET AVG	TB	IN 20	LG	BLK
Nick Harris	63	40.2	33.1	5	11	51	0

Interceptions Dre' Bly, 6

Sacks James Hall, Robert Porcher, 4.5

GREEN BAY PACKERS

Passing

Player	ATT	COMP	YDS	PCT COMP	YDS/ATT	TD	INT	Rating
Brett Favre	471	308	3,361	65.4	7.1	32	21	90.4

Rushing

Player	NO.	YDS	AVG	LG	TD
Ahman Green	355	1,883	5.3	98	15
Najeh Davenport	77	420	5.5	76	2
Tony Fisher	40	200	5.0	19	1

Receiving

Player	NO.	YDS	AVG	LG	TD
Javon Walker	41	716	17.5	66	9
Donald Driver	52	621	11.9	41	2
Robert Ferguson	38	520	13.7	47	4
Ahman Green	50	367	7.3	27	5
Bubba Franks	30	241	8.0	24	4
Wesley Walls	20	222	11.1	36	1
William Henderson	24	214	8.9	22	3
Tony Fisher	21	206	9.8	32	2

Kicking

Player	FGM	FGA	PCT COMP	XPM	XPA
Ryan Longwell	23	26	88.4	51	51

Punting

Player	NO.	AVG	NET AVG	TB	IN 20	LG	BLK
Josh Bidwell	69	41.7	35.1	7	16	60	0

Interceptions Darren Sharper, 5

Sacks Kabeer Gbaja-Biamila, 10

MINNESOTA VIKINGS

Passing

Player	ATT	COMP	YDS	PCT COMP	YDS/ATT	TD	INT	Rating
Daunte Culpepper	454	295	3,479	65.0	7.7	25	11	96.4
Gus Frerotte	65	38	690	58.5	10.6	7	2	118.1

Rushing

Player	NO.	YDS	AVG	LG	TD
Moe Williams	174	745	4.3	61	5
Onterrio Smith	107	579	5.4	47	5
Michael Bennett	90	447	5.0	28	1
Daunte Culpepper	73	422	5.8	42	4

Receiving

Player	NO.	YDS	AVG	LG	TD
Randy Moss	111	1,632	14.7	72	17
Moe Williams	65	644	9.9	42	3
Kelly Campbell	25	522	20.9	72	4
Nate Burleson	29	455	15.7	52	2
Jimmy Kleinsasser	46	401	8.7	19	4
D'Wayne Bates	15	151	10.1	18	1

Kicking

Player	FGM	FGA	PCT COMP	XPM	XPA
Aaron Elling	18	25	72.0	48	48

Punting

Player	NO.	AVG	NET AVG	TB	IN 20	LG	BLK
Eddie Johnson	56	39.1	32.6	5	12	55	0

Interceptions Brian Russell, 9

Sacks Kevin Williams, 10.5

NEW ORLEANS SAINTS

Passing

Player	ATT	COMP	YDS	PCT COMP	YDS/ATT	TD	INT	Rating
Aaron Brooks	518	306	3,546	59.1	6.8	24	8	88.8

Rushing

Player	NO.	YDS	AVG	LG	TD
Deuce McAllister	351	1,641	4.7	76	8
Aaron Brooks	54	175	3.2	15	2
Ki-Jana Carter	19	72	3.8	31	1

Receiving

Player	NO.	YDS	AVG	LG	TD
Joe Horn	78	973	12.5	50	10
Jerome Pathon	44	578	13.1	40	4
Deuce McAllister	69	516	7.5	39	0
Donte' Stallworth	25	485	19.4	76	3
Boo Williams	41	436	10.6	31	5
Ernie Conwell	26	290	11.2	32	2
Michael Lewis	12	226	18.8	39	1

Kicking

Player	FGM	FGA	PCT COMP	XPM	XPA
John Carney	23	30	76.6	36	37

Punting

Player	NO.	AVG	NET AVG	TB	IN 20	LG	BLK
Mitch Berger	71	44.3	38.2	5	28	59	0

Interceptions Fred Thomas, 4

Sacks Charles Grant, 10

NEW YORK GIANTS

Passing

Player	ATT	COMP	YDS	PCT COMP	YDS/ATT	TD	INT	Rating
Kerry Collins	500	284	3,110	56.8	6.2	13	16	70.7
Jesse Palmer	116	60	532	51.7	4.6	3	4	58.5

Rushing

Player	NO.	YDS	AVG	LG	TD
Tiki Barber	278	1,216	4.4	27	2
Dorsey Levens	68	197	2.9	17	3

Receiving

Player	NO.	YDS	AVG	LG	TD
Amani Toomer	63	1,057	16.8	77	5
Ike Hilliard	60	608	10.1	38	6
Jeremy Shockey	48	535	11.1	46	2
Tiki Barber	69	461	6.7	36	1
Tim Carter	26	309	11.9	30	0
David Tyree	16	211	13.2	48	0
Marcellus Rivers	17	155	9.1	27	0

Kicking

Player	FGM	FGA	PCT COMP	XPM	XPA
Matt Bryant	11	14	78.5	17	17
Brett Conway	9	12	75.0	6	6

Punting

Player	NO.	AVG	NET AVG	TB	IN 20	LG	BLK
Jeff Feagles	90	40.5	33.9	6	31	59	0

Interceptions Ralph Brown, Johnnie Harris, Frank Walker, Will Allen, 2

Sacks Michael Strahan, 18.5

PHILADELPHIA EAGLES

Passing

Player	ATT	COMP	YDS	PCT COMP	YDS/ATT	TD	INT	Rating
Donovan McNabb	478	275	3,216	57.5	6.7	16	11	79.6

Rushing

Player	NO.	YDS	AVG	LG	TD
Brian Westbrook	117	613	5.2	62	7
Correll Buckhalter	126	542	4.3	64	8
Duce Staley	96	463	4.8	22	5
Donovan McNabb	71	355	5.0	34	3

Receiving

Player	NO.	YDS	AVG	LG	TD
Todd Pinkston	36	575	16.0	59	2
James Thrash	49	558	11.4	51	1
Freddie Mitchell	35	498	14.2	39	2
Duce Staley	36	382	10.6	52	2
Brian Westbrook	37	332	9.0	38	4
L.J. Smith	27	321	11.9	36	1
Chad Lewis	23	293	12.7	29	1
Correll Buckhalter	10	133	13.3	27	1

Kicking

Player	FGM	FGA	PCT COMP	XPM	XPA
David Akers	24	29	82.7	42	42

Punting

Player	NO.	AVG	NET AVG	TB	IN 20	LG	BLK
Dirk Johnson	79	40.6	34.6	10	27	60	0

Interceptions Michael Lewis, Troy Vincent, 3

Sacks Corey Simon, 7.5

SAN FRANCISCO 49ERS

Passing

Player	ATT	COMP	YDS	PCT COMP	YDS/ATT	TD	INT	Rating
Jeff Garcia	392	225	2,704	57.4	6.9	18	13	80.1
Tim Rattay	118	73	856	61.9	7.3	7	2	96.6

Rushing

Player	NO.	YDS	AVG	LG	TD
Kevan Barlow	201	1,024	5.1	78	6
Garrison Hearst	178	768	4.3	36	3
Jeff Garcia	56	319	5.7	21	7
Jamal Robertson	32	136	4.3	23	0

Receiving

Player	NO.	YDS	AVG	LG	TD
Terrell Owens	80	1,102	13.8	75	9
Tai Streets	47	595	12.7	41	7
Jed Weaver	35	437	12.5	30	1
Cedrick Wilson	35	396	11.3	29	2
Kevan Barlow	35	307	8.8	48	1
Brandon Lloyd	14	212	15.1	44	2
Garrison Hearst	25	211	8.4	26	1
Fred Beasley	19	184	9.7	32	1
Aaron Walker	8	116	14.5	26	1

Kicking

Player	FGM	FGA	PCT COMP	XPM	XPA
Todd Peterson	12	15	80.0	22	23
Owen Pochman	8	15	53.3	9	10
Jeff Chandler	6	7	85.7	7	8

Punting

Player	NO.	AVG	NET AVG	TB	IN 20	LG	BLK
Bill Lafleur	68	38.7	33.5	3	17	56	0

Interceptions Tony Parrish, 9

Sacks Andre Carter, 6.5

SEATTLE SEAHAWKS

Passing

Player	ATT	COMP	YDS	PCT COMP	YDS/ATT	TD	INT	Rating
Matt Hasselbeck	513	313	3,841	61.0	7.5	26	15	88.8

Rushing

Player	NO.	YDS	AVG	LG	TD
Shaun Alexander	326	1,435	4.4	55	14
Maurice Morris	38	239	6.3	43	0
Mack Strong	37	174	4.7	21	1
Matt Hasselbeck	36	125	3.5	18	2

Receiving

Player	NO.	YDS	AVG	LG	TD
Darrell Jackson	68	1,137	16.7	80	9
Koren Robinson	65	896	13.8	38	4
Bobby Engram	52	637	12.3	34	6
Itula Mili	46	492	10.7	46	4
Shaun Alexander	42	295	7.0	22	2
Mack Strong	29	216	7.4	32	0

Kicking

Player	FGM	FGA	PCT COMP	XPM	XPA
Josh Brown	22	30	73.3	48	48

Punting

Player	NO.	AVG	NET AVG	TB	IN 20	LG	BLK
Tom Rouen	67	41.2	37.1	3	29	61	0

Interceptions Reggie Tongue, 4

Sacks Chike Okeafor, 8

ST. LOUIS RAMS

Passing

Player	ATT	COMP	YDS	PCT COMP	YDS/ATT	TD	INT	Rating
Marc Bulger	532	336	3,845	63.2	7.2	22	22	81.4
Kurt Warner	65	38	365	58.5	5.6	1	1	72.9

Rushing

Player	NO.	YDS	AVG	LG	TD
Marshall Faulk	209	818	3.9	52	10
Lamar Gordon	71	298	4.2	20	1
Arlen Harris	85	255	3.0	18	4
Marc Bulger	29	75	2.6	28	4

Receiving

Player	NO.	YDS	AVG	LG	TD
Torry Holt	117	1,696	14.5	48	12
Isaac Bruce	69	981	14.2	41	5
Dane Looker	47	495	10.5	41	3
Marshall Faulk	45	290	6.4	30	1
Brandon Manumaleuna	29	238	8.2	39	2
Mike Furrey	20	189	9.5	24	0
Cameron Cleeland	10	145	14.5	29	0
Arlen Harris	15	102	6.8	26	0

Kicking

Player	FGM	FGA	PCT COMP	XPM	XPA
Jeff Wilkins	39	42	92.8	46	46

Punting

Player	NO.	AVG	NET AVG	TB	IN 20	LG	BLK
Sean Landeta	59	42.8	32.9	5	14	57	0

Interceptions Travis Fisher, Jerametrius Butler, Aeneas Williams, Tommy Polley, 4

Sacks Leonard Little, 12.5

TAMPA BAY BUCCANEERS

Passing

Player	ATT	COMP	YDS	PCT COMP	YDS/ATT	TD	INT	Rating
Brad Johnson	570	354	3,811	62.1	6.7	26	21	81.5

Rushing

Player	NO.	YDS	AVG	LG	TD
Michael Pittman	187	751	4.0	17	0
Thomas Jones	137	627	4.6	61	3
Aaron Stecker	37	125	3.4	15	0
Mike Alstott	27	77	2.9	29	2
Brad Johnson	25	33	1.3	13	0

Receiving

Player	NO.	YDS	AVG	LG	TD
Keenan McCardell	84	1,174	14.0	76	8
Keyshawn Johnson	45	600	13.3	39	3
Michael Pittman	75	597	8.0	68	2
Charles Lee	33	432	13.1	72	2
Ken Dilger	22	244	11.1	48	1
Thomas Jones	24	180	7.5	29	0
Jameel Cook	20	120	6.0	19	1
Joe Jurevicius	12	118	9.8	22	2

Kicking

Player	FGM	FGA	PCT COMP	XPM	XPA
Martin Gramatica	16	26	61.5	33	34

Punting

Player	NO.	AVG	NET AVG	TB	IN 20	LG	BLK
Tom Tupa	83	43.3	35.9	6	26	60	0

Interceptions Dwight Smith, 5

Sacks Simeon Rice, 15

WASHINGTON REDSKINS

Passing

Player	ATT	COMP	YDS	PCT COMP	YDS/ATT	TD	INT	Rating
Patrick Ramsey	337	179	2,166	53.1	6.4	14	9	75.8
Tim Hasselbeck	177	95	1,012	53.7	5.7	5	7	63.6

Rushing

Player	NO.	YDS	AVG	LG	TD
Trung Canidate	142	600	4.2	38	1
Rock Cartwright	107	411	3.8	22	4
Ladell Betts	77	255	3.3	13	2
Chad Morton	48	216	4.5	27	0
Patrick Ramsey	15	62	4.1	24	1

Receiving

Player	NO.	YDS	AVG	LG	TD
Laveranues Coles	82	1,204	14.7	64	6
Rod Gardner	59	600	10.2	35	5
Darnerien McCants	27	360	13.3	32	6
Chad Morton	15	187	12.5	36	1
Rock Cartwright	18	176	9.8	40	0
Patrick Johnson	15	170	11.3	31	1
Ladell Betts	15	167	11.1	34	0

Kicking

Player	FGM	FGA	PCT COMP	XPM	XPA
John Hall	25	33	75.7	26	27

Punting

Player	NO.	AVG	NET AVG	TB	IN 20	LG	BLK
Bryan Barker	84	40.2	34.3	5	24	69	0

Interceptions Fred Smoot, 4

Sacks Jessie Armstead, 6.5

Super Bowl Results

Super Bowl	Date	Winner	Loser	Score	Site	Attendance
XXXVIII	2-1-04	Patriots	Panthers	32–29	Houston, TX	71,525
XXXVII	1-26-03	Buccaneers	Raiders	48–21	San Diego, CA	67,603
XXXVI	2-3-02	Patriots	Rams	20–17	New Orleans, LA	72,922
XXXV	1-28-01	Ravens	Giants	34–7	Tampa, FL	71,921
XXXIV	1-30-00	Rams	Titans	23–16	Atlanta, GA	72,625
XXXIII	1-31-99	Broncos	Falcons	34–19	Miami, FL	74,803
XXXII	1-25-98	Broncos	Packers	31–24	San Diego, CA	68,912
XXXI	1-26-97	Packers	Patriots	35–21	New Orleans, LA	72,301
XXX	1-28-96	Cowboys	Steelers	27–17	Tempe, AZ	76,347
XXIX	1-29-95	49ers	Chargers	49–26	Miami, FL	74,107
XXVIII	1-30-94	Cowboys	Bills	30–13	Atlanta, GA	72,817
XXVII	1-31-93	Cowboys	Bills	52–17	Pasadena, CA	98,374
XXVI	1-26-92	Redskins	Bills	37–24	Minneapolis, MN	63,130
XXV	1-27-91	Giants	Bills	20–19	Tampa, FL	73,813
XXIV	1-28-90	49ers	Broncos	55–10	New Orleans, LA	72,919
XXIII	1-22-89	49ers	Bengals	20–16	Miami, FL	75,129
XXII	1-31-88	Redskins	Broncos	42–10	San Diego, CA	73,302
XXI	1-25-87	Giants	Broncos	39–20	Pasadena, CA	101,063
XX	1-26-86	Bears	Patriots	46–10	New Orleans, LA	73,818
XIX	1-20-85	49ers	Dolphins	38–16	Stanford, CA	84,059
XVIII	1-22-84	Raiders	Redskins	38–9	Tampa, FL	72,920
XVII	1-30-83	Redskins	Dolphins	27–17	Pasadena, CA	103,667
XVI	1-24-82	49ers	Bengals	26–21	Pontiac, MI	81,270
XV	1-25-81	Raiders	Eagles	27–10	New Orleans, LA	76,135
XIV	1-20-80	Steelers	Rams	31–19	Pasadena, CA	103,985
XIII	1-21-79	Steelers	Cowboys	35–31	Miami, FL	79,484
XII	1-15-78	Cowboys	Broncos	27–10	New Orleans, LA	76,400
XI	1-9-77	Raiders	Vikings	32–14	Pasadena, CA	103,438
X	1-18-76	Steelers	Cowboys	21–17	Miami, FL	80,187
IX	1-12-75	Steelers	Vikings	16–6	New Orleans, LA	80,997
VIII	1-13-74	Dolphins	Vikings	24–7	Houston, TX	71,882
VII	1-14-73	Dolphins	Redskins	14–7	Los Angeles, CA	90,182
VI	1-16-72	Cowboys	Dolphins	24–3	New Orleans, LA	81,023
V	1-17-71	Colts	Cowboys	16–13	Miami, FL	79,204
IV	1-11-70	Chiefs	Vikings	23–7	New Orleans, LA	80,562
III	1-12-69	Jets	Colts	16–7	Miami, FL	75,389
II	1-14-68	Packers	Raiders	33–14	Miami, FL	75,546
I	1-15-67	Packers	Chiefs	35–10	Los Angeles, CA	61,946

Super Bowl MVPs

Super Bowl	Player/Team	Position
XXXVIII	Tom Brady, Patriots	QB
XXXVII	Dexter Jackson, Buccaneers	S
XXXVI	Tom Brady, Patriots	QB
XXXV	Ray Lewis, Ravens	LB
XXXIV	Kurt Warner, Rams	QB
XXXIII	John Elway, Broncos	QB
XXXII	Terrell Davis, Broncos	RB
XXXI	Desmond Howard, Packers	KR
XXX	Larry Brown, Cowboys	DB
XXIX	Steve Young, 49ers	QB
XXVIII	Emmitt Smith, Cowboys	RB
XXVII	Troy Aikman, Cowboys	QB
XXVI	Mark Rypien, Redskins	QB
XXV	Ottis Anderson, Giants	RB
XXIV	Joe Montana, 49ers	QB
XXIII	Jerry Rice, 49ers	WR
XXII	Doug Williams, Redskins	QB
XXI	Phil Simms, Giants	QB
XX	Richard Dent, Bears	DE
XIX	Joe Montana, 49ers	QB

Super Bowl	Player/Team	Position
XVIII	Marcus Allen, Raiders	RB
XVII	John Riggins, Redskins	RB
XVI	Joe Montana, 49ers	QB
XV	Jim Plunkett, Raiders	QB
XIV	Terry Bradshaw, Steelers	QB
XIII	Terry Bradshaw, Steelers	QB
XII (tie)	Randy White, Cowboys	DT
	Harvey Martin, Cowboys	DE
XI	Fred Biletnikoff, Raiders	WR
X	Lynn Swann, Steelers	WR
IX	Franco Harris, Steelers	RB
VIII	Larry Csonka, Dolphins	RB
VII	Jake Scott, Dolphins	S
VI	Roger Staubach, Cowboys	QB
V	Chuck Howley, Cowboys	LB
IV	Len Dawson, Chiefs	QB
III	Joe Namath, Jets	QB
II	Bart Starr, Packers	QB
I	Bart Starr, Packers	QB

KEY QB=quarterback; S=safety; LB=linebacker; RB=running back; KR=kick returner; DB=defensive back; WR=wide receiver; DE=defensive end; DT=defensive tackle

2003-04 TIME LINE

August 16, 2003: Quarterback Michael Vick of the Atlanta Falcons breaks his right leg on a first-quarter scramble in a pre-season game against the Baltimore Ravens. Vick's injury sidelines him until November 30 and hurts Atlanta's playoff hopes.

August 23, 2003: Another star quarterback bites the dust in a pre-season game. Chad Pennington of the New York Jets is out of action until October 26 after dislocating and breaking his left wrist in a pre-season game against the New York Giants.

September 4, 2003: The 84th NFL season kicks off with a Thursday night game featuring the Washington Redskins at home against the New York Jets. The Redskins win, 16–13, on a 33-yard field goal with eight seconds left in the game.

September 7, 2003: Two-time Super Bowl champion head coach Bill Parcells returns to the sideline as head coach of the Dallas Cowboys after a three-year absence from coaching. The Cowboys lose to the Falcons, 27–13.

September 14, 2003: Running back Jamal Lewis of the Baltimore Ravens breaks Corey Dillon's single-game NFL rushing record by ripping up the Cleveland Browns for 295 yards on 30 carries.

October 5, 2003: Emmitt Smith, who set the NFL's career rushing record as a member of the Dallas Cowboys, returns to Dallas now playing for the Arizona Cardinals. Smith's day is cut short when he suffers a broken shoulder blade in the second quarter. The Cowboys win, 24–7.

November 16, 2003: The Kansas City Chiefs' bid for a perfect season ends at 9–0 when they lose to the Cincinnati Bengals, 24–19. Bengal wide receiver Chad Johnson had guaranteed his team would win the game.

December 28, 2003: Running back Priest Holmes of the Kansas City Chiefs breaks Emmitt Smith's NFL record of 25 rushing touchdowns in a season with his 26th and 27th. He also breaks Marshall Faulk's single-season record for total touchdowns in a season (26).

January 4, 2004: Quarterback Peyton Manning of the Indianapolis Colts wins his first career playoff game after throwing for 377 yards and five touchdowns. The Colts defeat the Denver Broncos, 41–10.

January 18, 2004: The New England Patriots defeat the Indianapolis Colts, 24–14, and the Carolina Panthers defeat the Philadelphia Eagles, 14–3, to advance to Super Bowl XXXVIII.

February 1, 2004: Adam Vinatieri's 41-yard field goal gives the Patriots a 32–29 victory over the Panthers in Super Bowl XXXVIII.

February 5, 2004: A federal judge rules the NFL policy that forbids players from entering the draft until three years after graduation from high school violates U.S. antitrust laws. The ruling states that the league must allow Ohio State running back Maurice Clarett to enter the 2004 draft. The league appeals the ruling.

April 19, 2004: An appeals court blocks Maurice Clarett and wide receiver Mike Williams of USC from entering the draft.

April 24, 2004: Quarterback Eli Manning of Mississippi is chosen by the San Diego Chargers as the first pick in the 2004 NFL Draft. He is later traded to the New York Giants.

May 24, 2004: An appeals court says that federal labor policy allows the NFL to set rules for when players can enter the league, effectively barring Maurice Clarett and wide receiver Mike Williams of USC from the NFL in 2004.

Visit www.sikids.com for the latest sports stats and info.

Barry Sanders, Detroit Lions

DAMIAN STROHMEYER/SPORTS ILLUSTRATED

All-time NFL Individual Statistical Leaders—Career Leaders

Scoring

Player	YRS	TD	FG	PAT	PTS
Gary Anderson	22	0	521	783	2,346
†Morten Andersen	21	0	502	753	2,259
George Blanda	26	9	335	942	2,002
Norm Johnson	18	0	366	638	1,736
Nick Lowery	18	0	383	562	1,711
Jan Stenerud	19	0	373	580	1,699
Eddie Murray	19	0	352	538	1,594
Al Del Greco	17	0	347	543	1,584
Pat Leahy	18	0	304	558	1,470
Jim Turner	16	1	304	521	1,439
†John Carney	16	4	343	404	1,433
Matt Bahr	17	0	300	522	1,422
Mark Moseley	16	0	300	482	1,382
Jim Bakken	17	0	282	534	1,380
†Steve Christie	14	0	314	435	1,377
Fred Cox	15	0	282	519	1,365
†Matt Stover	13	3	321	401	1,364
Lou Groza	17	1	234	641	1,349
†Jason Elam	11	5	288	449	1,313
Jim Breech	14	0	243	517	1,246

Rushing

Player	YRS	ATT	YDS	AVG	LG	TD
†Emmitt Smith	14	4,142	17,418	4.2	75	155
Walter Payton	13	3,838	16,726	4.4	76	110
Barry Sanders	10	3,062	15,269	5.0	85	99
Eric Dickerson	11	2,996	13,259	4.4	85	90
Tony Dorsett	12	2,936	12,739	4.3	99	77
†Jerome Bettis	11	3,119	12,353	4.0	71	69
Jim Brown	9	2,359	12,312	5.2	80	106
Marcus Allen	16	3,022	12,243	4.1	61	123
Franco Harris	13	2,949	12,120	4.1	75	91
Thurman Thomas	13	2,877	12,074	4.2	80	65
†Curtis Martin	9	2,927	11,669	4.0	70	73
John Riggins	14	2,916	11,352	3.9	66	104
†Marshall Faulk	10	2,576	11,213	4.4	71	97
Ricky Watters	12	2,622	10,643	4.1	57	78
O.J. Simpson	11	2,223	10,539	4.9	94	59
Ottis Anderson	14	2,562	10,273	4.0	76	81
†Eddie George	8	2,733	10,009	3.7	76	64
Earl Campbell	8	2,187	9,407	4.3	81	74
Terry Allen	11	2,152	8,614	4.0	55	73
Jim Taylor	10	1,941	8,597	4.4	84	83

Touchdowns

Player	YRS	RUSH	REC	RET	TD
†Jerry Rice	19	10	194	1	205
†Emmitt Smith	14	155	11	0	166
Marcus Allen	16	123	21	1	145
†Marshall Faulk	10	97	34	0	131
Cris Carter	16	0	130	1	131
Jim Brown	9	106	20	0	126
Walter Payton	13	110	15	0	125
John Riggins	14	104	12	0	116
Lenny Moore	12	63	48	2	113
Barry Sanders	10	99	10	0	109
Don Hutson	11	3	99	3	105
†Tim Brown	16	1	99	4	104
Steve Largent	14	1	100	0	101
Franco Harris	13	91	9	0	100
Eric Dickerson	11	90	6	0	96
Jim Taylor	10	83	10	0	93
Tony Dorsett	12	77	13	1	91
Bobby Mitchell	11	18	65	8	91
Ricky Watters	11	78	13	0	91

Passing—Efficiency*

Player	YRS	ATT	COMP	PCT COMP	YDS	AVG GAIN	TD	INT	Rating
†Kurt Warner	6	1,688	1,121	66.4	14,447	8.56	102	65	97.2
Steve Young	15	4,149	2,667	64.3	33,124	7.98	232	107	96.8
Joe Montana	15	5,391	3,409	63.2	40,551	7.52	273	139	92.3
†Jeff Garcia	5	2,360	1,449	61.4	16,408	6.95	113	56	88.3
†Daunte Culpepper	4	1,843	1,160	62.9	13,881	7.53	90	63	88.0
†Brett Favre	13	6,464	3,960	61.2	45,646	7.06	346	209	86.7
Dan Marino	17	8,358	4,967	59.4	61,361	7.34	420	252	86.4
†Trent Green	6	2,266	1,336	59.0	17,016	7.51	106	65	86.1
†Tom Brady	4	1,544	955	61.9	10,233	6.63	69	38	85.9
†Peyton Manning	6	3,383	2,128	62.9	24,885	7.35	167	110	85.9

Passing—Yards

Player	YRS	ATT	COMP	PCT COMP	YDS
Dan Marino	17	8,358	4,967	59.4	61,361
John Elway	16	7,250	4,123	56.9	51,475
Warren Moon	17	6,823	3,988	58.4	49,325
Fran Tarkenton	18	6,467	3,686	57.0	47,003
†Brett Favre	13	6,464	3,960	61.2	45,646
Dan Fouts	15	5,604	3,297	58.8	43,040
†Vinny Testaverde	17	5,925	3,334	56.3	40,943
Joe Montana	15	5,391	3,409	63.2	40,551
Johnny Unitas	18	5,186	2,830	54.6	40,239
Dave Krieg	19	5,311	3,105	58.5	38,147
Boomer Esiason	14	5,205	2,969	57.0	37,920
Jim Kelly	11	4,779	2,874	60.1	35,467

KEY YRS=years; TD=touchdowns; FG=field goals; PAT=extra points; PTS=points; ATT=attempts; AVG=average; LG=long; RUSH=rushing; REC=receiving; RET=returns; COMP=completions; PCT COMP=completion percentage; AVG GAIN=average gain; INT=interceptions; COMP YDS=completion yards

*1,500 or more attempts. The passer ratings are based on performance standards established for completion percentage, interception percentage, touchdown percentage, and average gain. Passers are allocated points according to how their marks compare with those standards.

† Active in 2003

All-time NFL Individual Statistical Leaders (cont.)

Passing—Touchdowns

CRAIG HACKER/SPORTING NEWS/ICON SMI

Dan Marino, Miami Dolphins

Player	TD
Dan Marino	420
†Brett Favre	346
Fran Tarkenton	342
John Elway	300
Warren Moon	291
Johnny Unitas	290
Joe Montana	273
Dave Krieg	261
Sonny Jurgensen	255
Dan Fouts	254
†Vinny Testaverde	251
Boomer Esiason	247
Jim Kelly	237
Steve Young	232
John Brodie	214
Terry Bradshaw	212
Y.A. Tittle	212

Sacks

Player	Sacks
†Bruce Smith	200.0
Reggie White	198.0
Kevin Greene	160.0
Chris Doleman	150.5
Richard Dent	137.5

Note: Officially compiled since 1982

Interceptions

Player	YRS	NO.	YDS	AVG	LG	TD
Paul Krause	16	81	1,185	14.6	81	3
Emlen Tunnell	14	79	1,282	16.2	55	4
Rod Woodson	17	71	1,483	20.9	98	12
Dick "Night Train" Lane	14	68	1,207	17.8	80	5
Ronnie Lott	14	63	730	11.6	83	5

Receiving—Receptions

Player	YRS	NO.	YDS	AVG	LG	TD
†Jerry Rice	19	1,519	22,466	14.8	96	194
Cris Carter	16	1,101	13,899	12.6	80	130
†Tim Brown	16	1,070	14,734	13.7	80	99
Andre Reed	16	951	13,198	13.9	83	87
Art Monk	16	940	12,721	13.5	79	68
Irving Fryar	17	851	12,785	15.0	80	84
†Larry Centers	14	827	6,797	8.2	54	28
Steve Largent	14	819	13,089	16.0	74	100
†Shannon Sharpe	14	815	10,060	12.3	82	62
Henry Ellard	16	814	13,777	16.9	81	65
James Lofton	16	764	14,004	18.3	80	75
†Marvin Harrison	8	759	10,072	13.3	79	83

Receiving—Yards

Player	YDS
†Jerry Rice	22,466
†Tim Brown	14,734
James Lofton	14,004
Cris Carter	13,899
Henry Ellard	13,777
Andre Reed	13,198
Steve Largent	13,089
Irving Fryar	12,785
Art Monk	12,721
Charlie Joiner	12,146

† Active in 2003

Single-Season Leaders

Scoring—Points

Player	YEAR	TD	PAT	FG	PTS
Paul Hornung, Packers	1960	15	41	15	176
Gary Anderson, Vikings	1998	0	59	35	164
Jeff Wilkins, Rams	2003	0	46	39	163
Priest Holmes, Chiefs	2003	27	0	0	162
Mark Moseley, Redskins	1983	0	62	33	161
Marshall Faulk, Rams	2000	26	0	0	160
Gino Cappelletti, Patriots	1964	7	36	25	155
Emmitt Smith, Cowboys	1995	25	0	0	150
Chip Lohmiller, Redskins	1991	0	56	31	149
Gino Cappelletti, Patriots	1961	8	48	17	147

Note: Cappelletti's 1964 total includes a 2-point conversion.

Touchdowns

Player	YEAR	RUSH	REC	RET	TOTAL
Priest Holmes, Chiefs	2003	27	0	0	27
Marshall Faulk, Rams	2000	18	8	0	26
Emmitt Smith, Cowboys	1995	25	0	0	25
John Riggins, Redskins	1983	24	0	0	24
Priest Holmes, Chiefs	2002	21	3	0	24
O.J. Simpson, Bills	1975	16	7	0	23
Jerry Rice, 49ers	1987	1	22	0	23
Terrell Davis, Broncos	1998	21	2	0	23

Three tied with 22.

Field Goals

Player	YEAR	ATT	NO.
Jeff Wilkins, Rams	2003	42	39
Olindo Mare, Dolphins	1999	46	39
John Kasay, Panthers	1996	45	37
Mike Vanderjagt, Colts	2003	37	37
Cary Blanchard, Colts	1996	40	36
Al Del Greco, Titans	1998	39	36

Four tied with 35.

Rushing—Yards Gained

Player	YEAR	ATT	YDS	AVG
Eric Dickerson, Rams	1984	379	2,105	5.6
Jamal Lewis, Ravens	2003	387	2,066	5.3
Barry Sanders, Lions	1997	335	2,053	6.1
Terrell Davis, Broncos	1998	392	2,008	5.1
O.J. Simpson, Bills	1973	332	2,003	6.0
Earl Campbell, Oilers	1980	373	1,934	5.2
Jim Brown, Browns	1963	291	1,863	6.4
Barry Sanders, Lions	1994	331	1,883	5.7
Ahman Green, Packers	2003	355	1,883	5.3
Ricky Williams, Dolphins	2002	383	1,853	4.8
Walter Payton, Bears	1977	339	1,852	5.5

Single-Season Leaders (cont.)

Rushing—Average Gain

Player	YEAR	AVG
Beattie Feathers, Bears	1934	8.44
Randall Cunningham, Eagles	1990	7.98
Michael Vick, Falcons	2002	6.88
Bobby Douglass, Bears	1972	6.87

Minimum 100 attempts.

Rushing—Touchdowns

Player	YEAR	NO.
Priest Holmes, Chiefs	2003	27
Emmitt Smith, Cowboys	1995	25
John Riggins, Redskins	1983	24

Five tied with 21.

Passing—Yards Gained

Player	YEAR	ATT	COMP	PCT	YDS
Dan Marino, Dolphins	1984	564	362	64.2	5,084
Kurt Warner, Rams	2001	546	375	68.7	4,830
Dan Fouts, Chargers	1981	609	360	59.1	4,802
Dan Marino, Dolphins	1986	623	378	60.7	4,746
Dan Fouts, Chargers	1980	589	348	59.1	4,715
Warren Moon, Oilers	1991	655	404	61.7	4,690
Warren Moon, Oilers	1990	584	362	62.0	4,689
Rich Gannon, Raiders	2002	618	418	67.6	4,689
Neil Lomax, Cardinals	1984	560	345	61.6	4,614
Drew Bledsoe, Patriots	1994	691	400	57.9	4,555

Passer Rating

Player	YEAR	RATING
Steve Young, 49ers	1994	112.8
Joe Montana, 49ers	1989	112.4
Milt Plum, Browns	1960	110.4
Sammy Baugh, Redskins	1945	109.9
Kurt Warner, Rams	1999	109.2

Passing—Touchdowns

Player	YEAR	NO.
Dan Marino, Dolphins	1984	48
Dan Marino, Dolphins	1986	44
Kurt Warner, Rams	1999	41
Brett Favre, Packers	1996	39

Four tied with 36.

Receiving—Receptions

Player	YEAR	NO.	YDS
Marvin Harrison, Colts	2002	143	1,722
Herman Moore, Lions	1995	123	1,686
Cris Carter, Vikings	1994	122	1,256
Jerry Rice, 49ers	1995	122	1,848
Cris Carter, Vikings	1995	122	1,371
Isaac Bruce, Rams	1995	119	1,781
Torry Holt, Rams	2003	117	1,696
Jimmy Smith, Jaguars	1999	116	1,636
Marvin Harrison, Colts	1999	115	1,663
Rod Smith, Broncos	2001	113	1,343

Four tied with 112.

Receiving—Yards Gained

Player	YEAR	YDS
Jerry Rice, 49ers	1995	1,848
Isaac Bruce, Rams	1995	1,781
Charley Hennigan, Oilers	1961	1,746
Marvin Harrison, Colts	2002	1,722
Torry Holt, Lions	2003	1,696
Herman Moore, Lions	1995	1,686

Receiving—Touchdowns

Player	YEAR	NO.
Jerry Rice, 49ers	1987	22
Mark Clayton, Dolphins	1984	18
Sterling Sharpe, Packers	1994	18

Eight tied with 17.

Interceptions

Player	YEAR	NO.
Dick "Night Train" Lane, Rams	1952	14
Dan Sandifer, Redskins	1948	13
Spec Sanders, N.Y. Yankees	1950	13
Lester Hayes, Raiders	1980	13

Nine tied with 12.

Sacks

Player	YEAR	NO.
Michael Strahan, N.Y. Giants	2001	22.5
Mark Gastineau, Jets	1984	22
Reggie White, Eagles	1987	21
Chris Doleman, Vikings	1989	21
Lawrence Taylor, N.Y. Giants	1986	20.5

Pro Bowl Results

Date	Result
2-8-04	NFC 55, AFC 52
2-2-03	AFC 45, NFC 20
2-9-02	AFC 38, NFC 30
2-4-01	AFC 38, NFC 17
2-6-00	NFC 51, AFC 31
2-7-99	AFC 23, NFC 10
2-1-98	AFC 29, NFC 24
2-2-97	AFC 26, NFC 23
2-4-96	NFC 20, AFC 13
2-5-95	AFC 41, NFC 13
2-6-94	NFC 17, AFC 3
2-7-93	AFC 23, NFC 20
2-2-92	NFC 21, AFC 15
2-3-91	AFC 23, NFC 21
2-4-90	NFC 27, AFC 21
1-29-89	NFC 34, AFC 3
2-7-88	AFC 15, NFC 6
2-1-87	AFC 10, NFC 6
2-2-86	NFC 28, AFC 24
1-27-85	AFC 22, NFC 14
1-29-84	NFC 45, AFC 3
2-6-83	NFC 20, AFC 19
1-31-82	AFC 16, NFC 13
2-1-81	NFC 21, AFC 7
1-27-80	NFC 37, AFC 27

Pro Bowl Results (cont.)

Date	Result	Date	Result	Date	Result
1-29-79	NFC 13, AFC 7	1-22-67	NFL East 20, West 10	1-12-58	West 26, East 7
1-23-78	NFC 14, AFC 13	1-21-67	AFL East 30, West 23	1-13-57	West 19, East 10
1-17-77	AFC 24, NFC 14	1-15-66	NFL East 36, West 7	1-15-56	East 31, West 30
1-26-76	NFC 23, AFC 20	1-15-66	AFL All-Stars 30, Buffalo 19	1-16-55	West 26, East 19
1-20-75	NFC 17, AFC 10	1-16-65	AFL West 38, East 14	1-17-54	East 20, West 9
1-20-74	AFC 15, NFC 13	1-10-65	NFL West 34, East 14	1-10-53	N. Conf. 27, A. Conf. 7
1-21-73	AFC 33, NFC 28	1-19-64	AFL West 27, East 24	1-12-52	N. Conf. 30, A. Conf. 13
1-23-72	AFC 26, NFC 13	1-12-64	NFL West 31, East 17	1-14-51	A. Conf. 28, N. Conf. 27
1-24-71	NFC 27, AFC 6	1-13-63	NFL East 30, West 20	12-27-42	NFL All-Stars 17, Washington 14
1-18-70	NFL West 16, East 13	1-13-63	AFL West 21, East 14	1-4-42	Chi. Bears 35, NFL All-Stars 24
1-17-70	AFL West 26, East 3	1-14-62	NFL West 31, East 30	12-29-40	Chi. Bears 28, NFL All-Stars 14
1-19-69	NFL West 10, East 7	1-7-62	AFL West 47, East 27	1-14-40	Green Bay 16, NFL All-Stars 7
1-19-69	AFL West 38, East 25	1-15-61	West 35, East 31	1-15-39	N.Y. Giants 13, Pro All-Stars 10
1-21-68	NFL West 38, East 20	1-17-60	West 38, East 21		
1-21-68	AFL East 25, West 24	1-11-59	East 28, West 21		

2004 NFL Draft—First Round

April 24-25, 2004, New York, NY

Pick	Team	Player	Pos.	Ht.	Wt.	School
1	San Diego (rights traded to N.Y. Giants)	Eli Manning	QB	6-4	218	Mississippi
2	Oakland	Robert Gallyer	OT	6-7	323	Iowa
3	Arizona	Larry Fitzgerald	WR	6-2	223	Pittsburgh
4	N.Y. Giants (rights traded to San Diego)	Phillip Rivers	QB	6-4	226	North Carolina State
5	Washington	Sean Taylor	FS	6-2	231	Miami (Florida)
6	Cleveland (from Detroit)	Kellen Winslow	TE	6-4	243	Miami (Florida)
7	Detroit (from Cleveland)	Roy Williams	WR	6-2	212	Texas
8	Atlanta	DeAngelo Hall	CB	5-10	197	Virginia Tech
9	Jacksonville	Reggie Williams	WR	6-3	223	Washington
10	Houston	Dunta Robinson	CB	5-10	186	South Carolina
11	Pittsburgh	Ben Roethlisberger	QB	6-4	242	Miami (Ohio)
12	N.Y. Jets	Jonathan Vilma	ILB	6-1	223	Miami (Florida)
13	Buffalo	Lee Evans	WR	5-10	197	Wisconsin
14	Chicago	Tommie Harris	DT	6-2	289	Oklahoma
15	Tampa Bay	Michael Clayton	WR	6-3	197	LSU
16	Philadelphia (from San Francisco)	Shawn Andrews	OT	6-4	373	Arkansas
17	Denver (from Cincinnati)	D.J. Williams	OLB	6-0	247	Miami (Florida)
18	New Orleans	Will Smith	DE	6-3	267	Ohio State
19	Miami (from Minnesota)	Vernon Carey	G	6-4	363	Miami (Florida)
20	Minnesota (from Miami)	Kenechi Udeze	DE	6-3	287	USC
21	New England (from Baltimore)	Vince Wilfork	DT	6-1	344	Miami (Florida)
22	Buffalo (from Dallas)	J.P. Losman	QB	6-2	217	Tulane
23	Seattle	Marcus Tubbs	DT	6-3	324	Texas
24	St. Louis (from Denver through Cincinnati)	Steven Jackson	RB	6-2	233	Oregon State
25	Green Bay	Ahmad Carroll	CB	5-10	193	Arkansas
26	Cincinnati (from St. Louis)	Chris Perry	RB	6-0	224	Michigan
27	Houston (from Tennessee)	Jason Babin	DE	6-2	260	Western Michigan
28	Carolina (from Philadelphia through San Francisco)	Chris Gamble	CB	6-1	181	Ohio State
29	Atlanta (from Indianapolis)	Michael Jenkins	WR	6-4	217	Ohio State
30	Detroit (from Kansas City)	Kevin Jones	RB	5-11	221	Virginia Tech
31	San Francisco (from Carolina)	Rashaun Woods	WR	6-2	202	Oklahoma State
32	New England	Ben Watson	TE	6-3	253	Georgia

KEY QB=quarterback; OT=offensive tackle; WR=wide receiver; FS=free safety; TE=tight end; CB=cornerback; ILB=inside linebacker; DT=defensive tackle; OLB=outside linebacker DE=defensive end; G=guard; RB=running back

FOOTBALL

COLLEGE

The 2003 college football season will be remembered as much for what happened in the polls as for what happened on the field.

Division I-A football relies on a computer-based system called the Bowl Championship Series (BCS) to determine the two teams that play in the BCS national championship game. But the system failed in 2003: Two teams shared the title of national champion.

Controversy erupted over who deserved to play in the Sugar Bowl, the BCS title game. The USC Trojans, LSU Tigers, and Oklahoma Sooners finished the regular season with one loss apiece. The Trojans were ranked Number 1 in the Associated Press and Coaches' polls at the end of the regular season. But in December, they dropped to third in the final BCS poll and did not play in the championship game. (During the regular season, the AP and Coaches' polls are averaged into the BCS formula that decides the weekly Top 25 rankings.) Instead, LSU and Oklahoma faced off. The Tigers won the championship, 21–14. Three days earlier, the Trojans, still ranked Number 1 by AP, had defeated the Michigan Wolverines, 28–14, in the Rose Bowl to earn a share of the national title.

The awards season was dominated by Sooners. Quarterback Jason White won the Heisman Trophy. The award was made sweeter for White because he had come back from three torn knee ligaments the past two seasons. Teddy Lehman won the Butkus Award as the nation's best linebacker. Cornerback Derrick Strait won the Bronko Nagurski Trophy as defensive player of the year and the Jim Thorpe Award as best defensive back. Tommie Harris won the Lombardi Award as best lineman.

In February 2004, District Court Judge Shira Scheindlin ruled the NFL policy that kept players from entering the draft until they had been out of high school for three years violated U.S. antitrust laws. The ruling was the result of a lawsuit filed by Ohio State running back Maurice Clarett, who had challenged the rule to enter the 2004 draft. The NFL appealed the ruling, and on May 24, an appeals court said the NFL can set the rules for when players enter the league, keeping Clarett and wide receiver Mike Williams of USC out of the NFL in 2004.

Quarterback Matt Mauck led LSU to a 21–14 Sugar Bowl win over Oklahoma for a share of the national championship in 2003.

AL TIELEMANS/SPORTS ILLUSTRATED

Final 2003 College Football Polls

Associated Press

Team	Record	Points
1. USC	12–1	1,608
2. LSU	13–1	1,576
3. Oklahoma	12–2	1,476
4. Ohio St.	11–2	1,411
5. Miami (Florida)	11–2	1,329
6. Michigan	10–3	1,281
7. Georgia	11–3	1,255
8. Iowa	10–3	1,107
9. Washington St.	10–3	1,060
10. Miami (Ohio)	13–1	932
11. Florida St.	10–3	905
12. Texas	10–3	887
13. Mississippi	10–3	845
14. Kansas St.	11–4	833
15. Tennessee	10–3	695
16. Boise St.	13–1	645
17. Maryland	10–3	564
18. Purdue	9–4	526
19. Nebraska	10–3	520
20. Minnesota	10–3	368
21. Utah	10–2	308
22. Clemson	9–4	230
23. Bowling Green	11–3	189
24. Florida	8–5	165
25. TCU	11–2	126

ESPN/*USA Today* Coaches

Team	Record	Points
1. LSU	13–1	1,572
2. USC	12–1	1,514
3. Oklahoma	12–2	1,429
4. Ohio St.	11–2	1,370
5. Miami (Florida)	11–2	1,306
6. Georgia	11–3	1,183
7. Michigan	10–3	1,140
8. Iowa	10–3	1,119
9. Washington St.	10–3	983
10. Florida St.	10–3	929
11. Texas	10–3	894
12. Miami (Ohio)	13–1	800
13. Kansas St.	11–4	746
14. Mississippi	10–3	730
15. Boise St.	13–1	704
16. Tennessee	10–3	684
17. Minnesota	10–3	553
18. Nebraska	10–3	532
19. Purdue	9–4	510
20. Maryland	10–3	462
21. Utah	10–2	327
22. Clemson	9–4	219
23. Bowling Green	11–3	170
24. TCU	11–2	145
25. Florida	8–5	124

2003–04 College Bowl and Playoff Results

Bowl Games

Bowl	Date	Site	Result
Sugar	Jan. 4	New Orleans, Louisiana	LSU 21, Oklahoma 14
Fiesta	Jan. 2	Tempe, Arizona	Ohio St. 35, Kansas St. 28
Humanitarian	Jan. 3	Boise, Idaho	Georgia Tech 52, Tulsa 10
Orange	Jan. 1	Miami, Florida	Miami (Florida) 16, Florida St. 14
Cotton	Jan. 2	Dallas, Texas	Ole Miss 31, Oklahoma St. 28
Peach	Jan. 2	Atlanta, Georgia	Clemson 27, Tennessee 14
Rose	Jan. 1	Pasadena, California	USC 28, Michigan 14
Capital One	Jan. 1	Orlando, Florida	Georgia 34, Purdue 27 (OT)
Gator	Jan. 1	Jacksonville, Florida	Maryland 41, West Virginia 7
Outback	Jan. 1	Tampa, Florida	Iowa 37, Florida 17
San Francisco	Dec. 31	San Francisco, California	Boston College 35, Colorado St. 21
Liberty	Dec. 31	Memphis, Tennessee	Utah 17, Southern Miss 0
Sun	Dec. 31	El Paso, Texas	Minnesota 31, Oregon 30
Music City	Dec. 31	Nashville, Tennessee	Auburn 28, Wisconsin 14
Independence	Dec. 31	Shreveport, Louisiana	Arkansas 27, Missouri 14
Silicon Valley Classic	Dec. 30	San Jose, California	Fresno St. 17, UCLA 9
Holiday	Dec. 30	San Diego, California	Washington State 28, Texas 20
Houston	Dec. 30	Houston, Texas	Texas Tech 38, Navy 14
Alamo	Dec. 29	San Antonio, Texas	Nebraska 17, Michigan St. 3
Continental Tire	Dec. 27	Charlotte, North Carolina	Virginia 23, Pittsburgh 16
Insight	Dec. 26	Tempe, Arizona	Cal 52, Virginia Tech 49
Motor City	Dec. 26	Detroit, Michigan	Bowling Green 28, Northwestern 24
Hawaii	Dec. 25	Honolulu, Hawaii	Hawaii 54, Houston 48 (3OT)
Las Vegas	Dec. 24	Las Vegas, Nevada	Oregon St. 55, N. Mexico 14
Ft. Worth	Dec. 23	Ft. Worth, Texas	Boise St. 34, TCU 31
Tangerine	Dec. 22	Orlando, Florida	N.C. State 56, Kansas 26
GMAC	Dec. 18	Mobile, Alabama	Miami (Ohio) 49, Louisville 28
New Orleans	Dec. 16	New Orleans, Louisiana	Memphis 27, North Texas 17

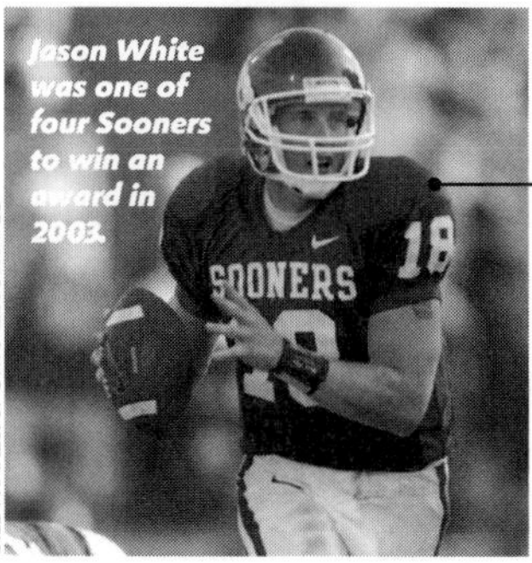

Jason White was one of four Sooners to win an award in 2003.

BILL FRAKES/SPORTS ILLUSTRATED

2003 Heisman Voting

Player, School	Position	1st	2nd	3rd	Total
Jason White, Oklahoma	QB	319	204	116	1,481
Larry Fitzgerald, Pittsburgh	WR	253	233	128	1,353
Eli Manning, Mississippi	QB	95	132	161	710
Chris Perry, Michigan	RB	27	66	128	341
Darren Sproles, Kansas St.	RB	15	30	29	134
Matt Leinart, USC	QB	5	27	58	127
Philip Rivers, N.C. St.	QB	18	20	24	118
Mike Williams, USC	WR	12	12	18	78
Ben Roethlisberger, Miami (Ohio)	QB	5	9	14	47
B.J. Symons, Texas Tech	QB	1	7	21	38

2003 AP All-America Team

Offense

QB Jason White, Oklahoma, senior
RB Chris Perry, Michigan, senior
Darren Sproles, Kansas St., junior
WR Larry Fitzgerald, Pittsburgh, sophomore
Mike Williams, USC, sophomore
TE Kellen Winslow, Jr., Miami (Florida), junior
C Jake Grove, Virginia Tech, senior
OL Shawn Andrews, Arkansas, junior
Alex Barron, Florida St., junior
Robert Gallery, Iowa, senior
Jacob Rogers, USC, senior
K Nate Kaeding, Iowa, senior
All-Purpose Antonio Perkins, Oklahoma, junior

Defense

DL Dave Ball, UCLA, senior
Tommie Harris, Oklahoma, junior
Chad Lavalais, LSU, senior
Kenechi Udeze, USC, junior
LB Derrick Johnson, Texas, junior
Teddy Lehman, Oklahoma, senior
Grant Wiley, West Virginia, senior
DB Will Allen, Ohio St., senior
Keiwan Ratliff, Florida, senior
Derrick Strait, Oklahoma, senior
Sean Taylor, Miami (Florida), junior
P Dustin Colquitt, Tennessee, junior

Fast Fact: In 1902, Michigan routed Stanford, 49–0, in the first Rose Bowl game. Tournament of Roses officials replaced football with polo in 1903, then chariot racing in 1904. Football did not return until 1916.

KEY QB=quarterback; RB=running back; WR=wide receiver; TE=tight end; C=center; OL=offensive lineman; K=kicker; DL=defensive lineman; LB=linebacker; DB=defensive back; P=punter

2003 NCAA Division I-A Conference Standings

Atlantic Coast Conference

	Conference				Overall			
Team	W	L	PF	PA	W	L	PF	PA
Florida State	7	1	269	138	10	2	405	201
Maryland	6	2	220	159	9	3	365	199
Clemson	5	3	210	158	8	4	338	236
North Carolina State	4	4	256	250	7	5	433	359
Virginia	4	4	216	181	7	5	341	249
Georgia Tech	4	4	151	178	6	6	222	256
Wake Forest	3	5	242	236	5	7	335	347
Duke	2	6	139	265	4	8	211	343
North Carolina	1	7	184	322	2	10	317	459

Big East Conference

	Conference				Overall			
Team	W	L	PF	PA	W	L	PF	PA
Miami (Florida)	6	1	193	113	10	2	345	182
West Virginia	6	1	248	158	8	4	369	256
Pittsburgh	5	2	206	183	8	4	373	288
Virginia Tech	4	3	216	152	8	4	411	247
Boston College	3	4	176	196	7	5	335	310
Syracuse	2	5	141	191	6	6	320	301
Rutgers	2	5	162	214	5	7	329	354
Temple	0	7	125	260	1	11	235	393

KEY W=win; L=loss; PF=points for; PA=points against

2003 NCAA Division I-A Conference Standings (cont.)

Big Ten Conference

Team	Conference W	Conference L	Conference PF	Conference PA	Overall W	Overall L	Overall PF	Overall PA
Michigan	7	1	286	150	10	2	446	191
Ohio State	6	2	175	124	10	2	287	201
Purdue	6	2	198	138	9	3	322	192
Iowa	5	3	198	160	9	3	336	193
Minnesota	5	3	285	204	9	3	472	255
Michigan State	5	3	249	191	8	4	360	276
Wisconsin	4	4	226	180	7	5	341	278
Northwestern	4	4	148	202	6	6	239	298
Penn State	1	7	154	190	3	9	233	255
Indiana	1	7	104	279	2	10	177	388
Illinois	0	8	112	317	1	11	203	398

Big 12 Conference

NORTH

Team	Conference W	Conference L	Conference PF	Conference PA	Overall W	Overall L	Overall PF	Overall PA
Kansas State	6	2	290	121	10	3	486	202
Nebraska	5	3	188	154	9	3	305	185
Missouri	4	4	250	198	8	4	385	260
Kansas	3	5	209	247	6	6	358	340
Colorado	3	5	228	255	5	7	319	398
Iowa State	0	8	71	343	2	10	173	437

SOUTH

Team	Conference W	Conference L	Conference PF	Conference PA	Overall W	Overall L	Overall PF	Overall PA
Oklahoma	8	0	412	90	12	0	580	158
Texas	7	1	308	182	10	2	513	252
Oklahoma State	5	3	241	259	9	3	439	295
Texas Tech	4	4	344	296	7	5	514	428
Texas A&M	2	6	205	356	4	8	304	465
Baylor	1	7	121	366	3	9	191	455

Conference USA

Team	Conference W	Conference L	Conference PF	Conference PA	Overall W	Overall L	Overall PF	Overall PA
Southern Mississippi	8	0	226	117	9	3	293	209
Texas Christian University (TCU)	7	1	269	202	11	1	349	242
Louisville	5	3	289	242	9	3	422	312
Memphis	5	3	217	138	8	4	366	233
South Florida	5	3	177	160	7	4	276	224
Houston	4	4	286	301	7	5	400	414
Alabama-Birmingham	4	4	189	190	5	7	245	287
Tulane	3	5	244	274	5	7	337	424
Cincinnati	2	6	190	216	5	7	303	319
East Carolina	1	7	174	280	1	11	217	428
Army	0	8	127	268	0	13	206	476

Mid-American Conference

EAST

Team	Conference W	Conference L	Conference PF	Conference PA	Overall W	Overall L	Overall PF	Overall PA
Miami (Ohio)	8	0	374	124	11	1	504	217
Marshall	6	2	230	170	8	4	350	278
Akron	5	3	257	246	7	5	435	353
Kent State	4	4	261	274	5	7	321	396
University of Central Florida (UCF)	2	6	131	221	3	9	224	373
Ohio	1	7	192	244	2	10	263	372
Buffalo	1	7	138	289	1	11	177	445

WEST

Team	Conference W	Conference L	Conference PF	Conference PA	Overall W	Overall L	Overall PF	Overall PA
Bowling Green	7	1	246	165	10	2	415	231
Northern Illinois	6	2	281	196	10	2	386	258
Toledo	6	2	280	189	8	4	389	285
Western Michigan	4	4	211	220	5	7	331	370
Ball State	3	5	173	249	4	8	261	386
Eastern Michigan	2	6	145	240	3	9	205	371
Central Michigan	1	7	154	246	3	9	277	428

2003 NCAA Division I-A Conference Standings (cont.)

Mountain West Conference

Team	Conference W	Conference L	Conference PF	Conference PA	Overall W	Overall L	Overall PF	Overall PA
Utah	6	1	213	144	9	2	327	229
New Mexico	5	2	206	138	8	4	377	235
Colorado State	4	3	216	162	7	5	360	283
Air Force	3	4	161	169	7	5	322	242
San Diego State	3	4	111	145	6	6	224	207
Brigham Young University (BYU)	3	4	114	161	4	8	196	310
University Nevada-Las Vegas (UNLV)	2	5	132	169	6	6	256	272
Wyoming	2	5	141	206	4	8	286	360

Pacific-Ten Conference

Team	Conference W	Conference L	Conference PF	Conference PA	Overall W	Overall L	Overall PF	Overall PA
University of Southern California (USC)	7	1	342	161	11	1	506	225
Washington State	6	2	245	169	9	3	366	237
Oregon	5	3	209	216	8	4	326	317
California	5	3	267	170	7	6	405	292
Oregon State	4	4	270	224	7	5	378	287
University of California-Los Angeles (UCLA)	4	4	175	200	6	6	239	288
Washington	4	4	203	233	6	6	312	316
Arizona State	2	6	203	246	5	7	298	328
Stanford	2	6	130	243	4	7	186	324
Arizona	1	7	109	291	2	10	181	429

Southeastern Conference

EAST

Team	Conference W	Conference L	Conference PF	Conference PA	Overall W	Overall L	Overall PF	Overall PA
Georgia	6	2	215	102	10	2	324	142
Tennessee	6	2	260	170	10	2	351	212
Florida	6	2	178	152	8	4	373	234
South Carolina	2	6	164	227	5	7	268	314
Kentucky	1	7	198	244	4	8	328	321
Vanderbilt	1	7	126	261	2	10	235	358

WEST

Team	Conference W	Conference L	Conference PF	Conference PA	Overall W	Overall L	Overall PF	Overall PA
Louisiana State University (LSU)	7	1	228	90	11	1	420	127
Mississippi	7	1	218	150	9	3	411	257
Auburn	5	3	190	148	7	5	314	198
Arkansas	4	4	247	223	8	4	409	291
Alabama	2	6	216	237	4	9	331	333
Mississippi State	1	7	93	329	2	10	225	471

Sun Belt Conference

Team	Conference W	Conference L	Conference PF	Conference PA	Overall W	Overall L	Overall PF	Overall PA
North Texas	7	0	237	142	9	3	341	258
Louisiana-Lafayette	4	3	225	228	4	8	266	415
Middle Tennessee State	4	3	213	204	4	8	332	375
Arkansas State	3	4	131	273	5	7	242	401
Idaho	3	4	191	171	3	9	248	314
Utah State	3	4	193	136	3	9	264	315
New Mexico State	2	5	154	172	3	9	262	341
Louisiana-Monroe	1	6	180	249	1	11	239	467

2003 NCAA Division I-A Conference Standings (cont.)

Western Athletic Conference

Team	Conference W	Conference L	Conference PF	Conference PA	Overall W	Overall L	Overall PF	Overall PA
Boise State	8	0	375	143	12	1	568	208
Tulsa	6	2	272	193	8	4	390	309
Fresno State	6	2	203	168	8	5	305	308
Hawaii	5	3	242	211	8	5	432	379
Rice	5	3	292	217	5	7	343	378
Nevada	4	4	195	251	6	6	282	338
Louisiana Tech	3	5	237	275	5	7	310	394
San Jose State	2	6	217	290	3	8	259	386
Texas-El Paso	1	7	195	332	2	11	288	498
Southern Methodist University (SMU)	0	8	98	246	0	12	134	386

Independents

Team	Overall W	Overall L	Overall PF	Overall PA
University of Connecticut	9	3	408	300
Navy	8	4	382	245
Troy State	6	6	185	272
Notre Dame	5	7	243	315

2003 NCAA Division I-AA Conference Standings

Atlantic 10 Conference

Team	Conference W	Conference L	Conference PF	Conference PA	Overall W	Overall L	Overall PF	Overall PA
Delaware	8	1	295	193	11	1	406	224
Massachusetts	8	1	276	209	10	2	361	276
Northeastern	6	3	265	185	8	4	414	219
Villanova	5	4	250	152	7	4	314	178
Maine	5	4	176	169	7	5	297	237
William & Mary	4	4	229	219	5	5	287	299
James Madison	4	5	214	228	6	6	307	284
New Hampshire	3	6	261	303	5	7	406	380
Rhode Island	3	6	230	278	4	8	309	381
Hofstra	2	7	161	249	2	10	247	368
Richmond	1	8	137	314	2	9	189	370

Big Sky Conference

Team	Conference W	Conference L	Conference PF	Conference PA	Overall W	Overall L	Overall PF	Overall PA
Montana	5	2	240	122	9	3	390	223
Northern Arizona	5	2	233	192	8	3	349	254
Montana State	5	2	197	118	7	5	316	180
Idaho State	4	3	224	260	8	4	394	423
Weber State	4	3	183	165	8	4	325	241
Eastern Washington	3	4	230	247	6	5	344	321
Portland State	1	6	105	214	4	7	220	327
Sacramento State	1	6	117	211	2	9	237	332

Big South Conference

Team	Conference W	Conference L	Conference PF	Conference PA	Overall W	Overall L	Overall PF	Overall PA
Gardner-Webb	4	0	148	59	8	4	335	254
Liberty	3	1	103	82	6	6	306	378
Virginia Military Institute	2	2	122	85	6	6	359	257
Coastal Carolina	1	3	96	109	6	5	309	253
Charleston Southern	0	4	27	161	1	11	148	513

2003 NCAA Division I-AA Conference Standings (cont.)

Gateway Conference

Team	Conference W	L	PF	PA	Overall W	L	PF	PA
Southern Illinois	6	1	231	153	10	1	430	181
Northern Iowa	6	1	195	144	9	2	348	195
Western Illinois	5	2	270	213	8	3	402	263
Western Kentucky	5	2	208	121	8	3	365	178
Illinois State	3	4	189	183	6	6	318	293
Youngstown State	2	5	148	228	5	7	281	283
Southwest Missouri State	1	6	169	210	4	7	288	276
Indiana State	0	7	107	265	3	9	170	356

Ivy League

Team	Conference W	L	PF	PA	Overall W	L	PF	PA
Pennsylvania	7	0	250	117	10	0	346	164
Harvard	4	3	212	151	7	3	317	221
Yale	4	3	211	188	6	4	354	284
Brown	4	3	193	192	5	5	244	246
Dartmouth	4	3	161	168	5	5	211	261
Columbia	3	4	135	189	4	6	211	283
Princeton	2	5	175	181	2	8	204	267
Cornell	0	7	65	216	1	9	130	304

Metro Atlantic Athletic Conference

Team	Conference W	L	PF	PA	Overall W	L	PF	PA
Duquesne	5	0	210	70	8	3	345	202
Iona	4	1	135	104	6	5	267	275
Marist	2	3	102	130	4	6	187	324
La Salle	2	3	121	164	3	8	233	353
Saint Peter's	2	3	86	114	2	8	144	304
Siena	0	5	65	137	0	11	109	345

Mid-Eastern Athletic Conference

Team	Conference W	L	PF	PA	Overall W	L	PF	PA
North Carolina A&T	6	1	182	133	10	2	284	205
Bethune-Cookman	5	2	235	168	9	2	352	220
Hampton	5	2	244	158	7	4	351	212
South Carolina State	5	2	237	150	8	4	364	229
Morgan State	4	3	223	185	6	5	318	318
Howard	2	5	117	156	4	7	208	265
Delaware State	1	6	120	236	1	10	182	348
Norfolk State	0	8	140	357	1	11	192	479
Florida A&M	0	0	0	0	6	6	278	280

Northeast Conference

Team	Conference W	L	PF	PA	Overall W	L	PF	PA
Monmouth (New Jersey)	6	1	121	73	10	2	247	102
Albany (New York)	6	1	216	69	7	4	299	185
Robert Morris	4	3	154	139	6	4	246	219
Stony Brook	4	3	201	165	6	4	284	237
Wagner	3	4	140	150	6	5	231	203
Sacred Heart	3	4	134	181	6	5	286	280
Central Connecticut	2	5	147	195	3	8	231	359
St. Francis (Pennsylvania)	0	7	109	250	1	9	168	367

2003 NCAA Division I-AA Conference Standings (cont.)

Ohio Valley Conference

Team	Conference W	Conference L	Conference PF	Conference PA	Overall W	Overall L	Overall PF	Overall PA
Jacksonville State	7	1	278	161	8	3	309	233
Eastern Kentucky	6	2	255	204	7	5	347	352
Samford	5	3	258	188	7	4	350	276
Tennessee State	5	3	236	210	7	5	348	285
Southeast Missouri State	5	3	239	207	5	7	262	290
Murray State	3	5	168	252	4	8	225	338
Eastern Illinois	3	5	162	187	4	8	210	268
Tennessee Tech	1	7	183	248	2	9	245	340
Tennessee-Martin	1	7	164	286	2	10	198	439

Patriot League

Team	Conference W	Conference L	Conference PF	Conference PA	Overall W	Overall L	Overall PF	Overall PA
Colgate	7	0	219	114	12	0	397	205
Lehigh	6	1	226	99	8	3	330	185
Fordham	4	3	179	158	9	3	386	251
Bucknell	4	3	175	197	6	6	284	300
Towson	3	4	118	142	6	6	271	265
Lafayette	2	5	170	175	5	6	315	249
Georgetown	1	6	126	223	4	8	271	328
Holy Cross	1	6	185	290	1	11	312	478

Pioneer Football League

NORTH

Team	Conference W	Conference L	Conference PF	Conference PA	Overall W	Overall L	Overall PF	Overall PA
San Diego	3	1	169	113	8	2	399	215
Valparaiso	3	1	146	132	8	4	406	333
Dayton	2	2	129	89	9	2	400	183
Drake	1	3	119	130	6	6	342	307
Butler	1	3	39	138	2	9	119	418

SOUTH

Team	Conference W	Conference L	Conference PF	Conference PA	Overall W	Overall L	Overall PF	Overall PA
Morehead State	3	0	104	26	8	3	327	185
Jacksonville (Florida)	1	2	75	57	5	6	268	307
Austin Peay	1	2	31	100	4	7	194	276
Davidson	1	2	68	95	3	8	246	364

Southern Conference

Team	Conference W	Conference L	Conference PF	Conference PA	Overall W	Overall L	Overall PF	Overall PA
Wofford	8	0	246	91	10	1	309	156
Appalachian State	6	2	204	123	7	4	252	219
Georgia Southern	5	3	224	163	7	4	311	232
Furman	4	4	185	110	6	5	278	155
Citadel	4	4	163	176	6	6	261	311
Western Carolina	3	5	144	197	5	7	251	301
Chattanooga	3	5	143	281	3	9	195	421
East Tennessee State	2	6	158	175	5	7	270	233
Elon	1	7	70	221	2	10	119	314

Southland Conference

Team	Conference W	Conference L	Conference PF	Conference PA	Overall W	Overall L	Overall PF	Overall PA
McNeese State	5	0	190	119	10	1	402	249
Stephen F. Austin	4	1	167	108	7	4	343	230
Nicholls State	3	2	152	146	5	6	389	280
Northwestern State	1	4	126	145	6	6	386	265
Texas State University	1	4	136	190	4	8	315	417
Sam Houston State	1	4	137	200	2	9	239	406

2003 NCAA Division I-AA Conference Standings (cont.)

Southwestern Athletic Conference

EAST	Conference				Overall			
Team	**W**	**L**	**PF**	**PA**	**W**	**L**	**PF**	**PA**
Alabama State	5	2	255	167	8	4	425	307
Alcorn State	5	2	213	163	7	5	361	318
Alabama A&M	4	3	210	161	8	4	398	194
Jackson State	2	5	139	203	2	10	201	338
Mississippi Valley State	1	6	108	211	2	9	181	331

WEST	Conference				Overall			
Team	**W**	**L**	**PF**	**PA**	**W**	**L**	**PF**	**PA**
Southern	6	1	307	143	11	1	500	186
Grambling	6	1	309	119	9	3	439	258
Texas Southern	3	4	151	167	5	6	213	331
Arkansas-Pine Bluff	3	4	125	166	4	7	211	291
Prairie View	0	7	44	361	1	9	99	522

Independents

	Overall			
Team	**W**	**L**	**PF**	**PA**
Northern Colorado	9	2	425	180
Florida Atlantic	10	2	332	245
California Polytechnic	7	4	316	241
University of California-Davis	6	4	295	184
Southeastern Louisiana	5	7	369	382
Southern Utah	4	7	240	283
Florida International	2	10	270	341
St. Mary's (California)	1	11	162	471
Savannah State	0	12	109	491

2003 NCAA Individual Leaders: Division I-A

Scoring

	TD	PTS
B.J. Symons, Texas Tech	57	342
Ryan Dinwiddie, Boise St.	43	258
Josh Harris, Bowling Green	41	246
Jason White, Oklahoma	41	246
Ben Roethlisberger, Miami (Ohio)	40	240
Rod Rutherford, Pittsburgh	39	234
Ell Roberson, Kansas St.	39	234
Matt Leinart, USC	39	234
Philip Rivers, North Carolina St.	37	222
J.P. Losman, Tulane	35	210

Field Goals

	FGM	FGA	PCT
Billy Bennett, Georgia	29	36	80.6
Drew Dunning, Washington St.	27	30	90.0
Nick Browne, TCU	27	32	84.4
Jonathan Nichols, Mississippi	24	28	85.7
Ben Jones, Purdue	23	28	82.1
Nick Novak, Maryland	22	28	78.6

Trivia Challenge

Which Division I-A team holds the record for wins?

The Michigan Wolverines, who had 833 victories through the end of the 2003-04 season.

KEY TD=touchdowns; PTS=points; FGM=field goals made; FGA=field goals attempted; PCT=percentage

Today's Stars

Matt Leinart, quarterback, b. May 11, 1983, Anaheim Hills, California. Replacing a Heisman Trophy winner isn't easy, but USC's Leinart made it seem like a piece of cake in 2003. He stepped in for 2002 Heisman winner Carson Palmer and passed for 3,556 yards and 38 touchdowns. He passed for at least two TDs in 12 of 13 games and had at least three TD tosses in eight games. In the Rose Bowl, he passed for 327 yards and three touchdowns, and caught a TD pass thrown by wide receiver Mike Williams. Leinart was named the game's MVP.

Quarterback Matt Leinart led USC to a 12–1 record in 2003 and a Rose Bowl victory over Michigan.

JOHN W. McDONOUGH/SPORTS ILLUSTRATED

Darren Sproles, running back, b. June 20, 1983, Waterloo, Iowa. The 5' 7" Sproles is like the little engine that could. In 2003, he led Division I-A in rushing yards (1,986) and all-purpose yards (2,735), and was ranked third in yards per game (132.4). In Kansas State's upset of Number 1 Oklahoma in the Big 12 championship game, Sproles rushed for 235 yards and caught a touchdown pass.

Chris Leak, quarterback, b. May 3, 1985, Charlotte, North Carolina. Leak played beyond his years as a true freshman for Florida in 2003. His .750 win percentage (6–2) was the highest of any freshman QB in the country. Leak was named the Southeastern Conference (SEC) Freshman of the Year. He joined Emmitt Smith (1987), Danny Wuerffel (1993), and Jabar Gaffney (2000) as the only Gators to earn the honor. He ranked second in SEC history in completions (168), passing yards (2,167), and touchdowns (14) by a true freshman. He was 6–1 as a starter in SEC games, including a 3–1 record against Top 15 teams.

2003 NCAA Individual Leaders: Division I-A (cont.)

Rushing

	G	Carries	YDS	AVG	TD
Darren Sproles, Kansas St.	15	306	1,986	6.5	16
Derrick Knight, Boston College	13	321	1,721	5.4	11
Patrick Cobbs, North Texas	11	307	1,680	5.5	19
Chris Perry, Michigan	13	338	1,674	5.0	18
Michael Turner, Northern Illinois	12	310	1,648	5.3	14
Kevin Jones, Virginia Tech	13	281	1,647	5.9	21
Steven Jackson, Oregon St.	13	350	1,545	4.4	19
Anthony Sherrell, Eastern Michigan	12	338	1,531	4.5	12
P.J. Daniels, Georgia Tech	13	283	1,447	5.1	10

▷Fast Fact: Since 1962, the Nebraska Cornhuskers have sold out an NCAA-record 262 straight home games.

Passing Efficiency

	ATTS	COMP PCT	YDS	INT	TD	Rating
Philip Rivers, North Carolina St.	483	72.0	4,491	7	34	170.5
Ben Roethlisberger, Miami (Ohio)	495	69.1	4,486	10	37	165.8
Matt Leinart, USC	402	63.4	3,556	9	38	164.5
Ryan Dinwiddie, Boise St.	446	61.9	4,356	7	31	163.7
Asad Abdul-Khaliq, Minnesota	250	63.2	2,401	5	17	162.3
Bruce Gradkowski, Toledo	389	71.2	3,210	7	28	160.7
Jason White, Oklahoma	451	61.6	3,846	10	40	158.1
Rod Rutherford, Pittsburgh	413	59.8	3,679	14	37	157.4
Bill Whittemore, Kansas	263	60.5	2,385	6	18	154.7
Kevin Kolb, Houston	360	61.1	3,131	6	25	153.8

KEY G=games; YDS=yards; AVG=average; TD=touchdowns; ATTS=attempts; COMP PCT=completion percentage; INT=interceptions

2003 NCAA Individual Leaders: Division I-A (cont.)

Receiving

	G	REC	YDS	YDS/G	TD
Larry Fitzgerald, Pittsburgh	13	92	1,672	128.6	22
Geoff McArthur, California	13	85	1,504	115.7	10
Martin Nance, Miami (Ohio)	14	90	1,498	107.0	11
Mark Clayton, Oklahoma	14	83	1,425	101.8	15
Jerricho Cotchery, North Carolina St.	13	86	1,369	105.3	10
Rashaun Woods, Oklahoma St.	13	77	1,367	105.2	15
Mike Williams, USC	13	95	1,314	101.1	16
James Newson, Oregon St.	12	81	1,306	108.8	3
David Anderson, Colorado St.	13	72	1,293	99.5	9
Kerry Wright, Middle Tennessee St.	12	73	1,280	106.7	9

Larry Fitzgerald of Pittsburgh was second in the Heisman Trophy voting in 2003.

Interceptions

	INT	YDS	TD
Josh Bullocks, Nebraska	10	154	0
Sean Taylor, Miami (Florida)	10	184	3
Keiwan Ratliff, Florida	9	182	2
Jonathan Burke, Arkansas St.	9	120	0
Derrick Ansley, Troy St.	9	74	1
Will Poole, USC	7	70	1
J.R. Reed, South Florida	7	45	0
Corey Webster, LSU	7	60	0
Janssen Patton, Bowling Green	7	84	0
Brodney Pool, Oklahoma	7	79	0

2003 NCAA Individual Leaders: Division I-AA

Scoring

	TD	PTS
Quincy Richard, Southern	44	264
David Macchi, Valparaiso	42	252
Bruce Eugene, Grambling	40	240
Jason Murrietta, Northern Arizona	35	210
Eric Rasmussen, San Diego	35	210
Andy Hall, Delaware	33	198
Martin Hankins, Southeastern Louisiana	30	180
Chris Brown, Colgate	30	180

Trivia Challenge

What were the names of Notre Dame's original "Four Horsemen"?

Elmer Layden (fullback), Don Miller (right halfback), Jim Crowley (left halfback), and Harry Stuhldreher (quarterback)

Field Goals

	FGM	FGA	PCT
Chris Snyder, Montana	25	30	83.3
Matt Lange, Western Kentucky	23	28	82.1
Paul Ernster, Northern Arizona	18	30	60.0
Jeremy Hershey, Idaho St.	18	26	69.2
Matt Sharpe, Virginia Military Institute	17	24	70.8

Rushing

	G	Carries	YDS	AVG	TD
Jamaal Branch, Colgate	16	450	2,326	145.4	29
Charles Anthony, Tennessee St.	12	322	1,708	142.3	12
Nick Chournos, Weber St.	12	297	1,649	137.4	13
Germaine Bennett, Delaware	16	323	1,625	101.6	21
Mike Hilliard, Duquesne	11	306	1,544	140.4	15
Gary Jones, Albany (New York)	11	211	1,524	138.5	18
Nick Hartigan, Brown	10	275	1,498	149.8	15
Lerron Moore, Western Kentucky	13	273	1,490	114.6	13
Jonathan Taylor, Drake	12	318	1,486	123.8	14
Evan Harney, San Diego	10	285	1,475	147.5	17

KEY G=games; REC=receptions; YDS=yards; YDS/G=yards per game; TD=touchdowns; INT=interceptions; PTS=points; FGM=field goals made; FGA=field goals attempted; PCT=percentage; AVG=average

2003 NCAA Individual Leaders: Division I-AA (cont.)

Passing Efficiency

	ATTS	COMP PCT	YDS	INT	TD	Rating
Eric Rasmussen, San Diego	318	61.3	2,982	3	35	174.5
Quincy Richard, Southern	389	65.8	3,427	15	33	160.1
David Macchi, Valparaiso	410	57.6	3,752	10	38	160.1
Jared Allen, Florida Atlantic	346	63.0	2,991	9	24	153.3
Scott Pendarvis, McNeese St.	244	58.2	2,186	6	18	152.9
Lang Campbell, William & Mary	285	63.9	2,296	7	22	152.1
Mike Mitchell, Pennsylvania	319	62.7	2,470	7	26	150.2
Chris Peterson, Cal Polytechnic	223	61.0	1,843	3	15	149.9
Kyle Keating, Lehigh	180	60.6	1,419	6	16	149.4
Jason Murrietta, Northern Arizona	412	59.0	3,472	12	29	147.2

Receiving

	G	REC	YDS	YDS/G	TD
Rob Giancola, Valparaiso	11	57	1,496	136.0	23
Javarus Dudley, Fordham	12	99	1,426	118.8	14
Efrem Hill, Samford	11	92	1,387	126.1	15
Jason Jones, Drake	12	75	1,267	105.6	14
Clarence Moore, Northern Arizona	13	64	1,197	92.1	12
Adam Hannula, San Diego	10	72	1,161	116.1	12
Michel Warfield, Duquesne	11	51	1,147	104.3	14
Johnny Marshall, Northern Arizona	13	80	1,146	88.2	7
Kevin Knutson, Valparaiso	12	74	1,139	94.9	5
Anthony Crissinger-Hill, Florida Atlantic	14	74	1,139	81.4	9

Interceptions

	INT	YDS	TD
Brandon Martin, Butler	8	76	0
Tyrone Parsons, Alcorn St.	7	157	1
Levy Brown, Florida A&M	7	90	0
Joe Glenn, Bucknell	7	126	1
Steve Costello, Massachusetts	6	24	0
Montreal Harkley, East Tennessee St.	6	75	1
Nick Collins, Bethune-Cookman	6	84	1
Matt Nelson, Wofford	6	61	1
Levernonte Turner, Alabama A&M	6	70	0
O'Keefe Henderson, Mississippi Valley St.	6	61	1

Did You Know?

Eight Heisman Trophy winners have played on Super Bowl-winning teams: wide receiver Desmond Howard, running backs Marcus Allen, George Rogers, Tony Dorsett, and Mike Garrett, quarterbacks Jim Plunkett, Roger Staubach, and Paul Hornung.

KEY ATTS=attempts; COMP PCT=completion percentage; YDS=yards; INT=interceptions; TD=touchdowns; G=games; REC=receptions; YDS/G=yards per game

National Championships

Year	Champion	Record	Head Coach
2003	USC	12–1–0	Pete Carroll
(split)	LSU	13–1–0	Nick Saban
2002	Ohio St.	14–0	Jim Tressel
2001	Miami (Florida)	12–0	Larry Coker
2000	Oklahoma	13–0	Bob Stoops
1999	Florida St.	12–0	Bobby Bowden
1998	Tennessee	13–0	Phillip Fulmer
1997	Michigan	12–0	Lloyd Carr
(split)	Nebraska (ESPN)	13–0	Tom Osborne
1996	Florida	12–1	Steve Spurrier
1995	Nebraska	12–0–0	Tom Osborne
1994	Nebraska	13–0–0	Tom Osborne
1993	Florida St.	12–1–0	Bobby Bowden
1992	Alabama	13–0–0	Gene Stallings
1991	Miami (Florida)	12–0–0	Dennis Erickson
(split)	Washington (CNN)	12–0–0	Don James
1990	Colorado	11–1–1	Bill McCartney
(split)	Georgia Tech (UPI)	11–0–1	Bobby Ross
1989	Miami (Florida)	11–1–0	Dennis Erickson
1988	Notre Dame	12–0–0	Lou Holtz
1987	Miami (Florida)	12–0–0	Jimmy Johnson
1986	Penn St.	12–0–0	Joe Paterno
1985	Oklahoma	11–1–0	Barry Switzer
1984	Brigham Young	13–0–0	LaVell Edwards
1983	Miami (Florida)	11–1–0	Howard Schnellenberger
1982	Penn St.	11–1–0	Joe Paterno
1981	Clemson	12–0–0	Danny Ford
1980	Georgia	12–0–0	Vince Dooley
1979	Alabama	12–0–0	Bear Bryant
1978	Alabama	11–1–0	Bear Bryant
(split)	USC (UPI)	12–1–0	John Robinson
1977	Notre Dame	11–1–0	Dan Devine
1976	Pittsburgh	12–0–0	Johnny Majors
1975	Oklahoma	11–1–0	Barry Switzer
1974	Oklahoma (AP)	11–0–0	Barry Switzer
(split)	USC (UPI)	10–1–1	John McKay
1973	Notre Dame	11–0–0	Ara Parseghian
(split)	Alabama (UPI)	11–1–0	Bear Bryant
1972	USC	12–0–0	John McKay
1971	Nebraska	13–0–0	Bob Devaney
1970	Nebraska	11–0–1	Bob Devaney
(split)	Texas (UPI)	10–1–0	Darrell Royal
1969	Texas	11–0–0	Darrell Royal
1968	Ohio St.	10–0–0	Woody Hayes
1967	USC	10–1–0	John McKay
1966	Notre Dame	9–0–1	Ara Parseghian
1965	Alabama	9–1–1	Bear Bryant
(split)	Michigan St. (UPI)	10–1–0	Duffy Daugherty
1964	Alabama	10–1–0	Bear Bryant
1963	Texas	11–0–0	Darrell Royal

Note: National Champion selectors: Helms Athletic Foundation (H), 1883–1935; The Dickinson System (D), 1924–40; The Associated Press (AP), 1936–present; United Press International (UPI), 1958–90; *USA Today*/CNN (CNN), 1991–96; *USA Today*/ESPN (ESPN), 1997–present.

National Championships (cont.)

Year	Champion	Record	Head Coach
1962	USC	11-0-0	John McKay
1961	Alabama	11-0-0	Bear Bryant
1960	Minnesota	8-2-0	Murray Warmath
1959	Syracuse	11-0-0	Ben Schwartzwalder
1958	Louisiana St.	11-0-0	Paul Dietzel
1957	Auburn	10-0-0	Shug Jordan
(split)	Ohio St. (UPI)	9-1-0	Woody Hayes
1956	Oklahoma	10-0-0	Bud Wilkinson
1955	Oklahoma	11-0-0	Bud Wilkinson
1954	Ohio St.	10-0-0	Woody Hayes
(split)	UCLA (UPI)	9-0-0	Red Sanders
1953	Maryland	10-1-0	Jim Tatum
1952	Michigan St.	9-0-0	Biggie Munn
1951	Tennessee	10-0-0	Robert Neyland
1950	Oklahoma	10-1-0	Bud Wilkinson
1949	Notre Dame	10-0-0	Frank Leahy
1948	Michigan	9-0-0	Bennie Oosterbaan
1947	Notre Dame	9-0-0	Frank Leahy
(split)	Michigan	10-0-0	Fritz Crisler
1946	Notre Dame	8-0-1	Frank Leahy
1945	Army	9-0-0	Red Blaik
1944	Army	9-0-0	Red Blaik
1943	Notre Dame	9-1-0	Frank Leahy
1942	Ohio St.	9-1-0	Paul Brown
1941	Minnesota	8-0-0	Bernie Bierman
1940	Minnesota	8-0-0	Bernie Bierman
1939	Texas A&M (AP)	11-0-0	Homer Norton
(split)	USC (D)	8-0-2	Howard Jones
1938	TCU (AP)	11-0-0	Dutch Meyer
(split)	Notre Dame (D)	8-1-0	Elmer Layden
1937	Pittsburgh	9-0-1	Jock Sutherland
1936	Minnesota	7-1-0	Bernie Bierman
1935	Minnesota (H)	8-0-0	Bernie Bierman
(split)	SMU (D)	12-1-0	Matty Bell
1934	Minnesota	8-0-0	Bernie Bierman
1933	Michigan	8-0-0	Harry Kipke
1932	USC (H)	10-0-0	Howard Jones
(split)	Michigan (D)	8-0-0	Harry Kipke
1931	USC	10-1-0	Howard Jones
1930	Notre Dame	10-0-0	Knute Rockne
1929	Notre Dame	9-0-0	Knute Rockne
1928	Georgia Tech (H)	10-0-0	Bill Alexander
(split)	USC (D)	9-0-1	Howard Jones
1927	Illinois	7-0-1	Bob Zuppke
1926	Alabama (H)	9-0-1	Wallace Wade
(split)	Stanford (D)(H)	10-0-1	Pop Warner
1925	Alabama (H)	10-0-0	Wallace Wade
(split)	Dartmouth (D)	8-0-0	Jesse Hawley
1924	Notre Dame	10-0-0	Knute Rockne
1923	Illinois	8-0-0	Bob Zuppke
1922	Cornell	8-0-0	Gil Dobie
1921	Cornell	8-0-0	Gil Dobie
1920	California	9-0-0	Andy Smith
1919	Harvard	9-0-1	Bob Fisher
1918	Pittsburgh	4-1-0	Pop Warner
1917	Georgia Tech	9-0-0	John Heisman
1916	Pittsburgh	8-0-0	Pop Warner
1915	Cornell	9-0-0	Al Sharpe
1914	Army	9-0-0	Charley Daly
1913	Harvard	9-0-0	Percy Haughton
1912	Harvard	9-0-0	Percy Haughton
1911	Princeton	8-0-2	Bill Roper
1910	Harvard	8-0-1	Percy Haughton
1909	Yale	12-1-0	Howard Jones
1908	Pennsylvania	11-0-1	Sol Metzger
1907	Yale	9-0-1	Bill Knox
1906	Princeton	9-0-1	Bill Roper
1905	Chicago	10-0-0	Amos Alonzo Stagg
1904	Pennsylvania	12-0-0	Carl Williams
1903	Princeton	11-0-0	Art Hillebrand
1902	Michigan	11-0-0	Fielding Yost
1901	Michigan	11-0-0	Fielding Yost
1900	Yale	12-0-0	Malcolm McBride
1899	Harvard	10-0-1	Benjamin H. Dibblee
1898	Harvard	11-0-0	W. Cameron Forbes
1897	Pennsylvania	15-0-0	George W. Woodruff
1896	Princeton	10-0-1	Garrett Cochran
1895	Pennsylvania	14-0-0	George W. Woodruff
1894	Yale	16-0-0	William C. Rhodes
1893	Princeton	11-0-0	Tom Trenchard
1892	Yale	13-0-0	Walter Camp
1891	Yale	13-0-0	Walter Camp
1890	Harvard	11-0-0	G. Stewart/G.Adams
1889	Princeton	10-0-0	Edgar Poe
1888	Yale	13-0-0	Walter Camp
1887	Yale	9-0-0	Harry W. Beecher
1886	Yale	9-0-1	Robert N. Corwin
1885	Princeton	9-0-0	Charles DeCamp
1884	Yale	8-0-1	Eugene L. Richards
1883	Yale	8-0-0	Ray Tompkins

Major Bowl Game Results

Rose Bowl

Date	Result
2004	USC 28, Michigan 14
2003	Oklahoma 34, Washington St. 14
2002	Miami 37, Nebraska 14
2001	Washington 34, Purdue 24
2000	Wisconsin 17, Stanford 9
1999	Wisconsin 38, UCLA 31
1998	Michigan 21, Washington St. 16
1997	Ohio St. 20, Arizona St. 17
1996	USC 41, Northwestern 32
1995	Penn St. 38, Oregon 20
1994	Wisconsin 21, UCLA 16
1993	Michigan 38, Washington 31
1992	Washington 34, Michigan 14
1991	Washington 46, Iowa 34
1990	USC 17, Michigan 10
1989	Michigan 22, USC 14
1988	Michigan St. 20, USC 17
1987	Arizona St. 22, Michigan 15
1986	UCLA 45, Iowa 28
1985	USC 20, Ohio St. 17
1984	UCLA 45, Illinois 9
1983	UCLA 24, Michigan 14
1982	Washington 28, Iowa 0
1981	Michigan 23, Washington 6
1980	USC 17, Ohio St. 16
1979	USC 17, Michigan 10

Major Bowl Game Results (cont.)

Rose Bowl (cont.)

Date	Result
1978	Washington 27, Michigan 20
1977	USC 14, Michigan 6
1976	UCLA 23, Ohio St. 10
1975	USC 18, Ohio St. 17
1974	Ohio St. 42, USC 21
1973	USC 42, Ohio St. 17
1972	Stanford 13, Michigan 12
1971	Stanford 27, Ohio St. 17
1970	USC 10, Michigan 3
1969	Ohio St. 27, USC 16
1968	USC 14, Indiana 3
1967	Purdue 14, USC 13
1966	UCLA 14, Michigan St. 12
1965	Michigan 34, Oregon St. 7
1964	Illinois 17, Washington 7
1963	USC 42, Wisconsin 37
1962	Minnesota 21, UCLA 3
1961	Washington 17, Minnesota 7
1960	Washington 44, Wisconsin 8
1959	Iowa 38, California 12
1958	Ohio St. 10, Oregon 7
1957	Iowa 35, Oregon St. 19
1956	Michigan St. 17, UCLA 14
1955	Ohio St. 20, USC 7
1954	Michigan St. 28, UCLA 20
1953	USC 7, Wisconsin 0
1952	Illinois 40, Stanford 7
1951	Michigan 14, California 6
1950	Ohio St. 17, California 14
1949	Northwestern 20, California 14
1948	Michigan 49, USC 0
1947	Illinois 45, UCLA 14

Date	Result
1946	Alabama 34, USC 14
1945	USC 25, Tennessee 0
1944	USC 29, Washington 0
1943	Georgia 9, UCLA 0
1942	Oregon St. 20, Duke 16
1941	Stanford 21, Nebraska 13
1940	USC 14, Tennessee 0
1939	USC 7, Duke 3
1938	California 13, Alabama 0
1937	Pittsburgh 21, Washington 0
1936	Stanford 7, SMU 0
1935	Alabama 29, Stanford 13
1934	Columbia 7, Stanford 0
1933	USC 35, Pittsburgh 0
1932	USC 21, Tulane 12
1931	Alabama 24, Washington St. 0
1930	USC 47, Pittsburgh 14
1929	Georgia Tech 8, California 7
1928	Stanford 7, Pittsburgh 6
1927	Stanford 7, Alabama 7
1926	Alabama 20, Washington 19
1925	Notre Dame 27, Stanford 10
1924	Washington 14, Navy 14
1923	USC 14, Penn St. 3
1922	California 0, Washington & Jefferson 0
1921	California 28, Ohio St. 0
1920	Harvard 7, Oregon 6
1919	Great Lakes 17, Mare Island 0
1918	Mare Island 19, Camp Lewis 7
1917	Oregon 14, Pennsylvania 0
1916	Washington St. 14, Brown 0
1902	Michigan 49, Stanford 0

Note: From 1903–15, no Rose Bowl football game was held. In 1903, polo replaced football. From 1904–1915, chariot races were held. Football returned in 1916.

Orange Bowl

Date	Result
January 1, 2004	Miami (Florida) 16, Florida St. 14
January 2, 2003	USC 38, Iowa 17
January 2, 2002	Florida 56, Maryland 23
January 3, 2001	Oklahoma 13, Florida St. 2
January 1, 2000	Michigan 35, Alabama 34 (OT)
January 2, 1999	Florida 31, Syracuse 10
January 2, 1998	Nebraska 42, Tennessee 17
December 31, 1996	Nebraska 41, Virginia Tech 21
January 1, 1996	Florida St. 31, Notre Dame 26
January 1, 1995	Nebraska 24, Miami (Florida) 17
January 1, 1994	Florida St. 18, Nebraska 16
January 1, 1993	Florida St. 27, Nebraska 14
January 1, 1992	Miami (Florida) 22, Nebraska 0
January 1, 1991	Colorado 10, Notre Dame 9
January 1, 1990	Notre Dame 21, Colorado 6
January 2, 1989	Miami (Florida) 23, Nebraska 3
January 1, 1988	Miami (Florida) 20, Oklahoma 14
January 1, 1987	Oklahoma 42, Arkansas 8
January 1, 1986	Oklahoma 25, Penn St. 10
January 1, 1985	Washington 28, Oklahoma 17
January 2, 1984	Miami (Florida) 31, Nebraska 30
January 1, 1983	Nebraska 21, LSU 20
January 1, 1982	Clemson 22, Nebraska 15
January 1, 1981	Oklahoma 18, Florida St. 17
January 1, 1980	Oklahoma 24, Florida St. 7
January 1, 1979	Oklahoma 31, Nebraska 24
January 2, 1978	Arkansas 31, Oklahoma 0
January 1, 1977	Ohio St. 27, Colorado 10
January 1, 1976	Oklahoma 14, Michigan 6
January 1, 1975	Notre Dame 13, Alabama 11

Date	Result
January 1, 1974	Penn St. 16, LSU 9
January 1, 1973	Nebraska 40, Notre Dame 6
January 1, 1972	Nebraska 38, Alabama 6
January 1, 1971	Nebraska 17, LSU 12
January 1, 1970	Penn St. 10, Missouri 3
January 1, 1969	Penn St. 15, Kansas 14
January 1, 1968	Oklahoma 26, Tennessee 24
January 2, 1967	Florida 27, Georgia Tech 12
January 1, 1966	Alabama 39, Nebraska 28
January 1, 1965	Texas 21, Alabama 17
January 1, 1964	Nebraska 13, Auburn 7
January 1, 1963	Alabama 17, Oklahoma 0
January 1, 1962	LSU 25, Colorado 7
January 2, 1961	Missouri 21, Navy 14
January 1, 1960	Georgia 14, Missouri 0
January 1, 1959	Oklahoma 21, Syracuse 6
January 1, 1958	Oklahoma 48, Duke 21
January 1, 1957	Colorado 27, Clemson 21
January 2, 1956	Oklahoma 20, Maryland 6
January 1, 1955	Duke 34, Nebraska 7
January 1, 1954	Oklahoma 7, Maryland 0
January 1, 1953	Alabama 61, Syracuse 6
January 1, 1952	Georgia Tech 17, Baylor 14
January 1, 1951	Clemson 15, Miami (Florida) 14
January 2, 1950	Santa Clara 21, Kentucky 13
January 1, 1949	Texas 41, Georgia 28
January 1, 1948	Georgia Tech 20, Kansas 14
January 1, 1947	Rice 8, Tennessee 0
January 1, 1946	Miami (Florida) 13, Holy Cross 6
January 1, 1945	Tulsa 26, Georgia Tech 12

Major Bowl Game Results (cont.)

Orange Bowl (cont.)

Date	Result
January 1, 1944	LSU 19, Texas A&M 14
January 1, 1943	Alabama 37, Boston College 21
January 1, 1942	Georgia 40, TCU 26
January 1, 1941	Mississippi St. 14, Georgetown 7
January 1, 1940	Georgia Tech 21, Missouri 7
January 2, 1939	Tennessee 17, Oklahoma 0
January 1, 1938	Auburn 6, Michigan St. 0
January 1, 1937	Duquesne 13, Mississippi St. 12
January 1, 1936	Catholic 20, Mississippi 19
January 1, 1935	Bucknell 26, Miami (Florida) 0

Sugar Bowl

Date	Result
January 4, 2004	LSU 21, Oklahoma 14
January 1, 2003	Georgia 26, Florida St. 13
January 1, 2002	LSU 47, Illinois 34
January 2, 2001	Miami (Florida) 37, Florida 20
January 4, 2000	Florida St. 46, Virginia Tech 29
January 1, 1999	Ohio St. 24, Texas A&M 14
January 1, 1998	Florida St. 31, Ohio St. 14
January 2, 1997	Florida 52, Florida St. 20
December 31, 1995	Virginia Tech 28, Texas 10
January 2, 1995	Florida St. 23, Florida 17
January 1, 1994	Florida 41, West Virginia 7
January 1, 1993	Alabama 34, Miami (Florida) 13
January 1, 1992	Notre Dame 39, Florida 28
January 1, 1991	Tennessee 23, Virginia 22
January 1, 1990	Miami (Florida) 33, Alabama 25
January 2, 1989	Florida St. 13, Auburn 7
January 1, 1988	Auburn 16, Syracuse 16
January 1, 1987	Nebraska 30, LSU 15
January 1, 1986	Tennessee 35, Miami (Florida) 7
January 1, 1985	Nebraska 28, LSU 10
January 2, 1984	Auburn 9, Michigan 7
January 1, 1983	Penn St. 27, Georgia 23
January 1, 1982	Pittsburgh 24, Georgia 20
January 1, 1981	Georgia 17, Notre Dame 10
January 1, 1980	Alabama 24, Arkansas 9
January 1, 1979	Alabama 14, Penn St. 7
January 2, 1978	Alabama 35, Ohio St. 6
January 1, 1977	Pittsburgh 27, Georgia 3
December 31, 1975	Alabama 13, Penn St. 6
December 31, 1974	Nebraska 13, Florida 10
December 31, 1973	Notre Dame 24, Alabama 23
December 31, 1972	Oklahoma 14, Penn St. 0
January 1, 1972	Oklahoma 40, Auburn 22
January 1, 1971	Tennessee 34, Air Force 13
January 1, 1970	Mississippi 27, Arkansas 22
January 1, 1969	Arkansas 16, Georgia 2
January 1, 1968	LSU 20, Wyoming 13
January 2, 1967	Alabama 34, Nebraska 7
January 1, 1966	Missouri 20, Florida 18
January 1, 1965	LSU 13, Syracuse 10
January 1, 1964	Alabama 12, Mississippi 7
January 1, 1963	Mississippi 17, Arkansas 3
January 1, 1962	Alabama 10, Arkansas 3
January 2, 1961	Mississippi 14, Rice 6
January 1, 1960	Mississippi 21, LSU 0
January 1, 1959	LSU 7, Clemson 0
January 1, 1958	Mississippi 39, Texas 7
January 1, 1957	Baylor 13, Tennessee 7
January 2, 1956	Georgia Tech 7, Pittsburgh 0
January 1, 1955	Navy 21, Mississippi 0
January 1, 1954	Georgia Tech 42, West Virginia 19
January 1, 1953	Georgia Tech 24, Mississippi 7
January 1, 1952	Maryland 28, Tennessee 13
January 1, 1951	Kentucky 13, Oklahoma 7
January 2, 1950	Oklahoma 35, LSU 0
January 1, 1949	Oklahoma 14, North Carolina 6
January 1, 1948	Texas 27, Alabama 7
January 1, 1947	Georgia 20, North Carolina 10
January 1, 1946	Oklahoma St. 33, Saint Mary's (Colorado) 13
January 1, 1945	Duke 29, Alabama 26
January 1, 1944	Georgia Tech 20, Tulsa 18
January 1, 1943	Tennessee 14, Tulsa 7
January 1, 1942	Fordham 2, Missouri 0
January 1. 1941	Boston College 19, Tennessee 13
January 1, 1940	Texas A&M 14, Tulane 13
January 2, 1939	TCU 15, Carnegie Mellon 7
January 1, 1938	Santa Clara 6, LSU 0
January 1, 1937	Santa Clara 21, LSU 14
January 1, 1936	TCU 3, LSU 2
January 1, 1935	Tulane 20, Temple 14

Cotton Bowl

Date	Result
January 2, 2004	Mississippi 31, Oklahoma St. 28
January 1, 2003	Texas 35, LSU 20
January 1, 2002	Oklahoma 10, Arkansas 3
January 1, 2001	Kansas St. 35, Tennessee 21
January 1, 2000	Arkansas 27, Texas 6
January 1, 1999	Texas 38, Mississippi St. 11
January 1, 1998	UCLA 29, Texas A&M 23
January 1, 1997	BYU 19, Kansas St. 15
January 1, 1996	Colorado 38, Oregon 6
January 2, 1995	USC 55, Texas Tech 14
January 1, 1994	Notre Dame 24, Texas A&M 21
January 1, 1993	Notre Dame 28, Texas A&M 3
January 1, 1992	Florida St. 10, Texas A&M 2
January 1, 1991	Miami (Florida) 46, Texas 3
January 1, 1990	Tennessee 31, Arkansas 27
January 2, 1989	UCLA 17, Arkansas 3
January 1, 1988	Texas A&M 35, Notre Dame 10
January 1, 1987	Ohio St. 28, Texas A&M 12
January 1, 1986	Texas A&M 36, Auburn 16
January 1, 1985	Boston College 45, Houston 28
January 2, 1984	Georgia 10, Texas 9

Legends

Vincent "Bo" Jackson, running back, b. November 30, 1962, Bessemer, Alabama. Bo knows college football. The gridiron legend left Auburn with school records for rushing yards (4,303) and rushing touchdowns (43). He averaged a whopping 6.6 yards per carry for his four-year career. In 1985, Jackson became the third player in SEC history to top 4,000 career yards. He also won the Heisman Trophy that season.

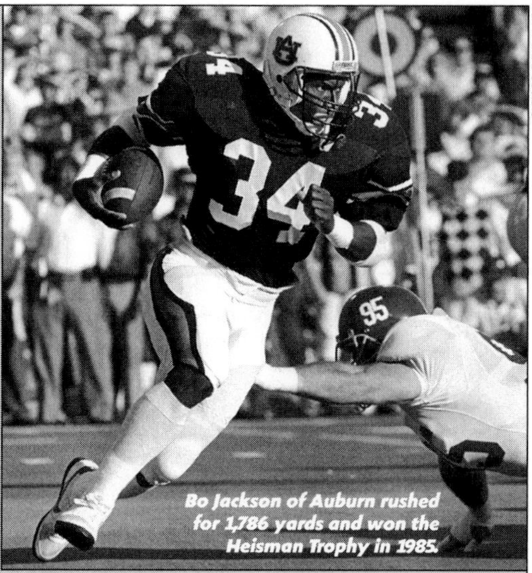

BETTMAN/CORBIS

Bo Jackson of Auburn rushed for 1,786 yards and won the Heisman Trophy in 1985.

Herschel Walker, running back, b. March 3, 1962, Wrightsville, Georgia. This Georgia Dawg is one of the greatest players in college football history. Walker rushed for 5,259 yards and scored 52 touchdowns in his three college seasons. He held 11 NCAA records, 16 SEC records, and 41 Georgia records when he left to play in the United States Football League (USFL) in 1983. Walker set the NCAA single-season record for most rushing yards by a freshman (1,616). The next season, he set the NCAA single-season record for most rushing yards by a sophomore (1,891). Walker never rushed for less than 1,600 yards during his career and averaged 1,753 yards per season. He won the Heisman Trophy in 1982.

Doug Flutie, quarterback, b. October 23, 1962, Manchester, Maryland. The Boston College QB won the Heisman Trophy in 1984 and left the school after four seasons as the Division I-A leader in career passing yards (10,579). But he will always be remembered for making one of the greatest plays in college football history. As time expired in a 1984 game against Miami, he threw a 48-yard touchdown pass that defeated the Hurricanes, 47–45.

Major Bowl Game Results (cont.)

Cotton Bowl (cont.)

Date	Result
January 1, 1983	SMU 7, Pittsburgh 3
January 1, 1982	Texas 14, Alabama 12
January 1, 1981	Alabama 30, Baylor 2
January 1, 1980	Houston 17, Nebraska 14
January 1, 1979	Notre Dame 35, Houston 34
January 2, 1978	Notre Dame 38, Texas 10
January 1, 1977	Houston 30, Maryland 21
January 1, 1976	Arkansas 31, Georgia 10
January 1, 1975	Penn St. 41, Baylor 20
January 1, 1974	Nebraska 19, Texas 3
January 1, 1973	Texas 17, Alabama 13
January 1, 1972	Penn St. 30, Texas 6
January 1, 1971	Notre Dame 24, Texas 11
January 1, 1970	Texas 21, Notre Dame 17
January 1, 1969	Texas 36, Tennessee 13
January 1, 1968	Texas A&M 20, Alabama 16
December 31, 1966	Georgia 24, SMU 9
January 1, 1966	LSU 14, Arkansas 7
January 1, 1965	Arkansas 10, Nebraska 7
January 1, 1964	Texas 28, Navy 6

Date	Result
January 1, 1963	LSU 13, Texas 0
January 1, 1962	Texas 12, Mississippi 7
January 2, 1961	Duke 7, Arkansas 6
January 1, 1960	Syracuse 23, Texas 14
January 1, 1959	TCU 0, Air Force 0
January 1, 1958	Navy 20, Rice 7
January 1, 1957	TCU 28, Syracuse 27
January 2, 1956	Mississippi 14, TCU 13
January 1, 1955	Georgia Tech 14, Arkansas 6
January 1, 1954	Rice 28, Alabama 6
January 1, 1953	Texas 16, Tennessee 0
January 1, 1952	Kentucky 20, TCU 7
January 1, 1951	Tennessee 20, Texas 14
January 2, 1950	Rice 27, North Carolina 13
January 1, 1949	SMU 21, Oregon 13
January 1, 1948	SMU 13, Penn St. 13
January 1, 1947	Arkansas 0, LSU 0
January 1, 1946	Texas 40, Missouri 27
January 1, 1945	Oklahoma St. 34, TCU 0
January 1, 1944	Texas 7, Randolph Field 7

Major Bowl Game Results (cont.)

Cotton Bowl (cont.)

Date	Result
January 1, 1943	Texas 14, Georgia Tech 7
January 1, 1942	Alabama 29, Texas A&M 21
January 1, 1941	Texas A&M 13, Fordham 12
January 1, 1940	Clemson 6, Boston College 3
January 2, 1939	St. Mary's (Calif.) 20, Texas Tech 13
January 1, 1938	Rice 28, Colorado 14
January 1, 1937	TCU 16, Marquette 6

Fiesta Bowl

Date	Result
January 2, 2004	Ohio St. 35, Kansas St. 28
January 3, 2003	Ohio St. 31, Miami 24
January 1, 2002	Oregon 38, Colorado 16
January 1, 2001	Oregon St. 41, Notre Dame 9
January 2, 2000	Nebraska 31, Tennessee 21
January 4, 1999	Tennessee 23, Florida St. 16
December 31, 1997	Kansas St. 35, Syracuse 18
January 1, 1997	Penn St. 38, Texas 15
January 2, 1996	Nebraska 62, Florida 24
January 2, 1995	Colorado 41, Notre Dame 24
January 1, 1994	Arizona 29, Miami (Florida) 0
January 1, 1993	Syracuse 26, Colorado 22
January 1, 1992	Penn St. 42, Tennessee 17
January 1, 1991	Louisville 34, Alabama 7
January 1, 1990	Florida St. 41, Nebraska 17
January 2, 1989	Notre Dame 34, West Virginia 21
January 1, 1988	Florida St. 31, Nebraska 28
January 2, 1987	Penn St. 14, Miami (Florida) 10
January 1, 1986	Michigan 27, Nebraska 23
January 1, 1985	UCLA 39, Miami (Florida) 37
January 2, 1984	Ohio St. 28, Pittsburgh 23
January 1, 1983	Arizona St. 32, Oklahoma 21
January 1, 1982	Penn St. 26, USC 10
December 26, 1980	Penn St. 31, Ohio St. 19
December 25, 1979	Pittsburgh 16, Arizona 10
December 25, 1978	Arkansas 10, UCLA 10
December 25, 1977	Penn St. 42, Arizona St. 30
December 25, 1976	Oklahoma 41, Wyoming 7
December 26, 1975	Arizona St. 17, Nebraska 14
December 28, 1974	Oklahoma St. 16, BYU 6
December 21, 1973	Arizona St. 28, Pittsburgh 7
December 23, 1972	Arizona St. 49, Missouri 35
December 27, 1971	Arizona St. 45, Florida St. 38

NCAA Division I-AA Championships

Year	Winner	Runner-up	Score
2003	Delaware	Colgate	40–0
2002	Western Kentucky	McNeese St.	34–14
2001	Montana	Furman	13–6
2000	Georgia Southern	Montana	27–25
1999	Georgia Southern	Youngstown St.	59–24
1998	Massachusetts	Georgia Southern	55–43
1997	Youngstown St.	McNeese St.	10–9
1996	Marshall	Montana	49–29
1995	Montana	Marshall	22–20
1994	Youngstown St.	Boise St.	28–14
1993	Youngstown St.	Marshall	17–5
1992	Marshall	Youngstown St.	31–28
1991	Youngstown St.	Marshall	25–17
1990	Georgia Southern	Nevada-Reno	36–13
1989	Georgia Southern	Stephen F. Austin	37–34
1988	Furman	Georgia Southern	17–12
1987	Northeast Louisiana	Marshall	43–42
1986	Georgia Southern	Arkansas St.	48–21
1985	Georgia Southern	Furman	44–42
1984	Montana St.	Louisiana Tech	19–6
1983	Southern Illinois	Western Carolina	43–7
1982	Eastern Kentucky	Delaware	17–14
1981	Idaho St.	Eastern Kentucky	34–23
1980	Boise St.	Eastern Kentucky	31–29
1979	Eastern Kentucky	Lehigh	30–7
1978	Florida A&M	Massachusetts	35–28

Heisman Memorial Trophy

Awarded to the nation's best college player by the Downtown Athletic Club (DAC) of New York City. The trophy is named after John W. Heisman, who coached Georgia Tech to the national championship in 1917 and later served as DAC athletic director.

Year	Winner, College	Runner-up, College
2003	Jason White, Oklahoma	Larry Fitzgerald, Pittsburgh
2002	Carson Palmer, USC	Brad Banks, Iowa
2001	Eric Crouch, Nebraska	Rex Grossman, Florida
2000	Chris Weinke, Florida St.	Josh Heupel, Oklahoma
1999	Ron Dayne, Wisconsin	Joe Hamilton, Georgia Tech
1998	Ricky Williams, Texas	Michael Bishop, Kansas St.

Heisman Memorial Trophy (cont.)

Year	Winner, College	Runner-up, College
1997	† Charles Woodson, Michigan	Peyton Manning, Tennessee
1996	† Danny Wuerffel, Florida	Troy Davis, Iowa St.
1995	Eddie George, Ohio St.	Tommie Frazier, Nebraska
1994	Rashaan Salaam, Colorado	Ki-Jana Carter, Penn St.
1993	† Charlie Ward, Florida St.	Heath Shuler, Tennessee
1992	Gino Torretta, Miami (Florida)	Marshall Faulk, San Diego St.
1991	* Desmond Howard, Michigan	Casey Weldon, Florida St.
1990	* Ty Detmer, BYU	Raghib Ismail, Notre Dame
1989	* Andre Ware, Houston	Anthony Thompson, Indiana
1988	* Barry Sanders, Oklahoma St.	Rodney Peete, USC
1987	Tim Brown, Notre Dame	Don McPherson, Syracuse
1986	Vinny Testaverde, Miami (Florida)	Paul Palmer, Temple
1985	Bo Jackson, Auburn	Chuck Long, Iowa
1984	Doug Flutie, Boston College	Keith Byars, Ohio St.
1983	Mike Rozier, Nebraska	Steve Young, BYU
1982	* Herschel Walker, Georgia	John Elway, Stanford
1981	Marcus Allen, USC	Herschel Walker, Georgia
1980	George Rogers, South Carolina	Hugh Green, Pittsburgh
1979	Charles White, USC	Billy Sims, Oklahoma
1978	* Billy Sims, Oklahoma	Chuck Fusina, Penn St.
1977	Earl Campbell, Texas	Terry Miller, Oklahoma St.
1976	† Tony Dorsett, Pittsburgh	Ricky Bell, USC
1975	Archie Griffin, Ohio St.	Chuck Muncie, California
1974	* Archie Griffin, Ohio St.	Anthony Davis, USC
1973	John Cappelletti, Penn St.	John Hicks, Ohio St.
1972	Johnny Rodgers, Nebraska	Greg Pruitt, Oklahoma
1971	Pat Sullivan, Auburn	Ed Marinaro, Cornell
1970	Jim Plunkett, Stanford	Joe Theismann, Notre Dame
1969	Steve Owens, Oklahoma	Mike Phipps, Purdue
1968	O.J. Simpson, USC	Leroy Keyes, Purdue
1967	Gary Beban, UCLA	O.J. Simpson, USC
1966	Steve Spurrier, Florida	Bob Griese, Purdue
1965	Mike Garrett, USC	Howard Twilley, Tulsa
1964	John Huarte, Notre Dame	Jerry Rhome, Tulsa
1963	* Roger Staubach, Navy	Billy Lothridge, Georgia Tech
1962	Terry Baker, Oregon St.	Jerry Stovall, LSU
1961	Ernie Davis, Syracuse	Bob Ferguson, Ohio St.
1960	Joe Bellino, Navy	Tom Brown, Minnesota
1959	Billy Cannon, LSU	Rich Lucas, Penn St.
1958	Pete Dawkins, Army	Randy Duncan, Iowa
1957	John David Crow, Texas A&M	Alex Karras, Iowa
1956	Paul Hornung, Notre Dame	Johnny Majors, Tennessee
1955	Howard Cassady, Ohio St.	Jim Swink, TCU
1954	Alan Ameche, Wisconsin	Kurt Burris, Oklahoma
1953	John Lattner, Notre Dame	Paul Giel, Minnesota
1952	Billy Vessels, Oklahoma	Jack Scarbath, Maryland
1951	Dick Kazmaier, Princeton	Hank Lauricella, Tennessee
1950	* Vic Janowicz, Ohio St.	Kyle Rote, SMU
1949	† Leon Hart, Notre Dame	Charlie Justice, North Carolina
1948	* Doak Walker, SMU	Charlie Justice, North Carolina
1947	† John Lujack, Notre Dame	Bob Chappius, Michigan
1946	Glenn Davis, Army	Charley Trippi, Georgia
1945	*† Doc Blanchard, Army	Glenn Davis, Army
1944	Les Horvath, Ohio St.	Glenn Davis, Army
1943	Angelo Bertelli, Notre Dame	Bob Odell, Pennsylvania
1942	Frank Sinkwich, Georgia	Paul Governali, Columbia
1941	† Bruce Smith, Minnesota	Angelo Bertelli, Notre Dame
1940	Tom Harmon, Michigan	John Kimbrough, Texas A&M
1939	Nile Kinnick, Iowa	Tom Harmon, Michigan
1938	† Davey O'Brien, TCU	Marshall Goldberg, Pittsburgh
1937	Clint Frank, Yale	Byron White, Colorado
1936	Larry Kelley, Yale	Sam Francis, Nebraska
1935	Jay Berwanger, Chicago	Monk Meyer, Army

*Juniors (all others were Seniors)
†Winners who played for national championship teams the same year
Note: Former Heisman winners and members of the national media cast votes with ballots allowing for three names (3 points for first, 2 points for second, and 1 point for third).

Maxwell Award

Given to the nation's outstanding college football player by the Maxwell Football Club of Philadelphia.

Year	Player, College	Year	Player, College
2003	Eli Manning, Mississippi	1969	Mike Reid, Penn St.
2002	Larry Johnson, Penn St.	1968	O.J. Simpson, USC
2001	Ken Dorsey, Miami (Florida)	1967	Gary Beban, UCLA
2000	Drew Brees, Purdue	1966	Jim Lynch, Notre Dame
1999	Ron Dayne, Wisconsin	1965	Tommy Nobis, Texas
1998	Ricky Williams, Texas	1964	Glenn Ressler, Penn St.
1997	Peyton Manning, Tennessee	1963	Roger Staubach, Navy
1996	Danny Wuerffel, Florida	1962	Terry Baker, Oregon St.
1995	Eddie George, Ohio St.	1961	Bob Ferguson, Ohio St.
1994	Kerry Collins, Penn St.	1960	Joe Bellino, Navy
1993	Charlie Ward, Florida St.	1959	Rich Lucas, Penn St.
1992	Gino Torretta, Miami (Florida)	1958	Pete Dawkins, Army
1991	Desmond Howard, Michigan	1957	Bob Reifsnyder, Navy
1990	Ty Detmer, BYU	1956	Tommy McDonald, Oklahoma
1989	Anthony Thompson, Indiana	1955	Howard Cassady, Ohio St.
1988	Barry Sanders, Oklahoma St.	1954	Ron Beagle, Navy
1987	Don McPherson, Syracuse	1953	John Lattner, Notre Dame
1986	Vinny Testaverde, Miami (Florida)	1952	John Lattner, Notre Dame
1985	Chuck Long, Iowa	1951	Dick Kazmaier, Princeton
1984	Doug Flutie, Boston College	1950	Reds Bagnell, Pennsylvania
1983	Mike Rozier, Nebraska	1949	Leon Hart, Notre Dame
1982	Herschel Walker, Georgia	1948	Chuck Bednarik, Pennsylvania
1981	Marcus Allen, USC	1947	Doak Walker, SMU
1980	Hugh Green, Pittsburgh	1946	Charley Trippi, Georgia
1979	Charles White, USC	1945	Doc Blanchard, Army
1978	Chuck Fusina, Penn St.	1944	Glenn Davis, Army
1977	Ross Browner, Notre Dame	1943	Bob Odell, Pennsylvania
1976	Tony Dorsett, Pittsburgh	1942	Paul Governali, Columbia
1975	Archie Griffin, Ohio St.	1941	Bill Dudley, Virginia
1974	Steve Joachim, Temple	1940	Tom Harmon, Michigan
1973	John Cappelletti, Penn St.	1939	Nile Kinnick, Iowa
1972	Brad Van Pelt, Michigan St.	1938	Davey O'Brien, TCU
1971	Ed Marinaro, Cornell	1937	Clint Frank, Yale
1970	Jim Plunkett, Stanford		

Davey O'Brien National Quarterback Award

Given to the nation's top quarterback by the Davey O'Brien Educational and Charitable Trust of Fort Worth. Named for TCU Hall of Fame quarterback Davey O'Brien (1936-38).

Year	Player, College	Year	Player, College
2003	Jason White, Oklahoma	1991	Ty Detmer, BYU
2002	Brad Banks, Iowa	1990	Ty Detmer, BYU
2001	Eric Crouch, Nebraska	1989	Andre Ware, Houston
2000	Chris Weinke, Florida St.	1988	Troy Aikman, UCLA
1999	Joe Hamilton, Georgia Tech	1987	Don McPherson, Syracuse
1998	Michael Bishop, Kansas St.	1986	Vinny Testaverde, Miami (Florida)
1997	Peyton Manning, Tennessee	1985	Chuck Long, Iowa
1996	Danny Wuerffel, Florida	1984	Doug Flutie, Boston College
1995	Danny Wuerffel, Florida	1983	Steve Young, BYU
1994	Kerry Collins, Penn St.	1982	Todd Blackledge, Penn St.
1993	Charlie Ward, Florida St.	1981	Jim McMahon, BYU
1992	Gino Torretta, Miami (Florida)		

Did You Know?

The Auburn-Alabama rivalry got its "Iron Bowl" nickname because the city of Birmingham, Alabama, was built around large iron ore deposits.

Vince Lombardi/Rotary Award

Given to the outstanding college lineman of the year. The award is sponsored by the Rotary Club of Houston, Texas.

Year	Player, College	Year	Player, College
2003	Tommie Harris, Oklahoma	1986	Cornelius Bennett, Alabama
2002	Terrell Suggs, Arizona St.	1985	Tony Casillas, Oklahoma
2001	Julius Peppers, North Carolina	1984	Tony Degrate, Texas
2000	Jamal Reynolds, Florida St.	1983	Dean Steinkuhler, Nebraska
1999	Corey Moore, Virginia Tech	1982	Dave Rimington, Nebraska
1998	Dat Nguyen, Texas A&M	1981	Kenneth Sims, Texas
1997	Grant Wistrom, Nebraska	1980	Hugh Green, Pittsburgh
1996	Orlando Pace, Ohio St.	1979	Brad Budde, USC
1995	Orlando Pace, Ohio St.	1978	Bruce Clark, Penn St.
1994	Warren Sapp, Miami (Florida)	1977	Ross Browner, Notre Dame
1993	Aaron Taylor, Notre Dame	1976	Wilson Whitley, Houston
1992	Marvin Jones, Florida St.	1975	Lee Roy Selmon, Oklahoma
1991	Steve Emtman, Washington	1974	Randy White, Maryland
1990	Chris Zorich, Notre Dame	1973	John Hicks, Ohio St.
1989	Percy Snow, Michigan St.	1972	Rich Glover, Nebraska
1988	Tracy Rocker, Auburn	1971	Walt Patulski, Notre Dame
1987	Chris Spielman, Ohio St.	1970	Jim Stillwagon, Ohio St.

2003-04 TIME LINE

September 27, 2003: The third-ranked USC Trojans suffer their only loss of the season when the unranked California Golden Bears defeat them, 34–31, in triple overtime.

October 11, 2003: The sixth-ranked LSU Tigers lose their only game of the season when they are upset at home by the unranked Florida Gators, 19–7.

October 25, 2003: The Florida State Seminoles' 48–24 win over Wake Forest pushes Bobby Bowden past Penn State coach Joe Paterno as the head coach with the most victories in Division I-A history (339). Bowden finishes the season with 342 career wins.

November 1, 2003: Pittsburgh wideout Larry Fitzgerald sets the NCAA record for consecutive games with a touchdown catch (14), against Boston College. Fitzgerald extends the record to 18 games by the end of the season.

December 7, 2003: USC finishes the regular season ranked Number 1 in both the AP and Coaches' polls. But the final BCS poll ranks Oklahoma first, LSU second, and the Trojans third.

December 13, 2003: Quarterback Jason White of the Oklahoma Sooners wins the 69th Heisman Trophy.

January 1, 2004: USC defeats Michigan, 28–14, in the Rose Bowl to earn a share of the national championship.

January 4, 2004: LSU defeats Oklahoma, 21–14, in the Sugar Bowl to win the BCS national championship.

February 5, 2004: A federal judge rules that the NFL must allow Ohio State running back Maurice Clarett to enter the league's 2004 draft. The ruling states that the league's policy of not allowing players into the draft until they have been out of high school for three years violates U.S. antitrust laws. The NFL appeals the ruling.

April 19, 2004: An appeals court rules that the NFL does not have to allow Maurice Clarett of Ohio State and sophomore Mike Williams of USC in the 2004 NFL draft.

May 24, 2004: An appeals court rules that federal labor policy allows the NFL to set rules for when players can enter the league, effectively keeping Clarett and Williams out of the NFL in 2004.

BASEBALL

The Florida Marlins snuck by the New York Yankees in 2003 to win their second World Series in seven years.

The 2003 major league baseball regular season was filled with milestones. Outfielder Sammy Sosa of the Chicago Cubs and first baseman Rafael Palmeiro of the Texas Rangers joined the 500-home-run club. Roger Clemens of the New York Yankees became the first pitcher since 1990 to win his 300th career game.

The post-season was exciting and heart-wrenching, especially for Boston Red Sox and Chicago Cubs fans. Both teams reached their league championship series, and it looked as if they might meet in the World Series. (The Red Sox haven't won the Series since 1918; the Cubs haven't won it since 1908.) But both teams lost seven-game heartbreakers in their league championship series.

The Florida Marlins were the most unlikely World Series candidates. Seven weeks into the season, they were 19–29, but they reached the playoffs as the wild card with a 91–71 record. The team proved they were neither too young (average age of starters: 25) nor too old (manager Jack McKeon was 72) to knock off powerhouse teams. The Marlins became the post-season's comeback kids. They rallied from one game down in the division series to beat the National League West champion San Francisco Giants in four games. In the National League Championship Series, they were down three games to one but won the National League pennant and a World Series berth by defeating the Cubs, 4 games to 3. They faced the New York Yankees and overcame a 2-games-to-1 deficit to win the title. Josh Beckett, the Marlins' 23-year-old pitching ace, was named the Series MVP.

The Yankees won their 39th American League pennant with a seven-game triumph over the Boston Red Sox. In the off-season, the Red Sox beefed up their roster by acquiring starting pitcher Curt Schilling and closer Keith Foulke. The Yankees answered by adding starters Kevin Brown and Javier Vazquez and outfielder Gary Sheffield. But New York made its biggest move over the weekend of February 14-15, 2004, when it acquired reigning A.L. MVP Alex Rodriguez from the Texas Rangers.

When spring training opened, the talk was of big names in new places. But a steroid controversy soon grabbed all the headlines and threatened to severely damage the game when several of baseball's biggest stars, including Barry Bonds of the Giants, were forced to answer questions about alleged steroid use as part of an ongoing investigation by the FBI.

2003 Major League Baseball Final Standings

National League

EASTERN DIVISION

Team	Won	Lost	Pct	GB	Home	Away
Braves	101	61	.623	—	55–26	46–35
†Marlins	91	71	.562	10.0	53–28	38–43
Phillies	86	76	.531	15.0	49–32	37–44
Expos	83	79	.512	18.0	52–29	31–50
Mets	66	95	.410	34.5	34–46	32–49

CENTRAL DIVISION

Team	Won	Lost	Pct	GB	Home	Away
Cubs	88	74	.543	—	44–37	44–37
Astros	87	75	.537	1.0	48–33	39–42
Cardinals	85	77	.525	3.0	48–33	37–44
Pirates	75	87	.463	13.0	39–42	36–45
Reds	69	93	.426	19.0	35–46	34–47
Brewers	68	94	.420	20.0	31–50	37–44

WESTERN DIVISION

Team	Won	Lost	Pct	GB	Home	Away
Giants	100	61	.621	—	57–24	43–37
Dodgers	85	77	.525	15.5	46–35	39–42
Diamondbacks	84	78	.519	16.5	45–36	39–42
Rockies	74	88	.457	26.5	49–32	25–56
Padres	64	98	.395	36.5	35–46	29–52

†Wild-card team

American League

EASTERN DIVISION

Team	Won	Lost	Pct	GB	Home	Away
Yankees	101	61	.623	—	50–32	51–29
†Red Sox	95	67	.586	6.0	53–28	42–39
Blue Jays	86	76	.531	15.0	41–40	45–36
Orioles	71	91	.438	30.0	40–40	31–51
Devil Rays	63	99	.389	38.0	36–45	27–54

CENTRAL DIVISION

Team	Won	Lost	Pct	GB	Home	Away
Twins	90	72	.556	—	48–33	42–39
White Sox	86	76	.531	4.0	51–30	35–46
Royals	83	79	.512	7.0	40–40	43–39
Indians	68	94	.420	22.0	38–43	30–51
Tigers	43	119	.265	47.0	23–58	20–61

WESTERN DIVISION

Team	Won	Lost	Pct	GB	Home	Away
A's	96	66	.593	—	57–24	39–42
Mariners	93	69	.574	3.0	50–31	43–38
Angels	77	85	.475	19.0	45–37	32–48
Rangers	71	91	.438	25.0	43–38	28–53

†Wild-card team

MLB TEAMS

NATIONAL LEAGUE

Arizona Diamondbacks
Atlanta Braves
Chicago Cubs
Cincinnati Reds
Colorado Rockies
Florida Marlins
Houston Astros
Los Angeles Dodgers
Milwaukee Brewers
Montreal Expos
New York Mets
Philadelphia Phillies
Pittsburgh Pirates
San Diego Padres
San Francisco Giants
St. Louis Cardinals

AMERICAN LEAGUE

Anaheim Angels
Baltimore Orioles
Boston Red Sox
Chicago White Sox
Cleveland Indians
Detroit Tigers
Kansas City Royals
Minnesota Twins
New York Yankees
Oakland Athletics
Seattle Mariners
Tampa Bay Devil Rays
Texas Rangers
Toronto Blue Jays

Pitcher Josh Beckett of the Marlins gave up five hits in nine innings of Game 6 and was named World Series MVP.

JOHN IACONO/SPORTS ILLUSTRATED

MLB 2003 Playoffs

National League Division Series

September 30	Marlins 0 at Giants 2	October 3	Giants 3 at Marlins 4 (11 innings)
October 1	Marlins 9 at Giants 5	October 4	Giants 6 at Marlins 7

(Florida Marlins won series, 3–1)

September 30	Cubs 4 at Braves 2	October 4	Braves 6 at Cubs 4
October 1	Cubs 3 at Braves 5	October 5	Cubs 5 at Braves 1
October 3	Braves 1 at Cubs 3		

(Chicago Cubs won series, 3–2)

National League Championship Series

October 7	Marlins 9 at Cubs 8 (11 innings)	October 12	Cubs 0 at Marlins 4
October 8	Marlins 3 at Cubs 12	October 14	Marlins 8 at Cubs 3
October 10	Cubs 5 at Marlins 4 (11 innings)	October 15	Marlins 9 at Cubs 6
October 11	Cubs 8 at Marlins 3		

(Florida Marlins won series, 4–3)

GAME 1

Marlins	0 0 5	0 0 1	0 0 2	0 1 **9**
Cubs	4 0 0	0 0 2	0 0 2	0 0 **8**

W— Urbina. **L—** Guthrie. **SV—** Looper.
E— FLA: Gonzalez; CHI: Grudzielanek. **LOB—** FLA: 8; CHI: 6. **2B—** FLA: Castillo, Hollandsworth; CHI: Gonzalez, Simon, Miller, Lofton. **3B—** FLA: Conine, Pierre; CHI: Grudzielanek, Ramirez. **HR—** FLA: Rodriguez, Cabrera, Encarnacion, Lowell; CHI: Alou, Gonzalez, Sosa. **SF—** FLA: Conine. **S—** CHI: Lofton. **PB—** CHI: Bako. **SB—** FLA: Castillo 2. **CS—** FLA: Pierre. **GIDP—** CHI: Alou. **T—** 3:44. **A—** 39,567.

Recap: The Marlins were down four runs early, but thanks to Ivan Rodriguez, who had a homer and five RBIs, they came back. Sammy Sosa hit a ninth-inning, game-tying two-run homer, but it wasn't enough for the Cubs. Mike Lowell led off the 11th inning with a pinch-hit home run to pull out the win for the Marlins. The game featured seven homers, four triples and six doubles.

GAME 2

Marlins	0 0 0	0 0 2	0 1 0	**3**
Cubs	2 3 3	0 3 1	0 0 x	**12**

W— Prior. **L—** Penny.
E— FLA: Conine; CHI: Simon. **LOB—** FLA: 8; CHI: 8. **2B—** FLA: Encarnacion, Conine; CHI: Bako, Simon, Grudzielanek. **HR—** FLA: Lee, Cabrera; CHI: Sosa, Ramirez, Gonzalez. **S—** CHI: Prior. **SB—** CHI: Lofton. **WP—** FLA: Bump, Helling. **GIDP—** FLA: Encarnacion. **T—** 3:02. **A—** 39,562.

Recap: The Cubs came out strong at the plate — and the mound. Sammy Sosa hit a two-run shot in the second inning, Alex Gonzalez homered twice, and Aramis Ramirez also went yard. The Cubs were up 11–0 by the fifth inning. Cubs pitcher Mark Prior kept his cool — and the team's lead.

GAME 3

Cubs	1 1 0	0 0 0	0 2 0	0 1 **5**
Marlins	0 1 0	0 0 0	2 1 0	0 0 **4**

W— Borowski. **L—** Tejera. **SV—** Remlinger.
LOB— CHI: 12; FLA: 12. **2B—** CHI: Alou; FLA: Gonzalez. **3B—** CHI: Goodwin, Glanville. **HR—** CHI: Simon. **S—** CHI: Grudzielanek, Wood; FLA: Pierre, Mordecai, Castillo. **SF—** CHI: Wood. **SB—** FLA: Pierre. **WP—** CHI: Remlinger. **GIDP—** CHI: Alou. **T—** 4:16. **A—** 65,115.

Recap: The second extra-inning game of the series had a wild finish. Doug Glanville of the Cubs lined a pinch-hit triple in the 11th inning to put the Cubs ahead. Then the Marlins were at bat. Luis Castillo struck out but got to first base when the ball went through Cubs catcher Paul Bako's legs for a wild pitch. Castillo reached second on a groundout, then Derrek Lee hit a grounder to third. Castillo started running, thinking Cubs third baseman Aramis Ramirez would field it and throw to first. But Ramirez bobbled the ball and Castillo hesitated. He was caught in a rundown for the last out.

GAME 4

Cubs	4 0 2	1 0 0	1 0 0	**8**
Marlins	0 0 0	0 2 0	0 1 0	**3**

W— Clement. **L—** Willis.
E— FLA: Rodriguez. **LOB—** CHI: 8; FLA: 4. **2B—** FLA: Rodriguez. **HR—** CHI: Ramirez. **WP—** FLA: Helling. **GIDP—** FLA: Cabrera. **CS—** FLA: Pierre. **T—** 2:58. **A—** 65,829.

Recap: Aramis Ramirez hit the first grand slam in Cubs' post-season history in the first inning. He added another homer and drove in six runs as the Cubs came within one game of going to their first World Series since 1945. Rookie pitcher Dontrelle Willis of the Marlins had a rough night, walking a career-high five batters.

GAME 5

Cubs	0 0 0	0 0 0	0 0 0	**0**
Marlins	0 0 0	0 2 0	1 1 x	**4**

W— Beckett. **L—** Zambrano.
LOB— CHI: 3; FLA: 9. **HR—** FLA: Lowell, Rodriguez, Conine. **GIDP—** FLA: Lee. **WP—** CHI: Zambrano. **T—** 2:42. **A—** 65,279.

Recap: Pitcher Josh Beckett of the Marlins shut down the Cubs as he struck out 11 in the first complete game of his 51 starts in the major leagues. Rodriguez, Lowell, and Conine homered for the Marlins, spoiling the Cubs' chance at closing out the Series.

KEY W=winning pitcher; L=losing pitcher; SV=save; E=errors; LOB=left on base; SF=sacrifice fly; S=single; 2B=double; 3B=triple; HR=home run; SAC=sacrifice; SB=stolen bases; CS=caught stealing; HBP=hit by pitch; GIDP=grounded into double plays; WP=wild pitch; PB=passed ball; T=time; A=attendance

National League Championship Series (cont.)

GAME 6

Marlins	0 0 0	0 0 0	0 8 0	**8**
Cubs	1 0 0	0 0 1	1 0 0	**3**

W— Fox. **L—** Prior.
E— CHI: Grudzielanek, Gonzalez. **LOB—** FLA: 6; CHI: 7. **2B—** FLA: Pierre, Lee, Mordecai; CHI: Sosa. **S—** CHI: Grudzielanek, Prior. **SF—** FLA: Conine. **GIDP—** CHI: Simon, Ramirez. **WP—** FLA: Willis; CHI: Prior. **PB—** CHI: Bako. **CS—** FLA: Pierre. **T—** 3:00. **A—** 39,577.

Recap: The Cubs cruised into the eighth inning with a 3-0 lead. But then the lovable losers lost it. Luis Castillo hit a fly ball to left field where a fan interfered as Moises Alou tried to grab it. The Marlins went on to score eight runs in the inning and shocked the Cubs.

GAME 7

Marlins	3 0 0	0 3 1	2 0 0	**9**
Cubs	0 3 2	0 0 0	1 0 0	**6**

W— Penny. **L—** Wood. **SV—** Urbina.
LOB— FLA: 6; CHI: 2. **2B—** FLA: Rodriguez, Gonzalez, Lee. CHI: Gonzalez. **3B—** FLA: Pierre. **HR—** FLA: Cabrera; CHI: Wood, Alou, O'Leary. **SB—** FLA: Lee. **T—** 3:11. **A—** 39,574.

Recap: At 72, Marlins manager Jack McKeon became the oldest manager to reach the World Series as his Florida Marlins capped a stunning comeback to win the NLCS. They became the sixth team to overcome a 3-1 deficit in the best-of-seven series. Pitcher Kerry Wood of the Cubs couldn't hold an early lead as the Marlins scored three runs in the fifth inning, one in the sixth, and two insurance runs in the seventh. And the curse of the Chicago Cubs continued.

MLB 2003 Playoffs

American League Division Series

September 30	Twins 3 at Yankees 1	October 4	Yankees 3 at Twins 1
October 2	Twins 1 at Yankees 4	October 5	Yankees 8 at Twins 1

(New York Yankees won series, 3-1)

October 1	Red Sox 4 at A's 5 (12 innings)	October 5	A's 4 at Red Sox 5
October 2	Red Sox 1 at A's 5	October 6	Red Sox 4 at A's 3
October 4	A's 1 at Red Sox 3 (11 innings)		

(Boston Red Sox won series, 3-2)

American League Championship Series

October 8	Red Sox 5 at Yankees 2	October 14	Yankees 4 at Red Sox 2
October 9	Red Sox 2 at Yankees 6	October 15	Red Sox 9 at Yankees 6
October 11	Yankees 4 at Red Sox 3	October 16	Red Sox 5 at Yankees 6 (11 innings)
October 13	Yankees 2 at Red Sox 3		

(New York Yankees won series, 4-3)

GAME 1

Red Sox	0 0 0	2 2 0	1 0 0	**5**
Yankees	0 0 0	0 0 0	2 0 0	**2**

W— Wakefield. **L—** Mussina. **SV—** Williamson.
LOB— Bos: 10; NY: 3. **2B—** NY: Posada. **HR—** Bos: Ortiz, Walker, Ramirez. **SF—** NY: Matsui. **CS—** Bos: Jackson. **WP—** NY: Contreras. **HBP—** Bos: Ortiz. **T—** 3:20. **A—** 56,281.

Recap: Tim Wakefield's knuckleball frustrated the Yankees. He retired 14 straight batters starting in the second inning. The Red Sox offense came through, taking a five-run lead into the seventh inning. Yankee pitcher Mike Mussina looked shaky on the mound as he gave up three homers.

GAME 2

Red Sox	0 1 0	0 0 1	0 0 0	**2**
Yankees	0 2 1	0 1 0	2 0 x	**6**

W— Pettitte. **L—** Lowe.
E— Bos: Jackson. **LOB—** Bos: 8; NY: 8. **2B—** Bos: Varitek; NY: Williams, Posada. **HR—** Bos: Varitek. **GIDP—** Bos: Kapler. **PB—** Bos: Varitek. **SB—** Bos: Nixon; NY: Boone. **CS—** Bos: Kapler. **HBP—** NY: Boone, Soriano. **T—** 3:05. **A—** 56,295.

Recap: Yankee pitcher Andy Pettitte struggled early as seven of Boston's first nine batters reached base. But the Red Sox only got one run in the first two innings despite having six hits. Pettitte left in the sixth inning, allowing two runs and nine hits. Nick Johnson jump-started the Yankee offense with a two-run shot in the second inning.

GAME 3

Yankees	0 1 1	2 0 0	0 0 0	**4**
Red Sox	2 0 0	0 0 0	1 0 0	**3**

W— Clemens. **L—** Martinez. **SV—** Rivera.
LOB— Bos: 3; NY: 3. **2B—** Bos: Walker; NY: Posada, Matsui. **HR—** NY: Jeter. **GIDP—** Bos: Ramirez, Nixon; NY: Soriano, Matsui. **CS—** Bos: Ramirez. **HBP—** NY: Garcia. **T—** 3:09. **A—** 34,209.

Recap: Game 3 featured two bench-clearing brawls, including one involving 72-year-old Yankee coach Don Zimmer and Red Sox pitcher Pedro Martinez. But pitcher Roger Clemens kept his cool to lead the Yankees to a 2-1 advantage in the Series. He retired 13 of 14 batters after giving up a two-run single to Manny Ramirez in the first inning.

GAME 4

Yankees	0 0 0	0 1 0	0 0 1	**2**
Red Sox	0 0 0	1 1 0	1 0 x	**3**

W— Wakefield. **L—** Mussina. **SV—** Williamson.
E— NY: Boone. **LOB—** Bos: 3; NY: 8. **2B—** Bos: Nixon; NY: Jeter. **HR—** Bos: Walker, Nixon; NY: Sierra. **GIDP—** Bos: Ortiz, Garciaparra. **PB—** Bos: Mirabelli. **HBP—** Bos: Walker; NY: Dellucci. **SB—** NY: Dellucci. **CS—** Bos: Nixon. **T—** 2:49. **A—** 34,559.

Recap: Tim Wakefield's baffling pitching befuddled the Yankees again in Game 4. Boston's offense, which struggled in the post-season, managed three homers. After Scott Williamson of the Red Sox took over the mound in the ninth, Ruben Sierra pulled New York to within one run. Williamson struck out the last two batters to earn the save.

American League Championship Series (cont.)

GAME 5

Yankees	0	3	0	0	0	0	0	1	0	**4**
Red Sox	0	0	0	1	0	0	0	1	0	**2**

W— Wells. **L—** Lowe. **SV—** Rivera.
E— Bos: Millar; NY: Soriano. **LOB—** Bos: 7; NY: 7. **3B—** Bos: Walker. **HR—** Bos: Ramirez. **GIDP—** Bos: Millar; NY: Posada. **HBP—** Bos: Nixon. **CS—** NY: Boone. **T—** 3:04. **A—** 34,619.

Recap: David Wells allowed four hits and just one run in seven innings to bring the Yankees to within one game of the World Series. Derek Lowe struggled on the mound for Boston, losing his second game of the series. The Red Sox went 0-for-5 with runners in scoring position.

GAME 6

Red Sox	0	0	4	0	0	0	3	0	2	**9**
Yankees	1	0	0	4	1	0	0	0	0	**6**

W— Embree. **L—** Contreras. **SV—** Williamson.
E— Bos: Garciaparra; NY: Boone, Matsui. **LOB—** Bos: 11; NY: 8. **2B—** Bos: Mueller, Ramirez, Damon; NY: Johnson, Soriano. **3B—** Bos: Garciaparra. **HR—** Bos: Varitek, Nixon. **GIDP—** Bos: Mueller, Ramirez; NY: Johnson. **PB—** Bos: Varitek. **SB—** Bos: Damon; NY: Soriano, Jeter. **WP—** NY: Contreras, Heredia. **T—** 3:57. **A—** 56,277.

Recap: Slumping Nomar Garciaparra had four hits for the Red Sox as Boston forced a Game 7. A swirling wind made it tough for fielders to catch twisting balls. Red Sox pitcher Scott Williamson earned his third save of the series.

GAME 7

Red Sox	0	3	0	1	0	0	0	1	0	0	**5**
Yankees	0	0	0	0	1	0	1	3	0	1	**6**

W— Rivera. **L—** Wakefield.
E— NY: Wilson. **LOB—** Bos: 7; NY: 8. **2B—** Bos: Varitek, Ortiz; NY: Matsui, Posada, Jeter. **HR—** Bos: Nixon, Millar, Ortiz; NY: Giambi, Boone. **GIDP—** Bos: Damon. **T—** 3:56. **A—** 56,279.

Recap: Aaron Boone hit a leadoff home run in the eleventh inning to give New York a 6–5 win over the Red Sox in Game 7. The Yankees trailed 4–0 in the fourth inning but came back. Jason Giambi started the rally with homers in the fifth and seventh innings. Yankee reliever Mariano Rivera didn't allow a run in his three-inning appearance and was named the ALCS MVP.

2003 World Series

October 18	Marlins 3 at Yankees 2
October 19	Marlins 1 at Yankees 6
October 21	Yankees 6 at Marlins 1
October 22	Yankees 3 at Marlins 4 (12 innings)
October 23	Yankees 4 at Marlins 6
October 25	Marlins 2 at Yankees 0

(Florida Marlins won series, 4–2)

GAME 1

Marlins	1	0	0	0	2	0	0	0	0	**3**
Yankees	0	0	1	0	0	1	0	0	0	**2**

W— Penny. **L—** Wells. **SV—** Urbina.
E— Fla: Cabrera. **LOB—** Fla: 8; NY: 9. **HR—** NY: Williams. **S—** Fla: Gonzalez. **SF—** Fla: Rodriguez. **SB—** Fla: Castillo, Pierre; NY: Soriano, Posada. **GIDP—** Fla: Gonzalez; NY: Giambi, Soriano. **HBP—** Fla: Pierre. **T—** 3:43. **A—** 55,769.

Recap: The Florida Marlins proved they were no fluke as they won Game 1 of the World Series, ending New York's record of 10 straight home Series wins. Florida showed its speed early with a lead-off bunt single by outfielder Juan Pierre. New York tried to rally in the ninth, drawing a pair of walks, but the Marlins held on.

GAME 2

Marlins	0	0	0	0	0	0	0	0	1	**1**
Yankees	3	1	0	2	0	0	0	0	x	**6**

W— Pettitte. **L—** Redman.
E— NY: Boone, 2. **LOB—** Fla: 5; NY: 6. **2B—** NY: Rivera, Johnson, Giambi. **HR—** NY: Matsui, Soriano. **GIDP—** Fla: Rodriguez. **CS—** Fla: Castillo; NY: Posada, Soriano. **WP—** Fla: Redman. **HBP—** NY: Giambi. **T—** 2:56. **A—** 55,750.

Recap: Working on just three days rest, Andy Pettitte pitched into the ninth inning as the Yankees shut down the Marlins. He improved his lifetime post-season record to 13–7. The Yankee bats came alive, with outfielder Nick Johnson contributing three hits for the night.

GAME 3

Yankees	0	0	0	1	0	0	0	1	4	**6**
Marlins	1	0	0	0	0	0	0	0	0	**1**

W— Mussina. **L—** Beckett. **SV—** Rivera.
E— NY: Boone. **LOB—** Fla: 8; NY: 8. **2B—** Fla: Pierre, Gonzalez, Rodriguez; NY: Jeter. **HR—** NY: Boone, Williams. **S—** Fla: Beckett. **CS—** Fla: Pierre. **HBP—** NY: Matsui, Jeter. **PB—** NY: Posada. **T—** 3:21 (plus rain delay totaling 39 minutes in the fifth inning). **A—** 65,731.

Recap: New York pitcher Mike Mussina had been 0–3 in this post-season, but managed to come out on top in Game 3. A 39-minute rain delay in the fifth inning didn't seem to rattle him. Mussina gave up one run and seven hits, struck out nine, and walked one. Again, the Yankee offense backed up the pitching. Shortstop Derek Jeter had three hits and outfielder Bernie Williams hit his 19th post-season homer.

GAME 4

Yankees	0	1	0	0	0	0	0	0	2	0	0	0	**3**
Marlins	3	0	0	0	0	0	0	0	0	0	0	1	**4**

W— Looper. **L—** Weaver.
LOB— Fla: 7; NY: 10. **2B—** Fla: Rodriguez; NY: Jeter, Williams. **3B—** NY: Sierra. **HR—** Fla: Cabrera, Gonzalez. **S—** Fla: Castillo, Pavano; NY: Dellucci. **SF—** NY: Boone. **GIDP—** NY: Jeter. **T—** 4:03. **A—** 65,934.

Recap: The Florida Marlins spoiled Roger Clemens's possible last appearance at the plate for the Yankees by squeaking out a win in 12 innings. At 12:28 A.M.,

World Series (cont.)

Marlin shortstop Alex Gonzalez hit a low line drive off Yankee reliever Jeff Weaver. It barely cleared the wall but was enough for the victory. Gonzalez had been slumping in this post-season, going just 5 for 53.

GAME 5

Yankees	1	0	0	0	0	0	1	0	2	**4**
Marlins	0	3	0	1	2	0	0	0	x	**6**

W— Penny. **L—** Contreras. **SV—** Urbina.
E— Fla: Lee; NY: Wilson. **LOB—** Fla: 6; NY: 9. **2B—** Fla: Gonzalez, Conine, Pierre; NY: Wilson. **HR—** NY: Giambi. **S—** Fla: Penny. **SF—** NY: Williams. **GIDP—** Fla: Lee; NY: Wilson. **CS—** Fla: Gonzalez. **T—** 3:05. **A—** 65,975.

Recap: Pitcher Brad Penny of the Marlins won for the second time in this Series and even had a two-run single as Florida charged out to a 6-1 lead. Injuries took their toll on the Yankees. Jason Giambi was pulled from the starting lineup because of a bad left knee, and pitcher David Wells left the game after the first inning due to back spasms. The loss marked the first time since 1981 that the Yankees faced elimination at home in the World Series.

GAME 6

Marlins	0	0	0	0	1	1	0	0	0	**2**
Yankees	0	0	0	0	0	0	0	0	0	**0**

W— Beckett. **L—** Pettitte.
E— NY: Jeter. **LOB—** Fla: 9; NY: 5. **2B—** Fla: Lowell; NY: Williams, Posada. **S—** NY: Boone. **SF—** Fla: Encarnacion. **GIDP—** NY: Williams, Johnson. **T—** 2:57. **A—** 55,773.

Recap: The wild-card Marlins knocked off the powerhouse Yankees behind the strong arm of 23-year-old pitcher Josh Beckett. He was named the World Series MVP for his efforts. Beckett gave up five hits in nine innings as the Marlins won their second World Series championship in seven seasons.

Today's Stars

Derek Jeter dislocated his left shoulder on Opening Day 2003, but rebounded to bat .324 for the season.

CHUCK SOLOMON/SPORTS ILLUSTRATED

Derek Jeter, shortstop, b. June 26, 1974, Pequannock, New Jersey. The five-time All-Star shortstop's smooth glove, fast legs, and dangerous bat make him one of the game's best all-around players. The New York Yankee captain's .317 lifetime batting average ranks fifth in Yankee history, behind Hall of Famers Babe Ruth (first), Lou Gehrig (second), Earle Combs (third), and Joe DiMaggio (fourth). In eight full seasons in the Bronx, Jeter has led New York to the American League pennant six times and the World Series championship four times. He was MVP of the 2000 World Series and has a .314 post-season average.

Albert Pujols, first baseman, b. January 16, 1980, Santo Domingo, Dominican Republic. The St. Louis Cardinals' "Big Bird" is a two-time All-Star capable of playing five positions. In 2003, at age 23, Pujols won the National League batting championship (.359) and was the runner-up in the league's MVP voting. A career .334 hitter, he has averaged 38 home runs, 127 RBIs, and 122 runs scored in his three big-league seasons. In 2003, he was the National League's top vote-getter for the All-Star Game.

Pedro Martinez, pitcher, b. October 25, 1971, Manoguyabo, Dominican Republic. Though small (5' 11", 180 pounds), Martinez is one of baseball's biggest pitchers. In 2003, he led the American League in ERA (2.22) for the second-straight season. Martinez first reached the majors in 1992 with the Los Angeles Dodgers, where he pitched with his brother Ramon. He gained stardom with the Montreal Expos when he won the N.L. Cy Young Award in 1997. Martinez was traded to Boston in November 1997 and has since won the award twice more, in 1999 and 2000, making him one of only two pitchers to win the award in both leagues. (Randy Johnson has also accomplished this feat.) In six seasons with the Red Sox, Martinez has won 78 percent of his decisions and recorded a 2.26 ERA.

MLB 2003 Playoffs Composite Box Scores

National League Championship Series

CHICAGO CUBS

BATTING	AB	R	H	HR	RBI	BA
Lofton	31	8	10	0	2	.323
Grudzielanek	30	2	6	0	3	.200
Alou	29	4	9	2	5	.310
Gonzalez	28	5	8	3	7	.286
Ramirez	26	4	6	3	7	.231
Sosa	26	7	8	2	6	.308
Simon	17	3	5	1	4	.294
Bako	16	4	4	0	1	.250
Karros	13	2	3	0	0	.231
Miller	10	0	2	0	1	.200
Clement	4	0	0	0	0	.000
Goodwin	4	1	1	0	0	.250
Martinez	4	0	0	0	0	.000
Prior	4	0	0	0	0	.000
O'Leary	3	1	1	1	1	.333
Wood	3	1	1	1	3	.333
Zambrano	3	0	0	0	0	.000
Glanville	1	0	1	0	1	1.000

PITCHING	G	IP	H	BB	SO	ERA
Prior	2	14 ⅓	14	5	11	3.14
Wood	2	12 ⅓	14	7	13	7.30
Zambrano	2	11	14	5	8	5.73
Clement	1	7 ⅔	5	2	3	3.52
Borowski	3	5 ⅔	5	3	1	1.59
Farnsworth	5	5 ⅓	6	2	7	10.13
Remlinger	5	3 ⅓	3	1	2	2.70
Veres	3	3	4	1	0	3.00
Alfonseca	3	2 ⅓	2	2	0	0.00
Guthrie	2	1	1	0	0	9.00

FLORIDA MARLINS

BATTING	AB	R	H	HR	RBI	BA
Pierre	33	5	10	0	1	.303
Lee	32	2	6	1	4	.188
Cabrera	30	9	10	3	6	.333
Castillo	28	3	6	0	2	.214
Rodriguez	28	5	9	2	10	.321
Conine	24	4	11	1	3	.458
Gonzalez	24	1	3	0	4	.125
Lowell	20	5	4	2	3	.200
Encarnacion	12	1	3	1	1	.250
Beckett	8	0	2	0	0	.250
Mordecai	5	1	1	0	3	.200
Hollandsworth	3	2	3	0	2	1.000
Harris	2	0	0	0	0	.000
Pavano	2	0	0	0	0	.000
Redman	2	0	0	0	0	.000
Banks	1	1	0	0	0	.000
Helling	1	0	0	0	0	.000
Penny	1	0	0	0	0	.000
Redmond	0	1	0	0	0	.000

PITCHING	G	IP	H	BB	SO	ERA
Beckett	3	19 ⅓	11	2	19	3.26
Redman	2	9 ⅔	13	4	4	6.52
Pavano	3	7 ⅔	8	1	8	2.35
Helling	2	5 ⅔	7	4	5	6.35
Penny	3	4	9	3	0	15.75
Fox	3	3 ⅓	5	2	2	5.40
Willis	2	3 ⅓	4	6	4	18.90
Bump	2	3	3	0	3	6.00
Looper	2	1 ⅔	1	1	1	0.00
Tejera	2	1 ⅓	2	0	1	6.75

American League Championship Series

BOSTON RED SOX

BATTING	AB	R	H	HR	RBI	BA
Garciaparra	29	2	7	0	1	.241
Millar	29	3	7	1	3	.241
Ramirez	29	6	9	2	4	.310
Mueller	27	1	6	0	0	.222
Walker	27	5	10	2	2	.370
Ortiz	26	4	7	2	6	.269
Nixon	24	3	8	3	5	.333
Damon	20	1	4	0	1	.200
Varitek	20	4	6	2	3	.300
Kapler	8	0	1	0	0	.125
Mirabelli	7	0	2	0	0	.286
Jackson	3	0	1	0	1	.333
McCarty	1	0	0	0	0	.000

PITCHING	G	IP	H	BB	SO	ERA
Martinez	2	14 ⅓	16	2	14	5.65
Lowe	2	14	14	7	5	6.43
Wakefield	3	14	8	6	10	2.57
Timlin	5	5 ⅓	1	2	6	0.00
Embree	5	4 ⅔	3	0	1	0.00
Burkett	1	3 ⅔	7	0	1	7.36
Arroyo	3	3 ⅓	2	2	5	2.70
Williamson	3	3	1	0	6	3.00
Jones	1	⅓	1	1	1	0.00
Sauerbeck	1	⅓	1	1	0	0.00

NEW YORK YANKEES

BATTING	AB	R	H	HR	RBI	BA
Jeter	30	3	7	1	2	.233
Soriano	30	0	4	0	3	.133
Posada	27	5	8	1	6	.296
Giambi	26	4	6	3	3	.231
Johnson	26	4	6	1	3	.231
Matsui	26	3	8	0	4	.308
Williams	26	5	5	0	2	.192
Boone	17	2	3	1	2	.176
Garcia	16	1	4	0	3	.250
Wilson	7	0	1	0	0	.143
Dellucci	3	2	1	0	0	.333
Rivera	2	0	0	0	0	.000
Sierra	2	1	1	1	1	.500

PITCHING	G	IP	H	BB	SO	ERA
Mussina	3	15 ⅓	16	4	17	4.11
Pettitte	2	11 ⅔	17	4	10	4.63
Clemens	2	9	11	2	8	5.00
Rivera	4	8	5	0	6	1.13
Wells	2	7 ⅔	5	2	5	2.35
Contreras	4	4 ⅔	6	2	7	5.79
Nelson	4	3	4	0	3	6.00
Heredia	5	2 ⅔	0	3	3	3.38
White	2	2	4	0	1	4.50

KEY AB=at-bats; R=runs; H=hits; HR=home runs; RBI=runs batted in; BA=batting average; G=games; IP=innings pitched; H=hits; BB=bases on balls; SO=strikeouts; ERA=earned run average

2003 World Series Composite Box Score

FLORIDA MARLINS

BATTING	AB	R	H	HR	RBI	BA
Castillo	26	1	4	0	1	.154
Cabrera	24	1	4	1	3	.167
Lee	24	2	5	0	2	.208
Lowell	23	1	5	0	2	.217
Gonzalez	22	3	6	1	2	.273
Rodriguez	22	2	6	0	1	.273
Conine	21	4	7	0	0	.333
Pierre	21	2	7	0	3	.333
Encarnacion	11	1	2	0	1	.182
Beckett	2	0	0	0	0	.000
Hollandsworth	2	0	0	0	0	.000
Pavano	2	0	0	0	0	.000
Penny	2	0	1	0	2	.500
Redmond	1	0	0	0	0	.000
Fox	0	0	0	0	0	.000
Looper	0	0	0	0	0	.000
Willis	0	0	0	0	0	.000

PITCHING	G	IP	H	BB	SO	ERA
Beckett	2	16⅓	8	5	19	1.10
Penny	2	12⅓	15	5	7	2.19
Pavano	2	9	8	1	6	1.00
Looper	4	3⅔	6	0	4	9.82
Willis	3	3⅔	4	2	3	0.00
Fox	3	3	4	4	4	6.00
Helling	1	2⅔	2	0	2	6.75
Redman	1	2⅓	5	2	2	15.43

NEW YORK YANKEES

BATTING	AB	R	H	HR	RBI	BA
Jeter	26	5	9	0	2	.346
Williams	25	5	10	2	5	.400
Matsui	23	1	6	1	4	.261
Soriano	22	2	5	1	2	.227
Boone	21	1	3	1	2	.143
Posada	19	0	3	0	1	.158
Giambi	17	2	4	1	1	.235
Johnson	17	3	5	0	0	.294
Garcia	14	1	4	0	0	.286
Rivera	6	0	1	0	1	.167
Sierra	4	0	1	0	2	.250
Wilson	4	0	2	0	1	.500
Mussina	3	0	0	0	0	.000
Clemens	2	0	1	0	0	.500
Dellucci	2	1	0	0	0	.000
Flaherty	2	0	0	0	0	.000
Contreras	0	0	0	0	0	.000
Hammond	0	0	0	0	0	.000
Nelson	0	0	0	0	0	.000
Rivera	0	0	0	0	0	.000
Weaver	0	0	0	0	0	.000
Wells	0	0	0	0	0	.000

PITCHING	G	IP	H	BB	SO	ERA
Pettitte	2	15⅔	12	4	14	0.57
Wells	2	8	6	2	1	3.38
Clemens	1	7	8	0	5	3.86
Mussina	1	7	7	1	9	1.29
Contreras	4	6⅓	5	5	10	5.68
Nelson	3	4	4	2	5	0.00
Rivera	2	4	2	0	4	0.00
Hammond	1	2	2	0	0	0.00
Weaver	1	1	1	0	0	9.00

Trivia Challenge

In 2003, Alex Rodriguez became the first American League player on a last-place team to win the MVP award. Who is the only National League MVP from a last-place team?

Outfielder Andre Dawson of the Chicago Cubs (1987)

2003 MLB Individual leaders

National League Batting

BATTING AVERAGE	
Albert Pujols, StL	.359
Todd Helton, Col	.358
Barry Bonds, SF	.341
Edgar Renteria, StL	.330
Gary Sheffield, Atl	.330
Jason Kendall, Pit	.325
Marcus Giles, Atl	.316
Luis Castillo, Fla	.314
Mark Grudzielanek, Chi	.314
Mark Loretta, SD	.314
Scott Podsednik, Mil	.314

HITS	
Albert Pujols, StL	212
Todd Helton, Col	209
Juan Pierre, Fla	204
Edgar Renteria, StL	194
Jason Kendall, Pit	191
Gary Sheffield, Atl	190
Luis Castillo, Fla	187
Orlando Cabrera, Mon	186
Mark Loretta, SD	185
Jay Payton, Col	181

DOUBLES	
Albert Pujols, StL	51
Marcus Giles, Atl	49
Shawn Green, LA	49
Todd Helton, Col	49
Scott Rolen, StL	49

TRIPLES	
Steve Finley, Ariz	10
Rafael Furcal, Atl	10
Kenny Lofton, Chi	8
Scott Podsednik, Mil	8

Four tied with 7.

HOME RUNS	
Jim Thome, Phil	47
Barry Bonds, SF	45
Richie Sexson, Mil	45
Javier Lopez, Atl	43
Albert Pujols, StL	43
Sammy Sosa, Chi	40
Jeff Bagwell, Hou	39
Jim Edmonds, StL	39
Gary Sheffield, Atl	39
Andruw Jones, Atl	36
Preston Wilson, Col	36

RUNS SCORED	
Albert Pujols, Stl	137
Todd Helton, Col	135
Rafael Furcal, Atl	130
Gary Sheffield, Atl	126
Barry Bonds, SF	111
Jim Thome, Phil	111
Lance Berkman, Hou	110
Jeff Bagwell, Hou	109
Chipper Jones, Atl	103
Craig Biggio, Hou	102

TOTAL BASES	
Albert Pujols, StL	394
Todd Helton, Col	367
Gary Sheffield, Atl	348
Richie Sexson, Mil	332
Jim Thome, Phi	331

STOLEN BASES	
Juan Pierre, Fla	65
Scott Podsednik, Mil	43
Dave Roberts, LA	40
Edgar Renteria, StL	34
Kenny Lofton, Chi	30
Eric Young, SF	28

RUNS BATTED IN	
Preston Wilson, Col	141
Gary Sheffield, Atl	132
Jim Thome, Phil	131
Albert Pujols, StL	124
Richie Sexson, Mil	124
Todd Helton, Col	117
Andruw Jones Atl	116
Javier Lopez, Atl	109
Chipper Jones, Atl	106
Aramis Ramirez, Chi	106

SLUGGING PERCENTAGE	
Barry Bonds, SF	.749
Albert Pujols, StL	.667
Todd Helton, Col	.630
Jim Edmonds, StL	.617
Gary Sheffield, Atl	.604

ON-BASE PERCENTAGE	
Barry Bonds, SF	.529
Todd Helton, Col	.458
Albert Pujols, StL	.439
Brian Giles, SD	.427
Larry Walker, Col	.422

BASES ON BALLS	
Barry Bonds, SF	148
Todd Helton, Col	111
Jim Thome, Phil	111
Bobby Abreu, Phil	109
Lance Berkman, Hou	107

Juan Pierre

CHUCK SOLOMON/SPORTS ILLUSTRATED

National League Pitching

EARNED RUN AVERAGE	
Jason Schmidt, SF	2.34
Kevin Brown, LA	2.39
Mark Prior, Chi	2.43
Brandon Webb, Ariz	2.84
Curt Schilling, Ariz	2.95
Hideo Nomo, LA	3.09
Carlos Zambrano, Chi	3.11
Livan Hernandez, Mtl	3.20
Kerry Wood, Chi	3.20
Javier Vazquez, Mtl	3.24

SAVES	
Eric Gagne, LA	55
John Smoltz, Atl	45
Billy Wagner, Hou	44
Tim Worrell, SF	38
Rocky Biddle, Mtl	34
Joe Borowski, Chi	33
Matt Mantei, Ari	29
Braden Looper, Fla	28
Mike Williams, Phil	28
Jose Mesa, Phil	24

Note: Players listed under batting average must have had at least 3.1 plate appearances per game.

WINS	
Russ Ortiz, Atl	21
Mark Prior, Chi	18
Woody Williams, StL	18
Jason Schmidt, SF	17
Greg Maddux, Atl	16
Hideo Nomo, LA	16
Steve Trachsel, NY	16
Randy Wolf, Phil	16

Three tied with 15.

GAMES PITCHED	
Paul Quantrill, LA	89
Oscar Villarreal, Ariz	86
Ray King, Atl	80
Tom Martin, LA	80

Four tied with 78.

INNINGS PITCHED	
Livan Hernandez, Mtl	233⅓
Javier Vazquez, Mtl	230⅔
Kevin Millwood, Phil	222
Ben Sheets, Mil	220⅔
Woody Williams, StL	220⅔
Greg Maddux, Atl	218⅓
Hideo Nomo, LA	218⅓

STRIKEOUTS	
Kerry Wood, Chi	266
Mark Prior, Chi	245
Javier Vazquez, Mtl	241
Jason Schmidt, SF	208
Curt Schilling, Ariz	194
Kevin Brown, LA	185
Livan Hernandez, Mtl	178
Hideo Nomo, LA	177
Randy Wolf, Phil	177
Brandon Webb, Ariz	172

COMPLETE GAMES	
Livan Hernandez, Mtl	8
Kevin Millwood, Phil	5
Matt Morris, StL	5
Jason Schmidt, SF	5

SHUTOUTS	
Kevin Millwood, Phil	3
Matt Morris, StL	3
Jason Schmidt, SF	3

Seven tied with 2.

2003 MLB Individual leaders

American League Batting

BATTING AVERAGE	
Bill Mueller, Bos	.326
Manny Ramirez, Bos	.325
Derek Jeter, NY	.324
Maggio Ordonez, Chi	.317
Vernon Wells, Tor	.317
Garret Anderson, Ana	.315
A.J. Pierzynski, Min	.312
Ichiro Suzuki, Sea	.312
Aubrey Huff, TB	.311
Carlos Beltran, KC	.307

HITS	
Vernon Wells, Tor	215
Ichiro Suzuki, Sea	212
Michael Young, Tex	204
Garret Anderson, Ana	201
Nomar Garciaparra, Bos	198
Aubrey Huff, TB	198
Alfonso Soriano, NY	198
Magglio Ordonez Chi	192
Manny Ramirez, Bos	185
Rocco Baldelli, Atl	184

DOUBLES	
Garret Anderson, Ana	49
Vernon Wells, Tor	49
Aubrey Huff, TB	47
Magglio Ordonez, Chi	46
Eric Hinske, Tor	45
Bill Mueller, Bos	45

TRIPLES	
Cristian Guzman, Min	14
Nomar Garciaparra, Bos	13
Carlos Beltran, KC	10
Eric Byrnes, Oak	9
Carl Crawford, TB	9
Luis Rivas, TB	9
Michael Young, Tex	9

HOME RUNS	
Alex Rodriguez, Tex	47
Carlos Delgado, Tor	42
Frank Thomas, Chi	42
Jason Giambi, NY	41
Rafael Palmeiro, Tex	38
Alfonso Soriano, NY	38
Manny Ramirez, Bos	37
Bret Boone, Sea	35
Aubrey Huff, TB	34
Vernon Wells, Tor	33

RUNS SCORED	
Alex Rodriguez, Tex	124
Nomar Garciaparra, Bos	120
Vernon Wells, Tor	118
Carlos Delgado, Tor	117
Manny Ramirez, Bos	117
Alfonso Soriano, NY	114
Bret Boone, Sea	111
Ichiro Suzuki, Sea	111
Michael Young, Tex	106
Johnny Damon, Bos	103
Randy Winn, Sea	103

TOTAL BASES	
Vernon Wells, Tor	373
Alex Rodriguez, Tex	364
Alfonso Soriano, NY	358
Aubrey Huff, TB	353
Garret Anderson, Ana	345
Nomar Garciaparra, Bos	345

STOLEN BASES	
Carl Crawford, TB	55
Alex Sanchez, Det	44
Carlos Beltran, KC	41
Alfonso Soriano, NY	35
Ichiro Suzuki, Sea	34

RUNS BATTED IN	
Carlos Delgado, Tor	145
Alex Rodriguez, Tex	118
Bret Boone, Sea	117
Vernon Wells, Tor	117
Garret Anderson, Ana	116
Carlos Lee, Chi	113
Rafael Palmeiro, Tex	112
Jason Giambi, NY	107
Aubrey Huff, TB	107

SLUGGING PERCENTAGE	
Alex Rodriguez, Tex	.600
Carlos Delgado, Tor	.593
David Ortiz, Bos	.592
Manny Ramirez, Bos	.587
Trot Nixon, Bos	.578

ON-BASE PERCENTAGE	
Manny Ramirez, Bos	.427
Carlos Delgado, Tor	.426
Jason Giambi, NY	.412
Edgar Martinez, Sea	.406
Jorge Posada, NY	.405

BASES ON BALLS	
Jason Giambi, NY	129
Carlos Delgado, Tor	109
Erubiel Durazo, Oak	100
Frank Thomas, Chi	100
Manny Ramirez, Bos	97

Carlos Delgado

TOM DIPACE

American League Pitching

EARNED RUN AVERAGE	
Pedro Martinez, Bos	2.22
Tim Hudson, Oak	2.70
Esteban Loaiza, Chi	2.90
Mark Mulder, Oak	3.13
Roy Halladay, Tor	3.25
Jamie Moyer, Sea	3.27
Barry Zito, Oak	3.30
Mike Mussina, NY	3.40
Ryan Franklin, Sea	3.57
C.C. Sabathia, Cle	3.60

SAVES	
Keith Foulke, Oak	43
Eddie Guardado, Min	41
Mariano Rivera, NY	40
Jorge Julio, Bal	36
Troy Percival, Ana	33
Mike MacDougal, KC	27
Lance Carter, TB	26
Ugueth Urbina, Tex	26
Danys Baez, Cle	25
Shigetoshi Hasegawa, Sea	16

WINS	
Roy Halladay, Tor	22
Esteban Loaiza, Chi	21
Jamie Moyer, Sea	21
Andy Pettitte, NY	21
Roger Clemens, NY	17
Derek Lowe, Bos	17
Mike Mussina, NY	17
Tim Hudson, Oak	16
Ramon Ortiz, Ana	16
Joel Pineiro, Sea	16

Three tied with 15.

GAMES PITCHED	
Trever Miller, Tor	79
Jamie Walker, Det	78
Jason Grimsley, KC	76
B.J. Ryan, Bal	76
LaTroy Hawkins, Min	74

Three tied with 73.

INNINGS PITCHED	
Roy Halladay, Tor	266.0
Bartolo Colon, Chi	242.0
Tim Hudson, Oak	240.0
Barry Zito, Oak	231.2
Mark Buehrle, Chi	230.1

STRIKEOUTS	
Esteban Loaiza, Chi	207
Pedro Martinez, Bos	206
Roy Halladay, Tor	204
Mike Mussina, NY	195
Roger Clemens, NY	190
Andy Pettitte, NY	180
Bartolo Colon, Chi	173
Johan Santana, Min	169
Tim Wakefield, Bos	169
Tim Hudson, Oak	162

COMPLETE GAMES	
Bartolo Colon, Chi	9
Roy Halladay, Tor	9
Mark Mulder, OAK	9

Three tied with 4.

SHUTOUTS	
Roy Halladay, Tor	2
Tim Hudson, Oak	2
John Lackey, Ana	2

Twenty-one tied with 1.

2003 Regular Season Team Stats

National League

TEAM BATTING	G	AB	R	H	2B	3B	HR	RBI	TB	BB	SO	SB	OBP	SLG	BA
Atlanta	162	5,670	907	1,608	321	31	235	872	2,696	545	933	68	.349	.475	.284
St. Louis	162	5,672	876	1,580	342	32	196	827	2,574	580	952	82	.350	.454	.279
Colorado	162	5,518	853	1,472	330	31	198	814	2,458	619	1,134	63	.344	.445	.267
Pittsburgh	162	5,581	753	1,492	275	45	163	711	2,346	529	1,049	86	.338	.420	.267
Florida	162	5,490	751	1,459	292	44	157	709	2,310	515	978	150	.333	.421	.266
San Francisco	161	5,456	755	1,440	281	29	180	713	2,319	593	980	53	.338	.425	.264
Arizona	162	5,570	717	1,467	303	47	152	696	2,320	531	1,006	76	.330	.417	.263
Houston	162	5,583	805	1,466	308	30	191	763	2,407	557	1,021	66	.336	.431	.263
Philadelphia	162	5,543	791	1,448	325	27	166	757	2,325	651	1,155	72	.343	.419	.261
San Diego	162	5,531	678	1,442	257	32	128	641	2,147	565	1,073	76	.333	.388	.261
Chicago	162	5,519	724	1,431	302	24	172	691	2,297	492	1,158	73	.323	.416	.259
Montreal	162	5,437	711	1,404	294	25	144	682	2,180	522	990	100	.326	.401	.258
Milwaukee	162	5,548	714	1,423	266	24	196	685	2,325	547	1,221	99	.329	.419	.256
New York	161	5,341	642	1,317	262	24	124	607	1,999	489	1,035	70	.314	.374	.247
Cincinnati	162	5,509	694	1,349	239	21	182	669	2,176	524	1,326	80	.318	.395	.245
Los Angeles	162	5,458	574	1,328	260	25	124	544	2,010	407	985	80	.303	.368	.243

TEAM PITCHING	W	L	ERA	CG	Sho	SV	Inn	H	R	ER	BB	SO
Los Angeles	85	77	3.16	3	17	58	1,457⅔	1,254	556	511	526	1,289
San Francisco	100	61	3.73	7	10	43	1,437⅓	1,349	638	595	546	1,006
Chicago	88	74	3.83	13	14	36	1,456⅓	1,304	683	619	617	1,404
Arizona	84	78	3.84	7	11	42	1,455	1,379	685	621	526	1,291
Houston	87	75	3.86	1	5	50	1,450	1,350	677	622	565	1,139
Montreal	83	79	4.01	15	10	42	1,437⅔	1,467	716	640	463	1,028
Florida	91	71	4.04	7	11	36	1,445⅓	1,415	692	648	530	1,132
Philadelphia	86	76	4.04	9	13	33	1,443⅔	1,386	697	648	536	1,060
Atlanta	101	61	4.10	4	7	51	1,456⅓	1,425	740	663	555	992
New York	66	95	4.48	3	10	38	1,413⅓	1,497	754	704	576	907
St. Louis	85	77	4.60	9	10	41	1,463⅔	1,544	796	748	508	969
Pittsburgh	75	87	4.64	7	10	44	1,444⅓	1,527	801	744	502	926
San Diego	64	98	4.87	2	10	31	1,431⅓	1,458	831	774	611	1,091
Milwaukee	68	94	5.02	5	3	44	1,452	1,590	873	810	575	1,034
Cincinnati	69	93	5.09	4	5	38	1,446⅓	1,578	886	818	590	932
Colorado	74	88	5.20	3	4	34	1,420	1,629	892	821	552	866

American League

TEAM BATTING	G	AB	R	H	2B	3B	HR	RBI	TB	BB	SO	SB	OBP	SLG	BA
Boston	162	5,769	961	1,667	371	40	238	932	2,832	620	943	88	.360	.491	.289
Toronto	162	5,661	894	1,580	357	33	190	853	2,573	546	1,081	37	.349	.455	.279
Minnesota	162	5,655	801	1,567	318	45	155	755	2,440	512	1,027	94	.341	.431	.277
Kansas City	162	5,568	836	1,526	288	39	162	781	2,378	476	926	120	.336	.427	.274
New York	163	5,605	877	1,518	304	14	230	845	2,540	684	1,042	98	.356	.453	.271
Seattle	162	5,561	795	1,509	290	33	139	759	2,282	586	989	108	.344	.410	.271
Anaheim	162	5,487	736	1,473	276	33	150	687	2,265	476	838	129	.330	.413	.268
Baltimore	163	5,665	743	1,516	277	24	152	695	2,297	431	902	89	.323	.405	.268
Texas	162	5,664	826	1,506	274	36	239	799	2,569	488	1,052	65	.330	.454	.266
Tampa Bay	162	5,654	715	1,501	298	38	137	678	2,286	420	1,030	142	.320	.404	.265
Chicago	162	5,487	791	1,445	303	19	220	766	2,446	519	916	77	.331	.446	.263
Cleveland	162	5,572	699	1,413	296	26	158	660	2,235	466	1,062	86	.316	.401	.254
Oakland	162	5,497	768	1,398	317	24	176	742	2,291	556	898	48	.327	.417	.254
Detroit	162	5,466	591	1,312	201	39	153	553	2,050	443	1,099	98	.300	.375	.240

TEAM PITCHING	W	L	ERA	CG	Sho	SV	Inn	H	R	ER	BB	SO
Oakland	96	66	3.63	16	14	48	1,441⅔	1,336	643	582	499	1,018
Seattle	93	69	3.76	8	15	38	1,441	1,340	637	602	466	1,001
New York	101	61	4.02	8	12	49	1,462	1,512	716	653	375	1,119
Chicago	86	76	4.17	12	4	36	1,431	1,364	715	663	518	1,056
Cleveland	68	94	4.21	5	7	34	1,459⅓	1,477	778	682	501	943
Anaheim	77	85	4.28	5	9	39	1,431⅓	1,444	743	680	486	980
Minnesota	90	72	4.41	7	8	45	1,462	1,526	758	716	402	997
Boston	95	67	4.48	5	6	36	1,464⅔	1,503	809	729	488	1,141
Toronto	86	76	4.69	14	6	36	1,435	1,560	826	748	485	984
Baltimore	71	91	4.76	9	3	41	1,449⅔	1,579	820	767	526	981
Tampa Bay	63	99	4.93	7	7	30	1,436⅔	1,454	852	787	639	877
Kansas City	83	79	5.05	7	10	36	1,438⅔	1,569	867	808	566	865
Detroit	43	119	5.30	3	5	27	1,438⅔	1,616	928	847	557	764
Texas	71	91	5.67	4	3	43	1,433⅓	1,625	969	903	603	1,009

KEY G=games; AB=at bat; R=run; H=hit; 2B=double; 3B=triple; HR=home run; RBI=run batted in; TB=total bases; BB=walk; SO=strikeout; SB=stolen base; OBP=on-base percentage; SLG=slugging percentage; BA=batting average; W=win; L=loss; ERA=earned run average; CG=complete game; Sho=shutout; Inn=innings; ER=earned run

NATIONAL LEAGUE TEAM-BY-TEAM STATS

ARIZONA DIAMONDBACKS

BATTING	G	AB	R	H	2B	3B	HR	RBI	TB	BB	SO	SB	OBP	SLG	BA
Carlos Baerga	105	207	31	71	13	0	4	39	96	18	20	1	.396	.464	.343
Alex Cintron	117	448	70	142	26	6	13	51	219	29	33	2	.359	.489	.317
Luis Gonzalez	156	579	92	176	46	4	26	104	308	94	67	5	.402	.532	.304
Raul Mondesi	45	162	27	49	8	1	8	22	83	18	31	5	.372	.512	.302
Steve Finley	147	516	82	148	24	10	22	70	258	57	94	15	.363	.500	.287
Robby Hammock	65	195	30	55	10	2	8	28	93	17	44	3	.343	.477	.282
Lyle Overbay	86	254	23	70	20	0	4	28	102	35	67	1	.365	.402	.276
Danny Bautista	88	284	29	78	16	3	4	36	112	21	50	3	.330	.394	.275
Chad Moeller	78	239	29	64	17	1	7	29	104	23	59	1	.335	.435	.268
Shea Hillenbrand	85	330	40	88	18	1	17	59	159	17	44	0	.302	.482	.267
Matt Kata	78	288	42	74	16	5	7	29	121	25	53	3	.315	.420	.257
Junior Spivey	106	365	52	93	22	2	13	50	158	33	95	4	.326	.433	.255
Matt Williams	44	134	17	33	9	0	4	16	54	16	26	0	.327	.403	.246
David Dellucci	70	165	18	40	11	3	2	19	63	19	45	9	.328	.382	.242
Craig Counsell	89	303	40	71	6	3	3	21	92	41	32	11	.328	.304	.234

PITCHING	W–L	ERA	G	GS	CG	SV	Inn	H	R	ER	BB	SO
Mike Koplove	3–0	2.15	31	0	0	0	37⅔	31	11	9	10	27
Jose Valverde	2–1	2.15	54	0	0	10	50⅓	24	16	12	26	71
Oscar Villarreal	10–7	2.57	86	1	0	0	98	80	40	28	46	80
Matt Mantei	5–4	2.62	50	0	0	29	55	37	17	16	18	68
Brandon Webb	10–9	2.84	29	28	1	0	180⅔	140	65	57	68	172
Curt Schilling	8–9	2.95	24	24	3	0	168	144	58	55	32	194
Miguel Batista	10–9	3.54	36	29	2	0	193⅓	197	85	76	60	142
Byung-Hyun Kim	1–5	3.56	7	7	0	0	43	34	17	17	15	33
Stephen Randolph	8–1	4.05	50	0	0	0	60	50	28	27	43	50
Randy Johnson	6–8	4.26	18	18	1	0	114	125	61	54	27	125
Chris Capuano	2–4	4.64	9	5	0	0	33	27	19	17	11	23

ATLANTA BRAVES

BATTING	G	AB	R	H	2B	3B	HR	RBI	TB	BB	SO	SB	OBP	SLG	BA
Gary Sheffield	155	576	126	190	37	2	39	132	348	86	55	18	.419	.604	.330
Javy Lopez	129	457	89	150	29	3	43	109	314	33	90	0	.378	.687	.328
Marcus Giles	145	551	101	174	49	2	21	69	290	59	80	14	.390	.526	.316
Chipper Jones	153	555	103	169	33	2	27	106	287	94	83	2	.402	.517	.305
Julio Franco	103	197	28	58	12	2	5	31	89	25	43	0	.372	.452	.294
Rafael Furcal	156	664	130	194	35	10	15	61	294	60	76	25	.352	.443	.292
Vinny Castilla	147	542	65	150	28	3	22	76	250	26	86	1	.310	.461	.277
Andruw Jones	156	595	101	165	28	2	36	116	305	53	125	4	.338	.513	.277
Robert Fick	126	409	52	110	26	1	11	80	171	42	47	1	.335	.418	.269
Mark DeRosa	103	266	40	70	14	0	6	22	102	16	49	1	.316	.383	.263
Matt Franco	112	134	11	33	5	0	3	15	47	11	26	0	.299	.351	.246

PITCHING	W–L	ERA	G	GS	CG	SV	Inn	H	R	ER	BB	SO
John Smoltz	0–2	1.12	62	0	0	45	64⅓	48	9	8	8	73
Will Cunnane	2–2	2.70	20	0	0	3	20	14	6	6	6	20
Ray King	3–4	3.51	80	0	0	0	59	46	30	23	27	43
Russ Ortiz	21–7	3.81	34	34	1	0	212⅓	177	101	90	102	149
Mike Hampton	14–8	3.84	31	31	1	0	190	186	91	81	78	110
Kevin Gryboski	6–4	3.86	64	0	0	0	44⅓	44	22	19	23	32
Greg Maddux	16–11	3.96	36	36	1	0	218⅓	225	112	96	33	124
Horacio Ramirez	12–4	4.00	29	29	1	0	182⅓	181	91	81	72	100
Darren Holmes	1–2	4.29	48	0	0	0	42	47	22	20	11	46
Roberto Hernandez	5–3	4.35	66	0	0	0	60	61	36	29	43	45
Trey Hodges	3–3	4.66	52	1	0	0	65⅔	69	38	34	31	66
Jung Bong	6–2	5.05	44	0	0	1	57	56	32	32	31	47
Shane Reynolds	11–9	5.43	30	29	0	0	167⅓	191	104	101	59	94

CHICAGO CUBS

BATTING	G	AB	R	H	2B	3B	HR	RBI	TB	BB	SO	SB	OBP	SLG	BA
Kenny Lofton	56	208	39	68	13	4	3	20	98	18	22	12	.381	.471	.327
Mark Grudzielanek	121	481	73	151	38	1	3	38	200	30	64	6	.366	.416	.314
Corey Patterson	83	329	49	98	17	7	13	55	168	15	77	16	.329	.511	.298
Tom Goodwin	87	171	26	49	10	0	1	12	62	11	33	19	.328	.363	.287
Eric Karros	114	336	37	96	16	1	12	40	150	28	46	1	.340	.446	.286
Ramon Martinez	108	293	30	83	16	1	3	34	110	24	50	0	.333	.375	.283
Randall Simon	33	103	13	29	3	0	6	21	50	4	7	0	.318	.485	.282
Moises Alou	151	565	83	158	35	1	22	91	261	63	67	3	.357	.462	.280
Sammy Sosa	137	517	99	144	22	0	40	103	286	62	143	0	.358	.553	.279
Aramis Ramirez	63	232	31	60	7	1	15	39	114	17	31	1	.314	.491	.259
Damian Miller	114	352	34	82	19	1	9	36	130	39	91	1	.310	.369	.233
Alex Gonzalez	152	536	71	122	37	0	20	59	219	47	123	3	.295	.409	.228
Troy O'Leary	93	174	18	38	9	0	5	28	62	14	31	3	.275	.356	.218

PITCHING	W-L	ERA	G	GS	CG	SV	Inn	H	R	ER	BB	SO
Mark Prior	18-6	2.43	30	30	3	0	211⅓	183	67	57	50	245
Joe Borowski	2-2	2.63	68	0	0	33	68⅓	53	23	20	19	66
Mark Guthrie	2-3	2.74	65	0	0	0	42⅔	40	14	13	22	24
Carlos Zambrano	13-11	3.11	32	32	3	0	214	188	88	74	94	168
Kerry Wood	14-11	3.20	32	32	4	0	211	152	77	75	100	266
Kyle Farnsworth	3-2	3.30	77	0	0	0	76⅓	53	31	28	36	92
Mike Remlinger	6-5	3.65	73	0	0	0	69	54	30	28	39	83
Matt Clement	14-12	4.11	32	32	2	0	201⅔	169	100	92	79	171
Shawn Estes	8-11	5.73	29	28	1	0	152⅓	182	113	97	83	103

CINCINNATI REDS

BATTING	G	AB	R	H	2B	3B	HR	RBI	TB	BB	SO	SB	OBP	SLG	BA
Jose Guillen	91	315	52	106	21	1	23	63	198	17	63	1	.318	.629	.337
Sean Casey	147	573	71	167	19	3	14	80	234	51	58	4	.333	.408	.291
D'Angelo Jimenez	73	290	34	84	13	2	7	31	122	34	43	7	.350	.421	.290
Ryan Freel	43	137	23	39	6	1	4	12	59	9	13	9	.365	.431	.285
Barry Larkin	70	241	39	68	16	1	2	18	92	22	32	2	.344	.382	.282
Aaron Boone	106	403	61	110	19	3	18	65	189	35	74	15	.345	.469	.273
Austin Kearns	82	292	39	77	11	0	15	58	133	41	68	5	.395	.455	.264
Juan Castro	113	320	28	81	14	1	9	33	124	18	58	2	.290	.388	.253
Ken Griffey, Jr.	53	166	34	41	12	1	13	26	94	27	44	1	.370	.566	.247
Ruben Mateo	74	207	16	50	9	0	3	18	68	12	53	0	.290	.329	.242
Ray Olmedo	79	230	24	55	6	1	0	17	63	13	46	1	.280	.274	.239
Jason LaRue	118	379	52	87	23	1	16	50	160	33	111	3	.321	.422	.230
Adam Dunn	116	381	70	82	12	1	27	57	177	74	126	8	.354	.465	.215

PITCHING	W-L	ERA	G	GS	CG	SV	Inn	H	R	ER	BB	SO
Felix Heredia	5-2	3.00	57	0	0	1	72	61	27	24	28	41
Scott Williamson	5-3	3.19	42	0	0	21	42⅓	34	15	15	25	53
Scott Sullivan	6-0	3.62	50	0	0	0	49⅔	39	22	20	26	43
Brian Reith	2-3	4.11	42	1	0	1	61⅓	61	32	28	36	39
Chris Reitsma	9-5	4.29	57	3	0	12	84	92	41	40	19	53
John Bale	1-2	4.47	10	9	0	0	46⅓	50	24	23	12	37
Paul Wilson	8-10	4.64	28	28	0	0	166⅔	190	97	86	50	93
John Riedling	2-3	4.90	55	8	0	1	101	107	61	55	47	65
Danny Graves	4-15	5.33	30	26	2	2	169	204	108	100	41	60
Jimmy Haynes	2-12	6.30	18	18	1	0	94⅓	118	74	66	57	49
Ryan Dempster	3-7	6.54	22	20	0	0	115⅔	134	89	84	70	84

COLORADO ROCKIES

BATTING	G	AB	R	H	2B	3B	HR	RBI	TB	BB	SO	SB	OBP	SLG	BA
Todd Helton	160	583	135	209	49	5	33	117	367	111	72	0	.458	.630	.358
Jay Payton	157	600	93	181	32	5	28	89	307	43	77	6	.354	.512	.302
Larry Walker	143	454	86	129	25	7	16	79	216	98	87	7	.422	.476	.284
Preston Wilson	155	600	94	169	43	1	36	141	322	54	139	14	.343	.537	.282
Ronnie Belliard	116	447	73	124	31	2	8	50	183	49	71	7	.351	.409	.277
Greg Norton	114	179	19	47	15	0	6	31	80	16	47	2	.325	.447	.263
Rene Reyes	53	116	13	30	7	1	2	7	45	5	19	2	.287	.388	.259
Mark Sweeney	67	97	13	25	9	0	2	14	40	9	27	0	.321	.412	.258
Chris Stynes	138	443	71	113	31	3	11	73	183	48	76	3	.335	.413	.255
Juan Uribe	87	316	45	80	19	3	10	33	135	17	60	7	.297	.427	.253
Mark Bellhorn	99	249	27	55	10	1	2	26	73	50	78	5	.353	.293	.221
Charles Johnson	108	356	49	82	20	0	20	61	162	49	84	1	.320	.455	.230
Gabe Kapler	39	67	10	15	2	0	0	4	17	8	18	2	.307	.254	.224

PITCHING	W-L	ERA	G	GS	CG	SV	Inn	H	R	ER	BB	SO
Brian Fuentes	3-3	2.75	75	0	0	4	75⅓	64	24	23	34	82
Steve Reed	5-3	3.27	67	0	0	0	63⅓	59	24	23	26	39
Javier Lopez	4-1	3.70	75	0	0	1	58⅓	58	25	24	12	40
Justin Speier	3-1	4.05	72	0	0	9	73⅓	73	37	33	23	66
Shawn Chacon	11-8	4.60	23	23	0	0	137	124	73	70	58	93
Darren Oliver	13-11	5.04	33	32	1	0	180⅓	201	108	101	61	88
Jason Jennings	12-13	5.11	32	32	1	0	181⅓	212	115	103	88	119
Jose Jimenez	2-10	5.22	63	7	0	20	101⅔	137	62	59	32	45
Denny Stark	3-3	5.83	17	13	0	0	78⅔	98	57	51	33	30
Aaron Cook	4-6	6.02	43	16	1	0	124	160	89	83	57	43

FLORIDA MARLINS

BATTING	G	AB	R	H	2B	3B	HR	RBI	TB	BB	SO	SB	OBP	SLG	BA
Luis Castillo	152	595	99	187	19	6	6	39	236	63	60	21	.381	.397	.314
Juan Pierre	162	668	100	204	28	7	1	41	249	55	35	65	.361	.373	.305
Ivan Rodriguez	144	511	90	152	36	3	16	85	242	55	92	10	.369	.474	.297
Ramon Castro	40	53	6	15	2	0	5	8	32	4	11	0	.333	.604	.283
Mike Lowell	130	492	76	136	27	1	32	105	261	56	78	3	.350	.530	.276
Derrek Lee	155	539	91	146	31	2	31	92	274	88	131	21	.379	.508	.271
Juan Encarnacion	156	601	80	162	37	6	19	94	268	37	82	19	.313	.446	.270
Miguel Cabrera	87	314	39	84	21	3	12	62	147	25	84	0	.325	.468	.268
Alex Gonzalez	150	528	52	135	33	6	18	77	234	33	106	0	.313	.443	.256
Todd Hollandsworth	93	228	32	58	23	3	3	20	96	22	55	2	.317	.421	.254
Brian Banks	92	149	14	35	6	2	4	23	57	25	38	2	.348	.383	.235

PITCHING	W-L	ERA	G	GS	CG	SV	Inn	H	R	ER	BB	SO
Josh Beckett	9-8	3.04	24	23	0	0	142	132	54	48	56	152
Dontrelle Willis	14-6	3.30	27	27	2	0	160⅔	148	61	59	58	142
Mark Redman	14-9	3.59	29	29	3	0	190⅔	172	82	76	61	151
Braden Looper	6-4	3.68	74	0	0	28	80⅔	82	34	33	29	56
Tommy Phelps	3-2	4.00	27	7	0	0	63	70	32	28	23	43
Brad Penny	14-10	4.13	32	32	0	0	196⅓	195	96	90	56	138
Carl Pavano	12-13	4.30	33	32	2	0	201	204	99	96	49	133
Michael Tejera	3-4	4.67	50	6	0	2	81	82	44	42	36	58

BASEBALL

HOUSTON ASTROS

BATTING	G	AB	R	H	2B	3B	HR	RBI	TB	BB	SO	SB	OBP	SLG	BA
Richard Hidalgo	141	514	91	159	43	4	28	88	294	58	104	9	.385	.572	.309
Jeff Kent	130	505	77	150	39	1	22	93	257	39	85	6	.351	.509	.297
Morgan Ensberg	127	385	69	112	15	1	25	60	204	48	60	7	.377	.530	.291
Lance Berkman	153	538	110	155	35	6	25	93	277	107	108	5	.412	.515	.288
Jeff Bagwell	160	605	109	168	28	2	39	100	317	88	119	11	.373	.524	.278
Craig Biggio	153	628	102	166	44	2	15	62	259	57	116	8	.350	.412	.264
Geoff Blum	123	420	51	110	19	0	10	52	159	20	50	0	.295	.379	.262
Adam Everett	128	387	51	99	18	3	8	51	147	28	66	8	.320	.380	.256
Jose Vizcaino	91	189	14	47	7	3	3	26	69	8	22	0	.281	.365	.249
Brian L. Hunter	56	98	13	23	6	1	0	13	31	6	21	0	.278	.316	.235
Orlando Merced	123	212	20	49	17	2	3	26	79	15	33	3	.283	.373	.231
Brad Ausmus	143	450	43	103	12	2	4	47	131	46	66	5	.303	.291	.229

PITCHING	W-L	ERA	G	GS	CG	SV	Inn	H	R	ER	BB	SO
Billy Wagner	1-4	1.78	78	0	0	44	86	52	18	17	23	105
Octavio Dotel	6-4	2.48	76	0	0	4	87	53	25	24	31	97
Roy Oswalt	10-5	2.97	21	21	0	0	127⅓	116	48	42	29	108
Mike Gallo	1-0	3.00	32	0	0	0	30	28	10	10	10	16
Brad Lidge	6-3	3.60	78	0	0	1	85	60	36	34	42	97
Tim Redding	10-14	3.68	33	32	0	0	176	179	85	72	65	116
Ricky Stone	6-4	3.69	65	0	0	1	83	76	36	34	31	47
Jared Fernandez	3-3	3.99	12	6	0	0	38⅓	37	17	17	12	19
Wade Miller	14-13	4.13	33	33	1	0	187⅓	168	96	86	77	161
Ron Villone	6-6	4.13	19	19	0	0	106⅔	91	51	49	48	91
Pete Munro	3-4	4.67	40	2	0	0	54	63	30	28	26	27
Jeriome Robertson	15-9	5.10	32	31	0	0	160⅔	180	98	91	64	99

LOS ANGELES DODGERS

BATTING	G	AB	R	H	2B	3B	HR	RBI	TB	BB	SO	SB	OBP	SLG	BA
Brian Jordan	66	224	28	67	9	0	6	28	94	23	30	1	.372	.420	.299
Jolbert Cabrera	128	347	43	98	32	2	6	37	152	17	62	6	.332	.438	.282
Shawn Green	160	611	84	171	49	2	19	85	281	68	112	6	.355	.460	.280
Paul Lo Duca	147	568	64	155	34	2	7	52	214	44	54	0	.335	.377	.273
Dave Ross	140	124	19	32	7	0	10	18	69	13	42	0	.336	.556	.258
Cesar Izturis	158	558	47	140	21	6	1	40	176	25	70	10	.282	.315	.251
Dave Roberts	107	388	56	97	6	5	2	16	119	43	39	40	.331	.307	.250
Alex Cora	148	477	39	119	24	3	4	34	161	16	59	4	.287	.338	.249
Fred McGriff	86	297	32	74	14	0	13	40	127	31	66	0	.322	.428	.249
Adrian Beltre	158	559	50	134	30	2	23	80	237	37	103	2	.290	.424	.240
Robin Ventura	49	109	11	24	5	1	5	13	46	18	25	0	.331	.422	.220
Jeromy Burnitz	61	230	25	47	4	0	13	32	90	14	57	4	.252	.391	.204

PITCHING	W-L	ERA	G	GS	CG	SV	Inn	H	R	ER	BB	SO
Eric Gagne	2-3	1.20	77	0	0	55	82⅓	37	12	11	20	137
Paul Quantrill	2-5	1.75	89	0	0	1	77⅓	61	18	15	15	44
Guillermo Mota	6-3	1.97	76	0	0	1	105	78	23	23	26	99
Wilson Alvarez	6-2	2.37	21	12	1	1	95	80	27	25	23	82
Kevin Brown	14-9	2.39	32	32	0	0	211	184	67	56	56	185
Edwin Jackson	2-1	2.45	4	3	0	0	22	17	6	6	11	19
Paul Shuey	6-4	3.00	62	0	0	0	69	50	24	23	33	60
Hideo Nomo	16-13	3.09	33	33	2	0	218⅓	175	82	75	98	177
Kazuhisa Ishii	9-7	3.86	27	27	0	0	147	129	72	63	101	140
Odalis Perez	12-12	4.52	30	30	0	0	185⅓	191	98	93	46	141
Andy Ashby	3-10	5.18	21	12	0	0	73	90	42	42	17	41

MILWAUKEE BREWERS

BATTING	G	AB	R	H	2B	3B	HR	RBI	TB	BB	SO	SB	OBP	SLG	BA
Scott Podsednik	154	558	100	175	29	8	9	58	247	56	91	43	.379	.443	.314
Brooks Kieschnick	69	70	12	21	1	0	7	12	43	6	13	0	.355	.614	.300
Geoff Jenkins	124	487	81	144	30	2	28	95	262	58	120	0	.375	.538	.296
Alex Sanchez	43	163	15	46	10	3	0	10	62	7	28	8	.316	.380	.282
Brady Clark	128	315	33	86	21	1	6	40	127	21	40	13	.330	.403	.273
Richie Sexson	162	606	97	165	28	2	45	124	332	98	151	2	.379	.548	.272
Eddie Perez	107	350	26	95	17	1	11	45	147	17	47	0	.304	.420	.271
Bill Hall	52	142	23	37	9	2	5	20	65	7	28	1	.298	.458	.261
Wes Helms	134	476	56	124	21	0	23	67	214	43	131	0	.330	.450	.261
Eric Young	109	404	71	105	18	1	15	31	170	48	34	25	.344	.421	.260
Keith Ginter	127	358	51	92	15	2	14	44	153	37	87	1	.352	.427	.257
John Vander Wal	117	327	50	84	25	1	14	45	153	46	104	1	.350	.468	.257
Keith Osik	80	241	22	60	12	0	2	21	78	31	44	0	.342	.324	.249
Royce Clayton	146	483	49	110	16	1	11	39	161	49	92	5	.301	.333	.228
Jeffrey Hammonds	10	38	2	6	2	0	1	3	11	3	7	0	.220	.289	.158

PITCHING	W-L	ERA	G	GS	CG	SV	Inn	H	R	ER	BB	SO
Danny Kolb	1–2	1.96	37	0	0	21	41⅓	34	10	9	19	39
Doug Davis	3–2	2.58	8	8	1	0	52⅓	49	18	15	21	35
Dave Burba	1–1	3.53	17	2	0	0	43⅓	42	19	17	19	35
Matt Ford	0–3	4.33	25	4	0	0	43⅔	46	23	21	21	26
Leo Estrella	7–3	4.36	58	0	0	3	66	75	32	32	21	25
Ben Sheets	11–13	4.45	34	34	1	0	220⅔	232	122	109	43	157
Wes Obermueller	2–5	5.07	12	11	0	0	65⅔	81	40	37	25	34
Matt Kinney	10–13	5.19	33	31	1	0	190⅔	201	121	110	80	152
Wayne Franklin	10–13	5.50	36	34	1	0	194⅔	201	129	119	94	116
Glendon Rusch	1–12	6.42	32	19	1	1	123⅓	171	93	88	45	93

MONTREAL EXPOS

BATTING	G	AB	R	H	2B	3B	HR	RBI	TB	BB	SO	SB	OBP	SLG	BA
Vladimir Guerrero	112	394	71	130	20	3	25	79	231	63	53	9	.426	.586	.330
Jose Vidro	144	509	77	158	36	0	15	65	239	69	50	3	.397	.470	.310
Orlando Cabrera	162	626	95	186	47	2	17	80	288	52	64	24	.347	.460	.297
Wil Cordero	130	436	57	121	27	0	16	71	196	49	90	1	.354	.450	.278
Brad Wilkerson	146	504	78	135	34	4	19	77	234	89	155	13	.380	.464	.268
Jamey Carroll	105	227	31	59	10	1	1	10	74	19	39	5	.323	.326	.260
Todd Zeile	34	113	11	29	2	2	5	19	50	10	18	1	.331	.442	.257
Endy Chavez	141	483	66	121	25	5	5	47	171	31	59	18	.294	.354	.251
Edwards Guzman	52	146	15	35	5	0	1	14	43	5	17	0	.263	.295	.240
Henry Mateo	100	154	29	37	3	1	0	7	42	11	38	11	.304	.273	.240
Jose Macias	111	272	31	65	15	2	4	22	96	11	45	4	.273	.353	.239
Ron Calloway	126	340	36	81	17	1	9	52	127	20	80	9	.282	.374	.238
Brian Schneider	108	335	34	77	26	1	9	46	132	37	75	0	.309	.394	.230
Michael Barrett	70	226	33	47	9	2	10	30	90	21	37	0	.280	.398	.208

PITCHING	W-L	ERA	G	GS	CG	SV	Inn	H	R	ER	BB	SO
Luis Ayala	10–3	2.92	65	0	0	5	71	65	27	23	13	46
Joey Eischen	2–2	3.06	70	0	0	1	53	57	27	18	13	40
Livan Hernandez	15–10	3.20	33	33	8	0	233⅓	225	92	83	57	178
Javier Vazquez	13–12	3.24	34	34	4	0	230⅔	198	93	83	57	241
Scott Stewart	3–1	3.98	51	0	0	0	43	52	22	19	13	29
Tomo Ohka	10–12	4.16	34	34	2	0	199	233	106	92	45	118
Zach Day	9–8	4.18	23	23	1	0	131⅓	132	64	61	59	61
Claudio Vargas	6–8	4.34	23	20	0	0	114	111	59	55	41	62
Rocky Biddle	5–8	4.65	73	0	0	34	71⅔	71	43	37	40	54
T.J. Tucker	2–3	4.73	45	7	0	0	80	90	49	42	20	47

NEW YORK METS

BATTING	G	AB	R	H	2B	3B	HR	RBI	TB	BB	SO	SB	OBP	SLG	BA
Jose Reyes	69	274	47	84	12	4	5	32	119	13	36	13	.334	.434	.307
Jackson Phillips	119	403	45	120	25	0	11	58	178	39	50	0	.373	.442	.298
Cliff Floyd	108	365	57	106	25	2	18	68	189	51	66	3	.376	.518	.290
Mike Piazza	68	234	37	67	13	0	11	34	113	35	40	0	.377	.483	.286
Jeromy Burnitz	65	234	38	64	18	0	18	45	136	21	55	1	.344	.581	.274
Timo Perez	127	346	32	93	21	0	4	42	126	18	29	5	.301	.364	.269
Roger Cedeno	148	484	70	129	25	4	7	37	183	38	86	14	.320	.378	.267
Roberto Alomar	73	263	34	69	17	1	2	22	94	29	40	6	.336	.357	.262
Ty Wigginton	156	573	73	146	36	6	11	71	227	46	124	12	.318	.396	.255
Vance Wilson	96	268	28	65	9	1	8	39	100	15	56	1	.293	.373	.243
Joe McEwing	119	278	31	67	11	0	1	16	81	25	57	3	.309	.291	.241
Tony Clark	125	254	29	59	13	0	16	43	120	24	73	0	.300	.472	.232
Raul Gonzalez	107	217	28	50	12	2	2	21	72	27	34	3	.317	.332	.230
Rey Sanchez	56	174	11	36	3	1	0	12	41	8	18	1	.240	.236	.207

PITCHING	W-L	ERA	G	GS	CG	SV	Inn	H	R	ER	BB	SO
John Franco	0-3	2.62	38	0	0	2	34⅓	35	11	10	13	16
Dave Weathers	1-6	3.08	77	0	0	7	87⅔	87	33	30	40	75
Armando Benitez	3-3	3.10	45	0	0	21	49⅓	41	18	17	24	50
Graeme Lloyd	1-2	3.31	36	0	0	0	35⅓	39	16	13	7	17
Pedro Feliciano	0-0	3.35	23	0	0	0	48⅓	52	21	18	21	43
Dan Wheeler	1-3	3.71	35	0	0	2	51	49	23	21	17	35
Steve Trachsel	16-10	3.78	33	33	2	0	204⅔	204	90	86	65	111
Jae Weong Seo	9-12	3.82	32	31	0	0	188⅓	193	94	80	46	110
Al Leiter	15-9	3.99	30	30	1	0	180⅔	176	83	80	94	139
Tom Glavine	9-14	4.52	32	32	0	0	183⅓	205	94	92	66	82
Mike Stanton	2-7	4.57	50	0	0	5	45⅓	37	25	23	19	34
Aaron Heilman	2-7	6.75	14	13	0	0	65⅓	79	53	49	41	51

PHILADELPHIA PHILLIES

BATTING	G	AB	R	H	2B	3B	HR	RBI	TB	BB	SO	SB	OBP	SLG	BA
Jason Michaels	76	109	20	36	11	0	5	17	62	15	22	0	.416	.569	.330
Mike Lieberthal	131	508	68	159	30	1	13	81	230	38	59	0	.373	.453	.313
Marlon Byrd	135	495	86	150	28	4	7	45	207	44	94	11	.366	.418	.303
Bobby Abreu	158	577	99	173	35	1	20	101	270	109	126	22	.409	.468	.300
Placido Polanco	122	492	87	142	30	3	14	63	220	42	38	14	.352	.447	.289
Tyler Houston	54	97	7	27	6	0	2	14	39	6	19	0	.320	.402	.278
Jim Thome	159	578	111	154	30	3	47	131	331	111	182	0	.385	.573	.266
Tomas Perez	125	298	39	79	18	1	5	33	114	23	54	0	.316	.383	.265
Jimmy Rollins	156	628	85	165	42	6	8	62	243	54	113	20	.320	.387	.263
Ricky Ledee	121	255	37	63	15	2	13	46	121	34	59	0	.334	.475	.247
Pat Burrell	146	522	57	109	31	4	21	64	211	72	142	0	.309	.404	.209
David Bell	85	297	32	58	14	0	4	37	84	41	40	0	.296	.283	.195

PITCHING	W-L	ERA	G	GS	CG	SV	Inn	H	R	ER	BB	SO
Rheal Cormier	8-0	1.70	65	0	0	1	84⅔	54	18	16	25	67
Terry Adams	1-4	2.65	66	0	0	0	68	68	22	20	23	51
Dan Plesac	2-1	2.70	58	0	0	2	33⅓	29	12	10	11	37
Turk Wendall	3-3	3.38	56	0	0	1	64	54	24	24	28	27
Vicente Padilla	14-12	3.62	32	32	1	0	208⅔	196	94	84	62	133
Amaury Telemaco	1-4	3.97	8	8	0	0	45⅓	41	22	20	11	29
Kevin Millwood	14-12	4.01	35	35	5	0	222	210	103	99	68	169
Randy Wolf	16-10	4.23	33	33	2	0	200	176	101	94	78	177
Brett Myers	14-9	4.43	32	32	1	0	193	205	99	95	76	143
Carlos Silva	3-1	4.43	62	1	0	1	87⅓	92	43	43	37	48
Brandon Duckworth	4-7	4.94	24	18	0	0	93	98	58	51	44	68
Jose Mesa	5-7	6.52	61	0	0	24	58	71	44	42	31	45

PITTSBURGH PIRATES

BATTING	G	AB	R	H	2B	3B	HR	RBI	TB	BB	SO	SB	OBP	SLG	BA
Tike Redman	56	230	36	76	16	5	3	19	111	14	18	7	.374	.483	.330
Jason Kendall	150	587	84	191	29	3	6	58	244	49	40	8	.399	.416	.325
Brian Giles	105	388	70	116	30	4	16	70	202	85	48	0	.430	.521	.299
Matt Stairs	121	305	49	89	20	1	20	57	171	45	64	0	.389	.561	.292
Reggie Sanders	130	453	74	129	27	4	31	87	257	38	110	15	.345	.567	.285
Aramis Ramirez	96	375	44	105	25	1	12	67	168	25	68	1	.330	.448	.280
Kenny Lofton	84	339	58	94	19	4	9	26	148	28	29	18	.333	.437	.277
Randall Simon	91	307	34	84	14	0	10	51	128	12	30	0	.305	.417	.274
Rob Mackowiak	77	174	20	47	4	4	6	19	77	15	53	6	.342	.443	.270
Craig Wilson	116	309	49	81	15	4	18	48	158	35	89	3	.360	.511	.262
Jack Wilson	150	558	58	143	21	3	9	62	197	36	74	5	.303	.353	.256
Abraham Nunez	118	311	37	77	8	7	4	35	111	26	53	9	.310	.357	.248
Jeff Reboulet	93	261	37	63	10	2	3	25	86	27	47	2	.321	.330	.241

PITCHING	W-L	ERA	G	GS	CG	SV	Inn	H	R	ER	BB	SO
Kip Wells	10-9	3.28	31	31	1	0	197⅓	171	77	72	76	147
Nelson Figueroa	2-1	3.31	12	3	0	0	35⅓	28	13	13	13	23
Jeff Suppan	10-7	3.57	21	21	3	0	141	147	57	56	31	78
Julian Taverez	3-3	3.66	64	0	0	11	83⅔	75	37	34	27	39
Scott Sauerbeck	3-4	4.05	53	0	0	0	40	30	20	18	25	32
Brian Meadows	2-1	4.72	34	7	0	1	76⅓	91	45	40	11	38
Salomon Torres	7-5	4.76	41	16	0	2	121	128	65	64	42	84
Jeff D'Amico	9-16	4.77	29	29	2	0	175⅓	204	104	93	42	100
Pat Mahomes	0-1	4.84	9	1	0	0	22⅓	19	13	12	12	13
Kris Benson	5-9	4.97	18	18	0	0	105	127	67	58	36	68
Josh Fogg	10-9	5.26	26	26	1	0	142	166	90	83	40	71

ST. LOUIS CARDINALS

BATTING	G	AB	R	H	2B	3B	HR	RBI	TB	BB	SO	SB	OBP	SLG	BA
Albert Pujols	157	591	137	212	51	1	43	124	394	79	65	5	.439	.667	.359
Edgar Renteria	157	587	96	194	47	1	13	100	282	65	54	34	.394	.480	.330
J.D. Drew	100	287	60	83	13	3	15	42	147	36	48	2	.374	.512	.289
Scott Rolen	154	559	98	160	49	1	28	104	295	82	104	13	.382	.528	.286
Brett Tomko	32	63	4	18	1	0	0	9	19	4	15	0	.328	.302	.286
Eduardo Perez	105	253	47	72	16	0	11	41	121	29	53	5	.365	.478	.285
Bo Hart	77	296	46	82	13	5	4	28	117	12	64	3	.317	.395	.277
Jim Edmonds	137	447	89	123	32	2	39	89	276	77	127	1	.385	.617	.275
Tino Martinez	138	476	66	130	25	2	15	69	204	53	71	1	.352	.429	.273
Orlando Palmeiro	141	317	37	86	13	1	3	33	110	32	31	3	.336	.347	.271
Mike Matheny	141	441	43	111	18	2	8	47	157	44	81	1	.320	.356	.252

PITCHING	W-L	ERA	G	GS	CG	SV	Inn	H	R	ER	BB	SO
Jason Isringhausen	0-1	2.36	40	0	0	22	42	31	14	11	18	41
Kiko Calero	1-1	2.82	26	1	0	1	38⅓	29	12	12	20	51
Cal Eldred	7-4	3.74	62	0	0	8	67⅓	62	32	28	31	67
Matt Morris	11-8	3.76	27	27	5	0	172⅓	164	76	72	39	120
Sterling Hitchcock	5-1	3.79	8	6	0	0	38	34	17	16	14	32
Steve Kline	5-5	3.82	78	0	0	3	63⅔	56	29	27	30	31
Woody Williams	18-9	3.87	34	33	0	0	220⅔	220	101	95	55	153
Garrett Stephenson	7-13	4.59	32	27	1	0	174⅓	167	94	89	60	91
Danny Haren	3-7	5.08	14	14	0	0	72⅔	84	44	41	22	43
Brett Tomko	13-9	5.28	33	32	2	0	202⅔	252	126	119	57	114
Jason Simontacchi	9-5	5.56	46	16	1	1	126⅓	153	82	78	41	74
Jeff Fassero	1-7	5.68	62	6	0	3	77⅔	93	51	49	34	55

SAN DIEGO PADRES

BATTING	G	AB	R	H	2B	3B	HR	RBI	TB	BB	SO	SB	OBP	SLG	BA
Mark Loretta	154	589	74	185	28	4	13	72	260	54	62	5	.372	.441	.314
Brian Giles	29	104	23	31	4	2	4	18	51	20	10	4	.414	.490	.298
Sean Burroughs	146	517	62	148	27	6	7	58	208	44	75	7	.352	.402	.286
Phil Nevin	59	226	30	63	8	0	13	46	110	21	44	2	.339	.487	.279
Rondell White	115	413	49	115	17	3	18	66	192	25	71	1	.330	.465	.278
Lou Merloni	65	151	20	41	7	2	1	17	55	22	33	2	.362	.364	.272
Gary Matthews, Jr.	103	306	50	83	19	1	4	22	116	34	66	12	.346	.379	.271
Xavier Nady	110	371	50	99	17	1	9	39	145	24	74	6	.321	.391	.267
Mark Kotsay	128	482	64	128	28	4	7	38	185	56	82	6	.343	.384	.266
Brian Buchanan	115	198	29	52	10	2	8	29	90	24	51	6	.346	.455	.263
Ramon Vazquez	116	422	56	110	17	4	3	30	144	52	88	10	.342	.341	.261
Ryan Klesko	121	397	47	100	18	0	21	67	181	65	83	2	.354	.456	.252

PITCHING	W–L	ERA	G	GS	CG	SV	Inn	H	R	ER	BB	SO
Rod Beck	3–2	1.78	36	0	0	20	35⅓	25	7	7	11	32
Trevor Hoffman	0–0	2.00	9	0	0	0	9	7	2	2	3	11
Scott Linebrink	2–1	2.82	43	0	0	0	60⅔	55	22	19	22	51
Matt Herges	2–2	2.86	40	0	0	3	44	40	16	14	20	40
Adam Eaton	9–12	4.08	31	31	1	0	183	173	91	83	68	146
Jake Peavy	12–11	4.11	32	32	0	0	194⅔	173	94	89	82	156
Brian Lawrence	10–15	4.19	33	33	1	0	210⅔	206	106	98	57	116
Brandon Villafuerte	0–2	4.20	31	0	0	2	40⅔	39	20	19	26	34
Mike Matthews	6–4	4.45	77	0	0	0	64⅔	65	34	32	29	44
Jay Witasick	3–7	4.53	46	0	0	2	45⅔	42	24	23	25	42
Luther Hackman	2–2	5.17	65	0	0	0	76⅔	78	51	44	36	48
Oliver Perez	4–7	5.38	19	19	0	0	103⅔	103	65	62	65	117
Kevin Jarvis	4–8	5.87	16	16	0	0	92	113	65	60	32	49
Joe Roa	1–1	6.75	18	1	0	0	25⅓	34	20	19	6	18

SAN FRANCISCO GIANTS

BATTING	G	AB	R	H	2B	3B	HR	RBI	TB	BB	SO	SB	OBP	SLG	BA
Barry Bonds	130	390	111	133	22	1	45	90	292	148	58	7	.529	.749	.341
Andres Galarraga	110	272	36	82	15	0	12	42	133	19	61	1	.352	.489	.301
Marquis Grissom	149	587	82	176	33	3	20	79	275	20	82	11	.322	.468	.300
Ray Durham	110	410	61	117	30	5	8	33	181	50	82	7	.366	.441	.285
Benito Santiago	108	401	53	112	21	2	11	56	170	29	69	0	.329	.424	.279
Rich Aurilia	129	505	65	140	26	1	13	58	207	36	82	2	.325	.410	.277
Jeffrey Hammonds	36	94	20	26	10	0	3	10	56	13	21	1	.370	.479	.277
J.T. Snow	103	330	48	90	18	3	8	51	138	55	55	1	.387	.418	.273
Yorvit Torrealba	66	200	22	52	10	2	4	29	78	14	39	1	.312	.390	.260
Edgardo Alfonzo	142	514	56	133	25	2	13	81	201	58	41	5	.334	.391	.259
Neifi Perez	120	328	27	84	19	4	1	31	114	14	23	3	.285	.348	.256
Jose Cruz	158	539	90	135	26	1	20	68	223	102	121	5	.366	.414	.250
Pedro Feliz	95	235	31	58	9	3	16	48	121	10	53	2	.278	.515	.247
Eric Young	26	71	9	14	2	0	0	3	16	9	10	3	.293	.225	.197

PITCHING	W–L	ERA	G	GS	CG	SV	Inn	H	R	ER	BB	SO
Jason Schmidt	17–5	2.34	29	29	5	0	207⅔	152	56	54	46	208
Tim Worrell	4–4	2.87	76	0	0	38	78⅓	74	35	25	28	65
Joe Nathan	12–4	2.96	78	0	0	0	79	51	26	26	33	83
Felix Rodriguez	8–2	3.10	68	0	0	0	61	59	21	21	29	46
Jerome Williams	7–5	3.30	21	21	0	2	131	116	54	48	49	88
Scott Eyre	2–1	3.32	74	0	2	0	57	60	23	21	26	35
Jim Brower	8–5	3.96	51	5	0	2	100	90	48	44	33	65
Kirk Rueter	10–5	4.53	27	27	0	0	147	170	77	74	47	41
Damian Moss	9–7	4.70	21	20	0	0	115	121	62	60	63	57
Jesse Foppert	8–9	5.03	23	21	0	0	111	103	69	62	69	101

AMERICAN LEAGUE TEAM-BY-TEAM STATS

ANAHEIM ANGELS

BATTING	G	AB	R	H	2B	3B	HR	RBI	TB	BB	SO	SB	OBP	SLG	BA
Garret Anderson	159	638	80	201	49	4	29	116	345	31	83	6	.345	.541	.315
Chone Figgins	71	240	34	71	9	4	0	27	88	20	38	13	.345	.367	.296
Jeff DaVanon	123	330	56	93	16	1	12	43	147	42	59	17	.360	.445	.282
Bengie Molina	119	409	37	115	24	0	14	71	181	13	31	1	.304	.443	.281
Tim Salmon	148	528	78	145	35	4	19	72	245	77	93	3	.374	.464	.275
Eric Owens	111	241	29	65	6	0	1	20	74	10	24	11	.300	.307	.270
Adam Kennedy	143	449	71	121	17	1	13	49	179	45	73	22	.344	.399	.269
Scott Spezio	158	521	69	138	36	7	16	83	236	46	66	6	.326	.453	.265
David Eckstein	120	452	59	114	22	1	3	31	147	36	45	16	.325	.325	.252
Darin Erstad	67	258	35	65	7	1	4	17	86	18	40	9	.309	.333	.252
Troy Glaus	91	319	53	79	17	2	16	50	148	46	73	7	.343	.464	.248
Shawn Wooten	98	272	25	66	8	0	7	32	95	24	45	0	.303	.349	.243

PITCHING	W-L	ERA	G	GS	CG	SV	Inn	H	R	ER	BB	SO
Brendan Donnelly	2-2	1.58	63	0	0	3	74	55	14	13	24	79
Ben Weber	5-1	2.69	62	0	0	0	80⅓	84	26	24	22	46
Scot Shields	5-6	2.85	44	13	0	1	148⅓	138	56	47	38	111
Francisco Rodriguez	8-3	3.03	59	0	0	2	86	50	30	29	35	95
Troy Percival	0-5	3.47	52	0	0	33	49⅓	33	22	19	23	48
Jarrod Washburn	10-15	4.43	32	32	2	0	207⅓	205	106	102	54	118
John Lackey	10-16	4.63	33	33	2	0	204	223	117	105	66	151
Gary Glover	1-0	5.00	18	0	0	0	27	34	15	15	8	14
Ramon Ortiz	16-13	5.20	32	32	1	0	180	209	121	104	63	94
Kevin Appier	7-7	5.63	19	19	0	0	92⅔	105	60	58	36	50
Aaron Sele	7-11	5.77	25	25	0	0	121⅔	135	82	78	58	53

BALTIMORE ORIOLES

BATTING	G	AB	R	H	2B	3B	HR	RBI	TB	BB	SO	SB	OBP	SLG	BA
Melvin Mora	96	344	68	109	17	1	15	48	173	49	71	6	.418	.503	.317
Larry Bigbie	83	287	43	87	15	1	9	31	131	29	60	7	.365	.456	.303
Luis Matos	109	439	70	133	23	3	13	45	201	28	90	15	.353	.458	.303
B.J. Surhoff	93	319	32	94	20	0	5	41	129	29	29	2	.353	.404	.295
Jeff Conine	124	493	75	143	33	3	15	80	227	37	60	5	.338	.460	.290
Jay Gibbons	160	625	80	173	39	2	23	100	285	49	89	0	.330	.456	.277
Brook Fordyce	108	348	28	95	12	2	6	31	129	19	44	2	.311	.371	.273
Jerry Hairston, Jr.	58	218	25	59	12	2	2	21	81	23	25	14	.353	.372	.271
Brian Roberts	112	460	65	124	22	4	5	41	169	46	58	23	.337	.367	.270
David Segui	67	224	26	59	10	1	5	25	86	26	47	1	.341	.384	.263
Deivi Cruz	152	548	61	137	24	2	14	65	207	13	49	1	.269	.378	.250
Tony Batista	161	631	76	148	20	1	26	99	248	28	102	4	.270	.393	.235

PITCHING	W-L	ERA	G	GS	CG	SV	Inn	H	R	ER	BB	SO
Kerry Ligtenberg	4-2	3.34	68	0	0	1	59⅓	60	23	22	14	47
B.J. Ryan	4-1	3.40	76	0	0	0	50⅓	42	19	19	27	63
Sidney Ponson	14-6	3.77	21	21	4	0	148	147	65	62	43	100
Eric DuBose	3-6	3.79	17	10	1	0	73⅔	60	33	31	25	44
Pat Hentgen	7-8	4.09	28	22	1	1	160⅔	150	74	73	58	100
Jason Johnson	10-10	4.18	32	32	0	0	189⅔	216	100	88	80	118
Jorge Julio	0-7	4.38	64	0	0	36	61⅔	60	36	30	34	52
Rick Bauer	0-0	4.55	35	0	0	0	61⅓	58	36	31	24	43
Rick Helling	7-8	5.71	24	24	0	0	138⅔	156	90	88	40	86
Rodrigo Lopez	7-10	5.82	26	26	3	0	147	188	101	95	43	103
Omar Daal	4-11	6.34	19	17	0	0	93⅔	134	69	66	30	53

BOSTON RED SOX

BATTING	G	AB	R	H	2B	3B	HR	RBI	TB	BB	SO	SB	OBP	SLG	BA
Bill Mueller	146	524	85	171	45	5	19	85	283	59	77	1	.398	.540	.326
Manny Ramirez	154	569	117	185	36	1	37	104	334	97	94	3	.427	.587	.325
Trot Nixon	134	441	81	135	24	6	28	87	255	65	96	4	.396	.578	.306
Shea Hillenbrand	49	185	20	56	17	0	3	38	82	7	26	1	.335	.443	.303
Nomar Garciaparra	156	658	120	198	37	13	28	105	345	39	61	19	.345	.524	.301
Gabe Kapler	68	158	29	46	11	1	4	23	71	14	23	4	.349	.449	.291
David Ortiz	128	448	79	129	39	2	31	101	265	58	83	0	.369	.592	.288
Todd Walker	144	587	92	166	38	4	13	85	251	48	54	1	.333	.428	.283
Kevin Millar	148	544	83	150	30	1	25	96	257	60	108	3	.348	.472	.276
Johnny Damon	145	608	103	166	32	6	12	67	246	68	74	30	.345	.405	.273
Jason Varitek	142	451	63	123	31	1	25	85	231	51	106	3	.351	.512	.273
Damian Jackson	109	161	34	42	7	0	1	13	52	8	28	16	.294	.323	.261

PITCHING	W–L	ERA	G	GS	CG	SV	Inn	H	R	ER	BB	SO
Pedro Martinez	14–4	2.22	29	29	3	0	186⅔	147	52	46	47	206
Byung-Hyun Kim	8–5	3.18	49	5	0	16	79⅓	70	38	28	18	69
Mike Timlin	6–4	3.55	72	0	0	2	83⅔	77	37	33	9	65
Tim Wakefield	11–7	4.09	35	33	0	1	202⅓	193	106	92	71	169
Brandon Lyon	4–6	4.12	49	0	0	9	59	73	33	27	19	50
Alan Embree	4–1	4.25	65	0	0	1	55	49	26	26	16	45
Derek Lowe	17–7	4.47	33	33	1	0	203⅓	216	113	101	72	110
John Burkett	12–9	5.15	32	30	1	0	181⅔	202	108	104	47	107
Casey Fossum	6–5	5.47	19	14	0	1	79	82	55	48	34	63
Jeff Suppan	3–4	5.57	11	10	0	0	63	70	41	39	20	32
Ramiro Mendoza	3–5	6.75	37	5	0	0	66⅔	98	51	50	20	36

CHICAGO WHITE SOX

BATTING	G	AB	R	H	2B	3B	HR	RBI	TB	BB	SO	SB	OBP	SLG	BA
Magglio Ordonez	160	606	95	192	46	3	29	99	331	57	73	9	.380	.546	.317
Carl Everett	73	256	40	77	14	0	10	41	121	22	36	4	.377	.473	.301
Carlos Lee	158	623	100	181	35	1	31	113	311	37	91	18	.331	.499	.291
Aaron Rowand	93	157	22	45	8	0	6	24	71	7	21	0	.327	.452	.287
Sandy Alomar, Jr.	75	194	22	52	12	0	5	26	79	4	17	0	.281	.407	.268
Frank Thomas	153	546	87	146	35	0	42	105	307	100	115	0	.390	.562	.267
Joe Crede	151	536	68	140	31	2	19	75	232	32	75	1	.308	.433	.261
Tony Graffanino	90	250	51	65	15	3	7	23	107	24	37	8	.331	.428	.260
D'Angelo Jimenez	73	271	35	69	11	5	7	26	111	32	46	4	.332	.410	.255
Roberto Alomar	67	253	42	64	11	1	3	17	86	30	37	6	.330	.340	.253
Miguel Olivo	114	317	37	75	19	1	6	27	114	19	80	6	.287	.360	.237
Jose Valentin	144	503	79	119	26	2	28	74	233	54	114	8	.313	.463	.237
Paul Konerko	137	444	49	104	19	0	18	65	177	43	50	0	.305	.399	.234

PITCHING	W–L	ERA	G	GS	CG	SV	Inn	H	R	ER	BB	SO
Damaso Marte	4–2	1.58	71	0	0	11	79⅔	50	16	14	34	87
Kelly Wunsch	0–0	2.75	43	0	0	0	36	17	13	11	25	33
Esteban Loaiza	21–9	2.90	34	34	1	0	226⅓	196	75	73	56	207
Tom Gordon	7–6	3.16	66	0	0	12	74	57	29	26	31	91
Bartolo Colon	15–13	3.87	34	34	9	0	242	223	107	104	67	173
Mark Buehrle	14–14	4.14	35	35	2	0	230⅓	250	124	106	61	119
Scott Schoeneweis	2–1	4.50	20	0	0	0	26	26	16	13	9	27
Jon Garland	12–13	4.51	32	32	0	0	191⅔	188	103	96	74	108
Billy Koch	5–5	5.77	55	0	0	11	53	59	36	34	28	42
Dan Wright	1–7	6.15	20	15	0	1	86⅓	91	63	59	46	47
Rick White	1–2	6.61	34	0	0	1	47⅔	56	39	35	13	37

CLEVELAND INDIANS

BATTING	G	AB	R	H	2B	3B	HR	RBI	TB	BB	SO	SB	OBP	SLG	BA
Milton Bradley	101	377	61	121	34	2	10	56	189	64	73	17	.421	.501	.321
Victor Martinez	49	159	15	46	4	0	1	16	53	13	21	1	.345	.333	.289
Jody Gerut	127	480	66	134	33	2	22	75	237	35	70	4	.336	.494	.279
Shane Spencer	64	210	23	57	10	0	8	26	91	18	52	2	.328	.433	.271
Coco Crisp	99	414	55	110	15	6	3	27	146	23	51	15	.302	.353	.266
Ryan Ludwick	39	136	14	36	7	1	7	26	71	8	39	2	.306	.485	.265
Ellis Burks	55	198	27	52	11	1	6	28	83	27	46	1	.360	.419	.263
Casey Blake	152	557	80	143	35	0	17	67	229	38	109	7	.312	.411	.257
Travis Hafner	91	291	35	74	19	3	14	40	141	22	81	2	.327	.485	.254
Ben Broussard	116	386	53	96	21	3	16	55	171	32	75	5	.312	.443	.249
Matt Lawton	99	374	57	93	19	0	15	53	157	47	47	10	.343	.420	.249
Josh Bard	91	303	25	74	13	1	8	36	113	22	53	0	.293	.373	.244
Omar Vizquel	64	250	43	61	13	2	2	19	84	29	20	8	.321	.336	.244
Brandon Phillips	112	370	36	77	18	1	6	33	115	14	77	4	.242	.311	.208
Karim Garcia	24	93	8	18	1	0	5	14	34	5	20	0	.238	.366	.194

PITCHING	W-L	ERA	G	GS	CG	SV	Inn	H	R	ER	BB	SO
David Riske	2-2	2.29	68	0	0	8	74⅔	52	21	19	20	82
C.C. Sabathia	13-9	3.60	30	30	2	0	197⅔	190	85	79	66	141
Brian Anderson	9-10	3.71	25	24	0	0	148	162	88	61	32	72
Cliff Lee	3-3	3.61	9	9	0	0	52⅓	41	28	21	20	44
Danys Baez	2-9	3.81	73	0	0	25	75⅔	65	36	32	23	66
Jason Boyd	3-1	4.30	44	0	0	0	52⅓	38	25	25	26	31
Jake Westbrook	7-10	4.33	34	22	1	0	133	142	70	64	56	58
Jason Davis	8-11	4.68	27	27	1	0	165⅓	172	101	86	47	85
Terry Mulholland	3-4	4.91	43	3	0	0	99	117	60	54	37	42
Billy Traber	6-9	5.24	33	18	1	0	111⅔	132	67	65	40	88
Ricardo Rodriguez	3-9	5.73	15	15	0	0	81⅔	89	57	52	28	41

DETROIT TIGERS

BATTING	G	AB	R	H	2B	3B	HR	RBI	TB	BB	SO	SB	OBP	SLG	BA
Dmitri Young	155	562	78	167	34	7	29	85	302	58	130	2	.372	.537	.297
Alex Sanchez	101	394	43	114	13	5	1	22	140	18	46	44	.320	.355	.289
Warren Morris	97	346	37	94	13	2	6	37	129	23	42	4	.316	.373	.272
Kevin Witt	93	270	25	71	9	0	10	26	110	15	68	1	.301	.407	.263
Carlos Pena	131	452	51	112	21	6	18	50	199	53	123	4	.332	.440	.248
Craig Monroe	128	425	51	102	18	1	23	70	191	27	89	4	.287	.449	.240
Eric Munson	99	313	28	75	9	0	18	50	138	35	61	3	.312	.441	.240
Bobby Higginson	130	469	61	110	13	4	14	52	173	59	73	8	.320	.369	.235
Ramon Santiago	141	444	41	100	18	1	2	29	126	33	66	10	.292	.284	.225
Omar Infante	69	221	24	49	6	1	0	8	57	18	37	6	.278	.258	.222
Andres Torres	59	168	23	37	4	3	1	9	50	10	35	5	.263	.298	.220
Shane Halter	114	360	33	78	5	2	12	30	123	27	77	2	.269	.342	.217
Brandon Inge	104	330	32	67	15	3	8	30	112	24	79	4	.265	.339	.203

PITCHING	W-L	ERA	G	GS	CG	SV	Inn	H	R	ER	BB	SO
Jamie Walker	4-3	3.32	78	0	0	3	65	61	30	24	17	45
Nate Cornejo	6-17	4.67	32	32	2	0	194⅔	236	111	101	58	46
Chris Spurling	1-3	4.68	66	0	0	3	77	78	42	40	22	38
Steve Sparks	0-6	4.72	42	0	0	2	89⅔	95	57	47	34	49
Matt Roney	1-9	5.45	45	11	0	0	100⅔	102	67	61	48	47
Jeremy Bonderman	6-19	5.56	33	28	0	0	162	193	118	100	58	108
Mike Maroth	9-21	5.73	33	33	1	0	193⅓	231	131	123	50	87
Wilfredo Ledezma	3-7	5.79	34	8	0	0	84	99	55	54	35	49
Gary Knotts	3-8	6.04	20	18	0	0	95⅓	111	70	64	47	51
Franklyn German	2-4	6.04	45	0	0	5	44⅔	47	32	30	45	41
Adam Bernero	1-12	6.08	18	17	0	0	100⅔	104	68	68	51	54

KANSAS CITY ROYALS

BATTING	G	AB	R	H	2B	3B	HR	RBI	TB	BB	SO	SB	OBP	SLG	BA
Carlos Beltran	141	521	102	160	14	10	26	100	272	72	81	41	.389	.522	.307
Raul Ibanez	157	608	95	179	33	5	18	90	276	49	81	8	.345	.454	.294
Mike Sweeney	108	392	62	115	18	1	16	83	183	64	56	3	.391	.467	.293
Joe Randa	131	502	80	146	31	1	16	72	227	41	61	1	.348	.452	.291
Angel Berroa	158	567	92	163	28	7	17	73	256	29	100	21	.338	.451	.287
Aaron Guiel	99	354	63	98	30	0	15	52	173	27	63	3	.346	.489	.277
Mendy Lopez	52	94	13	26	5	1	3	11	42	4	28	2	.306	.447	.277
Ken Harvey	135	485	50	129	30	0	13	64	198	29	94	2	.313	.408	.266
Michael Tucker	104	389	61	102	20	5	13	55	171	39	88	8	.331	.440	.262
Mike DiFelice	62	189	29	48	16	1	3	25	75	9	30	1	.299	.397	.254
Desi Relaford	141	500	70	127	27	5	8	59	188	40	70	20	.315	.376	.254
Brent Mayne	113	372	39	91	17	1	6	36	128	32	59	0	.307	.344	.245
Carlos Febles	74	196	31	46	5	0	0	11	51	13	30	8	.299	.260	.235

PITCHING	W–L	ERA	G	GS	CG	SV	Inn	H	R	ER	BB	SO
Darrell May	10–8	3.77	35	32	2	0	210	197	98	88	53	115
Jeremy Affeldt	7–6	3.93	36	18	0	4	126	126	58	55	38	98
Brian Anderson	5–1	3.99	7	7	2	0	$49\frac{2}{3}$	50	22	22	11	15
Mike MacDougal	3–5	4.08	68	0	0	27	64	64	36	29	32	57
Kevin Appier	1–2	4.26	4	4	0	0	19	15	9	9	7	5
Jimmy Gobble	4–5	4.61	9	9	0	0	$52\frac{2}{3}$	56	32	27	15	31
Runelvys Hernandez	7–5	4.61	16	16	0	0	$91\frac{2}{3}$	87	51	47	37	48
D.J. Carrasco	6–5	4.82	50	2	0	2	$80\frac{1}{3}$	82	44	43	40	57
Jose Lima	8–3	4.91	14	14	0	0	$73\frac{1}{3}$	80	40	40	26	32
Jason Grimsley	2–6	5.16	76	0	0	0	75	88	47	43	36	58
Kyle Snyder	1–6	5.17	15	15	0	0	$85\frac{1}{3}$	94	52	49	21	39
Kris Wilson	6–3	5.33	29	4	0	0	$72\frac{2}{3}$	92	49	43	16	42
Chris George	9–6	7.11	18	18	0	0	$93\frac{2}{3}$	120	75	74	44	39

MINNESOTA TWINS

BATTING	G	AB	R	H	2B	3B	HR	RBI	TB	BB	SO	SB	OBP	SLG	BA
Shannon Stewart	65	270	43	87	22	0	6	38	127	25	36	3	.384	.470	.322
A.J. Pierzynski	137	487	63	152	35	3	11	74	226	24	55	3	.360	.464	.312
Jacque Jones	136	517	76	157	33	1	16	69	240	21	105	13	.333	.464	.304
Doug Mientkiewicz	142	487	67	146	38	1	11	65	219	74	55	4	.393	.450	.300
Corey Koskie	131	469	76	137	29	2	14	69	212	77	113	11	.393	.452	.292
Matthew LeCroy	107	345	39	99	19	0	17	64	169	25	82	0	.342	.490	.287
Cristian Guzman	143	534	78	143	15	14	3	53	195	30	79	18	.311	.365	.268
Luis Rivas	135	475	69	123	16	9	8	43	181	30	65	17	.308	.381	.259
Bobby Kielty	75	238	40	60	13	0	9	32	100	42	56	6	.370	.420	.252
Torii Hunter	154	581	83	145	31	4	26	102	262	50	106	6	.312	.451	.250
Dustan Mohr	121	348	50	87	22	0	10	36	139	33	106	5	.314	.399	.250

PITCHING	W–L	ERA	G	GS	CG	SV	Inn	H	R	ER	BB	SO
LaTroy Hawkins	9–3	1.86	74	0	0	2	$77\frac{1}{3}$	69	20	16	15	75
Eddie Guardado	3–5	2.89	66	0	0	41	$65\frac{1}{3}$	50	22	21	14	60
Johan Santana	12–3	3.07	45	18	0	0	$158\frac{1}{3}$	127	56	54	47	169
Juan Rincon	5–6	3.68	58	0	0	0	$85\frac{2}{3}$	74	38	35	38	63
Brad Radke	14–10	4.49	33	33	3	0	$212\frac{1}{3}$	242	111	106	28	120
Kenny Rogers	13–8	4.57	33	31	0	0	195	227	108	99	50	116
Kyle Lohse	14–11	4.61	33	33	2	0	201	211	107	103	45	130
J.C. Romero	2–0	5.00	73	0	0	0	63	66	37	35	42	50
Rick Reed	6–12	5.07	27	21	2	0	135	155	80	76	29	71
Joe Mays	8–8	6.30	31	21	0	0	130	159	92	91	39	50

NEW YORK YANKEES

BATTING	G	AB	R	H	2B	3B	HR	RBI	TB	BB	SO	SB	OBP	SLG	BA
Derek Jeter	119	482	87	156	25	3	10	52	217	43	88	11	.393	.450	.324
Karim Garcia	52	151	17	46	5	0	6	21	69	9	32	0	.342	.457	.305
Alfonso Soriano	156	682	114	198	36	5	38	91	358	38	130	35	.338	.525	.290
Hideki Matsui	163	623	82	179	42	1	16	106	271	63	86	2	.353	.435	.287
Nick Johnson	96	324	60	92	19	0	14	47	153	70	57	5	.422	.472	.284
Jorge Posada	142	481	83	135	24	0	30	101	249	93	110	2	.405	.518	.281
Ruben Sierra	63	174	19	48	8	1	6	31	76	13	20	1	.323	.437	.276
Juan Rivera	57	173	22	46	14	0	7	26	81	10	27	0	.304	.468	.266
Bernie Williams	119	445	77	117	19	1	15	64	183	71	61	5	.367	.411	.263
Raul Mondesi	98	361	56	93	23	3	16	49	170	38	66	17	.330	.471	.258
Aaron Boone	54	189	31	48	13	0	6	31	79	11	30	8	.302	.418	.254
Robin Ventura	89	283	31	71	13	0	9	42	111	40	62	0	.344	.392	.251
Jason Giambi	156	535	97	134	25	0	41	107	282	129	140	2	.412	.527	.250
Enrique Wilson	63	135	18	31	9	0	3	15	49	7	14	3	.276	.363	.230
Todd Zeile	66	186	29	39	8	0	6	23	65	24	36	0	.294	.349	.210

PITCHING	W-L	ERA	G	GS	CG	SV	Inn	H	R	ER	BB	SO
Mariano Rivera	5-2	1.66	64	0	0	40	70⅔	61	15	13	10	63
Chris Hammond	3-2	2.86	62	0	0	1	63	65	23	20	11	45
Jose Contreras	7-2	3.30	18	9	0	0	71	52	27	26	30	72
Mike Mussina	17-8	3.40	31	31	2	0	214⅔	192	86	81	40	195
Antonio Osuna	2-5	3.73	48	0	0	0	50⅔	58	22	21	20	47
Roger Clemens	17-9	3.91	33	33	1	0	211⅔	199	99	92	58	190
Andy Pettitte	21-8	4.02	33	33	1	0	208⅓	227	109	93	50	180
David Wells	15-7	4.14	31	30	4	0	213	242	101	98	20	101
Jeff Nelson	1-0	4.58	24	0	0	1	17⅔	17	9	9	10	21
Jeff Weaver	7-9	5.99	32	24	0	0	159⅓	211	113	106	47	93

OAKLAND ATHLETICS

BATTING	G	AB	R	H	2B	3B	HR	RBI	TB	BB	SO	SB	OBP	SLG	BA
Eric Chavez	156	588	94	166	39	5	29	101	302	62	89	8	.350	.514	.282
Miguel Tejada	162	636	98	177	42	0	27	106	300	53	65	10	.336	.472	.278
Ramon Hernanadez	140	483	70	132	24	1	21	78	221	33	79	0	.331	.458	.273
Billy McMillon	66	153	15	41	11	0	6	26	70	19	36	0	.354	.458	.268
Jose Guillen	45	170	25	45	7	1	8	23	78	7	32	0	.311	.459	.265
Eric Byrnes	121	414	64	109	27	9	12	51	190	42	71	10	.333	.459	.263
Erubiel Durazo	154	537	92	139	29	0	21	77	231	100	105	1	.374	.430	.259
Scott Hatteberg	147	541	63	137	34	0	12	61	207	66	53	0	.342	.383	.253
Mark Ellis	154	553	78	137	31	5	9	52	205	48	94	6	.313	.371	.248
Terrence Long	140	486	64	119	22	2	14	61	187	31	67	4	.293	.385	.245
Chris Singleton	120	306	38	75	24	1	1	36	104	26	55	7	.301	.340	.245
Jermaine Dye	65	221	28	38	6	0	4	20	56	25	42	1	.261	.253	.172

PITCHING	W-L	ERA	G	GS	CG	SV	Inn	H	R	ER	BB	SO
Keith Foulke	9-1	2.08	72	0	0	43	86⅔	57	21	20	20	88
Tim Hudson	16-7	2.70	34	34	3	0	240	197	84	72	61	162
Chad Bradford	7-4	3.04	72	0	0	2	77	67	28	26	30	62
Mark Mulder	15-9	3.13	26	26	9	0	186⅔	180	66	65	40	128
Ricardo Rincon	8-4	3.25	64	0	0	0	55⅓	45	21	20	32	40
Barry Zito	14-12	3.30	35	35	4	0	231⅔	186	98	85	88	146
John Halama	3-5	4.22	35	13	0	0	108⅔	117	68	51	36	51
Ted Lilly	12-10	4.34	32	31	0	0	178⅓	179	92	86	58	147
Rich Harden	5-4	4.46	15	13	0	0	74⅔	72	38	37	40	67

SEATTLE MARINERS

BATTING	G	AB	R	H	2B	3B	HR	RBI	TB	BB	SO	SB	OBP	SLG	BA
Ichiro Suzuki	159	679	111	212	29	8	13	62	296	36	69	34	.352	.436	.312
Randy Winn	157	600	103	177	37	4	11	75	255	41	108	23	.346	.425	.295
Bret Boone	159	622	111	183	35	5	35	117	333	68	125	16	.366	.535	.294
Edgar Martinez	145	497	72	146	25	0	24	98	243	92	95	0	.406	.489	.294
Rey Sanchez	46	170	22	50	5	1	0	11	57	8	21	1	.330	.335	.294
Greg Colbrunn	22	58	7	16	1	1	3	7	28	4	16	0	.323	.483	.276
Carlos Guillen	109	388	63	107	19	3	7	52	153	52	64	4	.359	.394	.276
John Olerud	152	539	64	145	35	0	10	83	210	84	67	0	.372	.390	.269
Mike Cameron	147	534	74	135	31	5	18	76	230	70	137	17	.344	.431	.253
Willie Bloomquist	89	196	30	49	7	2	1	14	63	19	39	4	.317	.321	.250
Dan Wilson	96	316	32	76	15	2	4	43	107	15	52	0	.372	.339	.241
Ben Davis	80	246	25	58	18	0	6	42	94	18	61	0	.284	.382	.236
Mark McLemore	99	309	34	72	15	2	2	37	97	38	71	5	.318	.314	.233
Jeff Cirillo	87	258	24	53	11	0	2	23	70	24	32	1	.284	.271	.205

PITCHING	W–L	ERA	G	GS	CG	SV	Inn	H	R	ER	BB	SO
Shigetoshi Hasegawa	2–4	1.48	63	0	0	16	73	62	12	12	18	32
Rafael Soriano	3–0	1.53	40	0	0	1	53	30	9	9	12	68
Julio Mateo	4–0	3.15	50	0	0	1	85⅔	69	32	30	13	71
Jamie Moyer	21–7	3.27	33	33	1	0	215	199	83	78	66	129
Jeff Nelson	3–2	3.35	46	0	0	7	37⅔	34	16	14	14	47
Ryan Franklin	11–13	3.57	32	32	2	0	212	199	93	84	61	99
Joel Pineiro	16–11	3.78	32	32	3	0	211⅔	192	94	89	76	151
Kazuhiro Sasaki	1–2	4.05	35	0	0	10	33⅓	31	17	15	15	29
Arthur Rhodes	3–3	4.17	67	0	0	3	54	53	25	25	18	48
Freddy Garcia	12–14	4.51	33	33	1	0	201⅓	196	109	101	71	144
Gil Meche	15–13	4.59	32	32	1	0	186⅓	187	97	95	63	130

TAMPA BAY DEVIL RAYS

BATTING	G	AB	R	H	2B	3B	HR	RBI	TB	BB	SO	SB	OBP	SLG	BA
Rey Ordonez	34	117	14	37	11	0	3	22	57	2	12	0	.328	.487	.316
Aubrey Huff	162	636	91	198	47	3	34	107	353	53	80	2	.367	.555	.311
Rocco Baldelli	156	637	89	184	32	8	11	78	265	30	128	27	.326	.416	.289
Carl Crawford	151	630	80	177	18	9	5	54	228	26	102	55	.309	.362	.281
Jason Tyner	46	90	12	25	7	0	0	6	32	10	12	2	.350	.356	.278
Travis Lee	145	542	75	149	37	3	19	70	249	64	97	6	.348	.459	.275
Julio Lugo	117	433	58	119	13	4	15	53	185	35	88	10	.333	.427	.275
Marlon Anderson	145	482	59	130	27	3	6	67	181	41	60	19	.328	.376	.270
Damian Rolls	107	373	43	95	20	0	7	46	136	19	84	11	.301	.365	.255
Toby Hall	130	463	50	117	23	0	12	47	176	23	40	0	.295	.380	.253
Al Martin	100	238	19	60	12	2	3	26	85	17	51	2	.306	.357	.252
Antonio Perez	48	125	19	31	6	1	2	12	45	18	34	4	.345	.360	.248
Ben Grieve	55	165	28	38	7	0	4	17	57	32	41	0	.371	.345	.230

PITCHING	W–L	ERA	G	GS	CG	SV	Inn	H	R	ER	BB	SO
Chad Gaudin	2–0	3.60	15	3	0	0	40	37	18	16	16	23
Travis Harper	4–8	3.77	61	0	0	1	93	86	45	39	31	64
Jeremi Gonzalez	6–11	3.91	25	25	2	0	156⅓	131	71	68	69	97
Victor Zambrano	12–10	4.21	34	28	1	0	188⅓	165	97	88	106	132
Lance Carter	7–5	4.33	62	0	0	26	79	72	39	38	19	47
Jesus Colome	3–7	4.50	54	0	0	2	74	69	37	37	46	69
Jorge Sosa	5–12	4.62	29	19	1	0	128⅔	137	71	66	60	72
Brandon Backe	1–1	5.44	28	0	0	0	44⅔	40	28	27	25	36
Rob Bell	5–4	5.52	19	18	0	0	101	103	64	62	39	44
Joe Kennedy	3–12	6.13	32	22	1	1	133⅔	167	101	91	47	77
Dewon Brazelton	1–6	6.89	10	10	0	0	48⅓	57	49	37	23	24

TEXAS RANGERS

BATTING	G	AB	R	H	2B	3B	HR	RBI	TB	BB	SO	SB	OBP	SLG	BA
Michael Young	160	666	106	204	33	9	14	72	297	36	103	13	.339	.446	.306
Hank Blalock	143	567	89	170	33	3	29	90	296	44	97	2	.350	.522	.300
Alex Rodriguez	161	607	124	181	30	6	47	118	364	87	126	17	.396	.600	.298
Juan Gonzalez	82	327	49	96	17	1	24	70	187	14	73	1	.329	.572	.294
Carl Everett	74	270	53	74	13	3	18	51	147	31	48	4	.356	.544	.274
Doug Glanville	52	195	22	53	5	0	4	14	70	6	25	4	.294	.359	.272
Ruben Sierra	43	133	14	35	9	0	3	12	53	14	27	1	.333	.398	.263
Rafael Palmeiro	154	561	92	146	21	2	38	112	285	84	77	2	.359	.508	.260
Mark Teixeira	146	529	66	137	29	5	26	84	254	44	120	1	.331	.480	.259
Einar Diaz	101	334	30	86	14	1	4	35	114	9	32	3	.294	.341	.257
Laynce Nix	53	184	25	47	10	0	8	30	81	9	53	3	.289	.440	.255
Todd Greene	62	205	25	47	10	1	10	20	89	2	47	0	.243	.434	.229
Shane Spencer	55	185	16	42	10	0	4	23	64	27	40	0	.329	.346	.227

PITCHING	W-L	ERA	G	GS	CG	SV	Inn	H	R	ER	BB	SO
Francisco Cordero	5-8	2.94	73	0	0	15	82⅔	70	33	27	38	90
Brian Shouse	0-1	3.10	62	0	0	1	61	62	24	21	14	40
Ron Mahay	3-3	3.18	35	0	0	0	45⅓	33	19	16	20	38
Erasmo Ramirez	3-1	3.86	34	0	0	0	49	46	21	21	9	28
Ugueth Urbina	0-4	4.19	39	0	0	26	38⅔	33	19	18	18	41
John Thomson	13-14	4.85	35	35	3	0	217	234	125	117	49	136
R.A. Dickey	9-8	5.09	38	13	1	1	116⅔	135	68	66	38	94
Aaron Fultz	1-3	5.21	64	0	0	0	67⅓	75	43	39	27	53
Joaquin Benoit	8-5	5.49	25	17	0	0	105	99	67	64	51	87
Rosman Garcia	1-2	6.02	46	0	0	0	46⅓	63	33	31	23	25
Ismael Valdes	8-8	6.10	22	22	0	0	115	148	83	78	29	47
Colby Lewis	10-9	7.30	26	26	0	0	127	163	104	103	70	88

TORONTO BLUE JAYS

BATTING	G	AB	R	H	2B	3B	HR	RBI	TB	BB	SO	SB	OBP	SLG	BA
Vernon Wells	161	678	118	215	49	5	33	117	373	42	80	4	.359	.550	.317
Greg Myers	121	329	51	101	19	0	15	52	165	37	57	0	.374	.502	.307
Carlos Delgado	161	570	117	172	38	1	42	145	338	109	137	0	.426	.593	.302
Frank Catalanatto	133	489	83	146	34	6	13	59	231	35	62	2	.351	.472	.299
Reed Johnson	114	412	79	121	21	2	10	52	176	20	67	5	.353	.427	.294
Shannon Stewart	71	303	47	89	22	2	7	35	136	27	30	1	.347	.449	.294
Mike Bordick	102	343	39	94	18	2	5	54	131	33	60	3	.340	.382	.274
Orlando Hudson	142	474	54	127	21	6	9	57	187	39	87	5	.328	.395	.268
Josh Phelps	119	396	57	106	18	1	20	66	186	39	115	1	.358	.470	.268
Chris Woodward	104	349	49	91	22	2	7	45	138	28	72	1	.316	.395	.261
Tom Wilson	96	256	37	66	19	0	5	35	100	28	80	0	.331	.391	.258
Dave Berg	61	161	26	41	6	1	4	18	61	11	34	0	.301	.379	.255
Eric Hinske	124	449	74	109	45	3	12	63	196	59	104	12	.329	.437	.243
Bobby Kielty	62	189	31	44	13	1	4	25	71	29	36	2	.342	.376	.233

PITCHING	W-L	ERA	G	GS	CG	SV	Inn	H	R	ER	BB	SO
Jason Kershner	3-3	3.17	40	0	0	0	54	43	21	19	15	32
Roy Halladay	22-7	3.25	36	36	9	0	266	253	111	96	32	204
Aquilino Lopez	1-3	3.42	72	0	0	14	73⅔	58	31	28	34	64
Kelvim Escobar	13-9	4.29	41	26	1	4	180⅓	189	94	86	78	159
Josh Towers	8-1	4.48	14	8	1	1	64⅓	67	34	32	7	42
Trever Miller	2-2	4.61	79	0	0	4	52⅔	46	30	27	28	44
Pete Walker	2-2	4.88	23	7	0	0	55⅓	59	31	30	24	29
Doug Davis	4-6	5.00	12	11	0	0	54	70	33	30	26	25
Mark Hendrickson	9-9	5.51	30	30	1	0	158⅓	207	111	97	40	76
Cory Lidle	12-15	5.75	31	31	2	0	192⅔	216	133	123	60	112
Tanyon Sturtze	7-6	5.94	40	8	0	0	89⅓	107	67	59	43	54

World Series All-time Results

2003	Florida (N) 4, New York (A) 2	1952	New York (A) 4, Brooklyn (N) 3
2002	Anaheim (A) 4, San Francisco (N) 3	1951	New York (A) 4, New York (N) 2
2001	Arizona (N) 4, New York (A) 3	1950	New York (A) 4, Philadelphia (N) 0
2000	New York (A) 4, New York (N) 1	1949	New York (A) 4, Brooklyn (N) 1
1999	New York (A) 4, Atlanta (N) 0	1948	Cleveland (A) 4, Boston (N) 2
1998	New York (A) 4, San Diego (N) 0	1947	New York (A) 4, Brooklyn (N) 3
1997	Florida (N) 4, Cleveland (A) 3	1946	St. Louis (N) 4, Boston (A) 3
1996	New York (A) 4, Atlanta (N) 2	1945	Detroit (A) 4, Chicago (N) 3
1995	Atlanta (N) 4, Cleveland (A) 2	1944	St. Louis (N) 4, St. Louis (A) 2
1994	Series canceled due to players' strike.	1943	New York (A) 4, St. Louis (N) 1
1993	Toronto (A) 4, Philadelphia (N) 2	1942	St. Louis (N) 4, New York (A) 1
1992	Toronto (A) 4, Atlanta (N) 2	1941	New York (A) 4, Brooklyn (N) 1
1991	Minnesota (A) 4, Atlanta (N) 3	1940	Cincinnati (N) 4, Detroit (A) 3
1990	Cincinnati (N) 4, Oakland (A) 0	1939	New York (A) 4, Cincinnati (N) 0
1989	Oakland (A) 4, San Francisco (N) 0	1938	New York (A) 4, Chicago (N) 0
1988	Los Angeles (N) 4, Oakland (A) 1	1937	New York (A) 4, New York (N) 1
1987	Minnesota (A) 4, St. Louis (N) 3	1936	New York (A) 4, New York (N) 2
1986	New York (N) 4, Boston (A) 3	1935	Detroit (A) 4, Chicago (N) 2
1985	Kansas City (A) 4, St. Louis (N) 3	1934	St. Louis (N) 4, Detroit (A) 3
1984	Detroit (A) 4, San Diego (N) 1	1933	New York (N) 4, Washington (A) 1
1983	Baltimore (A) 4, Philadelphia (N) 1	1932	New York (A) 4, Chicago (N) 0
1982	St. Louis (N) 4, Milwaukee (A) 3	1931	St. Louis (N) 4, Philadelphia (A) 3
1981	Los Angeles (N) 4, New York (A) 2	1930	Philadelphia (A) 4, St. Louis (N) 2
1980	Philadelphia (N) 4, Kansas City (A) 2	1929	Philadelphia (A) 4, Chicago (N) 1
1979	Pittsburgh (N) 4, Baltimore (A) 3	1928	New York (A) 4, St. Louis (N) 0
1978	New York (A) 4, Los Angeles (N) 2	1927	New York (A) 4, Pittsburgh (N) 0
1977	New York (A) 4, Los Angeles (N) 2	1926	St. Louis (N) 4, New York (A) 3
1976	Cincinnati (N) 4, New York (A) 0	1925	Pittsburgh (N) 4, Washington (A) 3
1975	Cincinnati (N) 4, Boston (A) 3	1924	Washington (A) 4, New York (N) 3
1974	Oakland (A) 4, Los Angeles (N) 1	1923	New York (A) 4, New York (N) 2
1973	Oakland (A) 4, New York (N) 3	1922	New York (N) 4, New York (A) 0; 1 tie
1972	Oakland (A) 4, Cincinnati (N) 3	1921	New York (N) 5, New York (A) 3
1971	Pittsburgh (N) 4, Baltimore (A) 3	1920	Cleveland (A) 5, Brooklyn (N) 2
1970	Baltimore (A) 4, Cincinnati (N) 1	1919	Cincinnati (N) 5, Chicago (A) 3
1969	New York (N) 4, Baltimore (A) 1	1918	Boston (A) 4, Chicago (N) 2
1968	Detroit (A) 4, St. Louis (N) 3	1917	Chicago (A) 4, New York (N) 2
1967	St. Louis (N) 4, Boston (A) 3	1916	Boston (A) 4, Brooklyn (N) 1
1966	Baltimore (A) 4, Los Angeles (N) 0	1915	Boston (A) 4, Philadelphia (N) 1
1965	Los Angeles (N) 4, Minnesota (A) 3	1914	Boston (N) 4, Philadelphia (A) 0
1964	St. Louis (N) 4, New York (A) 3	1913	Philadelphia (A) 4, New York (N) 1
1963	Los Angeles (N) 4, New York (A) 0	1912	Boston (A) 4, New York (N) 3; 1 tie
1962	New York (A) 4, San Francisco (N) 3	1911	Philadelphia (A) 4, New York (N) 2
1961	New York (A) 4, Cincinnati (N) 1	1910	Philadelphia (A) 4, Chicago (N) 1
1960	Pittsburgh (N) 4, New York (A) 3	1909	Pittsburgh (N) 4, Detroit (A) 3
1959	Los Angeles (N) 4, Chicago (A) 2	1908	Chicago (N) 4, Detroit (A) 1
1958	New York (A) 4, Milwaukee (N) 3	1907	Chicago (N) 4, Detroit (A) 0; 1 tie
1957	Milwaukee (N) 4, New York (A) 3	1906	Chicago (A) 4, Chicago (N) 2
1956	New York (A) 4, Brooklyn (N) 3	1905	New York (N) 4, Philadelphia (A) 1
1955	Brooklyn (N) 4, New York (A) 3	1904	No series
1954	New York (N) 4, Cleveland (A) 0	1903	Boston (A) 5, Pittsburgh (N) 3
1953	New York (A) 4, Brooklyn (N) 2		

Note: A=American League; N=National League

The World Series

Most Valuable Players

2003	Josh Beckett, Fla	1979	Willie Stargell, Pitt
2002	Troy Glaus, Ana	1978	Bucky Dent, NY (A)
2001	Randy Johnson, Ariz	1977	Reggie Jackson, NY (A)
	Curt Schilling, Ariz	1976	Johnny Bench, Cin
2000	Derek Jeter, NY (A)	1975	Pete Rose, Cin
1999	Mariano Rivera, NY (A)	1974	Rollie Fingers, Oak
1998	Scott Brosius, NY (A)	1973	Reggie Jackson, Oak
1997	Livan Hernandez, Fla	1972	Gene Tenace, Oak
1996	John Wetteland, NY (A)	1971	Roberto Clemente, Pitt
1995	Tom Glavine, Atl	1970	Brooks Robinson, Balt
1994	Series canceled due to labor dispute.	1969	Donn Clendenon, NY (N)
1993	Paul Molitor, Tor	1968	Mickey Lolich, Det
1992	Pat Borders, Tor	1967	Bob Gibson, StL
1991	Jack Morris, Minn	1966	Frank Robinson, Balt
1990	Jose Rijo, Cin	1965	Sandy Koufax, LA
1989	Dave Stewart, Oak	1964	Bob Gibson, StL
1988	Orel Hershiser, LA	1963	Sandy Koufax, LA
1987	Frank Viola, Minn	1962	Ralph Terry, NY (A)
1986	Ray Knight, NY (N)	1961	Whitey Ford, NY (A)
1985	Bret Saberhagen, KC	1960	Bobby Richardson, NY (A)
1984	Alan Trammell, Det	1959	Larry Sherry, LA
1983	Rick Dempsey, Balt	1958	Bob Turley, NY (A)
1982	Darrell Porter, StL	1957	Lew Burdette, Mil
1981	Ron Cey, LA; Steve Yeager, LA;	1956	Don Larsen, NY (A)
	Pedro Guerrero, LA	1955	Johnny Podres, Bklyn
1980	Mike Schmidt, Phil		

League Championship Series

	National League		American League
2003	Florida (WC) 4, Chicago (C) 3	2003	New York (E) 4, Boston (WC) 3
2002	San Francisco (WC) 4, St. Louis (C) 1	2002	Anaheim (WC) 4, Minnesota (C) 1
2001	Arizona (W) 4, Atlanta (E) 1	2001	New York (E) 4, Seattle (W) 1
2000	New York (WC) 4, St. Louis (C) 1	2000	New York (E) 4, Seattle (WC) 2
1999	Atlanta (E) 4, New York (WC) 2	1999	New York (E) 4, Boston (WC) 1
1998	San Diego (W) 4, Atlanta (E) 2	1998	New York (E) 4, Cleveland (C) 2
1997	Florida (WC) 4, Atlanta (E) 2	1997	Cleveland (C) 4, Baltimore (E) 2
1996	Atlanta (E) 4, St. Louis (C) 3	1996	New York (E) 4, Baltimore (WC) 1
1995	Atlanta (E) 4, Cincinnati (C) 0	1995	Cleveland (C) 4, Seattle (W) 2
1994	Playoffs canceled due to labor dispute.	1994	Playoffs canceled due to labor dispute.
1993	Philadelphia (E) 4, Atlanta (W) 2	1993	Toronto (E) 4, Chicago (W) 2
1992	Atlanta (W) 4, Pittsburgh (E) 3	1992	Toronto (E) 4, Oakland (W) 2
1991	Atlanta (W) 4, Pittsburgh (E) 3	1991	Minnesota (W) 4, Toronto (E) 1
1990	Cincinnati (W) 4, Pittsburgh (E) 2	1990	Oakland (W) 4, Boston (E) 0
1989	San Francisco (W) 4, Chicago (E) 1	1989	Oakland (W) 4, Toronto (E) 1
1988	Los Angeles (W) 4, New York (E) 3	1988	Oakland (W) 4, Boston (E) 0
1987	St. Louis (E) 4, San Francisco (W) 3	1987	Minnesota (W) 4, Detroit (E) 1
1986	New York (E) 4, Houston (W) 2	1986	Boston (E) 4, California (W) 3
1985	St. Louis (E) 4, Los Angeles (W) 2	1985	Kansas City (W) 4, Toronto (E) 3
1984	San Diego (W) 3, Chicago (E) 2	1984	Detroit (E) 3, Kansas City (W) 0
1983	Philadelphia (E) 3, Los Angeles (W) 1	1983	Baltimore (E) 3, Chicago (W) 1
1982	St. Louis (E) 3, Atlanta (W) 0	1982	Milwaukee (E) 3, California (W) 2
1981	Los Angeles (W) 3, Montreal (E) 2	1981	New York (E) 3, Oakland (W) 0
1980	Philadelphia (E) 3, Houston (W) 2	1980	Kansas City (W) 3, New York (E) 0
1979	Pittsburgh (E) 3, Cincinnati (W) 0	1979	Baltimore (E) 3, California (W) 1
1978	Los Angeles (W) 3, Philadelphia (E) 1	1978	New York (E) 3, Kansas City (W) 1
1977	Los Angeles (W) 3, Philadelphia (E) 1	1977	New York (E) 3, Kansas City (W) 2
1976	Cincinnati (W) 3, Philadelphia (E) 0	1976	New York (E) 3, Kansas City (W) 2
1975	Cincinnati (W) 3, Pittsburgh (E) 0	1975	Boston (E) 3, Oakland (W) 0
1974	Los Angeles (W) 3, Pittsburgh (E) 1	1974	Oakland (W) 3, Baltimore (E) 1
1973	New York (E) 3, Cincinnati (W) 2	1973	Oakland (W) 3, Baltimore (E) 2
1972	Cincinnati (W) 3, Pittsburgh (E) 2	1972	Oakland (W) 3, Detroit (E) 2
1971	Pittsburgh (E) 3, San Francisco (W) 1	1971	Baltimore (E) 3, Oakland (W) 0
1970	Cincinnati (W) 3, Pittsburgh (E) 0	1970	Baltimore (E) 3, Minnesota (W) 0
1969	New York (E) 3, Atlanta (W) 0	1969	Baltimore (E) 3, Minnesota (W) 0

Note: WC=wild-card team; W=Western Division; E=Eastern Division; C=Central Division

NLCS Most Valuable Player

2003	Ivan Rodriguez, Fla	1994	Playoffs canceled	1985	Ozzie Smith, StL
2002	Benito Santiago, SF	1993	Curt Schilling, Phil	1984	Steve Garvey, SD
2001	Craig Counsell, Ariz	1992	John Smoltz, Atl	1983	Gary Matthews, Phil
2000	Mike Hampton, NY	1991	Steve Avery, Atl	1982	Darrell Porter, StL
1999	Eddie Perez, Atl	1990	R. Myers/R. Dibble, Cin	1981	Burt Hooton, LA
1998	Sterling Hitchcock, SD	1989	Will Clark, SF	1980	Manny Trillo, Phil
1997	Livan Hernandez, Fla	1988	Orel Hershiser, LA	1979	Willie Stargell, Pitt
1996	Javier Lopez, Atl	1987	Jeffrey Leonard, SF	1978	Steve Garvey, LA
1995	Mike Devereaux, Atl	1986	Mike Scott, Hou	1977	Dusty Baker, LA

ALCS Most Valuable Player

2003	Mariano Rivera, NY	1995	Orel Hershiser, Clev	1987	Gary Gaetti, Minn
2002	Adam Kennedy, Ana	1994	Playoffs canceled	1986	Marty Barrett, Bos
2001	Andy Pettitte, NY	1993	Dave Stewart, Tor	1985	George Brett, KC
2000	David Justice, NY	1992	Roberto Alomar, Tor	1984	Kirk Gibson, Det
1999	Orlando Hernandez, NY	1991	Kirby Puckett, Minn	1983	Mike Boddicker, Balt
1998	David Wells, NY	1990	Dave Stewart, Oak	1982	Fred Lynn, Calif
1997	Marquis Grissom, Clev	1989	Rickey Henderson, Oak	1981	Graig Nettles, NY
1996	Bernie Williams, NY	1988	Dennis Eckersley, Oak	1980	Frank White, KC

All-Star Game

Date	Winner	Score	Site
7-13-04	American	9–4	Minute Maid Park, Hou
7-15-03	American	7–6	U.S. Cellular Field, Chi
7-9-02	Tie (11 inn)	7–7	Miller Park, Milwaukee
7-10-01	American	4–1	Safeco Field, Sea
7-11-00	American	6–3	Turner Field, Atl
7-13-99	American	4–1	Fenway Park, Bos
7-7-98	American	13–8	Coors Field, Col
7-8-97	American	3–1	Jacobs Field, Clev
7-9-96	National	6–0	Veterans Stadium, Phil
7-11-95	National	3–2	The Ballpark in Arlington, Tex
7-12-94	National	8–7	Three Rivers Stadium, Pitt
7-13-93	American	9–3	Camden Yards, Balt
7-14-92	American	13–6	Jack Murphy Stadium, SD
7-9-91	American	4–2	SkyDome, Tor
7-10-90	American	2–0	Wrigley Field, Chi
7-11-89	American	5–3	Anaheim Stadium, Cal
7-12-88	American	2–1	Riverfront Stadium, Cin
7-14-87	National	2–0	Oakland Coliseum, Oak
7-15-86	American	3–2	Astrodome, Hou
7-16-85	National	6–1	Metrodome, Minn
7-10-84	National	3–1	Candlestick Park, SF
7-6-83	American	13–3	Comiskey Park, Chi
7-13-82	National	4–1	Olympic Stadium, Mtl
8-9-81	National	5–4	Municipal Stadium, Clev
7-8-80	National	4–2	Dodger Stadium, LA
7-17-79	National	7–6	Kingdome, Sea
7-11-78	National	7–3	Jack Murphy Stadium, SD
7-19-77	National	7–5	Yankee Stadium, NY
7-13-76	National	7–1	Veterans Stadium, Phil
7-15-75	National	6–3	County Stadium, Mil
7-23-74	National	7–2	Three Rivers Stadium, Pitt
7-24-73	National	7–1	Royals Stadium, KC
7-25-72	National	4–3	Atlanta Stadium, Atl
7-13-71	American	6–4	Tiger Stadium, Det
7-14-70	National	5–4	Riverfront Stadium, Cin
7-23-69	National	9–3	R.F.K. Memorial Stadium, Wash
7-9-68	National	1–0	Astrodome, Hou
7-11-67	National	2–1	Anaheim Stadium, Cal
7-12-66	National	2–1	Busch Stadium, StL
7-13-65	National	6–5	Metropolitan Stadium, Minn
7-7-64	National	7–4	Shea Stadium, NY
7-9-63	National	5–3	Municipal Stadium, Clev
7-30-62	American	9–4	Wrigley Field, Chi
7-10-62	National	3–1	D.C. Stadium, Wash
7-31-61	Tie*	1–1	Fenway Park, Bos
7-11-61	National	5–4	Candlestick Park, SF
7-13-60	National	6–0	Yankee Stadium, NY
7-11-60	National	5–3	Municipal Stadium, KC
8-3-59	American	5–3	Memorial Coliseum, LA
7-7-59	National	5–4	Forbes Field, Pitt
7-8-58	American	4–3	Memorial Stadium, Balt
7-9-57	American	6–5	Sportsman's Park, StL
7-10-56	National	7–3	Griffith Stadium, Wash
7-12-55	National	6–5	County Stadium, Mil
7-13-54	American	11–9	Municipal Stadium, Clev
7-14-53	National	5–1	Crosley Field, Cin
7-8-52	National	3–2	Shibe Park, Phil
7-10-51	National	8–3	Briggs Stadium, Det
7-11-50	National	4–3	Comiskey Park, Chi
7-12-49	American	11–7	Ebbets Field, Bklyn
7-13-48	American	5–2	Sportsman's Park, StL
7-8-47	American	2–1	Wrigley Field, Chi
7-9-46	American	12–0	Fenway Park, Bos
1945	No game due to wartime travel restrictions.		
7-11-44	National	7–1	Forbes Field, Pitt
7-13-43	American	5–3	Shibe Park, Phil
7-6-42	American	3–1	Polo Grounds, NY
7-8-41	American	7–5	Briggs Stadium, Det
7-10-40	National	4–0	Sportsman's Park, StL
7-11-39	American	3–1	Yankee Stadium, NY
7-6-38	National	4–1	Crosley Field, Cin
7-7-37	American	8–3	Griffith Stadium, Wash
7-7-36	National	4–3	Braves Field, Bos
7-8-35	American	4–1	Municipal Stadium, Clev
7-10-34	American	9–7	Polo Grounds, NY
7-6-33	American	4–2	Comiskey Park, Chi

*Game called because of rain after nine innings.

Did You Know?

The American League East has had the exact same order of finish — Yankees, Red Sox, Blue Jays, Orioles, Devil Rays — for each of the past six seasons (1998 through 2003).

All-Star Game
Most Valuable Players

2004	Alfonso Soriano, Tex	AL	1989	Bo Jackson, KC	AL	1975	Jon Matlack, NY	NL
2003	Garret Anderson, Ana	AL	1988	Terry Steinbach, Oak	AL	1974	Steve Garvey, LA	NL
2002	Not selected		1987	Tim Raines, Mtl	NL	1973	Bobby Bonds, SF	NL
2001	Cal Ripken, Jr., Balt	AL	1986	Roger Clemens, Bos	AL	1972	Joe Morgan, Cin	NL
2000	Derek Jeter, NY	AL	1985	LaMarr Hoyt, SD	NL	1971	Frank Robinson, Balt	AL
1999	Pedro Martinez, Bos	AL	1984	Gary Carter, Mtl	NL	1970	Carl Yastrzemski, Bos	AL
1998	Roberto Alomar, Balt	AL	1983	Fred Lynn, Calif	AL	1969	Willie McCovey, SF	NL
1997	Sandy Alomar, Clev	AL	1982	Dave Concepcion, Cin	NL	1968	Willie Mays, SF	NL
1996	Mike Piazza, LA	NL	1981	Gary Carter, Mtl	NL	1967	Tony Perez, Cin	NL
1995	Jeff Conine, Fla	NL	1980	Ken Griffey, Cin	NL	1966	Brooks Robinson, Balt	AL
1994	Fred McGriff, Atl	NL	1979	Dave Parker, Pitt	NL	1965	Juan Marichal, SF	NL
1993	Kirby Puckett, Minn	AL	1978	Steve Garvey, LA	NL	1964	Johnny Callison, Phil	NL
1992	Ken Griffey, Jr., Sea	AL	1977	Don Sutton, LA	NL	1963	Willie Mays, SF	NL
1991	Cal Ripken, Jr., Balt	AL	1976	George Foster, Cin	NL	1962	Maury Wills, LA	NL
1990	Julio Franco, Tex	AL	1975	Bill Madlock, Chi	NL	1962	Leon Wagner, LA	AL

Barry Bonds

BRAD MANGIN

Trivia Challenge

The Florida Marlins have never lost a post-season series. Only three teams have never *won* a post-season series. Can you name them?

The Houston Astros, Texas Rangers, and Tampa Bay Devil Rays

Regular Season
Most Valuable Players

NATIONAL LEAGUE

Year	Name and Team	Position
2003	Barry Bonds, SF	Outfield
2002	Barry Bonds, SF	Outfield
2001	Barry Bonds, SF	Outfield
2000	Jeff Kent, SF	Second Base
1999	Chipper Jones, Atl	Third Base
1998	Sammy Sosa, Chi	Outfield
1997	Larry Walker, Col	Outfield
1996	Ken Caminiti, SD	Third Base
1995	Barry Larkin, Cin	Shortstop
1994	Jeff Bagwell, Hou	First Base
1993	Barry Bonds, SF	Outfield
1992	Barry Bonds, Pitt	Outfield
1991	Terry Pendleton, Atl	Third Base
1990	Barry Bonds, Pitt	Outfield
1989	Kevin Mitchell, SF	Outfield
1988	Kirk Gibson, LA	Outfield
1987	Andre Dawson, Chi	Outfield
1986	Mike Schmidt, Phil	Third Base
1985	Willie McGee, StL	Outfield
1984	Ryne Sandberg, Chi	Second Base
1983	Dale Murphy, Atl	Outfield
1982	Dale Murphy, Atl	Outfield
1981	Mike Schmidt, Phil	Third Base
1980	Mike Schmidt, Phil	Third Base
1979	Keith Hernandez, StL	First Base
	Willie Stargell, Pitt	First Base
1978	Dave Parker, Pitt	Outfield
1977	George Foster, Cin	Outfield
1976	Joe Morgan, Cin	Second Base
1975	Joe Morgan, Cin	Second Base
1974	Steve Garvey, LA	First Base
1973	Pete Rose, Cin	Outfield
1972	Johnny Bench, Cin	Catcher
1971	Joe Torre, StL	Third Base
1970	Johnny Bench, Cin	Catcher
1969	Willie McCovey, SF	First Base
1968	Bob Gibson, StL	Pitcher
1967	Orlando Cepeda, StL	First Base
1966	Roberto Clemente, Pitt	Outfield

Year	Name and Team	Position
1965	Willie Mays, SF	Outfield
1964	Ken Boyer, StL	Third Base
1963	Sandy Koufax, LA	Pitcher
1962	Maury Wills, LA	Shortstop
1961	Frank Robinson, Cin	Outfield
1960	Dick Groat, Pitt	Shortstop
1959	Ernie Banks, Chi	Shortstop
1958	Ernie Banks, Chi	Shortstop
1957	Hank Aaron, Mil	Outfield
1956	Don Newcombe, Bklyn	Pitcher
1955	Roy Campanella, Bklyn	Catcher
1954	Willie Mays, NY	Outfield
1953	Roy Campanella, Bklyn	Catcher
1952	Hank Sauer, Chi	Outfield
1951	Roy Campanella, Bklyn	Catcher
1950	Jim Konstanty, Phil	Pitcher
1949	Jackie Robinson, Bklyn	Second Base
1948	Stan Musial, StL	Outfield
1947	Bob Elliott, Bos	Third Base
1946	Stan Musial, StL	First Base, Outfield
1945	Phil Cavarretta, Chi	First Base
1944	Marty Marion, StL	Shortstop
1943	Stan Musial, StL	Outfield
1942	Mort Cooper, StL	Pitcher
1941	Dolph Camilli, Bklyn	First Base
1940	Frank McCormick, Cin	First Base
1939	Bucky Walters, Cin	Pitcher
1938	Ernie Lombardi, Cin	Catcher
1937	Joe Medwick, StL	Outfield
1936	Carl Hubbell, NY	Pitcher
1935	Gabby Hartnett, Chi	Catcher
1934	Dizzy Dean, StL	Pitcher
1933	Carl Hubbell, NY	Pitcher
1932	Chuck Klein, Phil	Outfield
1931	Frankie Frisch, StL	Second Base
1930	No selection	
1929	Rogers Hornsby, Chi	Second Base
1928	Jim Bottomley, StL	First Base

Regular Season
Most Valuable Players (cont.)

BRAD MANGIN

Alex Rodriguez of the Texas Rangers was A.L. MVP of 2003.

Year	Name and Team	Position
1927	Paul Waner, Pitt	Outfield
1926	Bob O'Farrell, StL	Catcher
1925	Rogers Hornsby, StL	Second Base, Manager
1924	Dazzy Vance, Bklyn	Pitcher
1915-23	No selections	
1914	Johnny Evers, Bos	Second Base
1913	Jake Daubert, Bklyn	First Base
1912	Larry Doyle, NY	Second Base
1911	Wildfire Schulte, Chi	Outfield

AMERICAN LEAGUE

Year	Name and Team	Position
2003	Alex Rodriguez, Tex	Shortstop
2002	Miguel Tejada, Oak	Shortstop
2001	Ichiro Suzuki, Sea	Outfield
2000	Jason Giambi, Oak	First Base
1999	Ivan Rodriguez, Tex	Catcher
1998	Juan Gonzalez, Tex	Outfield
1997	Ken Griffey, Jr., Sea	Outfield
1996	Juan Gonzalez, Tex	Outfield
1995	Mo Vaughn, Bos	First Base
1994	Frank Thomas, Chi	First Base
1993	Frank Thomas, Chi	First Base
1992	Dennis Eckersley, Oak	Pitcher
1991	Cal Ripken, Jr., Balt	Shortstop
1990	Rickey Henderson, Oak	Outfield
1989	Robin Yount, Mil	Outfield
1988	Jose Canseco, Oak	Outfield
1987	George Bell, Tor	Outfield
1986	Roger Clemens, Bos	Pitcher
1985	Don Mattingly, NY	First Base
1984	Willie Hernandez, Det	Pitcher
1983	Cal Ripken, Jr., Balt	Shortstop
1982	Robin Yount, Mil	Shortstop
1981	Rollie Fingers, Mil	Pitcher
1980	George Brett, KC	Third Base
1979	Don Baylor, Calif	Outfield, DH
1978	Jim Rice, Bos	Outfield, DH
1977	Rod Carew, Minn	First Base
1976	Thurman Munson, NY	Catcher
1975	Fred Lynn, Bos	Outfield
1974	Jeff Burroughs, Tex	Outfield
1973	Reggie Jackson, Oak	Outfield
1972	Dick Allen, Chi	First Base
1971	Vida Blue, Oak	Pitcher
1970	Boog Powell, Balt	First Base
1969	Harmon Killebrew, Minn	Third Base, First Ba
1968	Denny McLain, Det	Pitcher
1967	Carl Yastrzemski, Bos	Outfield
1966	Frank Robinson, Balt	Outfield
1965	Zoilo Versalles, Minn	Shortstop
1964	Brooks Robinson, Balt	Third Base
1963	Elston Howard, NY	Catcher
1962	Mickey Mantle, NY	Outfield
1961	Roger Maris, NY	Outfield
1960	Roger Maris, NY	Outfield
1959	Nellie Fox, Chi	Second Base
1958	Jackie Jensen, Bos	Outfield
1957	Mickey Mantle, NY	Outfield
1956	Mickey Mantle, NY	Outfield
1955	Yogi Berra, NY	Catcher
1954	Yogi Berra, NY	Catcher
1953	Al Rosen, Clev	Third Base
1952	Bobby Shantz, Phil	Pitcher
1951	Yogi Berra, NY	Catcher
1950	Phil Rizzuto, NY	Shortstop
1949	Ted Williams, Bos	Outfield
1948	Lou Boudreau, Clev	Shortstop
1947	Joe DiMaggio, NY	Outfield
1946	Ted Williams, Bos	Outfield
1945	Hal Newhouser, Det	Pitcher
1944	Hal Newhouser, Det	Pitcher
1943	Spud Chandler, NY	Pitcher
1942	Joe Gordon, NY	Second Base
1941	Joe DiMaggio, NY	Outfield
1940	Hank Greenberg, Det	Outfield
1939	Joe DiMaggio, NY	Outfield
1938	Jimmie Foxx, Bos	First Base
1937	Charlie Gehringer, Det	Second Base
1936	Lou Gehrig, NY	First Base
1935	Hank Greenberg, Det	First Base
1934	Mickey Cochrane, Det	Catcher
1933	Jimmie Foxx, Phil	First Base
1932	Jimmie Foxx, Phil	First Base
1931	Lefty Grove, Phil	Pitcher
1930	No selection	
1929	No selection	
1928	Mickey Cochrane, Phil	Catcher
1927	Lou Gehrig, NY	First Base
1926	George Burns, Clev	First Base
1925	Roger Peckinpaugh, Wash	Shortstop
1924	Walter Johnson, Wash	Pitcher
1923	Babe Ruth, NY	Outfield
1922	George Sisler, StL	First Base
1915–21	No selections	
1914	Eddie Collins, Phil	Second Base
1913	Walter Johnson, Wash	Pitcher
1912	Tris Speaker, Bos	Outfield
1911	Ty Cobb, Det	Outfield

The Regular Season
Rookies of the Year

NATIONAL LEAGUE

2003	Dontrelle Willis, Fla (P)
2002	Jason Jennings, Col (P)
2001	Albert Pujols, StL (OF)
2000	Rafael Furcal, Atl (SS)
1999	Scott Williamson, Cin (P)
1998	Kerry Wood, Chi (P)
1997	Scott Rolen, Phil (3B)
1996	Todd Hollandsworth, LA (OF)
1995	Hideo Nomo, LA (P)
1994	Raul Mondesi, LA (OF)
1993	Mike Piazza, LA (C)
1992	Eric Karros, LA (1B)
1991	Jeff Bagwell, Hou (3B)
1990	David Justice, Atl (OF)
1989	Jerome Walton, Chi (OF)
1988	Chris Sabo, Cin (3B)
1987	Benito Santiago, SD (C)
1986	Todd Worrell, StL (P)
1985	Vince Coleman, StL (OF)
1984	Dwight Gooden, NY (P)
1983	Darryl Strawberry, NY (OF)
1982	Steve Sax, LA (2B)
1981	Fernando Valenzuela, LA (P)
1980	Steve Howe, LA (P)
1979	Rick Sutcliffe, LA (P)
1978	Bob Horner, Atl (3B)
1977	Andre Dawson, Mtl (OF)
1976	Pat Zachry, Cin (P)
	Butch Metzger, SD (P)
1975	John Montefusco, SF (P)
1974	Bake McBride, StL (OF)
1973	Gary Matthews, SF (OF)
1972	Jon Matlack, NY (P)
1971	Earl Williams, Atl (C)
1970	Carl Morton, Mtl (P)
1969	Ted Sizemore, LA (2B)
1968	Johnny Bench, Cin (C)
1967	Tom Seaver, NY (P)
1966	Tommy Helms, Cin (2B)
1965	Jim Lefebvre, LA (2B)
1964	Dick Allen, Phil (3B)
1963	Pete Rose, Cin (2B)
1962	Ken Hubbs, Chi (2B)
1961	Billy Williams, Chi (OF)
1960	Frank Howard, LA (OF)
1959	Willie McCovey, SF (1B)
1958	Orlando Cepeda, SF (1B)
1957	Jack Sanford, Phil (P)
1956	Frank Robinson, Cin (OF)
1955	Bill Virdon, StL (OF)
1954	Wally Moon, StL (OF)
1953	Junior Gilliam, Bklyn (2B)
1952	Joe Black, Bklyn (P)
1951	Willie Mays, NY (OF)
1950	Sam Jethroe, Bos (OF)
1949	Don Newcombe, Bklyn (P)
*1948	Alvin Dark, Bos (SS)
*1947	Jackie Robinson, Bklyn (1B)

*Just one selection for both leagues

AMERICAN LEAGUE

2003	Angel Berroa, KC (SS)
2002	Eric Hinske, Tor (3B)
2001	Ichiro Suzuki, Sea (OF)
2000	Kazuhiro Sasaki, Sea (P)
1999	Carlos Beltran, KC (OF)
1998	Ben Grieve, Oak (OF)
1997	Nomar Garciaparra, Bos (SS)
1996	Derek Jeter, NY (SS)
1995	Marty Cordova, Minn (OF)
1994	Bob Hamelin, KC (DH)
1993	Tim Salmon, Calif (OF)
1992	Pat Listach, Mil (SS)
1991	Chuck Knoblauch, Minn (2B)
1990	Sandy Alomar, Jr., Clev (C)
1989	Gregg Olson, Balt (P)
1988	Walt Weiss, Oak (SS)
1987	Mark McGwire, Oak (1B)
1986	Jose Canseco, Oak (OF)
1985	Ozzie Guillen, Chi (SS)
1984	Alvin Davis, Sea (1B)
1983	Ron Kittle, Chi (OF)
1982	Cal Ripken, Jr., Balt (SS)
1981	Dave Righetti, NY (P)
1980	Joe Charboneau, Clev (OF)
1979	Alfredo Griffin, Tor (SS)
	John Castino, Minn (3B)
1978	Lou Whitaker, Det (2B)
1977	Eddie Murray, Balt (DH)
1976	Mark Fidrych, Det (P)
1975	Fred Lynn, Bos (OF)
1974	Mike Hargrove, Tex (1B)
1973	Al Bumbry, Balt (OF)
1972	Carlton Fisk, Bos (C)
1971	Chris Chambliss, Clev (1B)
1970	Thurman Munson, NY (C)
1969	Lou Piniella, KC (OF)
1968	Stan Bahnsen, NY (P)
1967	Rod Carew, Minn (2B)
1966	Tommie Agee, Chi (OF)
1965	Curt Blefary, Balt (OF)
1964	Tony Oliva, Minn (OF)
1963	Gary Peters, Chi (P)
1962	Tom Tresh, NY (SS)
1961	Don Schwall, Bos (P)
1960	Ron Hansen, Balt (SS)
1959	Bob Allison, Wash (OF)
1958	Albie Pearson, Wash (OF)
1957	Tony Kubek, NY (OF, SS)
1956	Luis Aparicio, Chi (SS)
1955	Herb Score, Clev (P)
1954	Bob Grim, NY (P)
1953	Harvey Kuenn, Det (SS)
1952	Harry Byrd, Phil (P)
1951	Gil McDougald, NY (3B)
1950	Walt Dropo, Bos (1B)
1949	Roy Sievers, StL (OF)

The Regular Season

Eric Gagne

Cy Young Award Winners

National League

Year	Pitcher	W–L	Sv	ERA
2003	Eric Gagne, LA	2–3	55	1.20
2002	Randy Johnson, Ariz	24–5	0	2.32
2001	Randy Johnson, Ariz	21–6	0	2.49
2000	Randy Johnson, Ariz	19–7	0	2.64
1999	Randy Johnson, Ariz	17–9	0	2.48
1998	Tom Glavine, Atl	20–6	0	2.47
1997	Pedro Martinez, Mtl	17–8	0	1.90
1996	John Smoltz, Atl	24–8	0	2.94
1995	Greg Maddux, Atl	19–2	0	1.63
1994	Greg Maddux, Atl	16–6	0	1.56
1993	Greg Maddux, Atl	20–10	0	2.36
1992	Greg Maddux, Chi	20–11	0	2.18
1991	Tom Glavine, Atl	20–11	0	2.55
1990	Doug Drabek, Pitt	22–6	0	2.76
1989	Mark Davis, SD	4–3	44	1.85
1988	Orel Hershiser, LA	23–8	1	2.26
1987	Steve Bedrosian, Phil	5–3	40	2.83
1986	Mike Scott, Hou	18–10	0	2.22
1985	Dwight Gooden, NY	24–4	0	1.53
1984	†Rick Sutcliffe, Chi	16–1	0	2.69
1983	John Denny, Phil	19–6	0	2.37
1982	Steve Carlton, Phil	23–11	0	3.10
1981	Fernando Valenzuela, LA	13–7	0	2.48
1980	Steve Carlton, Phil	24–9	0	2.34
1979	Bruce Sutter, Chi	6–6	37	2.23
1978	Gaylord Perry, SD	21–6	0	2.72
1977	Steve Carlton, Phil	23–10	0	2.64
1976	Randy Jones, SD	22–14	0	2.74
1975	Tom Seaver, NY	22–9	0	2.38
1974	Mike Marshall, LA	15–12	21	2.42
1973	Tom Seaver, NY	19–10	0	2.08
1972	Steve Carlton, Phil	27–10	0	1.97
1971	Ferguson Jenkins, Chi	24–13	0	2.77
1970	Bob Gibson, StL	23–7	0	3.12
1969	Tom Seaver, NY	25–7	0	2.21
1968	*Bob Gibson, StL	22–9	0	1.12
1967	Mike McCormick, SF	22–10	0	2.85

Year	Pitcher**	W–L	Sv	ERA
1966	Sandy Koufax, LA (NL)	27–9	0	1.73
1965	Sandy Koufax, LA (NL)	26–8	2	2.04
1964	Dean Chance, LA (AL)	20–9	4	1.65
1963	*Sandy Koufax, LA (NL)	25–5	0	1.88
1962	Don Drysdale, LA (NL)	25–9	1	2.83
1961	Whitey Ford, NY (AL)	25–4	0	3.21
1960	Vernon Law, Pitt (NL)	20–9	0	3.08
1959	Early Wynn, Chi (AL)	22–10	0	3.17
1958	Bob Turley, NY (AL)	21–7	1	2.97
1957	Warren Spahn, Mil (NL)	21–11	3	2.69
1956	*Don Newcombe, Bklyn (NL)	27–7	0	3.06

* Won the MVP and Cy Young awards in the same season.
** One award presented for both leagues.
† NL games only. Sutcliffe pitched 15 games with Cleveland before being traded to the Cubs.

American League

Year	Pitcher	W–L	Sv	ERA
2003	Roy Halladay, Tor	22–7	0	3.25
2002	Barry Zito, Oak	23–5	0	2.75
2001	Roger Clemens, NY	20–3	0	3.51
2000	Pedro Martinez, Bos	18–6	0	1.74
1999	Pedro Martinez, Bos	23–4	0	1.55
1998	Roger Clemens, Tor	20–6	0	2.65
1997	Roger Clemens, Tor	21–7	0	2.05
1996	Pat Hentgen, Tor	20–10	0	3.22
1995	Randy Johnson, Sea	18–2	0	2.48
1994	David Cone, KC	16–4	0	2.94
1993	Jack McDowell, Chi	22–10	0	3.37
1992	*Dennis Eckersley, Oak	7–1	51	1.91
1991	Roger Clemens, Bos	18–10	0	2.62
1990	Bob Welch, Oak	27–6	0	2.95
1989	Bret Saberhagen, KC	23–6	0	2.16
1988	Frank Viola, Minn	24–7	0	2.64
1987	Roger Clemens, Bos	20–9	0	2.97
1986	*Roger Clemens, Bos	24–4	0	2.48
1985	Bret Saberhagen, KC	20–6	0	2.87
1984	*Willie Hernandez, Det	9–3	32	1.92
1983	LaMarr Hoyt, Chi	24–10	0	3.66
1982	Pete Vuckovich, Mil	18–6	0	3.34
1981	*Rollie Fingers, Mil	6–3	28	1.04
1980	Steve Stone, Balt	25–7	0	3.23
1979	Mike Flanagan, Balt	23–9	0	3.08
1978	Ron Guidry, NY	25–3	0	1.74
1977	Sparky Lyle, NY	13–5	26	2.17
1976	Jim Palmer, Balt	22–13	0	2.51
1975	Jim Palmer, Balt	23–11	1	2.09
1974	Catfish Hunter, Oak	25–12	0	2.49
1973	Jim Palmer, Balt	22–9	1	2.40
1972	Gaylord Perry, Clev	24–16	1	1.92
1971	*Vida Blue, Oak	24–8	0	1.82
1970	Jim Perry, Minn	24–12	0	3.03
1969	Denny McLain, Det	24–9	0	2.80
	(tie) Mike Cuellar, Balt	23–11	0	2.38
1968	*Denny McLain, Det	31–6	0	1.96
1967	Jim Lonborg, Bos	22–9	0	3.16

Roy Halladay went 22–7 in 2003 and won the A.L. Cy Young Award.

The Regular Season

Career Individual Batting

GAMES	
Pete Rose	3,562
Carl Yastrzemski	3,308
Hank Aaron	3,298
*Rickey Henderson	3,081
Ty Cobb	3,034
Stan Musial	3,026
Eddie Murray	3,026
Cal Ripken, Jr.	3,001
Willie Mays	2,992
Dave Winfield	2,973
Rusty Staub	2,951
Brooks Robinson	2,896
Robin Yount	2,856
Al Kaline	2,834
Harold Baines	2,830
Eddie Collins	2,826
Reggie Jackson	2,820
Frank Robinson	2,808
Honus Wagner	2,794
Tris Speaker	2,789

HITS	
Pete Rose	4,256
Ty Cobb	4,189
Hank Aaron	3,771
Stan Musial	3,630
Tris Speaker	3,515
Carl Yastrzemski	3,419
Honus Wagner	3,414
Paul Molitor	3,319
Eddie Collins	3,315
Willie Mays	3,283
Eddie Murray	3,255
Nap Lajoie	3,242
Cal Ripken, Jr.	3,184
George Brett	3,154
Paul Waner	3,152
Robin Yount	3,142
Tony Gwynn	3,141
Dave Winfield	3,110
Rod Carew	3,053
*Rickey Henderson	3,055

DOUBLES	
Tris Speaker	792
Pete Rose	746
Stan Musial	725
Ty Cobb	724
George Brett	665
Nap Lajoie	657
Carl Yastrzemski	646
Honus Wagner	643
Hank Aaron	624
Paul Molitor	605
Paul Waner	605
Cal Ripken, Jr.	603
Robin Yount	583
Wade Boggs	578
Charlie Gehringer	574
Eddie Murray	560
Tony Gwynn	543
*Rafael Palmeiro	543
Harry Heilmann	542
Rogers Hornsby	541

AT-BATS	
Pete Rose	14,053
Hank Aaron	12,364
Carl Yastrzemski	11,988
Cal Ripken, Jr.	11,551
Ty Cobb	11,434
Eddie Murray	11,336
Robin Yount	11,008
Dave Winfield	11,003
Stan Musial	10,972
*Rickey Henderson	10,961
Willie Mays	10,881
Paul Molitor	10,835
Brooks Robinson	10,654
Honus Wagner	10,439
George Brett	10,349
Lou Brock	10,332
Luis Aparicio	10,230
Tris Speaker	10,195
Al Kaline	10,116
Rabbit Maranville	10,078

BATTING AVERAGE (5,000 AB)	
Ty Cobb	.366
Rogers Hornsby	.358
Ed Delahanty	.346
Tris Speaker	.345
Ted Williams	.344
Billy Hamilton	.344
Dan Brouthers	.342
Babe Ruth	.342
Harry Heilmann	.342
Willie Keeler	.341
Bill Terry	.341
George Sisler	.340
Lou Gehrig	.340
Jesse Burkett	.338
Tony Gwynn	.338
Nap Lajoie	.338
Al Simmons	.334
Paul Waner	.333
Eddie Collins	.333
Sam Thompson	.331

TRIPLES	
Sam Crawford	309
Ty Cobb	295
Honus Wagner	252
Jake Beckley	244
Roger Connor	233
Tris Speaker	222
Fred Clarke	220
Dan Brouthers	205
Joe Kelley	194
Paul Waner	191
Bid McPhee	189
Eddie Collins	187
Ed Delahanty	186
Sam Rice	184
Jesse Burkett	182
Edd Roush	182
Ed Konetchy	182
Buck Ewing	178
Rabbit Maranville	177
Stan Musial	177

HOME RUNS	
Hank Aaron	755
Babe Ruth	714
Willie Mays	660
*Barry Bonds	658
Frank Robinson	586
Mark McGwire	583
Harmon Killebrew	573
Reggie Jackson	563
Mike Schmidt	548
*Sammy Sosa	539
Mickey Mantle	536
Jimmie Foxx	534
*Rafael Palmeiro	528
Ted Williams	521
Willie McCovey	521
Eddie Mathews	512
Ernie Banks	512
Mel Ott	511
Eddie Murray	504
Lou Gehrig	493

RUNS	
*Rickey Henderson	2,295
Ty Cobb	2,246
Babe Ruth	2,174
Hank Aaron	2,174
Pete Rose	2,165
Willie Mays	2,062
Stan Musial	1,949
*Barry Bonds	1,941
Lou Gehrig	1,888
Tris Speaker	1,882
Mel Ott	1,859
Frank Robinson	1,829
Eddie Collins	1,821
Carl Yastrzemski	1,816
Ted Williams	1,798
Paul Molitor	1,782
Charlie Gehringer	1,774
Jimmie Foxx	1,751
Honus Wagner	1,739
Cap Anson	1,722

BASES ON BALLS	
*Rickey Henderson	2,190
*Barry Bonds	2,070
Babe Ruth	2,062
Ted Williams	2,019
Joe Morgan	1,865
Carl Yastrzemski	1,845
Mickey Mantle	1,733
Mel Ott	1,708
Eddie Yost	1,614
Darrell Evans	1,605
Stan Musial	1,599
Pete Rose	1,566
Harmon Killebrew	1,559
Lou Gehrig	1,508
Mike Schmidt	1,507
Eddie Collins	1,499
Willie Mays	1,464
Jimmie Foxx	1,452
Eddie Mathews	1,444
Frank Robinson	1,420

*Active in 2003.

Note: Stats were compiled after the 2003 season.

Regular Season
Career Individual Batting (cont.)

RUNS BATTED IN	
Hank Aaron	2,297
Babe Ruth	2,213
Lou Gehrig	1,995
Stan Musial	1,951
Ty Cobb	1,938
Jimmie Foxx	1,922
Eddie Murray	1,917
Willie Mays	1,903
Cap Anson	1,880
Mel Ott	1,860
Carl Yastrzemski	1,844
Ted Williams	1,839
Dave Winfield	1,833
Al Simmons	1,827
Frank Robinson	1,812
*Barry Bonds	1,742
Honus Wagner	1,732
Reggie Jackson	1,702
Cal Ripken, Jr.	1,695
*Rafael Palmeiro	1,687

SLUGGING AVERAGE (5,000 AB)	
Babe Ruth	.690
Ted Williams	.634
Lou Gehrig	.632
Jimmie Foxx	.609
Hank Greenberg	.605
*Barry Bonds	.602
Mark McGwire	.588
Joe DiMaggio	.579
Rogers Hornsby	.577
*Mike Piazza	.572
*Frank Thomas	.568
*Larry Walker	.567
Albert Belle	.564
*Juan Gonzalez	.563
*Ken Griffey, Jr.	.562
Johnny Mize	.562
Stan Musial	.559
Willie Mays	.557
Mickey Mantle	.557
Hank Aaron	.555

Rickey Henderson is the career leader in stolen bases (1,406).

STOLEN BASES	
*Rickey Henderson	1,406
Lou Brock	938
Billy Hamilton	914
Ty Cobb	892
*Tim Raines	808
Vince Coleman	752
Arlie Latham	742
Eddie Collins	741
Max Carey	738
Honus Wagner	723
Joe Morgan	689
Willie Wilson	668
Tom Brown	657
Bert Campaneris	649
Otis Nixon	620
George Davis	619
Dummy Hoy	596
Maury Wills	586
George Van Haltren	583
Ozzie Smith	580

ON-BASE PERCENTAGE (5,000 AB)	
Ted Williams	.482
Babe Ruth	.474
Billy Hamilton	.455
Lou Gehrig	.447
Rogers Hornsby	.434
Ty Cobb	.433
*Barry Bonds	.433
*Frank Thomas	.428
Jimmie Foxx	.428
Tris Speaker	.428
Eddie Collins	.424
*Edgar Martinez	.423
Dan Brouthers	.423
Mickey Mantle	.421
Mickey Cochrane	.419
Stan Musial	.417
Cupid Childs	.416
Jesse Burkett	.415
Wade Boggs	.415
*Jeff Bagwell	.411

TOTAL BASES	
Hank Aaron	6,856
Stan Musial	6,134
Willie Mays	6,066
Ty Cobb	5,854
Babe Ruth	5,793
Pete Rose	5,752
Carl Yastrzemski	5,539
Eddie Murray	5,397
Frank Robinson	5,373
*Barry Bonds	5,253
Dave Winfield	5,221
Cal Ripken, Jr.	5,168
Tris Speaker	5,101
Lou Gehrig	5,060
George Brett	5,044
Mel Ott	5,041
Jimmie Foxx	4,956
Ted Williams	4,884
Honus Wagner	4,870
Paul Molitor	4,854

STRIKEOUTS	
Reggie Jackson	2,597
*Andres Galarraga	2,000
*Sammy Sosa	1,977
Jose Canseco	1,942
Willie Stargell	1,936
Mike Schmidt	1,883
Tony Perez	1,867
*Fred McGriff	1,863
Dave Kingman	1,816
Bobby Bonds	1,757
Dale Murphy	1,748
Lou Brock	1,730
Mickey Mantle	1,710
Harmon Killebrew	1,699
Chili Davis	1,698
Dwight Evans	1,697
*Rickey Henderson	1,694
Dave Winfield	1,686
Gary Gaetti	1,602
Mark McGwire	1,596

*Active in 2003.

Regular Season

Career Individual Pitching

GAMES	
Jesse Orosco	1,252
Dennis Eckersley	1,071
Hoyt Wilhelm	1,070
*Dan Plesac	1,064
Kent Tekulve	1,050
*John Franco	1,036
Lee Smith	1,022
Goose Gossage	1,002
Lindy McDaniel	987
Mike Jackson	960
Rollie Fingers	944
Gene Garber	931
Cy Young	906
Sparky Lyle	899
Jim Kaat	898
Mike Stanton	885
Paul Assenmacher	884
Jeff Reardon	880
Don McMahon	874
Phil Niekro	864

LOSSES	
Cy Young	316
Pud Galvin	308
Nolan Ryan	292
Walter Johnson	279
Phil Niekro	274
Gaylord Perry	265
Don Sutton	256
Jack Powell	254
Eppa Rixey	251
Bert Blyleven	250
Robin Roberts	245
Warren Spahn	245
Steve Carlton	244
Early Wynn	244
Jim Kaat	237
Frank Tanana	236
Gus Weyhing	232
Tommy John	231
Bob Friend	230
Ted Lyons	230

EARNED RUN AVERAGE (2,000 IP)	
Ed Walsh	1.82
Addie Joss	1.89
Al Spalding	2.04
Three Finger Brown	2.06
John Ward	2.10
Christy Mathewson	2.13
Tommy Bond	2.14
Rube Waddell	2.16
Walter Johnson	2.17
Ed Reulbach	2.28
Will White	2.28
Eddie Plank	2.35
Larry Corcoran	2.36
Eddie Cicotte	2.38
Candy Cummings	2.39
Doc White	2.39
Nap Rucker	2.42
George Bradley	2.43
Jim McCormick	2.43
Chief Bender	2.46

INNINGS PITCHED	
Cy Young	7,356⅔
Pud Galvin	5,941⅓
Walter Johnson	5,914⅓
Phil Niekro	5,404⅓
Nolan Ryan	5,386
Gaylord Perry	5,350⅓
Don Sutton	5,282⅓
Warren Spahn	5,243⅔
Steve Carlton	5,217⅓
Grover Alexander	5,190
Kid Nichols	5,056⅓
Tim Keefe	5,049⅓
Bert Blyleven	4,970
Mickey Welch	4,802
Tom Seaver	4,782⅔
Christy Mathewson	4,780⅔
Tommy John	4,710⅓
Robin Roberts	4,688⅔
Early Wynn	4,564
John Clarkson	4,536⅓

WINNING PERCENTAGE**	
Al Spalding	.796
Spud Chandler	.717
*Pedro Martinez	.712
Whitey Ford	.690
Dave Foutz	.690
Bob Caruthers	.688
Don Gullett	.686
Lefty Grove	.680
Joe Wood	.671
*Randy Johnson	.668
Vic Raschi	.667
Larry Corcoran	.665
Christy Mathewson	.665
Sam Leever	.660
*Roger Clemens	.660
Sal Maglie	.658
Dick McBride	.656
Sandy Koufax	.655
Johnny Allen	.654
Ron Guidry	.651

SHUTOUTS	
Walter Johnson	110
Grover Alexander	90
Christy Mathewson	79
Cy Young	76
Eddie Plank	69
Warren Spahn	63
Nolan Ryan	61
Tom Seaver	61
Bert Blyleven	60
Don Sutton	58
Pud Galvin	57
Ed Walsh	57
Bob Gibson	56
Three Finger Brown	55
Steve Carlton	55
Jim Palmer	53
Gaylord Perry	53
Juan Marichal	52
Rube Waddell	50
Vic Willis	50

WINS	
Cy Young	511
Walter Johnson	417
Grover Alexander	373
Christy Mathewson	373
Warren Spahn	363
Pud Galvin	361
Kid Nichols	361
Tim Keefe	342
Steve Carlton	329
John Clarkson	328
Eddie Plank	326
Nolan Ryan	324
Don Sutton	324
Phil Niekro	318
Gaylord Perry	314
Tom Seaver	311
*Roger Clemens	310
Charley Radbourn	309
Mickey Welch	307
Lefty Grove	300
Early Wynn	300

SAVES	
Lee Smith	478
*John Franco	424
Dennis Eckersley	390
Jeff Reardon	367
*Trevor Hoffman	352
Randy Myers	347
Rollie Fingers	341
John Wetteland	330
*Roberto Hernandez	320
Rick Aguilera	318
*Robb Nen	314
Tom Henke	311
Goose Gossage	310
Jeff Montgomery	304
Doug Jones	303
Bruce Sutter	300
*Rod Beck	286
*Troy Percival	283
*Mariano Rivera	283
Todd Worrell	256

COMPLETE GAMES	
Cy Young	749
Pud Galvin	639
Tim Keefe	554
Kid Nichols	532
Walter Johnson	531
Mickey Welch	525
Charley Radbourn	488
John Clarkson	485
Tony Mullane	468
Jim McCormick	466
Gus Weyhing	448
Grover Alexander	437
Christy Mathewson	435
Jack Powell	422
Eddie Plank	410
Will White	394
Amos Rusie	393
Vic Willis	388
Tommy Bond	386
Warren Spahn	382

*Active in 2003. **Minimum 100 victories.

Regular Season

Career Individual Pitching (cont.)

STRIKEOUTS	
Nolan Ryan	5,714
Steve Carlton	4,136
*Roger Clemens	4,099
*Randy Johnson	3,871
Bert Blyleven	3,701
Tom Seaver	3,640
Don Sutton	3,574
Gaylord Perry	3,534
Walter Johnson	3,509
Phil Niekro	3,342
Ferguson Jenkins	3,192
Bob Gibson	3,117
Jim Bunning	2,855
Mickey Lolich	2,832
Cy Young	2,803
Frank Tanana	2,773
*Greg Maddux	2,765
*David Cone	2,655
Chuck Finley	2,610
Warren Spahn	2,583

BASES ON BALLS	
Nolan Ryan	2,795
Steve Carlton	1,833
Phil Niekro	1,809
Early Wynn	1,775
Bob Feller	1,764
Bobo Newsom	1,732
Amos Rusie	1,707
Charlie Hough	1,665
Gus Weyhing	1,566
Red Ruffing	1,541
Bump Hadley	1,442
Warren Spahn	1,434
Earl Whitehill	1,431
Tony Mullane	1,408
Sad Sam Jones	1,396
Jack Morris	1,390
Tom Seaver	1,390
Gaylord Perry	1,379
Roger Clemens	1,379
Bobby Witt	1,375

Fast Fact: The Chicago Cubs and Chicago White Sox were in first place in their divisions on September 8, 2003. It is the latest in the season both teams have been in first place since 1906, when they both won the pennant.

Individual Batting, Single Season

HITS	
George Sisler, 1920	257
Lefty O'Doul, 1929	254
Bill Terry, 1930	254
Al Simmons, 1925	253
Rogers Hornsby, 1922	250
Chuck Klein, 1930	250
Ty Cobb, 1911	248
George Sisler, 1922	246
Ichiro Suzuki, 2001	242
Heinie Manush, 1928	241
Babe Herman, 1930	241

BATTING AVERAGE	
Hugh Duffy, 1894	.440
Tip O'Neill, 1887	.435
Ross Barnes, 1876	.429
Nap Lajoie, 1901	.426
Willie Keeler, 1897	.424
Rogers Hornsby, 1924	.424
George Sisler, 1922	.420
Ty Cobb, 1911	.420
Sam Thompson, 1894	.415
Fred Dunlap, 1884	.412

DOUBLES	
Earl Webb, 1931	67
George Burns, 1926	64
Joe Medwick, 1936	64
Hank Greenberg, 1934	63
Paul Waner, 1932	62
Charlie Gehringer, 1936	60
Tris Speaker, 1923	59
Chuck Klein, 1930	59
Todd Helton, 2000	59
Billy Herman, 1936	57
Billy Herman, 1935	57
Carlos Delgado, 2000	57

TRIPLES	
Chief Wilson, 1912	36
Dave Orr, 1886	31
Heinie Reitz, 1894	31
Perry Werden, 1893	29
Harry Davis, 1897	28
Sam Thompson, 1894	28
George Davis, 1893	27
Sam Thompson, 1894	27
Jimmy Williams, 1899	27
John Reilly, 1890	26
George Treadway, 1894	26
Joe Jackson, 1912	26
Sam Crawford, 1914	26
Kiki Cuyler, 1925	26

HOME RUNS	
Barry Bonds, 2001	73
Mark McGwire, 1998	70
Sammy Sosa, 1998	66
Mark McGwire, 1999	65
Sammy Sosa, 2001	64
Sammy Sosa, 1999	63
Roger Maris, 1961	61
Babe Ruth, 1927	60
Babe Ruth, 1921	59
Jimmie Foxx, 1932	58
Hank Greenberg, 1938	58
Mark McGwire, 1997	58

TOTAL BASES	
Babe Ruth, 1921	457
Rogers Hornsby, 1922	450
Lou Gehrig, 1927	447
Chuck Klein, 1930	445
Jimmie Foxx, 1932	438
Stan Musial, 1948	429
Sammy Sosa, 2001	425
Hack Wilson, 1930	423
Chuck Klein, 1932	420
Luis Gonzalez, 2001	419
Lou Gehrig, 1930	419

RUNS BATTED IN	
Hack Wilson, 1930	190
Lou Gehrig, 1931	184
Hank Greenberg, 1937	183
Lou Gehrig, 1927	175
Jimmie Foxx, 1938	175
Lou Gehrig, 1930	174
Babe Ruth, 1921	171
Chuck Klein, 1930	170
Hank Greenberg, 1935	170
Jimmie Foxx, 1932	169

STRIKEOUTS	
Bobby Bonds, 1970	189
Jose Hernandez, 2002	188
Bobby Bonds, 1969	187
Preston Wilson, 2000	187
Rob Deer, 1987	186
Jose Hernandez, 2001	185
Jim Thome, 2001	185
Pete Incaviglia, 1986	185
Cecil Fielder, 1990	182
Mo Vaughn, 2000	181

RUNS	
Billy Hamilton, 1894	198
Tom Brown, 1891	177
Babe Ruth, 1921	177
Tip O'Neill, 1887	167
Lou Gehrig, 1936	167
Billy Hamilton, 1895	166
Willie Keeler, 1894	165
Joe Kelley, 1894	165
Arlie Latham, 1887	163
Babe Ruth, 1928	163
Lou Gehrig, 1931	163

Regular Season

Individual Batting, Single Season (cont.)

STOLEN BASES	
Hugh Nicol, 1887	138
Rickey Henderson, 1982	130
Arlie Latham, 1887	129
Lou Brock, 1974	118
Charlie Comiskey, 1887	117
John Ward, 1887	111
Billy Hamilton, 1889	111
Billy Hamilton, 1891	111
Vince Coleman, 1985	110
Arlie Latham, 1888	109
Vince Coleman, 1987	109

BASES ON BALLS	
Barry Bonds, 2002	198
Barry Bonds, 2001	177
Babe Ruth, 1923	170
Ted Williams, 1947	162
Ted Williams, 1949	162
Mark McGwire, 1998	162
Ted Williams, 1946	156
Eddie Yost, 1956	151
Barry Bonds, 1996	151
Babe Ruth, 1920	150

SLUGGING AVERAGE	
Barry Bonds, 2001	.863
Babe Ruth, 1920	.847
Babe Ruth, 1921	.846
Barry Bonds, 2002	.799
Babe Ruth, 1927	.772
Lou Gehrig, 1927	.765
Babe Ruth, 1923	.764
Rogers Hornsby, 1925	.756
Mark McGwire, 1998	.752
Jeff Bagwell, 1994	.750

Individual Pitching, Single Season

GAMES	
Mike Marshall, 1974	106
Kent Tekulve, 1979	94
Mike Marshall, 1973	92
Kent Tekulve, 1978	91
Wayne Granger, 1969	90
Mike Marshall, 1979	90
Kent Tekulve, 1987	90
Steve Kline, 2001	89
Mark Eichhorn, 1987	89
Paul Quantrill, 2003	89
Julian Tavarez, 1997	89

GAMES STARTED	
Will White, 1879	75
Jim Galvin, 1883	75
Jim McCormick, 1880	74
Charley Radbourn, 1884	73
Guy Hecker, 1884	73
Jim Galvin, 1884	72
John Clarkson, 1889	72
Bill Hutchison, 1892	71
John Clarkson, 1885	70
Matt Kilroy, 1887	69

INNINGS PITCHED	
Will White, 1878	680
Charley Radbourn, 1884	678⅔
Guy Hecker, 1884	670⅔
Jim McCormick, 1880	657⅔
Jim Galvin, 1883	656⅓
Jim Galvin, 1884	636⅓
Charley Radbourn, 1883	632⅓
Bill Hutchison, 1892	627
John Clarkson, 1885	623
Jim Devlin, 1876	622
Bill Hutchison, 1892	622

WINS	
Charley Radbourn, 1884	59
John Clarkson, 1885	53
Guy Hecker, 1884	52
John Clarkson, 1889	49
Charley Radbourn, 1883	48
Charlie Buffinton, 1884	48
Al Spalding, 1876	47
John Ward, 1879	47
Jim Galvin, 1883	46
Jim Galvin, 1884	46
Matt Kilroy, 1887	46

LOSSES	
John Coleman, 1883	48
Will White, 1880	42
Larry McKeon, 1884	41
George Bradley, 1879	40
Jim McCormick, 1879	40
Henry Porter, 1888	37
Kid Carsey, 1891	37
George Cobb, 1892	37
Stump Weidman, 1886	36
Bill Hutchison, 1892	36

WINNING PERCENTAGE	
Roy Face, 1959	.947
Johnny Allen, 1937	.938
Greg Maddux, 1995	.905
Randy Johnson, 1995	.900
Ron Guidry, 1978	.893
Freddie Fitzsimmons, 1940	.889
Lefty Grove, 1931	.886
Bob Stanley, 1978	.882
Preacher Roe, 1951	.880
Fred Goldsmith, 1880	.875
Tom Seaver, 1981	.875

SAVES	
Bobby Thigpen, 1990	57
Eric Gagne, 2003	55
John Smoltz, 2002	55
Randy Myers, 1993	53
Trevor Hoffman, 1998	53
Eric Gagne, 2002	52
Dennis Eckersley, 1992	51
Rod Beck, 1998	51
Mariano Rivera, 2001	50
Dennis Eckersley, 1990	48
Rod Beck, 1993	48
Jeff Shaw, 1998	48

EARNED RUN AVERAGE	
Tim Keefe, 1880	0.86
Dutch Leonard, 1914	0.96
Three Finger Brown, 1906	1.04
Bob Gibson, 1968	1.12
Christy Mathewson, 1909	1.14
Walter Johnson, 1913	1.14
Jack Pfiester, 1907	1.15
Addie Joss, 1908	1.16
Carl Lundgren, 1907	1.17
Denny Driscoll, 1882	1.21

SHUTOUTS	
George Bradley, 1876	16
Grover Alexander, 1916	16
Jack Coombs, 1910	13
Bob Gibson, 1968	13
Jim Galvin, 1884	12
Ed Morris, 1886	12
Grover Alexander, 1915	12
Tommy Bond, 1879	11
Charley Radbourn, 1884	11
Dave Foutz, 1886	11
Christy Mathewson, 1908	11
Ed Walsh, 1908	11
Walter Johnson, 1913	11
Sandy Koufax, 1963	11
Dean Chance, 1964	11

COMPLETE GAMES	
Will White, 1879	75
Charley Radbourn, 1884	73
Jim McCormick, 1880	72
Jim Galvin, 1883	72
Guy Hecker, 1884	72
Jim Galvin, 1884	71
Tim Keefe, 1883	68
John Clarkson, 1885	68
John Clarkson, 1889	68
Bill Hutchison, 1892	67

STRIKEOUTS	
Matt Kilroy, 1886	513
Toad Ramsey, 1886	499
Hugh Daily, 1884	483
Dupee Shaw, 1884	451
Charley Radbourn, 1884	441
Charlie Buffinton, 1884	417
Guy Hecker, 1884	385
Nolan Ryan, 1973	383
Sandy Koufax, 1965	382
Bill Sweeney, 1884	374

BASES ON BALLS	
Amos Rusie, 1890	289
Mark Baldwin, 1889	274
Amos Rusie, 1892	270
Amos Rusie, 1891	262
Mark Baldwin, 1890	249
Jack Stivetts, 1891	232
Mark Baldwin, 1891	227
Phil Knell, 1891	226
Bob Barr, 1890	219
Amos Rusie 1893	218

Regular Season

Individual Batting, Single Game

MOST RUNS		
7	Guy Hecker, Lou	Aug 15, 1886

MOST HITS		
7	Wilbert Robinson, Balt	June 10, 1892
	Rennie Stennett, Pitt	Sept 16, 1975

MOST HOME RUNS		
4	Bobby Lowe, Bos (N)	May 30, 1894
	Ed Delahanty, Phil	July 13, 1896
	Lou Gehrig, NY (A)	June 3, 1932
	Gil Hodges, Bklyn	Aug 31, 1950
	Joe Adcock, Mil (N)	July 31, 1954
	Rocky Colavito, Clev	June 10, 1959
	Willie Mays, SF	April 30, 1961
	Bob Horner, Atl	July 6, 1986
	Mark Whiten, StL	Sept 7, 1993
	Mike Cameron, Sea	May 2, 2002
	Shawn Green, LA	May 23, 2002

MOST GRAND SLAMS		
2	Tony Lazzeri, NY (A)	May 24, 1936
	Jim Tabor, Bos (A)	July 4, 1939
	Rudy York, Bos (A)	July 27, 1946
	Jim Gentile, Balt	May 9, 1961
	Tony Cloninger, Atl	July 3, 1966
	Jim Northrup, Det	June 24, 1968
	Frank Robinson, Balt	June 26, 1970
	Robin Ventura, Chi (A)	Sept 4, 1995
	Chris Hoiles, Balt	Aug 14, 1998
	Fernando Tatis, StL	Apr 23, 1999
	Nomar Garciaparra, Bos	May 10, 1999

MOST RBIs		
12	Jim Bottomley, StL	Sept 16, 1924
	Mark Whiten, StL	Sept 7, 1993

Individual Pitching, Single Game

MOST INNINGS PITCHED		
26	Leon Cadore, Bklyn	May 1, 1920, tie 1–1
	Joe Oeschger, Bos (N)	May 1, 1920, tie 1–1

MOST RUNS ALLOWED		
24	Al Travers, Det	May 18, 1912

MOST HITS ALLOWED		
36	Jack Wadsworth, Lou	Aug 17, 1894

MOST STRIKEOUTS		
20	Roger Clemens, Bos	April 29, 1986
20	Roger Clemens, Bos	Sept 18, 1996
20	Kerry Wood, Chi (N)	May 6, 1998
20	Randy Johnson, Ariz	May 8, 2001

MOST WALKS ALLOWED		
16	Bill George, NY (N)	May 30, 1887
	George Van Haltren, Chi (N)	June 27, 1887
	Henry Gruber, Clev	Apr 19, 1890
	Bruno Haas, Phil (A)	June 2, 1915

MOST WILD PITCHES		
6	J.R. Richard, Hou	April 10, 1979
	Phil Niekro, Atl	Aug 14, 1979
	Bill Gullickson, Mtl	April 10, 1982

Notable Achievements

No-Hit Games, Nine Innings or More

National League

Date		Pitcher and Game
1876	July 15	George Bradley, StL vs. Hart 2–0
1880	June 12	John Richmond, Wor vs. Clev 1–0 (perfect game)
	June 17	Monte Ward, Prov vs. Buff 5–0 (perfect game)
	Aug 19	Larry Corcoran, Chi vs. Bos 6–0
	Aug 20	Pud Galvin, Buff vs. Wor 1–0
1882	Sept 20	Larry Corcoran, Chi vs. Wor 5–0
	Sept 22	Tim Lovett, Bklyn vs. NY 4–0
1883	July 25	Hoss Radbourn, Prov vs. Clev 8–0
	Sept 13	Hugh Daily, Clev vs. Phil 1–0
1884	June 27	Larry Corcoran, Chi vs. Prov 6–0
	Aug 4	Pud Galvin, Buff vs. Det 18–0
1885	July 27	John Clarkson, Chi vs. Prov 4–0
	Aug 29	Charles Ferguson, Phil vs. Prov 1–0
1891	June 22	Tom Lovett, Bklyn vs. NY 4–0
	July 31	Amos Rusie, NY vs. Bklyn 6–0
1892	Aug 6	Jack Stivetts, Bos vs. Bklyn 11–0
	Aug 22	Alex Sanders, Lou vs. Balt 6–2
	Oct 15	Bumpus Jones, Cin vs. Pitt 7–1 (first major league game)
1893	Aug 16	Bill Hawke, Balt vs. Wash 5–0
1897	Sept 18	Cy Young, Clev vs. Cin 6–0
1898	Apr 22	Ted Breitenstein, Cin vs. Pitt 11–0
	Apr 22	Jim Hughes, Balt vs. Bos 8–0
	July 8	Frank Donahue, Phil vs. Bos 5–0
	Aug 21	Walter Thornton, Chi vs. Bklyn 2–0
1899	May 25	Deacon Phillippe, Lou vs. NY 7–0
	Aug 7	Vic Willis, Bos vs. Wash 7–1
1900	July 12	Noodles Hahn, Cin vs. Phil 4–0
1901	July 15	Christy Mathewson, NY vs. StL 5–0
1903	Sept 18	Chick Fraser, Phil vs. Chi 10–0
1904	June 11	Bob Wicker, Chi vs. NY 1–0 (hit in 10th; won in 12th)

Notable Achievements

No-Hit Games, Nine Innings or More (cont.)

National League

Date		Pitcher and Game
1905	June 13	Christy Mathewson, NY vs. Chi 1–0
1906	May 1	John Lush, Phil vs. Bklyn 6–0
	July 20	Mal Eason, Bklyn vs. StL 2–0
	Aug 1	Harry McIntire, Bklyn vs. Pitt 0–1 (hit in 11th; lost in 13th)
1907	May 8	Frank Pfeffer, Bos vs. Cin 6–0
	Sept 20	Nick Maddox, Pitt vs. Bklyn 2–1
1908	July 4	George Wiltse, NY vs. Phil 1–0 (10 innings)
	Sept 5	Nap Rucker, Bklyn vs. Bos 6–0
1909	Apr 15	Leon Ames, NY vs. Bklyn 0–3 (hit in 10th; lost in 13th)
1912	Sept 6	Jeff Tesreau, NY vs. Phil 3–0
1914	Sept 9	George Davis, Bos vs. Phil 7–0
1915	Apr 15	Rube Marquard, NY vs. Bklyn 2–0
	Aug 31	Jimmy Lavender, Chi vs. NY 2–0
1916	June 16	Tom Hughes, Bos vs. Pitt 2–0
1917	May 2	Jim Vaughn, Chi vs. Cin 0–1 (hit in 10th; lost in 10th)
	May 2	Fred Toney, Cin vs. Chi 1–0 (10 innings)
1919	May 11	Hod Eller, Cin vs. StL 6–0
1922	May 7	Jesse Barnes, NY vs. Phil 6–0
1924	July 17	Jesse Haines, StL vs. Bos 5–0
1925	Sept 13	Dazzy Vance, Bklyn vs. Phil 10–1
1929	May 8	Carl Hubbell, NY vs. Pitt 11–0
1934	Sept 21	Paul Dean, StL vs. Bklyn 3–0
1938	June 11	Johnny Vander Meer, Cin vs. Bos3-0
	June 15	Johnny Vander Meer, Cin vs. Bklyn 6-0
1940	Apr 30	Tex Carleton, Bklyn vs. Cin, 3–0
1941	Aug 30	Lon Warneke, StL vs. Cin 2–0
1944	Apr 27	Jim Tobin, Bos vs. Bklyn 2–0
	May 15	Clyde Shoun, Cin vs. Bos 1–0
1946	Apr 23	Ed Head, Bklyn vs. Bos 5–0
1947	June 18	Ewell Blackwell, Cin vs. Bos 6–0
1948	Sept 9	Rex Barney, Bklyn vs. NY 2–0
1950	Aug 11	Vern Bickford, Bos vs. Bklyn 7–0
1951	May 6	Cliff Chambers, Pitt vs. Bos 3–0
1952	June 19	Carl Erskine, Bklyn vs. Chi 5–0
1954	June 12	Jim Wilson, Mil vs. Phil 2–0
1955	May 12	Sam Jones, Chi vs. Pitt 4–0
1956	May 12	Carl Erskine, Bklyn vs. NY 3–0
	Sept 25	Sal Maglie, Bklyn vs. Phil 5–0
1959	May 26	Harvey Haddix, Pitt vs. Mil 0–1 (hit in 13th; lost in 13th)
1960	May 15	Don Cardwell, Chi vs. StL 4–0
	Aug 18	Lew Burdette, Mil vs. Phil 1–0
	Sept 16	Warren Spahn, Mil vs. Phil 4–0
1961	Apr 28	Warren Spahn, Mil vs. SF 1–0
1962	June 30	Sandy Koufax, LA vs. NY 5–0
1963	May 11	Sandy Koufax, LA vs. SF 8–0
	May 17	Don Nottebart, Hou vs. Phil 4–1
	June 15	Juan Marichal, SF vs. Hou 1–0
1964	Apr 23	Ken Johnson, Hou vs. Cin 0–1
	June 4	Sandy Koufax, LA vs. Phil 3–0
	June 21	Jim Bunning, Phil vs. NY 6–0 (perfect game)
1965	June 14	Jim Maloney, Cin vs. NY 0–1 (hit in 11th; lost in 11th)
	Aug 19	Jim Maloney, Cin vs. Chi 1–0 (10 innings)
	Sept 9	Sandy Koufax, LA vs. Chi 1–0 (perfect game)
1967	June 18	Don Wilson, Hou vs. Atl 2–0
1968	July 29	George Culver, Cin vs. Phil 6–1
	Sept 17	Gaylord Perry, SF vs. StL 1–0
	Sept 18	Ray Washburn, StL vs. SF 2–0

Date		Pitcher and Game
1969	Apr 17	Bill Stoneman, Mtl vs. Phil 7–0
	Apr 30	Jim Maloney, Cin vs. Hou 10–0
	May 1	Don Wilson, Hou vs. Cin 4–0
	Aug 19	Ken Holtzman, Chi vs. Atl 3–0
	Sept 20	Bob Moose, Pitt vs. NY 4–0
1970	June 12	Dock Ellis, Pitt vs. SD 2–0
	July 20	Bill Singer, LA vs. Phil 5–0
1971	June 3	Ken Holtzman, Chi vs. Cin 1–0
	June 23	Rick Wise, Phil vs. Cin 4–0
	Aug 14	Bob Gibson, StL vs. Pitt 11–0
1972	Apr 16	Burt Hooton, Chi vs. Phil 4–0
	Sept 2	Milt Pappas, Chi vs. SD 8–0
	Oct 2	Bill Stoneman, Mtl vs. NY 7–0
1973	Aug 5	Phil Niekro, Atl vs. SD 9–0
1975	Aug 24	Ed Halicki, SF vs. NY 6–0
1976	July 9	Larry Dierker, Hou vs. Mtl 6–0
	Aug 9	John Candelaria, Pitt vs. LA 2–0
	Sept 29	John Montefusco, SF vs. Atl 9–0
1978	Apr 16	Bob Forsch, StL vs. Phil 5–0
	June 16	Tom Seaver, Cin vs. StL 4–0
1979	Apr 7	Ken Forsch, Hou vs. Atl 6–0
1980	June 27	Jerry Reuss, LA vs. SF 8–0
1981	May 10	Charlie Lea, Mtl vs. SF 4–0
	Sept 26	Nolan Ryan, Hou vs. LA 5–0
1983	Sept 26	Bob Forsch, StL vs. Mtl 3–0
1986	Sept 25	Mike Scott, Hou vs. SF 2–0
1988	Sept 16	Tom Browning, Cin vs. LA 1–0 (perfect game)
1990	June 29	Fernando Valenzuela, LA vs. StL 6–0
	Aug 15	Terry Mulholland, Phil vs. SF 6–0
1991	May 23	Tommy Greene, Phil vs. Mtl 2–0
	July 26	Mark Gardner, Mtl vs. LA 0–1 (hit in 10th, lost in 10th)
	July 28	Dennis Martinez, Mtl vs. LA 2–0 (perfect game)
	Sept 11	Kent Mercker (6), Mark Wohlers (2), and Alejandro Pena (1), Atl vs. SD 1–0
1992	Aug 17	Kevin Gross, LA vs. SF 2–0
1993	Sept 8	Darryl Kile, Hou vs. NY 7–1
1994	Apr 8	Kent Mercker, Atl vs. LA 6–0
1995	June 3	Pedro Martinez, Mtl vs. SD 1–0 (perfect through nine, hit in 10th)
	July 14	Ramon Martinez, LA vs. Fla 7–0
1996	May 11	Al Leiter, Fla vs. Col 11–0
	Sept 17	Hideo Nomo, LA vs. Col 9–0
1997	June 10	Kevin Brown, Fla vs. SF 9–0
	July 12	Francisco Cordova (9) and Ricardo Rincon (1), Pitt vs. Col 3–0
1999	June 25	Jose Jimenez, StL vs. Ariz 1–0
2001	May 12	A.J. Burnett, Fla vs. SD 3–0
	Sept 3	Bud Smith, StL vs. SD 4–0
2003	April 27	Kevin Millwood, Phil vs. SF 1–0
	June 11	Roy Oswalt (1), Pete Munro ($2\frac{2}{3}$), Kirk Saarloos ($1\frac{1}{3}$), Brad Lidge (2), Octavio Dotel (1), and Billy Wagner (1), Hou vs. NY 6–0

Fast Fact: On July 25, 2003, Chin-hui Tsao of the Colorado Rockies became the first native of Taiwan to pitch in the major leagues. He gave up three hits in $6\frac{1}{3}$ innings as the Rockies defeated the Milwaukee Brewers, 7–3. Tsao got the win.

Notable Achievements

No-Hit Games, Nine Innings or More (cont.)

American League

Date		Pitcher and Game
1901	May 9	Earl Moore, Clev vs. Chi 2–4 (hit in 10th; lost in 10th)
1902	Sept 20	Jimmy Callahan, Chi vs. Det 3–0
1904	May 5	Cy Young, Bos vs. Phil 3–0 (perfect game)
	Aug 17	Jesse Tannehill, Bos vs. Chi 6–0
1905	July 22	Weldon Henley, Phil vs. StL 6–0
	Sept 6	Frank Smith, Chi vs. Det 15–0
	Sept 27	Bill Dinneen, Bos vs. Chi 2–0
1908	June 30	Cy Young, Bos vs. NY 8–0
	Sept 18	Bob Rhoades, Clev vs. Bos 2–1
	Sept 20	Frank Smith, Chi vs. Phil 1–0
	Oct 2	Addie Joss, Clev vs. Chi 1–0 (perfect game)
1910	Apr 20	Addie Joss, Clev vs. Chi 1–0
	May 12	Chief Bender, Phil vs. Clev 4–0
	Aug 30	Tom Hughes, NY vs. Clev 0–5 (hit in 10th; lost in 11th)
1911	July 29	Joe Wood, Bos vs. StL 5–0
	Aug 27	Ed Walsh, Chi vs. Bos 5–0
1912	July 4	George Mullin, Det vs. StL 7–0
	Aug 30	Earl Hamilton, StL vs. Det 5–1
1914	May 14	Jim Scott, Chi vs. Wash 0–1 (hit in 10th; lost in 10th)
	May 31	Joe Benz, Chi vs. Clev 6–1
1916	June 21	George Foster, Bos vs. NY 2–0
	Aug 26	Joe Bush, Phil vs. Clev 5–0
	Aug 30	Dutch Leonard, Bos vs. StL 4–0
1917	Apr 14	Ed Cicotte, Chi vs. StL 11–0
	Apr 24	George Mogridge, NY vs. Bos 2–1
	May 5	Ernie Koob, StL vs. Chi 1–0
	May 6	Bob Groom, StL vs. Chi 3–0
	June 23	Ernie Shore, Bos vs. Wash 4–0 (perfect game)
1918	June 3	Dutch Leonard, Bos vs. Det 5–0
1919	Sept 10	Ray Caldwell, Clev vs. NY 3–0
1920	July 1	Walter Johnson, Wash vs. Bos 1–0
1922	Apr 30	Charlie Robertson, Chi vs. Det 2–0 (perfect game)
1923	Sept 4	Sam Jones, NY vs. Phil 2–0
	Sept 7	Howard Ehmke, Bos vs. Phil 4–0
1926	Aug 21	Ted Lyons, Chi vs. Bos 6–0
1931	Apr 29	Wes Ferrell, Clev vs. StL 9–0
	Aug 8	Bob Burke, Wash vs. Bos 5–0
1934	Sept 18	Bobo Newsom, StL vs. Bos 1–2 (hit in 10th; lost in 10th)
1935	Aug 31	Vern Kennedy, Chi vs. Clev 5–0
1937	June 1	Bill Dietrich, Chi vs. StL 8–0
1938	Aug 27	Mtle Pearson, NY vs. Clev 13–0
1940	Apr 16	Bob Feller, Clev vs. Chi 1–0 (opening day)
1945	Sept 9	Dick Fowler, Phil vs. StL 1–0
1946	Apr 30	Bob Feller, Clev vs. NY 1–0
1947	July 10	Don Black, Clev vs. Phil 3–0
	Sep 3	Bill McCahan, Phil vs. Wash 3–0
1948	June 30	Bob Lemon, Clev vs. Det 2–0
1951	July 1	Bob Feller, Clev vs. Det 2–1
	July 12	Allie Reynolds, NY vs. Clev 1–0
	Sept 28	Allie Reynolds, NY vs. Bos 8–0
1952	May 15	Virgil Trucks, Det vs. Wash 1–0
	Aug 25	Virgil Trucks, Det vs. NY 1–0
1953	May 6	Bobo Holloman, StL vs. Phil 6–0 (first major league start)
1956	July 14	Mel Parnell, Bos vs. Chi 4–0
	Oct 8	Don Larsen, NY (A) vs. Bklyn (N) 2–0 (World Series) (perfect game)
1957	Aug 20	Bob Keegan, Chi vs. Wash 6–0
1958	July 20	Jim Bunning, Det vs. Bos 3–0
	Sept 20	Hoyt Wilhelm, Balt vs. NY 1–0
1962	May 5	Bo Belinsky, LA vs. Balt 2–0
	June 26	Earl Wilson, Bos vs. LA 2–0
	Aug 1	Bill Monbouquette, Bos vs. Chi 1–0
	Aug 26	Jack Kralick, Minn vs. KC 1–0
1965	Sept 16	Dave Morehead, Bos vs. Clev 2–0
1966	June 10	Sonny Siebert, Clev vs. Wash 2–0
1967	Apr 30	Steve Barber ($8\frac{2}{3}$) and Stu Miller ($\frac{1}{3}$), Balt vs. Det 1–2
	Aug 25	Dean Chance, Minn vs. Clev 2–1
	Sept 10	Joel Horlen, Chi vs. Det 6–0
1968	Apr 27	Tom Phoebus, Balt vs. Bos 6–0
	May 8	Catfish Hunter, Oak vs. Minn 4–0 (perfect game)
1969	Aug 13	Jim Palmer, Balt vs. Oak 8–0
1970	July 3	Clyde Wright, Cal vs. Oak 4–0
	Sept 21	Vida Blue, Oak vs. Minn 6–0
1973	Apr 27	Steve Busby, KC vs. Det 3–0
	May 15	Nolan Ryan, Cal vs. KC 3–0
	July 15	Nolan Ryan, Cal vs. Det 6–0
	July 30	Jim Bibby, Tex vs. Oak 6–0
1974	June 19	Steve Busby, KC vs. Mil 2–0
	July 19	Dick Bosman, Clev vs. Oak 4–0
	Sept 28	Nolan Ryan, Cal vs. Minn 4–0
1975	June 1	Nolan Ryan, Cal vs. Balt 1–0
	Sept 28	Vida Blue (5), Glenn Abbott and Paul Lindblad (1), Rollie Fingers (2), Oak vs. Cal 5–0
1976	July 28	John Odom (5) and Francisco Barrios (4), Chi vs. Oak 2–1
1977	May 14	Jim Colborn, KC vs. Tex 6–0
	May 30	Dennis Eckersley, Clev vs. Cal 1–0
	Sept 22	Bert Blyleven, Tex vs. Cal 6–0
1981	May 15	Len Barker, Clev vs. Tor 3–0 (perfect game)
1983	July 4	Dave Righetti, NY vs. Bos 4–0
	Sept 29	Mike Warren, Oak vs. Chi 3–0
1984	Apr 7	Jack Morris, Det vs. Chi 4–0
	Sept 30	Mike Witt, Cal vs. Tex 1–0 (perfect game)
1986	Sept 19	Joe Cowley, Chi vs. Cal 7–1
1987	Apr 15	Juan Nieves, Mil vs. Balt 7–0
1990	Apr 11	Mark Langston (7), Mike Witt (2), Cal vs. Sea 1–0
	June 2	Randy Johnson, Sea vs. Det 2–0
	June 11	Nolan Ryan, Tex vs. Oak 5–0
	June 29	Dave Stewart, Oak vs. Tor 5–0
1990	July 1	Andy Hawkins, NY vs. Chi 0–4 (pitched eight of nine-innning game)
	Sept 2	Dave Stieb, Tor vs. Clev 3–0
1991	May 1	Nolan Ryan, Tex vs. Tor 3–0
	July 13	Bob Milacki (6), Mike Flanagan (1), Mark Williamson (1), and Gregg Olson (1), Balt vs. Oak 2–0

Notable Achievements

No-Hit Games, Nine Innings or More (cont.)

American League

Date		Pitcher and Game
	Aug 11	Wilson Alvarez, Chi vs. Balt 7–0
	Aug 26	Bret Saberhagen, KC vs. Chi 7–0
1993	Apr 22	Chris Bosio, Sea vs. Bos 7–0
	Sept 4	Jim Abbott, NY vs. Clev 4–0
1994	Apr 27	Scott Erickson, Minn vs. Mil 6–0
	July 28	Kenny Rogers, Texas vs. Cal 4–0 (perfect game)
1996	May 14	Dwight Gooden, NY vs. Sea 2–0
1998	May 17	David Wells, NY vs. Minn 4–0 (perfect game)
1999	July 18	David Cone, NY vs. Mtl 6–0 (perfect game)
	Sept 11	Eric Milton, Minn vs. Ana 7–0
2001	Apr 4	Hideo Nomo, Bos vs. Balt 3–0
2002	Apr 27	Derek Lowe, Bos vs. TB 10–0

Longest Hitting Streaks

National League

Player and Team	Year	G
Willie Keeler, Balt	1897	44
Pete Rose, Cin	1978	44
Bill Dahlen, Chi	1894	42
Tommy Holmes, Bos	1945	37
Billy Hamilton, Phil	1894	36
Luis Castillo, Fla	2002	35
Fred Clarke, Lou	1895	35
Benito Santiago, SD	1987	34
George Davis, NY	1893	33
Rogers Hornsby, StL	1922	32

American League

Player and Team	Year	G
Joe DiMaggio, NY	1941	56
George Sisler, StL	1922	41
Ty Cobb, Det	1911	40
Paul Molitor, Mil	1987	39
Ty Cobb, Det	1917	35
Ty Cobb, Det	1912	34
George Sisler, StL	1925	34
John Stone, Det	1930	34
George McQuinn, StL	1938	34
Dom DiMaggio, Bos	1949	34

Triple Crown Winners*

National League

Player and Team	Year	HR	RBI	BA
Paul Hines, Prov	1878	4	50	.358
Hugh Duffy, Bos	1894	18	145	.438
Heinie Zimmerman, Chi**	1912	14	103	.372
Rogers Hornsby, StL	1922	42	152	.401
Rogers Hornsby, StL	1925	39	143	.403
Chuck Klein, Phil	1933	28	120	.368
Joe Medwick, StL	1937	31	154	.374

American League

Player and Team	Year	HR	RBI	BA
Nap Lajoie, Phil	1901	14	125	.422
Ty Cobb, Det	1909	9	115	.377
Jimmie Foxx, Phil	1933	48	163	.356
Lou Gehrig, NY	1934	49	165	.363
Ted Williams, Bos	1942	36	137	.356
Ted Williams, Bos	1947	32	114	.343
Mickey Mantle, NY	1956	52	130	.353
Frank Robinson, Balt	1966	49	122	.316
Carl Yastrzemski, Bos	1967	44	121	.326

*Player who leads in three categories: home runs, RBIs, and batting average.
**Zimmerman ranked first in RBIs as calculated by Ernie Lanigan, but only third as calculated by Information Concepts Inc.

Triple Crown Pitchers***

National League

Player and Team	Year	W	L	SO	ERA
Tommy Bond, Bos	1877	40	17	170	2.11
Hoss Radbourn, Prov	1884	60	12	441	1.38
Tim Keefe, NY	1888	35	12	333	1.74
John Clarkson, Bos	1889	49	19	284	2.73
Amos Rusie, NY	1894	36	13	195	2.78
Christy Mathewson, NY	1905	31	8	206	1.27
Christy Mathewson, NY	1908	37	11	259	1.43
Grover Alexander, Phil	1915	31	10	241	1.22
Grover Alexander, Phil	1916	33	12	167	1.55
Grover Alexander, Phil	1917	30	13	201	1.86
Hippo Vaughn, Chi	1918	22	10	148	1.74
Grover Alexander, Chi	1920	27	14	173	1.91
Dazzy Vance, Bklyn	1924	28	6	262	2.16
Bucky Walters, Cin	1939	27	11	137	2.29
Sandy Koufax, LA	1963	25	5	306	1.88
Sandy Koufax, LA	1965	26	8	382	2.04
Sandy Koufax, LA	1966	27	9	317	1.73
Steve Carlton, Phil	1972	27	10	310	1.97
Dwight Gooden, NY	1985	24	4	268	1.53
Randy Johnson, Ariz	2002	24	5	334	2.32

American League

Player and Team	Year	W	L	SO	ERA
Cy Young, Bos	1901	33	10	158	1.62
Rube Waddell, Phil	1905	26	11	287	1.48
Walter Johnson, Wash	1913	36	7	303	1.09
Walter Johnson, Wash	1918	23	13	162	1.27
Walter Johnson, Wash	1924	23	7	158	2.72
Lefty Grove, Phil	1930	28	5	209	2.54
Lefty Grove, Phil	1931	31	4	175	2.06
Lefty Gomez, NY	1934	26	5	158	2.33
Lefty Gomez, NY	1937	21	11	194	2.33
Hal Newhouser, Det	1945	25	9	212	1.81
Roger Clemens, Tor	1997	21	7	292	2.05
Roger Clemens, Tor	1998	20	6	271	2.64
Pedro Martinez, Bos	1999	23	4	313	2.07

***Pitcher who leads in three categories: ERA, wins, and strikeouts.

Notable Achievements

Consecutive Games Played, 500 or More Games

Cal Ripken, Jr.	2,632
Lou Gehrig	2,130
Everett Scott	1,307
Steve Garvey	1,207
Billy Williams	1,117
Joe Sewell	1,103
Stan Musial	895
Eddie Yost	829
Gus Suhr	822
Nellie Fox	798
Pete Rose	745
Dale Murphy	740
Richie Ashburn	730
Ernie Banks	717
Pete Rose	678
Earl Averill	673
Frank McCormick	652
Sandy Alomar, Sr.	648
Eddie Brown	618
Roy McMillan	585
George Pinckney	577
Steve Brodie	574
Aaron Ward	565
Candy LaChance	540
Buck Freeman	535
Fred Luderus	533
Clyde Milan	511
Charlie Gehringer	511
Vada Pinson	508
Tony Cuccinello	504
Charlie Gehringer	504
Omar Moreno	503

Unassisted Triple Play

Player and Team	Date	Pos	Opp	Opp Batter
Neal Ball, Clev	7-19-09	SS	Bos	Amby McConnell
Bill Wambsganss, Clev	10-10-20	2B	Bklyn	Clarence Mitchell
George Burns, Bos	9-14-23	1B	Clev	Frank Brower
Ernie Padgett, Bos	10-6-23	SS	Phil	Walter Holke
Glenn Wright, Pitt	5-7-25	SS	StL	Jim Bottomley
Jimmy Cooney, Chi	5-30-27	SS	Pitt	Paul Waner
Johnny Neun, Det	5-31-27	1B	Clev	Homer Summa
Ron Hansen, Wash	7-30-68	SS	Clev	Joe Azcue
Mickey Morandini, Phil	9-20-92	2B	Pitt	Jeff King
John Valentin, Bos	7-15-94	SS	Minn	Marc Newfield
Randy Velarde, Oak	5-29-00	2B	NYY	Shane Spencer
Rafael Furcal, Atl	5-10-03	SS	StL	Woody Williams

National League

Pennant Winners (past 50 years)

Year	Team	Manager	W	L	Pct	GA
2003	††Florida Marlins (WC)	Jack McKeon	91	71	.562	-10
2002	††San Francisco (WC)	Dusty Baker	95	66	.590	-2½
2001	††Arizona (W)	Bob Brenly	92	70	.568	2
2000	††New York Mets (WC)	Bobby Valentine	94	68	.580	-6½
1999	††Atlanta Braves (E)	Bobby Cox	103	59	.636	6½
1998	††San Diego (W)	Bruce Bochy	98	64	.605	9½
1997	††Florida (WC)	Jim Leyland	92	70	.568	-9
1996	††Atlanta (E)	Bobby Cox	96	66	.593	8
1995	††Atlanta (E)	Bobby Cox	90	54	.625	21
1994	Season ended Aug. 11 due to labor dispute.					
1993	††Philadelphia (E)	Jim Fregosi	97	65	.599	3
1992	††Atlanta (W)	Bobby Cox	98	64	.605	8
1991	††Atlanta (W)	Bobby Cox	94	68	.580	1
1990	††Cincinnati (W)	Lou Piniella	91	71	.562	5
1989	††San Francisco (W)	Roger Craig	92	70	.568	3
1988	††Los Angeles (W)	Tommy Lasorda	94	67	.584	7
1987	††St. Louis (E)	Whitey Herzog	95	67	.586	3
1986	††New York (E)	Dave Johnson	108	54	.667	21½
1985	††St. Louis (E)	Whitey Herzog	101	61	.623	3
1984	††San Diego (W)	Dick Williams	92	70	.568	12
1983	††Philadelphia (E)	Pat Corrales/Paul Owens	90	72	.556	6
1982	††St. Louis (E)	Whitey Herzog	92	70	.568	3
1981	††Los Angeles (W)	Tommy Lasorda	63	47	.573	**
1980	††Philadelphia (E)	Dallas Green	91	71	.562	1
1979	††Pittsburgh (E)	Chuck Tanner	98	64	.605	2
1978	††Los Angeles (W)	Tommy Lasorda	95	67	.586	2½
1977	††Los Angeles (W)	Tommy Lasorda	98	64	.605	10
1976	††Cincinnati (W)	Sparky Anderson	102	60	.630	10
1975	††Cincinnati (W)	Sparky Anderson	108	54	.667	20

††Won championship series.

Legends

Cal Ripken, Jr., shortstop/third baseman, b. August 24, 1960, Havre de Grace, Maryland. Ripken used his 6 ' 4 " frame and athleticism to dominate the game both at the plate and in the field. He led his hometown Baltimore Orioles to the World Series title in 1983 and was named the American League Rookie of the Year in 1982 and its MVP in 1983 and 1991. Ripken appeared in the All-Star Game 19 times during his 20-year career and won the Gold Glove twice. He will be remembered most for playing 2,632 games in a row, a streak that shattered Lou Gehrig's record of 2,130, which many considered unbreakable.

Cal Ripken, Jr. is the seventh major leaguer to collect 3,000 hits and 400 homers.

GENE SWEENEY, JR.

Sandy Koufax, pitcher, b. December 30, 1935, Brooklyn, New York. Considered by many to be the greatest left-handed pitcher of all time, Sandy Koufax of the Los Angeles Dodgers enjoyed the most dominating five-year run of any pitcher in baseball in the last 80 years. Between 1962 and 1966, he won the Cy Young Award three times (when it was awarded to just one major league pitcher), the ERA title five times in a row, and at least 25 games three times. He also had 300 or more strikeouts in a season three times and pitched four no-hitters, including a perfect game in 1965. Arm trouble caused him to retire after the 1966 season, in which he had a 27–9 record and 1.63 ERA. Koufax was inducted into the Hall of Fame in 1972.

Joe DiMaggio, outfielder, b. November 25, 1914, Martinez, California; d. March 8, 1999, Hollywood, Florida. Remembered as one of the game's most graceful and complete players, DiMaggio led the New York Yankees to the American League pennant 10 times and the World Series championship nine times in his 13 full seasons. His 56-game hitting streak in 1941 is one of sports' most remarkable and enduring achievements. "The Yankee Clipper" won the MVP award three times and retired after the 1951 season with a .325 lifetime batting average and just eight more strikeouts (369) than home runs (361). He was inducted into the Hall of Fame in 1955 and named baseball's Greatest Living Player in 1969.

National League

Pennant Winners (cont.)

Year	Team	Manager	W	L	Pct	GA
1974	††Los Angeles (W)	Walt Alston	102	60	.630	4
1973	††New York (E)	Yogi Berra	82	79	.509	1½
1972	††Cincinnati (W)	Sparky Anderson	95	59	.617	10½
1971	††Pittsburgh (E)	Danny Murtaugh	97	65	.599	7
1970	††Cincinnati (W)	Sparky Anderson	102	60	.630	14½
1969	††New York (E)	Gil Hodges	100	62	.617	8
1968	St. Louis	Red Schoendienst	97	65	.599	9
1967	St. Louis	Red Schoendienst	101	60	.627	10½
1966	Los Angeles	Walt Alston	95	67	.586	1½
1965	Los Angeles	Walt Alston	97	65	.599	2
1964	St. Louis	Johnny Keane	93	69	.574	1
1963	Los Angeles	Walt Alston	99	63	.611	6
1962	#San Francisco	Al Dark	103	62	.624	1
1961	Cincinnati	Fred Hutchinson	93	61	.604	4
1960	Pittsburgh	Danny Murtaugh	95	59	.617	7
1959	‡Los Angeles	Walt Alston	88	68	.564	2
1958	Milwaukee	Fred Haney	92	62	.597	8
1957	Milwaukee	Fred Haney	95	59	.617	8
1956	Brooklyn	Walt Alston	93	61	.604	1
1955	Brooklyn	Walt Alston	98	55	.641	13½
1954	New York	Leo Durocher	97	57	.630	5

††Won championship series. #Defeated Los Angeles, two games to one, in playoff for pennant. ‡Defeated Milwaukee, two games to none, in playoff for pennant.

American League
Pennant Winners (past 50 years)

Year	Team	Manager	W	L	Pct	GA
2003	‡New York (E)	Joe Torre	101	61	.623	–
2002	‡Anaheim (WC)	Mike Scioscia	99	63	.611	-4
2001	‡New York (E)	Joe Torre	95	65	.594	13 ½
2000	‡New York (E)	Joe Torre	87	74	.540	2 ½
1999	‡New York (E)	Joe Torre	98	64	.605	4
1998	‡New York (E)	Joe Torre	114	48	.704	22
1997	‡Cleveland (C)	Mike Hargrove	86	75	.534	6
1996	‡New York (E)	Joe Torre	92	70	.568	4
1995	‡Cleveland (C)	Mike Hargrove	100	44	.694	30
1994	Season ended Aug. 11 due to labor dispute.					
1993	‡Toronto	Cito Gaston	95	67	.586	7
1992	‡Toronto	Cito Gaston	96	66	.593	4
1991	‡Minnesota (W)	Tom Kelly	95	67	.586	8
1990	‡Oakland (W)	Tony La Russa	103	59	.636	9
1989	‡Oakland (W)	Tony La Russa	99	63	.611	7
1988	‡Oakland (W)	Tony La Russa	104	58	.642	13
1987	‡Minnesota (W)	Tom Kelly	85	77	.525	2
1986	‡Boston (E)	John McNamara	95	66	.590	5 ½
1985	‡Kansas City (W)	Dick Howser	91	71	.562	1
1984	‡Detroit (E)	Sparky Anderson	104	58	.642	15
1983	‡Baltimore (E)	Joe Altobelli	98	64	.605	6
1982	‡Milwaukee (E)	Buck Rodgers, Harvey Kuenn	95	67	.586	1
1981	‡New York (E)	Gene Michael, Bob Lemon	59	48	.551	#
1980	‡Kansas City (W)	Jim Frey	97	65	.599	14
1979	‡Baltimore (E)	Earl Weaver	102	57	.642	8
1978	†‡New York (E)	Billy Martin, Bob Lemon	100	63	.613	1
1977	‡New York (E)	Billy Martin	100	62	.617	2 ½
1976	‡New York (E)	Billy Martin	97	62	.610	10 ½
1975	‡Boston (E)	Darrell Johnson	95	65	.594	4 ½
1974	‡Oakland (W)	Al Dark	90	72	.556	5
1973	‡Oakland (W)	Dick Williams	94	68	.580	6
1972	‡Oakland (W)	Dick Williams	93	62	.600	5 ½
1971	‡Baltimore (E)	Earl Weaver	101	57	.639	12
1970	‡Baltimore (E)	Earl Weaver	108	54	.667	15
1969	‡Baltimore (E)	Earl Weaver	109	53	.673	19
1968	Detroit	Mayo Smith	103	59	.636	12
1967	Boston	Dick Williams	92	70	.568	1
1966	Baltimore	Hank Bauer	97	63	.606	9
1965	Minnesota	Sam Mele	102	60	.630	7
1964	New York	Yogi Berra	99	63	.611	1
1963	New York	Ralph Houk	104	57	.646	10 ½
1962	New York	Ralph Houk	96	66	.593	5
1961	New York	Ralph Houk	109	53	.673	8
1960	New York	Casey Stengel	97	57	.630	8
1959	Chicago	Al Lopez	94	60	.610	5
1958	New York	Casey Stengel	92	62	.597	10
1957	New York	Casey Stengel	98	56	.636	8
1956	New York	Casey Stengel	97	57	.630	9
1955	New York	Casey Stengel	96	58	.623	3
1954	Cleveland	Al Lopez	111	43	.721	8

‡Won championship series.
†Defeated Boston in a one-game playoff.
#First half 34-22; second half 25-26, in season split by strike; defeated Milwaukee in playoff for Eastern Division title.

2003 Off-season Transactions

The following is a list of big-time players who switched teams for the 2004 season.

ROGER CLEMENS, pitcher, Houston Astros The 2003 season was one long victory lap for Clemens, who insisted it would be his final season. He won his 300th game in June, the same night he threw his 4,000th strikeout. When he walked off the mound in Game 4 of the World Series, everyone thought it was for good. Clemens ended his 80-day retirement in January and signed a one-year contract with Houston. He was lured by former New York Yankee teammate Andy Pettitte, who signed with the Astros in December, and enticed by the prospect of pitching in his home state. Clemens will be pitching in the National League for the first time in his 21-year career.

CURT SCHILLING, pitcher, Boston Red Sox Schilling developed into one of baseball's premier pitchers during his three-and-a-half-season stint with the Arizona Diamondbacks. He won a World Series ring in 2001 and had two 20-win seasons. But the cost-cutting D-Backs traded him to Boston in November 2003 for three prospects. Schilling is now teamed with Pedro Martinez, giving the Red Sox the American League's most potent 1-2 pitching punch. Some Red Sox fans believe Schilling may be the missing piece Boston has needed to win the team's first World Series championship since 1918.

VLADIMIR GUERRERO, outfielder, Anaheim Angels After eight seasons with the Montreal Expos, Guerrero signed a five-year, $70 million contract with the California Angels in January. As an Expo, he was feared for his right arm (84 outfield assists) and potent bat (.323 lifetime). From 1998 through 2002, he averaged 39 home runs and 116 RBIs, but back injuries caused him to slip to 25 HRs and 79 RBIs in 2003. His presence gives the Angels an even stronger lineup than they had in 2002, the year they won the World Series.

OTTO GRULE, JR./GETTY IMAGES

ALEX RODRIGUEZ, third baseman, New York Yankees On February 16, 2004, the Yankees announced they had traded second baseman Alfonso Soriano to the Texas Rangers for the man hailed as the best player in the game: A.L. MVP Alex Rodriguez. The former Ranger shortstop immediately moved to third base so that Derek Jeter could stay at shortstop. A trade that would have sent Rodriguez to the Boston Red Sox fell through in December 2003 when the players' union refused to allow his contract to be restructured.

2004 Rookies to Watch

JOHN IACONO/SPORTS ILLUSTRATED

KAZ MATSUI, shortstop, New York Mets The most interesting new player on the New York Mets in 2004 was a 5' 9" switch-hitter from Japan who has surprising power (at least 20 homers in four straight seasons), a good glove (a four-time Gold Glover in Japan's Pacific League) and blazing speed (he's considered the fastest player in the majors). He's also durable (1,143 consecutive games in Japan). Matsui batted .300 for seven straight seasons in Japan and hit .440 during a seven-game exhibition against major league All-Stars in November 2002.

GARY ROTHSTEIN/ICONSMI

JOE MAUER, catcher, Minnesota Twins Mauer was the Number 1 pick in the 2001 major league draft. He's a hometown kid (a native of St. Paul, Minnesota) who turned down a football scholarship to Florida State to sign with the Twins. As a minor leaguer in 2003, he hit .338 and threw out 52.2 percent of the runners who tried to steal on him. *Baseball America* ranked him as the best prospect in baseball in 2004. He is so good that the Twins made room for him by trading All-Star catcher A.J. Pierzynski to the San Francisco Giants.

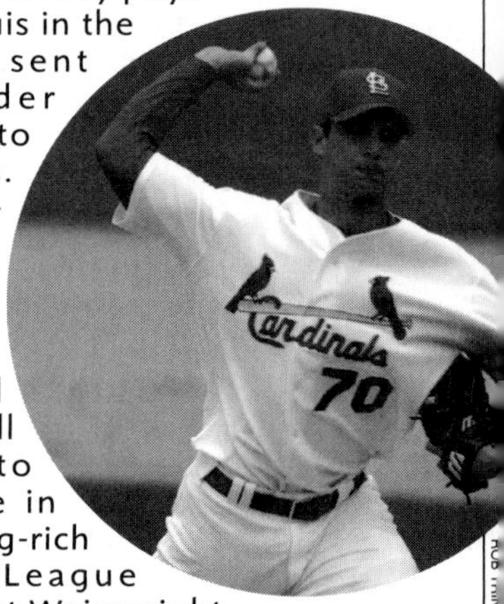

ADAM WAINWRIGHT, pitcher, St. Louis Cardinals Wainwright was drafted in 2000 by the Atlanta Braves. He was traded to the Cardinals in December 2003. Wainwright was the key player for St. Louis in the deal that sent rightfielder J.D. Drew to the Braves. The right-hander has a live arm and good control. The Cardinal starters will struggle to keep pace in the pitching-rich National League Central, but Wainwright may be counted on to bring depth to the starting rotation.

Did You Know?

In 2003, Mike Maroth of the Detroit Tigers became the first major league pitcher to lose 20 games since Brian Kingman of the Oakland A's lost 20 in 1980.

2003-04 TIME LINE

July 15, 2003: A new format grants the league whose team wins the All-Star Game home-field advantage in the World Series. The American League wins 7–6, on an eighth-inning home run by third baseman Hank Blalock of the Texas Rangers.

July 29, 2003: Third baseman Bill Mueller of the Boston Red Sox becomes the first player to hit a grand slam from each side of the plate in one game. Boston defeats the Texas Rangers, 14–7.

August 14, 2003: The New York Mets-San Francisco Giants game at Shea Stadium is postponed because of a blackout that affects part of the East Coast, the Midwest, and Canada.

September 2, 2003: Eric Gagne of the Los Angeles Dodgers sets the major league record for most saves in a row (55). The save comes in a 4–1 win over the Houston Astros. Gagne goes on to win the National League Cy Young Award.

September 21, 2003: Pitcher Greg Maddux of the Atlanta Braves sets the major league record for most seasons in a row with at least 15 wins. It is the 16th-straight season in which he has reached the mark.

October 6, 2003: After being down two games to none in the American League Division Series, the Boston Red Sox win Game 5, 4–3, knocking the Oakland A's out of the playoffs and advancing to the American League Championship Series.

October 14, 2003: The Chicago Cubs are five outs from a trip to the World Series for the first time in 58 years when a fan at Wrigley Field prevents Cub leftfielder Moises Alou from catching a foul ball. The incident opens the door for the Florida Marlins, who score eight runs in the eighth inning and win, 9–3. The next day, the Marlins win the National League pennant.

October 16, 2003: Five days after a bench-clearing brawl, the Yankees beat the Boston Red Sox, 6–5, in Game 7 of the American League Championship Series. Aaron Boone's walk-off home run in the 11th inning gives the Yanks the win.

October 25, 2003: The Florida Marlins win the World Series for the second time with a 2–0 rout of the New York Yankees in Game 6. Marlin right-hander Josh Beckett pitches a five-hitter and is named the Series MVP.

November 18, 2003: Barry Bonds of the San Francisco Giants wins the National League MVP award for the sixth time. No other player has won the award more than three times.

February 16, 2004: Less than two months after a trade to the Boston Red Sox falls through, the Texas Rangers send American League MVP Alex Rodriguez to the New York Yankees.

March 30, 2004: The first game of the 2004 major league season takes place in Tokyo, Japan. The Tampa Bay Devil Rays defeat the New York Yankees, 8–3.

April 13, 2004: Barry Bonds hits his 661st career home run in a game against the Milwaukee Brewers. Bonds passes Willie Mays for third place on the career home-run list.

May 5, 2004: Mike Piazza of the New York Mets breaks Carlton Fisk's major league record for home runs by a catcher, hitting number 352 against the Giants.

May 18, 2004: Randy Johnson of the Seattle Mariners, a five-time Cy Young Award-winner, becomes the oldest pitcher (40 years, 8 months, 8 days) in major league history to throw a perfect game. He retires all 27 hitters in a 2–0 victory over the Atlanta Braves. It is the 17th perfect game in major league history and the first since 1999.

BASKETBALL PRO

Before the 2003-04 season, fans and the media wondered how long it would take rookie phenom LeBron James of the Cleveland Cavaliers to become a dominant NBA player. The answer: one game.

"King James" fueled the enormous hype surrounding him by scoring 25 points in his first pro game, then averaged 20.9 points for the season. Fellow first-season sensation Carmelo Anthony averaged a rookie-leading 21 points per game and led the Denver Nuggets to their first playoff berth since 1994-95. James beat out Anthony for the Rookie of the Year Award.

While James and Anthony wowed fans with their youthful heroics, straight-from-high-school vet Kevin Garnett of the Minnesota Timberwolves was the NBA's best player, hands down. K.G. (24.2 points, 13.9 rebounds per game) won his first MVP Award. Most important, he carried the

DAVID MAXWELL/EPA

The Detroit Pistons earned their first NBA title since 1989-90 by defeating the Los Angeles Lakers, 4–1, in the 2003-04 NBA Finals.

NBA TEAMS

EASTERN CONFERENCE
Atlanta Hawks
Boston Celtics
Chicago Bulls
Cleveland Cavaliers
Detroit Pistons
Indiana Pacers
Miami Heat
Milwaukee Bucks
New Jersey Nets
New Orleans Hornets
New York Knicks
Orlando Magic
Philadelphia 76ers
Toronto Raptors
Washington Wizards

WESTERN CONFERENCE
Dallas Mavericks
Denver Nuggets
Golden State Warriors
Houston Rockets
Los Angeles Clippers
Los Angeles Lakers
Memphis Grizzlies
Minnesota Timberwolves
Phoenix Suns
Portland Trail Blazers
Sacramento Kings
San Antonio Spurs
Seattle SuperSonics
Utah Jazz

T-Wolves past the first round of the playoffs for the first time in the team's history.

The Detroit Pistons made the smartest acquisition of the season by picking up Rasheed Wallace from the Atlanta Hawks in February. The forward gave the Pistons the athletic low-post scoring threat they needed to complement defensive force Ben Wallace at center and sweet-shooting Richard Hamilton at guard.

The Indiana Pacers finished the regular season with the NBA's best record (61–21). But Pacer forward Jermaine O'Neal injured his knee in the playoffs, and Indiana fell to Detroit in the Eastern Conference Finals.

In the Western Conference, the Los Angeles Lakers knocked off the defending champion San Antonio Spurs in the second round, then beat Minnesota to advance to the Finals. The Lakers were the overwhelming favorites, but Detroit thoroughly outplayed them, winning the series 4–1. Piston point guard Chauncey Billups had 21 points per game and was named the Finals' MVP.

The summer of 2004 was packed with player movement, which intensified the anticipation for 2004-05. Among the big-time players who changed teams: guards Tracy McGrady (from Orlando to Houston), Steve Francis (from Houston to Orlando), and center Shaquille O'Neal (from Los Angeles to Miami).

Piston point guard Chauncey Billups was named 2003-04 NBA Finals' MVP.

JED JACOBSOHN/GETTY IMAGES

2003-04 NBA Final Standings

Eastern Conference

ATLANTIC	W	L	PCT	GB
a-Nets (2)	47	35	.573	0.0
x-Heat (4)	42	40	.512	5.0
x-Knicks (7)	39	43	.476	8.0
x-Celtics (8)	36	46	.439	11.0
76ers	33	49	.402	14.0
Wizards	25	57	.305	22.0
Magic	21	61	.256	26.0

CENTRAL	W	L	PCT	GB
e, c-Pacers (1)	61	21	.744	0.0
x-Pistons (3)	54	28	.659	7.0
x-Hornets (5)	41	41	.500	20.0
x-Bucks (6)	41	41	.500	20.0
Cavaliers	35	47	.427	26.0
Raptors	33	49	.402	28.0
Hawks	28	54	.349	33.0
Bulls	23	59	.280	38.0

Western Conference

MIDWEST	W	L	PCT	GB
w,m-Timberwolves (1)	58	24	.707	0.0
x-Spurs (3)	57	25	.695	1.0
x-Mavericks (5)	52	30	.634	6.0
x-Grizzlies (6)	50	32	.610	8.0
x-Rockets (7)	45	37	.549	13.0
x-Nuggets (8)	43	39	.524	15.0
Jazz	42	40	.512	16.0

PACIFIC	W	L	PCT	GB
p-Lakers (2)	56	26	.683	0.0
x-Kings (4)	55	27	.671	1.0
Trail Blazers	41	41	.500	15.0
Warriors	37	45	.451	19.0
SuperSonics	37	45	.451	19.0
Suns	29	53	.354	27.0
Clippers	28	54	.341	28.0

Note: Numbers in parentheses are seedings for the playoffs.

KEY x=clinched playoff berth; e=clinched Eastern Conference; a=clinched Atlantic Division; c=clinched Central Division; w=clinched Western Conference; m=clinched Midwest Division; p=clinched Pacific Division; W=wins; L=losses; PCT=winning percentage; GB=games back

2004 NBA Playoffs

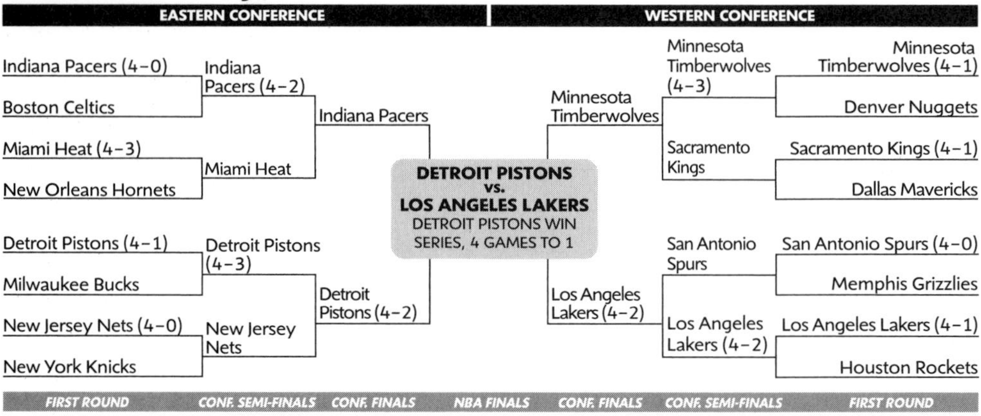

NBA Playoff Results

First Round

EASTERN CONFERENCE

Indiana Pacers vs. Boston Celtics
GAME 1 April 17, 2004: Indiana 104, Boston 88
GAME 2 April 20, 2004: Indiana 103, Boston 90
GAME 3 April 23, 2004: Indiana 108, Boston 85
GAME 4 April 25, 2004: Indiana 90, Boston 75
Indiana Pacers win series, 4–0

New Jersey Nets vs. New York Knicks
GAME 1 April 17, 2004: New Jersey 107, New York 83
GAME 2 April 20, 2004: New Jersey 99, New York 81
GAME 3 April 22, 2004: New Jersey 81, New York 78
GAME 4 April 25, 2004: New Jersey 100, New York 94
New Jersey Nets win series, 4–0

Detroit Pistons vs. Milwaukee Bucks
GAME 1 April 18, 2004: Detroit 108, Milwaukee 82
GAME 2 April 21, 2004: Milwaukee 92, Detroit 88
GAME 3 April 24, 2004: Detroit 95, Milwaukee 85
GAME 4 April 26, 2004: Detroit 109, Milwaukee 92
GAME 5 April 29, 2004: Detroit 91, Milwaukee 77
Detroit Pistons win series, 4–1

Miami Heat vs. New Orleans Hornets
GAME 1 April 18, 2004: Miami 81, New Orleans 79
GAME 2 April 21, 2004: Miami 93, New Orleans 63
GAME 3 April 24, 2004: New Orleans 77, Miami 71
GAME 4 April 27, 2004: New Orleans 96, Miami 85
GAME 5 April 30, 2004: Miami 87, New Orleans 83
GAME 6 May 2, 2004: New Orleans 89, Miami 83
GAME 7 May 4, 2004: Miami 85, New Orleans 77
Miami Heat win series, 4–3

WESTERN CONFERENCE

Minnesota Timberwolves vs. Denver Nuggets
GAME 1 April 18, 2004: Minnesota 106, Denver 92
GAME 2 April 21, 2004: Minnesota 95, Denver 81
GAME 3 April 24, 2004: Denver 107, Minnesota 86
GAME 4 April 27, 2004: Minnesota 84, Denver 82
GAME 5 April 30, 2004: Minnesota 102, Denver 91
Minnesota Timberwolves win series, 4–1

Los Angeles Lakers vs. Houston Rockets
GAME 1 April 17, 2004: Los Angeles 72, Houston 71
GAME 2 April 19, 2004: Los Angeles 98, Houston 84
GAME 3 April 23, 2004: Houston 102, Los Angeles 91
GAME 4 April 25, 2004: Los Angeles 92, Houston 88 (OT)
GAME 5 April 28, 2004: Los Angeles 97, Houston 78
Los Angeles Lakers win series, 4–1

San Antonio Spurs vs. Memphis Grizzlies
GAME 1 April 17, 2004: San Antonio 98, Memphis 74
GAME 2 April 19, 2004: San Antonio 87, Memphis 70
GAME 3 April 22, 2004: San Antonio 95, Memphis 93
GAME 4 April 25, 2004: San Antonio 110, Memphis 97
San Antonio Spurs win series, 4–0

Sacramento Kings vs. Dallas Mavericks
GAME 1 April 18, 2004: Sacramento 116, Dallas 105
GAME 2 April 20, 2004: Sacramento 83, Dallas 79
GAME 3 April 24, 2004: Dallas 104, Sacramento 79
GAME 4 April 26, 2004: Sacramento 94, Dallas 92
GAME 5 April 29, 2004: Sacramento 119, Dallas 118
Sacramento Kings win series, 4–1

Conference Semi-finals

EASTERN CONFERENCE

Indiana Pacers vs. Miami Heat
GAME 1 May 6, 2004: Indiana 94, Miami 81
GAME 2 May 8, 2004: Indiana 91, Miami 80
GAME 3 May 10, 2004: Miami 94, Indiana 87
GAME 4 May 12, 2004: Miami 100, Indiana 88
GAME 5 May 15, 2004: Indiana 94, Miami 83
GAME 6 May 18, 2004: Indiana 73, Miami 70
Indiana Pacers win series, 4–2

New Jersey Nets vs. Detroit Pistons
GAME 1 May 3, 2004: Detroit 78, New Jersey 56
GAME 2 May 7, 2004: Detroit 95, New Jersey 80
GAME 3 May 9, 2004: New Jersey 82, Detroit 64
GAME 4 May 11, 2004: New Jersey 94, Detroit 79
GAME 5 May 14, 2004: New Jersey 127, Detroit 120 (3OT)
GAME 6 May 16, 2004: Detroit 81, New Jersey 75
GAME 7 May 20, 2004: Detroit 90, New Jersey 69
Detroit Pistons win series, 4–3

NBA Playoff Results (cont.)

Conference Semi-finals (cont.)

WESTERN CONFERENCE

San Antonio Spurs vs. Los Angeles Lakers

GAME 1 May 2, 2004: San Antonio 88, Los Angeles 78
GAME 2 May 5, 2004: San Antonio 95, Los Angeles 85
GAME 3 May 9, 2004: Los Angeles 105, San Antonio 81
GAME 4 May 11, 2004: Los Angeles 98, San Antonio 90
GAME 5 May 13, 2004: Los Angeles 74, San Antonio 73
GAME 6 May 15, 2004: Los Angeles 88, San Antonio 76
Los Angeles Lakers win series, 4–2

Sacramento Kings vs. Minnesota Timberwolves

GAME 1 May 4, 2004: Sacramento 104, Minnesota 98
GAME 2 May 8, 2004: Minnesota 94, Sacramento 89
GAME 3 May 10, 2004: Minnesota 114, Sacramento 113 (OT)
GAME 4 May 12, 2004: Sacramento 87, Minnesota 81
GAME 5 May 14, 2004: Minnesota 86, Sacramento 74
GAME 6 May 16, 2004: Sacramento 104, Minnesota 87
GAME 7 May 19, 2004: Minnesota 83, Sacramento 80
Minnesota Timberwolves win series, 4–3

Did You Know?

A record eight high school players were chosen in the first round of the 2004 NBA Draft. A high school player has been taken with the Number 1 pick in the Draft in three of the past four years.

Conference Finals

EASTERN CONFERENCE

Indiana Pacers vs. Detroit Pistons

GAME 1 May 22, 2004: Indiana 78, Detroit 74
GAME 2 May 24, 2004: Detroit 72, Indiana 67
GAME 3 May 26, 2004: Detroit 85, Indiana 78
GAME 4 May 28, 2004: Indiana 83, Detroit 68
GAME 5 May 30, 2004: Detroit 83, Indiana 65
GAME 6 June 1, 2004: Detroit 69, Indiana 65
Detroit Pistons win series, 4–2

WESTERN CONFERENCE

Los Angeles Lakers vs. Minnesota Timberwolves

GAME 1 May 21, 2004: Los Angeles 97, Minnesota 88
GAME 2 May 23, 2004: Minnesota 89, Los Angeles 71
GAME 3 May 25, 2004: Los Angeles 100, Minnesota 89
GAME 4 May 27, 2004: Los Angeles 92, Minnesota 85
GAME 5 May 29, 2004: Minnesota 98, Los Angeles 96
GAME 6 May 31, 2004: Los Angeles 96, Minnesota 90
Los Angeles Lakers win series, 4–2

Finals

Detroit Pistons vs. Los Angeles Lakers

GAME 1 June 6, 2004: Detroit 87, Los Angeles 75
GAME 2 June 8, 2004: Los Angeles 99, Detroit 91 (OT)
GAME 3 June 10, 2004: Detroit 88, Los Angeles 68
GAME 4 June 13, 2004: Detroit 88, Los Angeles 80
GAME 5 June 15, 2004: Detroit 100, Los Angeles 87
Detroit Pistons win series, 4–1

NBA FINALS COMPOSITE BOX SCORE

LOS ANGELES LAKERS

		Field Goals		3-PT FG		Free Throws		Rebounds						
Player	**GP**	**FGM**	**PCT**	**FGM**	**PCT**	**FTM**	**PCT**	**OFF**	**TOTAL**	**A**	**STL**	**TO**	**BLK**	**AVG**
O'Neal	5	53	63.1	0	00.0	27	49.1	15	54	8	2	14	3	26.6
Bryant	5	43	38.1	4	17.4	23	92.0	2	14	22	9	18	3	22.6
Fisher	5	11	30.6	6	37.5	4	57.1	5	15	9	5	4	0	6.4
George	5	11	39.3	5	33.3	2	50.0	3	14	3	5	2	2	5.8
Malone	4	8	33.3	0	00.0	4	66.7	8	29	9	1	4	1	5.0
Payton	5	9	32.1	2	20.0	1	50.0	6	15	22	6	7	2	4.2
Medvedenko	5	6	35.3	0	00.0	6	75.0	6	18	3	0	2	1	3.6
Rush	5	7	31.8	4	25.0	0	00.0	0	5	2	1	5	0	3.6
Walton	4	5	38.5	1	16.7	2	100.0	3	12	18	6	7	2	3.3
Fox	3	4	57.1	0	00.0	0	00.0	0	3	7	0	1	0	2.7
Cook	3	1	16.7	0	00.0	2	100.0	3	8	0	1	2	0	1.3
Russell	3	0	00.0	0	00.0	0	00.0	1	1	0	0	0	0	.0
Totals	**5**	**158**	**41.6**	**22**	**24.7**	**71**	**64.0**	**52**	**188**	**103**	**36**	**68**	**14**	**81.8**

DETROIT PISTONS

		Field Goals		3-PT FG		Free Throws		Rebounds						
Player	**GP**	**FGM**	**PCT**	**FGM**	**PCT**	**FTM**	**PCT**	**OFF**	**TOTAL**	**A**	**STL**	**TO**	**BLK**	**AVG**
Hamilton	5	37	40.2	4	40.0	29	85.3	12	26	20	4	23	0	21.4
Billups	5	29	50.9	8	47.1	39	92.9	3	16	26	6	13	0	21.0
R. Wallace	5	24	45.3	3	25.0	14	77.8	7	39	7	2	4	8	13.0
B. Wallace	5	22	47.8	0	00.0	10	29.4	19	68	7	9	6	5	10.8
Prince	5	21	38.9	3	18.8	5	45.5	15	34	10	9	2	2	10.0
Williamson	5	6	40.0	0	00.0	9	90.0	4	12	1	0	4	0	4.2
Hunter	5	5	29.4	2	25.0	6	100.0	1	7	4	3	1	2	3.6
Campbell	5	6	37.5	0	00.0	5	50.0	6	13	8	5	3	3	3.4
Okur	4	4	44.4	1	100.0	2	50.0	1	6	2	0	4	0	2.8
James	5	2	50.0	0	00.0	0	00.0	2	4	4	0	1	0	.8
Ham	4	1	100.0	0	00.0	0	00.0	1	1	0	0	1	0	.5
Milicic	3	0	00.0	0	00.0	0	00.0	1	2	0	1	1	0	.0
Totals	**5**	**157**	**42.9**	**21**	**31.8**	**119**	**69.6**	**72**	**228**	**89**	**39**	**69**	**20**	**90.8**

KEY GP=games played; FGM=field goals made; PCT=percentage; FTM=free throws made; OFF=offensive; A=assists; STL=steals; TO=turnovers; BLK=blocks; AVG=average

NBA Finals Box Scores

Game 1

DETROIT PISTONS 87

	MIN	FG M-A	FT M-A	REB O-T	A	PF	STL	TO	PTS
Hamilton	43	5-16	2-4	3-7	5	0	1	6	12
Billups	39	8-14	4-4	1-3	4	1	3	2	22
Prince	35	5-10	0-0	1-6	4	3	2	0	11
R. Wallace	29	3-4	6-6	1-8	1	3	0	1	14
B. Wallace	41	4-8	1-2	1-8	0	1	1	2	9
Campbell	18	2-5	2-6	1-1	4	1	2	1	6
Hunter	13	1-5	2-2	0-1	0	2	0	1	5
Williamson	11	2-3	3-4	1-2	1	3	0	0	7
Okur	6	0-0	1-2	0-0	0	1	0	1	1
Ham	4	0-0	0-0	0-0	0	2	0	0	0
James	1	0-0	0-0	0-0	0	0	0	0	0
Milicic									DNP
Totals	**240**	**30-65**	**21-30**	**9-36**	**19**	**17**	**9**	**14**	**87**

Percentages: Field goals— 46.2%, Free throws— 70%, 3-point field goals— 6-12, 50% (Billups 2-4, Prince 1-4, R. Wallace 2-2, Hunter 1-2). Team rebounds: 11. Blocked shots: 4 (R. Wallace 1, B. Wallace 1, Campbell 2).

LOS ANGELES LAKERS 75

	MIN	FG M-A	FT M-A	REB O-T	A	PF	STL	TO	PTS
Bryant	47	10-27	4-4	1-4	4	2	4	3	25
Payton	31	1-4	0-0	1-2	3	5	2	2	3
Malone	44	2-9	0-0	3-11	3	1	0	0	4
George	27	2-5	0-0	0-3	0	2	1	1	5
O'Neal	45	13-16	8-12	5-11	1	4	0	6	34
Fisher	20	1-9	0-0	3-3	3	2	1	1	2
Rush	16	0-3	0-0	0-2	0	4	0	2	0
Medvedenko	6	0-0	2-2	0-1	0	3	0	0	2
Fox	4	0-0	0-0	0-0	1	2	0	0	0
Cook									DNP
Walton									DNP
Russell									DNP
Totals	**240**	**29-73**	**14-18**	**13-37**	**15**	**25**	**8**	**15**	**75**

Percentages: Field goals— 39.7%, Free throws— 77.8%, 3-point field goals— 3-13, 23.1% (Bryant 1-6, Payton 1-1, George 1-2, Fisher 0-2, Rush 0-2). Team rebounds: 8. Blocked shots: 4 (Bryant 2, Malone 1, O'Neal 1).

Game 2

LOS ANGELES LAKERS 99 (OT)

	MIN	FG M-A	FT M-A	REB O-T	A	PF	STL	TO	PTS
Bryant	49	14-27	4-5	0-4	7	5	2	5	33
Payton	28	1-3	0-0	1-3	3	4	1	3	2
Malone	39	3-9	3-4	3-9	2	3	1	1	9
George	21	3-7	0-0	0-2	1	2	1	0	7
O'Neal	48	10-20	9-14	3-7	3	5	0	3	29
Walton	27	3-3	0-0	1-5	8	3	0	0	7
Fisher	25	2-6	1-2	0-3	2	4	2	0	7
Rush	18	2-4	0-0	0-2	2	0	0	1	5
Medvedenko	9	0-1	0-0	1-3	0	1	0	0	0
Cook	1	0-0	0-0	0-0	0	0	0	1	0
Fox									DNP
Russell									DNP
Totals	**265**	**38-80**	**17-25**	**9-38**	**28**	**27**	**7**	**14**	**99**

Percentages: Field goals— 47.5%, Free throws— 68%, 3-point field goals— 6-17, 35.3% (Bryant 1-5, Payton 0-1, Malone 0-1, George 1-3, Walton 1-1, Fisher 2-4, Rush 1-2). Team rebounds: 13. Blocked shots: 3 (O'Neal 1, Walton 2).

DETROIT PISTONS 91

	MIN	FG M-A	FT M-A	REB O-T	A	PF	STL	TO	PTS
Hamilton	47	10-25	4-5	5-8	2	2	0	5	26
Billups	47	6-15	13-14	2-4	9	1	0	3	27
Prince	47	2-6	0-0	4-5	0	2	3	0	5
R. Wallace	34	5-14	1-2	1-7	3	4	0	0	11
B. Wallace	43	5-11	2-8	4-14	1	5	2	0	12
Okur	18	0-2	1-2	0-2	1	2	0	3	1
Hunter	12	2-4	0-0	0-0	2	1	1	0	5
Campbell	9	1-2	0-0	2-4	1	4	0	1	2
Williamson	7	1-2	0-0	1-2	0	2	0	2	2
James	1	0-0	0-0	0-0	0	0	0	0	0
Ham									DNP
Milicic									DNP
Totals	**265**	**32-81**	**21-31**	**19-46**	**19**	**23**	**6**	**14**	**91**

Percentages: Field goals— 39.5%, Free throws— 67.7%, 3-point field goals— 6-12, 50% (Hamilton 2-2, Billups 2-2, Prince 1-2, R. Wallace 0-3, Hunter 1-3). Team rebounds: 12. Blocked shots: 6 (Prince 2, R. Wallace 2, B. Wallace 2).

Game 3

DETROIT PISTONS 88

	MIN	FG M-A	FT M-A	REB O-T	A	PF	STL	TO	PTS
Hamilton	43	11-22	7-7	3-6	3	1	2	3	31
Billups	36	5-11	7-7	0-2	3	1	1	2	19
Prince	36	5-13	0-2	3-6	2	1	3	1	11
R. Wallace	26	1-4	1-4	2-10	1	3	0	1	3
B. Wallace	38	3-9	1-4	2-11	3	3	2	3	7
Hunter	16	1-3	0-0	1-5	2	4	0	0	2
Williamson	15	2-4	2-2	0-3	0	0	0	1	6
Campbell	13	1-4	3-4	2-2	1	3	3	0	5
Okur	8	1-4	0-0	1-4	1	0	0	0	2
James	4	0-0	0-0	1-1	1	0	0	0	0
Ham	3	1-1	0-0	0-0	0	0	0	0	2
Milicic	2	0-1	0-0	0-1	0	0	0	0	0
Totals	**240**	**31-76**	**21-30**	**15-51**	**17**	**16**	**11**	**11**	**88**

Percentages: Field goals— 40.8%, Free throws— 70%, 3-point field goals— 5-15, 33.3% (Hamilton 2-4, Billups 2-5, Prince 1-5, B. Wallace 0-1). Team rebounds: 8. Blocked shots: 4 (R. Wallace 2, Hunter 2).

LOS ANGELES LAKERS 68

	MIN	FG M-A	FT M-A	REB O-T	A	PF	STL	TO	PTS
Bryant	45	4-13	3-3	0-3	5	3	1	4	11
Payton	35	2-7	1-2	1-4	7	2	1	0	6
George	21	3-8	0-0	0-3	0	3	2	1	8
Malone	18	2-4	1-2	0-4	2	2	0	1	5
O'Neal	38	7-14	0-2	2-8	1	5	1	2	14
Medvedenko	21	1-3	1-2	2-8	1	4	0	1	3
Walton	19	1-5	2-2	1-3	2	4	1	2	4
Rush	18	3-8	0-0	0-1	0	2	1	2	8
Fisher	16	4-9	0-0	1-2	1	1	0	3	9
Cook	8	0-3	0-0	0-3	0	2	0	0	0
Russell	1	0-0	0-0	0-0	0	0	0	0	0
Fox									DNP
Totals	**240**	**27-74**	**8-13**	**7-39**	**19**	**28**	**7**	**16**	**68**

Percentages: Field goals— 36.5%, Free throws— 61.5%, 3-point field goals— 6-27, 22.2% (Bryant 0-4, Payton 1-5, George 2-6, Walton 0-2, Rush 2-7, Fisher 1-3). Team rebounds: 8. Blocked shots: 4 (Bryant 1, Payton 1, George 1, Medvedenko 1).

KEY MIN=minutes played; FG M-A=field goals made-attempted; FT M-A=free throws made-attempted; REB O-T=rebounds offensive-total; A=assists; PF=personal fouls; STL=steals; TO=turnovers; PTS=points; DNP=did not play

NBA Finals Box Scores (cont.)

Game 4

DETROIT PISTONS 88

	MIN	FG M-A	FT M-A	REB O-T	A	PF	STL	TO	PTS
Hamilton	44	5-11	7-7	1-2	6	5	0	5	17
Billups	37	7-12	7-9	0-4	4	3	2	3	23
R. Wallace	41	10-23	6-6	2-13	2	4	2	2	26
Prince	40	3-10	0-1	4-7	2	1	0	0	6
B. Wallace	39	2-5	4-14	2-13	2	3	1	1	8
Campbell	14	0-3	0-0	0-2	0	2	0	0	0
Hunter	11	0-1	4-4	0-0	0	1	0	0	4
James	6	2-2	0-0	0-2	0	0	0	1	4
Williamson	5	0-1	0-0	0-2	0	0	0	0	0
Ham	2	0-0	0-0	0-0	0	1	0	0	0
Milicic	1	0-0	0-0	0-0	0	0	0	0	0
Okur									DNP
Totals	**240**	**29-68**	**28-41**	**9-45**	**16**	**20**	**5**	**12**	**88**

Percentages: Field goals— 42.6%, Free throws— 68.3%, 3-point field goals— 2-13, 15.4% (Billups 2-5, R. Wallace 0-5, Prince 0-3). Team rebounds: 15. Blocked shots: 4 (R. Wallace 2, B. Wallace 1, Campbell 1).

LOS ANGELES LAKERS 80

	MIN	FG M-A	FT M-A	REB O-T	A	PF	STL	TO	PTS
Bryant	45	8-25	2-2	0-0	2	3	1	3	20
Payton	43	4-11	0-0	1-2	5	4	0	1	8
Malone	21	1-2	0-0	2-5	2	2	0	2	2
George	15	1-2	2-4	1-3	0	5	1	0	5
O'Neal	47	16-21	4-11	3-20	2	4	0	2	36
Fisher	21	1-6	2-3	1-5	2	4	0	0	4
Fox	16	1-4	0-0	0-1	6	3	0	0	2
Medvedenko	13	1-5	1-2	1-1	1	3	0	0	3
Walton	12	0-1	0-0	0-1	3	6	2	2	0
Rush	6	0-1	0-0	0-0	0	1	0	0	0
Russell	1	0-0	0-0	0-0	0	0	0	0	0
Cook									DNP
Totals	**240**	**33-78**	**11-22**	**9-38**	**23**	**35**	**4**	**10**	**80**

Percentages: Field goals— 42.3%, Free throws— 50%, 3-point field goals— 3-16, 18.8% (Bryant 2-6, Payton 0-2, George 1-2, Fisher 0-3, Fox 0-1, Walton 0-1, Rush 0-1). Team rebounds: 10. Blocked shots: 1 (O'Neal).

Game 5

DETROIT PISTONS 100

	MIN	FG M-A	FT M-A	REB O-T	A	PF	STL	TO	PTS
Hamilton	45	6-18	9-11	0-3	4	1	1	4	21
Billups	33	3-5	8-8	0-3	6	2	0	3	14
Prince	38	6-15	5-8	3-10	2	2	1	1	17
R. Wallace	21	5-8	0-0	1-1	0	5	0	0	11
B. Wallace	42	8-13	2-6	10-22	1	3	3	0	18
Campbell	14	2-2	0-0	1-4	2	3	0	1	4
Williamson	14	1-5	4-4	2-3	0	2	0	1	6
Hunter	13	1-4	0-0	0-1	0	3	2	0	2
James	10	0-2	0-0	1-1	3	2	0	0	0
Okur	7	3-3	0-0	0-0	0	4	0	0	7
Milicic	2	0-1	0-2	1-1	0	0	1	1	0
Ham	1	0-0	0-0	1-1	0	0	0	1	0
Totals	**240**	**35-76**	**28-39**	**20-50**	**18**	**27**	**8**	**12**	**100**

Percentages: Field goals— 46.1%, Free throws— 71.8%, 3-point field goals— 2-14, 14.3% (Hamilton 0-4, Billups 0-1, Prince 0-2, R. Wallace 1-2, B. Wallace 0-1, Hunter 0-3, Okur 1-1). Team rebounds: 10. Blocked shots: 2 (R. Wallace 1, B. Wallace 1).

LOS ANGELES LAKERS 87

	MIN	FG M-A	FT M-A	REB O-T	A	PF	STL	TO	PTS
Bryant	45	7-21	10-11	1-3	4	2	1	3	24
Payton	31	1-3	0-0	2-4	4	2	2	1	2
Medvedenko	23	4-8	2-2	2-5	1	1	0	1	10
George	20	2-6	0-0	2-3	2	4	0	0	4
O'Neal	35	7-13	6-16	2-8	1	4	1	1	20
Rush	20	2-6	0-0	0-0	0	3	0	0	5
Walton	19	1-4	0-0	1-3	5	2	3	3	2
Fisher	19	3-6	1-2	0-2	1	5	2	0	10
Cook	12	1-3	2-2	3-5	0	2	1	1	4
Fox	10	3-3	0-0	0-2	0	1	0	1	6
Russell	6	0-1	0-0	1-1	0	1	0	0	0
Malone									DNP
Totals	**240**	**31-75**	**21-33**	**14-36**	**18**	**27**	**10**	**11**	**87**

Percentages: Field goals— 41.3%, Free throws— 63.6%, 3-point field goals— 4-16, 25.0% (Bryant 0-2, Payton 0-1, George 0-2, Rush 1-4, Walton 0-2, Fisher 3-4, Russell 0-1). Team rebounds: 12. Blocked shots: 2 (Payton 1, George 1)

2003-04 NBA Individual Leaders

Jason Kidd, New Jersey Nets

Scoring	GP	PTS	AVG
Tracy McGrady, Orlando Magic	67	1,878	28.0
Predrag Stojakovic, Sacramento Kings	81	1,964	24.2
Kevin Garnett, Minnesota Timberwolves	82	1,987	24.2
Kobe Bryant, Los Angeles Lakers	65	1,557	24.0
Paul Pierce, Boston Celtics	80	1,836	23.0

Rebounds	GP	REB	AVG
Kevin Garnett, Minnesota Timberwolves	82	1,139	13.9
Ben Wallace, Detroit Pistons	81	1,006	12.4
Tim Duncan, San Antonio Spurs	69	859	12.4
Erick Dampier, Golden State Warriors	74	887	12.0
Carlos Boozer, Cleveland Cavaliers	75	857	11.4
Zach Randolph, Portland Trail Blazers	81	851	10.5

Assists	GP	A	AVG
Jason Kidd, New Jersey Nets	67	618	9.2
Stephon Marbury, Phoenix Suns/ New York Knicks	81	719	8.9
Steve Nash, Dallas Mavericks	78	687	8.8
Baron Davis, New Orleans Hornets	67	501	7.5
Sam Cassell, Minnesota Timberwolves	81	592	7.3

Field-goal Percentage	FGA	FGM	PCT
Shaquille O'Neal, Los Angeles Lakers	948	554	58.4
Mark Blount, Boston Celtics	604	342	56.6
Erick Dampier, Golden State Warriors	650	348	53.5
Antawn Jamison, Dallas Mavericks	913	488	53.5
Nenê, Denver Nuggets	630	334	53.0

Free-throw Percentage	FTA	FTM	PCT
Predrag Stojakovic, Sacramento Kings	425	394	92.7
Steve Nash, Dallas Mavericks	251	230	91.6
Allan Houston, New York Knicks	172	157	91.3
Ray Allen, Seattle SuperSonics	271	245	90.4
Reggie Miller, Indiana Pacers	165	146	88.5

KEY GP=games played; PTS=points; AVG=average; REB=rebounds; A=assists; FGA=field-goal attempts; FGM=field goals made; FTA=free-throw attempts; FTM=free throws made; PCT=percentage

2003-04 NBA Individual Leaders (cont.)

3-point Field-goal Percentage	FGA	FGM	PCT
Anthony Peeler, Sacramento Kings	141	68	48.2
Brent Barry, Seattle SuperSonics	252	114	45.2
Brian Cardinal, Golden State Warriors	124	55	44.4
Fred Hoiberg, Minnesota Timberwolves	172	76	44.2
Aaron McKie, Philadelphia 76ers	172	75	43.6

Steals	GP	STL	AVG
Baron Davis, New Orleans Hornets	67	158	2.36
Shawn Marion, Phoenix Suns	79	167	2.11
Ron Artest, Indiana Pacers	73	152	2.08
Andrei Kirilenko, Utah Jazz	78	150	1.92
Doug Christie, Sacramento Kings	82	151	1.84

Blocks	GP	BLK	AVG
Theo Ratliff, Atlanta Hawks/Portland Trail Blazers	85	307	3.61
Ben Wallace, Detroit Pistons	81	246	3.04
Andrei Kirilenko, Utah Jazz	78	215	2.76
Tim Duncan, San Antonio Spurs	69	185	2.68
Marcus Camby, Denver Nuggets	72	187	2.60

Theo Ratliff, Atlanta Hawks/ Portland Trail Blazers

ELISE AMENDOLA/AP

KEY GP=games played; STL=steals; BLK=blocks; AVG=average

Legends

Magic Johnson is third on the NBA's all-time assists list (10,141).

JOHN W. McDONOUGH/SPORTS ILLUSTRATED

Earvin "Magic" Johnson, guard, b. August 14, 1959, Lansing, Michigan. The 6' 9" Johnson revolutionized the point guard position with his keen passing ability, a rare skill in a man his size. He won the NBA championship five times with the Los Angeles Lakers (1979-80, 1981-82, 1984-85, 1986-87, 1987-88) in his 13-season career. He was also a three-time league MVP (1986-87, 1988-89, 1989-90), three-time Finals MVP (1979-80, 1981-82, 1986-87), and 12-time All-Star. Magic won a gold medal as a member of the original U.S. "Dream Team" at the 1992 Summer Olympics. He was named one of the NBA's 50 Greatest Players in 1996 and was elected to the Naismith Memorial Basketball Hall of Fame in 2002.

Walt "Clyde" Frazier, guard, b. March 29, 1945, Atlanta, Georgia. In 10 seasons with the New York Knicks (1966-67 through 1976-77), Frazier helped guide the team to the NBA championship in 1969-70 and 1972-73. The seven-time All-Star and seven-time All-Defensive First Team selection may be remembered best for his remarkable performance in Game 7 of the 1969-70 NBA Finals. Frazier scored 36 points and dished out 19 assists as the Knicks beat the Los Angeles Lakers, 113–99, to win the championship. He was elected to the Naismith Memorial Basketball Hall of Fame in 1987 and named one of the NBA's 50 Greatest Players in 1996.

Julius Erving, forward, b. February 22, 1950, Roosevelt, New York. Erving began his career by playing five seasons in the American Basketball Association (ABA) with the Virginia Squires and New York Nets. In the ABA, he won the scoring title three times (1972-73, 1973-74, 1975-76), the MVP Award twice (1973-74, 1975-76), one co-MVP Award (1974-75), and the league championship twice (1973-74, 1975-76). "Dr. J" popularized playing the pro game "above the rim" with his high-flying dunks. He moved to the NBA in 1976 and spent 11 seasons with the Philadelphia 76ers. The 11-time NBA All-Star earned the league's MVP Award in 1980-81 and won his only NBA championship in 1982-83. Erving was elected to the Naismith Memorial Basketball Hall of Fame in 1993 and named one of the NBA's 50 Greatest Players in 1996.

2003-04 TIME LINE

July 16, 2003: The Los Angeles Lakers sign forward Karl Malone and guard Gary Payton. The All-Star additions put as many as four future Hall of Famers into the Laker starting lineup and make the team an early favorite to win its fourth NBA title in five seasons.

October 24, 2003: Pat Riley resigns as head coach of the Miami Heat after eight seasons. He is replaced by his top assistant, Stan Van Gundy. Less than three weeks later, Van Gundy and the Heat face the Houston Rockets, who are coached by his brother Jeff. It is only the second coaching matchup between brothers in NBA history.

October 29, 2003: Number-1 draft pick LeBron James makes his NBA debut with the Cleveland Cavaliers in a game against the Sacramento Kings. He leads the team in points (25), assists (9), steals (4), field goals (12), and minutes (42). The Cavs lose, 106–92.

November 5, 2003: LeBron James and fellow rookie Carmelo Anthony of the Denver Nuggets face each other for the first time. Anthony and the Nuggets spoil James's first home game with a 93–89 win. 'Melo scores 14 points to LeBron's 7.

January 27, 2004: Jim O'Brien resigns as head coach of the Boston Celtics. With his departure, no Eastern Conference team has the same head coach it had at the beginning of the 2002-03 season.

February 15, 2004: The Western Conference defeats the Eastern Conference, 136–132, in the NBA All-Star Game. Center Shaquille O'Neal of the Los Angeles Lakers contributes 24 points and 11 rebounds off the bench and is named the game's MVP.

February 19, 2004: The Detroit Pistons give up two first-round draft picks to acquire forward Rasheed Wallace in a three-team deal. Wallace becomes a star for the Pistons and helps them win the 2003-04 NBA championship.

February 25, 2004: The New Jersey Nets lose to the Minnesota Timberwolves, 81–68. It is the first NBA loss for Lawrence Frank, the team's new head coach. He won his first 13 games as an NBA head coach, a league record.

March 10, 2004: Guard Tracy McGrady of the Orlando Magic scores 62 points against the Washington Wizards in the Magic's 108–99 win. It becomes the highest single-game point total by any player in 2003-04.

May 13, 2004: With 0.4 of a second left on the clock in Game 5 of a second-round playoff game, guard Derek Fisher of the Los Angeles Lakers receives an inbounds pass, turns, shoots, and scores. The shot defeats the San Antonio Spurs, 74–73, breaking a 2–2 tie between the teams. The Lakers go on to defeat the Spurs, 4–2, and cruise to the NBA Finals.

June 15, 2004: The Detroit Pistons win their first NBA championship since 1989-90 with a 100–87 victory over the Los Angeles Lakers in Game 5 of the NBA Finals. Piston point guard Chauncey Billups is named series MVP.

June 24, 2004: The Orlando Magic select 6' 11" high school forward Dwight Howard with the Number 1 pick of the NBA Draft. In 2003-04, Howard averaged 25 points and 18 rebounds for Southwest Atlanta Christian Academy, in Georgia.

June 29, 2004: Tracy McGrady is traded to the Houston Rockets in a seven-player deal. The two-time NBA scoring champ (2002-03, 2003-04) joins 7' 6" center Yao Ming, creating a potent inside-outside threat for the Rockets.

TEAM-BY-TEAM STATS

ATLANTA HAWKS

			Field Goals		3-PT FG	Free Throws		Rebounds						
Player	GP	MIN	FGM	PCT	FGA-FGM	FTM	PCT	OFF	TOTAL	A	STL	TO	BLK	AVG
Stephen Jackson	80	2,940	536	42.5	427-145	233	78.5	97	370	244	142	223	20	18.1
Jason Terry	81	3,018	499	41.7	421-146	215	82.7	49	336	437	124	229	16	16.8
Jason Collier	20	545	79	47.9	4-1	67	78.8	36	111	17	11	31	11	11.3
Chris Crawford	56	1,207	211	44.8	113-44	103	86.6	58	175	45	37	55	20	10.2
Bob Sura	80	1,663	202	41.6	79-21	171	75.7	100	326	233	62	105	14	7.5
Wesley Person	58	1,037	126	40.1	138-55	31	79.5	16	117	66	19	38	9	5.8
Boris Diaw	76	1,919	140	44.7	26-6	56	60.2	111	342	182	59	126	37	4.5
Alan Henderson	6	68	10	47.6	0-0	4	66.7	11	21	2	1	3	2	4.0
Zeljko Rebraca	24	273	34	44.2	0-0	23	76.7	23	58	6	5	17	11	3.8
Jacque Vaughn	71	1,271	107	38.6	20-3	53	77.9	12	116	195	44	84	2	3.8
Mamadou N'diaye	28	366	27	39.1	0-0	44	74.6	43	112	0	8	18	25	3.5
Travis Hansen	41	507	46	35.4	30-9	22	81.5	30	70	19	10	15	9	3.0
Joel Przybilla	17	347	18	36.0	0-0	13	41.9	32	111	7	5	18	17	2.9
Hiram Fuller	4	43	3	37.5	0-0	2	33.3	4	11	2	0	4	1	2.0
Josh Davis	4	23	2	40.0	2-0	1	100.0	1	5	0	0	2	0	1.3
Michael Bradley	16	98	7	46.7	0-0	1	50.0	6	23	1	3	7	0	.9
Team Totals	**82**	**19,905**	**2,829**	**43.3**	**1,249-419**	**1,534**	**77.6**	**996**	**3,503**	**1,648**	**627**	**1,350**	**408**	**92.8**
Opponents	**82**	**–**	**2,968**	**44.0**	**1,345-482**	**1,574**	**76.0**	**1,048**	**3,533**	**1,803**	**731**	**1,151**	**416**	**97.5**

BOSTON CELTICS

			Field Goals		3-PT FG	Free Throws		Rebounds						
Player	GP	MIN	FGM	PCT	FGA-FGM	FTM	PCT	OFF	TOTAL	A	STL	TO	BLK	AVG
Paul Pierce	80	3,099	602	40.2	384-115	517	81.9	69	522	410	131	303	52	23.0
Ricky Davis	79	2,474	446	46.9	140-52	196	71.8	77	358	259	96	189	22	14.4
Mark Blount	82	2,402	342	56.6	0-0	159	71.9	207	589	75	80	150	106	10.3
Jiri Welsch	81	2,179	262	42.8	181-69	153	74.3	60	296	183	101	129	7	9.2
Chucky Atkins	64	1,544	192	39.7	241-81	73	75.3	9	93	223	45	92	2	8.4
Walter McCarty	77	1,900	203	38.8	366-137	62	75.6	28	239	124	72	91	22	7.9
Raef LaFrentz	17	328	57	46.0	40-8	10	76.9	30	79	24	8	11	13	7.8
Chris Mihm	76	1,330	186	48.8	0-0	110	66.3	156	413	21	37	90	63	6.3
Dana Barros	1	11	2	66.7	0-0	2	100.0	0	0	0	0	0	0	6.0
Marcus Banks	81	1,385	177	40.0	86-27	99	75.6	30	133	175	88	125	13	5.9
Brandon Hunter	36	406	53	45.7	3-0	19	44.2	50	118	19	13	22	1	3.5
Jumaine Jones	42	373	33	34.4	44-13	14	60.9	24	68	14	12	19	9	2.2
Kendrick Perkins	10	35	8	53.3	0-0	6	66.7	5	14	3	0	5	2	2.2
Michael Stewart	25	147	5	41.7	0-0	3	75.0	8	29	0	2	3	10	.5
Team Totals	**82**	**19,705**	**2,843**	**44.3**	**1,599-553**	**1,572**	**75.0**	**851**	**3,291**	**1,683**	**770**	**1,332**	**331**	**95.3**
Opponents	**82**	**–**	**2,894**	**43.7**	**1,534-555**	**1,587**	**73.6**	**1,069**	**3,593**	**1,882**	**719**	**1,406**	**408**	**96.7**

KEY GP=games played; MIN=minutes played; FGM=field goals made; PCT=percentage; FGA=field goals attempted; FTM=free throws made; OFF=offensive; A=assists; STL=steals; TO=turnovers; BLK=blocks; AVG=average

CHICAGO BULLS

			Field Goals		3-PT FG	Free Throws		Rebounds						
Player	**GP**	**MIN**	**FGM**	**PCT**	**FGA-FGM**	**FTM**	**PCT**	**OFF**	**TOTAL**	**A**	**STL**	**TO**	**BLK**	**AVG**
Jamal Crawford	80	2,811	509	38.6	521-165	200	83.3	46	283	405	111	193	29	17.3
Eddy Curry	73	2,154	417	49.6	1-1	235	67.1	143	451	68	24	177	83	14.7
Kirk Hinrich	76	2,706	318	38.6	369-144	135	80.4	42	259	517	101	204	21	12.0
Kendall Gill	56	1,411	215	39.2	38-9	100	73.5	61	190	89	65	83	16	9.6
Antonio Davis	80	2,570	266	40.3	0-0	176	76.5	207	671	137	37	114	65	8.9
Marcus Fizer	46	738	134	38.3	17-2	90	75.0	61	202	43	16	51	8	7.8
Eddie Robinson	51	1,024	157	48.2	5-1	28	65.1	27	104	58	33	45	10	6.7
Jannero Pargo	31	479	81	40.7	62-22	23	85.2	8	37	70	13	47	6	6.7
Jerome Williams	68	1,637	158	47.0	8-0	106	68.4	177	475	72	90	74	8	6.2
Ronald Dupree	47	893	111	39.4	9-4	66	62.9	55	167	55	32	51	18	6.2
Tyson Chandler	35	782	67	42.4	1-0	79	66.9	82	270	23	17	38	43	6.1
Scottie Pippen	23	412	53	37.9	48-13	17	63.0	20	68	50	21	29	9	5.9
Linton Johnson III	41	734	72	35.5	33-7	22	59.5	59	183	27	37	37	32	4.2
Chris Jefferies	21	195	27	37.5	42-17	13	65.0	5	29	7	4	19	7	4.0
Rick Brunson	40	412	40	38.1	23-11	27	87.1	9	37	82	25	33	3	3.0
Paul Shirley	7	86	10	43.5	1-0	1	33.3	8	16	4	1	9	1	3.0
Team Totals	**82**	**19,830**	**2,798**	**41.4**	**1,256-429**	**1,330**	**72.5**	**1,048**	**3,567**	**1,793**	**659**	**1,321**	**396**	**89.7**
Opponents	**82**	**-**	**2,882**	**43.6**	**1,235-439**	**1,673**	**74.8**	**1,011**	**3,693**	**1,890**	**694**	**1,250**	**446**	**96.0**

CLEVELAND CAVALIERS

			Field Goals		3-PT FG	Free Throws		Rebounds						
Player	**GP**	**MIN**	**FGM**	**PCT**	**FGA-FGM**	**FTM**	**PCT**	**OFF**	**TOTAL**	**A**	**STL**	**TO**	**BLK**	**AVG**
LeBron James	79	3,122	622	41.7	217-63	347	75.4	99	432	465	130	273	58	20.9
Carlos Boozer	75	2,592	471	52.3	6-1	219	76.8	230	857	148	74	134	55	15.5
Zydrunas Ilgauskas	81	2,539	466	48.3	7-2	303	74.6	279	653	109	39	163	201	15.3
Jeff McInnis	70	2,365	334	44.7	127-46	114	79.7	33	176	430	72	120	6	11.8
Eric Williams	71	1,886	231	38.6	127-35	215	76.0	65	286	120	70	88	9	10.0
Dajuan Wagner	44	708	112	36.6	86-31	32	68.1	9	58	51	26	41	7	6.5
Lee Nailon	57	780	147	45.0	3-0	47	81.0	64	143	38	15	45	8	6.0
Tony Battie	73	1,478	170	44.3	9-2	66	74.2	118	359	58	26	63	67	5.6
Kedrick Brown	55	969	117	46.1	99-38	17	63.0	41	146	64	30	29	7	5.3
Kevin Ollie	82	1,401	95	37.0	9-4	147	83.5	23	170	234	51	81	8	4.2
Ira Newble	64	1,245	108	39.1	19-2	36	78.3	65	155	72	25	54	19	4.0
Mateen Cleaves	4	92	7	30.4	1-0	1	50.0	1	7	19	4	5	2	3.8
Jason Kapono	41	427	52	40.3	44-21	20	83.3	19	55	14	13	21	2	3.5
DeSagana Diop	56	730	57	38.8	0-0	12	60.0	72	199	34	26	29	51	2.3
Jelani McCoy	2	12	0	00.0	0-0	0	00.0	1	4	0	0	1	0	.0
Team Totals	**82**	**19,855**	**2,922**	**43.3**	**786-247**	**1,528**	**75.3**	**1,182**	**3,737**	**1,808**	**585**	**1,216**	**537**	**92.9**
Opponents	**82**	**-**	**2,956**	**43.7**	**1,162-431**	**1,491**	**74.9**	**971**	**3,446**	**1,783**	**635**	**1,071**	**434**	**95.5**

DALLAS MAVERICKS

			Field Goals		3-PT FG	Free Throws		Rebounds						
Player	GP	MIN	FGM	PCT	FGA-FGM	FTM	PCT	OFF	TOTAL	A	STL	TO	BLK	AVG
Dirk Nowitzki	77	2,915	605	46.2	290-99	371	87.7	90	670	207	92	135	104	21.8
Michael Finley	72	2,778	514	44.3	370-150	164	85.0	78	325	212	84	83	39	18.6
Antawn Jamison	82	2,376	488	53.5	40-16	220	74.8	233	520	70	83	81	30	14.8
Steve Nash	78	2,612	397	47.0	257-104	230	91.6	59	232	687	67	209	8	14.5
Antoine Walker	82	2,840	483	42.8	305-82	103	55.4	198	684	369	65	202	65	14.0
Josh Howard	67	1,589	229	43.0	66-20	97	70.3	149	368	97	69	67	54	8.6
Marquis Daniels	56	1,039	203	49.4	36-11	60	76.9	66	146	116	53	44	12	8.5
Tony Delk	33	509	70	38.0	66-20	37	84.1	16	59	28	27	17	7	6.0
Scott Williams	43	527	90	48.4	3-2	16	59.3	38	132	17	20	16	16	4.6
Danny Fortson	56	625	71	51.1	0-0	75	81.5	114	250	9	12	37	11	3.9
Shawn Bradley	66	773	89	47.3	1-0	41	83.7	72	173	20	33	17	74	3.3
Eduardo Najera	58	720	72	44.4	4-2	30	65.2	67	156	25	35	29	19	3.0
Travis Best	61	762	64	37.2	20-3	40	87.0	17	68	112	31	33	4	2.8
Team Totals	**82**	**19,805**	**3,322**	**45.9**	**1,456-507**	**1,475**	**79.6**	**1,174**	**3,712**	**1,963**	**656**	**1,000**	**437**	**105.2**
Opponents	**82**	**–**	**3,133**	**45.9**	**1,471-534**	**1,462**	**74.6**	**1,009**	**3,571**	**1,937**	**582**	**1,242**	**382**	**100.8**

DENVER NUGGETS

			Field Goals		3-PT FG	Free Throws		Rebounds						
Player	GP	MIN	FGM	PCT	FGA-FGM	FTM	PCT	OFF	TOTAL	A	STL	TO	BLK	AVG
Carmelo Anthony	82	2,995	624	42.6	214-69	408	77.7	183	498	227	97	247	41	21.0
Andre Miller	82	2,838	430	45.7	65-12	342	83.2	127	366	501	142	215	25	14.8
Voshon Lenard	73	2,233	394	42.2	289-106	144	79.1	46	200	151	61	101	12	14.2
Nenê	77	2,504	334	53.0	2-0	240	68.2	154	503	168	116	183	41	11.8
Earl Boykins	82	1,849	321	41.9	171-55	142	87.7	42	143	295	51	100	3	10.2
Marcus Camby	72	2,162	262	47.7	2-0	98	72.1	211	727	132	86	98	187	8.6
Rodney White	72	985	215	45.9	87-33	78	75.0	44	165	60	32	78	20	7.5
Jon Barry	57	1,101	120	40.4	138-51	60	84.5	25	123	147	57	53	8	6.2
Michael Doleac	72	1,029	140	43.5	0-0	45	86.5	88	265	44	23	48	36	4.5
Francisco Elson	62	875	94	47.2	1-0	30	66.7	65	203	32	35	35	39	3.5
Chris Andersen	71	1,029	90	44.3	1-0	63	58.9	89	298	35	34	48	114	3.4
Nikoloz Tskitishvili	39	307	40	32.8	11-3	23	79.3	24	63	10	6	17	8	2.7
Jeff Trepagnier	11	96	10	26.3	4-2	3	50.0	6	15	4	3	6	0	2.3
Ryan Bowen	52	392	18	34.0	0-0	10	83.3	39	87	18	18	6	16	.9
Mark Pope	4	20	1	50.0	0-0	0	00.0	0	3	0	1	3	0	.5
Team Totals	**82**	**19,730**	**2,993**	**44.3**	**985-331**	**1,655**	**76.7**	**1,083**	**3,470**	**1,794**	**745**	**1,278**	**520**	**97.2**
Opponents	**82**	**–**	**3,019**	**45.3**	**1,056-376**	**1,470**	**72.8**	**1,056**	**3,521**	**1,931**	**664**	**1,399**	**479**	**96.1**

DETROIT PISTONS

Player	GP	MIN	Field Goals FGM	PCT	3-PT FG FGA-FGM	Free Throws FTM	PCT	Rebounds OFF	TOTAL	A	STL	TO	BLK	AVG
Richard Hamilton	78	2,772	530	45.5	68-18	297	86.8	78	279	310	103	210	17	17.6
Chauncey Billups	78	2,758	392	39.4	335-130	404	87.8	35	276	446	84	189	8	16.9
Rasheed Wallace	68	2,390	425	43.6	248-82	156	73.6	102	459	156	61	119	122	16.0
Tayshaun Prince	82	2,701	338	46.7	157-57	108	76.6	93	390	191	63	119	69	10.3
Mehmet Okur	71	1,580	251	46.3	48-18	162	77.5	160	421	69	36	101	63	9.6
Ben Wallace	81	3,050	315	42.1	8-1	142	49.0	324	1,006	138	143	123	246	9.5
Corliss Williamson	79	1,574	304	50.5	0-0	144	73.1	88	256	57	30	113	20	9.5
Mike James	81	2,196	272	41.4	281-106	103	81.1	28	234	339	96	124	3	9.3
Elden Campbell	65	892	138	43.9	0-0	85	68.5	52	209	45	21	63	50	5.6
Lindsey Hunter	33	661	49	34.3	50-14	5	62.5	13	67	85	39	34	6	3.5
Darvin Ham	54	484	37	49.3	2-1	21	60.0	47	93	16	13	31	8	1.8
Darko Milicic	34	159	17	26.2	1-0	14	58.3	11	43	7	7	13	15	1.4
Tremaine Fowlkes	36	261	15	31.3	8-1	13	72.2	18	53	14	9	12	3	1.2
Team Totals	**82**	**19,780**	**2,747**	**43.5**	**968-333**	**1,561**	**75.3**	**1,014**	**3,506**	**1,702**	**659**	**1,241**	**570**	**90.1**
Opponents	**82**	**-**	**2,633**	**41.3**	**1,180-356**	**1,287**	**74.4**	**980**	**3,333**	**1,561**	**649**	**1,310**	**410**	**84.3**

GOLDEN STATE WARRIORS

Player	GP	MIN	Field Goals FGM	PCT	3-PT FG FGA-FGM	Free Throws FTM	PCT	Rebounds OFF	TOTAL	A	STL	TO	BLK	AVG
Jason Richardson	78	2,936	563	43.8	273-77	258	68.4	124	524	226	86	196	41	18.7
Nick Van Exel	39	1,255	187	39.0	150-46	70	70.7	16	104	206	20	78	2	12.6
Erick Dampier	74	2,403	348	53.5	2-0	217	65.4	344	887	60	33	131	137	12.3
Clifford Robinson	82	2,846	366	38.7	314-112	123	71.1	54	322	271	68	173	73	11.8
Mike Dunleavy	75	2,336	323	44.9	254-94	137	74.1	87	442	220	68	143	13	11.7
Speedy Claxton	60	1,595	224	42.7	22-4	182	81.3	38	156	267	97	102	9	10.6
Troy Murphy	28	610	107	44.0	17-5	60	75.0	48	173	20	12	34	17	10.0
Brian Cardinal	76	1,634	220	47.2	124-55	238	87.8	100	317	103	66	84	20	9.6
Calbert Cheaney	79	2,067	278	48.1	10-0	47	61.0	77	260	136	60	85	12	7.6
Mickael Pietrus	53	748	96	41.6	105-35	52	69.3	48	119	27	32	40	12	5.3
Avery Johnson	46	637	80	40.2	3-0	52	66.7	3	33	111	26	51	3	4.6
Sean Lampley	10	63	13	65.0	0-0	8	66.7	2	11	2	0	3	1	3.4
Adonal Foyle	44	572	59	45.4	0-0	19	54.3	54	167	17	6	21	46	3.1
J.R. Bremer	36	443	43	27.2	74-19	13	65.0	9	36	51	18	24	4	3.3
Cherokee Parks	12	64	4	40.0	0-0	4	66.7	4	10	1	0	2	3	1.0
Rusty LaRue	4	22	1	33.3	1-1	1	50.0	0	3	2	2	4	0	1.0
Popeye Jones	5	10	0	00.0	0-0	0	00.0	1	1	0	0	0	0	.0
Team Totals	**82**	**19,855**	**2,875**	**44.2**	**1,283-429**	**1,470**	**72.5**	**1,002**	**3,535**	**1,681**	**576**	**1,211**	**389**	**93.3**
Opponents	**82**	**-**	**2,948**	**44.5**	**1,107-414**	**1,399**	**74.6**	**981**	**3,513**	**1,762**	**666**	**1,145**	**418**	**94.0**

HOUSTON ROCKETS

Player	GP	MIN	Field Goals FGM	PCT	3-PT FG FGA-FGM	Free Throws FTM	PCT	Rebounds OFF	TOTAL	A	STL	TO	BLK	AVG
Yao Ming	82	2,692	535	52.2	2-0	361	80.9	197	735	122	22	204	156	17.5
Steve Francis	79	3,194	450	40.3	250-73	337	77.5	116	433	493	139	294	35	16.6
Cuttino Mobley	80	3,229	460	42.6	420-164	176	81.1	40	362	258	107	180	33	15.8
Jim Jackson	80	3,119	382	42.4	405-162	107	84.3	52	487	226	86	175	23	12.9
Maurice Taylor	75	2,081	367	48.0	2-0	128	73.6	131	384	107	43	149	47	11.5
Kelvin Cato	69	1,743	161	44.7	0-0	96	67.6	153	472	72	52	84	96	6.1
Clarence Weatherspoon	52	868	104	49.3	1-0	53	73.6	74	204	30	30	35	15	5.0
Eric Piatkowski	49	703	72	37.7	122-43	14	87.5	10	73	26	16	29	5	4.1
Scott Padgett	58	547	74	44.3	65-28	24	75.0	46	139	23	12	22	13	3.4
Bostjan Nachbar	45	516	47	35.6	63-23	21	72.4	8	70	30	14	23	14	3.1
Mark Jackson	42	577	34	34.0	41-7	28	71.8	10	70	119	17	53	1	2.5
Mike Wilks	26	145	17	47.2	10-6	10	83.3	3	16	17	3	7	0	1.9
Alton Ford	9	41	6	54.5	0-0	3	50.0	3	11	3	0	3	1	1.7
Charles Oakley	7	25	2	33.3	0-0	5	83.3	0	5	2	0	1	0	1.3
Adrian Griffin	19	133	5	27.8	2-1	0	00.0	1	19	10	7	3	2	.6
Team Totals	**82**	**19,930**	**2,738**	**44.2**	**1,406-515**	**1,371**	**77.3**	**847**	**3,494**	**1,579**	**560**	**1,373**	**443**	**89.8**
Opponents	**82**	**-**	**2,636**	**41.2**	**1,227-457**	**1,491**	**73.7**	**907**	**3,258**	**1,689**	**710**	**1,103**	**359**	**88.0**

INDIANA PACERS

Player	GP	MIN	Field Goals FGM	PCT	3-PT FG FGA-FGM	Free Throws FTM	PCT	Rebounds OFF	TOTAL	A	STL	TO	BLK	AVG
Jermaine O'Neal	78	2,788	608	43.4	18-2	348	75.7	193	778	164	59	181	199	20.1
Ron Artest	73	2,714	468	42.1	242-75	322	73.3	100	385	272	152	202	50	18.3
Al Harrington	79	2,441	421	46.3	77-21	185	73.4	163	508	131	80	163	22	13.3
Reggie Miller	80	2,254	260	43.8	334-134	146	88.5	18	188	249	65	68	11	10.0
Jamaal Tinsley	52	1,378	153	41.4	207-77	49	73.1	28	136	303	84	110	17	8.3
Jonathan Bender	21	271	50	47.2	22-9	39	83.0	9	40	9	5	33	11	7.0
Anthony Johnson	73	1,598	167	40.6	122-41	75	79.8	28	130	202	64	75	8	6.2
Jeff Foster	82	1,961	197	54.4	4-0	103	66.9	248	610	64	71	60	27	6.1
Kenny Anderson	44	905	113	44.1	4-1	35	72.9	19	81	125	26	50	5	6.0
Austin Croshere	77	1,051	119	38.8	144-56	93	89.4	60	243	52	24	55	14	5.0
Fred Jones	81	1,508	123	39.5	89-27	124	83.2	25	126	173	65	73	18	4.9
Jamison Brewer	13	160	13	37.1	14-5	1	16.7	2	11	17	7	10	0	2.5
Scot Pollard	61	678	47	41.2	0-0	12	57.1	67	164	10	23	22	26	1.7
Primoz Brezec	18	72	12	46.2	0-0	4	66.7	5	15	3	0	6	3	1.6
James Jones	6	26	2	22.2	4-1	2	100.0	0	2	0	1	0	0	1.2
Team Totals	**82**	**19,805**	**2,753**	**43.5**	**1,281-449**	**1,538**	**76.4**	**965**	**3,417**	**1,774**	**726**	**1,182**	**411**	**91.4**
Opponents	**82**	**-**	**2,671**	**43.2**	**1,014-329**	**1,350**	**75.0**	**867**	**3,290**	**1,649**	**582**	**1,301**	**512**	**85.6**

LOS ANGELES CLIPPERS

			Field Goals		3-PT FG	Free Throws		Rebounds						
Player	GP	MIN	FGM	PCT	FGA-FGM	FTM	PCT	OFF	TOTAL	A	STL	TO	BLK	AVG
Corey Maggette	73	2,628	453	44.7	231-76	526	84.8	96	430	224	65	207	16	20.7
Elton Brand	69	2,670	484	49.3	1-0	411	77.3	269	714	227	64	193	154	20.0
Quentin Richardson	65	2,338	425	39.8	341-120	151	74.0	146	414	139	67	141	19	17.2
Chris Wilcox	65	1,340	227	52.1	1-0	105	70.0	125	305	51	29	80	20	8.6
Marko Jaric	58	1,760	185	38.8	150-51	74	73.3	44	175	281	93	115	20	8.5
Bobby Simmons	56	1,376	147	39.4	12-2	141	83.4	115	262	96	51	73	17	7.8
Eddie House	60	1,188	161	35.9	136-51	36	80.0	28	138	148	65	63	4	6.8
Pedrag Drobnjak	61	954	149	39.3	36-11	73	84.9	54	196	39	22	48	24	6.3
Keyon Dooling	58	1,137	137	38.9	46-8	78	83.0	17	79	130	45	65	6	6.2
Chris Kaman	82	1,843	200	46.0	2-0	99	69.7	126	461	85	23	155	73	6.1
Matt Barnes	38	719	63	45.7	13-2	43	70.5	53	151	48	27	44	3	4.5
Doug Overton	61	1,033	99	40.4	23-3	23	74.2	16	86	138	26	58	2	3.7
Melvin Ely	42	510	66	43.1	1-0	25	59.5	48	101	22	9	20	17	3.7
Glen Rice	18	262	22	28.9	28-5	17	100.0	9	41	24	6	13	0	3.7
Randy Livingston	4	48	2	20.0	3-0	4	66.7	2	7	4	2	4	0	2.0
Olden Polynice	2	12	0	00.0	0-0	0	00.0	1	2	1	1	4	0	.0
Team Totals	**82**	**19,805**	**2,817**	**42.8**	**1,024-329**	**1,808**	**78.5**	**1,149**	**3,565**	**1,653**	**594**	**1,344**	**376**	**94.8**
Opponents	**82**	**-**	**3,075**	**46.0**	**1,256-452**	**1,545**	**74.1**	**1,033**	**3,391**	**1,874**	**693**	**1,122**	**437**	**99.4**

LOS ANGELES LAKERS

			Field Goals		3-PT FG	Free Throws		Rebounds						
Player	GP	MIN	FGM	PCT	FGA-FGM	FTM	PCT	OFF	TOTAL	A	STL	TO	BLK	AVG
Kobe Bryant	65	2,447	516	43.8	217-71	454	85.2	103	359	330	112	171	28	24.0
Shaquille O'Neal	67	2,464	554	58.4	0-0	331	49.0	246	769	196	34	195	166	21.5
Gary Payton	82	2,825	482	47.1	165-55	180	71.4	72	342	449	96	151	19	14.6
Karl Malone	42	1,373	193	48.3	1-0	168	74.7	61	367	163	50	103	20	13.2
Stanislav Medvedenko	68	1,442	237	44.1	3-0	89	76.7	148	343	57	38	59	18	8.3
Devean George	82	1,951	233	40.8	186-65	73	76.0	87	332	112	81	88	38	7.4
Derek Fisher	82	1,769	203	35.2	179-52	122	79.7	30	152	187	103	79	4	7.1
Kareem Rush	72	1,244	190	44.0	138-48	31	59.6	20	97	59	33	48	20	6.4
Rick Fox	38	846	73	39.2	61-15	22	73.3	29	102	98	29	48	4	4.8
Brian Cook	35	442	67	47.5	5-0	21	75.0	31	101	20	16	17	16	4.4
Horace Grant	55	1,106	92	41.1	1-0	39	72.2	79	233	71	24	29	21	4.1
Bryon Russell	72	945	98	40.2	112-43	50	76.9	32	146	71	32	37	12	4.0
Jamal Sampson	10	130	11	47.8	0-0	7	58.3	23	52	7	2	6	4	2.9
Luke Walton	72	730	65	42.5	39-13	31	70.5	39	127	113	28	44	8	2.4
Ime Udoka	4	28	3	33.3	1-0	2	50.0	1	5	2	2	3	1	2.0
Team Totals	**82**	**19,855**	**3,028**	**45.4**	**1,115-365**	**1,631**	**69.3**	**1,001**	**3,536**	**1,948**	**682**	**1,132**	**379**	**98.2**
Opponents	**82**	**-**	**2,920**	**44.0**	**1,247-420**	**1,472**	**74.9**	**922**	**3,480**	**1,708**	**616**	**1,254**	**308**	**94.3**

MEMPHIS GRIZZLIES

			Field Goals		3-PT FG	Free Throws		Rebounds						
Player	**GP**	**MIN**	**FGM**	**PCT**	**FGA-FGM**	**FTM**	**PCT**	**OFF**	**TOTAL**	**A**	**STL**	**TO**	**BLK**	**AVG**
Pau Gasol	78	2,458	506	48.2	15-4	365	71.4	206	600	198	44	187	132	17.7
James Posey	82	2,451	368	47.8	290-112	278	83.0	92	403	122	137	112	40	13.7
Bonzi Wells	72	1,872	363	42.7	69-22	138	75.4	78	260	139	91	161	19	12.3
Mike Miller	65	1,770	270	43.8	215-80	102	72.3	42	216	232	59	107	14	11.1
Jason Williams	72	2,115	290	40.7	364-120	82	83.7	25	147	492	92	136	5	10.9
Stromile Swift	77	1,528	268	46.9	4-1	190	72.5	141	378	38	56	88	118	9.4
Lorenzen Wright	65	1,674	257	43.9	5-0	96	73.3	144	445	71	45	77	58	9.4
Shane Battier	79	1,947	242	44.6	186-65	120	73.2	102	303	101	101	56	58	8.5
Earl Watson	81	1,669	172	37.1	106-26	90	65.2	49	178	402	91	146	19	5.7
Bo Outlaw	82	1,606	159	51.0	4-0	61	52.6	125	342	90	73	69	70	4.6
Jake Tsakalidis	40	533	67	50.4	0-0	36	59.0	37	128	18	9	23	22	4.3
Theron Smith	20	178	16	37.2	12-6	6	75.0	13	41	7	5	14	5	2.2
Dahntay Jones	20	154	15	28.3	4-1	5	45.5	7	23	12	5	12	6	1.8
Troy Bell	6	34	4	22.2	4-0	3	100.0	3	4	4	1	6	0	1.8
Ryan Humphrey	2	11	1	25.0	1-0	0	00.0	2	3	1	1	2	0	1.0
Team Totals	**82**	**19,880**	**2,963**	**44.5**	**1,314-447**	**1,557**	**72.7**	**1,047**	**3,428**	**1,915**	**795**	**1,226**	**565**	**96.7**
Opponents	**82**	**-**	**2,859**	**43.6**	**1,091-369**	**1,643**	**76.4**	**1,099**	**3,607**	**1,674**	**673**	**1,395**	**461**	**94.3**

MIAMI HEAT

			Field Goals		3-PT FG	Free Throws		Rebounds						
Player	**GP**	**MIN**	**FGM**	**PCT**	**FGA-FGM**	**FTM**	**PCT**	**OFF**	**TOTAL**	**A**	**STL**	**TO**	**BLK**	**AVG**
Eddie Jones	81	2,998	473	40.9	479-177	278	83.5	38	308	258	92	129	34	17.3
Lamar Odom	80	3,003	485	43.0	205-61	340	74.2	160	776	327	85	236	71	17.1
Dwyane Wade	61	2,126	371	46.5	53-16	233	74.7	85	247	275	86	196	34	16.2
Rafer Alston	82	2,581	287	37.6	434-161	103	76.9	26	226	372	114	128	18	10.2
Caron Butler	68	2,030	240	38.0	42-10	133	75.6	92	326	126	75	91	13	9.2
Brian Grant	76	2,303	289	47.1	1-0	86	78.2	174	524	69	51	82	35	8.7
Udonis Haslem	75	1,795	205	45.9	3-0	140	76.5	189	473	51	33	74	24	7.3
Rasual Butler	45	675	119	47.6	108-50	16	76.2	4	61	23	10	28	13	6.8
John Wallace	37	368	61	42.1	13-5	31	77.5	12	59	14	5	24	8	4.3
Malik Allen	45	616	83	41.9	0-0	25	75.8	42	119	16	12	27	28	4.2
Samaki Walker	33	418	38	38.4	2-0	29	65.9	42	112	6	9	15	11	3.2
Loren Woods	38	506	44	45.8	0-0	33	60.0	65	134	10	11	26	19	3.2
Wang Zhizhi	16	114	17	37.0	14-4	9	90.0	4	18	2	3	6	5	2.9
Tyrone Hill	5	38	3	60.0	0-0	3	75.0	5	8	0	0	2	1	1.8
Kirk Penney	2	18	1	16.7	3-1	0	00.0	0	1	1	1	3	0	1.5
Bimbo Coles	22	170	12	35.3	0-0	4	66.7	2	10	15	3	9	0	1.3
Jerome Beasley	2	5	1	33.3	0-0	0	00.0	0	1	0	0	0	0	1.0
Team Totals	**82**	**19,755**	**2,729**	**42.5**	**1,357-485**	**1,459**	**76.2**	**940**	**3,399**	**1,565**	**590**	**1,137**	**313**	**90.3**
Opponents	**82**	**-**	**2,658**	**42.8**	**1,256-431**	**1,612**	**76.8**	**892**	**3,378**	**1,526**	**578**	**1,207**	**439**	**89.7**

MILWAUKEE BUCKS

			Field Goals		3-PT FG	Free Throws		Rebounds						
Player	GP	MIN	FGM	PCT	FGA-FGM	FTM	PCT	OFF	TOTAL	A	STL	TO	BLK	AVG
Michael Redd	82	3,021	633	44.0	363-127	383	86.8	118	407	185	81	116	6	21.7
Keith Van Horn	72	2,340	410	45.4	233-93	249	85.9	149	501	120	68	169	33	16.1
Desmond Mason	82	2,534	409	47.2	39-9	356	76.9	93	359	152	60	148	24	14.4
Joe Smith	76	2,254	311	43.9	5-1	207	85.9	230	643	78	47	82	94	10.9
Brian Skinner	56	1,577	255	49.7	0-0	79	57.2	119	411	49	30	78	61	10.5
Toni Kukoc	73	1,522	211	41.7	168-49	145	72.9	60	271	200	59	110	21	8.4
T.J. Ford	55	1,472	153	38.4	21-5	80	81.6	37	177	356	60	139	3	7.1
Damon Jones	82	2,016	210	40.1	273-98	55	76.4	15	170	478	30	103	4	7.0
Dan Gadzuric	75	1,260	183	52.4	1-0	58	49.2	126	346	28	51	45	105	5.7
Erick Strickland	43	571	79	40.3	66-29	44	86.3	13	71	90	26	54	2	5.4
Brevin Knight	56	1,037	105	42.7	8-2	49	75.4	14	112	204	84	72	1	4.7
Daniel Santiago	54	708	78	47.9	0-0	61	67.8	35	132	24	19	32	21	4.0
Marcus Haislip	31	263	36	48.6	2-1	20	71.4	21	53	4	6	9	12	3.0
Dan Langhi	6	37	5	35.7	2-1	2	100.0	0	4	0	0	2	0	2.2
Team Totals	**82**	**19,780**	**2,970**	**44.7**	**1,145-401**	**1,698**	**77.5**	**960**	**3,462**	**1,872**	**554**	**1,110**	**383**	**98.0**
Opponents	**82**	**-**	**3,034**	**45.2**	**1,296-456**	**1,428**	**73.9**	**983**	**3,504**	**1,870**	**615**	**1,164**	**406**	**97.0**

MINNESOTA TIMBERWOLVES

			Field Goals		3-PT FG	Free Throws		Rebounds						
Player	GP	MIN	FGM	PCT	FGA-FGM	FTM	PCT	OFF	TOTAL	A	STL	TO	BLK	AVG
Kevin Garnett	82	3,231	804	49.9	43-11	368	79.1	245	1,139	409	120	212	178	24.2
Sam Cassell	81	2,838	620	48.8	186-74	289	87.3	44	271	592	102	220	18	19.8
Latrell Sprewell	82	3,100	518	40.9	299-99	240	81.4	56	310	286	88	158	21	16.8
Wally Szczerbiak	28	622	106	44.9	46-20	53	82.8	24	88	33	12	28	1	10.2
Troy Hudson	29	503	80	38.6	77-31	27	81.8	4	35	70	7	34	0	7.5
Fred Hoiberg	79	1,804	178	46.5	172-76	98	84.5	21	268	109	66	44	10	6.7
Michael Olowokandi	43	925	121	42.5	0-0	36	59.0	78	245	24	16	54	68	6.5
Gary Trent	68	1,025	155	47.3	6-0	69	75.8	83	216	49	12	54	17	5.6
Trenton Hassell	81	2,264	177	46.5	13-4	48	78.7	68	257	133	36	46	54	5.0
Mark Madsen	72	1,246	101	49.5	6-0	57	48.3	134	272	28	33	47	18	3.6
Derrick Martin	16	172	20	29.9	26-6	9	100.0	2	7	23	2	7	1	3.4
Keith McLeod	33	391	27	32.9	10-1	33	76.7	5	34	59	16	29	1	2.7
Oliver Miller	48	506	53	53.0	1-0	15	65.2	46	130	36	19	33	26	2.5
Ervin Johnson	66	965	55	53.4	1-0	17	60.7	61	232	24	27	30	43	1.9
Quincy Lewis	14	65	7	35.0	5-2	0	00.0	1	7	2	2	3	2	1.1
Ndudi Ebi	17	32	6	42.9	0-0	1	25.0	2	3	3	0	3	4	.8
Team Totals	**82**	**19,755**	**3,033**	**46.2**	**897-326**	**1,361**	**78.1**	**875**	**3,520**	**1,890**	**561**	**1,043**	**462**	**94.5**
Opponents	**82**	**-**	**2,741**	**41.4**	**1,181-395**	**1,426**	**75.3**	**1,001**	**3,401**	**1,701**	**547**	**1,106**	**296**	**89.1**

NEW JERSEY NETS

			Field Goals		3-PT FG	Free Throws		Rebounds						
Player	**GP**	**MIN**	**FGM**	**PCT**	**FGA-FGM**	**FTM**	**PCT**	**OFF**	**TOTAL**	**A**	**STL**	**TO**	**BLK**	**AVG**
Richard Jefferson	82	3,133	555	49.8	132-48	357	76.3	109	464	315	92	198	28	18.5
Kenyon Martin	65	2,252	439	48.8	25-7	201	68.4	133	617	160	95	168	82	16.7
Jason Kidd	67	2,450	368	38.4	293-94	206	82.7	85	428	618	122	214	14	15.5
Kerry Kittles	82	2,842	434	45.3	276-97	107	78.7	56	327	206	125	95	40	13.1
Alonzo Mourning	12	215	33	46.5	0-0	30	88.2	8	27	8	2	10	6	8.0
Rodney Rogers	69	1,409	207	41.0	152-50	75	76.5	100	307	137	59	98	27	7.8
Lucious Harris	69	1,504	187	40.4	101-38	66	84.6	39	140	135	41	53	2	6.9
Aaron Williams	72	1,337	172	50.3	3-1	105	67.7	101	294	81	34	89	46	6.3
Jason Collins	78	2,220	163	42.4	2-0	136	73.9	143	400	153	67	97	56	5.9
Brian Scalabrine	69	928	86	39.4	41-10	58	82.9	42	173	65	21	42	14	3.5
Zoran Planinic	49	473	53	41.1	32-9	38	63.3	14	55	68	13	36	3	3.1
Brandon Armstrong	56	434	65	37.1	52-19	2	50.0	12	43	14	12	24	2	2.7
Tamar Slay	22	165	21	35.0	12-4	7	50.0	10	25	14	7	11	1	2.4
Robert Pack	26	220	22	42.3	0-0	5	83.3	4	18	27	12	16	1	1.9
Anthony Goldwire	11	85	7	31.8	8-2	1	100.0	1	7	11	5	3	0	1.5
Damone Brown	3	17	1	10.0	0-0	1	50.0	3	5	0	2	1	0	1.0
Hubert Davis	17	78	1	9.10	0-1	2	100.0	2	8	4	2	3	0	.2
Team Totals	**82**	**19,705**	**2,813**	**44.1**	**1,123-377**	**1,398**	**75.3**	**862**	**3,335**	**2,009**	**709**	**1,209**	**322**	**90.3**
Opponents	**82**	**–**	**2,693**	**42.7**	**1,193-418**	**1,392**	**76.1**	**873**	**3,344**	**1,627**	**656**	**1,321**	**374**	**87.8**

NEW ORLEANS HORNETS

			Field Goals		3-PT FG	Free Throws		Rebounds						
Player	**GP**	**MIN**	**FGM**	**PCT**	**FGA-FGM**	**FTM**	**PCT**	**OFF**	**TOTAL**	**A**	**STL**	**TO**	**BLK**	**AVG**
Baron Davis	67	2,686	554	39.5	582-187	237	67.3	66	287	501	158	215	27	22.9
Jamal Mashburn	19	730	156	39.2	67-19	65	81.3	19	117	47	14	37	5	20.8
David Wesley	61	2,001	311	38.9	285-92	137	75.3	28	134	175	71	100	14	14.0
Jamaal Magloire	82	2,777	383	47.3	1-0	353	75.1	268	847	86	43	201	101	13.6
Darrell Armstrong	79	2,247	291	39.5	429-135	123	85.4	63	226	311	133	155	16	10.6
P.J. Brown	80	2,753	339	47.6	1-0	158	85.4	237	690	155	78	101	73	10.5
Stacey Augmon	69	1,416	143	41.2	7-1	110	79.1	52	174	85	55	76	15	5.8
Robert Traylor	71	942	145	50.5	5-2	70	54.7	106	262	43	39	62	37	5.1
Steve Smith	71	929	119	40.6	107-43	77	92.8	27	81	56	15	42	6	5.0
George Lynch	78	1,701	149	39.7	139-43	34	66.7	96	312	117	48	64	18	4.8
Shammond Williams	53	763	87	37.5	100-30	51	87.9	9	60	116	37	47	2	4.8
Maurice Carter	10	110	11	31.4	11-4	16	80.0	2	11	4	0	9	0	4.2
David West	71	930	108	47.4	2-0	57	71.3	117	297	60	27	48	28	3.8
Tierre Brown	3	17	2	50.0	0-0	2	50.0	0	1	2	0	7	0	2.0
Bryce Drew	15	78	4	22.2	7-1	3	100.0	0	6	13	4	8	0	.8
Team Totals	**82**	**19,830**	**2,772**	**42.0**	**1,666-531**	**1,454**	**75.1**	**1,091**	**3,509**	**1,716**	**708**	**1,228**	**346**	**91.8**
Opponents	**82**	**–**	**2,843**	**44.1**	**1,301-444**	**1,407**	**75.0**	**972**	**3,449**	**1,790**	**613**	**1,282**	**429**	**91.9**

NEW YORK KNICKS

Player	GP	MIN	Field Goals FGM	PCT	3-PT FG FGA-FGM	Free Throws FTM	PCT	Rebounds OFF	TOTAL	A	STL	TO	BLK	AVG
Stephon Marbury	81	3,254	598	43.1	274-87	356	81.7	58	263	719	129	249	9	20.2
Allan Houston	50	1,799	340	43.5	202-87	157	91.3	20	121	99	38	102	2	18.5
Tim Thomas	66	2,089	363	44.6	194-73	171	78.4	64	320	124	64	116	20	14.7
Kurt Thomas	80	2,548	392	47.3	3-0	106	83.5	145	662	149	56	132	80	11.1
Vin Baker	54	1,313	208	48.1	3-1	114	72.6	112	280	66	29	77	32	9.8
Anfernee Hardaway	76	2,095	279	41.1	79-30	111	80.4	69	287	176	70	107	20	9.2
Shandon Anderson	80	1,974	238	42.2	128-36	123	76.4	53	222	122	68	118	17	7.9
Nazr Mohammed	80	1,611	246	52.1	0-0	100	59.2	178	474	36	55	96	52	7.4
Dikembe Mutombo	65	1,494	141	47.8	0-0	81	68.1	145	437	25	17	54	123	5.6
DerMarr Johnson	21	287	36	37.1	36-13	28	90.3	5	39	11	8	16	7	5.4
Othella Harrington	56	872	100	49.5	0-0	58	74.4	58	177	29	12	65	14	4.6
Mike Sweetney	42	494	69	49.3	1-0	42	72.4	68	157	14	18	32	12	4.3
Frank Williams	56	714	80	38.5	60-18	41	85.4	8	53	121	25	63	6	3.9
Moochie Norris	66	847	80	36.9	58-20	54	76.1	10	65	121	44	64	5	3.5
Bruno Sundov	5	33	4	40.0	0-0	3	50.0	2	10	1	0	3	0	2.2
Cezary Trybanski	7	15	0	00.0	0-0	1	50.0	0	1	0	1	2	1	.1
Team Totals	**82**	**19,880**	**2,881**	**44.2**	**1,115-406**	**1,374**	**79.3**	**950**	**3,493**	**1,695**	**608**	**1,289**	**391**	**92.0**
Opponents	**82**	**-**	**2,785**	**42.9**	**1,228-415**	**1,678**	**76.3**	**950**	**3,394**	**1,676**	**675**	**1,132**	**383**	**93.5**

ORLANDO MAGIC

Player	GP	MIN	Field Goals FGM	PCT	3-PT FG FGA-FGM	Free Throws FTM	PCT	Rebounds OFF	TOTAL	A	STL	TO	BLK	AVG
Tracy McGrady	67	2,675	653	41.7	513-174	398	79.6	95	402	370	93	179	42	28.0
Juwan Howard	81	2,877	529	45.3	1-0	318	80.9	171	570	158	54	178	22	17.0
Drew Gooden	79	2,134	369	44.5	42-9	167	63.7	160	516	89	62	126	72	11.6
DeShawn Stevenson	80	2,444	376	43.2	71-19	138	67.6	79	298	158	52	120	17	11.4
Tyronn Lue	76	2,332	309	43.3	209-80	101	77.1	26	187	317	61	124	5	10.5
Keith Bogans	73	1,787	183	40.3	187-67	65	63.1	106	317	98	46	75	10	6.8
Zaza Pachulia	59	664	68	38.9	0-0	58	64.4	69	174	13	21	34	12	3.3
Andrew DeClercq	71	1,211	93	47.7	0-0	44	81.5	131	317	44	47	54	32	3.2
Desmond Penigar	10	89	14	50.0	0-0	4	100.0	6	24	3	2	6	2	3.2
Steven Hunter	59	789	82	52.9	0-0	23	33.3	54	170	12	5	29	73	3.2
Derrick Dial	9	86	9	32.1	9-2	6	75.0	5	13	2	6	1	0	2.9
Sean Rooks	55	595	54	35.8	1-0	33	89.2	24	97	29	14	22	10	2.6
Britton Johnsen	20	290	17	28.8	12-1	7	43.8	15	45	12	7	14	1	2.1
Reece Gaines	38	364	25	29.1	10-3	16	64.0	8	39	40	11	18	2	1.8
Pat Garrity	2	22	1	33.3	0-0	0	00.0	0	0	1	0	0	0	1.0
Team Totals	**82**	**19,830**	**2,904**	**42.9**	**1,248-429**	**1,474**	**73.7**	**1,003**	**3,353**	**1,584**	**547**	**1,123**	**308**	**94.0**
Opponents	**82**	**-**	**3,169**	**46.6**	**1,301-491**	**1,458**	**74.2**	**1,072**	**3,642**	**2,004**	**625**	**1,111**	**450**	**101.1**

PHILADELPHIA 76ers

			Field Goals		3-PT FG	Free Throws		Rebounds						
Player	**GP**	**MIN**	**FGM**	**PCT**	**FGA-FGM**	**FTM**	**PCT**	**OFF**	**TOTAL**	**A**	**STL**	**TO**	**BLK**	**AVG**
Allen Iverson	48	2,040	435	38.7	199-57	339	74.5	34	178	324	115	209	5	26.4
Glenn Robinson	42	1,336	275	44.8	100-34	114	83.2	46	189	57	42	106	9	16.6
Kenny Thomas	74	2,699	381	46.9	5-1	243	75.2	261	750	111	82	172	33	13.6
Eric Snow	82	2,966	295	41.3	18-2	252	79.7	62	281	563	97	187	6	10.3
Marc Jackson	22	598	71	41.5	1-0	64	79.0	45	126	18	12	24	6	9.4
Aaron McKie	75	2,112	265	45.9	172-75	84	75.7	45	253	195	85	103	23	9.2
Derrick Coleman	34	843	107	41.3	36-8	49	75.4	45	192	46	23	57	26	8.0
Samuel Dalembert	82	2,198	270	54.1	1-0	112	64.4	194	626	21	44	86	189	8.0
Willie Green	53	767	143	40.1	61-19	59	72.8	16	65	53	26	59	5	6.9
John Salmons	77	1,603	161	38.7	147-50	71	77.2	38	196	134	62	77	16	5.8
Kyle Korver	74	882	115	35.2	207-81	19	79.2	30	111	40	25	41	8	4.5
Zendon Hamilton	45	472	51	53.7	0-0	67	69.8	49	146	13	8	27	8	3.8
Greg Buckner	53	703	66	37.7	44-12	20	74.1	28	103	45	21	34	4	3.1
Amal McCaskill	59	636	47	40.2	1-0	19	70.4	48	133	20	12	25	20	1.9
Team Totals	**82**	**19,855**	**2,682**	**42.8**	**992-339**	**1,512**	**75.3**	**941**	**3,349**	**1,640**	**654**	**1,307**	**358**	**88.0**
Opponents	**82**	**–**	**2,751**	**43.2**	**1,329-443**	**1,474**	**74.4**	**996**	**3,394**	**1,747**	**678**	**1,245**	**463**	**90.5**

PHOENIX SUNS

			Field Goals		3-PT FG	Free Throws		Rebounds						
Player	**GP**	**MIN**	**FGM**	**PCT**	**FGA-FGM**	**FTM**	**PCT**	**OFF**	**TOTAL**	**A**	**STL**	**TO**	**BLK**	**AVG**
Amare Stoudemire	55	2,025	411	47.5	5-1	310	71.3	157	496	78	64	177	89	20.6
Shawn Marion	79	3,217	590	44.0	265-90	228	85.1	212	737	214	167	156	104	19.0
Joe Johnson	82	3,331	555	43.0	272-83	174	75.0	80	385	362	93	199	26	16.7
Leandro Barbosa	70	1,500	210	44.7	210-83	47	77.0	23	123	165	93	120	7	7.9
Howard Eisley	67	1,457	166	36.8	163-52	76	85.4	20	129	273	56	98	5	6.9
Antonio McDyess	42	927	126	47.0	0-0	38	55.1	70	257	36	37	57	24	6.9
Jake Voskuhl	66	1,606	152	50.7	0-0	134	74.0	123	343	57	42	77	25	6.6
Casey Jacobsen	78	1,828	150	41.7	180-75	91	82.0	42	201	98	48	68	9	6.0
Maciej Lampe	21	224	43	48.9	4-0	10	76.9	9	44	9	3	15	3	4.6
Jahidi White	62	865	99	52.1	0-0	63	50.0	97	261	7	25	66	51	4.2
Zarko Cabarkapa	49	570	81	41.1	32-6	35	66.0	26	99	40	10	54	13	4.1
Donnell Harvey	60	783	89	44.3	3-0	61	73.5	48	164	21	24	45	27	4.0
Team Totals	**82**	**19,730**	**2,958**	**44.3**	**1,202-415**	**1,392**	**74.6**	**924**	**3,330**	**1,586**	**734**	**1,249**	**383**	**94.2**
Opponents	**82**	**–**	**2,975**	**44.6**	**1,374-479**	**1,601**	**76.5**	**1,038**	**3,588**	**1,760**	**649**	**1,304**	**431**	**97.9**

PORTLAND TRAIL BLAZERS

			Field Goals		3-PT FG	Free Throws		Rebounds						
Player	GP	MIN	FGM	PCT	FGA-FGM	FTM	PCT	OFF	TOTAL	A	STL	TO	BLK	AVG
Zach Randolph	81	3,067	663	48.5	5-1	299	76.1	242	851	163	68	247	41	20.1
Shareef Abdur-Rahim	85	2,684	501	47.5	34-9	373	86.9	189	639	174	68	184	37	16.3
Derek Anderson	51	1,810	230	37.6	259-79	155	82.4	26	182	228	66	90	3	13.6
Damon Stoudamire	82	3,118	408	40.1	427-156	127	87.6	52	308	500	99	180	9	13.4
Darius Miles	79	2,079	365	48.5	40-7	124	64.2	112	359	162	67	130	61	10.9
Theo Ratliff	85	2,664	266	48.5	0-0	140	64.5	195	614	71	54	120	307	7.9
Ruben Patterson	73	1,651	200	50.6	12-2	105	55.3	129	268	139	84	105	21	6.9
Dale Davis	76	1,682	133	47.3	0-0	65	61.3	158	398	72	43	40	62	4.4
Qyntel Woods	62	673	88	37.1	29-10	38	63.3	46	136	46	20	52	14	3.6
Vladimir Stepania	42	453	43	41.7	0-0	22	61.1	50	125	23	11	19	15	2.6
Kaniel Dickens	3	12	3	100.0	0-0	1	50.0	2	2	0	0	1	0	2.3
Eddie Gill	22	157	15	41.7	8-3	17	85.0	4	17	16	9	12	1	2.3
Dan Dickau	43	294	37	37.8	30-10	11	78.6	7	26	38	17	26	0	2.2
Desmond Ferguson	7	32	5	41.7	8-3	0	00.0	0	4	1	0	1	0	1.9
Tracy Murray	7	35	3	25.0	5-2	0	00.0	3	5	1	1	2	0	1.1
Travis Outlaw	8	19	3	42.9	0-0	2	50.0	2	4	1	1	1	0	1.0
Omar Cook	17	139	7	25.9	1-0	0	00.0	3	6	24	10	10	0	.8
Slavko Vranes	1	3	0	00.0	0-0	0	00.0	0	0	0	0	0	0	.0
Team Totals	**82**	**19,980**	**2,898**	**44.8**	**1,102-381**	**1,263**	**73.1**	**1,040**	**3,416**	**1,768**	**613**	**1,213**	**443**	**90.7**
Opponents	**82**	**-**	**2,954**	**45.0**	**1,222-417**	**1,219**	**75.3**	**1,016**	**3,308**	**1,912**	**657**	**1,120**	**390**	**92.0**

SACRAMENTO KINGS

			Field Goals		3-PT FG	Free Throws		Rebounds						
Player	GP	MIN	FGM	PCT	FGA-FGM	FTM	PCT	OFF	TOTAL	A	STL	TO	BLK	AVG
Predrag Stojakovic	81	3,264	665	48.0	554-240	394	92.7	91	508	173	108	153	14	24.2
Chris Webber	23	831	174	41.3	5-1	81	71.1	48	200	105	31	60	20	18.7
Mike Bibby	82	2,980	527	45.0	378-148	304	81.5	67	277	444	112	175	18	18.4
Brad Miller	72	2,621	373	51.0	38-12	256	77.8	191	743	312	68	144	86	14.1
Bobby Jackson	50	1,185	263	44.4	219-81	82	75.2	55	174	105	49	63	8	13.8
Doug Christie	82	2,780	317	46.1	142-49	148	86.0	69	329	347	151	155	41	10.1
Vlade Divac	81	2,317	314	47.0	13-2	170	65.4	136	463	432	57	173	77	9.9
Anthony Peeler	75	1,391	156	44.8	141-68	51	83.6	31	153	120	56	77	10	5.7
Darius Songaila	73	976	133	48.7	0-0	71	80.7	91	225	48	42	43	12	4.6
Tony Massenburg	59	789	104	47.5	1-0	43	68.3	57	188	29	14	45	18	4.3
Jabari Smith	31	168	26	37.1	3-0	12	60.0	11	31	11	2	7	6	2.1
Gerald Wallace	37	337	32	36.0	2-0	11	45.8	35	74	19	14	8	14	2.0
Rodney Buford	22	141	19	33.9	2-0	3	50.0	6	15	7	6	4	1	1.9
Team Totals	**82**	**19,780**	**3,103**	**46.2**	**1,498-601**	**1,626**	**79.6**	**888**	**3,380**	**2,152**	**710**	**1,137**	**325**	**102.8**
Opponents	**82**	**-**	**3,140**	**45.4**	**1,205-409**	**1,333**	**74.9**	**1,080**	**3,601**	**1,743**	**651**	**1,225**	**413**	**97.8**

Fast Fact: In 2003-04, LeBron James of the Cleveland Cavaliers became the youngest NBA player (age 19) to win the NBA's Rookie of the Year Award.

SAN ANTONIO SPURS

Player	GP	MIN	Field Goals		3-PT FG	Free Throws		Rebounds		A	STL	TO	BLK	AVG
			FGM	PCT	FGA-FGM	FTM	PCT	OFF	TOTAL					
Tim Duncan	69	2,527	592	50.1	12-2	352	59.9	227	859	213	62	183	185	22.3
Tony Parker	75	2,577	423	44.7	199-62	191	70.2	43	237	411	61	179	7	14.7
Emanuel Ginobili	77	2,260	330	41.8	245-88	239	80.2	86	344	291	136	161	16	12.8
Hidayet Turkoglu	80	2,073	262	40.6	241-101	114	70.8	52	358	154	80	94	32	9.2
Radoslav Nesterovic	82	2,353	328	46.9	0-0	54	47.4	257	633	114	51	107	165	8.7
Malik Rose	67	1,256	173	42.8	3-0	183	81.3	110	320	69	36	112	24	7.9
Bruce Bowen	82	2,624	211	42.0	212-77	66	57.9	45	253	113	84	90	33	6.9
Charlie Ward	71	1,252	160	41.0	206-84	20	74.1	12	144	215	64	96	11	6.0
Ron Mercer	39	516	90	42.7	7-2	13	76.5	10	49	22	14	26	5	5.0
Robert Horry	81	1,290	141	40.5	108-41	69	64.5	108	272	101	48	55	49	4.8
Anthony Carter	5	87	11	29.7	3-0	0	00.0	2	11	12	4	12	0	4.4
Devin Brown	58	627	85	43.4	14-4	60	81.1	38	130	33	15	38	4	4.0
Shane Heal	6	72	7	29.2	18-4	4	80.0	1	4	5	1	5	0	3.7
Kevin Willis	48	373	70	46.7	1-0	24	61.5	37	98	11	21	32	9	3.4
Jason Hart	53	660	71	44.7	9-2	33	76.7	10	79	81	28	29	5	3.3
Alex Garcia	2	13	1	14.3	0-0	1	50.0	0	0	0	2	1	0	1.5
Matt Carroll	16	70	7	43.8	3-1	4	66.7	1	6	2	1	6	0	1.2
Team Totals	**82**	**19,755**	**2,842**	**44.2**	**1,140-408**	**1,409**	**68.1**	**1,029**	**3,698**	**1,676**	**661**	**1,203**	**537**	**91.5**
Opponents	**82**	**-**	**2,613**	**40.9**	**951-311**	**1,372**	**74.4**	**909**	**3,368**	**1,419**	**635**	**1,254**	**380**	**84.3**

SEATTLE SUPERSONICS

Player	GP	MIN	Field Goals		3-PT FG	Free Throws		Rebounds		A	STL	TO	BLK	AVG
			FGM	PCT	FGA-FGM	FTM	PCT	OFF	TOTAL					
Ray Allen	56	2,152	447	44.0	378-148	245	90.4	69	286	268	71	156	11	23.0
Rashard Lewis	80	2,931	535	43.5	386-145	206	76.3	133	518	175	99	135	54	17.8
Ronald Murray	82	2,021	389	42.5	229-67	168	71.5	45	204	205	81	149	28	12.4
Vladimir Radmanovic	77	2,321	345	42.5	377-140	95	74.8	104	406	142	80	109	42	12.0
Brent Barry	59	1,803	215	50.4	252-114	91	82.7	21	204	342	85	139	16	10.8
Antonio Daniels	71	1,512	187	47.0	116-42	155	84.2	23	142	298	45	61	6	8.0
Vitaly Potapenko	65	1,419	200	48.9	0-0	59	64.1	101	289	53	22	77	28	7.1
Luke Ridnour	69	1,114	145	41.4	80-27	65	82.3	35	108	163	52	80	7	5.5
Jerome James	65	990	129	49.8	0-0	66	66.0	78	230	32	20	82	60	5.0
Calvin Booth	71	1,206	135	46.6	2-0	75	79.8	86	280	28	17	45	101	4.9
Ansu Sesay	57	583	81	45.5	21-6	32	69.6	43	92	19	19	23	20	3.5
Richie Frahm	54	469	63	45.3	92-34	23	88.5	12	56	24	16	7	4	3.4
Reggie Evans	75	1,280	67	40.6	3-0	83	56.1	156	408	33	54	65	10	2.9
Leon Smith	1	4	1	50.0	0-0	0	00.0	1	2	0	0	0	0	2.0
Team Totals	**82**	**19,805**	**2,939**	**44.6**	**1,936-723**	**1,363**	**76.5**	**907**	**3,225**	**1,782**	**661**	**1,188**	**387**	**97.1**
Opponents	**82**	**-**	**2,980**	**45.0**	**1,394-486**	**1,570**	**77.4**	**1,068**	**3,498**	**1,728**	**629**	**1,211**	**387**	**97.8**

Trivia Challenge

Which of the following stars played four seasons of college ball before entering the NBA: Elton Brand, Kenyon Martin, or Stephon Marbury?

Kenyon Martin

TORONTO RAPTORS

			Field Goals		3-PT FG	Free Throws		Rebounds						
Player	GP	MIN	FGM	PCT	FGA-FGM	FTM	PCT	OFF	TOTAL	A	STL	TO	BLK	AVG
Vince Carter	73	2,785	608	41.7	243-93	336	80.6	95	349	348	88	223	65	22.5
Jalen Rose	66	2,497	383	40.2	202-69	187	81.0	34	266	329	51	208	22	15.5
Donyell Marshall	82	2,988	470	46.1	325-131	134	73.6	210	808	122	93	117	124	14.7
Chris Bosh	75	2,510	327	45.9	14-5	202	70.1	191	557	78	59	107	106	11.5
Dion Glover	69	1,643	230	39.0	119-40	120	76.9	58	266	130	50	102	19	9.0
Alvin Williams	56	1,730	201	40.5	89-26	66	77.6	18	150	224	55	78	10	8.8
Morris Peterson	82	2,148	238	40.5	340-126	76	80.9	35	261	113	88	69	14	8.3
Rod Strickland	61	1,197	150	42.5	36-10	72	73.5	34	155	244	35	85	11	6.3
Lamond Murray	33	518	76	35.3	60-21	24	68.6	14	90	28	15	38	7	6.0
Milt Palacio	59	1,211	104	34.9	26-4	45	66.2	15	102	184	41	87	11	4.4
Corie Blount	62	1,050	115	45.5	3-0	15	55.6	98	275	55	49	43	24	4.0
Roger Mason, Jr.	26	328	32	32.7	39-13	19	86.4	1	31	26	11	20	6	3.7
Michael Curry	70	1,229	76	38.8	15-3	49	84.5	22	87	53	23	48	5	2.9
Jerome Moiso	35	417	40	47.6	1-0	22	57.9	41	113	8	17	25	12	2.9
Robert Archibald	32	256	9	27.3	0-0	14	45.2	21	52	13	14	10	3	1.0
Team Totals	**82**	**19,980**	**2,654**	**41.8**	**1,294-461**	**1,237**	**75.0**	**830**	**3,249**	**1,574**	**604**	**1,164**	**402**	**85.4**
Opponents	**82**	**-**	**2,722**	**42.8**	**889-273**	**1,536**	**74.7**	**1,034**	**3,696**	**1,518**	**590**	**1,196**	**333**	**88.5**

UTAH JAZZ

			Field Goals		3-PT FG	Free Throws		Rebounds						
Player	GP	MIN	FGM	PCT	FGA-FGM	FTM	PCT	OFF	TOTAL	A	STL	TO	BLK	AVG
Andrei Kirilenko	78	2,895	412	44.3	201-68	392	79.0	226	629	244	150	215	215	16.5
Matt Harpring	31	1,134	193	47.1	33-8	108	68.8	91	247	63	22	65	2	16.2
Carlos Arroyo	71	2,008	339	44.1	117-38	181	80.4	41	185	355	63	156	5	12.6
Gordan Giricek	73	2,041	316	43.6	152-60	135	85.4	51	226	122	56	103	15	11.3
Raja Bell	82	2,020	329	40.9	166-62	195	78.6	60	241	107	63	111	13	11.2
Raul Lopez	82	1,617	223	43.1	85-25	101	86.3	24	155	305	62	174	2	7.0
Greg Ostertag	78	2,153	208	47.6	1-0	113	57.9	221	578	123	30	99	139	6.8
Jarron Collins	81	1,732	147	49.8	1-0	188	71.8	117	316	77	26	79	18	6.0
Maurice Williams	57	772	115	38.0	39-10	44	78.6	23	72	76	28	51	2	5.0
Aleksandar Pavlovic	79	1,144	149	39.6	70-19	65	77.4	44	159	60	41	67	16	4.8
Mikki Moore	32	395	50	50.5	0-0	30	85.7	29	84	19	7	22	13	4.1
Ben Handlogten	17	172	25	53.2	0-0	18	66.7	22	55	6	3	10	4	4.0
Curtis Borchardt	16	258	22	39.3	1-0	14	77.8	13	54	15	4	18	14	3.6
Tom Gugliotta	55	819	70	34.5	4-1	20	71.4	65	187	63	31	39	12	2.9
Paul Grant	10	98	11	47.8	0-0	3	37.5	7	17	3	1	7	1	2.5
Michael Ruffin	41	733	38	32.5	0-0	16	42.1	78	207	41	22	42	21	2.2
Team Totals	**82**	**19,780**	**2,690**	**43.6**	**786-252**	**1,639**	**74.6**	**1,103**	**3,375**	**1,671**	**583**	**1,365**	**494**	**88.7**
Opponents	**82**	**-**	**2,541**	**43.2**	**1,209-415**	**1,874**	**77.1**	**868**	**2,999**	**1,528**	**666**	**1,262**	**530**	**89.9**

WASHINGTON WIZARDS

Player	GP	MIN	Field Goals FGM	Field Goals PCT	3-PT FG FGA-FGM	Free Throws FTM	Free Throws PCT	Rebounds OFF	Rebounds TOTAL	A	STL	TO	BLK	AVG
Gilbert Arenas	55	2,066	358	39.2	333-125	237	74.8	55	254	275	103	226	12	19.6
Larry Hughes	61	2,061	401	39.7	232-79	267	79.7	96	326	148	95	152	26	18.8
Jerry Stackhouse	26	774	128	39.9	65-23	83	80.6	16	94	103	24	88	3	13.9
Kwame Brown	74	2,239	288	48.9	2-1	228	68.3	178	550	112	66	140	52	10.9
Jarvis Hayes	70	2,044	278	40.0	131-40	77	78.6	71	264	106	71	110	11	9.6
Juan Dixon	71	1,478	247	38.8	198-59	111	79.9	30	148	137	82	104	4	9.4
Etan Thomas	79	1,901	257	48.9	0-0	191	64.7	183	528	68	36	113	123	8.9
Brendan Haywood	77	1,484	200	51.5	1-0	137	58.5	186	387	43	32	80	100	7.0
Steve Blake	75	1,392	157	38.6	202-75	55	82.1	18	117	209	57	128	7	5.9
Christian Laettner	48	984	119	46.5	21-6	40	80.0	50	232	89	37	42	28	5.9
Jared Jeffries	82	1,913	177	37.7	30-5	105	61.4	180	424	93	48	107	28	5.7
Lonny Baxter	62	766	103	49.3	3-1	44	57.9	64	187	20	17	38	29	4.0
Mitchell Butler	41	552	54	43.5	30-11	15	62.5	24	71	32	22	24	4	3.3
Chris Whitney	16	186	17	37.8	18-8	5	100.0	3	15	14	6	6	2	2.9
Torraye Braggs	15	154	16	48.5	0-0	8	66.7	18	39	7	4	13	2	2.7
Team Totals	**82**	**19,830**	**2,758**	**42.1**	**1,269-433**	**1,579**	**71.4**	**1,115**	**3,507**	**1,537**	**733**	**1,439**	**406**	**91.8**
Opponents	**82**	**-**	**3,061**	**45.4**	**1,238-424**	**1,444**	**77.1**	**1,048**	**3,568**	**1,966**	**786**	**1,321**	**448**	**97.4**

Today's Stars

LeBron James, forward, b. December 30, 1984, Akron, Ohio. The Cleveland Cavaliers chose James as the Number 1 pick in the 2003 NBA Draft. He became the third NBA player with more than 20 points, 5 rebounds, and 5 assists per game as a rookie. (Oscar Robertson and Michael Jordan were the others.) The 19-year-old also became the league's youngest Rookie of the Year. He finished in the Top 5 among rookies in every major statistical category, including first in steals (1.65) and second in scoring (20.9 points) per game.

LeBron James led the Cleveland Cavaliers in scoring (20.9 points per game) and steals (1.65) in 2003-04.

KEVORK DJANSEZIAN/AP

Carmelo Anthony, forward, b. May 29, 1984, Baltimore, Maryland. The super-smooth forward for the Denver Nuggets led all NBA rookies in points per game (21) in 2003-04. 'Melo also finished third among rookies in rebounds (6.1) and second in minutes (36.5) per game and powered the Nuggets to their first playoff appearance since 1994-95. He was drafted by Denver third overall in June 2003 after leading Syracuse to its first NCAA championship as a freshman.

Zach Randolph, forward, b. July 16, 1981, Marion, Indiana. Randolph's dramatic improvement from the 2002-03 season (he more than doubled his per game averages in points and rebounds) earned him the 2003-04 NBA Most Improved Player Award. The 6′ 9″ bruiser for the Portland Trail Blazers became a force in the paint in his third season, with 20.1 points and 10.5 rebounds per game, and was fifth in the league in double-doubles (43).

NBA Champions

Season	Champion	Series	Runner-up	Winning Coach	Finals MVP
2003-04	Detroit	4-1	L.A. Lakers	Larry Brown	Chauncey Billups, Det
2002-03	San Antonio	4-2	New Jersey	Gregg Popovich	Tim Duncan, SA
2001-02	L.A. Lakers	4-0	New Jersey	Phil Jackson	Shaquille O'Neal, L.A.
2000-01	L.A. Lakers	4-1	Philadelphia	Phil Jackson	Shaquille O'Neal, L.A.
1999-00	L.A. Lakers	4-2	Indiana	Phil Jackson	Shaquille O'Neal, L.A.
1998-99	San Antonio	4-1	New York	Gregg Popovich	Tim Duncan, SA
1997-98	Chicago	4-2	Utah	Phil Jackson	Michael Jordan, Chi
1996-97	Chicago	4-2	Utah	Phil Jackson	Michael Jordan, Chi
1995-96	Chicago	4-2	Seattle	Phil Jackson	Michael Jordan, Chi
1994-95	Houston	4-0	Orlando	Rudy Tomjanovich	Hakeem Olajuwon, Hou
1993-94	Houston	4-3	New York	Rudy Tomjanovich	Hakeem Olajuwon, Hou
1992-93	Chicago	4-2	Phoenix	Phil Jackson	Michael Jordan, Chi
1991-92	Chicago	4-2	Portland	Phil Jackson	Michael Jordan, Chi
1990-91	Chicago	4-1	L.A. Lakers	Phil Jackson	Michael Jordan, Chi
1989-90	Detroit	4-1	Portland	Chuck Daly	Isiah Thomas, Det
1988-89	Detroit	4-0	L.A. Lakers	Chuck Daly	Joe Dumars, Det
1987-88	L.A. Lakers	4-3	Detroit	Pat Riley	James Worthy, L.A.
1986-87	L.A. Lakers	4-2	Boston	Pat Riley	Magic Johnson, L.A.
1985-86	Boston	4-2	Houston	K.C. Jones	Larry Bird, Bos
1984-85	L.A. Lakers	4-2	Boston	Pat Riley	Kareem Abdul-Jabbar, L.A.
1983-84	Boston	4-3	L.A. Lakers	K.C. Jones	Larry Bird, Bos
1982-83	Philadelphia	4-0	L.A. Lakers	Billy Cunningham	Moses Malone, Phil
1981-82	L.A. Lakers	4-2	Philadelphia	Pat Riley	Magic Johnson, L.A.
1980-81	Boston	4-2	Houston	Bill Fitch	Cedric Maxwell, Bos
1979-80	L.A. Lakers	4-2	Philadelphia	Paul Westhead	Magic Johnson, L.A.
1978-79	Seattle	4-1	Washington	Lenny Wilkens	Dennis Johnson, Sea
1977-78	Washington	4-3	Seattle	Dick Motta	Wes Unseld, Wash
1976-77	Portland	4-2	Philadelphia	Jack Ramsay	Bill Walton, Port
1975-76	Boston	4-2	Phoenix	Tom Heinsohn	Jo Jo White, Bos
1974-75	Golden State	4-0	Washington	Al Attles	Rick Barry, GS
1973-74	Boston	4-3	Milwaukee	Tom Heinsohn	John Havlicek, Bos
1972-73	New York	4-1	L.A. Lakers	Red Holzman	Willis Reed, N.Y.
1971-72	L.A. Lakers	4-1	New York	Bill Sharman	Wilt Chamberlain, L.A.
1970-71	Milwaukee	4-0	Baltimore	Larry Costello	Kareem Abdul-Jabbar, Mil
1969-70	New York	4-3	L.A. Lakers	Red Holzman	Willis Reed, N.Y.
1968-69	Boston	4-3	L.A. Lakers	Bill Russell	Jerry West, L.A.
1967-68	Boston	4-2	L.A. Lakers	Bill Russell	—
1966-67	Philadelphia	4-2	San Francisco	Alex Hannum	—
1965-66	Boston	4-3	L.A. Lakers	Red Auerbach	—
1964-65	Boston	4-1	L.A. Lakers	Red Auerbach	—
1963-64	Boston	4-1	San Francisco	Red Auerbach	—
1962-63	Boston	4-2	L.A. Lakers	Red Auerbach	—
1961-62	Boston	4-3	L.A. Lakers	Red Auerbach	—
1960-61	Boston	4-1	St. Louis	Red Auerbach	—
1959-60	Boston	4-3	St. Louis	Red Auerbach	—
1958-59	Boston	4-0	Minneapolis	Red Auerbach	—
1957-58	St. Louis	4-2	Boston	Alex Hannum	—
1956-57	Boston	4-3	St. Louis	Red Auerbach	—
1955-56	Philadelphia	4-1	Ft. Wayne	George Senesky	—
1954-55	Syracuse	4-3	Ft. Wayne	Al Cervi	—
1953-54	Minneapolis	4-3	Syracuse	John Kundla	—
1952-53	Minneapolis	4-1	New York	John Kundla	—
1951-52	Minneapolis	4-3	New York	John Kundla	—
1950-51	Rochester	4-3	New York	Les Harrison	—
1949-50	Minneapolis	4-2	Syracuse	John Kundla	—
1948-49	Minneapolis	4-2	Washington	John Kundla	—
1947-48	Baltimore	4-2	Philadelphia	Buddy Jeannette	—
1946-47	Philadelphia	4-1	Chicago	Ed Gottlieb	—

Note: The NBA did not name a Finals MVP from 1946-47 to 1967-68.

All-time Individual Leaders

Scoring

Most Points, Career	PTS	AVG
Kareem Abdul-Jabbar	38,387	24.6
Karl Malone	36,928	25.0
Michael Jordan	32,292	30.1
Wilt Chamberlain	31,419	30.1
Moses Malone	27,409	20.6
Elvin Hayes	27,313	21.0
Hakeem Olajuwon	26,946	21.8
Oscar Robertson	26,710	25.7
Dominique Wilkins	26,668	24.8
John Havlicek	26,395	20.8

Highest Scoring Average, Career

Michael Jordan	30.1	1,072 games
Wilt Chamberlain	30.1	1,045 games
Elgin Baylor	27.4	846 games
Shaquille O'Neal	27.1	809 games
Jerry West	27.0	932 games
Allen Iverson	27.0	535 games
Bob Pettit	26.4	792 games
George Gervin	26.2	791 games
Oscar Robertson	25.7	1,040 games
Karl Malone	25.0	1,476 games

Note: Minimum 400 games or 10,000 points.

Most Points, Game		Opponent	Date
100	Wilt Chamberlain, Phil	N.Y.	3/2/62
78	Wilt Chamberlain, Phil	L.A.	12/8/61
73	Wilt Chamberlain, Phil	Chi	1/13/62
73	Wilt Chamberlain, SF	N.Y.	11/16/62
73	David Thompson, Den	Det	4/9/78
72	Wilt Chamberlain, SF	L.A.	11/3/62
71	Elgin Baylor, L.A.	N.Y.	11/15/60
71	David Robinson, SA	LAC	4/24/94
70	Wilt Chamberlain, SF	Syr	3/10/63
69	Michael Jordan, Chi	Clev	3/28/90

Highest Field-goal Percentage, Career

.599 Artis Gilmore

Note: Minimum 2,000 field goals made.

Highest Free-throw Percentage, Career

.904 Mark Price

Note: Minimum 1,200 free throws made.

3-point Field Goals

Most 3-point Field Goals, Career:
2,464 Reggie Miller, Indiana
Highest 3-point Field-goal Percentage, Career:
.454 Steve Kerr, San Antonio
Most 3-point Field Goals, Game:
12 Kobe Bryant, L.A. Lakers vs. Seattle, 1/7/03

Note: First year of shot: 1979-80.

KEY PTS=points; AVG=average; NO=number; YRS=years

Kareem Abdul-Jabbar, Los Angeles Lakers

TONY TOMSIC/SPORTS ILLUSTRATED

Steals

Most Steals, Career: 3,265 John Stockton, Utah
Most Steals, Game: 11 Kendall Gill, New Jersey vs. Miami, 4/3/99; Larry Kenon, San Antonio vs. Kansas City, 12/26/76

Rebounds

Most Rebounds, Career	NO	YRS	AVG
Wilt Chamberlain	23,924	14	22.9
Bill Russell	21,620	13	22.5
Kareem Abdul-Jabbar	17,440	20	11.2
Elvin Hayes	16,279	16	12.5
Moses Malone	16,212	19	12.2
Karl Malone	14,968	19	10.1
Robert Parish	14,715	21	9.1
Nate Thurmond	14,464	14	15.0
Walt Bellamy	14,241	14	13.7
Wes Unseld	13,769	13	14.0

Most Rebounds, Game

NO	PLAYER, TEAM	OPPONENT	DATE
55	Wilt Chamberlain, Phil	Bos	11/24/60
51	Bill Russell, Bos	Syr	2/5/60
49	Bill Russell, Bos	Phil	11/16/57
49	Bill Russell, Bos	Det	3/11/65
45	Wilt Chamberlain, Phil	Syr	2/6/60
45	Wilt Chamberlain, Phil	L.A.	1/21/61

Assists

Most Assists, Career

John Stockton	15,806
Mark Jackson	10,334
Magic Johnson	10,141
Oscar Robertson	9,887
Isiah Thomas	9,061

Most Assists, Game

30 Scott Skiles, Orlando vs. Denver, 12/30/90

John Stockton, Utah Jazz

KEVORK DJANSEZIAN/AP

Blocks

Most Blocks, Career

Hakeem Olajuwon	3,830
Kareem Abdul-Jabbar	3,189
Mark Eaton	3,064
Dikembe Mutombo	2,996
David Robinson	2,954

Most Blocks, Game

17 Elmore Smith, L.A. Lakers vs. Portland, 10/28/73

Did You Know?

In March 2004, the Detroit Pistons held opponents below 70 points per game in five straight games, an NBA record.

Most Valuable Player: Maurice Podoloff Trophy

Season	Player, Team
2003–04	Kevin Garnett, Minnesota
2002–03	Tim Duncan, San Antonio
2001–02	Tim Duncan, San Antonio
2000–01	Allen Iverson, Philadelphia
1999–00	Shaquille O'Neal, L.A. Lakers
1998–99	Karl Malone, Utah
1997–98	Michael Jordan, Chicago
1996–97	Karl Malone, Utah
1995–96	Michael Jordan, Chicago
1994–95	David Robinson, San Antonio
1993–94	Hakeem Olajuwon, Houston
1992–93	Charles Barkley, Phoenix
1991–92	Michael Jordan, Chicago
1990–91	Michael Jordan, Chicago
1989–90	Magic Johnson, L.A. Lakers
1988–89	Magic Johnson, L.A. Lakers
1987–88	Michael Jordan, Chicago
1986–87	Magic Johnson, L.A. Lakers
1985–86	Larry Bird, Boston
1984–85	Larry Bird, Boston
1983–84	Larry Bird, Boston
1982–83	Moses Malone, Philadelphia
1981–82	Moses Malone, Houston
1980–81	Julius Erving, Philadelphia
1979–80	Kareem Abdul-Jabbar, L.A. Lakers
1978–79	Moses Malone, Houston
1977–78	Bill Walton, Portland
1976–77	Kareem Abdul-Jabbar, L.A. Lakers
1975–76	Kareem Abdul-Jabbar, L.A. Lakers
1974–75	Bob McAdoo, Buffalo
1973–74	Kareem Abdul-Jabbar, Milwaukee
1972–73	Dave Cowens, Boston
1971–72	Kareem Abdul-Jabbar, Milwaukee
1970–71	Kareem Abdul-Jabbar, Milwaukee
1969–70	Willis Reed, New York
1968–69	Wes Unseld, Baltimore
1967–68	Wilt Chamberlain, Philadelphia
1966–67	Wilt Chamberlain, Philadelphia
1965–66	Wilt Chamberlain, Philadelphia
1964–65	Bill Russell, Boston
1963–64	Oscar Robertson, Cincinnati
1962–63	Bill Russell, Boston
1961–62	Bill Russell, Boston
1960–61	Bill Russell, Boston
1959–60	Wilt Chamberlain, Philadelphia
1958–59	Bob Pettit, St. Louis
1957–58	Bill Russell, Boston
1956–57	Bob Cousy, Boston
1955–56	Bob Pettit, St. Louis

Rookie of the Year: Eddie Gottlieb Trophy

Season	Player, Team
2003–04	LeBron James, Cleveland
2002–03	Amare Stoudemire, Phoenix
2001–02	Pau Gasol, Memphis
2000–01	Mike Miller, Orlando
1999–00	Steve Francis, Houston
	Elton Brand, Chicago
1998–99	Vince Carter, Toronto
1997–98	Tim Duncan, San Antonio
1996–97	Allen Iverson, Philadelphia
1995–96	Damon Stoudamire, Toronto
1994–95	Jason Kidd, Dallas
	Grant Hill, Detroit
1993–94	Chris Webber, Golden State
1992–93	Shaquille O'Neal, Orlando
1991–92	Larry Johnson, Charlotte
1990–91	Derrick Coleman, New Jersey
1989–90	David Robinson, San Antonio
1988–89	Mitch Richmond, Golden State
1987–88	Mark Jackson, New York
1986–87	Chuck Person, Indiana
1985–86	Patrick Ewing, New York
1984–85	Michael Jordan, Chicago
1983–84	Ralph Sampson, Houston
1982–83	Terry Cummings, San Diego
1981–82	Buck Williams, New Jersey
1980–81	Darrell Griffith, Utah
1979–80	Larry Bird, Boston
1978–79	Phil Ford, Kansas City
1977–78	Walter Davis, Phoenix
1976–77	Adrian Dantley, Buffalo
1975–76	Alvan Adams, Phoenix
1974–75	Keith Wilkes, Golden State
1973–74	Ernie DiGregorio, Buffalo
1972–73	Bob McAdoo, Buffalo
1971–72	Sidney Wicks, Portland
1970–71	Dave Cowens, Boston
	Geoff Petrie, Portland
1969–70	Kareem Abdul-Jabbar, Milwaukee
1968–69	Wes Unseld, Baltimore
1967–68	Earl Monroe, Baltimore
1966–67	Dave Bing, Detroit
1965–66	Rick Barry, San Francisco
1964–65	Willis Reed, New York
1963–64	Jerry Lucas, Cincinnati
1962–63	Terry Dischinger, Chicago
1961–62	Walt Bellamy, Chicago
1960–61	Oscar Robertson, Cincinnati
1959–60	Wilt Chamberlain, Philadelphia
1958–59	Elgin Baylor, Minneapolis
1957–58	Woody Sauldsberry, Philadelphia
1956–57	Tom Heinsohn, Boston
1955–56	Maurice Stokes, Rochester
1954–55	Bob Pettit, Milwaukee
1953–54	Ray Felix, Baltimore
1952–53	Don Meineke, Ft. Wayne

Note: There were co-winners in 1999–00, 1994–95, and 1970–71.

Defensive Player of the Year

Ron Artest, Indiana Pacers

JOHN BIEVER/SPORTS ILLUSTRATED

Season	Player, Team
2003–04	Ron Artest, Indiana
2002–03	Ben Wallace, Detroit
2001–02	Ben Wallace, Detroit
2000–01	Dikembe Mutombo, Philadelphia/Atlanta
1999–00	Alonzo Mourning, Miami
1998–99	Alonzo Mourning, Miami
1997–98	Dikembe Mutombo, Atlanta
1996–97	Dikembe Mutombo, Atlanta
1995–96	Gary Payton, Seattle
1994–95	Dikembe Mutombo, Denver
1993–94	Hakeem Olajuwon, Houston
1992–93	Hakeem Olajuwon, Houston
1991–92	David Robinson, San Antonio
1990–91	Dennis Rodman, Detroit
1989–90	Dennis Rodman, Detroit
1988–89	Mark Eaton, Utah
1987–88	Michael Jordan, Chicago
1986–87	Michael Cooper, L.A. Lakers
1985–86	Alvin Robertson, San Antonio
1984–85	Mark Eaton, Utah
1983–84	Sidney Moncrief, Milwaukee
1982–83	Sidney Moncrief, Milwaukee

Sixth Man Award

Season	Player, Team
2003–04	Antawn Jamison, Dallas
2002–03	Bobby Jackson, Sacramento
2001–02	Corliss Williamson, Detroit
2000–01	Aaron McKie, Philadelphia
1999–00	Rodney Rogers, Phoenix
1998–99	Darrell Armstrong, Orlando
1997–98	Danny Manning, Phoenix
1996–97	John Starks, New York
1995–96	Toni Kukoc, Chicago
1994–95	Anthony Mason, New York
1993–94	Dell Curry, Charlotte
1992–93	Clifford Robinson, Portland
1991–92	Detlef Schrempf, Indiana
1990–91	Detlef Schrempf, Indiana
1989–90	Ricky Pierce, Milwaukee
1988–89	Eddie Johnson, Phoenix
1987–88	Roy Tarpley, Dallas
1986–87	Ricky Pierce, Milwaukee
1985–86	Bill Walton, Boston
1984–85	Kevin McHale, Boston
1983–84	Kevin McHale, Boston
1982–83	Bobby Jones, Philadelphia

Most Improved Player

Season	Player, Team
2003–04	Zach Randolph, Portland
2002–03	Gilbert Arenas, Golden State
2001–02	Jermaine O'Neal, Indiana
2000–01	Tracy McGrady, Orlando
1999–00	Jalen Rose, Indiana
1998–99	Darrell Armstrong, Orlando
1997–98	Alan Henderson, Atlanta
1996–97	Isaac Austin, Miami
1995–96	Gheorghe Muresan, Washington
1994–95	Dana Barros, Philadelphia
1993–94	Don MacLean, Washington
1992–93	Mahmoud Abdul-Rauf, Denver
1991–92	Pervis Ellison, Washington
1990–91	Scott Skiles, Orlando
1989–90	Rony Seikaly, Miami
1988–89	Kevin Johnson, Phoenix
1987–88	Kevin Duckworth, Portland
1986–87	Dale Ellis, Seattle
1985–86	Alvin Robertson, San Antonio

Zach Randolph, Portland Trail Blazers

BILL FRAKES/SPORTS ILLUSTRATED

Trivia Challenge

Guard Tracy McGrady won the NBA scoring title in 2002-03 and 2003-04. Who was the last NBA player before T-Mac to win back-to-back scoring titles?

Guard Allen Iverson of the Philadelphia 76ers, who won the title in 2000-01 and 2001-02.

Fast Fact: The Memphis Grizzlies became the ninth NBA team to go from at least 50 losses in a season (28–54, in 2002-03) to at least 50 wins the following season (50–32, in 2003-04).

All-Star Game Results

Year	Result	Site	Winning Coach	Most Valuable Player
2004	West 136, East 132	Los Angeles, CA	Flip Saunders	Shaquille O'Neal, L.A. Lakers
2003	West 155, East 145 (2OT)	Atlanta, GA	Rick Adelman	Kevin Garnett, Minnesota
2002	West 135, East 120	Philadelphia, PA	Don Nelson	Kobe Bryant, L.A. Lakers
2001	East 111, West 110	Washington, DC	Larry Brown	Allen Iverson, Philadelphia
2000	West 137, East 126	Oakland, CA	Phil Jackson	Shaquille O'Neal, L.A. Lakers/Tim Duncan, San Antonio
1999	Cancelled due to lockout			
1998	East 135, West 114	New York, NY	Larry Bird	Michael Jordan, Chicago
1997	East 132, West 120	Cleveland, OH	Doug Collins	Glen Rice, Charlotte
1996	East 129, West 118	San Antonio, TX	Phil Jackson	Michael Jordan, Chicago
1995	West 139, East 112	Phoenix, AZ	Paul Westphal	Mitch Richmond, Sacramento
1994	East 127, West 118	Minneapolis, MN	Lenny Wilkens	Scottie Pippen, Chicago
1993	West 135, East 132	Salt Lake City, UT	Paul Westphal	Karl Malone/John Stockton, Utah
1992	West 153, East 113	Orlando, FL	Don Nelson	Magic Johnson, L.A. Lakers
1991	East 116, West 114	Charlotte, NC	Chris Ford	Charles Barkley, Philadelphia
1990	East 130, West 113	Miami, FL	Chuck Daly	Magic Johnson, L.A. Lakers
1989	West 143, East 134	Houston, TX	Pat Riley	Karl Malone, Utah
1988	East 138, West 133	Chicago, IL	Mike Fratello	Michael Jordan, Chicago
1987	West 154, East 149 (OT)	Seattle, WA	Pat Riley	Tom Chambers, Seattle
1986	East 139, West 132	Dallas, TX	K.C. Jones	Isiah Thomas, Detroit
1985	West 140, East 129	Indianapolis, IN	Pat Riley	Ralph Sampson, Houston
1984	East 154, West 145 (OT)	Denver, CO	K.C. Jones	Isiah Thomas, Detroit
1983	East 132, West 123	Los Angeles, CA	Billy Cunningham	Julius Erving, Philadelphia
1982	East 120, West 118	East Rutherford, NJ	Bill Fitch	Larry Bird, Boston
1981	East 123, West 120	Cleveland, OH	Billy Cunningham	Nate Archibald, Boston
1980	East 144, West 135 (OT)	Washington, DC	Billy Cunningham	George Gervin, San Antonio
1979	West 134, East 129	Detroit, MI	Lenny Wilkens	David Thompson, Denver
1978	East 133, West 125	Atlanta, GA	Billy Cunningham	Randy Smith, Buffalo
1977	West 125, East 124	Milwaukee, WI	Larry Brown	Julius Erving, Philadelphia
1976	East 123, West 109	Philadelphia, PA	Tom Heinsohn	Dave Bing, Washington
1975	East 108, West 102	Phoenix, AZ	K.C. Jones	Walt Frazier, New York
1974	West 134, East 123	Seattle, WA	Larry Costello	Bob Lanier, Detroit
1973	East 104, West 84	Chicago, IL	Tom Heinsohn	Dave Cowens, Boston
1972	West 112, East 110	Los Angeles, CA	Bill Sharman	Jerry West, L.A. Lakers
1971	West 108, East 107	San Diego, CA	Larry Costello	Lenny Wilkens, Seattle
1970	East 142, West 135	Philadelphia, PA	Red Holzman	Willis Reed, New York
1969	East 123, West 112	Baltimore, MD	Gene Shue	Oscar Robertson, Cincinnati
1968	East 144, West 124	New York, NY	Alex Hannum	Hal Greer, Philadelphia
1967	West 135, East 120	San Francisco, CA	Fred Schaus	Rick Barry, San Francisco
1966	East 137, West 94	Cincinnati, OH	Red Auerbach	Adrian Smith, Cincinnati
1965	East 124, West 123	St. Louis, MO	Red Auerbach	Jerry Lucas, Cincinnati
1964	East 111, West 107	Boston, MA	Red Auerbach	Oscar Robertson, Cincinnati
1963	East 115, West 108	Los Angeles, CA	Red Auerbach	Bill Russell, Boston
1962	West 150, East 130	St. Louis, MO	Fred Schaus	Bob Pettit, St. Louis
1961	West 153, East 131	Syracuse, NY	Paul Seymour	Oscar Robertson, Cincinnati
1960	East 125, West 115	Philadelphia, PA	Red Auerbach	Wilt Chamberlain, Philadelphia
1959	West 124, East 108	Detroit, MI	Ed Macauley	Bob Pettit, St. Louis/Elgin Baylor, Minnesota
1958	East 130, West 118	St. Louis, MO	Red Auerbach	Bob Pettit, St. Louis
1957	East 109, West 97	Boston, MA	Red Auerbach	Bob Cousy, Boston
1956	West 108, East 94	Rochester, NY	Charley Eckman	Bob Pettit, St. Louis
1955	East 100, West 91	New York, NY	Al Cervi	Bill Sharman, Boston
1954	East 98, West 93 (OT)	New York, NY	Joe Lapchick	Bob Cousy, Boston
1953	West 79, East 75	Ft. Wayne, IN	John Kundla	George Mikan, Minnesota
1952	East 108, West 91	Boston, MA	Al Cervi	Paul Arizin, Philadelphia
1951	East 111, West 94	Boston, MA	Joe Lapchick	Ed Macauley, Boston

2004 NBA Draft—First Round

June 24, 2004, New York, NY

1. Dwight Howard, Orlando
2. Emeka Okafor, Charlotte (from L.A. Clippers)
3. Ben Gordon, Chicago
4. Shaun Livingston, L.A. Clippers (from Charlotte)
5. Devin Harris, Washington (traded to Dallas)
6. Josh Childress, Atlanta
7. Luol Deng, Phoenix (traded to Chicago)
8. Rafael Araujo, Toronto
9. Andre Iguodala, Philadelphia
10. Luke Jackson, Cleveland
11. Andris Biedrins, Golden State
12. Robert Swift, Seattle
13. Sebastian Telfair, Portland
14. Kris Humphries, Utah
15. Al Jefferson, Boston
16. Kirk Snyder, Utah (from New York via Phoenix)
17. Josh Smith, Atlanta (from Milwaukee via Denver and Detroit)
18. J.R. Smith, New Orleans
19. Dorell Wright, Miami
20. Jameer Nelson, Denver (traded to Orlando)
21. Pavel Podkolzine, Utah (from Houston; traded to Dallas)
22. Viktor Khryapa, New Jersey (traded to Portland)
23. Sergei Monia, Portland (from Memphis)
24. Delonte West, Boston (from Dallas)
25. Tony Allen, Boston (from Detroit)
26. Kevin Martin, Sacramento
27. Sasha Vujacic, L.A. Lakers
28. Beno Udrih, San Antonio
29. David Harrison, Indiana

World Championship of Basketball

Year	Winner	Runner-up	Score	Site
2002	Yugoslavia	Argentina	84–77 (OT)	Indianapolis, Indiana
1998	Yugoslavia	Russia	64–62	Athens, Greece
1994*	United States	Russia	137–91	Toronto, Ontario, Canada
1990	Yugoslavia	Soviet Union	92–75	Buenos Aires, Argentina
1986	United States	Soviet Union	87–85	Madrid, Spain
1982	Soviet Union	United States	95–94	Cali, Colombia
1978	Yugoslavia	Soviet Union	82–81 (OT)	Manila, Philippines
1974	Soviet Union	Yugoslavia	†	San Juan, Puerto Rico
1970	Yugoslavia	Brazil	†	Ljubljana, Yugoslavia
1967	Soviet Union	Yugoslavia	†	Montevideo, Uruguay
1963	Brazil	Yugoslavia	†	Rio de Janeiro, Brazil
1959	Brazil	United States	†	Santiago, Chile
1954	United States	Brazil	†	Rio de Janeiro, Brazil
1950	Argentina	United States	†	Rio de Janeiro, Brazil

* U.S. professionals began competing in 1994. In 1998, an NBA labor dispute resulted in a boycott of the World Championship by NBA stars. Players from the Continental Basketball Association, European professional leagues, and U.S. colleges were used to fill the U.S. team's roster.
† Result determined by overall record in final round of competition.

BASKETBALL *WOMEN'S*

Talented young stars dominated WNBA courts in 2003. For the first time in league history, the MVPs of the regular season, All-Star Game, and WNBA Finals were younger than 25 years old.

Forward-center Lauren Jackson of the Seattle Storm (age 23), was named the regular-season MVP after leading the league in scoring with 21.2 points per game. Guard Nikki Teasley of the Los Angeles Sparks (24) won the All-Star Game MVP award, and center Ruth Riley (23) of the Detroit Shock was named the Finals MVP.

Other 20-somethings recognized for their on-court performances were forward Michelle Snow (24) of the Houston Comets (Most Improved Player) and forward Cheryl Ford (23) of the Detroit Shock (Rookie of the Year).

It's fitting that the Shock, the league's youngest team (average age of the starting five: 24) had the league's best record (25–9) and won the championship. The Shock began the season by winning eight of their first nine games. Only the Sparks enjoyed a better start (9–0). The two teams met in the playoffs, where the Shock stunned the Sparks in an electrifying finals. A league-record 22,076 fans watched Ruth Riley drop a career-high 27 points in Game 3 to give the Shock their first WNBA crown.

WNBA vets weren't entirely forgotten.

Center Ruth Riley led the Shock to an upset victory over the Sparks in the WNBA Finals in 2003.

JESSE GARRABRANT/WNBAE/GETTY IMAGES

WNBA TEAMS

EASTERN CONFERENCE

Charlotte Sting
Cleveland Rockers*
Connecticut Sun
Detroit Shock
Indiana Fever
New York Liberty
Washington Mystics

WESTERN CONFERENCE

Houston Comets
Los Angeles Sparks
Minnesota Lynx
Phoenix Mercury
Sacramento Monarchs
San Antonio Silver Stars
Seattle Storm

*Team ceased operations in September 2003.

Trivia Challenge

Which college had four players selected among the first six picks in the WNBA draft in 2002?

University of Connecticut

After the 2003 season, the league allowed free agency for the first time. Players who had been in the league for six or more seasons and were not wanted by their current team were free to sign with any other team. The first big free-agent move occurred on February 4, 2004: Five-time All-Star guard Teresa Weatherspoon headed west, leaving the New York Liberty for the Los Angeles Sparks.

RON HOSKINS/WNBAE/GETTY IMAGES

Forward Chamique Holdsclaw of the Mystics led the WNBA in rebounds (10.9 per game) in 2003 for the second-straight season.

2003 WNBA Final Standings

Eastern Conference

TEAM	W	L	PCT	GB
Shock	25	9	.735	0.0
Sting	18	16	.529	7.0
Sun	18	16	.529	7.0
Rockers	17	17	.500	8.0
Fever	16	18	.471	9.0
Liberty	16	18	.471	9.0
Mystics	9	25	.265	16.0

Western Conference

TEAM	W	L	PCT	GB
Sparks	24	10	.706	0.0
Comets	20	14	.588	4.0
Monarchs	19	15	.559	5.0
Lynx	18	16	.529	6.0
Storm	18	16	.529	6.0
Silver Stars	12	22	.353	12.0
Mercury	8	26	.235	16.0

2003 WNBA Playoffs

EASTERN CONFERENCE				WESTERN CONFERENCE
CONF. SEMI-FINALS	**CONF. FINALS**	**FINALS**	**CONF. FINALS**	**CONF. SEMI-FINALS**
Detroit Shock (1)	Detroit Shock	**DETROIT SHOCK**	Los Angeles Sparks	Los Angeles Sparks (1)
Cleveland Rockers (4)				Minnesota Lynx (4)
Charlotte Sting (2)	Connecticut Sun	Los Angeles Sparks	Sacramento Monarchs	Houston Comets (2)
Connecticut Sun (3)				Sacramento Monarchs (3)

2003 WNBA Playoff Results

EASTERN CONFERENCE SEMI-FINALS

August 29: Shock 76 at Rockers 74
August 31: Rockers 66 at Shock 59
September 2: Rockers 63 at Shock 77
Detroit Shock won series, 2–1

August 28: Sting 66 at Sun 68
August 30: Sun 68 at Sting 62
Connecticut Sun won series, 2–0

WESTERN CONFERENCE SEMI-FINALS

August 28: Sparks 72 at Lynx 74
August 30: Lynx 69 at Sparks 80
September 1: Lynx 64 at Sparks 74
Los Angeles Sparks won series, 2–1

August 29: Comets 59 at Monarchs 65
August 31: Monarchs 48 at Comets 69
September 2: Monarchs 70 at Comets 68
Sacramento Monarchs won series, 2–1

EASTERN CONFERENCE FINALS

September 5: Shock 73 at Sun 63
September 7: Sun 73 at Shock 79
Detroit Shock won series, 2–0

WESTERN CONFERENCE FINALS

September 5: Sparks 69 at Monarchs 77
September 7: Monarchs 54 at Sparks 79
September 8: Monarchs 63 at Sparks 66
Los Angeles Sparks won series, 2–1

WNBA FINALS

September 12: Shock 63 at Sparks 75
September 14: Sparks 61 at Shock 62
September 16: Sparks 78 at Shock 83
Detroit Shock won series, 2–1

WNBA FINALS COMPOSITE BOX SCORE

DETROIT SHOCK

						REBOUNDS								
PLAYER	GP	MPG	FG%	3P%	FT%	OFF	DEF	TOTAL	APG	SPG	BPG	TO	PF	PPG
Deanna Nolan	3	30.7	.429	.375	1.000	.70	2.00	2.70	3.0	1.67	.33	2.00	2.30	15.3
Ruth Riley	3	32.3	.419	.000	.800	1.70	3.30	5.00	3.0	.00	3.33	1.67	3.30	14.7
Swin Cash	3	38.7	.341	.000	.769	2.70	4.70	7.30	5.3	.00	.33	2.00	1.30	12.7
Cheryl Ford	3	33.0	.333	.000	.900	3.70	6.30	10.00	.7	1.67	1.67	1.33	3.30	9.7
Kedra Holland-Corn	3	18.7	.429	.583	1.000	.30	1.30	1.70	1.3	1.67	.00	2.33	.30	9.7
Elaine Powell	3	28.0	.333	.000	.500	1.00	3.70	4.70	3.0	1.33	.67	1.00	2.30	3.7
Barbara Farris	3	14.0	.286	.000	1.000	.70	1.70	2.30	1.0	.00	.00	1.67	1.30	2.7
Sheila Lambert	2	4.0	.333	.500	.000	.00	.50	.50	.0	.00	.00	.50	.50	1.5
Ayana Walker	1	1.0	.000	.000	.000	.00	.00	.00	.0	.00	.00	.00	.00	.0
TEAM AVERAGES	3	200.0	.379	.389	.868	10.7	23.7	34.3	17.3	6.3	6.3	12.7	14.7	69.3

LOS ANGELES SPARKS

						REBOUNDS								
PLAYER	GP	MPG	FG%	3P%	FT%	OFF	DEF	TOTAL	APG	SPG	BPG	TO	PF	PPG
DeLisha Milton-Jones	3	38.3	.383	.667	.875	2.30	4.00	6.30	2.3	2.33	1.67	2.33	4.00	18.7
Lisa Leslie	3	39.7	.420	.000	.750	3.30	9.30	12.70	2.3	2.00	2.33	3.00	4.30	18.0
Mwadi Mabika	3	39.3	.381	.300	1.000	1.00	5.30	6.30	2.3	1.33	.33	2.00	2.00	14.0
Tamecka Dixon	3	35.3	.419	.286	1.000	.70	2.00	2.70	2.0	.67	.67	1.00	3.70	12.3
Nikki Teasley	3	37.0	.273	.263	.667	1.30	3.70	5.00	8.0	1.00	.00	1.33	3.00	6.3
Vanessa Nygaard	1	4.0	1.000	1.000	.000	1.00	1.00	2.00	.0	.00	.00	.00	.00	3.0
Nicky McCrimmon	2	2.5	.333	.333	.000	.00	.00	.00	.0	.00	.00	.00	.50	1.5
Jennifer Gillom	1	1.0	.000	.000	.000	.00	.00	.00	.0	.00	.00	.00	1.00	.0
Sophia Witherspoon	2	4.0	.000	.000	.000	.00	1.00	1.00	.0	.00	.00	.50	.00	.0
TEAM AVERAGES	3	200.0	.380	.340	.863	10.0	25.3	35.3	17.0	7.3	5.3	10.3	19.0	71.3

KEY GP=games played; MPG=minutes per game; FG%=field-goal percentage; 3P%=three-point percentage; FT%=free-throw percentage; OFF=offensive; DEF=defensive; APG=assists per game; SPG=steals per game; BPG=blocks per game; TO=turnovers; PF=personal fouls; PPG=points per game

WNBA FINALS GAME 1 **Sparks 75, Shock 63** Time of Game: 1:54 Attendance: 10,264

9/12/2003 STAPLES Center, Los Angeles, CA Officials: Bob Trammell, June Courteau, Lisa Mattingly

SHOCK

						REBOUNDS								
PLAYER	POS	MIN	FGM-A	3GM-A	FTM-A	OFF	DEF	TOT	A	STL	BLK	TO	PF	PTS
Deanna Nolan	G	36	6-13	1-5	2-2	1	4	5	2	1	0	2	1	15
Elaine Powell	G	20	1-5	0-1	0-0	1	4	5	3	1	0	1	1	2
Swin Cash	F	40	5-15	0-0	6-6	4	3	7	4	0	1	1	1	16
Cheryl Ford	F	37	3-14	0-0	5-6	7	5	12	0	2	3	2	2	11
Ruth Riley	C	32	2-10	0-0	2-2	1	5	6	1	0	3	3	5	6
Kedra Holland-Corn		17	2-8	2-5	2-2	1	0	1	1	3	0	4	0	8
Barbara Farris		11	0-2	0-0	2-2	1	3	4	3	0	0	2	1	2
Sheila Lambert		7	1-3	1-2	0-0	0	1	1	0	0	0	0	1	3
TOTAL		200	20-70 (28.6%)	4-13 (30.8%)	19-20 (95.0%)	16	25	41	14	7	7	15	12	63

SPARKS

						REBOUNDS								
PLAYER	POS	MIN	FGM-A	3GM-A	FTM-A	OFF	DEF	TOT	A	STL	BLK	TO	PF	PTS
Nikki Teasley	G	40	2-11	1-10	1-1	2	5	7	11	1	0	1	4	6
Tamecka Dixon	G	34	4-11	2-4	5-5	1	2	3	1	1	1	2	4	15
Mwadi Mabika	F	39	4-11	1-5	0-0	1	4	5	4	2	0	3	2	9
Delisha Milton	F	39	6-16	2-3	5-6	2	7	9	3	2	2	1	5	19
Lisa Leslie	C	40	10-18	0-0	3-4	2	10	12	3	1	3	4	5	23
Vanessa Nygaard		4	1-1	1-1	0-0	1	1	2	0	0	0	0	0	3
Lynn Pride		3	0-1	0-0	0-0	1	0	1	0	0	0	0	1	0
Nicky McCrimmon		1	0-0	0-0	0-0	0	0	0	0	0	0	0	0	0
TOTAL		200	27-69 (39.1%)	7-23 (30.4%)	14-16 (87.5%)	10	29	39	22	7	6	11	21	75

FINAL	1	2	T
Shock	21	42	63
Sparks	42	33	75

WNBA FINALS GAME 2 **Shock 62, Sparks 61** Time of Game: 1:54 Attendance: 17,846

9/14/2003 The Palace at Auburn Hills, Auburn Hills, MI Officials: Sally Bell, Roy Gulbeyan, Matthew Boland

SPARKS

						REBOUNDS								
PLAYER	POS	MIN	FGM-A	3GM-A	FTM-A	OFF	DEF	TOT	A	STL	BLK	TO	PF	PTS
Tamecka Dixon	G	36	4-9	0-0	0-0	0	2	2	1	0	1	1	2	8
Nikki Teasley	G	36	3-5	3-5	1-2	1	4	5	6	1	0	1	2	10
Mwadi Mabika	F	39	1-11	0-2	2-2	0	5	5	1	1	1	1	1	4
Delisha Milton	F	36	6-18	2-3	4-4	2	1	3	3	3	1	3	3	18
Lisa Leslie	C	40	6-13	0-1	6-8	4	11	15	1	3	2	3	2	18
Nicky McCrimmon		4	1-3	1-3	0-0	0	0	0	0	0	0	0	1	3
Sophia Witherspoon		4	0-1	0-1	0-0	0	2	2	0	0	0	1	0	0
Lynn Pride		4	0-0	0-0	0-0	1	0	1	0	0	0	1	0	0
Jennifer Gillom		1	0-0	0-0	0-0	0	0	0	0	0	0	0	1	0
TOTAL		200	21-60 (35%)	6-15 (40%)	13-16 (81.3%)	8	25	33	12	8	5	11	12	61

SHOCK

						REBOUNDS								
PLAYER	POS	MIN	FGM-A	3GM-A	FTM-A	OFF	DEF	TOT	A	STL	BLK	TO	PF	PTS
Deanna Nolan	G	30	5-11	2-5	2-2	0	2	2	3	3	0	3	2	14
Elaine Powell	G	29	1-4	0-0	0-0	2	6	8	1	1	1	0	3	2
Swin Cash	F	36	4-12	0-2	1-1	1	2	3	3	0	0	2	1	9
Cheryl Ford	F	33	4-9	0-0	0-0	2	5	7	2	2	1	1	4	8
Ruth Riley	C	31	5-14	0-0	1-2	0	3	3	5	0	4	2	2	11
Kedra Holland-Corn		22	6-11	4-5	0-0	0	4	4	3	1	0	1	0	16
Barbara Farris		14	1-2	0-0	0-0	0	2	2	0	0	0	2	2	2
Stacey Thomas		4	0-0	0-0	0-0	0	1	1	0	0	0	0	0	0
Ayana Walker		1	0-0	0-0	0-0	0	0	0	0	0	0	0	0	0
TOTAL		200	26-63 (41.3%)	6-12 (50%)	4-5 (80%)	5	25	30	17	7	6	11	14	62

FINAL	1	2	T
Sparks	22	39	61
Shock	38	24	62

KEY POS=position; MIN=minutes; FGM-A=field goals made-attempts; 3GM-A=three-point field goals made-attempts; FTM-A=free throws made-attempts; TOT=total; A=assists; STL=steals; BLK=blocks; PTS=points

WNBA FINALS GAME 3 Shock 83, Sparks 78 Time of Game: 2:01 Attendance: 22,076

9/16/2003 The Palace at Auburn Hills, Auburn Hills, MI Officials: June Courteau, Lisa Mattingly, Michael Price

SPARKS

PLAYER	POS	MIN	FGM-A	3GM-A	FTM-A	REBOUNDS OFF	REBOUNDS DEF	TOT	A	STL	BLK	TO	PF	PTS
Tamecka Dixon	G	36	5-11	0-3	4-4	1	2	3	4	1	0	0	5	14
Nikki Teasley	G	35	1-6	1-4	0-0	1	2	3	7	1	0	2	3	3
Mwadi Mabika	F	40	11-20	2-3	5-5	2	7	9	2	1	0	2	3	29
Delisha Milton	F	40	6-13	2-3	5-6	3	4	7	1	2	2	3	4	19
Lisa Leslie	C	39	5-19	0-0	3-4	4	7	11	3	2	2	2	6	13
Lynn Pride		6	0-0	0-0	0-0	1	0	1	0	0	1	0	3	0
Sophia Witherspoon		4	0-2	0-2	0-0	0	0	0	0	0	0	0	0	0
TOTAL		200	28-71 (39.4%)	5-15 (33.3%)	17-19 (89.5%)	12	22	34	17	7	5	9	24	78

SHOCK

PLAYER	POS	MIN	FGM-A	3GM-A	FTM-A	REBOUNDS OFF	REBOUNDS DEF	TOT	A	STL	BLK	TO	PF	PTS
Elaine Powell	G	36	3-6	0-2	1-2	0	1	1	5	2	1	2	3	7
Deanna Nolan	G	26	4-11	3-6	6-6	1	0	1	4	1	1	1	4	17
Swin Cash	F	40	5-14	0-1	3-6	3	9	12	9	0	0	3	2	13
Cheryl Ford	F	29	3-7	0-0	4-4	2	9	11	0	1	1	1	4	10
Ruth Riley	C	33	11-19	0-0	5-6	4	2	6	3	0	3	0	3	27
Kedra Holland-Corn		18	1-2	1-2	2-2	0	0	0	0	1	0	2	1	5
Barbara Farris		16	1-3	0-0	2-2	1	0	1	0	0	0	1	1	4
Stacey Thomas		1	0-0	0-0	0-0	0	0	0	0	0	0	0	0	0
Sheila Lambert		1	0-0	0-0	0-0	0	0	0	0	0	0	1	0	0
TOTAL		200	28-62 (45.2%)	4-11 (36.4%)	23-28 (82.1%)	11	21	32	21	5	6	11	18	83

FINAL	1	2	T
Sparks	37	41	78
Shock	42	41	83

Award Winners

YEAR	MVP	ROOKIE	DEFENSIVE	IMPROVED	SPORTSMANSHIP	COACH
2003	Lauren Jackson	Cheryl Ford	Sheryl Swoopes	Michelle Snow	Edna Campbell	Bill Laimbeer
2002	Sheryl Swoopes	Tamika Catchings	Sheryl Swoopes	Coco Miller	Jennifer Gillom	Marianne Stanley
2001	Lisa Leslie	Jackie Stiles	Debbie Black	Janeth Arcain	Sue Wicks	Dan Hughes
2000	Sheryl Swoopes	Betty Lennox	Sheryl Swoopes	Tari Phillips	Susie McConnell Serio	Michael Cooper
1999	Yolanda Griffith	Chamique Holdsclaw	Yolanda Griffith	N/A	Dawn Staley	Van Chancellor
1998	Cynthia Cooper	Tracy Reid	Teresa Weatherspoon	N/A	Susie McConnell Serio	Van Chancellor
1997	Cynthia Cooper	N/A	Teresa Weatherspoon	N/A	Haixia Zheng	Van Chancellor

NEWCOMER*

1998 Susie McConnell Serio
1999 Yolanda Griffith
*No longer awarded

Trivia Challenge

Who is the only player to win the WNBA Finals MVP award four times?

Guard Cynthia Cooper of the Houston Comets

WNBA Champions

YEAR	CHAMPION	RUNNER-UP	MVP
2003	Detroit Shock	Los Angeles Sparks	Ruth Riley
2002	Los Angeles Sparks	New York Liberty	Lisa Leslie
2001	Los Angeles Sparks	Charlotte Sting	Lisa Leslie
2000	Houston Comets	New York Liberty	Cynthia Cooper
1999	Houston Comets	New York Liberty	Cynthia Cooper
1998	Houston Comets	Phoenix Mercury	Cynthia Cooper
1997	Houston Comets	New York Liberty	Cynthia Cooper

TEAM-BY-TEAM STATS

CHARLOTTE STING

			FIELD GOALS		3-PT FG		FREE THROWS		REBOUNDS						
PLAYER	GP	MIN	FGM	PCT	FGA	FGM	FTM	PCT	OFF	TOTAL	A	STL	TO	BLK	AVG
Allison Feaster	34	1,096	142	37.6	205	72	66	84.6	37	113	73	52	72	9	12.4
Andrea Stinson	34	1,000	147	45.8	75	23	60	75.9	28	140	97	48	75	5	11.1
Shalonda Enis	29	613	82	43.6	62	26	62	80.5	62	125	16	29	41	2	8.7
Tammy Sutton-Brown	34	864	98	42.1	0	0	90	68.7	73	201	15	19	59	50	8.4
Dawn Staley	34	1,086	90	41.7	72	28	61	83.6	14	58	174	49	78	4	7.9
Kelly Miller	34	523	68	40.7	52	22	31	77.5	20	53	47	18	35	2	5.6
Rushia Brown	34	483	53	45.7	2	0	19	82.6	34	83	16	29	35	10	3.7
Charlotte Smith-Taylor	27	443	31	31.6	32	9	24	66.7	23	60	18	10	24	2	3.5
Teana McKiver	31	341	41	52.6	1	0	23	74.2	37	91	6	14	27	24	3.4
Tynesha Lewis	23	234	26	41.9	13	7	11	91.7	11	33	20	10	16	6	3.0
Marla Brumfield	25	123	6	37.5	3	0	6	100.0	1	10	14	1	6	1	.7
Erin Buescher	14	44	3	37.5	0	0	3	75.0	2	4	3	0	2	0	.6
STING	**34**	**6,850**	**787**	**41.8**	**517**	**187**	**456**	**77.3**	**342**	**971**	**499**	**279**	**497**	**115**	**65.2**
OPPONENTS	**34**	**-**	**790**	**41.5**	**407**	**138**	**477**	**71.5**	**386**	**1,007**	**491**	**264**	**469**	**104**	**64.6**

CLEVELAND ROCKERS

			FIELD GOALS		3-PT FG		FREE THROWS		REBOUNDS						
PLAYER	GP	MIN	FGM	PCT	FGA	FGM	FTM	PCT	OFF	TOTAL	A	STL	TO	BLK	AVG
Chasity Melvin	34	1,061	159	47.7	11	3	123	69.9	82	215	52	28	67	22	13.1
Penny Taylor	34	898	143	42.1	99	34	78	82.1	44	148	80	38	60	10	11.7
LaToya Thomas	32	852	137	46.3	6	0	71	78.9	63	164	37	28	42	13	10.8
Betty Lennox	34	560	100	37.2	103	32	26	72.2	19	89	32	14	58	4	7.6
Deanna Jackson	34	763	83	41.9	70	29	50	71.4	37	89	51	20	33	13	7.2
Merlakia Jones	34	672	66	33.7	13	4	28	71.8	18	97	44	22	36	3	4.8
Helen Darling	34	832	44	30.8	71	23	30	73.2	25	87	128	39	74	6	4.1
Lucienne Berthieu	22	201	27	51.9	1	0	30	65.2	20	42	6	10	22	4	3.8
Pollyanna Johns Kimbrough	30	416	35	55.6	0	0	19	55.9	31	82	19	12	19	10	3.0
Jennifer Rizzotti	33	525	20	27.8	51	10	9	56.3	4	42	65	14	35	0	1.8
Tracy Henderson	11	45	1	7.70	0	0	0	00.0	6	14	3	1	4	1	.2
ROCKERS	**34**	**6,825**	**815**	**41.3**	**425**	**135**	**464**	**72.2**	**349**	**1,069**	**517**	**226**	**466**	**86**	**65.6**
OPPONENTS	**34**	**-**	**809**	**42.0**	**355**	**127**	**465**	**76.6**	**300**	**1,004**	**510**	**223**	**467**	**135**	**65.0**

KEY FGM=field goals made; PCT=percentage; FGA=field-goal attempts; FTM=free throws made; A=assists; STL=steals; BLK=blocks, AVG=average

CONNECTICUT SUN

			FIELD GOALS		3-PT FG		FREE THROWS		REBOUNDS						
PLAYER	GP	MIN	FGM	PCT	FGA	FGM	FTM	PCT	OFF	TOTAL	A	STL	TO	BLK	AVG
Nykesha Sales	34	1,106	194	41.5	114	44	116	80.6	27	145	92	46	73	13	16.1
Shannon Johnson	34	1,107	138	43.3	73	19	125	73.1	39	134	196	44	107	3	12.4
Katie Douglas	28	843	120	43.8	123	47	49	72.1	33	106	56	31	28	11	12.0
Taj McWilliams-Franklin	34	983	133	44.2	43	12	76	74.5	78	227	49	43	54	33	10.4
Adrienne Johnson	34	584	69	35.4	49	17	18	75.0	23	58	18	17	21	1	5.1
Wendy Palmer	32	433	58	39.5	46	10	23	82.1	29	106	16	11	35	3	4.7
Brooke Wyckoff	34	755	55	38.7	70	20	26	72.2	48	146	35	33	39	19	4.6
Jessie Hicks	27	253	37	46.3	0	0	24	96.0	23	48	6	11	26	9	3.6
Rebecca Lobo	25	297	25	28.4	28	7	2	22.2	9	52	5	6	14	15	2.4
Courtney Coleman	20	141	11	55.0	0	0	14	46.7	8	22	1	8	13	2	1.8
Debbie Black	34	373	24	35.3	3	1	6	66.7	16	51	46	20	18	2	1.6
SUN	**34**	**6,875**	**864**	**41.1**	**549**	**177**	**479**	**74.1**	**333**	**1,095**	**520**	**270**	**434**	**111**	**70.1**
OPPONENTS	**34**	**–**	**864**	**41.1**	**536**	**172**	**509**	**75.6**	**366**	**1,178**	**553**	**252**	**476**	**88**	**70.9**

DETROIT SHOCK

			FIELD GOALS		3-PT FG		FREE THROWS		REBOUNDS						
PLAYER	GP	MIN	FGM	PCT	FGA	FGM	FTM	PCT	OFF	TOTAL	A	STL	TO	BLK	AVG
Swin Cash	33	1,097	195	45.3	40	12	146	68.2	65	193	119	43	108	23	16.6
Deanna Nolan	32	954	136	43.6	114	48	76	79.2	12	107	83	41	69	14	12.4
Cheryl Ford	32	956	128	47.4	0	0	88	68.2	99	334	27	32	79	31	10.8
Ruth Riley	34	995	115	49.8	0	0	97	76.4	59	201	64	25	82	58	9.6
Kedra Holland-Corn	34	694	107	46.1	124	50	48	76.2	12	57	63	36	59	3	9.2
Elaine Powell	33	938	105	45.1	20	7	79	74.5	43	106	129	45	79	9	9.0
Barbara Farris	34	522	43	43.4	0	0	41	65.1	29	82	23	10	41	4	3.7
Sheila Lambert	27	187	24	36.4	16	7	32	78.0	10	28	14	5	29	0	3.2
Stacy Thomas	30	269	20	32.3	27	7	14	51.9	15	43	15	20	16	9	2.0
Astou Ndiaye-Diatta	11	70	10	47.6	0	0	0	00.0	5	14	1	3	9	1	1.8
Ayana Walker	34	271	24	34.3	0	0	8	38.1	34	71	10	10	19	11	1.6
Petra Ujhelyi	14	68	2	25.0	0	0	0	00.0	3	12	3	0	10	1	.3
SHOCK	**34**	**6,900**	**902**	**45.0**	**323**	**125**	**624**	**70.7**	**379**	**1,230**	**545**	**263**	**608**	**158**	**75.1**
OPPONENTS	**34**	**–**	**911**	**39.9**	**541**	**161**	**412**	**74.1**	**390**	**1,064**	**504**	**309**	**497**	**129**	**70.4**

HOUSTON COMETS

PLAYER	GP	MIN	FIELD GOALS FGM	FIELD GOALS PCT	3-PT FG FGA	3-PT FG FGM	FREE THROWS FTM	FREE THROWS PCT	REBOUNDS OFF	REBOUNDS TOTAL	A	STL	TO	BLK	AVG
Tina Thompson	28	974	176	41.3	114	39	81	77.9	39	165	47	18	69	23	16.9
Cynthia Cooper	4	144	16	42.1	18	7	25	89.3	2	10	22	4	14	1	16.0
Sheryl Swoopes	31	1,084	175	40.3	79	24	110	88.7	32	143	121	77	73	26	15.6
Janeth Arcain	34	1,136	151	46.6	37	9	79	84.0	24	136	67	41	50	1	11.5
Michelle Snow	34	1,025	126	49.8	1	0	62	72.9	76	263	42	35	68	62	9.2
Dominique Canty	32	648	55	37.9	1	0	62	66.7	36	100	56	22	49	1	5.4
Ukari Figgs	34	952	52	419	69	26	19	86.4	11	81	82	26	59	1	4.4
Tiffani Johnson	22	359	30	48.4	0	0	17	73.9	19	63	13	3	20	7	3.5
Mfon Udoka	25	251	32	50.0	1	0	16	69.6	22	51	4	4	21	2	3.2
Kelley Gibson	26	209	14	33.3	24	10	0	00.0	4	16	8	1	9	5	1.5
Octavia Blue	16	37	1	25.0	0	0	2	50.0	1	2	2	0	2	0	.3
Itoro Umoh-Coleman	3	6	0	00.0	0	0	0	00.0	0	0	1	0	1	0	.0
COMETS	**34**	**6,825**	**828**	**43.2**	**344**	**115**	**473**	**78.8**	**266**	**1,030**	**465**	**231**	**450**	**129**	**66.0**
OPPONENTS	**34**	**-**	**824**	**40.6**	**500**	**169**	**325**	**72.5**	**298**	**1,006**	**516**	**227**	**430**	**122**	**63.0**

INDIANA FEVER

PLAYER	GP	MIN	FIELD GOALS FGM	FIELD GOALS PCT	3-PT FG FGA	3-PT FG FGM	FREE THROWS FTM	FREE THROWS PCT	REBOUNDS OFF	REBOUNDS TOTAL	A	STL	TO	BLK	AVG
Tamika Catchings	34	1,210	221	43.2	191	74	155	84.7	82	272	114	72	102	35	19.7
Natalie Williams	34	1,054	176	48.5	1	0	105	70.9	109	255	46	43	70	21	13.4
Stephanie White	28	577	60	34.7	84	29	45	93.8	14	41	58	34	37	6	6.9
Kristen Rasmussen	33	814	94	47.0	15	7	31	79.5	44	115	64	24	48	15	6.8
Coretta Brown	30	522	61	37.2	100	36	28	84.8	11	41	31	21	36	4	6.2
Kelly Schumacher	34	480	81	47.9	9	4	23	85.2	40	99	20	7	32	24	5.6
Niele Ivey	27	651	45	38.8	84	33	12	70.6	5	32	71	29	28	7	5.0
Nikki McCray	34	734	52	37.7	32	7	20	83.3	18	51	49	37	44	2	3.9
Coquese Washington	20	348	19	28.4	48	14	11	84.6	2	29	48	14	30	2	3.2
Zuzi Klimesova	1	3	0	00.0	0	0	2	100.0	0	0	0	0	0	0	2.0
Bridget Pettis	31	148	15	28.8	27	6	13	76.5	5	19	8	4	8	1	1.6
Leigh Aziz	7	44	4	28.6	0	0	2	50.0	2	9	1	0	3	4	1.4
Sonja Henning	24	295	11	25.6	9	0	2	25.0	2	25	29	15	13	0	1.0
FEVER	**34**	**6,875**	**839**	**41.7**	**600**	**210**	**449**	**79.8**	**334**	**988**	**539**	**299**	**474**	**121**	**68.7**
OPPONENTS	**34**	**-**	**837**	**43.9**	**421**	**157**	**490**	**76.8**	**309**	**986**	**570**	**227**	**512**	**170**	**68.3**

LOS ANGELES SPARKS

			FIELD GOALS		3-PT FG		FREE THROWS		REBOUNDS						
PLAYER	**GP**	**MIN**	**FGM**	**PCT**	**FGA**	**FGM**	**FTM**	**PCT**	**OFF**	**TOTAL**	**A**	**STL**	**TO**	**BLK**	**AVG**
Lisa Leslie	23	792	165	44.2	37	12	82	61.7	76	231	46	31	65	63	18.4
Mwadi Mabika	32	1,042	158	40.7	106	28	97	86.6	34	141	82	30	74	18	13.8
Tamecka Dixon	30	1,042	159	43.7	52	11	83	88.3	41	126	89	35	69	10	13.7
DeLisha Milton	31	1,086	139	42.4	61	23	115	80.4	59	220	64	49	79	41	13.4
Nikki Teasley	34	1,189	112	38.9	165	70	98	87.5	30	175	214	39	108	15	11.5
Latasha Byears	5	72	10	40.0	1	0	8	72.7	12	21	2	0	2	2	5.6
Vanessa Nygaard	11	168	16	44.4	17	6	3	75.0	11	19	5	3	4	0	3.7
Jennifer Gillom	33	397	40	41.2	26	7	16	76.2	18	55	21	16	9	3	3.1
Rhonda Mapp	24	255	30	50.0	1	0	2	50.0	26	68	6	7	12	6	2.6
Sophia Witherspoon	23	235	17	32.1	29	10	12	85.7	6	19	4	7	7	0	2.4
Nicky McCrimmon	33	299	28	44.4	12	5	7	87.5	7	29	32	19	17	1	2.1
Shaquala Williams	25	229	19	35.8	16	1	10	71.4	11	32	19	6	7	0	2.0
Lynn Pride	17	94	7	36.8	0	0	4	50.0	11	23	1	3	11	1	1.1
Chandra Johnson	8	45	1	20.0	5	1	3	75.0	2	6	3	0	4	1	.8
Jenny Mowe	1	21	0	00.0	0	0	0	00.0	0	1	0	0	1	1	.0
SPARKS	**34**	**6,900**	**894**	**41.8**	**528**	**174**	**537**	**79.2**	**336**	**1,149**	**587**	**242**	**470**	**161**	**73.5**
OPPONENTS	**34**	**–**	**866**	**40.3**	**540**	**196**	**504**	**71.8**	**316**	**1,105**	**572**	**241**	**468**	**127**	**71.5**

MINNESOTA LYNX

			FIELD GOALS		3-PT FG		FREE THROWS		REBOUNDS						
PLAYER	**GP**	**MIN**	**FGM**	**PCT**	**FGA**	**FGM**	**FTM**	**PCT**	**OFF**	**TOTAL**	**A**	**STL**	**TO**	**BLK**	**AVG**
Katie Smith	34	1,185	208	45.7	200	78	126	88.1	40	138	84	25	67	6	18.2
Sheri Sam	34	953	138	38.3	73	24	74	70.5	46	142	88	38	48	6	11.0
Svetlana Abrosimova	30	792	112	39.3	82	25	69	70.4	44	141	82	44	90	11	10.6
Tamika Williams	34	1,121	129	66.8	2	0	45	48.4	92	209	44	34	58	10	8.9
Janell Burse	29	438	76	49.0	2	0	54	77.1	40	108	19	13	42	28	7.1
Michele Van Gorp	31	528	70	43.2	1	0	35	67.3	32	107	17	10	56	20	5.6
Teresa Edwards	34	854	63	37.5	80	24	31	77.5	24	105	148	41	92	11	5.3
Jordan Adams	10	96	13	39.4	12	5	2	100.0	10	23	4	2	10	3	3.3
Kristi Harrower	31	499	32	36.8	43	16	8	61.5	9	39	72	18	39	3	2.8
Shaunzinski Gortman	25	200	21	42.9	20	5	3	75.0	9	32	14	11	20	1	2.0
Georgia Schweitzer	16	118	6	35.3	9	3	0	00.0	7	18	7	3	8	1	.9
LYNX	**34**	**6,850**	**875**	**44.2**	**524**	**180**	**450**	**72.1**	**361**	**1,079**	**580**	**242**	**558**	**101**	**70.0**
OPPONENTS	**34**	**–**	**878**	**42.5**	**446**	**141**	**473**	**74.7**	**337**	**989**	**528**	**271**	**471**	**126**	**69.7**

NEW YORK LIBERTY

			FIELD GOALS		3-PT FG		FREE THROWS		REBOUNDS						
PLAYER	**GP**	**MIN**	**FGM**	**PCT**	**FGA**	**FGM**	**FTM**	**PCT**	**OFF**	**TOTAL**	**A**	**STL**	**TO**	**BLK**	**AVG**
Becky Hammon	11	257	50	57.5	49	23	39	95.1	1	21	18	10	27	1	14.7
Vickie Johnson	32	1,042	158	45.8	96	35	79	85.9	30	95	75	29	55	7	13.4
Crystal Robinson	33	1,078	143	43.9	168	62	47	83.9	13	70	63	40	43	13	12.0
Tari Phillips	33	1,033	142	39.7	5	1	87	64.9	99	280	56	56	92	28	11.3
Elena Baranova	33	850	107	41.6	91	33	31	88.6	45	181	64	36	62	43	8.4
Tamika Whitmore	33	823	110	45.5	3	1	50	65.8	38	122	25	35	57	22	8.2
Linda Frohlich	26	214	31	43.1	13	7	14	63.6	11	36	15	6	14	8	3.2
K.B. Sharp	30	398	28	39.4	24	7	31	79.5	11	32	37	14	26	0	3.1
Teresa Weatherspoon	34	824	37	38.5	4	0	24	75.0	19	97	149	28	62	5	2.9
Erin Thorn	23	181	13	31.0	33	8	10	100.0	3	11	16	4	13	1	1.9
Lindsey Yamasaki	24	148	6	22.2	14	4	0	00.0	1	12	9	4	5	0	.7
Bethany Donaphin	1	2	0	00.0	0	0	0	00.0	0	0	0	0	0	0	.0
LIBERTY	**34**	**6,850**	**825**	**42.9**	**500**	**181**	**412**	**76.7**	**271**	**957**	**527**	**262**	**470**	**128**	**66.0**
OPPONENTS	**34**	**–**	**821**	**41.9**	**467**	**155**	**459**	**79.0**	**326**	**1,062**	**506**	**269**	**480**	**96**	**66.4**

PHOENIX MERCURY

			FIELD GOALS		3-PT FG		FREE THROWS		REBOUNDS						
PLAYER	**GP**	**MIN**	**FGM**	**PCT**	**FGA**	**FGM**	**FTM**	**PCT**	**OFF**	**TOTAL**	**A**	**STL**	**TO**	**BLK**	**AVG**
Anna DeForge	34	1,065	147	41.2	148	61	50	72.5	32	105	72	51	53	12	11.9
Adrian Williams	34	985	141	40.2	1	0	52	61.2	68	252	31	57	73	19	9.8
Tamicha Jackson	34	958	124	34.3	99	35	17	81.0	24	82	146	52	76	4	8.8
Slobodanka Tuvic	17	365	45	38.8	4	0	37	80.4	31	67	12	10	32	15	7.5
Kayte Christensen	30	659	78	48.4	0	0	50	60.2	61	126	16	25	39	16	6.9
Plenette Pierson	33	602	67	37.9	2	0	64	63.4	37	80	22	19	42	13	6.0
Lisa Harrison	33	838	74	41.3	3	0	35	68.6	42	118	36	29	34	6	5.5
Iziane Castro Marques	16	178	25	35.2	27	8	11	61.1	6	12	9	6	10	1	4.3
Edwina Brown	34	524	41	27.0	3	0	36	81.8	29	71	62	30	47	7	3.5
Nevriye Yilmaz	5	34	7	46.7	0	0	0	00.0	3	3	2	0	4	0	2.8
Tamara Moore	26	176	19	45.2	9	0	16	84.2	6	28	12	9	16	6	2.1
Edniesha Curry	20	205	13	37.1	22	5	2	66.7	1	11	24	9	15	0	1.7
Felicia Ragland	3	39	1	8.30	5	1	2	100.0	0	2	2	2	3	0	1.7
Sonja Mallory	6	44	4	44.4	0	0	2	100.0	4	10	0	1	6	4	1.7
Dalma Ivanyi	4	34	3	37.5	2	0	0	00.0	2	4	2	0	2	1	1.5
Tracy Reid	2	12	1	33.3	0	0	0	00.0	1	1	1	2	1	0	1.0
Michaela Pavlickova	8	29	3	42.9	0	0	0	00.0	1	4	1	1	2	0	.8
Grace Daley	3	28	1	20.0	2	0	0	00.0	1	2	3	0	3	1	.7
Gergana Slavtcheva	2	12	0	00.0	2	0	0	00.0	0	0	1	0	1	0	.0
Charmin Smith	4	17	0	00.0	2	0	0	00.0	1	4	1	0	0	0	.0
MERCURY	**34**	**6,925**	**801**	**38.2**	**349**	**116**	**379**	**68.2**	**357**	**1,000**	**461**	**310**	**479**	**111**	**61.7**
OPPONENTS	**34**	**–**	**834**	**44.7**	**371**	**136**	**466**	**74.4**	**303**	**1,114**	**509**	**275**	**610**	**146**	**66.8**

SACRAMENTO MONARCHS

			FIELD GOALS		3-PT FG		FREE THROWS		REBOUNDS						
PLAYER	GP	MIN	FGM	PCT	FGA	FGM	FTM	PCT	OFF	TOTAL	A	STL	TO	BLK	AVG
Yolanda Griffith	34	1,015	161	48.5	2	0	147	77.4	92	248	46	57	75	39	13.8
Tangela Smith	34	986	188	44.0	49	13	41	70.7	61	187	52	43	56	32	12.6
DeMya Walker	34	740	111	45.9	15	2	83	58.0	61	149	47	25	69	23	9.0
Edna Campbell	34	724	98	40.2	111	46	25	75.8	17	70	43	21	43	5	7.9
Kara Lawson	34	769	89	39.2	135	54	31	77.5	30	107	56	15	42	5	7.7
Ticha Penicheiro	34	1,089	62	30.2	60	15	44	57.9	29	119	229	61	81	1	5.4
Ruthie Bolton	33	521	55	31.4	98	19	20	76.9	15	57	35	33	21	2	4.5
Lady Grooms	34	470	45	40.2	1	0	21	80.8	15	46	29	17	21	5	3.3
Hamchetou Maiga	22	190	17	32.7	0	0	8	40.0	13	37	14	18	14	2	1.9
Chantelle Anderson	26	171	19	43.2	0	0	4	33.3	7	24	5	5	17	5	1.6
La'Keshia Frett	24	150	17	36.2	2	1	1	50.0	9	23	12	2	10	3	1.5
MONARCHS	**34**	**6,825**	**862**	**40.9**	**473**	**150**	**425**	**67.9**	**349**	**1,067**	**568**	**297**	**461**	**122**	**67.6**
OPPONENTS	**34**	**-**	**816**	**41.0**	**467**	**149**	**435**	**72.9**	**345**	**1,096**	**516**	**224**	**576**	**141**	**65.2**

SAN ANTONIO SILVER STARS

			FIELD GOALS		3-PT FG		FREE THROWS		REBOUNDS						
PLAYER	GP	MIN	FGM	PCT	FGA	FGM	FTM	PCT	OFF	TOTAL	A	STL	TO	BLK	AVG
Marie Ferdinand	34	1,116	139	36.2	52	16	176	78.9	28	127	90	58	85	6	13.8
Margo Dydek	34	926	156	45.1	1	0	94	72.3	45	251	58	19	80	100	11.9
Adrienne Goodson	33	969	141	39.5	36	8	81	79.4	74	185	71	24	85	6	11.2
Gwen Jackson	33	975	114	39.9	30	5	56	63.6	86	205	20	15	46	17	8.8
Jennifer Azzi	34	1,136	85	40.3	97	39	51	78.5	10	91	111	27	61	9	7.6
Sylvia Crawley	33	564	50	38.5	0	0	15	68.2	39	105	19	18	40	19	3.5
Semeka Randall	33	339	32	35.6	1	0	24	53.3	25	53	23	11	44	0	2.7
LaQuanda Quick	26	168	21	26.6	52	15	2	100.0	8	33	5	1	10	3	2.3
Tausha Mills	29	185	20	40.8	0	0	18	58.1	27	55	7	4	23	2	2.0
LaTonya Johnson	31	279	18	25.4	23	6	16	72.7	7	25	9	3	14	1	1.9
Tai Dillard	24	168	16	24.6	23	4	5	83.3	1	15	15	7	14	4	1.7
SILVER STARS	**34**	**6,825**	**792**	**38.3**	**315**	**93**	**538**	**73.1**	**350**	**1,145**	**428**	**187**	**513**	**167**	**65.1**
OPPONENTS	**34**	**-**	**867**	**39.8**	**482**	**149**	**544**	**73.0**	**389**	**1,172**	**530**	**275**	**424**	**140**	**71.4**

SEATTLE STORM

PLAYER	GP	MIN	FIELD GOALS FGM	PCT	3-PT FG FGA	FGM	FREE THROWS FTM	PCT	REBOUNDS OFF	TOTAL	A	STL	TO	BLK	AVG
Lauren Jackson	33	1,109	254	48.3	123	39	151	82.5	82	307	62	38	69	64	21.2
Sue Bird	34	1,136	155	42.1	140	49	61	88.4	22	113	221	48	110	1	12.4
Kamila Vodichkova	28	709	101	47.4	5	0	82	81.2	55	143	31	20	53	21	10.1
Sandy Brondello	34	975	117	41.5	48	21	25	80.6	19	56	69	31	37	2	8.2
Adia Barnes	16	396	32	38.1	31	12	12	57.1	26	65	23	11	18	7	5.5
Amanda Lassiter	32	733	60	38.5	73	24	19	63.3	33	112	42	27	42	26	5.1
Simone Edwards	34	577	61	45.5	0	0	35	62.5	54	133	16	10	31	9	4.6
Alisa Burras	27	270	35	46.7	0	0	19	70.4	27	61	5	5	25	5	3.3
Rita Williams	32	381	28	37.3	43	11	11	73.3	3	22	41	14	27	0	2.4
LaTonya Massaline	24	222	20	31.7	20	6	7	100.0	12	21	8	5	10	0	2.2
Tully Bevilaqua	31	252	17	33.3	21	8	16	76.2	9	26	32	14	20	1	1.9
Jung Sun-Min	17	118	13	40.6	7	0	4	100.0	1	10	1	5	5	0	1.8
Mactabene Amachree	7	47	3	30.0	0	0	2	50.0	4	14	0	5	9	2	1.1
Danielle McCulley	7	26	1	16.7	1	0	0	00.0	0	1	0	0	4	0	.3
STORM	**34**	**6,850**	**890**	**43.5**	**500**	**166**	**442**	**78.0**	**342**	**1,074**	**548**	**232**	**465**	**138**	**70.2**
OPPONENTS	**34**	**-**	**844**	**41.4**	**437**	**145**	**441**	**74.6**	**352**	**1,041**	**456**	**245**	**459**	**104**	**66.9**

WASHINGTON MYSTICS

PLAYER	GP	MIN	FIELD GOALS FGM	PCT	3-PT FG FGA	FGM	FREE THROWS FTM	PCT	REBOUNDS OFF	TOTAL	A	STL	TO	BLK	AVG
Chamique Holdsclaw	27	948	204	42.5	35	6	140	90.3	72	294	89	34	72	15	20.5
Coco Miller	33	1,076	172	45.0	89	32	37	69.8	55	127	86	39	53	7	12.5
Stacey Dales-Schuman	34	998	122	40.9	160	57	39	70.9	44	101	114	29	72	12	10.0
Asjha Jones	34	748	121	43.4	17	7	41	74.5	62	135	52	16	63	25	8.5
Murriel Page	34	850	83	37.7	12	5	42	75.0	62	152	35	18	41	24	6.3
Annie Burgess	34	841	50	37.3	58	16	15	60.0	24	79	112	27	52	1	3.9
Aiysha Smith	31	422	41	34.2	34	5	17	50.0	21	65	10	11	26	9	3.4
Helen Luz	20	165	19	35.8	40	12	9	90.0	2	10	21	6	11	2	3.0
Jocelyn Penn	30	288	31	39.7	13	2	22	66.7	19	52	16	15	20	1	2.9
Nakia Sanford	17	134	20	50.0	0	0	9	45.0	10	26	1	3	14	2	2.9
Kiesha Brown	27	269	24	33.3	33	10	2	66.7	6	32	28	13	22	1	2.2
Zuzana Zirkova	6	30	2	50.0	2	1	6	100.0	0	2	1	0	2	0	1.8
MYSTICS	**34**	**6,875**	**896**	**40.9**	**505**	**157**	**381**	**75.1**	**382**	**1,085**	**568**	**213**	**462**	**99**	**68.5**
OPPONENTS	**34**	**-**	**909**	**44.7**	**482**	**171**	**509**	**73.7**	**334**	**1,115**	**591**	**251**	**468**	**119**	**73.5**

Did You Know?

Van Chancellor has been the Houston Comets' head coach since 1997, the league's first season. He's the only one of the WNBA's 13 head coaches who has run the same team since the league's debut. He coached the Comets to the WNBA championship four seasons in a row (1997 through 2000).

Sheryl Swoopes was named Defensive Player of the Year in 2003 after leading the WNBA in steals (2.48 per game).

2003 WNBA Individual Leaders

POINTS	GP	PTS	AVG
Lauren Jackson, Seattle Storm	33	698	21.2
Chamique Holdsclaw, Washington Mystics	27	554	20.5
Tamika Catchings, Indiana Fever	34	671	19.7
Lisa Leslie, Los Angeles Sparks	23	424	18.4
Katie Smith, Minnesota Lynx	34	620	18.2

REBOUNDS	GP	REB	AVG
Chamique Holdsclaw, Washington Mystics	27	294	10.9
Cheryl Ford, Detroit Shock	32	334	10.4
Lisa Leslie, Los Angeles Sparks	23	231	10.0
Lauren Jackson, Seattle Storm	33	307	9.3
Tari Phillips, New York Liberty	33	280	8.5

ASSISTS	GP	A	AVG
Ticha Penicheiro, Sacramento Monarchs	34	229	6.7
Sue Bird, Seattle Storm	34	221	6.5
Nikki Teasley, Los Angeles Sparks	34	214	6.3
Shannon Johnson, Connecticut Sun	34	196	5.8
Dawn Staley, Charlotte Sting	34	174	5.1

FIELD-GOAL PERCENTAGE	FGA	FGM	PCT
Tamika Williams, Minnesota Lynx	193	129	66.8
Michelle Snow, Houston Comets	253	126	49.8
Ruth Riley, Detroit Shock	231	115	49.8
Yolanda Griffith, Sacramento Monarchs	332	161	48.5
Natalie Williams, Indiana Fever	363	176	48.5

FREE-THROW PERCENTAGE	FTA	FTM	PCT
Becky Hammon, New York Liberty	41	39	95.1
Stephanie White, Indiana Fever	48	45	93.8
Chamique Holdsclaw, Washington Mystics	155	140	90.3
Sheryl Swoopes, Houston Comets	124	110	88.7
Sue Bird, Seattle Storm	69	61	88.4

3-POINT FIELD-GOAL PERCENTAGE	FGA	FGM	PCT
Becky Hammon, New York Liberty	49	23	46.9
Sandy Brondello, Seattle Storm	48	21	43.8
Nikki Teasley, Los Angeles Sparks	165	70	42.4
Kelly Miller, Charlotte Sting	52	22	42.3
Deanna Nolan, Detroit Shock	114	48	42.1

STEALS	GP	STL	AVG
Sheryl Swoopes, Houston Comets	31	77	2.48
Tamika Catchings, Indiana Fever	34	72	2.12
Ticha Penicheiro, Sacramento Monarchs	34	61	1.79
Marie Ferdinand, San Antonio Silver Stars	34	58	1.71
Tari Phillips, New York Liberty	33	56	1.70

BLOCKS	GP	BLK	AVG
Margo Dydek, San Antonio Silver Stars	34	100	2.94
Lisa Leslie, Los Angeles Sparks	23	63	2.74
Lauren Jackson, Seattle Storm	33	64	1.94
Michelle Snow, Houston Comets	34	62	1.82
Ruth Riley, Detroit Shock	34	58	1.71

Today's Stars

Lauren Jackson, forward-center, b. May 11, 1981, Albury, Australia. In 2003, Jackson became the first international player named the WNBA MVP. The Seattle Storm's three-time All-Star led the league in points (21.2 per game) and was third in blocks (1.94) and fourth in rebounds (9.3). Jackson won a silver medal at the Summer Olympics in 2000 as a member of Australia's national team. She had 20 points and 13 rebounds in the 76–54 loss to the U.S. in the gold-medal game.

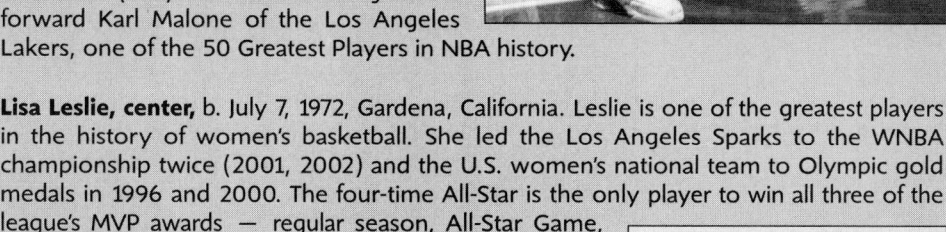

Lauren Jackson of the Storm was the WNBA's points leader (21.2 per game) and MVP in 2003.

JEFF REINKING/WNBAE/GETTY IMAGES

Cheryl Ford, forward, b. June 6, 1981, Homer, Louisiana. In April 2003, the Detroit Shock selected Ford with the third overall pick in the draft. Five months later, she was named Rookie of the Year and helped the Shock win their first WNBA championship. Ford led the league in double-doubles (15), total rebounds (334), and defensive rebounds (235). She is the daughter of forward Karl Malone of the Los Angeles Lakers, one of the 50 Greatest Players in NBA history.

Lisa Leslie, center, b. July 7, 1972, Gardena, California. Leslie is one of the greatest players in the history of women's basketball. She led the Los Angeles Sparks to the WNBA championship twice (2001, 2002) and the U.S. women's national team to Olympic gold medals in 1996 and 2000. The four-time All-Star is the only player to win all three of the league's MVP awards — regular season, All-Star Game, and WNBA Finals — in a single season (2001). In 2002, Leslie became the first player to dunk in a WNBA game and the first to reach 3,000 career points.

Fast Fact: The first brother and sister to play in the NBA and WNBA, respectively, are guard-forward Ime Udoka and his sister, forward Mfon. Ime played in six pre-season games for the Los Angeles Lakers during training camp in 2003. Mfon played in 25 games for the Houston Comets in 2003.

WNBA All-Star Game Results

YEAR	RESULT	SITE	WINNING COACH	MVP
2003	West 84, East 75	New York, NY	Michael Cooper	Nikki Teasley, Los Angeles Sparks
2002	West 81, East 76	Washington, D.C.	Michael Cooper	Lisa Leslie, Los Angeles Sparks
2001	West 80, East 72	Orlando, FL	Van Chancellor	Lisa Leslie, Los Angeles Sparks
2000	West 73, East 61	Phoenix, AZ	Van Chancellor	Tina Thompson, Houston Comets
1999	West 79, East 61	New York, NY	Van Chancellor	Lisa Leslie, Los Angeles Sparks

2004 WNBA Draft

April 17, 2004, Secaucus, NJ

FIRST ROUND

PICK	TEAM	NAME/POSITION	SCHOOL
1.	Phoenix	Diana Taurasi, G	Connecticut
2.	Washington	Alana Beard, G	Duke
3.	Charlotte	Nicolle Powell, G/F	Stanford
4.	Connecticut	Lindsay Whalen, G	Minnesota
5.	New York	Shameka Christon, G/F	Arkansas
6.	Minnesota	Nicole Ohide, C	Kansas State
7.	Minnesota	Vanessa Hayden, C	Florida
8.	Phoenix	Chandi Jones, G/F	Houston
9.	Indiana	Ebony Hoffman, C	USC
10.	Sacramento	Rebekkah Brunson, F	Georgetown
11.	Detroit	Iciss Tillis, C/F	Duke
12.	Los Angeles	Christi Thomas, F	Georgia
13.	Detroit	Shereka Wright, F	Purdue

KEY G=guard; F=forward; C=center

Legends

Teresa Edwards, guard, b. July 19, 1964, Cairo, Georgia. Edwards is the only U.S. basketball player to compete in the Summer Olympics five times. From 1981 through 2000, the three-time USA Basketball Female Athlete of the Year won 14 gold medals (including four in Olympic competition), three bronze medals, and one silver medal with 19 different U.S. teams. Edwards spent seven years playing pro hoops overseas before competing in the American Basketball League from 1996 through 1998. (That pro league folded in 1998.) In 2003, she joined the Minnesota Lynx as the WNBA's oldest rookie (38).

Teresa Edwards has won 14 gold medals with 19 different U.S. national teams since 1981.

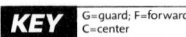

Carol Blazejowski, forward, b. September 29, 1956, Elizabeth, New Jersey. As a senior at Montclair State, Blazejowski won the first Wade Trophy as the Women's Basketball Player of the Year, in 1977-78. That same season, she set the NCAA women's single-season record for points per game (38.6). In 1980-81, "Blaze" was named MVP of the Women's Basketball League. That pro league folded in 1981. She was inducted into the Basketball Hall of Fame in 1994. Today, Blazejowski is the senior vice president and general manager of the New York Liberty.

Ann Meyers, guard, b. March 26, 1955, San Diego, California. At UCLA, Meyers was the first player to earn Kodak All-America honors four years in a row (1974-78). In 1978, she won the Broderick Cup as the nation's outstanding female player and led UCLA to the national title of the Association of Intercollegiate Athletics for Women (AIAW). (This was before the NCAA was involved in women's sports.) Meyers won a silver medal in 1976 with the first U.S. Women's Olympic Basketball Team. In 1979, she became the first and only woman to sign a contract with an NBA team, the Indiana Pacers. (She didn't make the team.) Meyers was inducted into the Basketball Hall of Fame in 1993.

Fast Fact: Center Ruth Riley is the only woman named Most Outstanding Player at the NCAA Women's Division I Final Four (2001, with Notre Dame) and MVP at the WNBA Finals (2003, with the Detroit Shock).

2003-04 TIME LINE

May 22, 2003: The WNBA approves the use of instant replay to review last-second plays at the end of each half and overtime period.

June 7, 2003: Forward-center Lauren Jackson of the Seattle Storm becomes the youngest WNBA player (age 22) to reach 1,000 career points.

July 12, 2003: The Western Conference beats the Eastern Conference, 84–75, to remain undefeated in the All-Star Game (5–0). Guard Nikki Teasley of the Los Angeles Sparks is named the game's MVP. She has 10 points, 6 assists, 6 rebounds, and 5 steals.

September 6, 2003: The Detroit Shock win their first league championship by upsetting the Los Angeles Sparks in Game 3 of the WNBA Finals. Shock center Ruth Riley is named the Finals MVP. The game sets a league attendance record (22,076).

October 19, 2003: The WNBA Select Team, featuring 10 of the league's youngest and brightest stars, finishes second in the FIBA Women's World Cup. The WNBA squad is defeated by Volgaburmash-Samara of Russia, 72–68.

April 17, 2004: The Phoenix Mercury chooses guard Diana Taurasi of Connecticut with the first pick in the WNBA Draft.

May 20, 2004: The WNBA tips off its eighth regular season with six teams in action.

Did You Know?

The Detroit Shock went from having the WNBA's worst record (9–23) in 2002 to having its best record (25–9) and winning the league championship in 2003.

World Championship All-time Results

YEAR	WINNER	RUNNER-UP	SCORE	SITE
2002	United States	Russia	79–74	China
1998	United States	Russia	71–65	Germany
1994	Brazil	China	96–87	Australia
1990	United States	Yugoslavia	88–78	Malaysia
1986	United States	Soviet Union	108–88	Soviet Union
1983	Soviet Union	United States	84–82	Brazil
1979	United States	South Korea	77–61	South Korea
1975	Soviet Union	Japan	106–75	Colombia
1971	Soviet Union	Czechoslovakia	88–69	Brazil
1967	Soviet Union	South Korea	83–50	Czechoslovakia
1964	Soviet Union	Czechoslovakia	70–35	Peru
1959*	Soviet Union	Bulgaria	51–38	Soviet Union
1957	United States	Soviet Union	51–48	Brazil
1953	United States	Chile	49–36	Chile

*The U.S. did not compete in 1959 because the worlds were held in Moscow, Soviet Union.

BASKETBALL MEN'S COLLEGE

Emeka Okafor (number 50) powered UConn past Georgia Tech, 82–73, in the 2004 NCAA championship game.

The UConn Huskies finished the 2003-04 season exactly where they started: Number 1 in the country. The team was ranked first in the pre-season in November and won the national championship in April. The last men's team to start the season ranked Number 1 and win the national championship was the Kentucky Wildcats, in 1995-96.

The Huskies also had the nation's top big man, junior center Emeka Okafor, who averaged 17.5 points, 11.5 rebounds, and 4.1 blocks per game for the season. He shared National Player of the Year honors with senior point guard Jameer Nelson of Saint Joseph's. Nelson led the Hawks to the first undefeated regular season in the men's game since 1990-91. Stanford lost its regular-season finale at Washington and finished 26–1.

UConn, Saint Joseph's, Stanford, Florida, Kansas, and Duke each held the AP's Number 1 ranking during the season, tying the record for most teams to hold the spot in a season. Kentucky was named the top seed in the NCAA tournament, but the Wildcats lost to Alabama-Birmingham (UAB) in the second round.

In the end, it was the heavyweights of college hoops who reached the Final Four. Duke, the only top seed still in the running, joined Big East tourney champ UConn, Big 12 tourney champ Oklahoma State, and ACC power Georgia Tech.

Okafor's 24 points and 15 rebounds in the national championship game helped push the Huskies past Tech with an 82–73 victory. It was the second time in five seasons the Huskies had won the national title.

Did You Know?

Dean Smith set the Division I record for most wins (879) by a head coach in his 36 seasons (1961-62 through 1996-97) at North Carolina.

Fast Fact: Four players have won the Division I national championship and been the Number 1 pick in the NBA Draft in the same year: Danny Manning (Kansas, 1988), James Worthy (North Carolina, 1982), Earvin "Magic" Johnson (Michigan State, 1979), and Lew Alcindor (UCLA, 1969).

NCAA Men's Division I Championship Box Score

CONNECTICUT HUSKIES 82

Player	POS	MIN	FG M-A	3-PT M-A	FT M-A	PF	PTS
Josh Boone	F	29	4-6	0-0	1-4	2	9
Rashad Anderson	G	31	5-10	2-7	6-8	1	18
Emeka Okafor	C	38	10-17	0-0	4-8	3	24
Ben Gordon	G	30	5-17	3-8	8-9	4	21
Taliek Brown	G	37	2-6	0-0	5-8	3	9
Charlie Villanueva		7	0-0	0-0	0-0	1	0
Hilton Armstrong		7	0-1	0-0	1-2	1	1
Shamon Tooles		2	0-0	0-0	0-0	0	0
Denham Brown		19	0-4	0-2	0-0	3	0
Totals			**26-61** (42.6%)	**5-17** (29.4%)	**25-39** (64.1%)	**18**	**82**

GEORGIA TECH YELLOW JACKETS 73

Player	POS	MIN	FG M-A	3-PT M-A	FT M-A	PF	PTS
Marvin Lewis	G	23	3-9	0-5	0-0	3	6
Anthony McHenry	G	20	1-3	1-1	0-0	4	3
Luke Schenscher	C	28	4-7	0-0	1-2	2	9
Barry (B.J.) Elder	G	28	4-15	3-8	3-4	4	14
Jarrett Jack	G	26	1-8	0-1	5-6	3	7
Isma'il Muhammad		16	5-12	0-0	0-0	3	10
Will Bynum		23	6-11	3-6	2-6	4	17
Robert Brooks		1	0-0	0-0	0-0	0	0
Clarence Moore		24	3-5	0-1	1-3	2	7
Theodis Tarver		11	0-1	0-0	0-0	1	0
Totals			**27-71** (38%)	**7-22** (31.8%)	**12-21** (57.1%)	**26**	**73**

KEY POS=position; MIN=minutes played; FG M-A=field goals made-attempted; 3-PT M-A=3-point field goals made-attempted; FT M-A=free throws made-attempted; PF=personal fouls; PTS=points; F=forward; G=guard; C=center

B.J. Elder led Georgia Tech in scoring in 2003-04 (14.9 points per game).

DOUG PENSINGER/GETTY IMAGES

USA TODAY/ESPN Top 25 Final Poll

Rank	School	Final Record	Points
1	Connecticut	31-6	775
2	Duke	31-5	722
3	Georgia Tech	27-9	721
4	Oklahoma State	31-3	688
5	Saint Joseph's	30-2	644
6	Stanford	30-2	553
7	Pittsburgh	31-5	544
8	Kentucky	27-5	522
9	Kansas	24-9	465
10	Texas	25-8	437
11	Illinois	26-7	419
12	Gonzaga	28-3	415
13	Mississippi State	26-4	373
14	Xavier	26-11	361
15	Wake Forest	21-10	357
16	Wisconsin	25-7	334
17	Alabama	20-13	248
18	Cincinnati	25-7	239
19	Syracuse	23-8	218
20	North Carolina St.	21-10	157
21	Nevada	25-9	156
22	North Carolina	19-11	135
23	Alabama-Birmingham	22-10	124
24	Maryland	20-12	119
25	Vanderbilt	23-10	102

Trivia Challenge

Two Big East schools won the national championship the past two seasons: Syracuse (2002-03) and Connecticut (2003-04). When was the last time the Big East won consecutive national championships?

In 1983-84 (Georgetown) and 1984-85 (Villanova)

NCAA Men's Division I Individual Leaders

Scoring

Player	Class	GP	FG	3FG	FT	PTS	AVG
Keydren Clark, St. Peter's	So.	29	233	112	197	775	26.7
Kevin Martin, Western Carolina	Jr.	27	208	51	206	673	24.9
David Hawkins, Temple	Sr.	29	224	84	177	709	24.4
Taylor Coppenrath, Vermont	Jr.	24	203	14	159	579	24.1
Luis Flores, Manhattan	Sr.	31	234	68	208	744	24.0
Michael Watson, Missouri-Kansas City	Sr.	29	225	96	134	680	23.4
Mike Helms, Oakland	Sr.	30	224	79	168	695	23.2
Odell Bradley, IUPUI	Sr.	29	235	31	170	671	23.1
Ike Diogu, Arizona State	So.	27	179	14	243	615	22.8
Derrick Tarver, Akron	Sr.	27	196	47	173	612	22.7

KEY GP=games played; FG=field goals; 3FG=3-point field goals; FT=free throws; PTS=points; AVG=average; So.=sophomore; Jr.=junior; Sr.=senior

2004 NCAA Division I Men's Basketball Tournament

ST. LOUIS

FIRST ROUND

Kentucky (96–76)
Florida A&M

Washington
Alabama-Birmingham (102–100)

Providence
Pacific (66–58)

Kansas (77–53)
Illinois-Chicago

Boston College (58–51)
Utah

Georgia Tech (65–60)
Northern Iowa

Michigan State
Nevada (72–66)

Gonzaga (76–49)
Valparaiso

SECOND ROUND

Kentucky
UAB (76–75)

Pacific
Kansas (78–63)

Boston College
Georgia Tech (57–54)

Nevada (91–72)
Gonzaga

REGIONALS

UAB
Kansas (100–74)

Georgia Tech (72–67)
Nevada

Kansas
Georgia Tech (79–71 OT)

EAST RUTHERFORD

FIRST ROUND

St. Joseph's (82–63)
Liberty

Texas Tech (76–73)
Charlotte

Florida
Manhattan (75–60)

Wake Forest (79–78)
Virginia Commonwealth

Wisconsin (76–64)
Richmond

Pittsburgh (53–44)
Central Florida

Memphis (59–43)
South Carolina

Oklahoma State (75–56)
Eastern Washington

SECOND ROUND

St. Joseph's (70–65)
Texas Tech

Manhattan
Wake Forest (84–80)

Wisconsin
Pittsburgh (59–55)

Memphis
Oklahoma State (70–53)

REGIONALS

St. Joseph's (84–80)
Wake Forest

Pittsburgh
Oklahoma State (63–51)

St. Joseph's
Oklahoma State (64–62)

FINAL FOUR

Georgia Tech (67–65)
Oklahoma State

Duke
UConn (79–78)

NATIONAL CHAMPIONSHIP
Connecticut (82–73)
Georgia Tech

ATLANTA

FIRST ROUND

Duke (96–61)
Alabama State

Seton Hall (80–76)
Arizona

Illinois (72–53)
Murray State

Cincinnati (80–77)
East Tennessee State

North Carolina (63–52)
Air Force

Texas (66–49)
Princeton

Xavier (80–70)
Louisville

Mississippi State (85–52)
Monmouth

SECOND ROUND

Duke (90–62)
Seton Hall

Illinois (92–68)
Cincinnati

North Carolina
Texas (78–75)

Xavier (89–74)
Mississippi State

REGIONALS

Duke (72–62)
Illinois

Texas
Xavier (79–71)

Duke (66–63)
Xavier

PHOENIX

FIRST ROUND

Stanford (71–45)
Texas-San Antonio

Alabama (65–64)
Southern Illinois

Syracuse (80–75)
Brigham Young

Maryland (86–83)
Texas-El Paso

Vanderbilt (71–58)
Western Michigan

North Carolina State (61–52)
Louisiana-Lafayette

DePaul (76–69 2OT)
Dayton

UConn (70–53)
Vermont

SECOND ROUND

Stanford
Alabama (70–67)

Syracuse (72–70)
Maryland

Vanderbilt (75–73)
North Carolina State

DePaul
UConn (72–55)

REGIONALS

Alabama (80–71)
Syracuse

Vanderbilt
UConn (73–53)

Alabama
UConn (87–71)

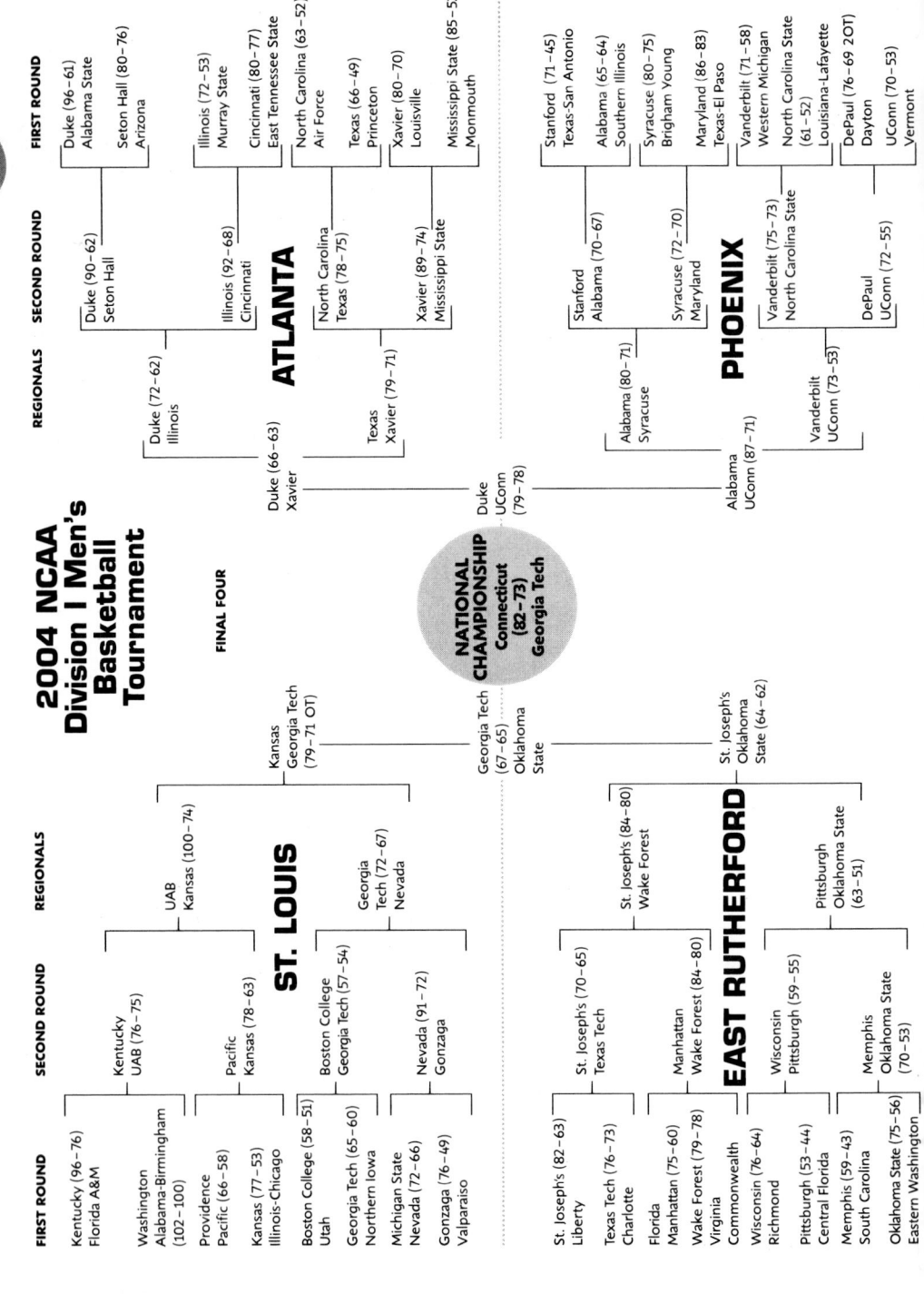

Being 'Melo

Guard LeBron James of the Cleveland Cavaliers got most of the rookie hype entering the 2003-04 NBA season. But forward Carmelo Anthony of the Denver Nuggets proved he deserved the same level of acclaim as "King James." 'Melo had 19.4 points per game and had led the Nuggets to 31 wins by the All-Star break. Denver had only 17 wins for the entire 2002-03 season. Anthony was also named the Western Conference Rookie of the Month in each of the season's first three months.

Taking It to the Street

Skateboarder Ryan Sheckler won the Slam City Jam, the first stop of the Vans Triple Crown tour, in May 2003. He was just 13, the youngest skater to win a pro contest. Sheckler continued to roll in 2003, winning the Park event at the Summer X Games and the Street event at the Gravity Games.

MATT A. BROWN/NEWSPORT

SIMON BRUTY/SPORTS ILLUSTRATED

Mighty Mia

The U.S. team finished a disappointing third in the Women's World Cup in 2003, but star forward Mia Hamm showed why she is one of the greatest women's players in the world. She had five assists (second-most in the tournament) and two goals in five games and was named to the World Cup All-Star team. The two-time FIFA Player of the Year (2001 and 2002) was a runner-up in 2003.

Piping Hot

At just 16 years old, Hannah Teter rose to the top of women's snowboarding in 2003-04. She placed first in Superpipe and second in Slopestyle at the first stop of the Vans Triple Crown tour. She also won a gold medal in Superpipe at the Winter X Games in 2004.

TOM ZIKAS

Panther on the Prowl

The weekly circus catches of University of Pittsburgh wide receiver Larry Fitzgerald made almost every highlight show in 2003. The sophomore set the NCAA record for consecutive games with a touchdown reception (18), tied the single-season record for consecutive games with a TD catch (12), and finished second in the Heisman Trophy voting. He also led Division I-A in receiving yards (1,672) and TD catches (22).

ICON SMI

Duchess of Hoops

Alana Beard is one of the Top 10 female athletes in ACC history. The 5' 11" senior guard/forward is the only female basketball player whose jersey number has been retired at Duke, where she owns the record for career points. Beard was the consensus National Freshman of the Year in 2000-01 and the National Player of the Year in 2002-03.

Icy Hot

It took less than three seasons for left wing Ilya Kovalchuk of the Atlanta Thrashers to establish himself as one of the NHL's elite players. Halfway through the 2003-04 season, he was fourth in the league in scoring (57 points). He was also named a starter for the Eastern Conference All-Star team in 2004. It was his first All-Star Game appearance.

JAMIE SABAU

ALEX LIVESEY/GETTY IMAGES

Roddick on a Roll

Andy Roddick of the United States won six championships in 2003, including the U.S. Open, his first career Grand Slam. Known for blistering serves that have reached 150 miles per hour, Roddick became the youngest U.S. player (21 years, 2 months) to finish Number 1 in the year-end ATP ranking.

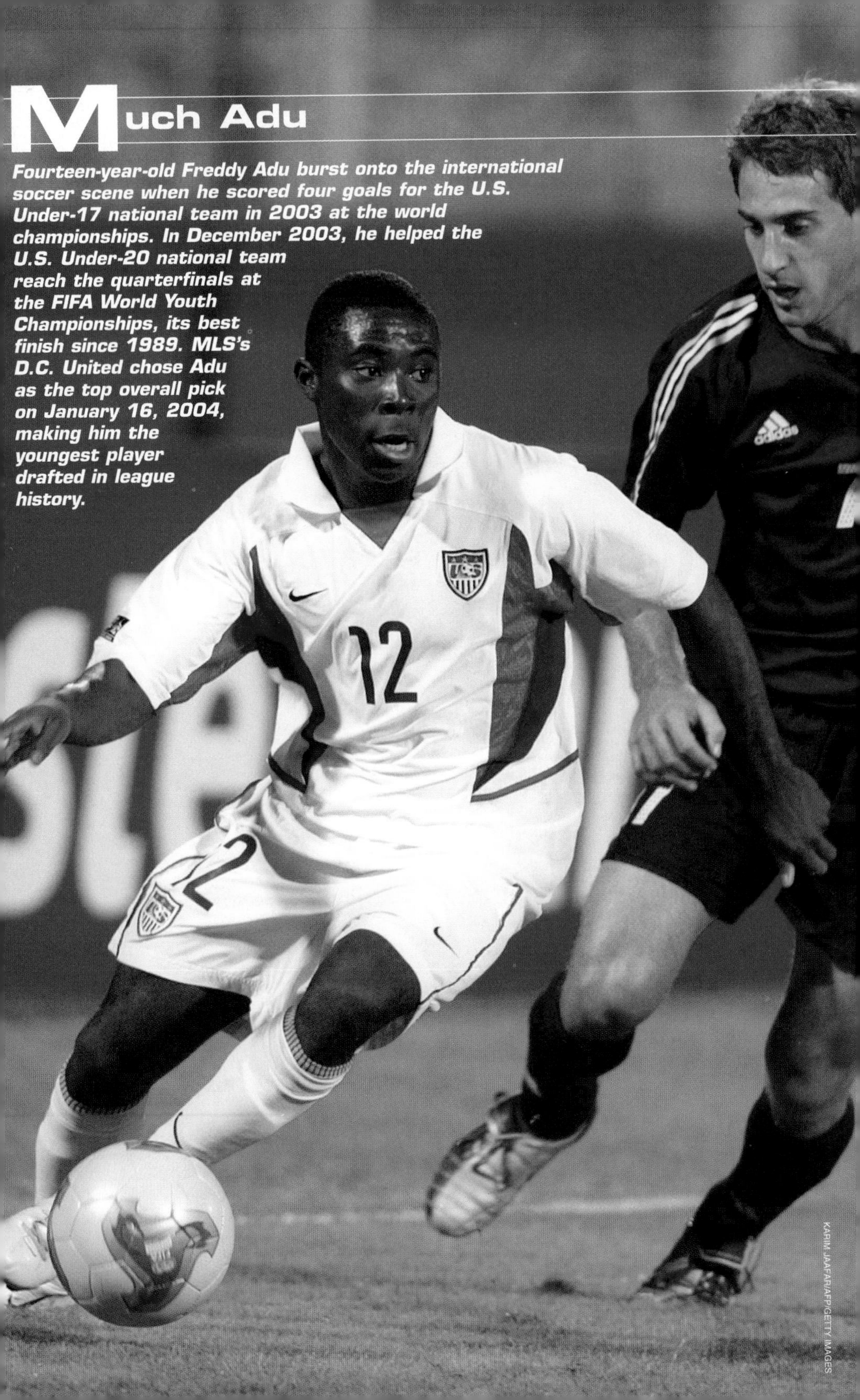

Much Adu

Fourteen-year-old Freddy Adu burst onto the international soccer scene when he scored four goals for the U.S. Under-17 national team in 2003 at the world championships. In December 2003, he helped the U.S. Under-20 national team reach the quarterfinals at the FIFA World Youth Championships, its best finish since 1989. MLS's D.C. United chose Adu as the top overall pick on January 16, 2004, making him the youngest player drafted in league history.

KARIM JAAFAR/AFP/GETTY IMAGES

CHUCK SOLOMON/SPORTS ILLUSTRATED

Man, She's Good!

On January 15, 2004, Michelle Wie became the youngest female golfer (age 14) to play in a PGA Tour (men's) event, the Sony Open. She missed the cut by one stroke, but "The Big Wiesy" impressed opponents with her powerful drives and accurate putts. In 2003, the 6-foot teenager won the U.S. Women's Amateur Public Links Championship. She was 13, the youngest winner in the event's 27-year history.

AL BELLO/GETTY IMAGES

Big East Beast

Forward/center Emeka Okafor led the Connecticut Huskies to the NCAA championship in 2003-04. He had 24 points and 15 rebounds in UConn's 82–73 victory over Georgia Tech in the title game and was named the Final Four's Most Outstanding Player. The victory made UConn the first team since the Kentucky Wildcats (1995-96) to win the title after being ranked Number 1 in the pre-season.

Riding the Wave

Andy Irons won the Association of Surfing Professionals world championship in 2003 for the second-straight season. Heading into the tour's last event, the Xbox Gerry Lopez Pipeline Masters, he was neck-and-neck in the standings with six-time world champion Kelly Slater. Irons held Slater off, despite breaking two boards during the competition. For the season, Irons won five of 12 events, topping his four first-place finishes of 2002.

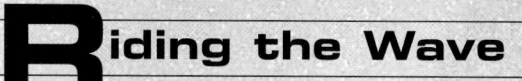

Ford Tough

Forward Cheryl Ford of the Detroit Shock was named the WNBA Rookie of the Year in 2003. She led all rookies in rebounds (10.4 per game), was tied for first among rookies in scoring (10.8), and helped the Shock earn the league's best record (25–9) and the team's first WNBA championship. Ford's father is forward Karl Malone of the Los Angeles Lakers.

Big Chief

All-Pro running back Priest Holmes of the Kansas City Chiefs set the NFL single-season records for rushing touchdowns and total touchdowns (27) in 2003. He helped the Chiefs blaze to a 9–0 start and finish the season with a 13–3 record. Holmes had at least two touchdowns in 10 games and failed to score in only three games. He was ranked fifth in the AFC in rushing yards (1,420).

The Last Champion

Matt Kenseth was the Winston Cup champion in 2003, despite earning only one victory. Consistency was his key to the title. He led the points standings for 33 straight weeks, led the series in Top 10 finishes (25), and was tied for seventh in Top 5 finishes (11). Kenseth was the last driver to be called the "Winston Cup" champion. The tour's name was changed to the Nextel Cup Series for the 2004 season.

DARRYL GRAHAM/AP; WORTH CANOY/ICON SMI (INSET)

Phenomenal Phelps

At the FINA World Championships, in Barcelona, Spain, in 2003, Michael Phelps of the U.S. became the first swimmer to break five world records in one meet. The 18-year-old set the record in the 100-meter butterfly, 200-meter fly, 200-meter individual medley (he broke the record in the semi-finals and again in the finals), and the 400-meter IM.

Wild Card

Leftfielder Albert Pujols of the St. Louis Cardinals won the National League batting championship in 2003 (.359 average). The best young slugger in baseball also led the N.L. in hits (212), doubles (51), and runs (137). He's the first major league player to hit .300, with at least 30 home runs, 100 runs scored, and 100 RBIs in each of his first three seasons.

NCAA Men's Division I Individual Leaders (cont.)

Field-Goal Percentage

Player	Class	GP	FGM	FGA	PCT
Nigel Dixon, Western Kentucky	Sr.	28	179	264	67.8
Sean Finn, Dayton	Sr.	33	175	264	66.3
Adam Mark, Belmont	Sr.	30	233	352	66.2
David Harrison, Colorado	Jr.	29	186	295	63.1
Cuthbert Victor, Murray State	Sr.	34	190	302	62.9
Jon Bentley, Eastern Kentucky	Sr.	29	154	245	62.9
Michael Harris, Rice	Jr.	33	217	360	60.3
Dominick Martin, Yale	Jr.	27	138	229	60.3
Emeka Okafor, UConn	Jr.	36	261	436	59.9
Jai Lewis, George Mason	So.	33	187	313	59.7

Note: Minimum five field goals made per game.

Free-Throw Percentage

Player	Class	GP	FTM	FTA	PCT
Blake Ahearn, Southwest Missouri State	Fr.	33	117	120	97.5
J.J. Redick, Duke	So.	37	143	150	95.3
Jake Sullivan, Iowa State	Sr.	33	83	89	93.3
Chris Hernandez, Stanford	So.	30	96	105	91.4
Steve Drabyn, Belmont	Sr.	30	96	105	91.4
Scooter McFadgon, Tennessee	Jr.	28	134	147	91.2
Terry Williams, Georgia Southern	Jr.	29	81	90	90.0
Delonte West, St. Joseph's	Jr.	32	124	139	89.2
Antoine Jordan, Siena	So.	25	63	71	88.7
Leon Pattman, Dartmouth	Fr.	26	70	79	88.6

Note: Minimum 2.5 free throws made per game.

J.J. Redick, Duke

Rebounds

Player	Class	GP	REB	AVG
Paul Millsap, Louisiana Tech	Fr.	30	374	12.5
Jaime Lloreda, LSU	Sr.	22	256	11.6
Emeka Okafor, UConn	Jr.	36	415	11.5
Nate Lofton, Southeastern Louisiana	Jr.	29	315	10.9
Nigel Wyatte, Wagner	Sr.	28	292	10.4
Charles Gaines, Southern Mississippi	Sr.	28	290	10.4
Nigel Dixon, Western Kentucky	Sr.	28	287	10.3
Cuthbert Victor, Murray State	Sr.	34	347	10.2
Odartey Blankson, UNLV	Jr.	31	315	10.2

Assists

Player	Class	GP	A	APG
Greg Davis, Troy State	Sr.	31	256	8.3
Martell Bailey, Illinois-Chicago	Sr.	32	250	7.8
Aaron Miles, Kansas	Jr.	33	242	7.3
Andres Rodriguez, American	Sr.	31	225	7.3
Raymond Felton, North Carolina	So.	30	212	7.1

3-Point Field-Goal Percentage

Player	Class	GP	3FGM	3FGA	PCT
Brad Lechtenberg, San Diego	Sr.	23	71	139	51.1
James Odoms, Mercer	Jr.	23	59	121	48.8
Tyson Dorsey, Samford	Sr.	28	74	152	48.7
Antonio Burks, Stephen F. Austin	Sr.	30	78	164	47.6
Trey Guidry, Illinois State	Jr.	29	86	187	46.0

Note: Minimum 2.5 three-point field goals made per game.

KEY GP=games played; FGM=field goals made; FGA=field goals attempted; PCT=percentage; FTM=free throws made; FTA=free throws attempted; REB=rebounds; AVG=average; A=assists; APG=assists per game; 3FGM=3-point field goals made; 3FGA=3-point field goals attempted

NCAA Men's Division I Individual Leaders (cont.)

Steals

Player	Class	GP	STL	SPG
Marques Green, St. Bonaventure	Sr.	27	107	4.0
Obie Trotter, Alabama A&M	So.	29	88	3.0
Chakowby Hicks, Norfolk State	Jr.	29	86	3.0
Zakee Wadood, East Tennessee State	Sr.	33	92	2.8
Jameer Nelson, St. Joseph's	Sr.	32	89	2.8
Louis Ford, Howard	So.	28	77	2.8
Jamon Gordon, Virginia Tech	Fr.	24	66	2.8

Marques Green, St. Bonaventure

Blocks

Player	Class	GP	BLK	BPG
Emeka Okafor, UConn	Jr.	36	147	4.1
Anwar Ferguson, Houston	Sr.	27	111	4.1
D'or Fischer, West Virginia	Jr.	31	124	4.0
Gerrick Morris, South Florida	Sr.	27	108	4.0
Nick Billings, Binghamton	Jr.	30	105	3.5

KEY GP=games played; STL=steals; SPG=steals per game; BLK=blocks; BPG=blocks per game

2003-04 TIME LINE

April 14, 2003: One week after coaching Kansas in the national championship game (an 81–78 loss to Syracuse), Roy Williams leaves the Jayhawks to become the head coach at his alma mater, North Carolina.

November 13, 2003: In the season's first game, Number 20 Wake Forest defeats unranked Memphis, 85–76, in the Coaches Versus Cancer Classic at Madison Square Garden, in New York.

January 29, 2004: Loyola's 63–57 win over Marist ends the school's losing streak at 31 games, two short of the NCAA Division I record. It is the Greyhounds' only win of the season.

February 8, 2004: In the regular season's most exciting finish, Stanford forward Nick Robinson hits a 35-foot shot at the buzzer to cap a wild comeback over Arizona. The Cardinal's 80–77 victory keeps the team undefeated at 20–0.

March 2, 2004: Led by co-National Player of the Year Jameer Nelson, St. Joseph's defeats St. Bonaventure, 82–50, to finish the regular season 27–0. St. Joseph's, a small school in Philadelphia, Pennsylvania, becomes the first team with a perfect regular season since 1990-91, when the Runnin' Rebels of Nevada-Las Vegas went 27–0.

March 28, 2004: Georgia Tech earns its first Final Four appearance since 1990 with a 79–71 win over Kansas. The Yellow Jackets join Duke, Oklahoma State, and UConn in the Final Four.

April 1, 2004: Michigan defeats Rutgers, 62–55, to win the National Invitation Tournament (NIT).

April 3, 2004: In the closest Final Four semi-final games since 1977, UConn rallies for a 79–78 win over Duke, and Georgia Tech defeats Oklahoma State, 67–65.

April 5, 2004: Led by Emeka Okafor, UConn dismantles Georgia Tech, 82–73, in the national championship game. It is the Huskies' second title in five years. Okafor is named the Final Four's Most Outstanding Player.

NCAA Men's Division I Championship Results

Year	Winner	Score	Runner-up	Third Place	Fourth Place	Winning Coach
2004	UConn	82–73	Georgia Tech	*Duke	*Oklahoma State	Jim Calhoun
2003	Syracuse	81–78	Kansas	*Texas	*Marquette	Jim Boeheim
2002	Maryland	64–52	Indiana	*Kansas	*Oklahoma	Gary Williams
2001	Duke	82–72	Arizona	*Maryland	*Michigan St.	Mike Krzyzewski
2000	Michigan St.	89–76	Florida	*Wisconsin	*North Carolina	Tom Izzo
1999	UConn	77–74	Duke	*Michigan St.	*Ohio St.	Jim Calhoun
1998	Kentucky	78–69	Utah	*Stanford	*North Carolina	Tubby Smith
1997	Arizona	84–79 (OT)	Kentucky	*Minnesota	*North Carolina	Lute Olson
1996	Kentucky	76–67	Syracuse	‡Vacated	Mississippi St.	Rick Pitino
1995	UCLA	89–78	Arkansas	*North Carolina	*Oklahoma St.	Jim Harrick
1994	Arkansas	76–72	Duke	*Arizona	*Florida	Nolan Richardson
1993	North Carolina	77–71	‡Vacated	*Kansas	*Kentucky	Dean Smith
1992	Duke	71–51	‡Vacated	*Cincinnati	*Indiana	Mike Krzyzewski
1991	Duke	72–65	Kansas	*UNLV	*North Carolina	Mike Krzyzewski
1990	UNLV	103–73	Duke	*Arkansas	*Georgia Tech	Jerry Tarkanian
1989	Michigan	80–79 (OT)	Seton Hall	*Duke	*Illinois	Steve Fisher
1988	Kansas	83–79	Oklahoma	*Arizona	*Duke	Larry Brown
1987	Indiana	74–73	Syracuse	*UNLV	*Providence	Bobby Knight
1986	Louisville	72–69	Duke	*Kansas	*Louisiana St.	Denny Crum
1985	Villanova	66–64	Georgetown	St. John's (N.Y.)	‡Vacated	Rollie Massimino
1984	Georgetown	84–75	Houston	*Kentucky	*Virginia	John Thompson
1983	North Carolina St.	54–52	Houston	*Georgia	*Louisville	Jim Valvano
1982	North Carolina	63–62	Georgetown	*Houston	*Louisville	Dean Smith
1981	Indiana	63–50	North Carolina	Virginia	Louisiana St.	Bobby Knight
1980	Louisville	59–54	‡Vacated	Purdue	Iowa	Denny Crum
1979	Michigan St.	75–64	Indiana St.	DePaul	Penn	Jud Heathcote
1978	Kentucky	94–88	Duke	Arkansas	Notre Dame	Joe Hall
1977	Marquette	67–59	North Carolina	UNLV	NC-Charlotte	Al McGuire
1976	Indiana	86–68	Michigan	UCLA	Rutgers	Bobby Knight
1975	UCLA	92–85	Kentucky	Louisville	Syracuse	John Wooden
1974	North Carolina St.	76–64	Marquette	UCLA	Kansas	Norm Sloan
1973	UCLA	87–66	Memphis St.	Indiana	Providence	John Wooden
1972	UCLA	81–76	Florida St.	North Carolina	Louisville	John Wooden
1971	UCLA	68–62	‡Vacated	‡Vacated	Kansas	John Wooden
1970	UCLA	80–69	Jacksonville	New Mexico St.	St. Bonaventure	John Wooden
1969	UCLA	92–72	Purdue	Drake	North Carolina	John Wooden
1968	UCLA	78–55	North Carolina	Ohio St.	Houston	John Wooden
1967	UCLA	79–64	Dayton	Houston	North Carolina	John Wooden
1966	Texas Western	72–65	Kentucky	Duke	Utah	Don Haskins
1965	UCLA	91–80	Michigan	Princeton	Wichita St.	John Wooden
1964	UCLA	98–83	Duke	Michigan	Kansas St.	John Wooden
1963	Loyola (Illinois)	60–58 (OT)	Cincinnati	Duke	Oregon St.	George Ireland
1962	Cincinnati	71–59	Ohio St.	Wake Forest	UCLA	Edwin Jucker
1961	Cincinnati	70–65 (OT)	Ohio St.	‡Vacated	Utah	Edwin Jucker
1960	Ohio St.	75–55	California	Cincinnati	NYU	Fred Taylor
1959	California	71–70	West Virginia	Cincinnati	Louisville	Pete Newell
1958	Kentucky	84–72	Seattle	Temple	Kansas St.	Adolph Rupp
1957	North Carolina	54–53 (3OT)	Kansas	San Francisco	Michigan St.	Frank McGuire
1956	San Francisco	83–71	Iowa	Temple	SMU	Phil Woolpert
1955	San Francisco	77–63	La Salle	Colorado	Iowa	Phil Woolpert
1954	La Salle	92–76	Bradley	Penn St.	USC	Kenneth Loeffler
1953	Indiana	69–68	Kansas	Washington	Louisiana St.	Branch McCracken
1952	Kansas	80–63	St. John's (N.Y.)	Illinois	Santa Clara	Forrest Allen
1951	Kentucky	68–58	Kansas St.	Illinois	Oklahoma St.	Adolph Rupp
1950	CCNY	71–68	Bradley	North Carolina St.	Baylor	Nat Holman
1949	Kentucky	46–36	Oklahoma St.	Illinois	Oregon St.	Adolph Rupp
1948	Kentucky	58–42	Baylor	Holy Cross	Kansas St.	Adolph Rupp
1947	Holy Cross	58–47	Oklahoma	Texas	CCNY	Alvin Julian
1946	Oklahoma A&M	43–40	North Carolina	Ohio St.	California	Hank Iba
1945	Oklahoma A&M	49–45	NYU	*Arkansas	*Ohio St.	Hank Iba
1944	Utah	42–40 (OT)	Dartmouth	*Iowa St.	*Ohio St.	Vadal Peterson
1943	Wyoming	46–34	Georgetown	*Texas	*DePaul	Everett Shelton
1942	Stanford	53–38	Dartmouth	*Colorado	*Kentucky	Everett Dean
1941	Wisconsin	39–34	Washington St.	*Pittsburgh	*Arkansas	Harold Foster
1940	Indiana	60–42	Kansas	*Duquesne	*USC	Branch McCracken
1939	Oregon	46–33	Ohio St.	*Oklahoma	*Villanova	Howard Hobson

* Tied for third place. ‡Student-athletes representing St. Joseph's (Pa.) in 1961, Villanova in 1971, Western Kentucky in 1971, UCLA in 1980, Memphis State in 1985, Michigan in 1992 and 1993, and Massachusetts in 1996 were declared ineligible subsequent to the tournament. Under NCAA rules, the teams' and ineligible student-athletes' records were deleted, and the teams' places in the standings were vacated.

Today's Stars

Charlie Villanueva will move into the UConn starting lineup in 2004-05.

JOHN W. McDONOUGH/SPORTS ILLUSTRATED

Charlie Villanueva, center, b. August 24, 1984, Queens, New York. Villanueva declared himself eligible for the 2003 NBA Draft, but changed his mind after a poor pre-draft showing and enrolled at UConn. As a freshman, he averaged 8.9 points, 5.3 rebounds, and 1.5 blocks in just 19 minutes per game and helped lead the Huskies to the national title. The 6' 10", 230-pounder could play inside or out and is Emeka Okafor's heir apparent in the middle. He'll move into the starting lineup in 2004-05, and the Huskies won't miss a step with him as their lead dog.

Wayne Simien, forward, b. March 9, 1983, Leavenworth, Kansas. The next in a line of great Kansas big men, Simien had 17.8 points and 9.3 rebounds per game in 2003-04 and led the Jayhawks to within one win of their third-straight Final Four berth. The 6' 9", 230-pound power forward earned third-team All-America and first-team All-Big 12 honors, after bouncing back from a shoulder injury that limited him to 16 games in 2002-03.

Chris Paul, guard, b. May 16, 1985, Winston-Salem, North Carolina. After his stellar freshman season at Wake Forest, Paul earned the nickname "the Mayor" because he grew up nearby and seemed to know everyone in town. He had 14.9 points and 5.9 assists per game, was named the ACC Rookie of the Year, and led the Demon Deacons to the Sweet 16 for the first time since 1996 with 25.5 points and 6.5 assists in two NCAA tournament wins.

NCAA Final Four Most Outstanding Players

Year	Winner, School
2004	Emeka Okafor, UConn
2003	Carmelo Anthony, Syracuse
2002	Juan Dixon, Maryland
2001	Shane Battier, Duke
2000	Mateen Cleaves, Michigan St.
1999	Richard Hamilton, UConn
1998	Jeff Sheppard, Kentucky
1997	Miles Simon, Arizona
1996	Tony Delk, Kentucky
1995	Ed O'Bannon, UCLA
1994	Corliss Williamson, Arkansas
1993	Donald Williams, North Carolina
1992	Bobby Hurley, Duke
1991	Christian Laettner, Duke
1990	Anderson Hunt, UNLV
1989	Glen Rice, Michigan
1988	Danny Manning, Kansas
1987	Keith Smart, Indiana
1986	Pervis Ellison, Louisville
1985	Ed Pinckney, Villanova
1984	Patrick Ewing, Georgetown
1983	* Akeem Olajuwon, Houston
1982	James Worthy, North Carolina
1981	Isiah Thomas, Indiana
1980	Darrell Griffith, Louisville
1979	Earvin Johnson, Michigan St.
1978	Jack Givens, Kentucky
1977	Butch Lee, Marquette
1976	Kent Benson, Indiana
1975	Richard Washington, UCLA
1974	David Thompson, North Carolina St.
1973	Bill Walton, UCLA
1972	Bill Walton, UCLA
1971	*† Howard Porter, Villanova
1970	Sidney Wicks, UCLA
1969	** Lew Alcindor, UCLA
1968	Lew Alcindor, UCLA
1967	Lew Alcindor, UCLA
1966	* Jerry Chambers, Utah
1965	* Bill Bradley, Princeton
1964	Walt Hazzard, UCLA
1963	Art Heyman, Duke
1962	Paul Hogue, Cincinnati
1961	* Jerry Lucas, Ohio St.
1960	Jerry Lucas, Ohio St.
1959	* Jerry West, West Virginia
1958	* Elgin Baylor, Seattle
1957	* Wilt Chamberlain, Kansas
1956	* Hal Lear, Temple
1955	Bill Russell, San Francisco
1954	Tom Gola, La Salle
1953	* B.H. Born, Kansas
1952	Clyde Lovellette, Kansas
1951	Bill Spivey, Kentucky
1950	Irwin Dambrot, CCNY
1949	Alex Groza, Kentucky
1948	Alex Groza, Kentucky
1947	George Kaftan, Holy Cross
1946	Bob Kurland, Oklahoma A&M
1945	Bob Kurland, Oklahoma A&M
1944	Arnie Ferrin, Utah
1943	Ken Sailors, Wyoming
1942	Howard Dallmar, Stanford
1941	John Kotz, Wisconsin
1940	Marv Huffman, Indiana
1939	* Jimmy Hull, Ohio St.

* Not a member of the championship-winning team.
† Record later vacated.
** Now known as Kareem Abdul-Jabbar.

National Invitation Tournament (NIT) Championship Results

Year	Winner	Score	Runner-up
2004	Michigan	62–55	Rutgers
2003	St. John's (N.Y.)	70–67	Georgetown
2002	Memphis	72–62	South Carolina
2001	Tulsa	79–60	Alabama
2000	Wake Forest	71–61	Notre Dame
1999	California	61–60	Clemson
1998	Minnesota	79–72	Penn St.
1997	Michigan	82–73	Florida St.
1996	Nebraska	60–56	St. Joseph's
1995	Virginia Tech	65–64 (OT)	Marquette
1994	Villanova	80–73	Vanderbilt
1993	Minnesota	62–61	Georgetown
1992	Virginia	81–76	Notre Dame
1991	Stanford	78–72	Oklahoma
1990	Vanderbilt	74–72	St. Louis
1989	St. John's (N.Y.)	73–65	St. Louis
1988	Connecticut	72–67	Ohio St.
1987	Southern Miss.	84–80	La Salle
1986	Ohio St.	73–63	Wyoming
1985	UCLA	65–62	Indiana
1984	Michigan	83–63	Notre Dame
1983	Fresno State	69–60	DePaul
1982	Bradley	67–58	Purdue
1981	Tulsa	86–84 (OT)	Syracuse
1980	Virginia	58–55	Minnesota
1979	Indiana	53–52	Purdue
1978	Texas	101–93	North Carolina St.
1977	St. Bonaventure	94–91	Houston
1976	Kentucky	71–67	North Carolina-Charlotte
1975	Princeton	80–69	Providence
1974	Purdue	87–81	Utah
1973	Virginia Tech	92–91 (OT)	Notre Dame
1972	Maryland	100–69	Niagara
1971	North Carolina	84–66	Georgia Tech
1970	Marquette	65–53	St. John's (N.Y.)
1969	Temple	89–76	Boston College
1968	Dayton	61–48	Kansas
1967	Southern Illinois	71–56	Marquette
1966	BYU	97–84	NYU
1965	St. John's (N.Y.)	55–51	Villanova
1964	Bradley	86–54	New Mexico
1963	Providence	81–66	Canisius
1962	Dayton	73–67	St. John's (N.Y.)
1961	Providence	62–59	St. Louis
1960	Bradley	88–72	Providence
1959	St. John's (N.Y.)	76–71 (OT)	Bradley
1958	Xavier	78–74 (OT)	Dayton
1957	Bradley	84–83	Memphis St.
1956	Louisville	93–80	Dayton
1955	Duquesne	70–58	Dayton
1954	Holy Cross	71–62	Duquesne
1953	Seton Hall	58–46	St. John's (N.Y.)
1952	La Salle	75–64	Dayton
1951	BYU	62–43	Dayton
1950	CCNY	69–61	Bradley
1949	San Francisco	48–47	Loyola (Illinois)
1948	St. Louis	65–52	NYU
1947	Utah	49–45	Kentucky
1946	Kentucky	46–45	Rhode Island
1945	DePaul	71–54	Bowling Green
1944	St. John's (N.Y.)	47–39	DePaul
1943	St. John's (N.Y.)	48–27	Toledo
1942	West Virginia	47–45	Western Kentucky
1941	Long Island Univ.	56–42	Ohio University
1940	Colorado	51–40	Duquesne
1939	Long Island Univ.	44–32	Loyola (Illinois)
1938	Temple	60–36	Colorado

Did You Know?

In 2004, UConn became the 12th school to win the NCAA championship at least twice.

Elvin Hayes, Houston

COURTESY OF UNIVERSITY OF HOUSTON SPORTS INFORMATION

NCAA Men's Division I Single-Season Leaders

Points

Player	Year	GP	FG	3FG	FT	PTS
Pete Maravich, LSU	1970	31	522	—	337	1,381
Elvin Hayes, Houston	1968	33	519	—	176	1,214
Frank Selvy, Furman	1954	29	427	—	355	1,209
Pete Maravich, LSU	1969	26	433	—	282	1,148
Pete Maravich, LSU	1968	26	432	—	274	1,138
Bo Kimble, Loyola Marymount	1990	32	404	92	231	1,131
Hersey Hawkins, Bradley	1988	31	377	87	284	1,125
Austin Carr, Notre Dame	1970	29	444	—	218	1,106
Austin Carr, Notre Dame	1971	29	430	—	241	1,101
Otis Birdsong, Houston	1977	36	452	—	186	1,090

Scoring Average

Player	Year	GP	FG	FT	PTS	AVG
Pete Maravich, LSU	1970	31	522	337	1,381	44.5
Pete Maravich, LSU	1969	26	433	282	1,148	44.2
Pete Maravich, LSU	1968	26	432	274	1,138	43.8
Frank Selvy, Furman	1954	29	427	355	1,209	41.7
Johnny Neumann, Mississippi	1971	23	366	191	923	40.1

KEY GP=games played; FG=field goals; 3FG=3-point field goals; FT=free throws; PTS=points; AVG=average

NCAA Men's Division I Single-Season Leaders (cont.)

Scoring Average (cont.)

Player	Year	GP	FG	FT	PTS	AVG
Freeman Williams, Portland St.	1977	26	417	176	1,010	38.8
Billy McGill, Utah	1962	26	394	221	1,009	38.8
Calvin Murphy, Niagara	1968	24	337	242	916	38.2
Austin Carr, Notre Dame	1970	29	444	218	1,106	38.1
Austin Carr, Notre Dame	1971	29	430	241	1,101	38.0

Rebound Average (before 1973)

Player	Year	GP	REB	AVG
Charlie Slack, Marshall	1955	21	538	25.6
Leroy Wright, Pacific	1959	26	652	25.1
Art Quimby, UConn	1955	25	611	24.4
Charlie Slack, Marshall	1956	22	520	23.6
Ed Conlin, Fordham	1953	26	612	23.5

Rebound Average (since 1973*)

Player	Year	GP	REB	AVG
Kermit Washington, American	1973	25	511	20.4
Marvin Barnes, Providence	1973	30	571	19.0
Marvin Barnes, Providence	1974	32	597	18.7
Pete Padgett, Nevada	1973	26	462	17.8
Jim Bradley, Northern Illinois	1973	24	426	17.8

*Freshmen became eligible for varsity play before the 1972-73 season.

Assists

Player	Year	GP	A
Mark Wade, UNLV	1987	38	406
Avery Johnson, Southern University	1988	30	399
Anthony Manuel, Bradley	1988	31	373
Avery Johnson, Southern University	1987	31	333
Mark Jackson, St. John's (N.Y.)	1986	32	328

Field-Goal Percentage

Player	Year	FGM	FGA	PCT
Steve Johnson, Oregon St.	1981	235	315	74.6
Dwayne Davis, Florida	1989	179	248	72.2
Keith Walker, Utica	1985	154	216	71.3
Steve Johnson, Oregon St.	1980	211	297	71.0
Adam Mark, Belmont	2002	150	212	70.8

Free-Throw Percentage

Player	Year	FTM	FTA	PCT
Blake Ahearn, Southwest Missouri State	2004	117	120	97.5
Craig Collins, Penn St.	1985	94	98	95.9
J.J. Redick, Duke	2004	143	150	95.3
Steve Drabyn, Belmont	2003	78	82	95.1
Rod Foster, UCLA	1982	95	100	95.0

3-Point Field-Goal Percentage

Player	Year	3FGM	3FGA	PCT
Glenn Tropf, Holy Cross	1988	52	82	63.4
Sean Wightman, Western Michigan	1992	48	76	63.2

KEY GP=games played; FG=field goals; FT=free throws; PTS=points; AVG=average; REB=rebounds; A=assists; FGM=field goals made; FGA=field goals attempted; PCT=percentage; FTM=free throws made; FTA=free throws attempted; 3FGM=3-point field goals made; 3FGA=3-point field goals attempted

Trivia Challenge

If Stanford hadn't lost its last 2003-04 regular-season game, the Cardinal would have joined St. Joseph's as an undefeated team. When was the last time two schools turned in perfect regular-season records?

Indiana State and Alcorn State were undefeated in 1978-79.

NCAA Men's Division I Single-Season Leaders (cont.)

3-Point Field-Goal Percentage (cont.)

Player	Year	3FGM	3FGA	PCT
Keith Jennings, East Tennessee St.	1991	84	142	59.2
Dave Calloway, Monmouth	1989	48	82	58.5
Steve Kerr, Arizona	1988	114	199	57.3

Steals

Player	Year	GP	STL
Desmond Cambridge, Alabama A&M	2002	29	160
Mookie Blaylock, Oklahoma	1988	39	150
Aldwin Ware, Florida A&M	1988	29	142
Darron Brittman, Chicago St.	1986	28	139
John Linehan, Providence	2002	31	139

David Robinson, Navy

MANNY MILLAN/SPORTS ILLUSTRATED

Blocks

Player	Year	GP	BLK
David Robinson, Navy	1986	35	207
Adonal Foyle, Colgate	1997	28	180
Keith Closs, Central Connecticut St.	1996	28	178
Shawn Bradley, BYU	1991	34	177
Wojciech Myrda, LA–Monroe	2002	32	172

KEY 3FGM=3-point field goals made; 3FGA=3-point field goals attempted; PCT=percentage; GP=games played; STL=steals; BLK=blocks

Fast Fact: UCLA played in the Final Four 14 times between 1961-62 and 1979-80. In the 24 seasons since 1980 the Bruins have appeared in the Final Four only once.

Legends

Michael Jordan averaged 17.7 points per game in three seasons at North Carolina.

HEINZ KLUETMEIER/SPORTS ILLUSTRATED

Michael Jordan, guard, b. February 17, 1963, Brooklyn, New York. North Carolina was where Jordan first displayed his dazzling dunks and wagging tongue. In three seasons in Chapel Hill, he was named ACC Rookie of the Year as a freshman, an All-America as a sophomore, and ACC Player of the Year and unanimous National Player of the Year as a junior. As a freshman in the 1981-82 NCAA championship game, Jordan nailed a 17-foot jump shot that gave the Tar Heels a 63–62 win over Georgetown.

Pete Maravich, guard, b. June 22, 1947, Aliquippa, Pennsylvania; d. January 5, 1988, Pasadena, California. As a kid, Maravich used to sleep with a basketball, and his skills were a dream to those who watched him play. In just three seasons at Louisiana State (freshmen were not eligible to play), he set the NCAA's scoring records: 3,667 total points, 44.2 points per game. Both records still stand. He was a three-time All-America and the 1969-70 National Player of the Year.

Lew Alcindor, center, b. April 16, 1947, New York, New York. Alcindor was the greatest college basketball player of all time. (He changed his name to Kareem Abdul-Jabbar in 1971.) He averaged 26.4 points and 15.5 rebounds in his three-season UCLA career (freshmen were not eligible to play) and led the school to an 88–2 record and the national championship three times (1966-67, 1967-68, 1968-69), winning the NCAA tournament's Most Outstanding Player honors each time. Alcindor was a three-time All-America and two-time National Player of the Year. He was so dominant that the college game outlawed the dunk in an effort to slow him down, but nothing — and no one — ever did.

BASKETBALL WOMEN'S COLLEGE

When the UConn Huskies women's team won its third consecutive national championship last April, a day after the men's team had claimed its own national title, the teams' hometown of Storrs, Connecticut, was proclaimed college basketball's capital. In truth, Storrs had long been the home of elite women's college hoops, and 2003-04 only confirmed the fact.

Led by senior guard Diana Taurasi, the reigning National Player of the Year, UConn came into 2003-04 with back-to-back national titles and was tabbed Number 1 in virtually every pre-season poll. The Huskies finished the regular season 25–4, but there were serious questions about their ability to three-peat. Their 69-game home winning streak ended in January when they blew a 14-point lead against Duke with less than four minutes to play, and they entered the NCAA Tournament with two losses in four games.

But despite its Number 2 seed in the East Regional, UConn used its home-court advantage to breeze to its NCAA-record fifth-straight Final Four, where it was joined by Tennessee, Minnesota, and LSU. The LSU Tigers earned their way to New Orleans without head coach Sue Gunter, who left the team in January because of a respiratory illness. Interim coach Pokey Chatman guided LSU to its first Final Four and a matchup with Tennessee, a perennial power and Southeastern Conference rival that was making its 15th Final Four appearance.

UConn senior Diana Taurasi won her third national championship in four seasons in 2003-04.

ELSA/GETTY IMAGES

The Lady Vols defeated the Tigers, 62–60, in their 2-point, down-to-the-wire win of the NCAA tournament. The Golden Gophers of Minnesota earned a berth in their first Final Four with an 82–76 win over Number 1-ranked Duke and National Player of the Year Alana Beard. But UConn ended the Gophers' tournament ride, 67–58.

In the championship game, UConn didn't give Tennessee the chance to duplicate its late-game magic. The Huskies sprinted to a 17-point first-half lead and never let the Lady Vols get closer than 2 points in the 70–61 win. The victory made UConn five for five in the NCAA title game. Four of the wins had come at Tennessee's expense.

Taurasi capped her four-year career — which included a 22–1 NCAA tournament record — by scoring 17 points and earning the Final Four's Most Outstanding Player award.

Trivia Challenge

In 2003-04, UConn became the first college to win the men's and women's Division I college hoops national championships in the same season. Which other schools have won both the men's title and women's title?

Stanford (men: 1941-42; women: 1989-90, 1991-92) and North Carolina (men: 1956-57, 1981-82, 1992-93; women: 1993-94)

NCAA Women's Division I Championship Box Score

UCONN HUSKIES 70

Player	MIN	FGM-A	FTM-A	OFF	REB	A	PF	PTS
Barbara Turner	33	4-12	3-6	1	9	4	2	12
Jessica Moore	30	6-9	2-2	6	9	1	3	14
Diana Taurasi	37	6-11	2-4	0	3	2	1	17
Maria Conlon	33	1-4	4-4	0	2	5	0	7
Ann Strother	37	5-8	3-3	0	2	2	1	14
Ashley Battle	15	1-4	0-0	0	1	0	1	3
Willnett Crockett	15	1-3	1-1	0	2	1	2	3
Totals		**24-51** (47.1%)	**15-20** (75%)	**7**	**28**	**15**	**10**	**70**

TENNESSEE VOLUNTEERS 61

Player	MIN	FGM-A	FTM-A	OFF	REB	A	PF	PTS
LaToya Davis	30	3-8	0-0	1	1	7	5	6
Shyra Ely	26	4-10	2-4	2	7	0	2	10
Ashley Robinson	39	6-10	1-4	4	7	1	1	13
Tasha Butts	32	1-10	6-6	3	6	2	2	8
Shanna Zolman	37	6-11	4-4	2	9	1	2	19
Sidney Spencer	14	0-1	0-0	0	1	0	4	0
Dominique Redding	3	0-1	0-0	0	0	1	0	0
Brittany Jackson	11	1-7	0-0	0	1	1	2	3
Tye'sha Fluker	8	1-3	0-0	1	1	0	0	2
Totals		**22-61** (36.1%)	**13-18** (72.2%)	**13**	**33**	**13**	**18**	**61**

KEY MIN=minutes played; FGM-A=field goals made-attempted; FTM-A=free throws made-attempted; OFF=offensive rebounds; REB=rebounds; A=assists; PF=personal fouls; PTS=points

Shyra Ely led Tennessee in scoring (14.5 points per game) in 2003-04.

WADE PAYNE/AP

Fast Fact: Forward Cindy Brown of Long Beach State set the women's Division I single-game scoring record (60 points), against San Jose State on February 16, 1987.

Did You Know?

Wofford, a small school in South Carolina, was the only Division I school in the country to go winless in 2003-04. The Lady Terriers finished 0–28.

USA TODAY/ESPN Top 25 Final Poll

Rank	Team	Record	Points
1.	UConn	30–4	1,000
2.	Tennessee	31–3	959
3.	LSU	27–8	895
4.	Minnesota	25–9	883
5.	Duke	30–4	787
6.	Penn State	28–6	769
7.	Stanford	27–7	759
8.	Georgia	25–10	678
9.	Purdue	29–4	644
10.	Texas	30–5	630
11.	Baylor	26–9	584
12.	Louisiana Tech	29–3	580
13.	Vanderbilt	26–8	521
14.	Boston College	27–7	464
15.	Kansas State	25–6	377
16.	Houston	28–4	342
17.	Texas Tech	25–8	314
18.	Oklahoma	24–9	281
19.	UC-Santa Barbara	27–7	266
20.	Notre Dame	21–11	173
21.	North Carolina	24–7	167
22.	TCU	25–7	157
23.	Auburn	22–9	138
24.	Colorado	22–8	119
25.	DePaul	23–7	100

2004 NCAA Division I Women's Basketball Tournament

EAST

FIRST ROUND

Penn State (79–42)
Hampton

Virginia Tech (89–76)
Iowa

Notre Dame (69–65 OT)
Southwest Missouri State

North Carolina
Middle Tennessee State (67–62)

Colorado
UC-Santa Barbara (76–49)

Houston (62–47)
Wisconsin-Green Bay

Auburn (79–59)
North Carolina State

UConn (91–55)
Pennsylvania

SECOND ROUND

Penn State (61–48)
Virginia Tech

Notre Dame (59–46)
Middle Tennessee State

UC-Santa Barbara (56–52)
Houston

Auburn
UConn (79–53)

REGIONALS

Penn State (55–49)
Notre Dame

UC-Santa Barbara
UConn (63–55)

Penn State
UConn (66–49)

MIDEAST

FIRST ROUND

Duke (103–51)
Northwestern State

Old Dominion
Marquette (67–64)

Louisiana Tech (81–77)
Montana

Texas Tech (60–50)
Maine

Ohio State (73–67)
West Virginia

Boston College (58–56)
Eastern Michigan

Minnesota (92–81)
UCLA

Kansas State (71–63)
Valparaiso

SECOND ROUND

Duke (76–67)
Marquette

Louisiana Tech (81–64)
Texas Tech

Ohio State
Boston College (63–48)

Minnesota (80–61)
Kansas State

REGIONALS

Duke (63–49)
Louisiana Tech

Boston College
Minnesota (76–63)

Duke
Minnesota (82–75)

FINAL FOUR

UConn (67–58)
Minnesota

Tennessee (52–50)
LSU

NATIONAL CHAMPIONSHIP
Connecticut (70–61)
Tennessee

MIDWEST

FIRST ROUND

Tennessee (77–54)
Colgate

George Washington
DePaul (83–46)

Florida (68–56)
New Mexico

Baylor (71–60)
Loyola Marymount

Stanford (68–44)
Missouri

Oklahoma (58–45)
Marist

Rutgers
Chattanooga (74–69)

Vanderbilt (76–45)
Lipscomb

SECOND ROUND

Tennessee (79–59)
DePaul

Florida
Baylor (91–76)

Stanford (68–43)
Oklahoma

Chattanooga
Vanderbilt (60–44)

REGIONALS

Tennessee (71–69)
Baylor

Stanford (57–55)
Vanderbilt

Tennessee (62–60)
Stanford

WEST

FIRST ROUND

Texas (92–57)
Southern

Michigan State (72–60)
Arizona

Miami (Florida)
Maryland (86–85)

LSU (83–66)
Austin Peay

TCU (70–57)
Temple

Georgia (78–53)
Liberty

Villanova (66–63)
Mississippi

Purdue (78–59)
St. Francis (Pennsylvania)

SECOND ROUND

Texas (80–61)
Michigan State

Maryland
LSU (76–61)

TCU
Georgia (85–71)

Villanova
Purdue (60–42)

REGIONALS

Texas
LSU (71–55)

Georgia (66–64)
Purdue

LSU (62–60)
Georgia

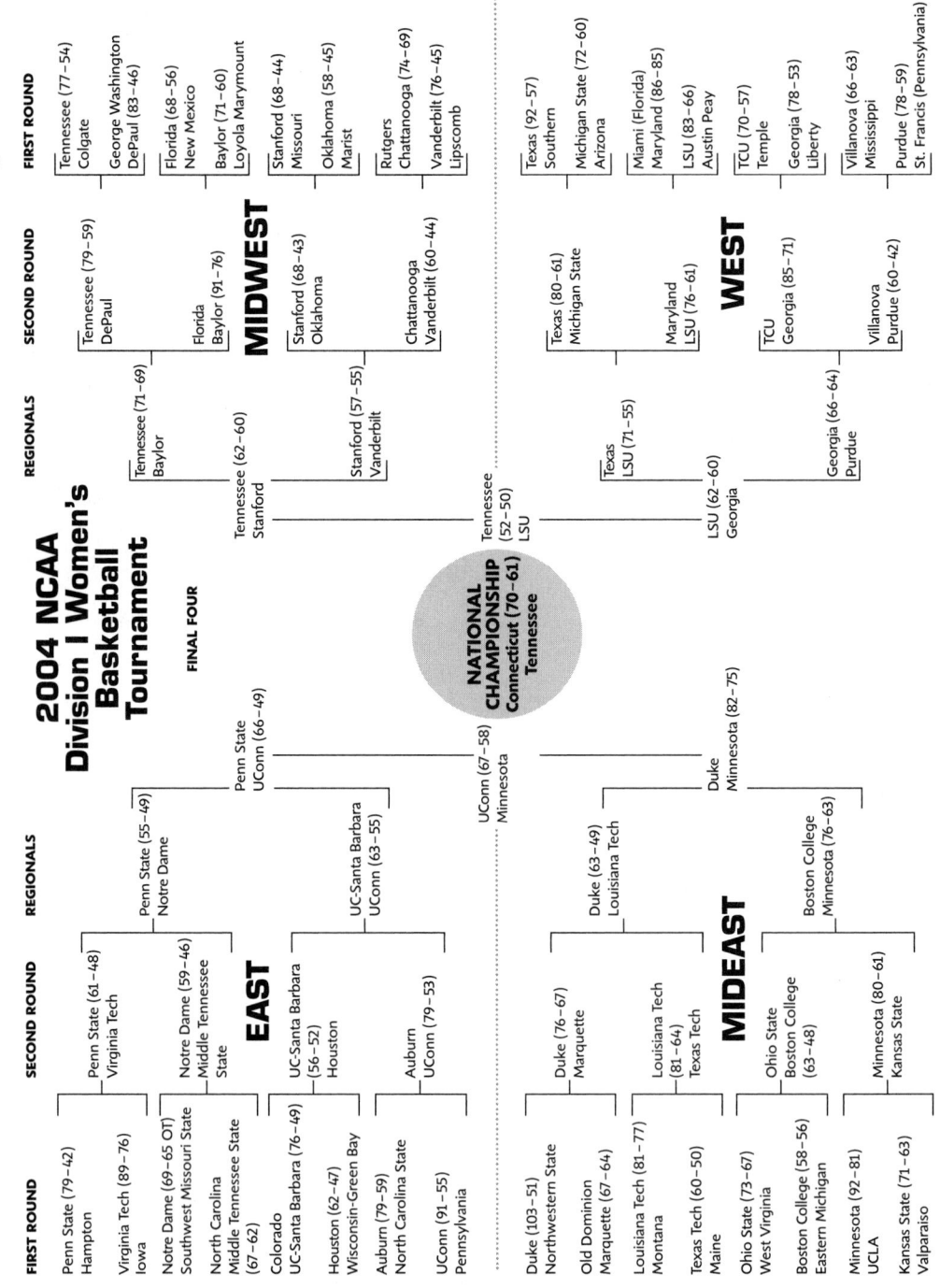

NCAA Women's Division I Individual Leaders

Scoring

Player	Class	GP	FG	3FG	FT	PTS	AVG
Emily Faurholt, Idaho	So.	29	261	43	172	737	25.4
Hana Peljito, Harvard	Sr.	27	246	37	112	641	23.7
Chandi Jones, Houston	Sr.	32	255	71	146	727	22.7
Cyndy Wilks, Virginia Commonwealth	Sr.	28	215	58	130	618	22.1
Shameka Christon, Arkansas	Sr.	28	219	47	126	611	21.8
Candace Futrell, Duquesne	Sr.	29	214	74	119	621	21.4
Giuliana Mendiola, Washington	Sr.	31	244	48	125	661	21.3
Jennifer Smith, Michigan	Sr.	31	218	13	210	659	21.3
Beth Swink, St. Francis (Pennsylvania)	Jr.	31	260	0	139	659	21.3
Katie Feenstra, Liberty	Jr.	32	291	0	92	674	21.1

KEY GP=games played; FG=field goals; 3FG=3-point field goals; FT=free throws; PTS=points; AVG=average

Legends

Jackie Stiles averaged 30.3 points per game as a senior at Southwest Missouri State in 2000-01.

CHRISTINA DICKEN/SPRINGFIELD NEWSLEADER/AP

Jackie Stiles, guard, b. December 21, 1978, Kansas City, Kansas. Stiles was a small guard (5' 8") at a small school, but she made a big impact on women's college basketball. At Southwest Missouri State, she was named conference Player of the Year three times, was an All-America twice, and led the Bears to the 2000-01 Final Four. Stiles holds the all-time career scoring record (3,393 points) in women's college hoops. She had 27 of the 30 top single-game scoring performances in Southwest Missouri history. The 2001-02 WNBA Rookie of the Year now plays for the Los Angeles Sparks.

Sheryl Swoopes, forward, b. March 21, 1971, Brownfield, Texas. Swoopes brought national attention to women's basketball in its pre-WNBA days and went on to become one of the most influential players in the sport. In 1992-93, the forward led Texas Tech to its first NCAA championship and set the college record for most points scored (47) by a male or female player in a national title game. She was also named the National Player of the Year that season. Swoopes now plays with the Houston Comets. She was the WNBA's MVP and Defensive Player of the Year in 2002.

Jennifer Azzi, guard, b. August 31, 1968, Oak Ridge, Tennessee. Azzi grew up in Tennessee but was never seriously recruited by the Lady Vols and attended Stanford. Four years later, she gave Tennessee fans a glimpse of what they had missed: The point guard led the Cardinal to an 88–81 win over Auburn in the 1989-90 national championship on Tennessee's home court. Azzi scored 17 points and was named the Final Four's Most Outstanding Player. The title capped a career in which she was a first-team All-Pac-10 selection three times, a conference Player of the Year twice, and the 1989-90 National Player of the Year. Azzi retired from basketball in 2004 after two and a half seasons in the American Basketball League (ABL) and five seasons in the WNBA.

NCAA Women's Division I Individual Leaders (cont.)

Field-Goal Percentage

Player	Class	GP	FGM	FGA	PCT
Katie Feenstra, Liberty	Jr.	32	291	443	65.7
Janel McCarville, Minnesota	Jr.	34	212	344	61.6
Gerlonda Hardin, Austin Peay	Sr.	31	223	367	60.8
Le'Coe Willingham, Auburn	Sr.	31	192	316	60.8
Khara Smith, DePaul	So.	30	261	430	60.7
Pam O'Connor, Eastern Illinois	Jr.	27	166	276	60.1
Colleen Fitzpatrick, Lafayette	Sr.	25	125	208	60.1
Beth Swink, St. Francis (Pennsylvania)	Jr.	31	260	433	60.0
Kate Flavin, Richmond	Jr.	33	251	424	59.2
Tera Bjorklund, Colorado	Sr.	30	211	359	58.8

Note: Minimum 5 field goals made per game.

Free-Throw Percentage

Player	Class	GP	FTM	FTA	PCT
Shanna Zolman, Tennessee	So.	35	88	92	95.7
Cyndi Valentin, Indiana	So.	29	99	107	92.5
Seimone Augustus, LSU	So.	35	100	111	90.1
Jill Marano, La Salle	Jr.	28	95	106	89.6
Kari Koch, Southwest Missouri State	So.	32	107	120	89.2
Kandi Brown, Morehead State	Sr.	28	104	117	88.9
Kate Murray, Loyola Marymount	Sr.	30	106	120	88.3
Lindsay Boyett, Birmingham-Southern	Sr.	30	81	92	88.0
Anne O'Neil, Iowa State	Sr.	33	127	145	87.6

Note: Minimum 2.5 free throws made per game.

Ashlee Kelly, Quinnipiac

COURTESY OF QUINNIPIAC UNIVERSITY

Rebounds

Player	Class	GP	REB	AVG
Ashlee Kelly, Quinnipiac	Sr.	29	392	13.5
Desire Almind, Bucknell	Sr.	29	390	13.4
Sandora Irvin, TCU	Jr.	30	366	12.2
Rebekkah Brunson, Georgetown	Sr.	28	336	12.0
Khara Smith, DePaul	So.	30	351	11.7
Rosalee Mason, Manhattan	Sr.	28	325	11.6
Crystal Kitt, Alabama State	Jr.	28	323	11.5
Angela Buckner, Wichita State	Sr.	28	318	11.4
Nicole Powell, Stanford	Sr.	31	346	11.2
Katie Feenstra, Liberty	Jr.	32	353	11.0

Assists

Player	Class	GP	A	APG
La'Terrica Dobin, Northwestern State	Sr.	26	249	9.6
Temeka Johnson, LSU	Sr.	35	289	8.3
Leah Cannon, Oral Roberts	So.	28	231	8.3
Yolanda Paige, West Virginia	Jr.	32	253	7.9
Brooklynn Lorenzen, Montana	Sr.	32	251	7.8
Toccara Williams, Texas A&M	Sr.	27	192	7.1
Tanara Golston, Brown	Sr.	27	188	7.0
Latesha Lee, Jackson State	Sr.	30	202	6.7
Malika Willoughby, Kent State	So.	29	194	6.7
Nancy Bowden, Butler	Sr.	29	193	6.7

KEY GP=games played; FGM=field goals made; FGA=field goals attempted; PCT=percentage; FTM=free throws made; FTA=free throws attempted; REB=rebounds; AVG=average; A=assists; APG=assists per game

Fast Fact: In 1994, Charlotte Smith of North Carolina hit the only championship-winning buzzer-beater in NCAA Division I history. Her 3-pointer at the horn gave the Tar Heels a 60–59 victory over Louisiana Tech.

NCAA Women's Division I Individual Leaders (cont.)

3-Point Field-Goal Percentage

Player	Class	GP	3FGM	3FGA	PCT
Marion Crandall, Eastern Michigan	Sr.	30	77	152	50.7
K.C. Cowgill, Southwest Missouri State	Jr.	32	65	138	47.1
Stephanie Collins, St. Bonaventure	Jr.	26	75	161	46.6
Tory Mauseth, Yale	Jr.	27	55	120	45.8
Cathy Joens, George Washington	Sr.	30	96	218	44.0
Chelsee Insell, Samford	So.	27	62	141	44.0
Emily Niemann, Baylor	Fr.	35	75	171	43.9
Laurie Koehn, Kansas State	Jr.	31	100	230	43.5

Note: Minimum 2 three-point field goals made per game.

Steals

Player	Class	GP	STL	SPG
Toccara Williams, Texas A&M	Sr.	27	111	4.1
Chanel Spriggs, American	Sr.	30	117	3.9
Nancy Bowden, Butler	Sr.	29	106	3.7
Keisha McClinic, Middle Tennessee	Sr.	32	112	3.5
Maria Jilian, Western Michigan	Jr.	32	110	3.4
Linda Sayavongchanh, Drake	So.	31	105	3.4
Antoinette Reese, Coppin State	Sr.	29	98	3.4
Melanie Boeglin, Indiana State	So.	28	94	3.4
Cricket Williams, San Jose State	Sr.	28	94	3.4

Blocks

Player	Class	GP	BLK	BPG
Brooke McAfee, IUPUI	So.	27	130	4.8
Amie Williams, Jackson State	Sr.	30	127	4.2
Sandora Irvin, TCU	Jr.	30	117	3.9
Zane Teilane, Western Illinois	So.	29	112	3.9
Kate Beth Pate, Lipscomb	So.	31	113	3.6
Ashley Sparkman, Northwestern State	Jr.	31	110	3.5
Vanessa Hayden, Florida	Sr.	30	106	3.5
Ugo Oha, George Washington	Sr.	30	100	3.3
Jennyffer Vargas, Morgan State	So.	22	69	3.1

KEY 3FGM=3-point field goals made; 3FGA=3-point field goals attempted; PCT=percentage; STL=steals; SPG=steals per game; BLK=blocks; BPG=blocks per game

NCAA Women's Division I Championship Results

Year	Winner	Score	Runner-up	Winning Coach
2004	UConn	70–61	Tennessee	Geno Auriemma
2003	UConn	73–68	Tennessee	Geno Auriemma
2002	UConn	82–70	Oklahoma	Geno Auriemma
2001	Notre Dame	68–66	Purdue	Muffet McGraw
2000	UConn	71–52	Tennessee	Geno Auriemma
1999	Purdue	62–45	Duke	Carolyn Peck
1998	Tennessee	93–75	Louisiana Tech	Pat Summitt
1997	Tennessee	68–59	Old Dominion	Pat Summitt
1996	Tennessee	83–65	Georgia	Pat Summitt
1995	UConn	70–64	Tennessee	Geno Auriemma
1994	North Carolina	60–59	Louisiana Tech	Sylvia Hatchell
1993	Texas Tech	84–82	Ohio State	Marsha Sharp
1992	Stanford	78–62	Western Kentucky	Tara VanDerveer
1991	Tennessee	70–67(OT)	Virginia	Pat Summitt
1990	Stanford	88–81	Auburn	Tara VanDerveer
1989	Tennessee	76–60	Auburn	Pat Summitt
1988	Louisiana Tech	56–54	Auburn	Leon Barmore
1987	Tennessee	67–44	Louisiana Tech	Pat Summitt
1986	Texas	97–81	USC	Jody Conradt
1985	Old Dominion	70–65	Georgia	Marianne Stanley
1984	USC	72–61	Tennessee	Linda Sharp
1983	USC	69–67	Louisiana Tech	Linda Sharp
1982	Louisiana Tech	76–62	Cheyney	Sonja Hogg

2003-04 TIME LINE

January 3, 2004: Guard Jessica Foley of Duke hits a 3-pointer at the buzzer to lift the fourth-ranked Blue Devils past Number 1 UConn, 68–67. Duke trailed, 64–50, with 3:53 remaining but ended the Huskies' home-court win streak by outscoring them, 18–3, down the stretch. (The 69-game streak tied the women's NCAA Division I record.)

January 24, 2004: Number 2-ranked Tennessee goes to Durham, North Carolina, and regains the top ranking for the first time since February 2001 by stopping Number 1-ranked Duke, 72–69.

February 5, 2004: Tennessee and UConn, the powers in women's college basketball, meet in a rematch of their 2002-03 NCAA championship game. The result: The Huskies rout the top-ranked Lady Vols, 81–67, in a preview of their 2003-04 title match.

February 12, 2004: Sue Gunter of Louisiana State becomes the third head coach in women's basketball history to win 700 games when the Lady Tigers beat Arkansas, 92–65. Gunter misses the game because of a respiratory illness. The illness causes her to retire in April after 22 seasons at LSU.

March 29, 2004: High school senior Candace Parker of Naperville, Illinois, wins the slam-dunk contest at the McDonald's All-America game by defeating a field of male competitors. She is the first woman to win the event. Parker will play for Tennessee in 2004-05.

March 30, 2004: Minnesota becomes the first Number 7 seed to reach the Final Four when it completes a remarkable run through the Mideast Regional with an 82–75 upset over Number 1-seed Duke. The Golden Gophers knock off the Top 3 seeds on the way to their first Final Four appearance in school history.

April 2, 2004: Creighton defeats UNLV, 72–53, to win the Women's National Invitation Tournament (NIT).

April 4, 2004: Tennessee and UConn get set to meet in the NCAA championship game for the fourth time after the Lady Vols knock off Louisiana State and the Huskies down Minnesota. UConn and Tennessee met for the championship in 1994-95, 1999-00, and 2002-03.

April 6, 2004: Led by Diana Taurasi, UConn withstands Tennessee's second-half rally and wins its third-straight national title, 70–61. Taurasi is named the Final Four's Most Outstanding Player.

Did You Know?

Tennessee and UConn combined have won eight of the past 10 national championships.

Trivia Challenge

Tennessee lost the national championship game for the second-straight year in 2003-04. Which school is the only one in women's college basketball history to lose the national championship game three times in a row?

Auburn. The Tigers lost to Louisiana Tech in 1987-88, to Tennessee in 1988-89, and to Stanford in 1989-90.

NCAA Women's Division I All-time Individual Leaders

Points

Chamique Holdsclaw, Tennessee

TODD J. VAN EMST/OPELIKA-AUBURN NEWS/AP PHOTO

Player	YRS	GP	PTS
Jackie Stiles, SW Missouri St.	1997–01	129	3,393
Patricia Hoskins, Miss. Valley St.	1985–89	110	3,122
Lorri Bauman, Drake	1981–84	120	3,115
Chamique Holdsclaw, Tennessee	1995–99	148	3,025
Cheryl Miller, USC	1983–86	128	3,018
Cindy Blodgett, Maine	1994–98	118	3,005
LaToya Thomas, Mississippi St.	1999-03	125	2,981
Kelly Mazzante, Penn St.	2000-04	133	2,919
Valorie Whiteside, Appalachian St.	1984–88	116	2,944
Joyce Walker, Louisiana St.	1981–84	117	2,906

Scoring Average

Player	YRS	GP	FG	3FG	FT	PTS	AVG
Patricia Hoskins, Miss. Valley St.	1985–89	110	1,196	24	706	3,122	28.4
Sandra Hodge, New Orleans	1981–84	107	1,194	—	472	2,860	26.7
Jackie Stiles, SW Missouri St.	1997–01	129	1,160	221	852	3,393	26.3
Lorri Bauman, Drake	1981–84	120	1,104	—	907	3,115	26.0
Andrea Congreaves, Mercer	1989–93	108	1,107	153	429	2,796	25.9
Cindy Blodgett, Maine	1994–98	118	1,055	219	676	3,005	25.5
Valorie Whiteside, Appalachian St.	1984–88	116	1,153	0	638	2,944	25.4
Joyce Walker, LSU	1981–84	117	1,259	—	388	2,906	24.8
Tarcha Hollis, Grambling	1988–91	85	904	3	247	2,058	24.2
Korie Hlede, Duquesne	1994–98	109	1,045	162	379	2,631	24.1

Today's Stars

In 2003-04, Seimone Augustus led LSU to the school's first Final Four appearance.

BILL FEIG/AP

Seimone Augustus, guard, b. April 30, 1984, Baton Rouge, Louisiana. When the four-time state high school player of the year arrived at LSU, she was already expected to be the best player in LSU history. She lived up to those expectations in her first two seasons. The forward was named the 2002-03 National Freshman of the Year and was a first-team SEC and third-team All-America selection in 2003-04. In the 2003-04 NCAA tournament, Augustus was MVP of the regionals, averaging 29 points per game as she led the Lady Tigers to their first Final Four.

Janel McCarville, center, b. November 3, 1982, Stevens Point, Wisconsin. McCarville also carried her school, Minnesota, to its first Final Four in 2003-04. The 6' 2" junior center became one of just three non-seniors to earn Kodak All-America honors after averaging 16.1 points and 10.8 rebounds per game in 2003-04. She set the record for most rebounds (75) in a single NCAA tournament in 2003-04 and, like Augustus, will be one of the nation's top players in 2004-05.

Shyra Ely, forward, b. August 9, 1983, Indianapolis, Indiana. After coming off the bench for two seasons, Ely became a full-time starter as a junior in 2003-04 and quickly established herself as Tennessee's best all-around player. The forward had team highs in points (14.5) and rebounds (8) per game and led the Lady Vols to their third-straight Final Four. Ely earned first-team all-conference and third-team All-America honors.

HOCKEY

Goaltenders dominated NHL play in 2003-04, ringing up a league-record 192 regular-season shutouts. Many of the NHL's veteran stars struggled offensively, but several up-and-coming players, including gritty right wing Martin St. Louis of the Tampa Bay Lightning, produced brilliant offensive seasons and emerged as superstars.

The 5'9", 185-pound St. Louis won his first career scoring title (94 points) and made his second-straight All-Star appearance. He also won the Hart Trophy, as the regular-season MVP.

In the playoffs, St. Louis helped lead the Lightning to the franchise's first Stanley Cup championship. It was also the first time in league history that a Florida team won the Cup. St. Louis finished the post-season with 24 points

Martin St. Louis and the Tampa Bay Lightning defeated the Calgary Flames to win their first Stanley Cup championship, in 2003-04.

GARY BOGDON/EPS/SIPA

NHL TEAMS

EASTERN CONFERENCE
Atlanta Thrashers
Boston Bruins
Buffalo Sabres
Carolina Hurricanes
Florida Panthers
Montreal Canadiens
New Jersey Devils
New York Islanders
New York Rangers
Ottawa Senators
Philadelphia Flyers
Pittsburgh Penguins
Tampa Bay Lightning
Toronto Maple Leafs
Washington Capitals

WESTERN CONFERENCE
Anaheim Mighty Ducks
Calgary Flames
Chicago Blackhawks
Colorado Avalanche
Columbus Blue Jackets
Dallas Stars
Detroit Red Wings
Edmonton Oilers
Los Angeles Kings
Minnesota Wild
Nashville Predators
Phoenix Coyotes
San Jose Sharks
St. Louis Blues
Vancouver Canucks

and a playoff-leading 15 assists.

The Calgary Flames made their first Finals appearance since 1988-89 by defeating all three Western Conference division winners in the playoffs (Vancouver Canucks, Detroit Red Wings, San Jose Sharks). Led by superstar right wing Jarome Iginla, veteran left wing Martin Gelinas, and fourth-year goaltender Miikka Kiprusoff, the Flames pushed the Lightning to a deciding seventh game before losing, 2–1.

Lightning center Brad Richards earned playoff MVP honors after scoring a post-season-leading 26 points. Richards also set the NHL record for game-winning goals in the playoffs (7). Meanwhile, Tampa's 40-year-old captain, Dave Andreychuk, won his first Stanley Cup after 22 seasons and a total of 1,759 games in the NHL.

The NHL's collective bargaining agreement with its players was scheduled to expire before the start of the 2004-05 season. If the NHL and its players don't come up with a new labor agreement, there could be a lockout for the first time since 1994-95.

In 2003-04, Jarome Iginla of the Calgary Flames was tied for first in the NHL in goals (41).

DAVID E. KLUTHO/SPORTS ILLUSTRATED

NHL 2003-04 Final Standings

DIVISION STANDINGS

Atlantic Division

	GP	W	L	T	OTL	GF	GA	PTS
y-Flyers	82	40	21	15	6	229	186	101
x-Devils	82	43	25	12	2	213	164	100
x-Islanders	82	38	29	11	4	237	210	91
Rangers	82	27	40	7	8	206	250	69
Penguins	82	23	47	8	4	190	303	58

Northeast Division

	GP	W	L	T	OTL	GF	GA	PTS
y-Bruins	82	41	19	15	7	209	188	104
x-Maple Leafs	82	45	24	10	3	242	204	103
x-Senators	82	43	23	10	6	262	189	102
x-Canadiens	82	41	30	7	4	208	192	93
Sabres	82	37	34	7	4	220	221	85

Southeast Division

	GP	W	L	T	OTL	GF	GA	PTS
z-Lightning	82	46	22	8	6	245	192	106
Thrashers	82	33	37	8	4	214	243	78
Hurricanes	82	28	34	14	6	172	209	76
Panthers	82	28	35	15	4	188	221	75
Capitals	82	23	46	10	3	186	253	59

Central Division

	GP	W	L	T	OTL	GF	GA	PTS
p-Red Wings	82	48	21	11	2	255	189	109
x-Blues	82	39	30	11	2	191	198	91
x-Predators	82	38	29	11	4	216	217	91
Blue Jackets	82	25	45	8	4	177	238	62
Blackhawks	82	20	43	11	8	188	259	59

Northwest Division

	GP	W	L	T	OTL	GF	GA	PTS
y-Canucks	82	43	24	10	5	235	194	101
x-Avalanche	82	40	22	13	7	236	198	100
x-Flames	82	42	30	7	3	200	176	94
Oilers	82	36	29	12	5	221	208	89
Wild	82	30	29	20	3	188	183	83

Pacific Division

	GP	W	L	T	OTL	GF	GA	PTS
y-Sharks	82	43	21	12	6	219	183	104
x-Stars	82	41	26	13	2	194	175	97
Kings	82	28	29	16	9	205	217	81
Mighty Ducks	82	29	35	10	8	184	213	76
Coyotes	82	22	36	18	6	188	245	68

KEY GP=games played; W=win; L=loss; T=tie; OTL=overtime loss; GF=goals for; GA=goals against; PTS=points; x=clinched playoff spot; y=clinched division; z=clinched conference; p=clinched Presidents' Trophy (best record in NHL)

2004 Stanley Cup Playoffs

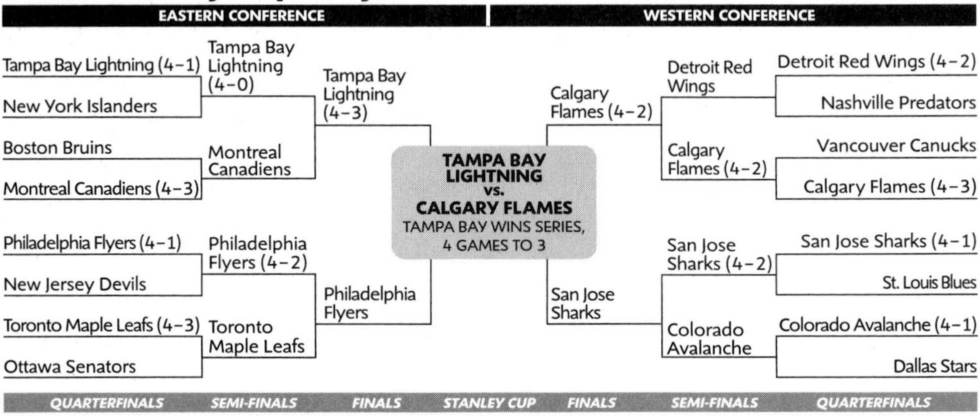

Stanley Cup Playoff Results

Conference Quarterfinals

EASTERN CONFERENCE

Tampa Bay Lightning vs. New York Islanders

GAME 1: April 8, 2004: Tampa Bay 3, New York 0
GAME 2: April 10, 2004: New York 3, Tampa Bay 0
GAME 3: April 12, 2004: Tampa Bay 3, New York 0
GAME 4: April 14, 2004: Tampa Bay 3, New York 0
GAME 5: April 16, 2004: Tampa Bay 3, New York 2 (OT)

Tampa Bay Lightning win series, 4–1

Boston Bruins vs. Montreal Canadiens

GAME 1: April 7, 2004: Boston 3, Montreal 0
GAME 2: April 9, 2004: Boston 2, Montreal 1 (OT)
GAME 3: April 11, 2004: Montreal 3, Boston 2
GAME 4: April 13, 2004: Boston 4, Montreal 3 (2OT)
GAME 5: April 15, 2004: Montreal 5, Boston 1
GAME 6: April 17, 2004: Montreal 5, Boston 2
GAME 7: April 19, 2004: Montreal 2, Boston 0

Montreal Canadiens win series, 4–3

Philadelphia Flyers vs. New Jersey Devils

GAME 1: April 8, 2004: Philadelphia 3, New Jersey 2
GAME 2: April 10, 2004: Philadelphia 3, New Jersey 2
GAME 3: April 12, 2004: New Jersey 4, Philadelphia 2
GAME 4: April 14, 2004: Philadelphia 3, New Jersey 0
GAME 5: April 17, 2004: Philadelphia 3, New Jersey 1

Philadelphia Flyers win series, 4–1

Toronto Maple Leafs vs. Ottawa Senators

GAME 1: April 8, 2004: Ottawa 4, Toronto 2
GAME 2: April 10, 2004: Toronto 2, Ottawa 0
GAME 3: April 12, 2004: Toronto 2, Ottawa 0
GAME 4: April 14, 2004: Ottawa 4, Toronto 1
GAME 5: April 16, 2004: Toronto 2, Ottawa 0
GAME 6: April 18, 2004: Ottawa 2, Toronto 1 (2OT)
GAME 7: April 20, 2004: Toronto 4, Ottawa 1

Toronto Maple Leafs win series, 4–3

WESTERN CONFERENCE

Detroit Red Wings vs. Nashville Predators

GAME 1: April 7, 2004: Detroit 3, Nashville 1
GAME 2: April 10, 2004: Detroit 2, Nashville 1
GAME 3: April 11, 2004: Nashville 3, Detroit 1
GAME 4: April 13, 2004: Nashville 3, Detroit 0
GAME 5: April 15, 2004: Detroit 4, Nashville 1
GAME 6: April 17, 2004: Detroit 2, Nashville 0

Detroit Red Wings win series, 4–2

Vancouver Canucks vs. Calgary Flames

GAME 1: April 7, 2004: Vancouver 5, Calgary 3
GAME 2: April 9, 2004: Calgary 2, Vancouver 1
GAME 3: April 11, 2004: Vancouver 2, Calgary 1
GAME 4: April 13, 2004: Calgary 4, Vancouver 0
GAME 5: April 15, 2004: Calgary 2, Vancouver 1
GAME 6: April 17, 2004: Vancouver 5, Calgary 4 (3OT)
GAME 7: April 19, 2004: Calgary 3, Vancouver 2 (OT)

Calgary Flames win series, 4–3

San Jose Sharks vs. St. Louis Blues

GAME 1: April 8, 2004: San Jose 1, St. Louis 0 (OT)
GAME 2: April 10, 2004: San Jose 3, St. Louis 1
GAME 3: April 12, 2004: St. Louis 4, San Jose 1
GAME 4: April 13, 2004: San Jose 4, St. Louis 3
GAME 5: April 15, 2004: San Jose 3, St. Louis 1

San Jose Sharks win series, 4–1

Colorado Avalanche vs. Dallas Stars

GAME 1: April 7, 2004: Colorado 3, Dallas 1
GAME 2: April 9, 2004: Colorado 5, Dallas 2
GAME 3: April 12, 2004: Dallas 4, Colorado 3 (OT)
GAME 4: April 14, 2004: Colorado 3, Dallas 2 (2OT)
GAME 5: April 17, 2004: Colorado 5, Dallas 1

Colorado Avalanche win series, 4–1

Stanley Cup Playoff Results (cont.)

Conference Semi-finals

EASTERN CONFERENCE

Tampa Bay Lightning vs. Montreal Canadiens

GAME 1: April 23, 2004: Tampa Bay 4, Montreal 0
GAME 2: April 25, 2004: Tampa Bay 3, Montreal 1
GAME 3: April 27, 2004: Tampa Bay 4, Montreal 3 (OT)
GAME 4: April 29, 2004: Tampa Bay 3, Montreal 1

Tampa Bay Lightning win series, 4–0

Philadelphia Flyers vs. Toronto Maple Leafs

GAME 1: April 22, 2004: Philadelphia 3, Toronto 1
GAME 2: April 25, 2004: Philadelphia 2, Toronto 1
GAME 3: April 28, 2004: Toronto 4, Philadelphia 1
GAME 4: April 30, 2004: Toronto 3, Philadelphia 1
GAME 5: May 2, 2004: Philadelphia 7, Toronto 2
GAME 6: May 4, 2004: Philadelphia 3, Toronto 2 (OT)

Philadelphia Flyers win series, 4–2

WESTERN CONFERENCE

Detroit Red Wings vs. Calgary Flames

GAME 1: April 22, 2004: Calgary 2, Detroit 1 (OT)
GAME 2: April 24, 2004: Detroit 5, Calgary 2
GAME 3: April 27, 2004: Calgary 3, Detroit 2
GAME 4: April 29, 2004: Detroit 4, Calgary 2
GAME 5: May 1, 2004: Calgary 1, Detroit 0
GAME 6: May 3, 2004: Calgary 1, Detroit 0 (OT)

Calgary Flames win series, 4–2

San Jose Sharks vs. Colorado Avalanche

GAME 1: April 22, 2004: San Jose 5, Colorado 2
GAME 2: April 24, 2004: San Jose 4, Colorado 1
GAME 3: April 26, 2004: San Jose 1, Colorado 0
GAME 4: April 28, 2004: Colorado 1, San Jose 0 (OT)
GAME 5: May 1, 2004: Colorado 2, San Jose 1 (OT)
GAME 6: May 4, 2004: San Jose 3, Colorado 1

San Jose Sharks wins series, 4–2

Eastern Finals

Tampa Bay Lightning vs. Philadelphia Flyers

GAME 1: May 8, 2004: Tampa Bay 3, Philadelphia 1
GAME 2: May 10, 2004: Philadelphia 6, Tampa Bay 2
GAME 3: May 13, 2004: Tampa Bay 4, Philadelphia 1
GAME 4: May 15, 2004: Philadelphia 3, Tampa Bay 2
GAME 5: May 18, 2004: Tampa Bay 4, Philadelphia 2
GAME 6: May 20, 2004: Philadelphia 5, Tampa Bay 4 (OT)
GAME 7: May 22, 2004: Tampa Bay 2, Philadelphia 1

Tampa Bay Lightning win series, 4–3

Western Finals

San Jose Sharks vs. Calgary Flames

GAME 1: May 9, 2004: Calgary 4, San Jose 3 (OT)
GAME 2: May 11, 2004: Calgary 4, San Jose 1
GAME 3: May 13, 2004: San Jose 3, Calgary 0
GAME 4: May 16, 2004: San Jose 4, Calgary 2
GAME 5: May 17, 2004: Calgary 3, San Jose 0
GAME 6 May 19, 2004: Calgary 3, San Jose 1

Calgary Flames win series, 4–2

Stanley Cup Finals

Tampa Bay Lightning vs. Calgary Flames

GAME 1: May 25, 2004: Calgary 4, Tampa Bay 1
GAME 2: May 27, 2004: Tampa Bay 4, Calgary 1
GAME 3: May 29, 2004: Calgary 3, Tampa Bay 0
GAME 4: May 31, 2004: Tampa Bay 1, Calgary 0
GAME 5: June 3, 2004: Calgary 3, Tampa Bay 2 (OT)
GAME 6: June 5, 2004: Tampa Bay 3, Calgary 2 (2OT)
GAME 7: June 7, 2004: Tampa Bay 2, Calgary 1

Tampa Bay Lightning win series, 4–3

Stanley Cup Championship Box Scores

GAME 1
May 25, 2004
CALGARY 4, TAMPA BAY 1

	1ST	2ND	3RD	TOTAL
CALGARY	1	2	1	4
TAMPA BAY	0	0	1	1

FIRST-PERIOD SCORING
Martin Gelinas, Calgary (3:02) Assists: Craig Conroy, Andrew Ference

SECOND-PERIOD SCORING
Jarome Iginla, Calgary (15:21), Stephane Yelle, Calgary (18:08)

THIRD-PERIOD SCORING
Martin St. Louis, Tampa Bay (4:13) Assists: Brad Richards, Dan Boyle
Chris Simon, Calgary (19:40) Assists: Oleg Saprykin, Robyn Regehr

GAME 2
May 27, 2004
TAMPA BAY 4, CALGARY 1

	1ST	2ND	3RD	TOTAL
CALGARY	0	0	1	1
TAMPA BAY	1	0	3	4

FIRST-PERIOD SCORING
Ruslan Fedotenko, Tampa Bay (7:10) Assists: Jassen Cullimore, Vincent Lecavalier

SECOND-PERIOD SCORING
None

THIRD-PERIOD SCORING
Brad Richards, Tampa Bay (2:51) Assists: Dave Andreychuk, Martin St. Louis
Dan Boyle, Tampa Bay (4:00) Assists: Brad Richards, Fredrik Modin
Martin St. Louis, Tampa Bay (5:58) Assists: Vincent Lecavalier, Dave Andreychuk
Ville Nieminen, Calgary (12:21) Assists: Shean Donovan, Robyn Regehr

GAME 3
May 29, 2004
CALGARY 3, TAMPA BAY 0

	1ST	2ND	3RD	TOTAL
TAMPA BAY	0	0	0	0
CALGARY	0	2	1	3

FIRST-PERIOD SCORING
None

SECOND-PERIOD SCORING
Chris Simon, Calgary (13:53) Assists: Jarome Iginla, Jordan Leopold
Shean Donovan, Calgary (17:09)

THIRD-PERIOD SCORING
Jarome Iginla, Calgary (18:28) Assists: Robyn Regehr, Chris Simon

Stanley Cup Championship Box Scores (cont.)

GAME 4
May 31, 2004
TAMPA BAY 1, CALGARY 0

	1ST	2ND	3RD	TOTAL
TAMPA BAY	1	0	0	1
CALGARY	0	0	0	0

FIRST-PERIOD SCORING
Brad Richards, Tampa Bay (2:48) Assists: Dave Andreychuk, Dan Boyle

SECOND-PERIOD SCORING
None

THIRD-PERIOD SCORING
None

GAME 5
June 3, 2004
CALGARY 3, TAMPA BAY 2 (OT)

	1ST	2ND	3RD	OT	TOTAL
CALGARY	1	1	0	1	3
TAMPA BAY	1	0	1	0	2

FIRST-PERIOD SCORING
Martin Gelinas, Calgary (2:13) Assists: Toni Lydman, Steve Montador
Martin St. Louis, Tampa Bay (19:26) Assists: Martin Cibak, Chris Dingman

SECOND-PERIOD SCORING
Jarome Iginla, Calgary (15:10)

THIRD-PERIOD SCORING
Fredrik Modin, Tampa Bay (:37) Assists: Brad Richards, Dave Andreychuk

OVERTIME SCORING
Oleg Saprykin, Calgary (14:40) Assists: Jarome Iginla, Marcus Nilson

GAME 6
June 5, 2004
TAMPA BAY 3, CALGARY 2 (2OT)

	1ST	2ND	3RD	OT	2OT	TOTAL
TAMPA BAY	0	2	0	0	1	3
CALGARY	0	2	0	0	0	2

FIRST-PERIOD SCORING
None

SECOND-PERIOD SCORING
Brad Richards, Tampa Bay (4:17) Assists: Martin St. Louis, Ruslan Fedotenko
Chris Clark, Calgary (9:05) Assists: Stephane Yelle, Ville Nieminen
Brad Richards, Tampa Bay (10:52)
Marcus Nilson, Calgary (17:49) Assists: Oleg Saprykin, Andrew Ference

THIRD-PERIOD SCORING
None

OVERTIME SCORING
None

SECOND OVERTIME SCORING
Martin St. Louis, Tampa Bay (:33) Assists: Brad Richards, Tim Taylor

GAME 7
June 7, 2003
TAMPA BAY 2, CALGARY 1

	1ST	2ND	3RD	TOTAL
CALGARY	0	0	1	1
TAMPA BAY	1	1	0	2

FIRST-PERIOD SCORING
Ruslan Fedotenko, Tampa Bay (13:31) Assists: Brad Richards, Fredrik Modin

SECOND-PERIOD SCORING
Ruslan Fedotenko, Tampa Bay (14:38) Assists: Vincent Lecavalier, Cory Stillman

THIRD-PERIOD SCORING
Craig Conroy, Calgary (9:21) Assist: Jordan Leopold

Rick Nash, Columbus Blue Jackets

2003-04 NHL Individual Leaders

Scoring

POINTS	GP	PTS
Martin St. Louis, Lightning	82	94
Ilya Kovalchuk, Thrashers	81	87
Joe Sakic, Avalanche	81	87
Markus Naslund, Canucks	78	84
Marian Hossa, Senators	81	82
Patrik Elias, Devils	82	81
Daniel Alfredsson, Senators	77	80
Cory Stillman, Lightning	81	80
Robert Lang, Red Wings	69	79
Brad Richards, Lightning	82	79
Alex Tanguay, Avalanche	69	79
Milan Hejduk, Avalanche	82	75
Mats Sundin, Maple Leafs	81	75

POINTS (cont.)	GP	PTS
Mark Recchi, Flyers	82	75
Jaromir Jagr, Rangers	77	74
Jarome Iginla, Flames	81	73
Steve Sullivan, Predators	80	73
Joe Thornton, Bruins	77	73
Keith Tkachuk, Blues	75	71
Scott Gomez, Devils	80	70

GOALS	GP	G
Rick Nash, Blue Jackets	80	41
Ilya Kovalchuk, Thrashers	81	41
Jarome Iginla, Flames	81	41
Martin St. Louis, Lightning	82	38

KEY GP=games played; PTS=points; G=goals

2003-04 NHL Individual Leaders (cont.)

GOALS (cont.)	GP	G
Patrik Elias, Devils	82	38
Marian Hossa, Senators	81	36
Markus Naslund, Canucks	78	35
Milan Hejduk, Avalanche	82	35
Bill Guerin, Stars	82	34
Joe Sakic, Avalanche	81	33
Keith Tkachuk, Blues	75	33

ASSISTS	GP	A
Martin St. Louis, Lightning	82	56
Scott Gomez, Devils	80	56
Cory Stillman, Lightning	81	55
Joe Sakic, Avalanche	81	54
Alex Tanguay, Avalanche	69	54
Brad Richards, Lightning	82	53
Doug Weight, Blues	75	51
Joe Thornton, Bruins	77	50
Markus Naslund, Canucks	78	49
Robert Lang, Red Wings	69	49
Mark Recchi, Flyers	82	49
Steve Sullivan, Predators	80	49

PLUS/MINUS	GP	+/-
Marek Malik, Canucks	78	35
Martin St. Louis, Lightning	82	35
Zdeno Chara, Senators	79	33
Fredrik Modin, Lightning	82	31
Nils Ekman, Sharks	82	30
Alex Tanguay, Avalanche	69	30
Adrian Aucoin, Islanders	81	29
Brad Lukowich, Lightning	79	29
Patrik Elias, Devils	82	26
Kenny Jonsson, Islanders	79	25

Note: +/-=plus minus rating (A player is awarded a plus (+1) each time he is on the ice when his team scores an even-strength or shorthanded goal. He receives a minus (-1) each time he is on the ice when the opposing team scores an even-strength or shorthanded goal. Power-play goals are not included in the rating.)

Goaltending

GOALS-AGAINST AVERAGE	GP	GAA
Miikka Kiprusoff, Flames	38	1.69
Dwayne Roloson, Wild	48	1.88
Marty Turco, Stars	73	1.98
Robert Esche, Flyers	40	2.04
Martin Brodeur, Devils	75	2.05
Andrew Raycroft, Bruins	57	2.05
Vesa Toskala, Sharks	28	2.06
John Grahame, Lightning	29	2.06
David Aebischer, Avalanche	62	2.09
Manny Legace, Red Wings	41	2.12
Martin Prusek, Senators	29	2.12
Ed Belfour, Maple Leafs	59	2.13
Evgeni Nabokov, Sharks	59	2.20
Chris Osgood, Blues	67	2.24
Martin Gerber, Mighty Ducks	32	2.26
Jose Theodore, Canadiens	67	2.27
Dan Cloutier, Canucks	60	2.27
Patrick Lalime, Senators	57	2.29
Jamie McLennan, Rangers	30	2.31
Kevin Weekes, Hurricanes	66	2.33
Nikolai Khabibulin, Lightning	55	2.33

SHUTOUTS	GP	W	L	T	SO
Martin Brodeur, Devils	75	38	26	11	11
Ed Belfour, Maple Leafs	59	34	19	6	10
Marty Turco, Stars	73	37	21	13	9
Evgeni Nabokov, Sharks	59	31	19	8	9
Roberto Luongo, Panthers	72	25	33	14	7
Jose Theodore, Canadiens	67	33	28	5	6
Kevin Weekes, Hurricanes	66	23	30	11	6

Seven tied with five.

SAVE PERCENTAGE	GP	GA	SA	SAVE PCT	W	L	T
Miikka Kiprusoff, Flames	38	65	966	.933	24	10	4
Dwayne Roloson, Wild	48	89	1,323	.933	19	18	11
Roberto Luongo, Panthers	72	172	2,475	.931	25	33	14
Vesa Toskala, Sharks	28	53	760	.930	12	8	4
Andrew Raycroft, Bruins	57	117	1,586	.926	29	18	9
David Aebischer, Avalanche	62	129	1,703	.924	32	19	9
Evgeni Nabokov, Sharks	59	127	1,610	.921	31	19	8
Manny Legace, Red Wings	41	82	1,019	.920	23	10	5
Jose Theodore, Canadiens	67	150	1,860	.919	33	28	5
Ed Belfour, Maple Leafs	59	122	1,483	.918	34	19	6
Marc Denis, Blue Jackets	66	162	1,970	.918	21	36	7
Martin Gerber, Mighty Ducks	32	64	785	.918	11	12	4
Jussi Markkanen, Oilers	33	65	793	.918	10	14	3

WINS	GP	W	L	T
Martin Brodeur, Devils	75	38	26	11
Marty Turco, Stars	73	37	21	13
Ed Belfour, Maple Leafs	59	34	19	6
Tomas Vokoun, Predators	73	34	29	10
Dan Cloutier, Canucks	60	33	21	6
Jose Theodore, Canadiens	67	33	28	5
David Aebischer, Avalanche	62	32	19	9
Evgeni Nabokov, Sharks	59	31	19	8
Chris Osgood, Blues	67	31	25	8
Andrew Raycroft, Bruins	57	29	18	9

Did You Know?

Wayne Gretzky, the NHL's all-time leading scorer (2,857 points), was so dominant that he would lead the career scoring list if he had never scored a goal. He holds the league record for career assists (1,963). (Goals and assists are each worth 1 point in the NHL.) Center Mark Messier is second on the career points list (1,887).

Trivia Challenge

Which NHL player scored 500 goals in the fewest number of games?

Right wing Mike Bossy of the New York Islanders scored his 500th goal in 1985-86, in his 752nd career NHL game. Only right wing Maurice Richard, center Mario Lemieux, and right wing Jaromir Jagr have reached the mark in fewer than 1,000 games.

KEY G=goals; A=assists; GAA=goals-against average; W=win; L=loss; T=tie; SO=shutout; GA=goals allowed; SA=shots allowed; SAVE PCT=save percentage

2003-04 NHL TEAM-BY-TEAM STATS

ANAHEIM MIGHTY DUCKS

	GP	G	A	PTS	+/-	PIM
Sergei Fedorov	80	31	34	65	-5	42
Vaclav Prospal	82	19	35	54	-9	54
Petr Sykora	81	23	29	52	-9	34
Steve Rucchin	82	20	23	43	-14	12
Joffrey Lupul	75	13	21	34	-6	28
Andy McDonald	79	9	21	30	-13	24
Rob Neidermayer	55	12	16	28	-6	34
Niclas Havelid	79	6	20	26	-28	28
Martin Skoula	79	4	21	25	5	32
Samuel Pahlsson	82	8	14	22	-2	52
Jason Krog	80	6	12	18	-4	16
Stanislav Chistov	56	2	16	18	-16	26
Vitaly Vishnevski	73	6	10	16	0	51
Sandis Ozolinsh	36	5	11	16	-7	24
Ruslan Salei	82	4	11	15	-1	110
Petr Schastlivy	65	4	4	8	-4	18
Keith Carney	69	2	5	7	-5	42
Chris Kunitz	21	0	6	6	1	12
Mike LeClerc	10	1	3	4	-1	4
Lance Ward	46	0	4	4	-1	94

	GP	G	A	PTS	+/-	PIM
Cam Severson	31	3	0	3	-3	50
Garrett Burnett	39	1	2	3	0	184
Mikael Holmqvist	21	2	0	2	-6	25
Tony Martensson	6	1	1	2	-2	0
Chris Armstrong	4	0	1	1	-1	0
Alexei Smirnov	8	0	1	1	0	2
Dan Bylsma	11	0	0	0	-3	0
Mark Popovic	1	0	0	0	0	0
Casey Hankinson	4	0	0	0	0	4

GOALIES	GP	W	L	T	GAA
Jean-Sebastien Giguere	55	17	31	6	2.62
Martin Gerber	32	11	12	4	2.26
Ilja Bryzgalov	1	1	0	0	2.00

ATLANTA THRASHERS

	GP	G	A	PTS	+/-	PIM
Ilya Kovalchuk	81	41	46	87	-10	63
Shawn McEachern	82	17	38	55	5	76
Vyacheslav Kozlov	76	20	32	52	-12	74
Marc Savard	45	19	33	52	-8	85
Patrik Stefan	82	14	26	40	-7	26
Randy Robitaille	69	11	26	37	-12	20
Ronald Petrovicky	78	16	15	31	-9	123
Frantisek Kaberle	67	3	26	29	2	30
Dany Heatley	31	13	12	25	-8	18
Serge Aubin	66	10	15	25	0	73
Andy Sutton	65	8	13	21	0	94
Daniel Tjarnqvist	68	5	15	20	-4	20
Jean-Pierre Vigier	70	10	8	18	-18	22
Ivan Majesky	63	3	7	10	-7	76
Yannick Tremblay	38	2	8	10	-13	13
Garnet Exelby	71	1	9	10	-10	134
Chris Tamer	38	2	5	7	-9	55
Brad Larsen	32	2	2	4	0	13
Shawn Heins	17	0	4	4	-1	16
Benjamin Simon	52	3	0	3	-10	28

	GP	G	A	PTS	+/-	PIM
Zdenek Blatny	16	3	0	3	0	6
Tommi Santala	33	1	2	3	-7	22
Francis Lessard	62	1	1	2	-5	181
Kip Brennan	23	1	0	1	-1	96
Brian Swanson	2	0	1	1	0	0
Karl Stewart	5	0	1	1	0	4
Daniel Corso	7	0	1	1	-2	0
Kyle Rossiter	6	0	1	1	0	7
Derek Mackenzie	12	0	1	1	0	10
Kurtis Foster	3	0	1	1	0	0

GOALIES	GP	W	L	T	GAA
Pasi Nurminen	64	25	30	7	2.78
Kari Lehtonen	4	4	0	0	1.25
Byron Dafoe	18	4	11	1	3.14
Frederic Cassivi	0	0	0	0	0.00

Note: Players are listed under the teams with which they finished the 2003-04 season.

KEY GP=games played; G=goals; A=assists; PTS=points; +/-=plus minus rating; PIM=penalty minutes; W=win; L=loss; T=tie; GAA=goals-against average

BOSTON BRUINS

	GP	G	A	PTS	+/-	PIM
Joe Thornton	77	23	50	73	18	98
Glen Murray	81	32	28	60	17	56
Sergei Gonchar	71	11	47	58	-14	56
Brian Rolston	82	19	29	48	9	40
Mike Knuble	82	21	25	46	19	32
Sergei Samsonov	58	17	23	40	12	4
Patrice Bergeron	71	16	23	39	5	22
Nick Boynton	81	6	24	30	17	98
Dan McGillis	80	5	23	28	-1	65
Jiri Slegr	52	6	20	26	11	35
Martin Lapointe	78	15	10	25	-5	67
P.J. Axelsson	68	6	14	20	2	42
Travis Green	64	11	5	16	-6	67
Michael Nylander	18	1	13	14	4	22
Ted Donato	63	6	5	11	2	18
Sean O'Donnell	82	1	10	11	10	110
Rob Zamuner	57	4	5	9	3	16
Hal Gill	82	2	7	9	16	99
Craig MacDonald	52	0	6	6	-5	33
Michal Grosek	33	3	2	5	1	33

	GP	G	A	PTS	+/-	PIM
Ian Moran	35	1	4	5	3	28
Andy Hilbert	18	2	0	2	1	9
Carl Corazzini	12	2	0	2	2	0
Doug Doull	35	0	1	1	2	132
Sergei Zinovjev	10	0	1	1	1	2
P.J. Stock	1	0	0	0	0	0
Kris Vernarsky	3	0	0	0	-1	0
Colton Orr	1	0	0	0	-1	0
Zdenek Kutlak	2	0	0	0	-1	0
Ivan Huml	7	0	0	0	-3	6

GOALIES	GP	W	L	T	GAA
Andrew Raycroft	57	29	18	9	2.05
Felix Potvin	28	12	8	6	2.50
Tim Thomas	0	0	0	0	0.00

BUFFALO SABRES

	GP	G	A	PTS	+/-	PIM
Daniel Briere	82	28	37	65	-7	70
Miroslav Satan	82	29	28	57	-15	30
Jean-Pierre Dumont	77	22	31	53	-9	40
Chris Drury	76	18	35	53	8	68
Jochen Hecht	64	15	37	52	17	49
Dmitri Kalinin	77	10	24	34	0	42
Maxim Afinogenov	73	17	14	31	-4	57
Mike Grier	82	9	20	29	-9	36
Alexei Zhitnik	68	4	24	28	-13	102
Ales Kotalik	62	15	11	26	-1	41
Taylor Pyatt	63	8	12	20	-7	25
Adam Mair	81	6	14	20	-3	146
Derek Roy	49	9	10	19	-8	12
Jeff Jillson	64	4	13	17	-4	54
Chris Taylor	54	6	6	12	-2	22
James Patrick	55	4	7	11	11	12
Rory Fitzpatrick	60	4	7	11	-5	44
Brian Campbell	53	3	8	11	-8	12
Henrik Tallinder	72	1	9	10	5	26
Milan Bartovic	23	1	8	9	1	18

	GP	G	A	PTS	+/-	PIM
Andy Delmore	37	2	5	7	-5	29
Jay McKee	43	2	3	5	6	41
Jason Botterill	19	2	1	3	0	14
Eric Boulton	44	1	2	3	-2	110
Brad Brown	43	0	3	3	2	66
Andrew Peters	42	2	0	2	-3	151
Domenic Pittis	4	0	0	0	-1	4
Jason Pominville	1	0	0	0	0	0
Norman Milley	2	0	0	0	0	2
Doug Janik	4	0	0	0	0	19

GOALIES	GP	W	L	T	GAA
Martin Biron	52	26	18	5	2.52
Mika Noronen	35	11	17	2	2.57
Ryan Miller	3	0	3	0	5.06

CALGARY FLAMES

	GP	G	A	PTS	+/-	PIM
Jarome Iginla	81	41	32	73	21	84
Craig Conroy	63	8	39	47	13	44
Shean Donovan	82	18	24	42	14	72
Martin Gelinas	76	17	18	35	10	70
Jordan Leopold	82	9	24	33	8	24
Dean McAmmond	64	17	13	30	9	18
Matthew Lombardi	79	16	13	29	4	32
Oleg Saprykin	69	12	17	29	1	41
Steven Reinprecht	44	7	22	29	1	4
Chris Simon	78	17	11	28	15	250
Chris Clark	82	10	15	25	-3	106
Marcus Nilson	83	11	13	24	-6	40
Ville Nieminen	79	5	16	21	-9	58
Toni Lydman	67	4	16	20	6	30
Robyn Regehr	82	4	14	18	14	74
Chuck Kobasew	70	6	11	17	-12	51
Stephane Yelle	53	4	13	17	1	24
Rhett Warrener	77	3	14	17	8	97
Andrew Ference	72	4	12	16	5	53
Denis Gauthier	80	1	15	16	4	113
Krzysztof Oliwa	65	3	2	5	-8	247
Blair Betts	20	1	2	3	-1	10
Steve Montador	26	1	2	3	-1	50
Dave Lowry	18	1	1	2	-6	11
Lynn Loyns	14	0	2	2	-3	2
Martin Sonnenberg	5	0	0	0	-2	2
Mike Commodore	12	0	0	0	-4	25

GOALIES	GP	W	L	T	GAA
Miikka Kiprusoff	38	24	10	4	1.69
Roman Turek	18	6	11	0	2.33
Brent Krahn	0	0	0	0	0.00
Dany Sabourin	4	0	3	0	3.55

CAROLINA HURRICANES

	GP	G	A	PTS	+/-	PIM
Josef Vasicek	82	19	26	45	-3	60
Justin Williams	79	11	33	44	12	64
Erik Cole	80	18	24	42	-4	93
Sean Hill	80	13	26	39	-2	84
Rod Brind'Amour	78	12	26	38	0	28
Jeff O'Neill	67	14	20	34	-12	60
Eric Staal	81	11	20	31	-6	40
Radim Vrbata	80	12	13	25	-10	24
Bret Hedican	81	7	17	24	-10	64
Kevyn Adams	73	10	12	22	6	43
Craig Adams	80	7	10	17	-5	69
Marty Murray	66	5	7	12	6	8
Niclas Wallin	57	3	7	10	-8	51
Pavel Brendl	18	5	3	8	0	8
Aaron Ward	49	3	5	8	1	37
Jesse Boulerice	76	6	1	7	-5	127
Ryan Bayda	44	3	3	6	-14	22
Glen Wesley	74	0	6	6	18	32
Jaroslav Svoboda	33	3	1	4	3	6
Allan Rourke	25	1	2	3	4	22
Michael Zigomanis	17	0	3	3	-1	2
Bruno St. Jacques	35	0	2	2	-7	31
Brad Fast	1	1	0	1	1	0
Damian Surma	1	0	1	1	1	0
Joey Tetarenko	2	0	0	0	0	0
Brett Lysak	2	0	0	0	0	2
Tomas Malec	2	0	0	0	-1	2
Tomas Kurka	3	0	0	0	0	0

GOALIES	GP	W	L	T	GAA
Kevin Weekes	66	23	30	11	2.33
Arturs Irbe	10	5	2	1	2.45
Jamie Storr	14	0	8	2	2.91

CHICAGO BLACKHAWKS

	GP	G	A	PTS	+/-	PIM
Tyler Arnason	82	22	33	55	-13	16
Bryan Berard	58	13	34	47	-24	53
Mark Bell	82	21	24	45	-14	106
Tuomo Ruutu	82	23	21	44	-31	58
Kyle Calder	66	21	18	39	-18	29
Brett McLean	76	11	20	31	-11	54
Eric Nickulas	65	8	12	20	-8	52
Scott Nichol	75	7	11	18	-16	145
Jim Vandermeer	46	5	12	17	-11	83
Igor Korolev	62	3	10	13	-15	22
Stephane Robidas	59	3	10	13	4	41
Eric Daze	19	4	7	11	-7	0
Deron Quint	51	4	7	11	-26	18
Igor Radulov	36	4	7	11	-2	18
Mikhail Yakubov	30	1	7	8	-12	8
Travis Moen	82	4	2	6	-17	142
Burke Henry	23	2	4	6	0	24
Ryan Vandenbussche	65	4	1	5	-10	120
Matt Keith	20	2	3	5	-5	10
Steve Poapst	53	2	2	4	-16	26
Jason Strudwick	54	1	3	4	-16	73
Pavel Vorobiev	18	1	3	4	1	4
Steve McCarthy	25	1	3	4	-9	8
Anton Babchuk	5	0	2	2	-1	2
Shawn Thornton	8	1	0	1	2	23
Johnathan Aitken	41	0	1	1	-9	70
Quintin Laing	3	0	1	1	1	0
Michal Barinka	9	0	1	1	-5	6
Lasse Kukkonen	10	0	1	1	-2	4
Matt Ellison	10	0	1	1	-3	0

GOALIES	GP	W	L	T	GAA
Craig Anderson	21	6	14	0	2.84
Michael Leighton	34	6	18	8	2.99
Jocelyn Thibault	14	5	7	2	2.85
Steve Passmore	9	2	6	0	2.89
Adam Munro	7	1	5	1	3.66
Matt Underhill	1	0	1	0	3.93

COLORADO AVALANCHE

	GP	G	A	PTS	+/-	PIM
Joe Sakic	81	33	54	87	11	42
Alex Tanguay	69	25	54	79	30	42
Milan Hejduk	82	35	40	75	19	20
Peter Forsberg	39	18	37	55	16	30
Rob Blake	74	13	33	46	6	61
Matthew Barnaby	82	16	25	41	18	157
Steve Konowalchuk	82	19	21	40	-3	70
Paul Kariya	51	11	25	36	-5	22
John-Michael Liles	79	10	24	34	7	28
Teemu Selanne	78	16	16	32	2	32
Chris Gratton	81	13	19	32	-18	111
Adam Foote	73	8	22	30	13	87
Karlis Skrastins	82	5	8	13	18	26
Andrei Nikolishin	49	5	7	12	3	24
Steve Moore	57	5	7	12	-5	37
Dan Hinote	59	4	7	11	-6	57
Travis Brigley	36	3	4	7	0	10
Ossi Vaananen	79	2	4	6	-14	89
Kurt Sauer	69	1	5	6	-11	51
Darby Hendrickson	34	2	3	5	-15	12
Cody McCormick	44	2	3	5	-4	73
Bob Boughner	54	0	5	5	-10	88
Peter Worrell	49	3	1	4	2	179
Jim Cummins	55	1	2	3	-5	147
Marek Svatos	4	2	0	2	1	0
Brett Clark	12	1	1	2	3	6
Charlie Stephens	6	0	2	2	-1	4
Riku Hahl	28	0	1	1	-7	12
Dennis Bonvie	1	0	0	0	0	0
Jordan Krestanovich	14	0	0	0	0	6

GOALIES	GP	W	L	T	GAA
David Aebischer	62	32	19	9	2.09
Tommy Salo	49	18	21	7	2.56
Phillipe Sauve	17	7	7	3	3.04

COLUMBUS BLUE JACKETS

	GP	G	A	PTS	+/-	PIM
Rick Nash	80	41	16	57	-35	87
David Vyborny	82	22	31	53	-26	40
Nikolai Zherdev	57	13	21	34	-11	54
Todd Marchant	77	9	25	34	-17	34
Trevor Letowski	73	15	17	32	-12	16
Anders Eriksson	66	7	20	27	-6	18
Andrew Cassels	58	6	20	26	-24	26
Manny Malhorta	65	12	13	25	-7	28
Brian Holzinger	74	7	15	22	-31	40
Jaroslav Spacek	58	5	17	22	-13	45
Tyler Wright	68	9	9	18	-19	63
Rostislav Klesla	47	2	11	13	-16	27
Alexander Svitov	40	2	9	11	-8	20
Derrick Walser	27	1	8	9	-6	22
Aaron Johnson	29	2	6	8	-2	32
Duvie Westcott	34	0	7	7	-15	39
Jody Shelley	76	3	3	6	-10	228
Luke Richardson	64	1	5	6	-11	48
Mark Hartigan	9	1	3	4	-2	6
Espen Knutsen	14	0	4	4	-5	2

	GP	G	A	PTS	+/-	PIM
Scott Lachance	77	0	4	4	-23	44
David Ling	50	1	2	3	-3	98
Tim Jackman	19	1	2	3	-7	16
Kent McDonell	29	1	2	3	-7	36
Andrej Nedorost	9	2	0	2	0	6
Brad Moran	2	1	1	2	-1	2
Donald MacLean	4	1	0	1	-1	0
Dan Fritsche	19	1	0	1	-5	12
Jeremy Reich	9	0	1	1	-3	20
Darrel Scoville	8	0	1	1	-4	6

GOALIES	GP	W	L	T	GAA
Marc Denis	66	21	36	7	2.56
Fred Brathwaite	21	4	11	1	3.37
Pascal Leclaire	2	0	2	0	3.53

DALLAS STARS

	GP	G	A	PTS	+/-	PIM
Bill Guerin	82	34	35	69	14	109
Jason Arnott	73	21	36	57	23	66
Valeri Bure	68	22	30	52	3	26
Brenden Morrow	81	25	24	49	10	121
Mike Modano	76	14	30	44	-21	46
Sergei Zubov	77	7	35	42	0	20
Pierre Turgeon	76	15	25	40	17	20
Stu Barnes	77	11	18	29	7	18
Jere Lehtinen	58	13	13	26	0	20
Rob DiMaio	69	9	15	24	2	52
Philippe Boucher	70	8	16	24	15	64
Richard Matvichuk	75	1	20	21	0	36
Teppo Numminen	62	3	14	17	-5	18
Scott Young	53	8	8	16	-15	14
David Oliver	36	7	5	12	6	12
Steve Ott	73	2	10	12	-2	152
Don Sweeney	63	0	11	11	22	18
Shayne Corson	17	5	5	10	12	29
Chris Therien	67	1	9	10	6	52
Jon Klemm	77	2	5	7	16	44

	GP	G	A	PTS	+/-	PIM
Niko Kapanen	67	1	5	6	-15	16
Trevor Daley	27	1	5	6	-6	14
Aaron Downey	37	1	1	2	2	77
Lubomir Sekeras	4	1	1	2	0	2
Mathias Tjarnqvist	18	1	1	2	-6	2
Antti Miettinen	16	1	0	1	-9	0
John Erskine	32	0	1	1	-9	84
Rob Valicevic	7	0	0	0	-1	2
Gavin Morgan	6	0	0	0	0	21
Jeff MacMillan	4	0	0	0	-2	0

GOALIES	GP	W	L	T	GAA
Marty Turco	73	37	21	13	1.98
Ron Tugnutt	11	3	7	0	2.41
Dan Ellis	1	1	0	0	3.00
Jason Bacashihua	0	0	0	0	0.00
Mike Smith	0	0	0	0	0.00

DETROIT RED WINGS

	GP	G	A	PTS	+/-	PIM
Robert Lang	69	30	49	79	4	24
Pavel Datsyuk	75	30	38	68	-2	35
Brett Hull	81	25	43	68	-4	12
Brendan Shanahan	82	25	28	53	15	117
Steve Yzerman	75	18	33	51	10	46
Mathieu Schneider	78	14	32	46	22	56
Henrik Zetterberg	61	15	28	43	15	14
Ray Whitney	67	14	29	43	7	22
Kris Draper	67	24	16	40	22	31
Nicklas Lidstrom	81	10	28	38	19	18
Kirk Maltby	79	14	19	33	24	80
Tomas Holmstrom	67	15	15	30	8	38
Steve Thomas	44	10	12	22	8	25
Chris Chelios	69	2	19	21	12	61
Jason Woolley	55	4	15	19	19	28
Jiri Fischer	81	4	15	19	0	75
Boyd Devereaux	61	6	9	15	-1	20
Jason Williams	49	6	7	13	1	15
Mathieu Dandenault	65	3	9	12	9	40
Darren McCarty	43	6	5	11	2	50
Mark Mowers	52	3	8	11	3	4
Jamie Rivers	50	3	4	7	9	41
Niklas Kronwall	20	1	4	5	5	16
Derian Hatcher	15	0	4	4	4	8
Jiri Hudler	12	1	2	3	-1	10
Darryl Bootland	22	1	1	2	-3	74
Kevin Miller	4	0	2	2	2	0
Anders Myrvold	8	0	1	1	-1	2
Ryan Barnes	2	0	0	0	0	0
Nathan Robinson	5	0	0	0	-1	2

GOALIES	GP	W	L	T	GAA
Manny Legace	41	23	10	5	2.12
Curtis Joseph	31	16	10	3	2.39
Dominik Hasek	14	8	3	2	2.20
Marc Lamothe	2	1	0	1	1.44
Joey MacDonald	0	0	0	0	0.00

EDMONTON OILERS

	GP	G	A	PTS	+/-	PIM
Ryan Smyth	82	23	36	59	11	70
Radek Dvorak	78	15	35	50	18	26
Petr Nedved	81	19	27	46	-8	46
Mike York	61	16	26	42	18	15
Shawn Horcoff	80	15	25	40	0	73
Raffi Torres	80	20	14	34	12	65
Ales Hemsky	71	12	22	34	-7	14
Ethan Moreau	81	20	12	32	7	96
Fernando Pisani	76	16	14	30	14	46
Steve Staios	82	6	22	28	17	86
Marc-Andre Bergeron	54	9	17	26	13	26
Eric Brewer	77	7	18	25	-6	67
Jarret Stoll	68	10	11	21	8	42
Cory Cross	68	7	14	21	9	56
Jason Smith	68	7	12	19	13	98
Brad Isbister	51	10	8	18	-2	54
Igor Ulanov	42	5	13	18	19	28
Adam Oates	60	2	16	18	0	8
Georges Laraque	66	6	11	17	7	99
Jason Chimera	60	4	8	12	-1	57
Marty Reasoner	17	2	6	8	5	10
Scott Ferguson	52	1	5	6	-5	80
Alexei Semenov	46	2	3	5	8	32
Mike Bishai	14	0	2	2	0	19
Peter Sarno	6	1	0	1	2	2
Tony Salmelainen	13	0	1	1	-1	4
Mikko Luoma	3	0	1	1	0	0
Jani Rita	2	0	0	0	0	0
Doug Lynch	2	0	0	0	0	0

GOALIES	GP	W	L	T	GAA
Ty Conklin	38	17	14	4	2.42
Jussi Markkanen	33	10	14	3	2.38
Tyler Moss	0	0	0	0	0.00
Michael Morrison	0	0	0	0	0.00

FLORIDA PANTHERS

	GP	G	A	PTS	+/-	PIM
Olli Jokinen	82	26	32	58	-16	81
Mike Van Ryn	79	13	24	37	-16	52
Kristian Huselius	76	10	21	31	-6	24
Stephen Weiss	50	12	17	29	-10	10
Juraj Kolnik	53	14	11	25	-7	14
Niklas Hagman	75	10	13	23	-5	22
Nathan Horton	55	14	8	22	-5	57
Donald Audette	51	9	12	21	-13	38
Jay Bouwmeester	61	2	18	20	-15	30
Matt Cullen	56	6	13	19	-2	24
Lyle Odelein	82	4	12	16	-7	88
Pavel Trnka	67	3	13	16	2	51
Mathieu Biron	57	3	10	13	-13	51
Byron Ritchie	50	5	6	11	-10	84
Christian Berglund	33	5	4	9	-6	14
Mikael Samuelsson	37	3	6	9	0	35
Vaclav Nedorost	32	4	3	7	-6	12
Andreas Lilja	79	3	4	7	-8	90
Lukas Krajicek	18	1	6	7	-2	12
Branislav Mezei	45	0	7	7	-4	80
Eric Beaudoin	30	2	4	6	-6	12
Darcy Hordichuk	57	3	1	4	-10	158
Eric Messier	21	0	3	3	-2	16
Kamil Piros	17	1	1	2	-4	4
Jaroslav Bednar	13	1	1	2	2	4
Josh Olson	5	1	0	1	1	0
Lee Goren	2	0	1	1	-4	0
Ty Jones	6	0	0	0	0	7
Denis Shvidki	2	0	0	0	0	0
Grant McNeill	3	0	0	0	0	5

GOALIES	GP	W	L	T	GAA
Roberto Luongo	72	25	33	14	2.43
Steve Shields	16	3	6	1	3.44
Travis Scott	0	0	0	0	0.00

LOS ANGELES KINGS

	GP	G	A	PTS	+/-	PIM
Luc Robitaille	80	22	29	51	4	56
Alexander Frolov	77	24	24	48	8	24
Trent Klatt	82	17	26	43	2	46
Zigmund Palffy	35	16	25	41	18	12
Jozef Stumpel	64	8	29	37	5	16
Derek Armstrong	57	14	21	35	4	33
Eric Belanger	81	13	20	33	-16	44
Nathan Dempsey	75	12	20	32	-12	32
Jaroslav Modry	79	5	27	32	11	44
Lubomir Visnovsky	58	8	21	29	8	26
Anson Carter	77	15	13	28	-15	20
Sean Avery	76	9	19	28	2	261
Jeff Cowan	71	11	16	27	1	92
Martin Straka	54	10	16	26	-25	20
Joseph Corvo	72	8	17	25	7	36
Ian LaPerriere	62	10	12	22	-4	58
Michael Cammalleri	31	9	6	15	1	20
Mattias Norstrom	74	1	13	14	-3	44
Scott Barney	19	5	6	11	3	4
Esa Pirnes	57	3	8	11	-9	12
Brad Chartrand	53	3	4	7	-3	30
Tim Gleason	47	0	7	7	1	21
Jason Holland	52	3	3	6	5	24
John Tripp	34	1	5	6	-4	33
Tomas Zizka	15	2	3	5	-4	12
Dustin Brown	31	1	4	5	0	16
Aaron Miller	35	1	2	3	-3	32
Pavel Rosa	2	1	1	2	1	0
Maxim Kuznetsov	16	0	1	1	-5	20
Jerred Smithson	8	0	1	1	0	4

GOALIES	GP	W	L	T	GAA
Roman Cechmanek	49	18	21	6	2.51
Cristobal Huet	41	10	16	10	2.43
Mathieu Chouinard	1	0	0	0	0.00
Milan Hnilicka	2	0	1	0	3.75

MINNESOTA WILD

	GP	G	A	PTS	+/-	PIM
Alexandre Daigle	78	20	31	51	-4	14
Andrew Brunette	82	15	34	49	3	12
Marian Gaborik	65	18	22	40	10	20
Antti Laaksonen	77	12	14	26	0	20
Pascal DuPuis	59	11	15	26	5	20
Richard Park	73	13	12	25	0	28
Wes Walz	57	12	13	25	5	32
Filip Kuba	77	5	19	24	-7	28
Jason Wiemer	75	8	14	22	-7	130
Pierre-Marc Bouchard	61	4	18	22	-7	22
Marc Chouinard	45	11	10	21	4	17
Andrei Zyuzin	65	8	13	21	4	48
Nick Schultz	79	6	10	16	12	16
Willie Mitchell	70	1	13	14	12	83
Eric Chouinard	48	6	4	10	-10	6
Stephane Veilleux	19	2	8	10	0	20
Rickard Wallin	15	5	4	9	1	14
Christoph Brandner	35	4	5	9	-2	8
Matt Johnson	57	7	1	8	4	177

	GP	G	A	PTS	+/-	PIM
Alex Henry	71	2	4	6	4	106
Brent Burns	36	1	5	6	-10	12
Zbynek Michalek	22	1	1	2	-7	4
Kyle Wanvig	6	0	1	1	-2	10
Travis Roche	5	0	1	1	-3	0

GOALIES	GP	W	L	T	GAA
Dwayne Roloson	48	19	18	11	1.88
Emmanuel Fernandez	37	11	14	9	2.49
Johan Holmqvist	0	0	0	0	0.00

MONTREAL CANADIENS

	GP	G	A	PTS	+/-	PIM
Mike Ribeiro	81	20	45	65	15	34
Michael Ryder	81	25	38	63	10	26
Saku Koivu	68	14	41	55	-5	52
Richard Zednik	81	26	24	50	5	63
Alex Kovalev	78	14	31	45	-9	66
Sheldon Souray	63	15	20	35	4	104
Yanic Perreault	69	16	15	31	-10	40
Patrice Brisebois	71	4	27	31	17	22
Jan Bulis	72	13	17	30	-8	30
Jim Dowd	69	7	22	29	12	44
Andrei Markov	69	6	22	28	-2	20
Pierre Dagenais	50	17	10	27	15	24
Niklas Sundstrom	66	8	12	20	3	18
Francis Bouillon	73	2	16	18	1	70
Steve Begin	52	10	5	15	6	41
Joe Juneau	70	5	10	15	-4	20
Jason Ward	53	5	7	12	3	21
Craig Rivet	80	4	8	12	-1	98
Andreas Dackell	60	4	8	12	8	10
Stephane Quintal	73	3	5	8	10	82

	GP	G	A	PTS	+/-	PIM
Michael Komisarek	46	0	4	4	4	34
Darren Langdon	64	0	3	3	-2	135
Ron Hainsey	11	1	1	2	3	4
Marcel Hossa	15	1	1	2	-3	8
Benoit Gratton	4	0	1	1	0	4
Karl Dykhuis	9	0	0	0	-2	2
Tomas Plekanec	2	0	0	0	0	0
Christopher Higgins	2	0	0	0	0	0
Gordie Dwyer	2	0	0	0	0	7

GOALIES	GP	W	L	T	GAA
Jose Theodore	67	33	28	5	2.27
Mathieu Garon	19	8	6	2	2.27

HOCKEY

NASHVILLE PREDATORS

	GP	G	A	PTS	+/-	PIM
Steve Sullivan	80	24	49	73	1	48
Scott Walker	75	25	42	67	4	94
Marek Zidlicky	82	14	39	53	-16	82
Martin Erat	76	16	33	49	10	38
David Legwand	82	18	29	47	9	46
Kimmo Timonen	77	12	32	44	-7	52
Vladimir Orszagh	82	16	21	37	-4	74
Scott Hartnell	59	18	15	33	-5	87
Greg Johnson	82	14	18	32	-21	33
Sergei Zholtok	70	14	17	31	2	19
Adam Hall	79	13	14	27	-8	37
Andreas Johansson	47	12	15	27	-2	26
Dan Hamhuis	80	7	19	26	-12	57
Denis Arkhipov	72	9	12	21	-2	22
Rem Murray	39	8	9	17	-1	12
Jason York	67	2	13	15	-4	64
Mark Eaton	75	4	9	13	16	26
Jeremy Stevenson	56	5	4	9	-3	105
Andrew Hutchinson	18	4	4	8	1	4
Jordin Tootoo	70	4	4	8	-6	137
Shane Hnidy	46	0	7	7	5	82
Wyatt Smith	18	3	1	4	2	2
Jim McKenzie	61	1	3	4	-13	88
Jason Morgan	19	0	4	4	1	4
Brad Bombardir	69	1	2	3	-9	25
Jamie Allison	47	0	3	3	-7	76
Robert Schnabel	20	0	3	3	6	34
Simon Gamache	9	1	1	2	-3	0
Stan Neckar	1	0	1	1	2	0
Scottie Upshall	7	0	1	1	-2	0

GOALIES	GP	W	L	T	GAA
Tomas Vokoun	73	34	29	10	2.53
Chris Mason	17	4	4	1	2.18
Wade Flaherty	0	0	0	0	0.00

NEW JERSEY DEVILS

	GP	G	A	PTS	+/-	PIM
Patrik Elias	82	38	43	81	26	44
Scott Gomez	80	14	56	70	18	70
Scott Niedermayer	81	14	40	54	20	44
Jeff Friesen	81	17	20	37	8	26
Brian Rafalski	69	6	30	36	6	24
John Madden	80	12	23	35	7	22
Sergei Brylin	82	14	19	33	10	20
Viktor Kozlov	59	13	20	33	-4	18
Jan Hrdina	68	12	21	33	-6	40
Brian Gionta	75	21	8	29	19	36
Turner Stevenson	61	14	13	27	0	76
Jay Pandolfo	82	13	13	26	5	14
Jamie Langenbrunner	53	10	16	26	9	43
Paul Martin	70	6	18	24	12	4
Grant Marshall	65	8	7	15	-9	67
Erik Rasmussen	69	7	6	13	5	41
Colin White	75	2	11	13	10	96
Scott Stevens	38	3	9	12	3	22
Igor Larionov	49	1	10	11	3	20
Tommy Albelin	45	1	3	4	7	4
David Hale	65	0	4	4	12	72
Raymond Giroux	11	0	3	3	-3	4
Sean Brown	39	0	3	3	5	44
Rob Skrlac	8	1	0	1	1	22
Jiri Bicek	12	0	1	1	0	0
Craig Darby	2	0	0	0	-1	0
Thomas Pihlman	2	0	0	0	0	2
Aleksander Suglobov	1	0	0	0	0	0

GOALIES	GP	W	L	T	GAA
Martin Brodeur	75	38	26	11	2.03
Scott Clemmensen	4	3	1	0	1.01
Corey Schwab	3	2	0	1	0.64
Ari Ahonen	0	0	0	0	0.00

NEW YORK ISLANDERS

	GP	G	A	PTS	+/-	PIM
Trent Hunter	77	25	26	51	23	16
Oleg Kvasha	81	15	36	51	4	48
Mariusz Czerkawski	81	25	24	49	8	16
Jason Blake	75	22	25	47	11	56
Adrian Aucoin	81	13	31	44	29	54
Michael Peca	76	11	29	40	17	71
Mark Parrish	59	24	11	35	8	18
Alexei Yashin	47	15	19	34	-1	10
Shawn Bates	69	9	23	32	-8	46
Roman Hamrlik	81	7	22	29	2	68
Kenny Jonsson	79	5	24	29	25	22
Janne Niinimaa	82	9	19	28	12	64
Dave Scatchard	61	9	16	25	12	78
Arron Asham	79	12	12	24	-12	92
Cliff Ronning	40	9	15	24	3	2
Mattias Weinhandl	55	8	12	20	9	26
Justin Papineau	64	8	5	13	4	8
Eric Cairns	72	2	6	8	-5	189
Alexander Karpovtsev	27	0	8	8	-16	18
Radek Martinek	47	4	3	7	-9	43

	GP	G	A	PTS	+/-	PIM
Sven Butenschon	41	1	6	7	-3	30
Justin Mapletoft	27	1	4	5	-1	6
Sean Bergenheim	18	1	1	2	-4	4
Eric Manlow	18	0	2	2	-2	2
Eric Godard	31	0	1	1	-2	97
Steve Webb	10	0	0	0	-4	4
Derek Bekar	4	0	0	0	0	2
Jeffrey Hamilton	1	0	0	0	0	0
Tomi Pettinen	4	0	0	0	-2	2

GOALIES	GP	W	L	T	GAA
Rick DiPietro	50	23	18	5	2.36
Garth Snow	39	14	15	5	2.80
Wade Dubielewicz	2	1	0	1	1.71
Dieter Kochan	0	0	0	0	0.00

NEW YORK RANGERS

	GP	G	A	PTS	+/-	PIM
Jaromir Jagr	77	31	43	74	-5	38
Bobby Holik	82	25	31	56	4	96
Mark Messier	76	18	25	43	3	42
Eric Lindros	39	10	22	32	7	60
Jan Hlavac	72	5	21	26	-8	16
Tom Poti	67	10	14	24	-1	47
Karel Rachunek	72	2	19	21	8	33
Boris Mironov	75	3	13	16	1	86
Josh Green	50	5	6	11	-3	32
Jamie Lundmark	56	2	8	10	-8	33
Darius Kasparaitis	44	1	9	10	11	48
Joel Bouchard	28	1	7	8	2	10
Dan LaCouture	59	5	2	7	-13	82
Fedor Tyutin	25	2	5	7	-4	14
Jed Ortmeyer	58	2	4	6	-10	16
Sandy McCarthy	50	4	1	5	-8	30
Jozef Balej	17	1	4	5	-1	4
Thomas Pock	6	2	2	4	-4	0
Mike Green	24	1	3	4	0	4
Dominic Moore	5	0	3	3	0	0

	GP	G	A	PTS	+/-	PIM
Dale Purinton	40	1	1	2	-9	117
Chad Wiseman	4	1	0	1	-1	0
Garth Murray	20	1	0	1	-5	24
Chris McAllister	46	0	1	1	-6	74
Cory LaRose	7	0	1	1	-2	4
Ken Gernander	2	0	0	0	-1	2
Bryce Lampman	8	0	0	0	-4	0
Benoit Dusablon	3	0	0	0	-1	2
Layne Ulmer	1	0	0	0	-1	0
Richard Scott	5	0	0	0	0	23

GOALIES	GP	W	L	T	GAA
Mike Dunham	57	16	30	6	3.03
Jamie McLennan	30	13	12	3	2.31
Stephen Valiquette	3	1	1	0	3.58
Jason LaBarbera	4	1	2	0	4.85
Phil Osaer	0	0	0	0	0.00

OTTAWA SENATORS

	GP	G	A	PTS	+/-	PIM
Marian Hossa	81	36	46	82	4	46
Daniel Alfredsson	77	32	48	80	12	24
Martin Havlat	68	31	37	68	12	46
Jason Spezza	78	22	33	55	22	71
Peter Bondra	77	26	23	49	-16	38
Bryan Smolinski	80	19	27	46	22	49
Radek Bonk	66	12	32	44	2	66
Wade Redden	81	17	26	43	21	65
Zdeno Chara	79	16	25	41	33	147
Peter Schaefer	81	15	24	39	22	26
Todd White	53	9	20	29	12	22
Chris Phillips	82	7	16	23	15	46
Josh Langfeld	38	7	10	17	6	16
Chris Neil	82	8	8	16	13	194
Greg De Vries	66	3	13	16	12	43
Antoine Vermette	57	7	7	14	5	16
Shaun Van Allen	73	2	10	12	6	80
Vaclav Varada	30	5	5	10	2	26
Mike Fisher	24	4	6	10	-3	39
Todd Simpson	62	4	4	8	-7	152
Brian Pothier	55	2	6	8	6	24
Curtis Leschyshyn	56	1	4	5	13	16
Anton Volchenkov	19	1	2	3	1	8
Rob Ray	6	1	0	1	0	14
Serge Payer	5	0	1	1	1	2
Jody Hull	1	0	0	0	0	0
Chris Kelly	4	0	0	0	-2	0
Julien Vauclair	1	0	0	0	1	2
Denis Hamel	5	0	0	0	-3	0

GOALIES	GP	W	L	T	GAA
Patrick Lalime	57	25	23	7	2.29
Martin Prusek	29	16	6	3	2.12
Ray Emery	3	2	0	0	2.38

PHILADELPHIA FLYERS

	GP	G	A	PTS	+/-	PIM
Mark Recchi	82	26	49	75	18	47
Michal Handzus	82	20	38	58	18	82
John Leclair	75	23	32	55	20	51
Tony Amonte	80	20	33	53	13	38
Jeremy Roenick	62	19	28	47	1	62
Simon Gagne	80	24	21	45	12	29
Kim Johnsson	80	13	29	42	16	26
Alexei Zhamnov	43	11	25	36	-1	28
Branko Radivojevic	77	10	22	32	-5	72
Sami Kapanen	74	12	18	30	9	14
Joni Pitkanen	71	8	19	27	15	44
Keith Primeau	54	7	15	22	11	80
Danny Markov	78	6	13	19	-6	95
Vladimir Malakhov	62	3	16	19	-6	55
Marcus Ragnarsson	70	7	9	16	12	58
Radovan Somik	53	4	10	14	-2	17
Donald Brashear	64	6	7	13	-1	212
Eric Desjardins	48	1	11	12	11	28
Claude Lapointe	42	5	3	8	2	32
Patrick Sharp	41	5	2	7	-3	55
Mattias Timander	39	2	5	7	15	21
Todd Fedoruk	49	1	4	5	-4	136
John Slaney	4	0	2	2	0	0
Kirby Law	6	0	1	1	0	2
Peter White	3	0	0	0	-1	2
Dennis Seidenberg	5	0	0	0	-4	2
Randy Jones	5	0	0	0	1	0
Frederick Meyer	1	0	0	0	0	0
Boyd Kane	7	0	0	0	-4	7
Mike Peluso	1	0	0	0	0	0

GOALIES	GP	W	L	T	GAA
Robert Esche	40	21	11	7	2.04
Sean Burke	47	16	20	7	2.73
Jeff Hackett	27	10	10	6	2.39
Antero Niittymaki	3	3	0	0	1.00
Neil Little	1	0	1	0	3.64

PHOENIX COYOTES

	GP	G	A	PTS	+/-	PIM
Shane Doan	79	27	41	68	-11	47
Ladislav Nagy	55	24	28	52	11	46
Daymond Langkow	81	21	31	52	4	40
Paul Mara	81	6	36	42	-11	48
Derek Morris	83	6	26	32	-1	49
Mike Comrie	49	12	12	24	-6	28
Radoslav Suchy	82	7	14	21	1	8
Cale Hulse	82	3	17	20	-4	123
Jeff Taffe	59	8	10	18	-8	20
Daniel Cleary	68	6	11	17	-8	42
Fredrik Sjostrom	57	7	6	13	-7	22
Michael Rupp	57	6	6	12	-4	47
David Tanabe	45	5	7	12	4	22
Krystofer Kolanos	41	4	6	10	-9	24
Mike Johnson	11	1	9	10	-1	10
Tyson Nash	69	3	5	8	-6	110
Ivan Novoseltsev	34	3	4	7	-13	14
Brad Ference	63	0	5	5	-19	103
Andrei Nazarov	33	1	2	3	-7	125
Erik Westrum	15	1	1	2	-3	20

	GP	G	A	PTS	+/-	PIM
Todd Reirden	7	0	2	2	-4	4
Bryan Helmer	17	0	1	1	-5	10
Jason Jaspers	3	0	0	0	-1	2
Goran Bezina	3	0	0	0	-1	2
Matthew Spiller	51	0	0	0	-11	54
Mike Stutzel	9	0	0	0	-4	0

GOALIES	GP	W	L	T	GAA
Brian Boucher	40	10	19	10	2.74
Brent Johnson	18	5	9	2	2.51
Jean-Marc Pelletier	4	1	1	0	4.11
Zac Bierk	4	0	1	2	3.79

PITTSBURGH PENGUINS

	GP	G	A	PTS	+/-	PIM
Dick Tarnstrom	80	16	36	52	-37	38
Aleksey Morozov	75	16	34	50	-24	24
Ryan Malone	81	22	21	43	-23	64
Milan Kraft	66	19	21	40	-22	18
Rico Fata	73	16	18	34	-46	54
Ric Jackman	54	9	21	30	-16	27
Konstantin Koltsov	82	9	20	29	-30	30
Tomas Surovy	47	11	12	23	-8	16
Tom Kostopoulos	60	9	13	22	-14	67
Lasse Pirjeta	70	8	14	22	-3	20
Mike Eastwood	82	4	15	19	-18	40
Jonathan Sim	63	8	10	18	-4	33
Matt Bradley	82	7	9	16	-27	65
Martin Strbak	49	5	11	16	-10	46
Landon Wilson	54	6	4	10	-3	47
Eric Meloche	25	3	7	10	-6	20
Brooks Orpik	79	1	9	10	-36	127
Mario Lemieux	10	1	8	9	-2	6
Josef Melichar	82	3	5	8	-17	62
Patrick Boileau	16	3	4	7	-16	8
Ramzi Abid	16	3	2	5	-5	27
Dan Focht	52	2	3	5	-23	105
Kelly Buchberger	71	1	3	4	-19	109
Matt Hussey	3	2	1	3	-1	0
Steve McKenna	49	1	2	3	-10	85

	GP	G	A	PTS	+/-	PIM
Robert Scuderi	13	1	2	3	2	4
Matt Murley	18	1	1	2	-6	14
Kris Beech	4	0	1	1	0	6
Reid Simpson	2	0	0	0	0	17

GOALIES	GP	W	L	T	GAA
Sebastien Caron	40	9	24	5	3.74
Jean-Sebastien Aubin	22	7	9	0	2.98
Marc-Andre Fleury	21	4	14	2	3.64
Andy Chiodo	8	3	4	1	3.46
Martin Brochu	1	0	0	0	1.82

SAN JOSE SHARKS

	GP	G	A	PTS	+/-	PIM
Patrick Marleau	80	28	29	57	-5	24
Nils Ekman	82	22	33	55	30	34
Jonathan Cheechoo	81	28	19	47	5	33
Alyn McCauley	82	20	27	47	23	28
Marco Sturm	64	21	20	41	0	36
Vincent Damphousse	82	12	29	41	-5	66
Brad Stuart	77	9	30	39	9	34
Alexander Korolyuk	63	19	18	37	20	18
Wayne Primeau	72	9	20	29	4	90
Scott Thornton	80	13	14	27	-6	84
Mike Ricci	71	7	19	26	8	40
Curtis Brown	80	11	14	25	3	36
Nicholas Dimitrakos	68	9	15	24	6	49
Kyle McLaren	64	2	22	24	10	60
Scott Hannan	82	6	15	21	10	48
Mike Rathje	80	2	17	19	17	46
Tom Preissing	69	2	17	19	8	12
Christian Ehrhoff	41	1	11	12	4	14
Todd Harvey	47	4	5	9	3	38
Jason Marshall	24	1	6	7	-2	26

	GP	G	A	PTS	+/-	PIM
Scott Parker	50	1	3	4	0	101
Mark Smith	36	1	3	4	-5	72
Rob Davison	55	0	3	3	-3	92
Jim Fahey	15	0	2	2	-2	18
Milan Michalek	2	1	0	1	1	4
Miroslav Zalesak	2	0	0	0	-1	0
Brad Boyes	1	0	0	0	-2	2
Pat Rissmiller	4	0	0	0	0	0

GOALIES	GP	W	L	T	GAA
Evgeni Nabokov	59	31	19	8	2.20
Vesa Toskala	28	12	8	4	2.06
Seamus Kotyk	0	0	0	0	0.00
Nolan Schaefer	0	0	0	0	0.00

ST. LOUIS BLUES

	GP	G	A	PTS	+/-	PIM
Keith Tkachuk	75	33	38	71	8	83
Doug Weight	75	14	51	65	-3	37
Pavol Demitra	68	23	35	58	1	18
Chris Pronger	80	14	40	54	-1	88
Dallas Drake	79	13	22	35	10	65
Brian Savage	74	16	16	32	-8	38
Scott Mellanby	68	14	17	31	-7	76
Petr Cajanek	70	12	14	26	12	16
Mike Sillinger	76	13	11	24	-10	68
Mark Rycroft	71	9	12	21	2	32
Eric Weinrich	80	4	15	19	12	46
Christian Backman	66	5	13	18	3	16
Mike Danton	68	7	5	12	-8	141
Jamal Mayers	80	6	5	11	-19	91
Ryan Johnson	69	4	7	11	-2	8
Eric Boguniecki	27	6	4	10	-1	20
Alexander Khavanov	48	3	7	10	2	18
Bryce Salvador	69	3	5	8	-4	47
Murray Baron	80	1	5	6	-6	61
Peter Sejna	20	2	2	4	-9	4

	GP	G	A	PTS	+/-	PIM
Pascal Rheaume	42	1	3	4	-6	9
Jeff Heerema	22	1	2	3	-5	4
Barret Jackman	15	1	2	3	-1	41
Al MacInnis	3	0	2	2	-1	6
Reed Low	57	0	2	2	-6	141
Steve Martins	25	1	0	1	-7	22
Jeff Finley	53	0	1	1	-9	34
Matt Walker	14	0	1	1	0	25
Christian Laflamme	16	0	1	1	-3	20
Scott Pellerin	2	0	0	0	-3	2

GOALIES	GP	W	L	T	GAA
Chris Osgood	67	31	25	8	2.24
Reinhard Divis	13	4	4	2	2.77
Curtis Sanford	0	0	0	0	0.00

TAMPA BAY LIGHTNING

	GP	G	A	PTS	+/-	PIM
Martin St. Louis	82	38	56	94	35	24
Cory Stillman	81	25	55	80	18	36
Brad Richards	82	26	53	79	14	12
Vincent Lecavalier	81	32	34	66	23	52
Fredrik Modin	82	29	28	57	31	32
Dave Andreychuk	82	21	18	39	-9	42
Ruslan Fedotenko	77	17	22	39	14	30
Dan Boyle	78	9	30	39	23	60
Pavel Kubina	81	17	18	35	9	85
Tim Taylor	82	7	15	22	-5	25
Darryl Sydor	80	3	19	22	-16	32
Brad Lukowich	79	5	14	19	29	24
Cory Sarich	82	3	16	19	5	89
Dimitry Afanasenkov	71	6	10	16	-4	12
Ben Clymer	66	2	8	10	5	50
Martin Cibak	63	2	7	9	-1	30
Jassen Cullimore	79	2	5	7	8	58
Chris Dingman	74	1	5	6	-9	140
Shane Willis	12	0	6	6	1	2
Nolan Pratt	58	1	3	4	11	42
Andre Roy	33	1	1	2	-5	78
Darren Rumble	5	0	0	0	-2	2
Eric Perrin	4	0	0	0	-1	0

GOALIES	GP	W	L	T	GAA
Nikolai Khabibulin	55	28	19	7	2.33
John Grahame	29	18	9	1	2.06

TORONTO MAPLE LEAFS

	GP	G	A	PTS	+/-	PIM
Mats Sundin	81	31	44	75	11	52
Bryan McCabe	75	16	37	53	22	86
Brian Leetch	72	15	36	51	6	34
Joe Nieuwendyk	64	22	28	50	7	26
Gary Roberts	72	28	20	48	9	84
Owen Nolan	65	19	29	48	4	110
Ron Francis	80	13	27	40	-9	14
Darcy Tucker	64	21	11	32	4	68
Nik Antropov	62	13	18	31	7	62
Tomas Kaberle	71	3	28	31	16	18
Robert Reichel	69	11	19	30	2	30
Alexander Mogilny	37	8	22	30	9	12
Ken Klee	66	4	25	29	-1	36
Alexei Ponikarovsky	73	9	19	28	14	44
Matt Stajan	69	14	13	27	7	22
Mikael Renberg	59	12	13	25	-1	50
Drake Berehowsky	56	6	18	24	-11	67
Tie Domi	80	7	13	20	-2	208
Karel Pilar	50	2	17	19	2	22
Tom Fitzgerald	69	7	10	17	-2	52
Aki Berg	79	2	7	9	-1	40
Chad Kilger	41	3	3	6	4	16
Calle Johansson	8	0	6	6	5	0
Bryan Marchment	75	1	3	4	4	106
Harold Druken	9	0	4	4	4	2
Nathan Perrott	40	1	2	3	-1	116
Wade Belak	34	1	1	2	0	109
Pierre Hedin	3	0	1	1	-1	0
Carlo Colaiacovo	2	0	1	1	1	2
Clarke Wilm	10	0	0	0	0	7

GOALIES	GP	W	L	T	GAA
Ed Belfour	59	34	19	6	2.13
Trevor Kidd	15	6	5	2	3.26
Mikael Tellqvist	11	5	3	2	2.87

VANCOUVER CANUCKS

	GP	G	A	PTS	+/-	PIM
Markus Naslund	78	35	49	84	24	58
Brendan Morrison	82	22	38	60	16	50
Todd Bertuzzi	69	17	43	60	21	122
Daniel Sedin	82	18	36	54	18	18
Martin Rucinsky	82	14	31	45	15	72
Henrik Sedin	76	11	31	42	23	32
Brent Sopel	80	10	32	42	11	36
Geoff Sanderson	80	16	20	36	-10	38
Trevor Linden	82	14	22	36	-6	26
Mattias Ohlund	82	14	20	34	14	73
Sami Salo	74	7	19	26	8	22
Matt Cooke	53	11	12	23	5	73
Ed Jovanovski	56	7	16	23	2	64
Jason King	47	12	9	21	0	8
Artem Chubarov	65	12	7	19	1	14
Marek Malik	78	3	16	19	35	45
Mike Keane	64	8	9	17	7	20
Magnus Arvedson	41	8	7	15	7	12
Jarkko Ruutu	71	6	8	14	-13	133
Brad May	70	5	6	11	-2	137
Marc Bergevin	61	1	10	11	-6	29

	GP	G	A	PTS	+/-	PIM
Bryan Allen	74	2	5	7	-10	94
Ryan Kesler	28	2	3	5	-2	16
Tyler Bouck	18	1	2	3	-4	23
Nolan Baumgartner	14	0	3	3	-4	4
Wade Brookbank	29	2	0	2	-1	133
Pat Kavanagh	3	1	0	1	0	0
Martin Grenier	7	1	0	1	3	9
Sean Pronger	3	0	1	1	-1	4
Fedor Fedorov	8	0	1	1	0	4

GOALIES	GP	W	L	T	GAA
Dan Cloutier	60	33	21	6	2.27
Johan Hedberg	21	8	6	2	2.51
Alexander Auld	6	2	2	2	2.06
Chris Levesque	0	0	0	0	0.00

WASHINGTON CAPITALS

	GP	G	A	PTS	+/-	PIM
Jeff Halpern	79	19	27	46	-21	56
Kip Miller	66	9	22	31	-10	8
Dainius Zubrus	54	12	15	27	-16	38
Alexander Semin	52	10	12	22	-2	36
Brian Willsie	49	10	5	15	-7	18
Josef Boumedienne	37	2	12	14	-10	30
Matt Pettinger	71	7	5	12	-9	37
Joel Kwiatkowski	80	6	6	12	-28	89
Brendan Witt	72	2	10	12	-22	123
Trent Whitfield	44	6	5	11	-2	14
Bates Battaglia	70	4	7	11	-24	42
Craig Johnson	64	2	9	11	-10	28
Jason Doig	65	2	9	11	-12	105
Shaone Morrisonn	33	1	7	8	10	10
Boyd Gordon	41	1	5	6	-9	8
Rick Berry	65	0	6	6	-5	108
Stephen Peat	64	5	0	5	-10	90
Jean-Luc Grand-Pierre	56	3	2	5	-12	52
Todd Rohloff	59	0	5	5	-17	26
Steve Eminger	41	0	4	4	-11	45

	GP	G	A	PTS	+/-	PIM
Brian Sutherby	30	2	0	2	-5	28
Ivan Ciernik	7	1	1	2	1	0
Brad Norton	36	0	2	2	-5	94
Darcy Verot	37	0	2	2	-6	135
John Gruden	11	1	0	1	-1	6
Roman Tvrdon	9	0	1	1	-3	2
Dwayne Zinger	7	0	1	1	2	9
Brooks Laich	5	0	1	1	-1	2
Owen Fussey	4	0	1	1	-1	0
Mel Angelstad	2	0	0	0	0	2

GOALIES	GP	W	L	T	GAA
Olaf Kolzig	63	19	35	9	2.89
Maxime Ouellet	6	2	3	1	3.12
Rastislav Stana	6	1	2	0	3.13
Matthew Yeats	5	1	3	0	3.02
Sebastien Charpentie	7	0	6	0	3.41

Legends

HEINZ KLUETMEIER/SPORTS ILLUSTRATED

In 25 NHL seasons, Gordie Howe scored 801 goals, second on the NHL's all-time list.

Gordie Howe, right wing, b. March 31, 1928, Floral, Saskatchewan, Canada. Nicknamed "Mr. Hockey," Howe led the NHL in scoring six times and finished in the Top 5 for 20 consecutive seasons. He won the Stanley Cup four times with the Detroit Red Wings (1949-50, 1951-52, 1953-54, 1954-55) and was a six-time league MVP and 23-time All-Star. He also played six seasons in the World Hockey Association (WHA) before retiring from pro hockey after the 1979-80 season. In 1,767 NHL games, Howe scored 801 goals and notched 1,049 assists. He is third all-time on the NHL points list (1,850), behind Wayne Gretzky (2,857) and Mark Messier (1,887).

Bobby Hull, left wing, b. January 3, 1939, Point Anne, Ontario, Canada. "The Golden Jet" was one of the league's most talented and tenacious offensive players. His booming slap shot was once clocked at 120 m.p.h. He starred for the Chicago Blackhawks for 15 seasons (1957-58 through 1971-72), then played seven seasons in the WHA. Hull led the Blackhawks to the Stanley Cup title in 1960-61 and led the league in goals seven times and total points three times. Bobby is the father of current NHL star right wing Brett Hull of the Detroit Red Wings. They are the only father-son duo in NHL history to score at least 600 goals apiece.

Tony Esposito, goaltender, b. April 23, 1943, Sault Ste. Marie, Ontario, Canada. After playing just 13 games with the Montreal Canadiens in 1968-69, Esposito was claimed by the Chicago Blackhawks in the 1969 Intra-League Draft. Over the next 15 seasons, the six-time All-Star became the most celebrated netminder in Chicago history. His league-high 38 wins and 15 shutouts in 1969-70 earned him the Rookie of the Year and Vezina awards. He won at least 20 games per season in all but two of his 15 seasons with the 'Hawks and ranks fourth all-time in wins by a goaltender (423). His brother, Phil, is the general manager of the Tampa Bay Lightning, the 2003-04 Stanley Cup champs.

Did You Know?

In 2003-04, goaltender Miikka Kiprusoff of the Calgary Flames had the lowest goals-against average (1.69) in the NHL's modern era.

The Stanley Cup

Awarded annually to the team that wins the NHL's best-of-seven final-round playoffs. The Stanley Cup is the oldest trophy for which professional athletes in North America compete. It was donated in 1893 by Frederick Arthur, Lord Stanley of Preston.

Season	Champion	Finalist	Games Played in Final
2003–04	Tampa Bay Lightning	Calgary Flames	7
2002–03	New Jersey Devils	Anaheim Mighty Ducks	7
2001–02	Detroit Red Wings	Carolina Hurricanes	5
2000–01	Colorado Avalanche	New Jersey Devils	7
1999–00	New Jersey Devils	Dallas Stars	6
1998–99	Dallas Stars	Buffalo Sabres	6
1997–98	Detroit Red Wings	Washington Capitals	4
1996–97	Detroit Red Wings	Philadelphia Flyers	4
1995–96	Colorado Avalanche	Florida Panthers	4
1994–95	New Jersey Devils	Detroit Red Wings	4
1993–94	New York Rangers	Vancouver Canucks	7
1992–93	Montreal Canadiens	Los Angeles Kings	5
1991–92	Pittsburgh Penguins	Chicago Blackhawks	4
1990–91	Pittsburgh Penguins	Minnesota North Stars	6
1989–90	Edmonton Oilers	Boston Bruins	5
1988–89	Calgary Flames	Montreal Canadiens	6
1987–88	Edmonton Oilers	Boston Bruins	4
1986–87	Edmonton Oilers	Philadelphia Flyers	7
1985–86	Montreal Canadiens	Calgary Flames	5
1984–85	Edmonton Oilers	Philadelphia Flyers	5
1983–84	Edmonton Oilers	New York Islanders	5
1982–83	New York Islanders	Edmonton Oilers	4
1981–82	New York Islanders	Vancouver Canucks	4
1980–81	New York Islanders	Minnesota North Stars	5
1979–80	New York Islanders	Philadelphia Flyers	6
1978–79	Montreal Canadiens	New York Rangers	5
1977–78	Montreal Canadiens	Boston Bruins	6
1976–77	Montreal Canadiens	Boston Bruins	4
1975–76	Montreal Canadiens	Philadelphia Flyers	4
1974–75	Philadelphia Flyers	Buffalo Sabres	6
1973–74	Philadelphia Flyers	Boston Bruins	6
1972–73	Montreal Canadiens	Chicago Blackhawks	6
1971–72	Boston Bruins	New York Rangers	6
1970–71	Montreal Canadiens	Chicago Blackhawks	7
1969–70	Boston Bruins	St. Louis Blues	4
1968–69	Montreal Canadiens	St. Louis Blues	4
1967–68	Montreal Canadiens	St. Louis Blues	4
1966–67	Toronto Maple Leafs	Montreal Canadiens	6
1965–66	Montreal Canadiens	Detroit Red Wings	6
1964–65	Montreal Canadiens	Chicago Blackhawks	7
1963–64	Toronto Maple Leafs	Detroit Red Wings	7
1962–63	Toronto Maple Leafs	Detroit Red Wings	5
1961–62	Toronto Maple Leafs	Chicago Blackhawks	6
1960–61	Chicago Blackhawks	Detroit Red Wings	6
1959–60	Montreal Canadiens	Toronto Maple Leafs	4
1958–59	Montreal Canadiens	Toronto Maple Leafs	5
1957–58	Montreal Canadiens	Boston Bruins	6
1956–57	Montreal Canadiens	Boston Bruins	5
1955–56	Montreal Canadiens	Detroit Red Wings	5
1954–55	Detroit Red Wings	Montreal Canadiens	7
1953–54	Detroit Red Wings	Montreal Canadiens	7
1952–53	Montreal Canadiens	Boston Bruins	5
1951–52	Detroit Red Wings	Montreal Canadiens	4
1950–51	Toronto Maple Leafs	Montreal Canadiens	5
1949–50	Detroit Red Wings	New York Rangers	7
1948–49	Toronto Maple Leafs	Detroit Red Wings	4
1947–48	Toronto Maple Leafs	Detroit Red Wings	4
1946–47	Toronto Maple Leafs	Montreal Canadiens	6
1945–46	Montreal Canadiens	Boston Bruins	5
1944–45	Toronto Maple Leafs	Detroit Red Wings	7

The Stanley Cup (cont.)

Season	Champion	Finalist	Games Played in Final
1943–44	Montreal Canadiens	Chicago Blackhawks	4
1942–43	Detroit Red Wings	Boston Bruins	4
1941–42	Toronto Maple Leafs	Detroit Red Wings	7
1940–41	Boston Bruins	Detroit Red Wings	4
1939–40	New York Rangers	Toronto Maple Leafs	6
1938–39	Boston Bruins	Toronto Maple Leafs	5
1937–38	Chicago Blackhawks	Toronto Maple Leafs	4
1936–37	Detroit Red Wings	New York Rangers	5
1935–36	Detroit Red Wings	Toronto Maple Leafs	4
1934–35	Montreal Maroons	Toronto Maple Leafs	3
1933–34	Chicago Blackhawks	Detroit Red Wings	4
1932–33	New York Rangers	Toronto Maple Leafs	4
1931–32	Toronto Maple Leafs	New York Rangers	3
1930–31	Montreal Canadiens	Chicago Blackhawks	5
1929–30	Montreal Canadiens	Boston Bruins	2
1928–29	Boston Bruins	New York Rangers	2
1927–28	New York Rangers	Montreal Maroons	5
1926–27	Ottawa Senators	Boston Bruins	4
1925–26	Montreal Maroons	Victoria Cougars	4
1924–25	Victoria Cougars	Montreal Canadiens	4
1923–24	Montreal Canadiens	Vancouver Maroons, Calgary Tigers	2, 2
1922–23	Ottawa Senators	Edmonton Eskimos, Vancouver Maroons	2, 4
1921–22	Toronto St. Pats	Vancouver Millionaires	5
1920–21	Ottawa Senators	Vancouver Millionaires	5
1919–20	Ottawa Senators	Seattle Metropolitans	5
1918–19	No decision*	No decision*	5
1917–18	Toronto Arenas	Vancouver Millionaires	5

*In 1918-19, the Montreal Canadiens traveled to meet the Seattle Metropolitans. After five games had been played — the teams were tied at two wins apiece and one tie — the series was called off by the local Department of Health because of an influenza epidemic and the death of Canadien defenseman Joe Hall from influenza.

2003-04 TIME LINE

October 9, 2003: Goaltender Dominik Hasek plays in his first game for the Detroit Red Wings since returning to the NHL after one season of retirement. He makes 21 saves in Detroit's 3–2 win over the Los Angeles Kings. But he plays only 14 games in 2003-04 because of an injury and finishes the season 8-3-2. He signs with the Ottawa Senators in the off-season.

November 4, 2003: Captain Mark Messier of the New York Rangers passes Gordie Howe for second place on the all-time scoring list when he scores a goal against the Dallas Stars for his 1,851st point.

February 8, 2004: Despite a hat trick by game MVP Joe Sakic, the Western Conference loses the 2003-04 NHL All-Star Game to the Eastern Conference, 6–4. Right wing Daniel Alfredsson has two goals and an assist for the East.

April 19, 2004: The Montreal Canadiens shut out the Boston Bruins, 2–0, to win their first-round playoff series. Montreal was down three games to one but rebounded to win the final three games of the best-of-seven series. It was the biggest playoff comeback in the Canadiens' storied history.

June 7, 2004: The Tampa Bay Lightning beat the Calgary Flames, four games to three, to win the Stanley Cup for the first time. Center Brad Richards scores 26 points in the playoffs and is awarded the Conn Smythe Trophy, as the playoff MVP.

June 10, 2004: For the second season in a row, Martin Brodeur of the New Jersey Devils wins the Vezina Trophy, as the league's top goaltender.

The Stanley Cup (cont.)

Season	Champion	Finalist	Games Played in Final
1916–17	Seattle Metropolitans	—	—
1915–16	Montreal Canadiens	—	—
1914–15	Vancouver Millionaires	—	—
1913–14	Toronto Blueshirts	—	—
1912–13	Quebec Bulldogs	—	—
1911–12	Quebec Bulldogs	—	—
1910–11	Ottawa Senators	—	—
1909–10	Montreal Wanderers	—	—
1908–09	Ottawa Senators	—	—
1907–08	Montreal Wanderers	—	—
1906–07	Montreal Wanderers (Mar.)	—	—
1906–07	Kenora Thistles (Jan.)	—	—
1905–06	Montreal Wanderers (Mar.)	—	—
1905–06	Ottawa Silver Seven (Feb.)	—	—
1904–05	Ottawa Silver Seven	—	—
1903–04	Ottawa Silver Seven	—	—
1902–03	Ottawa Silver Seven (Mar.)	—	—
1902–03	Montreal A.A.A. (Feb.)	—	—
1901–02	Montreal A.A.A. (Mar.)	—	—
1901–02	Winnipeg Victorias (Jan.)	—	—
1900–01	Winnipeg Victorias	—	—
1899–00	Montreal Shamrocks	—	—
1898–99	Montreal Shamrocks (Mar.)	—	—
1898–99	Montreal Victorias (Feb.)	—	—
1897–98	Montreal Victorias	—	—
1896–97	Montreal Victorias	—	—
1895–96	Montreal Victorias (Dec.)	—	—
1895–96	Winnipeg Victorias (Feb.)	—	—
1894–95	Montreal Victorias	—	—
1893–94	Montreal A.A.A.	—	—
1892–93	Montreal A.A.A.	—	—

Fast Fact: In 2003-04, the Nashville Predators, the league's second-youngest franchise, made their first post-season appearance. The Columbus Blue Jackets and Atlanta Thrashers are the only current NHL teams that have never been to the playoffs.

Conn Smythe Trophy (past 20 seasons)

Awarded to the Most Valuable Player of the Stanley Cup playoffs, as selected by the Professional Hockey Writers Association. The trophy was named for the former coach, general manager, president, and owner of the Toronto Maple Leafs.

Season	Player
2003-04	Brad Richards, Tampa Bay Lightning
2002-03	Jean-Sebastien Giguere, Anaheim Mighty Ducks
2001-02	Nicklas Lidstrom, Detroit Red Wings
2000-01	Patrick Roy, Colorado Avalanche
1999-00	Scott Stevens, New Jersey Devils
1998-99	Joe Nieuwendyk, Dallas Stars
1997-98	Steve Yzerman, Detroit Red Wings
1996-97	Mike Vernon, Detroit Red Wings
1995-96	Joe Sakic, Colorado Avalanche
1994-95	Claude Lemieux, New Jersey Devils

Season	Player
1993-94	Brian Leetch, New York Rangers
1992-93	Patrick Roy, Montreal Canadiens
1991-92	Mario Lemieux, Pittsburgh Penguins
1990-91	Mario Lemieux, Pittsburgh Penguins
1989-90	Bill Ranford, Edmonton Oilers
1988-89	Al MacInnis, Calgary Flames
1987-88	Wayne Gretzky, Edmonton Oilers
1986-87	Ron Hextall, Philadelphia Flyers
1985-86	Patrick Roy, Montreal Canadiens
1984-85	Wayne Gretzky, Edmonton Oilers

Hart Memorial Trophy (past 20 seasons)

Awarded annually "to the player adjudged to be the most valuable to his team." The original trophy was donated by Dr. David A. Hart, father of Cecil Hart, former manager-coach of the Montreal Canadiens.

Season	Winner
2003-04	Martin St. Louis, Tampa Bay Lightning
2002-03	Peter Forsberg, Colorado Avalanche
2001-02	Jose Theodore, Montreal Canadiens

Season	Winner
2000-01	Joe Sakic, Colorado Avalanche
1999-00	Chris Pronger, St. Louis Blues
1998-99	Jaromir Jagr, Pittsburgh Penguins

Hart Memorial Trophy (cont.)

Season	Winner	Season	Winner
1997-98	Dominik Hasek, Buffalo Sabres	1990-91	Brett Hull, St. Louis Blues
1996-97	Dominik Hasek, Buffalo Sabres	1989-90	Mark Messier, Edmonton Oilers
1995-96	Mario Lemieux, Pittsburgh Penguins	1988-89	Wayne Gretzky, Los Angeles Kings
1994-95	Eric Lindros, Philadelphia Flyers	1987-88	Mario Lemieux, Pittsburgh Penguins
1993-94	Sergei Fedorov, Detroit Red Wings	1986-87	Wayne Gretzky, Edmonton Oilers
1992-93	Mario Lemieux, Pittsburgh Penguins	1985-86	Wayne Gretzky, Edmonton Oilers
1991-92	Mark Messier, New York Rangers	1984-85	Wayne Gretzky, Edmonton Oilers

Art Ross Trophy (past 20 seasons)

Awarded annually "to the player who leads the league in scoring points at the end of the regular season." The trophy was presented to the NHL in 1947 by Arthur Howie Ross, former manager-coach of the Boston Bruins. If two or more players are tied, the tie-breakers, in order, are: (1) player with most goals, (2) player with fewer games played, (3) player who scored the first goal of the season.

Season	Winner	Points	Season	Winner	Points
2003-04	Martin St. Louis, Tampa Bay Lightning	94	1993-94	Wayne Gretzky, Los Angeles Kings	130
2002-03	Peter Forsberg, Colorado Avalanche	106	1992-93	Mario Lemieux, Pittsburgh Penguins	160
2001-02	Jarome Iginla, Calgary Flames	96	1991-92	Mario Lemieux, Pittsburgh Penguins	131
2000-01	Jaromir Jagr, Pittsburgh Penguins	121	1990-91	Wayne Gretzky, Los Angeles Kings	163
1999-00	Jaromir Jagr, Pittsburgh Penguins	96	1989-90	Wayne Gretzky, Los Angeles Kings	142
1998-99	Jaromir Jagr, Pittsburgh Penguins	127	1988-89	Mario Lemieux, Pittsburgh Penguins	199
1997-98	Jaromir Jagr, Pittsburgh Penguins	102	1987-88	Mario Lemieux, Pittsburgh Penguins	168
1996-97	Mario Lemieux, Pittsburgh Penguins	122	1986-87	Wayne Gretzky, Edmonton Oilers	183
1995-96	Mario Lemieux, Pittsburgh Penguins	161	1985-86	Wayne Gretzky, Edmonton Oilers	215
1994-95	Jaromir Jagr, Pittsburgh Penguins	70	1984-85	Wayne Gretzky, Edmonton Oilers	208

Lady Byng Memorial Trophy (past 20 seasons)

Awarded annually "to the player adjudged to have exhibited the best type of sportsmanship and gentlemanly conduct combined with a high standard of playing ability." Lady Byng, who first presented the trophy in 1925, was the wife of Canada's Governor-General. She donated a second trophy in 1936 because the first one was given permanently to Frank Boucher of the New York Rangers, who had won it seven times in eight seasons.

Season	Winner	Season	Winner
2003-04	Brad Richards, Tampa Bay Lightning	1993-94	Wayne Gretzky, Los Angeles Kings
2002-03	Alexander Mogilny, Toronto Maple Leafs	1992-93	Pierre Turgeon, New York Islanders
2001-02	Ron Francis, Carolina Hurricanes	1991-92	Wayne Gretzky, Los Angeles Kings
2000-01	Joe Sakic, Colorado Avalanche	1990-91	Wayne Gretzky, Los Angeles Kings
1999-00	Pavol Demitra, St. Louis Blues	1989-90	Brett Hull, St. Louis Blues
1998-99	Wayne Gretzky, New York Rangers	1988-89	Joe Mullen, Calgary Flames
1997-98	Ron Francis, Pittsburgh Penguins	1987-88	Mats Naslund, Montreal Canadiens
1996-97	Paul Kariya, Anaheim Mighty Ducks	1986-87	Joe Mullen, Calgary Flames
1995-96	Paul Kariya, Anaheim Mighty Ducks	1985-86	Mike Bossy, New York Islanders
1994-95	Ron Francis, Pittsburgh Penguins	1984-85	Jari Kurri, Edmonton Oilers

James Norris Memorial Trophy (past 20 seasons)

Awarded annually "to the defense player who demonstrates throughout the season the greatest all-around ability in the position." James Norris was the former owner-president of the Detroit Red Wings.

Season	Winner	Season	Winner
2003-04	Scott Niedermayer, New Jersey Devils	1993-94	Ray Bourque, Boston Bruins
2002-03	Nicklas Lidstrom, Detroit Red Wings	1992-93	Chris Chelios, Chicago Blackhawks
2001-02	Nicklas Lidstrom, Detroit Red Wings	1991-92	Brian Leetch, New York Rangers
2000-01	Nicklas Lidstrom, Detroit Red Wings	1990-91	Ray Bourque, Boston Bruins
1999-00	Chris Pronger, St. Louis Blues	1989-90	Ray Bourque, Boston Bruins
1998-99	Al MacInnis, St. Louis Blues	1988-89	Chris Chelios, Montreal Canadiens
1997-98	Rob Blake, Los Angeles Kings	1987-88	Ray Bourque, Boston Bruins
1996-97	Brian Leetch, New York Rangers	1986-87	Ray Bourque, Boston Bruins
1995-96	Chris Chelios, Chicago Blackhawks	1985-86	Paul Coffey, Edmonton Oilers
1994-95	Paul Coffey, Detroit Red Wings	1984-85	Paul Coffey, Edmonton Oilers

Calder Memorial Trophy (past 20 seasons)

Awarded annually "to the player selected as the most proficient in his first year of competition in the National Hockey League." Frank Calder was a former NHL president. Sergei Makarov, who won the award in 1989-90, was the oldest recipient of the trophy, at 31. If a player is 26 or older as of September 15 of a season, he is not eligible to win the award.

Season	Winner
2003-04	Andrew Raycroft, Boston Bruins
2002-03	Barret Jackman, St. Louis Blues
2001-02	Dany Heatley, Atlanta Thrashers
2000-01	Evgeni Nabokov, San Jose Sharks
1999-00	Scott Gomez, New Jersey Devils
1998-99	Chris Drury, Colorado Avalanche
1997-98	Sergei Samsonov, Boston Bruins
1996-97	Bryan Berard, New York Islanders
1995-96	Daniel Alfredsson, Ottawa Senators
1994-95	Peter Forsberg, Quebec Nordiques
1993-94	Martin Brodeur, New Jersey Devils
1992-93	Teemu Selanne, Winnipeg Jets
1991-92	Pavel Bure, Vancouver Canucks
1990-91	Ed Belfour, Chicago Blackhawks
1989-90	Sergei Makarov, Calgary Flames
1988-89	Brian Leetch, New York Rangers
1987-88	Joe Nieuwendyk, Calgary Flames
1986-87	Luc Robitaille, Los Angeles Kings
1985-86	Gary Suter, Calgary Flames
1984-85	Mario Lemieux, Pittsburgh Penguins

Fast Fact: In 2003-04, Florida Panther goaltender Roberto Luongo set the record for shots faced in the regular season (2,475).

Vezina Trophy (past 20 seasons)

Awarded annually "to the goalkeeper adjudged to be the best at his position." The trophy was named for Georges Vezina, an outstanding goalie for the Montreal Canadiens who collapsed during a game on November 28, 1925, and died four months later of tuberculosis. The general managers of the NHL teams vote on the award.

Season	Winner
2003-04	Martin Brodeur, New Jersey Devils
2002-03	Martin Brodeur, New Jersey Devils
2001-02	Jose Theodore, Montreal Canadiens
2000-01	Dominik Hasek, Buffalo Sabres
1999-00	Olaf Kolzig, Washington Capitals
1998-99	Dominik Hasek, Buffalo Sabres
1997-98	Dominik Hasek, Buffalo Sabres
1996-97	Dominik Hasek, Buffalo Sabres
1995-96	Jim Carey, Washington Capitals
1994-95	Dominik Hasek, Buffalo Sabres
1993-94	Dominik Hasek, Buffalo Sabres
1992-93	Ed Belfour, Chicago Blackhawks
1991-92	Patrick Roy, Montreal Canadiens
1990-91	Ed Belfour, Chicago Blackhawks
1989-90	Patrick Roy, Montreal Canadiens
1988-89	Patrick Roy, Montreal Canadiens
1987-88	Grant Fuhr, Edmonton Oilers
1986-87	Ron Hextall, Philadelphia Flyers
1985-86	John Vanbiesbrouck, New York Rangers
1984-85	Pelle Lindbergh, Philadelphia Flyers

Selke Trophy (past 20 seasons)

Awarded annually "to the forward who best excels in the defensive aspects of the game." The trophy was named for Frank J. Selke, the architect of the Montreal Canadiens dynasty that won the Stanley Cup five consecutive times in the late 1950's. The winner is selected by a vote of the Professional Hockey Writers Association.

Season	Winner
2003-04	Kris Draper, Detroit Red Wings
2002-03	Jere Lehtinen, Dallas Stars
2001-02	Michael Peca, New York Islanders
2000-01	John Madden, New Jersey Devils
1999-00	Steve Yzerman, Detroit Red Wings
1998-99	Jere Lehtinen, Dallas Stars
1997-98	Jere Lehtinen, Dallas Stars
1996-97	Michael Peca, Buffalo Sabres
1995-96	Sergei Fedorov, Detroit Red Wings
1994-95	Ron Francis, Pittsburgh Penguins
1993-94	Sergei Fedorov, Detroit Red Wings
1992-93	Doug Gilmour, Toronto Maple Leafs
1991-92	Guy Carbonneau, Montreal Canadiens
1990-91	Dirk Graham, Chicago Blackhawks
1989-90	Rick Meagher, St. Louis Blues
1988-89	Guy Carbonneau, Montreal Canadiens
1987-88	Guy Carbonneau, Montreal Canadiens
1986-87	Dave Poulin, Philadelphia Flyers
1985-86	Troy Murray, Chicago Blackhawks
1984-85	Craig Ramsay, Buffalo Sabres

Career Records

LOU CAPOZZOLA

Mark Messier, New York Rangers

All-time Points Leaders

Player	YRS	GP	G	A	PTS	PTS/GAME
Wayne Gretzky, Edm, LA, StL, NYR	20	1,487	894	1,963	2,857	1.921
*Mark Messier, Edm, Van, NYR	25	1,756	694	1,193	1,887	1.075
Gordie Howe, Det, Hart	26	1,767	801	1,049	1,850	1.047
*Ron Francis, Hart, Pitt, Car, Tor	23	1,731	549	1,249	1,798	1.039
Marcel Dionne, Det, LA, NYR	18	1,348	731	1,040	1,771	1.314

All-time Goal-Scoring Leaders

Player	YRS	GP	G	G/GAME
Wayne Gretzky, Edm, LA, StL, NYR	20	1,487	894	.601
Gordie Howe, Det, Hart	26	1,767	801	.453
*Brett Hull, Cal, StL, Dall, Det	19	1,264	741	.586
Marcel Dionne, Det, LA, NYR	18	1,348	731	.542
Phil Esposito, Chi, Bos, NYR	18	1,282	717	.559

All-time Assists Leaders

Player	YRS	GP	A	A/GAME
Wayne Gretzky, Edm, LA, StL, NYR	20	1,487	1,963	1.320
*Ron Francis, Hart, Pitt, Car, Tor	23	1,731	1,249	.721
*Mark Messier, Edm, NYR, Van	25	1,756	1,193	.679
Ray Bourque, Bos, Col	22	1,612	1,169	.725
Paul Coffey, eight teams	21	1,409	1,135	.806

GOALTENDING

All-time Win Leaders

Goaltender	W	L	T
Patrick Roy, Mtl, Col	551	315	131
Terry Sawchuk, Det, Bos, Tor, LA, NYR	447	330	172
Jacques Plante, Mtl, NYR, StL, Tor, Bos	435	247	145
Tony Esposito, Mtl, Chi	423	306	151
Glenn Hall, Det, Chi, StL	407	326	163

All-time Shutout Leaders

Goaltender	Team	YRS	GP	SO
Terry Sawchuk	Det, Bos, Tor, LA, NYR	21	971	103
George Hainsworth	Mtl, Tor	11	465	94
Glenn Hall	Det, Chi, StL	18	906	84
Jacques Plante	Mtl, NYR, StL, Tor, Bos	18	837	82
Tiny Thompson	Bos, Det	12	553	81
Alex Connell	Ott, Det, NYA, Mtl M	12	417	81

All-time Goals-Against Average Leaders (Pre-1950)

Goaltender	Team	YRS	GP	GA	GAA
George Hainsworth	Mtl, Tor	11	465	937	1.91
Alex Connell	Ott, Det, NYA, Mtl M	12	417	830	1.91
Chuck Gardiner	Chi	7	316	664	2.02
Lorne Chabot	NYR, Tor, Mtl, Chi, Mtl M, NYA	11	411	861	2.04
Tiny Thompson	Bos, Det	12	553	1,183	2.08

All-time Goals-Against Average Leaders (Post-1950)

w
sey
ils

Goaltender	Team	YRS	GP	GA	GAA
*Martin Brodeur	NJ	12	740	1,573	2.17
*Dominik Hasek	Chi, Buff, Det	13	595	1,284	2.23
Ken Dryden	Mtl	8	397	870	2.24
Jacques Plante	Mtl, NYR, StL, Tor, Bos	18	837	1,965	2.38
*Ed Belfour	Chi, SJ, Dall, Tor	15	856	2,006	2.43

Note: Minimum 350 games played. Goals-against average equals goals against per 60 minutes played.
*Active in 2003-04.

KEY YRS=years; GP=games played; G=goals; A=assists; PTS=points; PTS/GAME=points per game; G/Game=goals per game; A/GAME=assists per game; W=win; L=loss; T=tie; SO=shutout; GA=goals allowed; GAA=goals-against average

NHL All-Star Game

First played in 1947, this game was scheduled before the start of the regular season and used to match the defending Stanley Cup champions against a squad of NHL All-Stars from other teams. In 1966, the game was moved to mid-season, although there was no game that year. The format was changed to a conference-versus-conference showdown in 1969.

RESULTS

Year	Site	Score	MVP	Attendance
2004	St. Paul, MN	East 6, West 4	Joe Sakic, Col (West)	19,434
2003	Sunrise, FL	West 6, East 5	Dany Heatley, Atl (East)	19,250
2002	Los Angeles, CA	World 8, N America 5	Eric Daze, Chi (N America)	18,118
2001	Denver, CO	N America 14, World 12	Bill Guerin, Bos (N America)	18,646
2000	Toronto, ONT	World 9, N America 4	Pavel Bure, Fla (World)	19,300
1999	Tampa Bay, FL	N America 8, World 6	Wayne Gretzky, NYR (N America)	19,758
1998	Vancouver, BC	N America 8, World 7	Teemu Selanne, Ana (World)	18,422
1997	San Jose, CA	East 11, West 7	Mark Recchi, Mtl	17,422
1996	Boston, MA	East 5, West 4	Ray Bourque, Bos	17,565
1994	New York, NY	East 9, West 8	Mike Richter, NYR	18,200
1993	Montreal, QUE	Wales 16, Campbell 6	Mike Gartner, NYR	17,137
1992	Philadelphia, PA	Campbell 10, Wales 6	Brett Hull, StL	17,380
1991	Chicago, IL	Campbell 11, Wales 5	Vince Damphousse, Tor	18,472
1990	Pittsburgh, PA,	Wales 12, Campbell 7	Mario Lemieux, Pitt	16,236
1989	Edmonton, ALB	Campbell 9, Wales 5	Wayne Gretzky, LA	17,503
1988	St. Louis, MO	Wales 6, Campbell 5 (OT)	Mario Lemieux, Pitt	17,878
1986	Hartford, CT	Wales 4, Campbell 3 (OT)	Grant Fuhr, Edm	15,100
1985	Calgary, ALB	Wales 6, Campbell 4	Mario Lemieux, Pitt	16,825
1984	East Rutherford, NJ	Wales 7, Campbell 6	Don Maloney, NYR	18,939
1983	Uniondale, NY	Campbell 9, Wales 3	Wayne Gretzky, Edm	15,230
1982	Washington, DC	Wales 4, Campbell 2	Mike Bossy, NYI	18,130
1981	Los Angeles, CA	Campbell 4, Wales 1	Mike Liut, StL	15,761
1980	Detroit, MI	Wales 6, Campbell 3	Reg Leach, Phil	21,002
1978	Buffalo, NY	Wales 3, Campbell 2 (OT)	Billy Smith, NYI	16,433
1977	Vancouver, BC	Wales 4, Campbell 3	Rick Martin, Buff	15,607
1976	Philadelphia, PA	Wales 7, Campbell 5	Pete Mahovlich, Mtl	16,436
1975	Montreal, QUE	Wales 7, Campbell 1	Syl Apps Jr, Pitt	16,080
1974	Chicago, IL	West 6, East 4	Garry Unger, StL	16,426
1973	New York, NY	East 5, West 4	Greg Polis, Pitt	16,986
1972	Minneapolis, MN	East 3, West 2	Bobby Orr, Bos	15,423
1971	Boston, MA	West 2, East 1	Bobby Hull, Chi	14,790
1970	St. Louis, MO	East 4, West 1	Bobby Hull, Chi	16,587
1969	Montreal, QUE	East 3, West 3	Frank Mahovlich, Det	16,260
1968	Toronto, ONT	Toronto 4, All-Stars 3	Bruce Gamble, Tor	15,753
1967	Montreal, QUE	Montreal 3, All-Stars 0	Henri Richard, Mtl	14,284
1965	Montreal, QUE	All-Stars 5, Montreal 2	Gordie Howe, Det	13,529
1964	Toronto, ONT	All-Stars 3, Toronto 2	Jean Beliveau, Mtl	14,232
1963	Toronto, ONT	All-Stars 3, Toronto 3	Frank Mahovlich, Tor	14,034
1962	Toronto, ONT	Toronto 4, All-Stars 1	Eddie Shack, Tor	14,236
1961	Chicago, IL	All-Stars 3, Chicago 1	None named	14,534
1960	Montreal, QUE	All-Stars 2, Montreal 1	None named	13,949
1959	Montreal, QUE	Montreal 6, All-Stars 1	None named	13,818
1958	Montreal, QUE	Montreal 6, All-Stars 3	None named	13,989
1957	Montreal, QUE	All-Stars 5, Montreal 3	None named	13,003
1956	Montreal, QUE	All-Stars 1, Montreal 1	None named	13,095
1955	Detroit, MI	Detroit 3, All-Stars 1	None named	10,111
1954	Detroit, MI	All-Stars 2, Detroit 2	None named	10,689
1953	Montreal, QUE	All-Stars 3, Montreal 1	None named	14,153
1952	Detroit, MI	1st team 1, 2nd team 1	None named	10,680
1951	Toronto, ONT	1st team 2, 2nd team 2	None named	11,469
1950	Detroit, MI	Detroit 7, All-Stars 1	None named	9,166
1949	Toronto, ONT	All-Stars 3, Toronto 1	None named	13,541
1948	Chicago, IL	All-Stars 3, Toronto 1	None named	12,794
1947	Toronto, ONT	All-Stars 4, Toronto 3	None named	14,169

Note: The Challenge Cup, a series between the NHL All-Stars and the Soviet Union, was played instead of the All-Star Game in 1979. Eight years later, Rendez-Vous '87, a two-game series matching the Soviet Union and the NHL All-Stars, replaced the All-Star Game. The 1995 NHL All-Star Game was canceled because of a labor dispute. The 1998 NHL All-Star Game, billed as a preview to the 1998 Winter Olympics, in Nagano, Japan, matched North American-born All-Stars and All-Stars born elsewhere. NHL All-Star Games from 1999 through 2002 also followed this format.

Today's Stars

Markus Naslund finished in the Top 10 in points, goals, and assists in 2003-04.

ROBERT BECK/SPORTS ILLUSTRATED

Markus Naslund, left wing, b. July 30, 1973, Ornskoldsvik, Sweden. After riding the bench for nearly three seasons with the Pittsburgh Penguins, Naslund was traded to the Vancouver Canucks, in 1996. Since then, he has become the league's most dominant offensive player while helping the Canucks become regular playoff contenders. Naslund was runner-up to countryman Peter Forsberg for the 2002-03 scoring title (104 points) and led the league in game-winning goals (12) that season. In 2003-04, he finished fourth in the scoring race (84 points). Entering his 12th NHL season, Naslund was just 10 goals shy of 300 for his career.

Jarome Iginla, right wing, b. July 1, 1977, in Edmonton, Alberta, Canada. Iginla became the first black captain in NHL history when the Calgary Flames made him their leader in early 2003-04. He responded by tying for the league lead in goals (41), finishing second to Martin St. Louis in the MVP voting, and leading Calgary to the Stanley Cup finals. In just his second post-season appearance, he scored 22 points and a playoff-leading 13 goals in 26 games. Iginla was named MVP by NHL players in 2001-02, after leading the league in goals (52) and points (96).

Rick Nash, left wing, b. June 16, 1984, in Brampton, Ontario, Canada. Playing for the Columbus Blue Jackets in just his second NHL season, Nash was tied with right wing Jarome Iginla and left wing Ilya Kovalchuk of the Atlanta Thrashers for the league lead in goals (41) in 2003-04. He was 19, the youngest NHL player to finish first in goals scored. Nash led Columbus in points (57) and game-winning goals (7), and played in his first All-Star Game that season. As a rookie, in 2002-03, the 6 ' 4 " winger scored two goals in the Young Stars game, held during All-Star weekend. He was also a finalist for the league's Rookie of the Year Award.

Trivia Challenge

Which active NHL goaltender is tied with legend Jacques Plante for winning the Vezina Trophy the most times? (The trophy is awarded to the league's top goalie each season.)

Dominik Hasek won the award six times in eight seasons with the Buffalo Sabres.

Visit **www.sikids.com** for the latest sports stats and info.

SOCCER

MEN'S

The San Jose Earthquakes rumbled into the 2003 championship match of Major League Soccer (MLS) and came away with their second MLS Cup in three seasons. Led by forward Landon Donovan's two goals, the 'Quakes defeated the Chicago Fire, 4–2, at the brand new Home Depot Center, in Carson, California. Donovan was named MVP of the game.

Preki, the Kansas City Wizards' 40-year-old midfielder, won the MLS scoring title (41 points) and was named the regular-season MVP.

MLS continued to develop world-class talent and ship it overseas. MetroStars goalie Tim Howard made the leap in July when he signed with England's Manchester United. Defender Carlos Bocanegra and goalkeeper Zach Thornton of the Chicago Fire, and forward Brian McBride of the Columbus Crew also joined European clubs.

The biggest news in international soccer was the signing of two players. Megastar midfielder David Beckham left Manchester United after 12 years and signed a four-year deal with Spain's Real Madrid on July 1.

On November 18, MLS signed teen prodigy Freddy Adu of Potomac, Maryland, to a six-year contract. Several European soccer clubs were interested in the 14-year-old. The D.C. United forward is the league's highest paid player ($500,000 per season). Adu began his first MLS season in 2004 with huge expectations. "He's going to be one of the best players in the world," says D.C. coach Peter Nowak.

Forward Landon Donovan had 12 goals and 6 assists for the Earthquakes in 2003.

J. BRETT WHITESELL/ISI

Trivia Challenge

Which team won the first MLS Cup?

D.C. United. It defeated the Los Angeles Galaxy, 3–2 in overtime, in Foxboro, Massachusetts, on October 20, 1996.

MLS TEAMS

EASTERN CONFERENCE
Chicago Fire
Columbus Crew
D.C. United
MetroStars
New England Revolution

WESTERN CONFERENCE
Colorado Rapids
Dallas Burn
Kansas City Wizards
Los Angeles Galaxy
San Jose Earthquakes

HOWARD C. SMITH/ICON SMI

Damani Ralph (left) scored the lone goal in the Chicago Fire's U.S. Open Cup victory in 2003.

MLS CUP 2003

The Home Depot Center, Carson, California
November 23, 2003
Attendance: 27,000

	1st Half	2nd Half	Final
San Jose Earthquakes	2	2	4
Chicago Fire	0	2	2

Scoring Summary:
SJ: Ekelund (unassisted) 5
SJ: Donovan (Walker) 38
CHI: Beasley (Williams) 49
SJ: Mulrooney (Waibel) 50
CHI: own goal (Roner) 54
SJ: Donovan (De Rosario, Mullan) 71
Earthquakes: Pat Onstad, Eddie Robinson, Troy Dayak, Craig Waibel (Chris Roner 51), Jeff Agoos, Brian Mullan, Ronnie Ekelund, Richard Mulrooney, Manny Lagos (Ian Russell 70), Landon Donovan, Jamil Walker (Dwayne De Rosario 60)
Fire: Zach Thornton, Jim Curtin (Nate Jaqua 81), Evan Whitfield, Carlos Bocanegra, Orlando Perez (Kelly Gray 46), Andy Williams (Justin Mapp 70), Chris Armas, Jesse Marsch, DaMarcus Beasley, Ante Razov, Damani Ralph

Note: Numbers next to player names indicate time of game.

2003 MLS Final Standings

Eastern Conference

TEAM	GP	W	L	T	PTS	GF	GA
y-Fire	30	15	7	8	53	53	43
x-Revolution	30	12	9	9	45	55	47
x-MetroStars	30	11	10	9	42	40	40
x-United	30	10	11	9	39	38	36
z-Crew	30	10	12	8	38	44	44

Western Conference

TEAM	GP	W	L	T	PTS	GF	GA
y-Earthquakes	30	14	7	9	51	45	35
x-Wizards	30	11	10	9	42	48	44
x-Rapids	30	11	12	7	40	40	45
x-Galaxy	30	9	12	9	36	35	35
z-Burn	30	6	19	5	23	35	64

Note: Three points for a win. One point for a tie.
x=clinched playoffs; y=conference champion;
z=eliminated from playoffs.

KEY GP=games played; W=win; L=loss; T=tie; PTS=points; GF=goals for; GA=goals against

2003 MLS Playoffs

PLAYOFF LEADERS

SCORING	Games	Goals	Assists	Points
Landon Donovan, Earthquakes	4	4	2	10
Chris Klein, Wizards	3	2	1	5
Richard Mulrooney, Earthquakes	4	1	3	5
Ante Razov, Fire	4	2	1	5
Igor Simutenkov, Wizards	2	2	1	5
Ronnie Ekelund, Earthquakes	3	1	2	4
Brian Mullan, Earthquakes	4	1	2	4
Pat Noonan, Revolution	3	2	0	4
Carlos Ruiz, Galaxy	2	2	0	4
Jamil Walker, Earthquakes	4	1	2	4

Six tied with 3.

GOALS	Games	Goals
Landon Donovan, Earthquakes	4	4
Chris Klein, Wizards	3	2
Pat Noonan, Revolution	3	2
Ante Razov, Fire	4	2
Carlos Ruiz, Galaxy	2	2
Igor Simutenkov, Wizards	2	2

18 tied with 1.

ASSISTS	Games	Assists
Jose Cancela, Revolution	3	3
Richard Mulrooney, Earthquakes	4	3
Hong Myung-Bo, Galaxy	2	2
Ronnie Ekelund, Earthquakes	3	2
Troy Dayak, Earthquakes	4	2
Landon Donovan, Earthquakes	4	2
Brian Mullan, Earthquakes	4	2
Ian Russell, Earthquakes	4	2
Jamil Walker, Earthquakes	4	2

20 tied with 1.

GOALS-AGAINST AVERAGE	Games	GAA
Adin Brown, Revolution	3	0.64
Zach Thornton, Fire	4	0.97
Tony Meola, Wizards	3	1.21
Joe Cannon, Rapids	2	1.50
Jonny Walker, MetroStars	2	1.50
Pat Onstad, Earthquakes	4	1.83
Doug Warren, United	2	2.00
Kevin Hartman, Galaxy	2	2.42

Adin Brown, New England Revolution

Today's Stars

Fourteen-year-old Freddy Adu is the youngest player in MLS.

AL MESSERSCHMIDT/WIREIMAGE.COM

Freddy Adu, forward, b. June 2, 1989, Tema, Ghana. Adu became the youngest person (14 years, 10 months) to play in a top-level U.S. pro sports league in more than 100 years when he made his MLS debut with D.C. United in April 2004. Adu and his family moved to Potomac, Maryland, in 1997. U.S. Soccer discovered the phenom playing for school and club teams in 2001 and asked him to join the Under-14 national team. He later played for the Under-17 and Under-20 squads.

Taylor Twellman, forward, b. February 29, 1980, St. Louis, Missouri. Twellman finished 2003 tied for the MLS lead in goals (15), despite missing eight games for the New England Revolution because of injuries. He won the scoring title (52 points) in 2002 as a rookie after netting 23 goals and serving up six assists.

Carlos Ruiz, forward, b. September 15, 1979, Guatemala City, Guatemala. Ruiz tied Twellman for the league lead in goals (15) in 2003. He burst into MLS in 2002 as a rookie with the Los Angeles Galaxy and scored six goals in his first four games. He went on to pump in a league-leading 24 goals in 2002 and won the MLS MVP award. His overtime goal in the MLS Cup championship in 2002 beat the New England Revolution, 1–0.

Trivia Challenge

Which player has appeared in the most international matches for the U.S. men's team?

Forward Cobi Jones. He has played 159 matches for the U.S. team since 1992. He also plays for the Los Angeles Galaxy.

TEAM-BY-TEAM STATS

CHICAGO FIRE

PLAYER	GP	MIN	G	A	PTS	SHOTS	SOG
Ante Razov	26	2,270	14	6	34	119	67
Damani Ralph	25	1,985	11	6	28	91	36
DaMarcus Beasley	22	1,969	7	5	19	45	16
Andy Williams	20	1,360	2	7	11	22	7
Jesse Marsch	19	1,465	5	0	10	20	10
Justin Mapp	21	1,384	3	3	9	19	11
Chris Armas	25	2,267	2	4	8	19	7
Nate Jaqua	20	712	2	2	6	17	7
Kelly Gray	28	1,910	2	1	5	25	10
Carlos Bocanegra	19	1,784	1	2	4	10	5
Orlando Perez	21	1,635	2	0	4	12	5
Dipsy Selolwane	5	165	1	1	3	5	2
Evan Whitfield	27	2,329	1	1	3	14	8
Jonathan Bolanos	2	92	0	1	1	2	0
C.J. Brown	21	1,728	0	1	1	7	2
Jim Curtin	30	2,733	0	1	1	10	3
Ryan Futagaki	6	218	0	1	1	3	0
Craig Capano	5	122	0	0	0	0	0
*Rodrigo Faria	5	330	0	0	0	10	3
Logan Pause	23	1,354	0	0	0	4	1
FIRE			**53**	**42**	**148**	**454**	**200**
OPPONENTS			**43**	**48**	**134**	**365**	**176**

INDIVIDUAL GOALKEEPING

GOALKEEPER	GP	MIN	SHOTS	SVS	C/P	GA	GAA
Zach Thornton	30	2,728	165	123	82	37	1.22
Curtis Spiteri	1	45	10	4	1	6	12.00
Henry Ring	1	11	1	1	0	0	0.00
TOTALS	**30**	**2,784**	**176**	**133**	**84**	**43**	**1.39**

COLORADO RAPIDS

PLAYER	GP	MIN	G	A	PTS	SHOTS	SOG
John Spencer	27	2,265	14	5	33	81	37
Mark Chung	29	2,639	11	6	28	78	39
Chris Carrieri	30	2,458	3	8	14	54	27
Chris Henderson	26	2,180	4	6	14	47	17
Zizi Roberts	12	729	5	0	10	27	16
Kyle Beckerman	28	2,124	0	5	5	29	14
Ritchie Kotschau	26	2,333	1	1	3	17	3
Seth Trembly	16	1,112	1	1	3	16	6
Matt Crawford	16	750	1	0	2	3	2
Wes Hart	29	2,623	0	2	2	12	4
Zach Kingsley	12	480	0	2	2	4	3
Pablo Mastroeni	18	1,655	0	2	2	6	0
Casey Schmidt	13	363	0	2	2	4	0
Alex Blake	3	24	0	0	0	1	0
Nat Borchers	23	2,101	0	0	0	0	0
Robin Fraser	26	2,335	0	0	0	1	0
Steven Herdsman	3	198	0	0	0	0	0
Darryl Powell	5	335	0	0	0	1	1
Alberto Rizo	6	297	0	0	0	2	2
Jeff Stewart	8	608	0	0	0	1	1
RAPIDS			**40**	**40**	**120**	**384**	**172**
OPPONENTS			**45**	**41**	**131**	**370**	**145**

INDIVIDUAL GOALKEEPING

GOALKEEPER	GP	MIN	SHOTS	SVS	C/P	GA	GAA
Scott Garlick	26	2,346	123	83	97	38	1.46
Scott Vallow	4	380	22	14	12	7	1.66
Joe Cannon	1	45	0	0	5	0	0.00
TOTALS	**30**	**2,771**	**145**	**102**	**114**	**45**	**1.46**

*Played for more than one team.

KEY GP=games played; MIN=minutes played; G=goals; A=assists; PTS=points; SOG=shots on goal; SVS=saves; C/P=catches/punches; GA=goals allowed; GAA=goals-against average

COLUMBUS CREW

PLAYER	GP	MIN	G	A	PTS	SHOTS	SOG
Brian McBride	24	2,183	12	3	27	68	34
Edson Buddle	21	1,509	10	4	24	59	26
Jeff Cunningham	21	1,405	5	7	17	49	23
Ross Paule	25	2,212	4	7	15	27	15
Brian West	24	1,543	4	4	12	20	10
Freddy Garcia	22	1,278	1	6	8	41	12
Kyle Martino	22	1,765	2	4	8	25	13
Eric Denton	26	2,336	2	1	5	10	7
*Brian Dunseth	19	1,589	1	2	4	8	4
Frankie Hejduk	23	2,128	0	4	4	25	10
Brian Maisonneuve	23	1,730	1	0	2	9	3
*Jeff Matteo	6	286	1	0	2	2	1
*Alex Pineda Chacon	8	325	0	2	2	8	5
Jake Traeger	1	12	0	2	2	1	1
Diego Walsh	14	612	1	0	2	9	4
Mike Clark	29	2,673	0	1	1	10	2
Nelson Akwari	11	488	0	0	0	1	1
Chad McCarty	19	1,226	0	0	0	4	0
Duncan Oughton	23	1,717	0	0	0	16	8
*Trevor Perea	1	34	0	0	0	0	0
Michael Ritch	3	21	0	0	0	0	0
Daniel Torres	8	562	0	0	0	0	0
Mark Williams	5	391	0	0	0	3	0
CREW			**44**	**47**	**135**	**395**	**179**
OPPONENTS			**44**	**36**	**124**	**418**	**174**

INDIVIDUAL GOALKEEPING

GOALKEEPER	GP	MIN	SHOTS	SVS	C/P	GA	GAA
Jon Busch	24	2,194	144	104	88	35	1.44
Tom Presthus	7	613	30	21	28	9	1.32
TOTALS	**30**	**2,807**	**174**	**130**	**116**	**44**	**1.41**

DALLAS BURN

PLAYER	GP	MIN	G	A	PTS	SHOTS	SOG
Brad Davis	26	1,910	6	5	17	41	16
Jason Kreis	18	1,543	7	2	16	42	21
Toni Nhleko	11	792	2	4	8	22	7
Joselito Vaca	27	1,871	2	4	8	32	14
*Ronald Cerritos	15	852	3	1	7	15	10
Chad Deering	27	2,187	1	5	7	24	6
Edward Johnson	22	1,265	3	0	6	31	12
Oscar Pareja	24	1,982	1	4	6	20	3
Bobby Rhine	25	1,034	2	1	5	21	10
*Ali Curtis	8	474	1	2	4	9	5
Chris Gbandi	22	1,573	1	2	4	4	3
*Brian Dunseth	9	806	1	1	3	3	2
*Ezra Hendrickson	16	1,367	1	1	3	6	1
Ronnie O'Brien	6	317	1	0	2	10	5
*Ryan Suarez	12	1,110	1	0	2	9	3
Shavar Thomas	15	1,252	1	0	2	4	2
*Paul Broome	7	563	0	1	1	3	1
*Antonio Martinez	10	564	0	1	1	11	4
Matt Behncke	13	827	0	0	0	6	1
Tenywa Bonseu	20	1,789	0	0	0	4	2
*Gavin Glinton	10	273	0	0	0	4	2
Steve Morrow	17	1,484	0	0	0	6	2
Philip Salyer	8	491	0	0	0	3	0
Jordan Stone	16	1,057	0	0	0	1	0
Mandi Urbas	3	40	0	0	0	1	1
BURN			**35**	**34**	**104**	**332**	**133**
OPPONENTS			**64**	**63**	**191**	**439**	**213**

INDIVIDUAL GOALKEEPING

GOALKEEPER	GP	MIN	SHOTS	SVS	C/P	GA	GAA
D.J. Countess	24	2,193	173	115	88	48	1.97
Jeff Cassar	7	562	40	23	30	16	2.56
Chris Gbandi	1	1	0	0	0	0	0.00
TOTALS	**30**	**2,756**	**213**	**149**	**118**	**64**	**2.09**

*Played for more than one team.

D.C. UNITED

PLAYER	GP	MIN	G	A	PTS	SHOTS	SOG
Marco Etcheverry	25	2,006	6	7	19	27	13
Ben Olsen	26	2,239	4	7	15	31	13
Hristo Stoitchkov	21	901	5	5	15	30	12
Dema Kovalenko	26	2,401	6	0	12	26	14
Eliseo Quintanilla	18	1,179	3	3	9	23	13
Alecko Eskandarian	23	728	3	2	8	15	7
*Ali Curtis	17	1,035	1	4	6	19	6
Mike Petke	25	2,343	3	0	6	11	8
Bobby Convey	19	1,576	2	1	5	27	11
Santino Quaranta	12	738	1	3	5	14	8
Earnie Stewart	21	1,923	1	2	4	24	8
*Ronald Cerritos	10	915	1	1	3	15	6
Galin Ivanov	24	2,011	1	1	3	16	8
Ryan Nelsen	25	2,314	1	0	2	30	12
Jose Alegria	17	1,093	0	1	1	12	5
Bryan Namoff	22	1,665	0	1	1	3	1
Devin Barclay	3	113	0	0	0	0	0
Thiago Martins	5	359	0	0	0	7	3
*Trevor Perea	1	4	0	0	0	0	0
Brandon Prideaux	28	2,586	0	0	0	1	0
D.C. UNITED			**38**	**38**	**114**	**331**	**148**
OPPONENTS			**36**	**31**	**103**	**370**	**165**

INDIVIDUAL GOALKEEPING

GOALKEEPER	GP	MIN	SHOTS	SVS	C/P	GA	GAA
Nick Rimando	25	2,318	131	100	71	29	1.13
Doug Warren	5	404	33	26	19	6	1.34
*Clint Baumstark	1	100	1	0	5	1	0.90
TOTALS	**30**	**2,822**	**165**	**129**	**95**	**36**	**1.15**

KANSAS CITY WIZARDS

PLAYER	GP	MIN	G	A	PTS	SHOTS	SOG
Preki	30	2,678	12	17	41	92	34
Igor Simutenkov	21	1,435	7	3	17	43	25
Chris Klein	27	2,527	6	4	16	37	16
Eric Quill	27	2,261	3	7	13	33	17
Jimmy Conrad	30	2,777	4	1	9	18	8
Francisco Gomez	26	1,644	3	3	9	45	19
Davy Arnaud	18	818	3	0	6	11	5
*Chris Brown	18	1,189	2	2	6	29	13
Josh Wolff	13	872	2	1	5	14	9
Stephen Armstrong	23	1,102	2	0	4	17	9
Kerry Zavagnin	29	2,487	1	2	4	12	2
Chris Brunt	4	166	1	0	2	2	1
Alex Zotinca	20	1,239	1	0	2	11	5
Carey Talley	20	1,344	0	1	1	3	0
Jose Burciaga, Jr.	4	347	0	0	0	2	2
*Dario Fabbro	8	179	0	0	0	3	1
Nick Garcia	29	2,689	0	0	0	7	2
Taylor Graham	2	10	0	0	0	0	0
Diego Gutierrez	20	1,559	0	0	0	12	2
*Wolde Harris	10	560	0	0	0	20	10
Jack Jewsbury	2	61	0	0	0	0	0
WIZARDS			**48**	**41**	**137**	**411**	**180**
OPPONENTS			**44**	**38**	**126**	**370**	**172**

INDIVIDUAL GOALKEEPING

GOALKEEPER	GP	MIN	SHOTS	SVS	C/P	GA	GAA
Tony Meola	30	2,789	172	121	82	44	1.42
Bo Oshoniyi	1	8	0	0	0	0	0.00
TOTALS	**30**	**2,797**	**172**	**129**	**82**	**44**	**1.42**

*Played for more than one team.

LOS ANGELES GALAXY

PLAYER	GP	MIN	G	A	PTS	SHOTS	SOG
Carlos Ruiz	26	2,331	15	5	35	84	51
Alejandro Moreno	24	1,117	6	2	14	19	12
Cobi Jones	28	2,574	2	8	12	34	8
Chris Albright	27	1,966	3	4	10	48	24
Diego Serna	10	660	3	2	8	8	5
Sasha Victorine	20	1,797	2	1	5	30	17
Simon Elliott	24	2,141	1	2	4	39	16
*Gavin Glinton	9	399	1	1	3	12	8
Alexi Lalas	22	1,760	1	1	3	11	5
Danny Califf	23	2,162	0	2	2	13	5
Mauricio Cienfuegos	20	1,344	0	2	2	13	6
*Antonio Martinez	4	212	1	0	2	2	1
Hong Myung-Bo	25	2,296	0	2	2	7	0
Isaias Bardales, Jr.	1	21	0	0	0	0	0
*Paul Broome	4	186	0	0	0	0	0
Herculez Gomez	1	5	0	0	0	0	0
Guillermo Gonzalez	6	129	0	0	0	2	1
*Ezra Hendrickson	12	938	0	0	0	12	3
Ricky Lewis	13	798	0	0	0	0	0
Tyrone Marshall	25	1,882	0	0	0	9	0
Jesus Ochoa	10	571	0	0	0	5	0
*Alex Pineda Chacon	6	378	0	0	0	7	3
Jose Retiz	5	111	0	0	0	0	0
*Ryan Suarez	3	246	0	0	0	0	0
Arturo Torres	9	335	0	0	0	6	4
Peter Vagenas	20	1,724	0	0	0	7	3
Kevin Hartman	30	2,796	0	1	0	0	0
GALAXY			**35**	**33**	**103**	**367**	**171**
OPPONENTS			**35**	**34**	**104**	**434**	**190**

INDIVIDUAL GOALKEEPING

GOALKEEPER	GP	MIN	SHOTS	SVS	C/P	GA	GAA
Kevin Hartman	30	2,796	190	149	81	35	1.13
Dan Popik	1	16	0	0	0	0	0.00
TOTALS	**30**	**2,812**	**190**	**155**	**81**	**35**	**1.12**

METROSTARS

PLAYER	GP	MIN	G	A	PTS	SHOTS	SOG
Clint Mathis	22	2,019	9	1	19	84	35
Amado Guevara	25	2,264	3	10	16	72	37
Mike Magee	29	1,709	7	2	16	44	25
Mark Lisi	24	1,829	1	11	13	17	7
John Wolyniec	25	1,385	5	2	12	39	20
Steve Jolley	24	2,194	4	0	8	11	9
Ricardo Clark	28	2,590	3	1	7	38	15
Jacob LeBlanc	7	225	2	0	4	3	2
Jaime Moreno	11	517	2	0	4	10	6
Craig Ziadie	22	1,913	1	2	4	5	2
Eddie Gaven	12	691	1	1	3	13	9
Andrzej Juskowiak	5	160	1	0	2	7	3
Eddie Pope	20	1,724	0	2	2	15	6
Richie Williams	26	2,337	0	2	2	12	4
Joseph Addo	8	700	0	1	1	1	1
Kenny Arena	10	458	0	0	0	3	1
Edgar Bartolomeu	13	1,000	0	0	0	6	0
Joey DiGiamarino	18	1,446	0	0	0	4	2
Juan Forchetti	10	775	0	0	0	1	1
Jose Galvan	9	266	0	0	0	2	0
Chris Leitch	15	993	0	0	0	3	1
Mike Nugent	1	90	0	0	0	4	3
Tim Regan	15	747	0	0	0	5	2
METROSTARS			**40**	**35**	**115**	**399**	**191**
OPPONENTS			**40**	**40**	**120**	**421**	**190**

INDIVIDUAL GOALKEEPING

GOALKEEPER	GP	MIN	SHOTS	SVS	C/P	GA	GAA
Jonny Walker	14	1,325	70	55	44	14	0.95
Tim Howard	13	1,222	96	74	65	18	1.33
Paul Grafer	3	270	24	14	13	8	2.67
Eddie Gaven	1	1	0	0	0	0	0.00
TOTALS	**30**	**2,818**	**190**	**150**	**123**	**40**	**1.28**

*Played for more than one team.

NEW ENGLAND REVOLUTION

PLAYER	GP	MIN	G	A	PTS	SHOTS	SOG
Taylor Twellman	22	1,893	15	4	34	90	47
Pat Noonan	28	1,646	10	7	27	44	24
Brian Kamler	28	2,322	6	5	17	37	18
Joe-Max Moore	16	1,187	4	7	15	42	19
Steve Ralston	26	2,348	4	7	15	29	15
Jose Cancela	13	1,142	1	7	9	36	13
Jay Heaps	28	2,579	3	1	7	25	9
*Chris Brown	3	138	3	0	6	6	5
Joe Franchino	25	2,355	1	4	6	25	8
*Wolde Harris	17	856	2	2	6	26	13
Shalrie Joseph	28	2,466	2	2	6	46	17
*Dario Fabbro	8	511	2	0	4	7	4
Leo Cullen	26	1,564	0	2	2	7	2
Daniel Hernandez	9	520	0	2	2	8	2
*Jorge Vazquez	4	197	0	1	1	1	0
Chris Bagley	3	59	0	0	0	0	0
Daouda Kante	16	1,319	0	0	0	2	2
Ibrahim Kante	2	65	0	0	0	1	0
Marshall Leonard	10	550	0	0	0	2	0
Carlos Llamosa	24	2,001	0	0	0	0	0
Jason Moore	13	328	0	0	0	4	2
Rusty Pierce	21	1,878	0	0	0	2	1
REVOLUTION			**55**	**51**	**161**	**440**	**201**
OPPONENTS			**47**	**48**	**142**	**336**	**159**

INDIVIDUAL GOALKEEPING

GOALKEEPER	GP	MIN	SHOTS	SVS	C/P	GA	GAA
Adin Brown	25	2,347	136	95	115	37	1.42
Matt Reis	5	458	23	12	30	10	1.97
Shalrie Joseph	1	1	0	0	0	0	0.00
Kyle Singer	1	1	0	0	0	0	0.00
TOTALS	**30**	**2,807**	**159**	**114**	**146**	**47**	**1.51**

SAN JOSE EARTHQUAKES

PLAYER	GP	MIN	G	A	PTS	SHOTS	SOG
Landon Donovan	22	1,882	12	6	30	53	30
Brian Mullan	30	2,723	6	9	21	38	19
Brian Ching	15	1,235	6	2	14	39	17
Dwayne De Rosario	11	686	4	3	11	20	8
Manny Lagos	27	1,545	3	5	11	33	12
Todd Dunivant	30	2,778	1	6	8	19	11
Jamil Walker	19	365	4	0	8	18	13
Richard Mulrooney	25	2,330	0	7	7	24	7
Jeff Agoos	28	2,593	2	2	6	17	4
Chris Roner	23	1,939	2	2	6	16	8
Ronnie Ekelund	22	1,457	1	3	5	15	5
Ian Russell	18	1,339	0	5	5	14	5
Ramiro Corrales	25	2,080	1	2	4	39	14
Arturo Alvarez	15	655	1	1	3	6	2
Eddie Robinson	13	1,121	1	1	3	5	3
Craig Waibel	24	1,991	0	2	2	9	4
*Rodrigo Faria	4	249	0	1	1	8	1
Troy Dayak	9	785	0	0	0	2	0
Roger Levesque	3	43	0	0	0	0	0
EARTHQUAKES			**45**	**57**	**147**	**377**	**164**
OPPONENTS			**35**	**39**	**109**	**367**	**155**

INDIVIDUAL GOALKEEPING

GOALKEEPER	GP	MIN	SHOTS	SVS	C/P	GA	GAA
Pat Onstad	27	2,510	138	103	117	29	1.04
Jon Conway	3	280	18	11	10	6	1.93
TOTALS	**30**	**2,790**	**156**	**122**	**127**	**35**	**1.13**

*Played for more than one team.

VICTOR DECOLONGON/GETTY IMAGES

Carlos Ruiz, Los Angeles Galaxy

2003 MLS Statistical Leaders

SCORING	Games	Goals	Assists	Points
Preki, Wizards	30	12	17	41
Carlos Ruiz, Galaxy	26	15	5	35
Ante Razov, Fire	26	14	6	34
Taylor Twellman, Revolution	22	15	4	34
John Spencer, Rapids	27	14	5	33
Landon Donovan, Earthquakes	22	12	6	30
Mark Chung, Rapids	29	11	6	28
Damani Ralph, Fire	25	11	6	28
Brian McBride, Crew	24	12	3	27
Pat Noonan, Revolution	28	10	7	27

GOALS	Games	Goals
Carlos Ruiz, Galaxy	26	15
Taylor Twellman, Revolution	22	15
Ante Razov, Fire	26	14
John Spencer, Rapids	27	14
Landon Donovan, Earthquakes	22	12
Brian McBride, Crew	24	12
Preki, Wizards	30	12
Mark Chung, Rapids	29	11
Damani Ralph, Fire	25	11
Edson Buddle, Crew	21	10
Pat Noonan, Revolution	28	10

ASSISTS	Games	Assists
Preki, Wizards	30	17
Mark Lisi, MetroStars	24	11
Amado Guevara, MetroStars	25	10
Brian Mullan, Earthquakes	30	9
Chris Carrieri, Rapids	30	8
Cobi Jones, Galaxy	28	8

Eleven tied with 7.

GOALS-AGAINST AVERAGE	GAA
Jonny Walker, MetroStars	0.95
Pat Onstad, Earthquakes	1.04
Nick Rimando, United	1.13
Kevin Hartman, Galaxy	1.13
Zach Thornton, Fire	1.22
Tim Howard, MetroStars	1.33
Adin Brown, Revolution	1.42
Tony Meola, Wizards	1.42
Jon Busch, Crew	1.44
Scott Garlick, Rapids	1.46

United Soccer League Resu

2003 A-LEAGUE FINAL STANDINGS

Eastern Conference

Northeast Division

Team	GP	W	L	T
Montreal Impact	28	16	6	6
Rochester Raging Rhinos	28	15	7	6
Pittsburgh Riverhounds	28	15	9	4
Syracuse Salty Dogs	28	11	12	5
Toronto Lynx	28	11	13	4

Southeast Division

Team	GP	W	L	T
Charleston Battery	28	15	6	7
Virginia Beach Mariners	28	14	9	5
Richmond Kickers	28	12	9	7
Charlotte Eagles	28	6	15	7
Atlanta Silverbacks	28	4	17	7

Western Conference

Central Division

Team	GP	W	L	T
Milwaukee Wave United	28	18	10	0
Minnesota Thunder	28	17	9	2
El Paso Patriots	28	9	16	3
Cincinnati Riverhawks	28	9	19	0
Indiana Blast	28	3	23	2

Pacific Division

Team	GP	W	L	T
Seattle Sounders	28	16	7	5
Vancouver Whitecaps	28	15	6	7
Portland Timbers	28	15	11	2
Team Calgary	28	4	21	3

2003 A-LEAGUE CHAMPIONSHIP

Blackbaud Stadium, Charleston, South Carolina
September 20, 2003

Charleston Battery 3, Minnesota Thunder 0

Did You Know?

Bruce Arena has been the coach of the U.S. men's national team since 1998. Before then, he coached D.C. United to victory in the MLS Cup twice (1996, 1997). He also coached Virginia to the men's NCAA Division I championship five times (1989, 1991-94).

2003 U.S. Open Cup Results

The annual U.S. Open Cup is open to all amateur and professional teams in the U.S. The tournament is a single-elimination event running at the same time as the MLS season. The winner advances to the CONCACAF (Confederation of North, Central American, and Caribbean Association Football) Cup, a tournament of the top club teams from North and Central America and the Caribbean.

QUARTERFINALS

Los Angeles Galaxy 5, Seattle Sounders 1
D.C. United 1, Wilmington Hammerheads 0
Chicago Fire 2, Colorado Rapids 1
MetroStars 2, New England Revolution 1

SEMI-FINALS

Chicago Fire 3, Los Angeles Galaxy 2
MetroStars 3, D.C. United 2

2003 LAMAR HUNT
U.S. OPEN CUP FINAL RESULTS

October 15, 2003, East Rutherford, New Jersey
Chicago Fire 1, MetroStars 0
Scoring summary: Chicago — Damani Ralph, 68

Did You Know?

Forward Clint Mathis, formerly of the MetroStars, set the MLS record for most goals in a game (5) on August 26, 2000, against the Dallas Burn.

All-time MLS Cup Results

Year	Champion	Score	Runner-up
2003	San Jose Earthquakes	4–2	Chicago Fire
2002	Los Angeles Galaxy	1–0 (OT)	New England Revolution
2001	San Jose Earthquakes	2–1 (OT)	Los Angeles Galaxy
2000	Kansas City Wizards	1–0	Chicago Fire
1999	D.C. United	2–0	Los Angeles Galaxy
1998	Chicago Fire	2–0	D.C. United
1997	D.C. United	2–1	Colorado Rapids
1996	D.C. United	3–2 (OT)	Los Angeles Galaxy

Fast Fact: During MLS's first four seasons (1996-99), the official time of a match counted down, from 45:00 to 00:00 (45 minutes per half). In 2000, MLS adopted the international style of timekeeping, in which the clock counts up.

MLS All-Star Game Results

Year	Result	Site	MVP
2003	MLS 3, Guadalajara Chivas 1	Carson, California	Carlos Ruiz, Los Angeles Galaxy
2002	MLS 3, USA 2	Washington, D.C.	Marco Etcheverry, D.C. United
2001	East 6, West 6	San Jose, California	Landon Donovan, San Jose Earthquakes
2000	East 9, West 4	Columbus, Ohio	Mamadou Diallo, Tampa Bay Mutiny
1999	West 6, East 4	San Diego, California	Preki, Kansas City Wizards
1998	MLS USA 6, World 1	Orlando, Florida	Brian McBride, Columbus Crew
1997	East 5, West 4	East Rutherford, New Jersey	Carlos Valderrama, Tampa Bay Mutiny
1996	East 3, West 2	East Rutherford, New Jersey	Carlos Valderrama, Tampa Bay Mutiny

MLS Award Winners

Year	MVP	Scoring Champion	Goal of the Year	Coach
2003	Preki, Wizards	Preki, Wizards	Damani Ralph, Fire	Dave Sarachan, Fire
2002	Carlos Ruiz, Galaxy	Taylor Twellman, Revolution	Carlos Ruiz, Galaxy	Steve Nicol, Revolution
2001	Alex Pineda Chacon, Fusion	Alex Pineda Chacon, Fusion	Clint Mathis, MetroStars	Frank Yallop, Earthquakes
2000	Tony Meola, Wizards	Mamadou Diallo, Mutiny	Marcelo Balboa, Rapids	Bob Gansler, Wizards
1999	Jason Kreis, Burn	Jason Kreis, Burn	Marco Etcheverry, United	Sigi Schmid, Galaxy
1998	Marco Etcheverry, United	Stern John, Crew	Brian McBride, Crew	Bob Bradley, Fire
1997	Preki, Wizards	Preki, Wizards	Marco Etcheverry, United	Bruce Arena, United
1996	Carlos Valderrama, Mutiny	Roy Lassiter, Mutiny	Eric Wynalda, Clash	Thomas Rongen, Mutiny

Year	Goalkeeper	Defender	Rookie	Comeback Player
2003	Pat Onstad, Earthquakes	Carlos Bocanegra, Fire	Damani Ralph, Fire	Chris Armas, Fire
2002	Joe Cannon, Earthquakes	Carlos Bocanegra, Fire	Kyle Martino, Crew	Chris Klein, Wizards
2001	Tim Howard, MetroStars	Jeff Agoos, Earthquakes	Rodrigo Faria, MetroStars	Troy Dayak, Earthquakes
2000	Tony Meola, Wizards	Peter Vermes, Wizards	Carlos Bocanegra, Fire	Tony Meola, Wizards
1999	Kevin Hartman, Galaxy	Robin Fraser, Galaxy	Jay Heaps, Fusion	N/A
1998	Zach Thornton, Fire	Lubos Kubik, Fire	Ben Olsen, United	N/A
1997	Brad Friedel, Crew	Eddie Pope, United	Mike Duhaney, Mutiny	N/A
1996	Mark Dodd, Burn	John Doyle, Clash	Steve Ralston, Mutiny	N/A

A-League Results

Year	Champion	Score	Runner-up
2003	Charleston Battery	3–0	Minnesota Thunder
2002	Milwaukee Rampage	2–1 (2 OT)	Richmond Kickers
2001	Rochester Raging Rhinos	2–0	Vancouver Whitecaps
2000	Rochester Raging Rhinos	3–1	Minnesota Thunder
1999	Minnesota Thunder	2–1	Rochester Raging Rhinos
1998	Rochester Raging Rhinos	3–1	Minnesota Thunder
1997	Milwaukee Rampage	2–1 (SO)	Carolina Dynamo
1996	Seattle Sounders	2–0	Rochester Raging Rhinos
1995	Seattle Sounders	1–2 (SO), 3–0, 2–1 (SO)	Atlanta Ruckus
1994	Montreal Impact	1–0	Colorado Foxes
1993	Colorado Foxes	3–1 (OT)	Los Angeles Salsa
1992	Colorado Foxes	1–0	Tampa Bay Rowdies
1991	San Francisco Bay Blackhawks	1–3, 2–0 (1–0 on PKs)	Albany Capitals

U.S. Open Cup Results

YEAR	CHAMPION	YEAR	CHAMPION
2003	Chicago Fire (MLS)	1958	Los Angeles Kickers (CA)
2002	Columbus Crew (MLS)	1957	Kutis SC (St. Louis, MO)
2001	Los Angeles Galaxy (MLS)	1956	Harmarville SC (PA)
2000	Chicago Fire (MLS)	1955	Eintracht Sport Club (New York City)
1999	Rochester Rhinos (A-League)	1954	New York Americans (New York City)
1998	Chicago Fire (MLS)	1953	Falcons SC (Chicago, IL)
1997	Dallas Burn (MLS)	1952	Harmarville SC (PA)
1996	D.C. United (MLS)	1951	German Hungarian SC (New York City)
1995	Richmond Kickers (VA)	1950	Simpkins-Ford SC (St. Louis, MO)
1994	Greek American AC (San Francisco, CA)	1949	Morgan SC (PA)
1993	Club Deportivo Mexico (San Francisco, CA)	1948	Simpkins-Ford SC (St. Louis, MO)
1992	San Jose Oaks (CA)	1947	Ponta Delgada SC (Fall River, MA)
1991	Brooklyn Italians SC (East New York, NY)	1946	Chicago Viking FC (IL)
1990	AAC Eagles (Chicago, IL)	1945	Brookhattan FC (New York City)
1989	HRC Kickers (St. Petersburg, FL)	1944	Brooklyn Hispano SC (New York City)
1988	Busch SC (St. Louis, MO)	1943	Brooklyn Hispano SC (New York City)
1987	Club Espana (Washington, D.C.)	1942	Gallatin SC (PA)
1986	Kutis SC (St. Louis, MO)	1941	Pawtucket FC (RI)
1985	Greek American AC (San Francisco, CA)	1940	No winner
1984	AO Krete (New York City)	1939	St. Mary's Celtic SC (Brooklyn, NY)
1983	NY Pancyprian-Freedoms (New York City)	1938	Sparta A and BA (Chicago, IL)
1982	NY Pancyprian-Freedoms (New York City)	1937	New York American FC (New York City)
1981	Maccabee SC (Los Angeles, CA)	1936	German-Americans (Philadelphia, PA)
1980	NY Pancyprian-Freedoms (New York City)	1935	Central Breweries FC (Chicago, IL)
1979	Brooklyn Dodgers SC (New York City)	1934	Stix, Baer and Fuller FC (St. Louis, MO)
1978	Maccabee SC (Los Angeles, CA)	1933	Stix, Baer and Fuller FC (St. Louis, MO)
1977	Maccabee SC (Los Angeles, CA)	1932	New Bedford FC (MA)
1976	San Francisco AC (CA)	1931	Fall River FC (MA)
1975	Maccabee SC (Los Angeles, CA)	1930	Fall River FC (MA)
1974	Greek American AA (New York City)	1929	Hakoah All Stars SC (New York City)
1973	Maccabee SC (Los Angeles, CA)	1928	New York National FC (New York City)
1972	Elizabeth SC (Union, NJ)	1927	Fall River FC (MA)
1971	Hota SC (New York City)	1926	Bethlehem Steel FC (PA)
1970	Elizabeth SC (Union, NJ)	1925	Shawsheen FC (Andover, MA)
1969	Greek American AA (New York City)	1924	Fall River FC (MA)
1968	Greek American AA (New York City)	1923	Paterson FC (NJ)
1967	Greek American AA (New York City)	1922	Scullin Steel FC (St. Louis, MO)
1966	Ukrainian Nationals (Philadelphia, PA)	1921	Robbins Dry Dock FC (Brooklyn, NY)
1965	New York Hungaria (New York City)	1920	Ben Miller FC (St. Louis, MO)
1964	Los Angeles Kickers (CA)	1919	Bethlehem Steel FC (PA)
1963	Ukrainian Nationals (Philadelphia, PA)	1918	Bethlehem Steel FC (PA)
1962	New York Hungaria (New York City)	1917	Fall River Rovers (MA)
1961	Ukrainian Nationals (Philadelphia, PA)	1916	Bethlehem Steel FC (PA)
1960	Ukrainian Nationals (Philadelphia, PA)	1915	Bethlehem Steel FC (PA)
1959	McIlvaine Canvasbacks (Los Angeles, CA)	1914	Brooklyn Field Club (New York City)

Legends

In 1996, Tab Ramos became the first player signed by MLS.

Tab Ramos, midfielder, b. September 21, 1966, Montevideo, Uruguay. Ramos was the first player signed by MLS in the league's inaugural season (1996). The slick-passing midfielder played seven seasons with the MetroStars before retiring from pro soccer in May 2002 as the team's career assists leader (36). Before joining MLS, he played in first division club teams in Spain and Mexico from 1990 through 1996. Ramos is one of only three U.S. team players to compete in the World Cup three times (1990, 1994, 1998).

Eric Wynalda, forward, b. June 9, 1969, Fullerton, California. U.S. Soccer named Wynalda the Honda Player of the Decade (1990's) in 2000. He is the U.S. national team's all-time leader in goals (34) and appeared in the World Cup three times (1990, 1994, 1998). Wynalda played six MLS seasons, beginning in 1996. He scored the league's first goal, on April 6, 1996, as a member of the San Jose Clash (now the Earthquakes). Before joining MLS, Wynalda played four seasons in the Bundesliga, Germany's top league. He retired from pro soccer in 2002.

Preki, midfielder, b. June 24, 1963, Belgrade, Yugoslavia. Preki gets better with age. He won the MLS scoring crown in 2003, at age 40, after leading the league in assists (17). He also won the regular-season MVP award. Heading into the 2004 season, Preki was MLS's all-time leading scorer (264 points) and had started every MLS All-Star Game since 1996, the league's first season. He became a U.S. citizen in 1996.

Fast Fact: The North American Soccer League (NASL) was the top pro soccer league in the U.S. before MLS was created. NASL existed for 17 seasons (1968-84) and had as many as 24 teams at the height of its popularity. Tim Twellman played seven seasons (1977-83) in the league. The former midfielder and defender is the father of Taylor Twellman, the 2002 MLS goal-scoring champion.

All-time World Cup Results

Year	Champion	Score	Runner-up	Winning coach
2002	Brazil	2–0	Germany	Luis Felipe Scolari
1998	France	3–0	Brazil	Aime Jacquet
1994	Brazil	0–0 (3–2)	Italy	Carlos Alberto Parreira
1990	West Germany	1–0	Argentina	Franz Beckenbauer
1986	Argentina	3–2	West Germany	Carlos Bilardo
1982	Italy	3–1	West Germany	Enzo Bearzot
1978	Argentina	3–1	Netherlands	César Menotti
1974	West Germany	2–1	Netherlands	Helmut Schoen
1970	Brazil	4–1	Italy	Mario Zagalo
1966	England	4–2	West Germany	Alf Ramsey
1962	Brazil	3–1	Czechoslovakia	Aymore Moreira
1958	Brazil	5–2	Sweden	Vicente Feola
1954	West Germany	3–2	Hungary	Sepp Herberger
1950	Uruguay	2–1	Brazil	Juan Lopez
1938	Italy	4–2	Hungary	Vittorio Pozzo
1934	Italy	2–1	Czechoslovakia	Vittorio Pozzo
1930	Uruguay	4–2	Argentina	Alberto Supicci

All-time World Cup Scoring Leaders

GOALS

Player, Nation	Tournaments	Goals
Gerd Müller, West Germany	1970, 1974	14
Just Fontaine, France	1958	13
Pelé, Brazil	1958, 1962, 1966, 1970	12
Ronaldo, Brazil	1998, 2002	12
Sandor Kocsis, Hungary	1954	11
Teofilo Cubillas, Peru	1970, 1978	10
Gregorz Lato, Poland	1974, 1978, 1982	10
Helmut Rahn, West Germany	1954, 1958	10
Gary Lineker, England	1986, 1990	10
Ademir, Brazil	1950	9
Eusebio, Portugal	1966	9
Jairzinho, Brazil	1970, 1974	9
Paolo Rossi, Italy	1982, 1986	9
K.H. Rummenigge, West Germany	1978, 1982, 1986	9
Uwe Seeler, West Germany	1958, 1962, 1966, 1970	9
Vava, Brazil	1958, 1962	9

2003-04 TIME LINE

April 5, 2003: MLS kicks off its eighth season. The Columbus Crew hosts the Los Angeles Galaxy in the season's first game. The match ends in a 1–1 draw.

June 7, 2003: The Home Depot Center opens in Carson, California. The soccer-only stadium holds 27,000 fans. It is the home of the Los Angeles Galaxy and the training headquarters of U.S. Soccer national teams.

July 31, 2003: Former MetroStar goalkeeper Tim Howard appears in his first match for England's Manchester United. ManU defeats Juventus of Italy, 4–1, in an exhibition match at Giants Stadium, in East Rutherford, New Jersey. Howard makes 11 saves.

August 2, 2003: The eighth MLS All-Star Game is played, at The Home Depot Center in Carson, California. The MLS All-Stars defeat Chivas, a first division club from Mexico, 3–1.

August 30, 2003: Superstar midfielder David Beckham scores his first goal in Spanish league play for Real Madrid.

October 15, 2003: The Chicago Fire defeat the MetroStars, 1–0, in the final of the U.S. Open Cup, an annual tournament open to all amateur and pro teams in the U.S. Fire forward Damani Ralph notches the only goal of the match.

November 21, 2003: Midfielder Preki of the Kansas City Wizards is named the league MVP after leading MLS in points (41). At age 40, he is the oldest MVP winner in the history of MLS, the NHL, the NBA, the NFL, and Major League Baseball.

November 23, 2003: The San Jose Earthquakes defeat the Chicago Fire, 4–2, to win the MLS Cup for the second time in three seasons. 'Quake forward Landon Donovan scores two goals and is named MVP of the match.

January 16, 2004: Fourteen-year-old Freddy Adu is chosen first overall by D.C. United in the MLS SuperDraft.

February 10, 2004: The U.S. men's Under-23 team loses to Mexico, 4–0, in Guadalajara, Mexico, in a qualifying match for the 2004 Summer Olympics. It is the first time the U.S. fails to qualify for the Olympics since 1976.

April 17, 2004: Freddy Adu scores his first MLS goal in a 3–2 loss to the MetroStars, becoming the youngest goal scorer in league history.

SOCCER

WOMEN'S

When the Women's United Soccer Association (WUSA) kicked off its third season in April 2003, fans didn't know it would be the league's last. In September 2003, WUSA was forced to shut down because of dwindling sponsorship dollars, low TV ratings, and poor attendance. Since then, league organizers have been discussing ways to revive WUSA in 2005. Whether or not the league makes a comeback, one thing is certain: The players' on-field performances left lasting memories.

Briana Scurry won WUSA's Goalkeeper of the Year award. She helped the Atlanta Beat become the only team to play in all three WUSA post-seasons. Unfortunately, the third time wasn't the charm. The Beat lost the championship match, 2–1, to the Washington Freedom in overtime. Scurry had no answer for forward Abby Wambach of the Freedom, who scored twice to clinch her team's first Founder's Cup trophy and was named the game's MVP. Wambach had been a nightmare for goalies all season. She tied for first in the league in points (33) with teammate Mia Hamm and scored WUSA's Goal of the Year.

Nifty playmaker Maren Meinert of the Boston Breakers won the All-Star Game and regular-season MVP trophies. She scored two goals in the All-Star Game as the World team defeated the American team, 3–2. Meinert also led the Breakers to a league-best record (10-4-7) and the playoffs for the first time. Forward Christine Latham took home Rookie of the Year honors after helping the San Diego Spirit reach its

Forward Abby Wambach had 13 goals and 7 assists for the Freedom in 2003.

TONY QUINN

WUSA TEAMS

Atlanta Beat
Boston Breakers
Carolina Courage
New York Power
Philadelphia Charge
San Diego Spirit
San Jose CyberRays
Washington Freedom

Fast Fact: Midfielder Kristine Lilly of the Boston Breakers was fouled more times (151) than any other player in WUSA's three seasons (2001-03).

first post-season. Teammate Joy Fawcett was named Defensive Player of the Year.

After the 2003 season, the world's best women soccer players gathered for the 2003 FIFA World Cup (September 20-October 12). The tournament was relocated to the United States from China because of health threats from the SARS virus outbreak.

The U.S. was one of the favorites going into the tournament. But Germany stopped the U.S. in the semifinals, 3–0, then defeated Sweden, 2–1, to win its first World Cup championship.

2003 WUSA Final Standings

Team	GP	W	L	T	PTS	Home	Road
Boston Breakers	21	10	4	7	37	5-2-4	5-2-3
Atlanta Beat	21	9	4	8	35	7-2-2	2-2-6
San Diego Spirit	21	8	6	7	31	6-2-3	2-4-4
Washington Freedom	21	9	8	4	31	6-2-2	3-6-2
New York Power	21	7	9	5	26	3-4-3	4-5-2
San Jose CyberRays	21	7	10	4	25	4-3-3	3-7-1
Carolina Courage	21	7	10	4	25	3-6-2	4-4-2
Philadelphia Charge	21	5	11	5	20	3-4-3	2-7-2

KEY GP=games played; W=win; L=loss; T=tie; PTS=points

Trivia Challenge

Name the only U.S. city to field MLS and WUSA championship teams in the same season.

San Jose, California. In 2001, the Earthquakes won the MLS title and the CyberRays won the WUSA title. Both teams played their home games in San Jose.

Briana Scurry of the Beat was the Goalkeeper of the Year in 2003.

JAMIE SQUIRE/GETTY IMAGES

2003 PLAYOFFS

Washington Freedom 0, Boston Breakers 0
(Freedom wins, 3–1, on penalty kicks.)

Atlanta Beat 2, San Diego Spirit 1 (OT)

2003 FOUNDER'S CUP

San Diego, California August 24, 2003

Washington Freedom 2, Atlanta Beat 1 (OT)

	1st Half	2nd Half	OT	Final
Freedom	**1**	**0**	**1**	**2**
Beat	**1**	**0**	**0**	**1**

Scoring Summary:
WAS: Wambach (Minnert, Moore) 7
ATL: Hooper (penalty kick) 46
WAS: Wambach (Meier, J. Little) 96

Washington Freedom: Siri Mullinix, Jennifer Grubb, Sandra Minnert, Carrie Moore, Kelly Golebiowski (Jennifer Meier 64), Steffi Jones, Jacqui Little, Skylar Little, Lindsay Stoecker (Casey Zimny 70), Mia Hamm, Abby Wambach

Atlanta Beat: Briana Scurry, Nancy Augustyniak (ejected 94), Kylie Bivens, Leslie Gaston (Julie Augustyniak 91), Sharolta Nonen, Marci Miller (Kristin Warren 65), Cindy Parlow (Callie Withers 89), Homare Sawa, Nikki Serlenga (Maribel Dominguez 45), Charmaine Hooper, Conny Pohlers

Note: Numbers next to player names indicate time of game.

TEAM-BY-TEAM STATS

ATLANTA BEAT

PLAYER	GP	MIN	G	A	PTS	SHOTS	SOG
Charmaine Hooper	21	1,834	11	7	29	51	28
Maribel Dominguez	18	1,196	7	4	18	50	26
Conny Pohlers	17	1,121	4	5	13	29	14
Cindy Parlow	18	1,441	3	5	11	30	13
Homare Sawa	15	1,323	3	4	10	36	21
Abby Crumpton	18	657	3	2	8	20	11
Kylie Bivens	18	1,547	1	3	5	11	3
Nikki Serlenga	20	1,670	0	3	3	13	2
Ifeoma Dieke	13	756	1	0	2	8	2
Leslie Gaston	18	1,415	0	1	1	5	2
Sharolta Nonen	21	1,825	0	1	1	0	0
Katie Antongiovanni	1	9	0	0	0	0	0
Julie Augustyniak	13	669	0	0	0	1	0
Nancy Augustyniak	20	1,775	0	0	0	0	0
Emily Burt	3	13	0	0	0	0	0
Marci Miller	15	854	0	0	0	3	0
Tara Minnax	1	1	0	0	0	0	0
Kristin Warren	12	516	0	0	0	7	2
Callie Withers	12	224	0	0	0	2	2
Melinda Carter	0	0	0	0	0	0	0
BEAT	**21**	**1,890**	**34**	**36**	**104**	**266**	**126**
OPPONENTS	**21**	**1,890**	**19**	**14**	**52**	**236**	**100**

INDIVIDUAL GOALKEEPING

GOALKEEPER	GP	MIN	SOG	SVS	C/P	GA	GAA
Briana Scurry	19	1,710	88	70	73	18	0.95
Melanie Wilson	2	180	12	9	14	1	0.50
Ellen Dean	0	0	0	0	0	0	0.00
BEAT	**21**	**1,890**	**100**	**81**	**87**	**19**	**0.90**
OPPONENTS	**21**	**1,890**	**125**	**93**	**72**	**34**	**1.62**

BOSTON BREAKERS

PLAYER	GP	MIN	G	A	PTS	SHOTS	SOG
Dagny Mellgren	20	1,751	14	2	30	45	26
Maren Meinert	21	1,870	9	10	28	62	37
Kristine Lilly	19	1,678	3	4	10	47	16
Angela Hucles	17	1,424	1	4	6	24	8
Mary-Frances Monroe	12	778	1	3	5	8	5
Monica Gonzalez	14	1,068	1	2	4	1	1
Devvyn Hawkins	15	823	1	2	4	5	1
Jena Kluegel	20	1,665	0	4	4	3	0
Heather Aldama	19	1,521	1	1	3	4	2
Ragnhild Gulbrandsen	7	174	1	1	3	4	2
Kate Sobrero	19	1,710	0	3	3	2	2
Stephanie Mugneret-Beghe	17	1,273	0	2	2	7	1
Sarah Popper	14	889	0	2	2	7	4
Rebekah McDowell	10	488	0	1	1	2	0
Christine McCann	18	1,347	0	0	0	1	0
Erin O'Grady	9	319	0	0	0	3	2
Rebekah Splaine	1	9	0	0	0	0	0
Marica Wallis	3	97	0	0	0	3	1
BREAKERS	**21**	**1,890**	**33**	**41**	**107**	**228**	**108**
OPPONENTS	**21**	**1,890**	**29**	**36**	**94**	**250**	**123**

INDIVIDUAL GOALKEEPING

GOALKEEPER	GP	MIN	SOG	SVS	C/P	GA	GAA
Karina LeBlanc	21	1,890	123	91	66	29	1.38
Tracy Ducar	0	0	0	0	0	0	0.00
Kristin Slater	0	0	0	0	0	0	0.00
BREAKERS	**21**	**1,890**	**123**	**94**	**66**	**29**	**1.38**
OPPONENTS	**21**	**1,890**	**108**	**76**	**74**	**33**	**1.57**

TEAM-BY-TEAM STATS

CAROLINA COURAGE

PLAYER	GP	MIN	G	A	PTS	SHOTS	SOG
Birgit Prinz	20	1,790	11	3	25	64	35
Danielle Fotopoulos	12	1,029	7	6	20	28	18
Venus James	20	1,301	5	1	11	25	9
Nel Fettig	21	1,890	2	2	6	5	4
Unni Lehn	20	1,670	0	6	6	23	13
Erin Baxter	20	1,719	2	1	5	4	3
Danielle Slaton	18	1,154	2	1	5	25	10
Danielle Borgman	17	403	2	0	4	6	2
Staci Burt	21	1,832	0	4	4	2	1
Brooke O'Hanley	21	1,484	0	4	4	8	3
Breanna Boyd	16	1,180	0	2	2	2	1
Carla Overbeck	15	839	0	2	2	3	2
Tiffany Roberts	18	1,620	0	2	2	6	2
Robin McCullough	12	371	0	1	1	4	0
Kim Montgomery	7	168	0	1	1	6	2
Hege Riise	2	125	0	1	1	2	0
Marcia Wallis	8	204	0	0	0	6	2
Keri Sarver	0	0	0	0	0	0	0
COURAGE	**21**	**1,890**	**31**	**38**	**100**	**221**	**107**
OPPONENTS	**21**	**1,890**	**33**	**44**	**110**	**286**	**125**

INDIVIDUAL GOALKEEPING

GOALKEEPER	GP	MIN	SOG	SVS	C/P	GA	GAA
Kristin Luckenbill	18	1,575	98	68	72	25	1.43
Maite Zabala	3	225	19	13	10	6	2.40
COURAGE	**21**	**1,890**	**125**	**92**	**85**	**33**	**1.57**
OPPONENTS	**21**	**1,890**	**107**	**76**	**75**	**31**	**1.48**

NEW YORK POWER

PLAYER	GP	MIN	G	A	PTS	SHOTS	SOG
Tiffeny Milbrett	17	1,462	5	6	16	51	22
Christie Welsh	12	921	6	0	12	26	12
Margaret Tietjen	21	1,871	2	6	10	12	8
Shannon Boxx	21	1,868	1	8	10	29	9
Emily Janss	21	1,243	4	1	9	27	14
Krista Davey	17	531	3	2	8	5	4
Anita Rapp	19	1,389	2	4	8	22	9
Cheryl Salisbury	13	1,098	3	1	7	10	5
Joanne Peters	17	1,397	2	2	6	24	8
Justi Baumgardt	19	808	1	4	6	12	4
Jaclyn Ravela	20	1,761	2	1	5	6	5
Tammy Pearman	15	679	1	2	4	8	4
Heather Beem	12	735	1	0	2	10	6
Lindsey Jones	9	408	0	2	2	3	2
Lauren Orlandos	18	820	0	1	1	0	0
Christie Pearce	18	1,620	0	1	1	5	3
Keri Sarver	1	1	0	0	0	0	0
Kristy Whelchel	5	231	0	0	0	1	0
Sarah Whalen	0	0	0	0	0	0	0
POWER	**21**	**1,890**	**33**	**41**	**107**	**251**	**115**
OPPONENTS	**21**	**1,890**	**43**	**53**	**139**	**262**	**126**

INDIVIDUAL GOALKEEPING

GOALKEEPER	GP	MIN	SOG	SVS	C/P	GA	GAA
Saskia Webber	13	1,126	72	50	35	19	1.52
Carly Smolak	9	764	54	30	27	24	2.83
POWER	**21**	**1,890**	**126**	**86**	**62**	**43**	**2.05**
OPPONENTS	**21**	**1,890**	**115**	**82**	**77**	**33**	**1.57**

KEY GP=games played; MIN=minutes played; G=goals; A=assists; PTS=points; SOG=shots on goal; SVS=saves; C/P=catches/punches; GA=goals allowed; GAA=goals-against average

TEAM-BY-TEAM STATS

PHILADELPHIA CHARGE

PLAYER	GP	MIN	G	A	PTS	SHOTS	SOG
Marinette Pichon	18	1,583	14	3	31	77	37
Melanie Hoffman	20	1,640	5	5	15	33	12
Stacey Tullock	21	1,862	3	5	11	30	8
Emily Burt	15	998	2	2	6	19	8
Pavlina Scasna	7	319	1	2	4	5	1
Jennifer Tietjen-Prozzo	21	1,890	1	2	4	7	4
Deliah Arrington	5	313	1	1	3	7	3
Kelly Smith	6	242	1	1	3	10	3
Lorrie Fair	18	1,501	0	3	3	8	2
Rachel Kruze	15	1,054	0	2	2	3	1
Trina Maso de Moya	9	253	0	2	2	11	7
Erin Misaki	14	1,023	0	2	2	3	1
Heather Mitts	14	1,176	0	2	2	1	0
Jenny Benson	20	1,777	0	1	1	5	1
Mary McVeigh	18	1,477	0	1	1	2	1
Alexa Borisjuk	2	18	0	0	0	0	0
Karyn Hall	6	75	0	0	0	3	1
Anne Makinen	17	1,429	0	0	0	16	9
Mary-Frances Monroe	1	81	0	0	0	2	1
CHARGE	**21**	**1,890**	**30**	**35**	**95**	**243**	**102**
OPPONENTS	**21**	**1,890**	**40**	**51**	**131**	**237**	**116**

INDIVIDUAL GOALKEEPING

GOALKEEPER	GP	MIN	SOG	SVS	C/P	GA	GAA
Melissa Moore	13	1,170	81	50	51	30	2.31
Hope Solo	8	720	35	22	21	10	1.25
CHARGE	**21**	**1,890**	**116**	**76**	**72**	**40**	**1.90**
OPPONENTS	**21**	**1,890**	**102**	**73**	**56**	**30**	**1.43**

SAN DIEGO SPIRIT

PLAYER	GP	MIN	G	A	PTS	SHOTS	SOG
Julie Fleeting	18	1,538	11	4	26	67	44
Christine Latham	19	1,551	6	3	15	41	15
Julie Foudy	20	1,742	3	2	8	12	6
Aly Wagner	20	1,778	2	4	8	38	11
Zhang Ouying	20	1,196	1	4	6	26	13
Shannon MacMillan	6	461	1	3	5	16	8
Allie Sullivan	17	830	1	3	5	23	15
Daniela	17	1,075	0	3	3	23	6
Kerry Connors	21	1,830	0	2	2	11	6
Susan Bush	12	525	0	1	1	4	1
Joy Fawcett	18	1,535	0	1	1	4	3
Lisa Krzykowski	21	1,826	0	1	1	0	0
Jennifer Nielsen	16	623	0	1	1	8	2
Andrea Alfiler	2	68	0	0	0	0	0
Ronnie Fair	15	339	0	0	0	1	1
Kim Pickup	21	1,826	0	0	0	15	6
Shauna Rohbock	4	21	0	0	0	3	1
Rhiannon Tanaka	1	51	0	0	0	0	0
SPIRIT	**21**	**1,890**	**27**	**33**	**87**	**292**	**138**
OPPONENTS	**21**	**1,890**	**26**	**28**	**80**	**266**	**116**

INDIVIDUAL GOALKEEPING

GOALKEEPER	GP	MIN	SOG	SVS	C/P	GA	GAA
Jaime Pagliarulo	12	1,044	69	52	27	14	1.21
Jenni Branam	11	846	47	36	47	12	1.28
SPIRIT	**21**	**1,890**	**116**	**91**	**74**	**26**	**1.24**
OPPONENTS	**21**	**1,890**	**138**	**113**	**87**	**27**	**1.29**

TEAM-BY-TEAM STATS

SAN JOSE CYBERRAYS

PLAYER	GP	MIN	G	A	PTS	SHOTS	SOG
Pretinha	13	1,111	5	5	15	31	17
Katia	18	1,291	5	2	12	48	26
Sissi	20	1,404	3	5	11	35	16
Tisha Venturini-Hoch	20	1,161	3	2	8	22	12
Keri Sanchez	21	1,676	1	5	7	25	16
Brandi Chastain	15	1,269	1	4	6	24	11
Katie Barnes	18	882	2	1	5	29	9
Michelle French	21	1,806	0	4	4	6	2
Katie Antongiovanni	11	584	1	1	3	1	1
Dianne Alagich	11	764	1	0	2	4	1
Betsy Barr	20	1,703	1	0	2	12	4
Mandy Clemens	16	671	0	2	2	18	9
Christina Bell	10	285	0	1	1	6	3
Ann Cook	11	308	0	1	1	5	0
Amanda Cromwell	18	1,452	0	1	1	7	1
Thori Bryan	20	1,779	0	0	0	3	0
Melinda Carter	1	1	0	0	0	0	0
Kelly Lindsey	10	704	0	0	0	1	0
Kim Patrick	1	4	0	0	0	0	0
CYBERRAYS	**21**	**1,890**	**23**	**34**	**80**	**277**	**128**
OPPONENTS	**21**	**1,890**	**30**	**36**	**96**	**239**	**124**

INDIVIDUAL GOALKEEPING

GOALKEEPER	GP	MIN	SOG	SVS	C/P	GA	GAA
LaKeysia Beene	19	1,710	113	83	65	26	1.37
Dawn Greathouse	2	180	11	7	10	4	2.00
CYBERRAYS	**21**	**1,890**	**124**	**95**	**75**	**30**	**1.43**
OPPONENTS	**21**	**1,890**	**128**	**105**	**88**	**23**	**1.10**

WASHINGTON FREEDOM

PLAYER	GP	MIN	G	A	PTS	SHOTS	SOG
Abby Wambach	18	1,620	13	7	33	51	29
Mia Hamm	19	1,527	11	11	33	48	24
Jacqui Little	20	1,545	2	6	10	24	15
Lindsay Stoecker	21	1,636	4	1	9	20	10
Steffi Jones	21	1,831	2	4	8	27	9
Kelly Golebiowski	17	1,057	2	3	7	21	9
Jennifer Grubb	21	1,890	2	1	5	11	6
Lori Lindsey	19	991	2	1	5	14	4
Sandra Minnert	12	1,003	1	2	4	7	3
Casey Zimny	14	410	1	1	3	6	4
Skylar Little	20	1,741	0	2	2	0	0
Emmy Barr	11	889	0	1	1	2	0
Jennifer Meier	4	69	0	1	1	3	1
Carrie Moore	21	1,890	0	1	1	1	1
Sarah Kate Noftsinger	6	56	0	1	1	1	1
Laura Schott	7	163	0	1	1	1	0
Meredith Beard	14	487	0	0	0	12	4
FREEDOM	**21**	**1,890**	**40**	**46**	**126**	**251**	**121**
OPPONENTS	**21**	**1,890**	**31**	**42**	**104**	**253**	**115**

INDIVIDUAL GOALKEEPING

GOALKEEPER	GP	MIN	SOG	SVS	C/P	GA	GAA
Siri Mullinix	19	1,699	100	74	89	24	1.27
Nicci Wright	2	101	7	4	5	2	1.78
Erin Regan	1	90	8	3	5	5	5.00
FREEDOM	**21**	**1,890**	**115**	**84**	**99**	**31**	**1.48**
OPPONENTS	**21**	**1,890**	**121**	**81**	**91**	**40**	**1.90**

Mia Hamm, Washington Freedom

2003 WUSA Statistical Leaders

SCORING	GP	G	A	PTS
Mia Hamm, Freedom	19	11	11	33
Abby Wambach, Freedom	18	13	7	33
Marinette Pichon, Charge	18	14	3	31
Dagny Mellgren, Breakers	20	14	2	30
Charmaine Hooper, Beat	21	11	7	29
Maren Meinert, Breakers	21	9	10	28
Julie Fleeting, Spirit	18	11	4	26
Birgit Prinz, Courage	20	11	3	25
Danielle Fotopoulos, Courage	12	7	6	20
Maribel Dominguez, Beat	18	7	4	18

GOALS	GP	G
Marinette Pichon, Charge	18	14
Dagny Mellgren, Breakers	20	14
Abby Wambach, Freedom	18	13
Mia Hamm, Freedom	19	11
Charmaine Hooper, Beat	21	11
Julie Fleeting, Spirit	18	11
Birgit Prinz, Courage	20	11
Maren Meinert, Breakers	21	9
Danielle Fotopoulos, Courage	12	7
Maribel Dominguez, Beat	18	7

ASSISTS	GP	A
Mia Hamm, Freedom	19	11
Maren Meinert, Breakers	21	10
Shannon Boxx, Power	21	8
Abby Wambach, Freedom	18	7
Charmaine Hooper, Beat	21	7
Jacqui Little, Freedom	20	6
Unni Lehn, Courage	20	6
Danielle Fotopoulos, Courage	12	6
Margaret Tietjen, Power	21	6
Tiffeny Milbrett, Power	17	6

KEY GP=games played; G=goals; A=assists; PTS=points; GAA=goals-against average; SOG=shots on goal; SVS=saves; GPG=goals per game; GA=goals allowed

GOALS-AGAINST AVERAGE	GP	GAA
Melanie Wilson, Beat	2	0.50
Briana Scurry, Beat	19	0.95
Jaime Pagliarulo, Spirit	12	1.21
Hope Solo, Charge	8	1.25
Siri Mullinix, Freedom	19	1.27
Jenni Branam, Spirit	11	1.28
LaKeysia Beene, CyberRays	19	1.37
Karina LeBlanc, Breakers	21	1.38
Kristin Luckenbill, Courage	18	1.43
Saskia Webber, Power	13	1.52

SHOTS ON GOAL	GP	SOG
Julie Fleeting, Spirit	18	44
Marinette Pichon, Charge	18	37
Maren Meinert, Breakers	21	37
Birgit Prinz, Courage	20	35
Abby Wambach, Freedom	18	29
Charmaine Hooper, Beat	21	28
Katia, CyberRays	18	26
Dagny Mellgren, Breakers	20	26
Maribel Dominguez, Beat	18	26
Mia Hamm, Freedom	19	24

SAVES	GP	SVS
Karina LeBlanc, Breakers	21	91
LaKeysia Beene, CyberRays	19	83
Siri Mullinix, Freedom	19	74
Briana Scurry, Beat	19	70
Kristin Luckenbill, Courage	18	68
Jamie Pagliarulo, Spirit	12	52
Melissa Moore, Charge	13	50
Saskia Webber, Power	13	50
Jenni Branam, Spirit	11	36
Carly Smolak, Power	9	30

Karina LeBlanc, Boston Breakers

TEAM OFFENSE	GP	G	GPG
Washington Freedom	21	40	1.9
Atlanta Beat	21	34	1.6
New York Power	21	33	1.6
Boston Breakers	21	33	1.6
Carolina Courage	21	31	1.5
Philadelphia Charge	21	30	1.4
San Diego Spirit	21	27	1.3
San Jose CyberRays	21	23	1.1

TEAM DEFENSE	GP	GA	GAA
Atlanta Beat	21	19	0.9
San Diego Spirit	21	26	1.2
Boston Breakers	21	29	1.4
San Jose CyberRays	21	30	1.4
Washington Freedom	21	31	1.5
Carolina Courage	21	33	1.6
Philadelphia Charge	21	40	1.9
New York Power	21	43	2.0

CRAIG JONES/GETTY IMAGES

WUSA Award Winners

MVP

2003 Maren Meinert, Boston Breakers
2002 Marinette Pichon, Philadelphia Charge
2001 Tiffeny Milbrett, New York Power

Offensive Player of the Year

2002 Marinette Pichon, Philadelphia Charge
2001 Tiffeny Milbrett, New York Power

Defensive Player of the Year

2003 Joy Fawcett, San Diego Spirit
2002 Danielle Slaton, Carolina Courage
2001 Doris Fitschen, Philadelphia Charge

Goalkeeper of the Year

2003 Briana Scurry, Atlanta Beat
2002 Kristin Luckenbill, Carolina Courage
2001 LaKeysia Beene, San Jose CyberRays

Rookie of the Year

2003 Christine Latham, San Diego Spirit
2002 Abby Wambach, Washington Freedom

Goal of the Year

2003 Abby Wambach, Washington Freedom
2002 Katia, San Jose CyberRays

Today's Stars

Charmaine Hooper, forward, b. January 15, 1968, Georgetown, Guyana. In 2003, Hooper led the Atlanta Beat to its third-straight playoff appearance and became the only player to score goals in two WUSA championship games (2001, 2003). Hooper lives in Ottawa, Ontario, Canada. She leads the Canadian women's national team in international games played (94) and goals (56).

Dagny Mellgren, forward-midfielder, b. June 19, 1978, Stavanger, Norway. In 2003, Mellgren guided the Boston Breakers to WUSA's best record (10-4-7) and their first playoff appearance. She was tied for first in the league in goals (14) and hat tricks (3). At the Summer Olympics in 2000, Mellgren scored the "Golden Goal" that helped Norway defeat the U.S.,3–2, in the gold-medal game.

Charmaine Hooper had 11 goals and 7 assists for the Beat in 2003.

HOWARD SMITH/DIGITAL SPORTS ARCHIVE

Abby Wambach, forward, b. June 2, 1980, Pittsford, New York. In 2003, Wambach became the first and only player to score two goals in a WUSA championship game. She led the Washington Freedom to a 2–1 victory over the Atlanta Beat and was named the game's MVP. During the regular season, Wambach had 13 goals and 7 assists and was tied with teammate Mia Hamm for the league lead in points (33). Wambach was WUSA's Rookie of the Year and All-Star Game MVP in 2002.

Legends

Carin Jennings-Gabarra scored six goals in the 1991 Women's World Cup tournament.

DANIEL MOTZ

Carin Jennings-Gabarra, forward, b. January 9, 1965, East Orange, New Jersey. From 1987 through 1996, Jennings-Gabarra scored 53 goals in 117 international games with the U.S. team. In 1991, she led the U.S. to the gold medal at the first FIFA Women's World Cup. She was awarded the Golden Ball as the tournament's top player after registering the first hat trick in Women's World Cup history. The two-time U.S. Soccer Female Athlete of the Year also won an Olympic gold medal in 1996. In 2000, Jennings-Gabarra became the second female player inducted into the U.S. Soccer Hall of Fame.

Joy Fawcett, defender, b. February 8, 1968, Inglewood, California. Fawcett is one of the top defenders in women's soccer history. The 17-year member of the U.S. team won gold medals at the FIFA Women's World Cup (1991, 1999), Olympic Games (1996), Goodwill Games (1998), and Nike U.S. Women's Cup (1998). She holds the U.S. record for career goals by a defender (26). In 2003, Fawcett helped the San Diego Spirit make the playoffs for the first time. She earned the Defensive Player of the Year award and All-WUSA First Team honors.

Maren Meinert, forward-midfielder, b. August 5, 1973, Duisberg, Germany. In 2003, Meinert was named WUSA's MVP after finishing second in the league in assists (10) and sixth in goals (9). The Boston Breakers star also earned MVP honors at the All-Star Game by scoring two goals and an assist for the winning World team. After the season, Meinert helped Germany win its first FIFA Women's World Cup by scoring a goal in the championship game against Sweden. She retired after the 2003 World Cup.

Trivia Challenge

Which goalkeeper set the WUSA record for most saves in a game (13), against the Boston Breakers on June 1, 2002?

Siri Mullinix of the Washington Freedom

All-time Founder's Cup Results

Year	Champion	Score	Runner-up
2003	Washington Freedom	2–1 (OT)	Atlanta Beat
2002	Carolina Courage	3–2	Washington Freedom
2001	San Jose CyberRays	4–2 (on penalty kicks)	Atlanta Beat

SCOTT BALES/ICON SMI

Maren Meinert of the Breakers scored two goals in the 2003 All-Star Game and was named MVP.

Did You Know?

Midfielder Venus James and forward-midfielder Jacqui Little are the only women to play for two WUSA championship teams. James won the Founder's Cup with the Bay Area CyberRays in 2001 and Carolina Courage in 2002. Little won the Cup with the CyberRays in 2001 and Washington Freedom in 2003.

2003 ALL-STAR GAME

Cary, North Carolina June 19, 2003

World All-Stars 3
American All-Stars 2
MVP: Maren Meinert

	1st Half	2nd Half	Final
World All-Stars	2	1	3
American All-Stars	1	1	2

Scoring Summary:
American All-Stars: Chastain (Hamm, Milbrett) 29
World All-Stars: Meinert (Lehn, Prinz) 34
World All-Stars: Mellgren (Meinert, Dominguez) 40
World All-Stars: Meinert (Katia, Mellgren) 61
American All-Stars: Fotopoulos (Milbrett) 71

World All-Stars: Karina LeBlanc (LaKeysia Beene 41), Unni Lehn, Breanna Boyd, Sharolta Nonen (Monica Gonzalez 41), Kelly Golebiowski, Maribel Dominguez (Joanne Peters 48), Steffi Jones (Maribel Dominguez 68), Maren Meinert, Dagny Mellgren (Birgit Prinz 61), Birgit Prinz (Katia 41), Charmaine Hooper (Julie Fleeting 41)

American All-Stars: Briana Scurry (Siri Mullinix 41), Brandi Chastain, Joy Fawcett (Nancy Augustyniak 41), Jennifer Grubb (Abby Wambach 64), Tiffany Roberts (Heather Mitts 41), Mia Hamm (Cindy Parlow 41), Julie Foudy (Shannon Boxx 41), Aly Wagner (Julie Foudy 61), Kristine Lilly (Tiffany Roberts 61), Tiffeny Milbrett, Abby Wambach (Danielle Fotopoulos 41)

Note: Numbers next to player names indicate time of game.

2003 World Cup Results

2003 WORLD CUP GROUP STANDINGS

GROUP A

Country	GP	W	L	T	GF	GA	PTS
U.S.	3	3	0	0	11	1	9
Sweden	3	2	1	0	5	3	6
Korea DPR	3	1	2	0	3	4	3
Nigeria	3	0	3	0	0	11	0

GROUP B

Country	GP	W	L	T	GF	GA	PTS
Brazil	3	2	0	1	8	2	7
Norway	3	2	1	0	10	5	6
France	3	1	1	1	2	3	4
Korea Republic	3	0	3	0	1	11	0

GROUP C

Country	GP	W	L	T	GF	GA	PTS
Germany	3	3	0	0	13	2	9
Canada	3	2	1	0	7	5	6
Japan	3	1	2	0	7	6	3
Argentina	3	0	3	0	1	15	0

GROUP D

Country	GP	W	L	T	GF	GA	PTS
China	3	2	0	1	3	1	7
Russia	3	2	1	0	5	2	6
Ghana	3	1	2	0	2	5	3
Australia	3	0	2	1	3	5	1

KEY GP=games played; W=win; L=loss; T=tie; GF=goals for; GA=goals against; PTS=points

2003 World Cup Final Bracket

U.S. (1–0)
Norway
U.S.

Germany (7–1)
Russia
Germany (3–0)

Germany

GERMANY 2–1

Sweden

Sweden (2–1)
Canada

Brazil
Sweden (2–1)

China
Canada (1–0)

Group Play Scores

Group A

Korea DPR 3, Nigeria 0
U.S. 3, Sweden 1
Sweden 1, Korea DPR 0
U.S. 5, Nigeria 0
Sweden 3, Nigeria 0
U.S. 3, Korea DPR 0

Group C

Germany 4, Canada 1
Japan 6, Argentina 0
Germany 3, Japan 0
Canada 3, Argentina 0
Canada 3, Japan 1
Germany 6, Argentina 1

Group B

Norway 2, France 0
Brazil 3, Korea Republic 0
Brazil 4, Norway 1
France 1, Korea Republic 0
Norway 7, Korea Republic 1
France 1, Brazil 1

Group D

Russia 2, Australia 1
China 1, Ghana 0
Russia 3, Ghana 0
China 1, Australia 1
Ghana 2, Australia 1
China 1, Russia 0

2003 WORLD CUP FINAL

October 12, 2003
The Home Depot Center Carson, California

	1st Half	2nd Half	OT	Final
Germany	1	0	1	2
Sweden	1	0	0	1

Scoring Summary: Hanna Ljungberg (SWE) 41, Maren Meinert (GER) 46, Nia Kuenzer (GER) 98
Germany: Rottenberg, Stegemann, Lingor, Wunderlich (Kuenzer 88), Prinz, Wiegmann, Minnert, Meinert, Hingst, Garefrekes (Mueller 76), Gottschlich
Sweden: Joensson, Westberg, Toernqvist, Marklund, Mostroem, Larsson (Bengtsson 76), Andersson (Sjoegran 53), Ljungberg, Svensson, Sjoestroem (Fagerstoem), Oestberg
Referee: Ionescu (Romania)

Note: Numbers next to player names indicate time of game.

Individual Statistical Leaders

GOALS	Team	Total
Birgit Prinz	Germany	7
Maren Meinert	Germany	4
Kerstin Garefrekes	Germany	4
Katia	Brazil	4

Nine tied with 3.

ASSISTS	Team	Total
Maren Meinert	Germany	7
Mia Hamm	U.S.	5
Birgit Prinz	Germany	5
Victoria Svensson	Sweden	4

Ten tied with 2.

SAVES	Team	Total
Romina Ferro	Argentina	27
Andreia	Brazil	21
Briana Scurry	U.S.	19
Alla Volkova	Russia	19
Celine Marty	France	18
Taryn Swiatek	Canada	18
Precious Dede	Nigeria	18

All-time World Cup Results

Year	Champion	Score	Runner-up
2003	Germany	2–1	Sweden
1999	U.S.	5–4 (penalty kicks)	China
1995	Norway	2–0	Germany
1991	U.S.	2–1	Norway

All-time World Cup Scoring

Player	Nation	Tournaments	Goals
Michelle Akers	U.S.	1991, 1995, 1999	12
Ann Kristin Aarones	Norway	1995, 1999	10
Heidi Mohr	Germany	1991, 1995	10
Sun Wen	China	1991, 1995, 1999	10

TOM HAUCK/GETTY IMAGES

Michelle Akers is the all-time leading scorer in Women's World Cup history.

2003-04 TIME LINE

February 2, 2003: The San Diego Spirit selects midfielder Aly Wagner of Santa Clara University with the first overall pick in WUSA's draft.

June 19, 2003: The World All-Stars defeat the American All-Stars, 3–2, in the Hyundai WUSA All-Star Game. World captain Maren Meinert, representing the Boston Breakers, has two goals and an assist and is named the game's MVP.

July 19, 2003: Forward Abby Wambach of the Washington Freedom scores the WUSA Goal of the Year. She makes a diving header on teammate Mia Hamm's free kick that dips inside the box. The Freedom shuts out the New York Power, 2–0.

August 24, 2003: The Washington Freedom downs the Atlanta Beat in the WUSA championship match, 2–1, in overtime. Forward Abby Wambach scores both goals for the Freedom and earns MVP honors.

September 15, 2003: WUSA announces it must shut down.

October 12, 2003: Germany wins the FIFA Women's World Cup for the first time by defeating Sweden, 2–1, in overtime. Substitute defender Nia Kuenzer of Germany scores the game-winning goal.

December 11, 2003: WUSA plans to seek sponsorship dollars to revive the league in 2005.

February 25, 2004: The U.S. Women's National Team defeats Trinidad and Tobago, 7–0, in its first game of the women's Olympic qualifying tournament. Midfielder Shannon Boxx of the U.S. scores the first hat trick of her international career.

March 2, 2004: WUSA announces it will hold two women's soccer festivals in the hopes the league will return in 2005. One festival will be at the National Sports Center, in Blaine, Minnesota, from June 17 through 20, 2004. The second will be held at The Home Depot Center, in Carson, California, from June 24 through 27.

August 11, 2004: The women's soccer competition begins at the Summer Olympics, in Athens, Greece. The gold and bronze medal matches will be played on August 26.

Did You Know?

Tisha Venturini-Hoch of the San Jose CyberRays is one of three female soccer players to win the WUSA (2002), World Cup (1999), Summer Olympics (1996), and NCAA (1991, 1992, 1993, 1994) championships. Carla Overbeck and Tiffany Roberts are the other two.

ACTION SPORTS

The Summer X Games moved to a new city — Los Angeles, California — in 2003, but skateboarder Bucky Lasek was in a familiar spot: atop the medal podium. Lasek won his third Summer X Games gold medal in Vert, a record for the event. He went on to win gold in Vert Doubles, with partner Bob Burnquist. Lasek's medal haul didn't stop in L.A. In September, he snagged the Vert gold at the Gravity Games, in Cleveland, Ohio.

J. GRANT BRITTAIN/TRANSWORLD SKATEBOARDING

Bucky Lasek ruled vert skating in 2003, winning gold medals at the Summer X Games and Gravity Games.

While the veteran Lasek ruled vert skating, newcomer Ryan Sheckler owned the street. The then 13-year-old became the youngest competitor to win a gold medal in the Summer X Games' nine-year history when he finished first in Park. Like Lasek, Sheckler won at the Gravity Games, taking home the gold in Street.

Ryan Nyquist and Dave Mirra had a stranglehold on BMX hardware. Nyquist won gold medals in Dirt and Park at the Summer X Games, then won gold in Dirt and silver in Street at the Gravity Games. Mirra finished second in Vert and third in Park at the X Games but won Vert and Street at the Gravity Games.

In freestyle motocross, Brian Deegan and Travis Pastrana kept pushing the boundaries of motorcycle riding. Both riders pulled off-axis 360s at the Summer X Games. The trick helped Pastrana win in Freestyle, and Deegan nailed it to take home gold in Big Air. Unfortunately for Deegan, his success on dirt didn't carry over to snow. He attempted the same trick at the Winter X Games in 2004 and fell more than 40 feet, breaking both wrists and the femur bone in his left leg.

Snowboarder Hannah Teter had better luck at Winter X. The then 16-year-old won the Superpipe gold medal. (She finished third in 2003.) Elsewhere on the mountain, snowboarder Shaun White successfully defended his Slopestyle title and skier Tanner Hall won Slopestyle for the third-straight year.

The repeats continued in the ocean, where surfer Andy Irons earned his second-straight men's World Championship Tour (WCT) title by winning five events. Layne Beachley remained the dominant force in women's surfing. Her two victories helped secure her sixth consecutive WCT championship.

Winter X Games Results

Moto X

Year	Event	Gold	Silver	Bronze
2004	Best Trick	Caleb Wyatt, U.S.	Mike Metzger, U.S.	Nate Adams, U.S.
2003	Big Air	Mike Metzger, U.S.	Dane Kinnaird, Australia	Caleb Wyatt, U.S.
2002	Big Air	Brian Deegan, U.S.	Mike Jones, U.S.	Tommy Clowers, U.S.
2001	Big Air	Mike Jones, U.S.	Tommy Clowers, U.S.	Clifford Adoptante, U.S.

Skiing—Men

Year	Event	Gold	Silver	Bronze
2004	Skier X	Casey Puckett, U.S.	Lars Lewen, Sweden	Reggie Crist, U.S.
2003	Skier X	Lars Lewen, Sweden	Reggie Crist, U.S.	Enak Gavaggio, France
2002	Skier X	Reggie Crist, U.S.	Peter Lind, Sweden	Enak Gavaggio, France
2001	Skier X	Zach Crist, U.S.	Tomas Andersson, Sweden	Enak Gavaggio, France
2000	Skier X	Shaun Palmer, U.S.	Bill Hudson, U.S.	Zach Crist, U.S.
1999	Skier X	Enak Gavaggio, France	Shane McConkey, U.S.	Jeremy Nobis, U.S.
1998	Skier X	Denis Rey, France	Kent Kreitler, U.S.	Chris Davenport, U.S.
2004	Slopestyle	Tanner Hall, U.S.	Peter Olenick, U.S.	Jon Olsson, Sweden
2003	Slopestyle	Tanner Hall, U.S.	Pep Fujas, U.S.	Jon Olsson, Sweden
2002	Slopestyle	Tanner Hall, U.S.	C.R. Johnson, U.S.	Jon Olsson, Sweden
2004	Superpipe	Simon Dumont, U.S.	Jon Olsson, Sweden	Peter Olenick, U.S.
2003	Superpipe	Candide Thovex, France	Tanner Hall, U.S.	Jon Olsson, Sweden
2002	Superpipe	Jon Olsson, Sweden	Philippe Larose, Canada	Philippe Poirier, Canada
2001	Big Air	Tanner Hall, U.S.	Evan Raps, U.S.	C.R. Johnson, U.S.
2000	Big Air	Candide Thovex, France	Skogen Sprang, U.S.	Evan Raps, U.S.
1999	Big Air	J.F. Cusson, Canada	Jonny Moseley, U.S.	Vincent Dorion, Canada

Skiing—Women

Year	Event	Gold	Silver	Bronze
2004	Skier X	Karin Huttary, Austria	Aleisha Cline, Canada	Sanna Tidstrand, Sweden
2003	Skier X	Aleisha Cline, Canada	Karin Huttary, Austria	Cecilie Larsen, Norway
2002	Skier X	Aleisha Cline, Canada	Magdalena Jonsson, Sweden	Patti Sherman-Kauf, U.S.
2001	Skier X	Aleisha Cline, Canada	Magdalena Jonsson, Sweden	Chiara Lawrence, U.S.
2000	Skier X	Anik Demers, Canada	Chiara Lawrence, U.S.	Patti Sherman-Kauf, U.S.
1999	Skier X	Aleisha Cline, Canada	Darian Boyle, U.S.	Patti Sherman-Kauf, U.S.

Snowboarding—Men

Year	Event	Gold	Silver	Bronze
2004	Slopestyle	Shaun White, U.S.	Danny Kass, U.S.	Andreas Wiig, Norway
2003	Slopestyle	Shaun White, U.S.	Jussi Oksanen, Finland	Jimi Tomer, U.S.
2002	Slopestyle	Travis Rice, U.S.	Shaun White, U.S.	Todd Richards, U.S.
2001	Slopestyle	Kevin Jones, U.S.	Todd Richards, U.S.	Jussi Oksanen, Finland
2000	Slopestyle	Kevin Jones, U.S.	Todd Richards, U.S.	Peter Line, U.S.
1999	Slopestyle	Peter Line, U.S.	Kevin Jones, U.S.	Jimmy Halopoff, U.S.
1998	Slopestyle	Ross Powers, U.S.	Kevin Jones, U.S.	Rob Kingwill, U.S.
1997	Slopestyle	Daniel Franck, Norway	Jimmy Halopoff, U.S.	Bryan Iguchi, U.S.
2004	Snowboarder X	Ueli Kestenholz, Switzerland	Seth Wescott, U.S.	Xavier de le Rue, France
2003	Snowboarder X	Ueli Kestenholz, Switzerland	Xavier de le Rue, France	Michael Rosengren, U.S.
2002	Snowboarder X	Philippe Conte, Switzerland	Seth Wescott, U.S.	Berti Denervaud, Switzerland
2001	Snowboarder X	Scott Gaffney, Canada	Mark Schulz, U.S.	Seth Wescott, U.S.
2000	Snowboarder X	Drew Neilson, Canada	Scott Gaffney, Canada	Jason Ford, U.S.
1999	Snowboarder X	Shaun Palmer, U.S.	Drew Neilson, Canada	Scott Gaffney, Canada
1998	Snowboarder X	Shaun Palmer, U.S.	Jason Brown, U.S.	Seth Wescott, U.S.
1997	Snowboarder X	Shaun Palmer, U.S.	Berti Denervaud, Switzerland	Mike Basich, U.S.

Winter X Games Results (cont.)

Snowboarding—Men (cont.)

Year	Event	Gold	Silver	Bronze
2004	Superpipe	Steve Fisher, U.S.	Danny Kass, U.S.	Keir Dillon, U.S.
2003	Superpipe	Shaun White, U.S.	Danny Kass, U.S.	Markku Koski, Finland
2002	Superpipe	J.J. Thomas, U.S.	Shaun White, U.S.	Keir Dillon, U.S.
2001	Superpipe	Danny Kass, U.S.	Tommy Czeschin, U.S.	Ross Powers, U.S.
2000	Superpipe	Todd Richards, U.S.	Ross Powers, U.S.	Tommy Czeschin, U.S.
1999	Halfpipe	Jimi Scott, U.S.	Mike Michalchuk, Canada	Luke Wynen, U.S.
1998	Halfpipe	Ross Powers, U.S.	Guillaume Chastagnol, France	Todd Richards, U.S.
1997	Halfpipe	Todd Richards, U.S.	Daniel Franck, Norway	Fabien Rohrer, Switzerland
2001	Big Air	Jussi Oksanen, Finland	Todd Richards, U.S.	Josh Dirksen, U.S.
2000	Big Air	Peter Line, U.S.	Jason Borgstede, U.S.	Kevin Jones, U.S.
1999	Big Air	Kevin Sansalone, Canada	Peter Line, U.S.	Kevin Jones, U.S.
1998	Big Air	Jason Borgstede, U.S.	Ryan W. Williams, U.S.	Kevin Jones, U.S.
1997	Big Air	Jimmy Halopoff, U.S.	Steve Adkins, U.S.	Bjorn Leines, U.S.

Snowboarding—Women

Year	Event	Gold	Silver	Bronze
2004	Slopestyle	Janna Meyen, U.S.	Tara Dakides, U.S.	Jessica Dalpiaz, U.S.
2003	Slopestyle	Janna Meyen, U.S.	Hana Beaman, U.S.	Lindsey Jacobellis, U.S.
2002	Slopestyle	Tara Dakides, U.S.	Janna Meyen, U.S.	Barrett Christy, U.S.
2001	Slopestyle	Jaime MacLeod, U.S.	Shannon Dunn, U.S.	Marni Yamada, U.S.
2000	Slopestyle	Tara Dakides, U.S.	Jaime MacLeod, U.S.	Barrett Christy, U.S.
1999	Slopestyle	Tara Dakides, U.S.	Barrett Christy, U.S.	Jaime MacLeod, U.S.
1998	Slopestyle	Jennie Waara, Sweden	Barrett Christy, U.S.	Aurelie Sayres, U.S.
1997	Slopestyle	Barrett Christy, U.S.	Cara-Beth Burnside, U.S.	Jennie Waara, Sweden
2004	Snowboarder X	Lindsey Jacobellis, U.S.	Karine Ruby, France	Yvonne Mueller, Switzerland
2003	Snowboarder X	Lindsey Jacobellis, U.S.	Tanja Frieden, Switzerland	Yvonne Mueller, Switzerland
2002	Snowboarder X	Ine Poetzl, Austria	Erin Simmons, Canada	Tanja Frieden, Switzerland
2001	Snowboarder X	Line Oestvold, Norway	Erin Simmons, Canada	Amy Johnson, U.S.
2000	Snowboarder X	Leslee Olson, U.S.	Carlee Baker, Canada	Line Oestvold, Norway
1999	Snowboarder X	Maelle Ricker, Canada	Leslee Olson, U.S.	Candice Drouin, Canada
1998	Snowboarder X	Tina Dixon, U.S.	Corrie Rudishauser, U.S.	Katrina Warnick, U.S.
1997	Snowboarder X	Jennie Waara, Sweden	Hillary Maybery, U.S.	Aurelie Sayres, U.S.
2004	Superpipe	Hannah Teter, U.S.	Kelly Clark, U.S.	Doriane Vidal, France

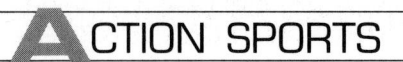

Hannah Teter won her first Winter X Games gold medal in 2004.

TOM ZIKAS

Fast Fact: Motocross racer James Stewart and Ken Griffey, Jr. of the Cincinnati Reds are good friends. Stewart rides motorcycles with Griffey's son, Trey.

Winter X Games Results (cont.)

Snowboarding—Women (cont.)

Year	Event	Gold	Silver	Bronze
2003	Superpipe	Gretchen Bleiler, U.S.	Kelly Clark, U.S.	Hannah Teter, U.S.
2002	Superpipe	Kelly Clark, U.S.	Stine Brun Kjeldaas, Norway	Natasza Zurek, Canada
2001	Superpipe	Shannon Dunn, U.S.	Natasza Zurek, Canada	Fabienne Reuteler, Switzerland
2000	Superpipe	Stine Brun Kjeldaas, Norway	Barrett Christy, U.S.	Natasza Zurek, Canada
1999	Halfpipe	Michelle Taggart, U.S.	Shannon Dunn, U.S.	Cara-Beth Burnside, U.S.
1998	Halfpipe	Cara-Beth Burnside, U.S.	Michelle Taggart, U.S.	Nicola Thost, Germany
1997	Halfpipe	Shannon Dunn, U.S.	Jennie Waara, Sweden	Nicole Angelrath, Switzerland
2001	Big Air	Tara Dakides, U.S.	Barrett Christy, U.S.	Jenna Murano, U.S.
2000	Big Air	Tara Dakides, U.S.	Leah Wagner, Canada	Jessica Dalpiaz, U.S.
1999	Big Air	Barrett Christy, U.S.	Tara Dakides, U.S.	Janet Matthews, Canada
1998	Big Air	Tina Basich, U.S.	Barrett Christy, U.S.	Tara Zwink, U.S.
1997	Big Air	Barrett Christy, U.S.	Tara Zwink, U.S.	Tina Basich, U.S.

Snowmobiling

Year	Event	Gold	Silver	Bronze
2004	SnoCross	Michael Island, Canada	Tucker Hibbert, U.S.	Blair Morgan, Canada
2003	SnoCross	Blair Morgan, Canada	D.J. Eckstrom, U.S.	Tucker Hibbert, U.S.
2002	SnoCross	Blair Morgan, Canada	Tucker Hibbert, U.S.	Tomi Ahmasalo, Finland
2001	SnoCross	Blair Morgan, Canada	Kent Ipsen, U.S.	D.J. Eckstrom, U.S.
2000	SnoCross	Tucker Hibbert, U.S.	Blair Morgan, Canada	T.J. Gulla, U.S.
1999	SnoCross	Chris Vincent, U.S.	Blair Morgan, Canada	Trevor John, U.S.
1998	SnoCross	Toni Haikonen, Finland	Dennis Burks, U.S.	Per Berggren, Sweden
2004	HillCross	Levi LaVallee, U.S.	Justin Tate, U.S.	Carl Kuster, Canada
2003	HillCross	T.J. Gulla, U.S.	Carl Kuster, Canada	Steve Martin, Canada
2002	HillCross	Carl Kuster, Canada	Steve Martin, Canada	Rick Ward, U.S.
2001	HillCross	Carl Kuster, Canada	Vinny Clark, Canada	Matt Luczynski, U.S.

Ultracross*

Year	Gold	Silver	Bronze
2004	Nate Holland, U.S.	Lars Lewen, Sweden	Xavier Kuhn, France
	Reggie Crist, U.S.	Xavier de le Rue, France	Drew Neilson, Canada
2003	Xavier de le Rue, France	Seth Wescott, U.S.	Ben Jacobellis, U.S.
	Kaj Zackrisson, Sweden	Peter Lind, Sweden	Lars Lewen, Sweden
2002	Seth Wescott, U.S.	Scott Gaffney, Canada	Rob Fagan, Canada
	Peter Lind, Sweden	Eric Archer, U.S.	Enak Gavaggio, France
2001	Shaun Palmer, U.S.	Jason Evans, U.S.	Pontus Staahlkloo, Sweden
	Hiroomi Takizawa, Japan	Isidor Gruener, Austria	Matt Murphy, U.S.
2000	Travis McLain, U.S.	Scott Gaffney, Canada	Terry Plum, U.S.
	Peter Lind, Sweden	Sverre Liliequist, Sweden	Mike Dill, U.S.

*First athlete listed in each category is a snowboarder; the second athlete is a skier.

U.S. Open Snowboarding Championships Results

Halfpipe—Men

Year	Gold	Silver	Bronze
2004	Danny Kass, U.S.	Steve Fisher, U.S.	Keir Dillon, U.S.
2003	Ross Powers, U.S.	Kazuhiro Kokubo, Japan	Daniel Franck, Norway
2002	Danny Kass, U.S.	Markku Koski, Finland	Keir Dillon, U.S.
2001	Danny Kass, U.S.	Abe Teter, U.S.	Daniel Franck, Norway
2000	Guillaume Morisset, Canada	Ross Powers, U.S.	Xavier Hoffman, Germany
1999	Ross Powers, U.S.	Xavier Hoffman, Germany	Tommy Czeschin, U.S.
1998	Rob Kingwill, U.S.	Terje Haakonsen, Norway	Todd Richards, U.S.
1997	Todd Richards, U.S.	Terje Haakonsen, Norway	Sebu Kuhlberg, Finland
1996	Jimi Scott, U.S.	Sami Hyry, Finland	Max Ploetzender, Austria
1995	Terje Haakonsen, Norway	Jason Evans, U.S.	J.J. Collier, U.S.
1994	Todd Richards, U.S.	Lael Gregory, U.S.	Jason Evans, U.S.

U.S. Open Snowboarding Championships Results (cont.)

Halfpipe—Men (cont.)

Year	Gold	Silver	Bronze
1993	Terje Haakonsen, Norway	Keith Wallace, U.S.	Sebu Kuhlberg, Finland
1992	Terje Haakonsen, Norway	Jeff Brushie, U.S.	Todd Richards, U.S.
1991	Jimi Scott, U.S.	Craig Kelly, U.S.	Shaun Palmer, U.S.
1990	Craig Kelly, U.S.	Shaun Palmer, U.S.	Jeff Brushie, U.S.
1989	Craig Kelly, U.S.	Bert Lamar, U.S.	Terry Kidwell, U.S.
1988	Terry Kidwell, U.S.	Bert Lamar, U.S.	Craig Kelly, U.S.

Halfpipe—Women

Year	Gold	Silver	Bronze
2004	Kelly Clark, U.S.	Tricia Byrnes, U.S.	Stine Brun Kjeldaas, Norway
2003	Gretchen Bleiler, U.S.	Natasza Zurek, Canada	Hannah Teter, U.S.
2002	Kelly Clark, U.S.	Tricia Byrnes, U.S.	Stine Brun Kjeldaas, Norway
2001	Natasza Zurek, Canada	Shannon Dunn, U.S.	Gretchen Bleiler, U.S.
2000	Natasza Zurek, Canada	Shannon Dunn, U.S.	Barrett Christy, U.S.
1999	Nicola Thost, Germany	Tricia Byrnes, U.S.	Shannon Dunn, U.S.
1998	Nicola Thost, Germany	Tricia Byrnes, U.S.	Tara Teigen, Canada
1997	Barrett Christy, U.S.	Tricia Byrnes, U.S.	Michelle Taggart, U.S.
1996	Satu Jarvela, Finland	Michelle Taggart, U.S.	Jennie Waara, Sweden
1995	Satu Jarvela, Finland	Nicole Angelrath, Switzerland	Jennie Waara, Sweden
1994	Shannon Dunn, U.S.	Tina Basich, U.S.	Sandra Farmand, Germany
1993	Shannon Dunn, U.S.	Janna Meyen, U.S.	Tricia Byrnes, U.S.
1992	Tricia Byrnes, U.S.	Nicole Angelrath, Switzerland	Tina Basich, U.S.
1991	Janna Meyen, U.S.	Tina Basich, U.S.	Michelle Taggart, U.S.
1990	Tina Basich, U.S.	Lisa Vinciguerra, U.S.	Jean Higgins, U.S.
1989	Jean Higgins, U.S.	Tara Eberhard, U.S.	Ashild Lofthus, Norway
1988	Petra Mussig, Germany	Jean Higgins, U.S.	Gayle Guerin, U.S.

Rail Jam—Men

Year	Gold	Silver	Bronze
2004	Rahm Klampert, U.S.	Travis Rice, U.S.	Chris Rotax, U.S.
2003	Travis Rice, U.S.	Shaun White, U.S.	Zach Leach, U.S.

Rail Jam—Women

Year	Gold	Silver	Bronze
2004	Leanne Pelosi, Canada	Erin Comstock, U.S.	Natasza Zurek, Canada

Slopestyle—Men

Year	Gold	Silver	Bronze
2004	Jake Blauvelt, U.S.	Travis Rice, U.S.	Christopher Schmidt, Germany
2003	Shaun White, U.S.	Travis Rice, U.S.	Nate Sheehan, U.S.
2002	Rahm Klampert, U.S.	Travis Rice, U.S.	Ryan Paris, U.S.

Slopestyle—Women

Year	Gold	Silver	Bronze
2004	Priscilla Levac, Canada	Kelly Clark, U.S.	Hana Beaman, U.S.
2003	Hana Beaman, U.S.	Priscilla Levac, Canada	Hannah Teter, U.S.
2002	Annie Boulanger, Canada	Hannah Teter, U.S.	Jaime MacLeod, U.S.

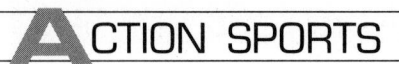

Summer X Games Results

Aggressive In-line—Men

Year	Event	Gold	Silver	Bronze
2003	Park	Bruno Lowe, Germany	Stephane Alfano, France	Sven Boekhorst, Netherlands
2002	Park	Jaren Grob, U.S.	Bruno Lowe, Germany	Blake Dennis, Australia
2001	Park	Jaren Grob, U.S.	Louie Zamora, U.S.	Franky Morales, U.S.
2000	Park	Sven Boekhorst, Netherlands	Jaren Grob, U.S.	Sam Fogarty, Australia
1999	Street	Nicky Adams, Canada	Blake Dennis, Australia	Aaron Feinberg, U.S.
1998	Street	Jonathan Bergeron, Canada	Marco Hintze, Mexico	Aaron Feinberg, U.S.
1997	Street	Aaron Feinberg, U.S.	Tim Ward, Australia	Chris Edwards, U.S.
1996	Street	Arlo Eisenberg, U.S.	Matt Mantz, U.S.	Chris Edwards, U.S.
1995	Street	Matt Salerno, Australia	Scott Bentley, New Zealand	Ryan Jacklone, U.S.
2003	Vert	Eito Yasutoko, Japan	Takeshi Yasutoko, Japan	Nel Martin, Spain
2002	Vert	Takeshi Yasutoko, Japan	Eito Yasutoko, Japan	Marc Englehart, U.S.
2001	Vert	Taig Khris, France	Takeshi Yasutoko, Japan	Shane Yost, Australia
2000	Vert	Eito Yasutoko, Japan	Takeshi Yasutoko, Japan	Cesar Mora, Australia
1999	Vert	Eito Yasutoko, Japan	Cesar Mora, Australia	Matt Salerno, Australia
1998	Vert	Cesar Mora, Australia	Matt Salerno, Australia	Taig Khris, France
1997	Vert	Tim Ward, Australia	Taig Khris, France	Chris Edwards, U.S.
1996	Vert	Rene Hulgreen, Denmark	Tom Fry, Australia	Chris Edwards, U.S.
1995	Vert	Tom Fry, Australia	Cesar Mora, Australia	Manuel Billiris, Australia
1999	Vert Triples	Sven Boekhorst, Netherlands Javier Bujanda, Spain Taig Khris, France	Mike Budnik, U.S. Cesar Mora, Australia Matt Salerno, Australia	Maki Komori, Japan Eito Yasutoko, Japan Takeshi Yasutoko, Japan
1998	Vert Triples	Paul Malina, Australia Viorel Popa, U.S. Sam Fogarty, Australia	Mike Budnik, U.S. Cesar Mora, Australia Matt Salerno, Australia	Sven Boekhorst, Netherlands Javier Bujanda, Spain Taig Khris, France
1996	Best Trick	Dion Antony, Australia	Ryan Jacklone, U.S.	Eric Schrijn, U.S.
1995	Best Trick	B. Hardin, U.S.	Ryan Jacklone, U.S.	Brooke Howard-Smith, New Zealand
1995	High Air	Chris Edwards, U.S.	Manuel Billiris, Australia	Ichi Komori, Japan

Aggressive In-line—Women

Year	Event	Gold	Silver	Bronze
2003	Park	Fabiola da Silva, Brazil	Jenny Logue, Great Britain	Martina Svobodova, Slovakia
2002	Park	Martina Svobodova, Slovakia	Jenna Downing, Great Britain	Fallon Heffernan, U.S.
2001	Park	Martina Svobodova, Slovakia	Fallon Heffernan, U.S.	Anneke Winter, Germany
2000	Park	Fabiola da Silva, Brazil	Martina Svobodova, Slovakia	Kelly Matthews, U.S.
1999	Street	Sayaka Yabe, Japan	Kelly Matthews, U.S.	Jenny Curry, U.S.
1998	Street	Jenny Curry, U.S.	Salima Sanga, Switzerland	Sayaka Yabe, Japan
1997	Street	Sayaka Yabe, Japan	Katie Brown, U.S.	True Otis, U.S.

M PAULSEN/SHAZAMM/ESPN

Eito Yasutoko has won four Summer X Games medals in Aggressive In-line Vert.

Did You Know?

At the 1999 Summer X Games, skateboarder Tony Hawk fell 10 times before landing the first 900 in skateboarding history.

Summer X Games Results (cont.)

Aggressive In-line—Women (cont.)

Year	Event	Gold	Silver	Bronze
2001	Vert	Fabiola da Silva, Brazil	Ayumi Kawasaki, Japan	N/A
2000	Vert	Fabiola da Silva, Brazil	Ayumi Kawasaki, Japan	Merce Borrull, Spain
1999	Vert	Ayumi Kawasaki, Japan	Fabiola da Silva, Brazil	Maki Komori, Japan
1998	Vert	Fabiola da Silva, Brazil	Ayumi Kawasaki, Japan	Maki Komori, Japan
1997	Vert	Fabiola da Silva, Brazil	Claudia Trachsel, Switzerland	Ayumi Kawasaki, Japan
1996	Vert	Fabiola da Silva, Brazil	Jodie Tyler, Australia	Tasha Hodgson, Australia
1995	Vert	Tasha Hodgson, Australia	Angie Walton, New Zealand	Laura Connery, U.S.

Barefoot Jumping

Year	Gold	Silver	Bronze
1998	Peter Fleck, U.S.	Ron Scarpa, U.S.	Massimiliano Colosio, Italy
1997	Peter Fleck, U.S.	Evan Berger, South Africa	Warren Fine, South Africa
1996	Ron Scarpa, U.S.	Jon Kretchman, U.S.	Rael Nurick, South Africa
1995	Justin Seers, Australia	Ron Scarpa, U.S.	Rael Nurick, South Africa

Bike Stunt

Year	Event	Gold	Silver	Bronze
2003	Dirt	Ryan Nyquist, U.S.	Corey Bohan, Australia	Chris Doyle, U.S.
2002	Dirt	Allan Cooke, U.S.	Ryan Nyquist, U.S.	Chris Doyle, U.S.
2001	Dirt	Stephen Murray, Great Britain	Ryan Nyquist, U.S.	T.J. Lavin, U.S.
2000	Dirt	Ryan Nyquist, U.S.	Cory Nastazio, U.S.	T.J. Lavin, U.S.
1999	Dirt	T.J. Lavin, U.S.	Brian Foster, U.S.	Ryan Nyquist, U.S.
1998	Dirt	Brian Foster, U.S.	Ryan Nyquist, U.S.	Joey Garcia, U.S.
1997	Dirt	T.J. Lavin, U.S.	Brian Foster, U.S.	Ryan Nyquist, U.S.
1996	Dirt	Joey Garcia, U.S.	T.J. Lavin, U.S.	Brian Foster, U.S.
1995	Dirt	Jay Miron, Canada	Taj Mihelich, U.S.	Joey Garcia, U.S.
2003	Flatland	Simon O'Brien, Australia	Nathan Penonzek, Canada	Trevor Meyer, U.S.
2002	Flatland	Martti Kuoppa, Finland	Michael Steingraeber, Germany	Phil Dolan, Great Britain
2001	Flatland	Martti Kuoppa, Finland	Phil Dolan, Great Britain	Matt Wilhelm, U.S.
2000	Flatland	Martti Kuoppa, Finland	Michael Steingraeber, Germany	Phil Dolan, Great Britain
1999	Flatland	Trevor Meyer, U.S.	Phil Dolan, Great Britain	Nathan Penonzek, Canada
1998	Flatland	Trevor Meyer, U.S.	Andrew Faris, Canada	Martti Kuoppa, Finland
1997	Flatland	Trevor Meyer, U.S.	Nate Hanson, U.S.	Andrew Faris, Canada
2003	Park	Ryan Nyquist, U.S.	Gary Young, U.S.	Dave Mirra, U.S.
2002	Park	Ryan Nyquist, U.S.	Alistair Whitton, Great Britain	Chad Kagy, U.S.

Ryan Nyquist has won medals at every Summer X Games since 1997.

MARK LOSEY

Trivia Challenge

Which snowboarder won the men's Halfpipe gold medal at the Winter Olympics in 2002?

Ross Powers of the United States

Today's Stars

Andy Irons won five of 12 events in 2003 to earn his second-straight World Championship Tour title.

PIERRE TOSTEE/ASP/REUTERS

Andy Irons, surfer, b. July 24, 1978, Kauai, Hawaii. In 2003, Irons became the fifth surfer to win the men's World Championship Tour (WCT) title in back-to-back years. He won five events and held off a strong charge from second-place finisher and six-time world champ Kelly Slater. With his win at the Xbox Pipeline Masters on Hawaii's North Shore, A.I. also joined Sunny Garcia as the only surfers to win the Vans Triple Crown title two years in a row.

Hannah Teter, snowboarder, b. January 27, 1987, Belmont, Vermont. After she finished first in Halfpipe at two United States Snowboard Association Grand Prix events, second at two Vans Triple Crown stops, and third at the Winter X Games and U.S. Open in 2002-03, big things were expected from Teter in 2003-04. She didn't disappoint. The baby girl of the Teter clan, which includes pro snowboarders Abe and Elijah, won gold in Superpipe at the X Games and the first stop of the Triple Crown in 2003-04. Teter also finished fourth in Halfpipe at the 2004 U.S. Open.

Ryan Nyquist, BMX rider, b. March 6, 1979, Los Gatos, California. Nyquist didn't share the wealth in 2003. He finished either first or second in every Park and Dirt event in which he competed. His domination included becoming the first rider at the Summer X Games to take home gold in BMX Dirt and Park in the same year. Nyquist has won 10 X Games medals (four gold, three silver, three bronze) and seven Gravity Games medals (three gold, four silver).

Summer X Games Results (cont.)

Bike Stunt (cont.)

Year	Event	Gold	Silver	Bronze
2001	Park	Bruce Crisman, U.S.	Alistair Whitton, Great Britain	Jay Miron, Canada
2000	Park	Dave Mirra, U.S.	Markus Wilke, Germany	Ryan Nyquist, U.S.
1999	Street	Dave Mirra, U.S.	Jay Miron, Canada	Chad Kagy, U.S.
1998	Street	Dave Mirra, U.S.	Jay Miron, Canada	Dennis McCoy, U.S.
1997	Street	Dave Mirra, U.S.	Dennis McCoy, U.S.	Dave Voelker, U.S.
1996	Street	Dave Mirra, U.S.	Jay Miron, Canada	Rob Nolli, U.S.
2003	Vert	Jamie Bestwick, Great Britain	Dave Mirra, U.S.	Kevin Robinson, U.S.
2002	Vert	Dave Mirra, U.S.	Mat Hoffman, U.S.	Simon Tabron, Great Britain
2001	Vert	Dave Mirra, U.S.	Jay Miron, Canada	Mat Hoffman, U.S.
2000	Vert	Jamie Bestwick, Great Britain	Dave Mirra, U.S.	Mat Hoffman, U.S.
1999	Vert	Dave Mirra, U.S.	Jay Miron, Canada	Simon Tabron, Great Britain
1998	Vert	Dave Mirra, U.S.	Dennis McCoy, U.S.	Simon Tabron, Great Britain
1997	Vert	Dave Mirra, U.S.	Dennis McCoy, U.S.	Mat Hoffman, U.S.
1996	Vert	Mat Hoffman, U.S.	Dave Mirra, U.S.	Jamie Bestwick, Great Britain
1995	Vert	Mat Hoffman, U.S.	Dave Mirra, U.S.	Jay Miron, Canada
1998	Vert Doubles	Dave Mirra, U.S. Dennis McCoy, U.S.	Jay Miron, Canada Dave Osato, Canada	Jason Davies, Great Britain John Parker, U.S.

Summer X Games Results (cont.)

Bungy

Year	Gold	Silver	Bronze
1996	Peter Bihun, Canada	Doug Anderson, Canada	Carolyn Anderson, Canada
1995	Doug Anderson, Canada	Mark Baldwin, U.S.	Todd Watkins, U.S.

Downhill BMX

Year	Gold	Silver	Bronze
2003	Brandon Meadows, U.S.	Kyle Bennett, U.S.	Michael Day, U.S.
2002	Robbie Miranda, U.S.	Kyle Bennett, U.S.	Robert de Wilde, Netherlands
2001	Brandon Meadows, U.S.	Brian Foster, U.S.	John Whipperman, U.S.

Downhill In-line—Men

Year		Gold	Silver	Bronze
1998		Patrick Naylor, U.S.	Jeremy Anderson, U.S.	Dane Lewis, U.S.
1997		Derek Downing, U.S.	Keith Turner, U.S.	B.J. Steketee, U.S.
1996		Dante Muse, U.S.	Derek Parra, U.S.	Jim Wiederhold, U.S.
1995	Combined	Derek Downing, U.S.	Jim Wiederhold, U.S.	Jondon Trevena, U.S.

Downhill In-line—Women

Year	Gold	Silver	Bronze
1998	Julie Brandt, U.S.	Aimee Sanderson, U.S.	Theresa Cliff, U.S.
1997	Gypsy Tidwell, U.S.	Julie Brandt, U.S.	Jessica Apgar, U.S.
1996	Gypsy Tidwell, U.S.	Jennifer Jones, U.S.	Desly Hill, Australia

Kiteskiing

Year	Gold	Silver	Bronze
1995	Cory Roessler, U.S.	Clarin Mustad, Norway	Thomas Jeltsch, Germany

Mountain Biking—Men

Year	Event	Gold	Silver	Bronze
1995	Dual Downhill	Robert Naughton, U.S.	Jurgen Beneke, Germany	Todd Tanner, U.S.
1995	Dual Slalom	Jimmy Knight, U.S.	Myles Rockwell, U.S.	Mike King, U.S.
1995	Observed Trials	Libor Karas, Czech Republic	Hans Rey, Germany	Marc Brooks, U.S.

Mountain Biking—Women

Year	Event	Gold	Silver	Bronze
1995	Dual Downhill	Cheri Elliott, U.S.	Kim Sonier, U.S.	Leigh Donovan, U.S.
1995	Dual Slalom	Leigh Donovan, U.S.	Cheri Elliott, U.S.	Giovanna Bonazzi, Italy

Moto X

Year	Event	Gold	Silver	Bronze
2003	Big Air	Brian Deegan, U.S.	Nate Adams, U.S.	Kenny Bartram, U.S.
2002	Big Air	Mike Metzger, U.S.	Carey Hart, U.S.	Brian Deegan, U.S.
2001	Big Air	Kenny Bartram, U.S.	Dustin Miller, U.S.	Brian Deegan, U.S.
2003	Freestyle	Travis Pastrana, U.S.	Nate Adams, U.S.	Brian Deegan, U.S.
2002	Freestyle	Mike Metzger, U.S.	Kenny Bartram, U.S.	Drake McElroy, U.S.
2001	Freestyle	Travis Pastrana, U.S.	Clifford Adoptante, U.S.	Jake Windham, U.S.
2000	Freestyle	Travis Pastrana, U.S.	Tommy Clowers, U.S.	Brian Deegan, U.S.
1999	Freestyle	Travis Pastrana, U.S.	Mike Cinqmars, U.S.	Brian Deegan, U.S.
2003	Step Up	Matt Buyten, U.S.	Tommy Clowers, U.S.	Ronnie Renner, U.S.

Moto X (cont.)

Year	Event	Gold	Silver	Bronze
2002	Step Up	Tommy Clowers, U.S.	Mike Metzger, U.S.	Brian Deegan, U.S.
2001	Step Up	Tommy Clowers, U.S.	Travis Pastrana, U.S.	Colin Morrison, U.S. (tie) Ronnie Renner, U.S. Kris Rourke, U.S. Jeremy Stenberg, U.S.
2000	Step Up	Tommy Clowers, U.S.	Kris Rourke, U.S.	Brian Deegan, U.S.

Skateboarding

Year	Event	Gold	Silver	Bronze
2003	Park	Ryan Sheckler, U.S.	Rodil de Araujo, Jr., Brazil	Chad Bartie, Australia
2002	Park	Rodil de Araujo, Jr., Brazil	Wagner Ramos, Brazil	Eric Koston, U.S.
2001	Park	Rodil de Araujo, Jr., Brazil	Kerry Getz, U.S.	Caine Gayle, U.S.
2000	Park	Eric Koston, U.S.	Rodil de Araujo, Jr., Brazil	Kerry Getz, U.S.
2003	Street	Eric Koston, U.S.	Rodil de Araujo, Jr., Brazil	Paul Rodriguez, U.S.
2002	Street	Rodil de Araujo, Jr., Brazil	Wagner Ramos, Brazil	Kyle Berard, U.S.
2001	Street	Kerry Getz, U.S.	Eric Koston, U.S.	Chris Senn, U.S.
1999	Street	Chris Senn, U.S.	Pat Channita, U.S.	Chad Fernandez, U.S.
1998	Street	Rodil de Araujo, Jr., Brazil	Andy Macdonald, U.S.	Chris Senn, U.S.
1997	Street	Chris Senn, U.S.	Andy Macdonald, U.S.	Brian Patch, U.S.
1996	Street	Rodil de Araujo, Jr., Brazil	Chris Senn, U.S.	Brian Patch, U.S.
1995	Street	Chris Senn, U.S.	Tony Hawk, U.S.	Willy Santos, U.S.
2003	Street Best Trick	Chad Muska, U.S.	Rodil de Araujo, Jr., Brazil	Wagner Ramos, Brazil
2002	Street Best Trick	Rodil de Araujo, Jr., Brazil	Wagner Ramos, Brazil	Dayne Brummet, U.S.
2001	Street Best Trick	Rick McCrank, Canada	Kerry Getz, U.S.	Eric Koston, U.S.
1996	Street Best Trick	Gershon Mosley, U.S.	Chris Senn, U.S.	Brian Patch, U.S.
1995	Street Best Trick	Jamie Thomas, U.S.	Gershon Mosley, U.S.	Kareem Campbell, U.S.
2003	Vert	Bucky Lasek, U.S.	Andy Macdonald, U.S.	Rune Glifberg, Denmark
2002	Vert	Pierre-Luc Gagnon, Canada	Bob Burnquist, Brazil	Rune Glifberg, Denmark
2001	Vert	Bob Burnquist, Brazil	Bucky Lasek, U.S.	Tas Pappas, Australia
2000	Vert	Bucky Lasek, U.S.	Pierre-Luc Gagnon, Canada	Colin McKay, Canada
1999	Vert	Bucky Lasek, U.S.	Andy Macdonald, U.S.	Tony Hawk, U.S.
1998	Vert	Andy Macdonald, U.S.	Giorgio Zattoni, Italy	Tony Hawk, U.S.
1997	Vert	Tony Hawk, U.S.	Rune Glifberg, Denmark	Bob Burnquist, Brazil
1996	Vert	Andy Macdonald, U.S.	Tony Hawk, U.S.	Tas Pappas, Australia
1995	Vert	Tony Hawk, U.S.	Neal Hendrix, U.S.	Rune Glifberg, Denmark
2003	Vert Best Trick	Tony Hawk, U.S.	Sandro Dias, Brazil	Andy Macdonald, U.S.
2002	Vert Best Trick	Pierre-Luc Gagnon, Canada	Sandro Dias, Brazil	Tony Hawk, U.S.
2001	Vert Best Trick	Matt Dove, U.S.	Tony Hawk, U.S.	Bob Burnquist, Brazil
2000	Vert Best Trick	Bob Burnquist, Brazil	Colin McKay, Canada	Andy Macdonald, U.S.
1999	Vert Best Trick	Tony Hawk, U.S.	Colin McKay, Canada	Bob Burnquist, Brazil
2003	Vert Doubles	Bucky Lasek, U.S. Bob Burnquist, Brazil	Rune Glifberg, Denmark Mike Crum, U.S.	Neal Hendrix, U.S. Buster Halterman, U.S.
2002	Vert Doubles	Tony Hawk, U.S. Andy Macdonald, U.S.	Bob Burnquist, Brazil Bucky Lasek, U.S.	Mike Crum, U.S. Rune Glifberg, Denmark
2001	Vert Doubles	Tony Hawk, U.S. Andy Macdonald, U.S.	Mike Crum, U.S. Chris Gentry, U.S.	Mike Frazier, U.S. Neal Hendrix, U.S.
2000	Vert Doubles	Tony Hawk, U.S. Andy Macdonald, U.S.	Pierre-Luc Gagnon, Canada Max Dufour, Canada	Sandro Dias, Brazil Cristiano Mateus, Brazil
1999	Vert Doubles	Tony Hawk, U.S. Andy Macdonald, U.S.	Bucky Lasek, U.S. Brian Patch, U.S.	Mike Crum, U.S. Rune Glifberg, Denmark
1998	Vert Doubles	Tony Hawk, U.S. Andy Macdonald, U.S.	Bucky Lasek, U.S. Brian Patch, U.S.	Bob Burnquist, Brazil Lincoln Ueda, Brazil
1997	Vert Doubles	Tony Hawk, U.S. Andy Macdonald, U.S.	Mike Frazier, U.S. Neal Hendrix, U.S.	Max Dufour, Canada Mathias Ringstrom, Sweden
1995	High Air	Danny Way, U.S.	Neal Hendrix, U.S.	Tas Pappas, Australia

Summer X Games Results (cont.)

Snowboarding—Men

Year	Event	Gold	Silver	Bronze
1999	Big Air	Peter Line, U.S.	Ben Hinkley, U.S.	Chris Engelsman, U.S.
1998	Big Air	Kevin Jones, U.S.	Ben Hinkley, U.S.	Jim Rippey, U.S.
1997	Big Air	Peter Line, U.S.	Kevin Jones, U.S.	Jason Borgstede, U.S.

Snowboarding—Women

Year	Event	Gold	Silver	Bronze
1999	Big Air	Barrett Christy, U.S.	Tina Dixon, U.S.	Janet Matthews, Canada
1998	Big Air	Janet Matthews, Canada	Tina Basich, U.S.	Tina Dixon, U.S.
1997	Big Air	Tina Dixon, U.S.	Hillary Maybery, U.S.	Shelly Ueckert, U.S.

Sport Climbing—Men

Year	Event	Gold	Silver	Bronze
2002	Speed	Maxim Stenkovoy, Ukraine	Alexandre Pechekhonov, Russia	Serguei Sinitsyn, Russia
2001	Speed	Maxim Stenkovoy, Ukraine	Vladimir Zakharov, Ukraine	Chris Bloch, U.S.
2000	Speed	Vladimir Zakharov, Ukraine	Chris Bloch, U.S.	Tomasz Oleksy, Poland
1999	Speed	Aaron Shamy, U.S.	Chris Bloch, U.S.	Vladimir Netsvetaev, Russia
1998	Speed	Vladimir Netsvetaev, Russia	Aaron Shamy, U.S.	Chris Bloch, U.S.
1997	Speed	Hans Florine, U.S.	Chris Bloch, U.S.	Jason Campbell, U.S.
1996	Speed	Hans Florine, U.S.	Chris Bloch, U.S.	Tim Fairfield, U.S.
1995	Speed	Hans Florine, U.S.	Salavat Rakhmetov, Russia	Yuji Hirayama, Japan
1999	Bouldering	Chris Sharma, U.S.	Francois Petit, France	Stephane Julien, France
1998	Difficulty	Christian Core, Italy	Francois Legrand, France	Vadim Vinokur, U.S.
1997	Difficulty	Francois Legrand, France	Yuji Hirayama, Japan	Chris Sharma, U.S.
1996	Difficulty	Arnaud Petit, France	Francois Lombard, France	Cristian Brenna, Italy
1995	Difficulty	Ian Vickers, Great Britain	Arnaud Petit, France	Francois Petit, France

Sport Climbing—Women

Year	Event	Gold	Silver	Bronze
2002	Speed	Tori Allen, U.S.	Olga Zakharova, Ukraine	Etti Hendrawati, Indonesia
2001	Speed	Elena Repko, Ukraine	Olga Zakharova, Ukraine	Alena Ostapenko, Ukraine
2000	Speed	Etti Hendrawati, Indonesia	Elena Repko, Ukraine	Olga Zakharova, Ukraine
1999	Speed	Renata Piszczek, Poland	Olga Zakharova, Ukraine	Etti Hendrawati, Indonesia
1998	Speed	Elena Ovchinnikova, U.S.	Yuyun Yuniar, Indonesia	Venera Tchereshneva, Russia
1997	Speed	Elena Ovchinnikova, U.S.	Abby Watkins, Australia	Mi Sun Go, South Korea
1996	Speed	Cecile Le Flem, France	Elena Choumilova, Russia	Natalie Richer, France
1995	Speed	Elena Ovchinnikova, Russia	Diane Russell, U.S.	Georgia Phipps-Franklin, U.S.
1999	Bouldering	Stephanie Bodet, France	Liv Sansoz, France	Elena Choumilova, Russia
1998	Difficulty	Katie Brown, U.S.	Mi Sun Go, South Korea	Elena Choumilova, Russia
1997	Difficulty	Katie Brown, U.S.	Liv Sansoz, France	Muriel Sarkany, Belgium
1996	Difficulty	Katie Brown, U.S.	Laurence Guyon, France	Liv Sansoz, France
1995	Difficulty	Robyn Erbesfield, U.S.	Elena Ovchinnikova, Russia	Mia Axon, U.S.

Street Luge

Year	Event	Gold	Silver	Bronze
2001	Super Mass	Brent DeKeyser, U.S.	David Rogers, U.S.	Dave Auld, U.S.
2000	Super Mass	Bob Pereyra, U.S.	Lee Dansie, Great Britain	John Rogers, U.S.
1999	Super Mass	David Rogers, U.S.	Biker Sherlock, U.S.	Sean Slate, U.S.

2003-04 TIME LINE

March 16, 2003: Snowboarder Shaun White wins his fourth major Slopestyle contest of 2002-03 by finishing first at the U.S. Open, in Stratton Mountain, Vermont.

May 3, 2003: Motocross racer Ricky Carmichael clinches his third consecutive 250cc Supercross championship. Four months later, he wins his fourth-straight 250cc Motocross title.

May 17, 2003: Dave Mirra's gold-medal win in BMX Park helps the U.S. win the first X Games Global Championship.

August 9, 2003: Surfing debuts at the Summer X Games. The East Coast team, led by Kelly Slater, defeats Rob Machado and the West Coast team.

August 16, 2003: Ryan Nyquist becomes the first rider in Summer X Games' history to win BMX Dirt and Park in the same year.

August 17, 2003: The Yasutoko brothers finish 1-2 in Aggressive In-line Vert for the third time in four years. This year, older brother Eito wins the gold medal and Takeshi takes the silver.

September 13, 2003: Less than a month after becoming the youngest person to win a gold medal at the Summer X Games, 13-year-old skateboarder Ryan Sheckler wins Street at the Gravity Games.

December 19, 2003: By winning the Xbox Pipeline Masters, surfer Andy Irons clinches his second-straight Vans Triple Crown overall championship and second-straight World Championship Tour title.

January 24, 2004: Snowboarder Hannah Teter wins her first Winter X Games gold medal, in Superpipe. Moto X rider Brian Deegan crashes while attempting an off-axis 360-degree spin. He breaks both wrists and the femur bone in his left leg.

January 25, 2004: With his victory in Slopestyle, skier Tanner Hall becomes the fourth person in Winter X Games history to win the same event three years in a row.

February 28, 2004: Motocross racer James Stewart wins his 14th career 125cc Supercross main event. The victory pushes him past Jeremy McGrath for most wins in Supercross history by a 125cc rider.

Summer X Games Results (cont.)

Street Luge (cont.)

Year	Event	Gold	Silver	Bronze
1998	Super Mass	Rat Sult, U.S.	Bob Pereyra, U.S.	Todd Lehr, U.S.
1997	Super Mass	Chris Ponseti, U.S.	Biker Sherlock, U.S.	Rat Sult, U.S.
2000	Dual	Bob Ozman, U.S.	Wade Sokol, U.S.	Bob Pereyra, U.S.
1999	Dual	Dennis Derammelaere, U.S.	Lee Dansie, Great Britain	Biker Sherlock, U.S.
1998	Dual	Biker Sherlock, U.S.	Stefan Wagner, Germany	Dave Auld, U.S.
1997	Dual	Biker Sherlock, U.S.	Dennis Derammelaere, U.S.	Darren Lott, U.S.
1996	Dual	Shawn Goulart, U.S.	Stefan Wagner, Germany	Dennis Derammelaere, U.S.
1995	Dual	Bob Pereyra, U.S.	Stefan Wagner, Germany	Shawn Goulart, U.S.
1998	Mass	Rat Sult, U.S.	Sean Slate, U.S.	Steve Fernando, U.S.
1997	Mass	Biker Sherlock, U.S.	Dennis Derammelaere, U.S.	Lee Dansie, Great Britain
1996	Mass	Biker Sherlock, U.S.	Daryl Thompson, U.S.	Dennis Derammelaere, U.S.
1995	Mass	Shawn Goulart, U.S.	Lee Dansie, Great Britain	Stefan Wagner, Germany

Summer X Games Results (cont.)

Surfing—Men

Year	Gold	Silver	Bronze
2003	East Coast	West Coast	N/A

Wakeboarding—Men

Year	Gold	Silver	Bronze
2003	Danny Harf, U.S.	Parks Bonifay, U.S.	Daniel Watkins, U.S.
2002	Danny Harf, U.S.	Darin Shapiro, U.S.	Shaun Murray, U.S.
2001	Danny Harf, U.S.	Darin Shapiro, U.S.	Erik Ruck, U.S.
2000	Darin Shapiro, U.S.	Shaun Murray, U.S.	Shane Bonifay, U.S.
1999	Parks Bonifay, U.S.	Darin Shapiro, U.S.	Brannan Johnson, U.S.
1998	Darin Shapiro, U.S.	Shaun Murray, U.S.	Zane Schwenk, U.S.
1997	Jeremy Kovak, Canada	Darin Shapiro, U.S.	Parks Bonifay, U.S.
1996	Parks Bonifay, U.S.	Jeremy Kovak, Canada	Scott Byerly, U.S.

Wakeboarding—Women

Year	Gold	Silver	Bronze
2003	Dallas Friday, U.S.	Melissa Marquardt, U.S.	Emily Copeland, U.S.
2002	Emily Copeland, U.S.	Dallas Friday, U.S.	Leslie Kent, U.S.
2001	Dallas Friday, U.S.	Emily Copeland, U.S.	Tara Hamilton, U.S.
2000	Tara Hamilton, U.S.	Dallas Friday, U.S.	Maeghan Major, U.S.
1999	Maeghan Major, U.S.	Emily Copeland, U.S.	Andrea Gaytan, Mexico
1998	Andrea Gaytan, Mexico	Dana Preble, U.S.	Tara Hamilton, U.S.
1997	Tara Hamilton, U.S.	Andrea Gaytan, Mexico	Jaime Necrason, U.S.

Windsurfing—Men

Year	Gold	Silver	Bronze
1995	Bjorn Dunkerbeck, Spain	Micah Buzianis, U.S.	Al Aguera, U.S.

Windsurfing—Women

Year	Gold	Silver	Bronze
1995	Angela Cochran, U.S.	Jayne Fenner-Benedict, U.S.	Jutta Mueller, Germany

X Venture Race

Year	Gold	Silver	Bronze
1997	**Team Presidio** Ian Adamson, Australia John Howard, New Zealand Andrea Spitzer, Germany	**Team Endeavour** Louise Cooper-Lovelace, U.S. Neil Jones, New Zealand Jeff Mitchell, New Zealand	**Team Red Hot** Sharyn Davis, Australia John Jacoby, Australia Tim Smallwood, Australia
1996	**Team Kobeer** Angelika Castaneda, U.S. John Howard, New Zealand Keith Murray, New Zealand	**Team Eco-Internet** Ian Adamson, Australia Robert Nagle, Ireland Vivienne Prince, U.S.	**Team Mirage** Kirk Boylston, U.S. Nancy Bristow, U.S. Steve Gurney, New Zealand
1995	**Team Thredbo** Jane Hall, Australia Andrew Hislop, Australia Rod Hislop, Australia John Jacoby, Australia Novak Thompson, Australia	**Twin Team** Angelika Castaneda, U.S. Adrian Crane, U.S. Tom Possert, U.S. Robert Rambach, U.S. Marshall Ulrich, U.S.	**Team Eco-Internet** Ian Adamson, Australia John Howard, New Zealand Keith Murray, New Zealand Robert Nagle, Ireland Cathy Sassin-Smith, U.S.

Gravity Games Results

Bike

Year	Event	Gold	Silver	Bronze
2003	Street	Dave Mirra, U.S.	Ryan Nyquist, U.S.	Steven McCann, Australia
2002	Street	Dave Mirra, U.S.	Ryan Nyquist, U.S.	Tom Haugen, U.S.
2001	Street	Ryan Nyquist, U.S.	Dave Osato, Canada	Chad Kagy, U.S.
2000	Street	Dave Osato, Canada	Ryan Nyquist, U.S.	Mike Laird, U.S.
1999	Street	Dave Mirra, U.S.	Ryan Nyquist, U.S.	Jay Miron, Canada
2003	Dirt	Ryan Nyquist, U.S.	Chris Doyle, U.S.	Steven McCann, Australia
2002	Dirt	Stephen Murray, Great Britain	Allan Cooke, U.S.	Chris Doyle, U.S.
2001	Dirt	Stephen Murray, Great Britain	Todd Walkowiak, U.S.	Chris Doyle, U.S.
2000	Dirt	T.J. Lavin, U.S.	Chris Doyle, U.S.	Ryan Jordan, U.S.
1999	Dirt	Ryan Nyquist, U.S.	Todd Walkowiak, U.S.	T.J. Lavin, U.S.
2003	Vert	Dave Mirra, U.S.	Kevin Robinson, U.S.	Simon Tabron, Great Britain
2002	Vert	Simon Tabron, Great Britain	Dave Mirra, U.S.	Jay Miron, Canada
2001	Vert	Jamie Bestwick, Great Britain	Kevin Robinson, U.S.	Simon Tabron, Great Britain
2000	Vert	Dave Mirra, U.S.	Jamie Bestwick, Great Britain	Jay Miron, Canada
1999	Vert	Jamie Bestwick, Great Britain	Jay Miron, Canada	John Parker, U.S.

Freestyle Motocross

Year	Gold	Silver	Bronze
2003	Nate Adams, U.S.	Travis Pastrana, U.S.	Ronnie Renner, U.S.
2002	Travis Pastrana, U.S.	Mike Metzger, U.S.	Kenny Bartram, U.S.
2001	Travis Pastrana, U.S.	Clifford Adoptante, U.S.	Tommy Clowers, U.S.
2000	Brian Deegan, U.S.	Mike Metzger, U.S.	Kenny Bartram, U.S.
1999	Travis Pastrana, U.S.	Brian Deegan, U.S.	Carey Hart, U.S.

Nate Adams won his first Gravity Games gold medal in 2003.

JED JACOBSOHN/GETTY IMAGES

Did You Know?

Tony Hawk and Andy Macdonald had won every Vert Doubles competition at the Summer X Games (1997-02) until Bucky Lasek and Bob Burnquist won the event, in 2003.

Visit **www.sikids.com** for the latest sports stats and info.

Gravity Games Results (cont.)

Skateboarding

Year	Event	Gold	Silver	Bronze
2003	Vert	Bucky Lasek, U.S.	Andy Macdonald, U.S.	Rune Glifberg, Denmark
2002	Vert	Bucky Lasek, U.S.	Bob Burnquist, Brazil	Pierre-Luc Gagnon, Canada
2001	Vert	Rune Glifberg, Denmark	Bucky Lasek, U.S.	Andy Macdonald, U.S.
2000	Vert	Andy Macdonald, U.S.	Bob Burnquist, Brazil	Pierre-Luc Gagnon, Canada
1999	Vert	Bob Burnquist, Brazil	Bucky Lasek, U.S.	Andy Macdonald, U.S.
2003	Vert Best Trick	Mathias Ringstrom, Sweden	Danny Mayer, U.S.	Sandro Diaz, Brazil
2002	Vert Best Trick	Pierre-Luc Gagnon, Canada	Bob Burnquist, Brazil	Sandro Diaz, Brazil
2003	Street	Ryan Sheckler, U.S.	Rick McCrank, Canada	Chris Senn, U.S.
2002	Street	Eric Koston, U.S.	Pat Channita, U.S.	Kerry Getz, U.S.
2001	Street	Eric Koston, U.S.	Rick McCrank, Canada	Kyle Berard, U.S.
2000	Street	Eric Koston, U.S.	Brian Anderson, U.S.	Kerry Getz, U.S.
1999	Street	Brian Anderson, U.S.	Rodil de Araujo, Jr., Brazil	Eric Koston, U.S.
2003	Street Best Trick	Chris Haslam, Canada	Daniel Vieira, Brazil	Chad Bartie, Australia
2002	Downhill, 2-person	Mark Golter, U.S.	Dane Van Bommel, U.S.	Alex Wenk, Switzerland
2001	Downhill, 2-person	Dane Van Bommel, U.S.	Gary Hardwick, U.S.	Mark Golter, U.S.
2000	Downhill, 2-person	Dane Van Bommel, U.S.	John Gwiazdowski, U.S.	Alex Wenk, Switzerland
1999	Downhill, 2-person	Lee Dansie, Great Britain	Biker Sherlock, U.S.	Dane Van Bommel, U.S.
2002	Downhill, 4-person	Darryl Freeman, U.S.	Mark Golter, U.S.	Dane Van Bommel, U.S.
2001	Downhill, 4-person	Dane Van Bommel, U.S.	Alex Wenk, Switzerland	Lee Dansie, Great Britain
2000	Downhill, 4-person	Dane Van Bommel, U.S.	John Gwiazdowski, U.S.	Alex Wenk, Switzerland
1999	Downhill, 4-person	Biker Sherlock, U.S.	Dane Van Bommel, U.S.	Emanuel Antuna, France

Aggressive In-line—Men

Year	Event	Gold	Silver	Bronze
2001	Street	Blake Dennis, Australia	Louie Zamora, U.S.	Aaron Feinberg, U.S.
2000	Street	Sven Boekhorst, Netherlands	Blake Dennis, Australia	Wilfried Rossignol, France
1999	Street	Sven Boekhorst, Netherlands	Den Bosch, Netherlands	Louie Zamora, U.S.
2003	Street Best Trick	Richie Velasquez, U.S.	Stephane Alfano, France	Brian Aragon, U.S.
2003	Vert	Eito Yasutoko, Japan	Marco de Santi, Brazil	Marc Englehart, U.S.
2002	Vert	Marc Englehart, U.S.	Takeshi Yasutoko, Japan	Shane Yost, Tasmania
2001	Vert	Taig Khris, France	Takeshi Yasutoko, Japan	Matt Lindenmuth, U.S.
2000	Vert	Matt Salerno, Australia	Taig Khris, France	Eito Yasutoko, Japan
1999	Vert	Taig Khris, France	Shane Yost, Australia	Cesar Mora, Australia

Aggressive In-line—Women

Year	Event	Gold	Silver	Bronze
2001	Street	Martina Svobodova, Slovakia	Fabiola da Silva, Brazil	Deborah West, U.S.
2000	Street	Martina Svobodova, Slovakia	Fabiola da Silva, Brazil	Kelly Matthews, U.S.
1999	Street	Fabiola da Silva, Brazil	Anneke Winter, Germany	Kelly Matthews, U.S.
2001	Vert	Ayumi Kawasaki, Japan	Fabiola da Silva, Brazil	N/A
2000	Vert	Fabiola da Silva, Brazil	Ayumi Kawasaki, Japan	Merce Borrull, Spain
1999	Vert	Fabiola da Silva, Brazil	Merce Borrull, Spain	Maki Komori, Japan

Wakeboarding—Men

Year	Gold	Silver	Bronze
2003	Parks Bonifay, U.S.	Shane Bonifay, U.S.	Brett Eisenhauer, Australia
2002	Mark Kenney, U.S.	Danny Harf, U.S.	Darin Shapiro, U.S.
2001	Darin Shapiro, U.S.	Parks Bonifay, U.S.	Daniel Watkins, Australia
2000	Parks Bonifay, U.S.	Darin Shapiro, U.S.	Ryan Wynne, U.S.
1999	Shaun Murray, U.S.	Parks Bonifay, U.S.	Rob Struharik, U.S.

Legends

Darin Shapiro, wakeboarder, b. October 25, 1973, Fort Lauderdale, Florida. Shapiro has ruled wakeboarding since he began riding in 1991. He has won the Pro Wakeboard Tour season championship six times (1992-95, 1997, 2000) and has finished worse than second only twice. (He finished third in 1999 and did not compete in 1996 because of an injury.) The 13-year veteran still had it going in 2003, when he won the World Cup title for the fourth time. Shapiro has also won six Summer X Games medals (two gold, four silver).

MIKE ISLER/ICON SMI

Darin Shapiro has won the Pro Wakeboard Tour championship six times in his 13-year career.

Todd Richards, snowboarder, b. December 28, 1969, Worcester, Massachusetts. When Richards began riding, in 1985, snowboarding wasn't even allowed at most ski resorts. Today the sport is hugely popular, thanks in part to Richards and his trick and style innovations. He has appeared on the cover of *Transworld Snowboarding* a record three times. He has also won seven Winter X Games medals (two gold, three silver, two bronze) in three different disciplines (Slopestyle, Halfpipe, and Big Air) and in 1998 was a member of the first U.S. Olympic snowboard team.

Mike Metzger, freestyle motocross rider, b. November 19, 1975, Huntington Beach, California. Metzger got his first motorcycle when he was 3 years old. His longtime dedication to and progression of the sport earned him the nickname "The Godfather" of freestyle motocross. He was the first rider to pull a backflip in competition. He quickly followed that up with variations, such as the backflip no-footer. Metzger has won five medals (three gold, two silver) at the Summer X and Winter X Games.

Gravity Games Results (cont.)

Wakeboarding—Women

Year	Gold	Silver	Bronze
2003	Emily Copeland-Durham, U.S.	Tara Hamilton, U.S.	Leslie Kent, U.S.
2002	Emily Copeland, U.S.	Melissa Marquardt, U.S.	Dallas Friday, U.S.
2001	Dallas Friday, U.S.	Tara Hamilton, U.S.	Christy Smith, U.S.
2000	Maeghan Major, U.S.	Tara Hamilton, U.S.	Lauren Loe, U.S.
1999	Andrea Gaytan, Mexico	Tara Hamilton, U.S.	Christy Smith, U.S.

Street Luge

Year	Event	Gold	Silver	Bronze
2002	4-person	Mike McIntyre, U.S.	John Rogers, U.S.	Dave Rogers, U.S.
2001	4-person	Rat Sult, U.S.	Biker Sherlock, U.S.	John Fryer, U.S.
1999	4-person	Sean Mallard, U.S.	Biker Sherlock, U.S.	George Orton, U.S.
2002	6-person	Dave Rogers, U.S.	Mike McIntyre, U.S.	John Rogers, U.S.
2001	6-person	Rat Sult, U.S.	Kurtis Head, U.S.	David Kelly, U.S.
1999	6-person	Biker Sherlock, U.S.	Sean Slate, U.S.	Wade Sokol, U.S.

Layne Beachley has won the world championship six times, the record among female surfers.

Surfing—All-time Results

Association of Surfing Professionals (ASP) World Champions

Year	Men
2003	Andy Irons, U.S.
2002	Andy Irons, U.S.
2001	C.J. Hobgood, U.S.
2000	Sunny Garcia, U.S.
1999	Mark Occhilupo, Australia
1998	Kelly Slater, U.S.
1997	Kelly Slater, U.S.
1996	Kelly Slater, U.S.
1995	Kelly Slater, U.S.
1994	Kelly Slater, U.S.
1993	Derek Ho, U.S.
1992	Kelly Slater, U.S.
1991	Damien Hardman, Australia
1990	Tom Curren, U.S.
1989	Martin Potter, Great Britain
1988	Barton Lynch, Australia
1987	Damien Hardman, Australia
1986	Tom Curren, U.S.
1985	Tom Curren, U.S.
1984	Tom Carroll, Australia
1983	Tom Carroll, Australia
1982	Mark Richards, Australia
1981	Mark Richards, Australia
1980	Mark Richards, Australia
1979	Mark Richards, Australia
1978	Wayne Bartholomew, Australia
1977	Shaun Tomson, South Africa
1976	Peter Townend, Australia

Year	Women
2003	Layne Beachley, Australia
2002	Layne Beachley, Australia
2001	Layne Beachley, Australia
2000	Layne Beachley, Australia
1999	Layne Beachley, Australia
1998	Layne Beachley, Australia
1997	Lisa Andersen, U.S.
1996	Lisa Andersen, U.S.
1995	Lisa Andersen, U.S.
1994	Lisa Andersen, U.S.
1993	Pauline Menczer, Australia
1992	Wendy Botha, Australia
1991	Wendy Botha, Australia
1990	Pam Burridge, Australia
1989	Wendy Botha, Australia
1988	Freida Zamba, U.S.
1987	Wendy Botha, South Africa
1986	Freida Zamba, U.S.
1985	Freida Zamba, U.S.
1984	Freida Zamba, U.S.
1983	Kim Mearig, U.S.
1982	Debbie Beacham, U.S.
1981	Margo Oberg, U.S.
1980	Margo Oberg, U.S.
1979	Lynne Boyer, U.S.
1978	Lynne Boyer, U.S.
1977	Margo Oberg, U.S.

Year	Longboard
2003	Beau Young, Australia
2002	Colin McPhillips, U.S.
2001	Colin McPhillips, U.S.
2000	Beau Young, Australia
1999	Colin McPhillips, U.S.
1998	Joel Tudor, U.S.
1997	Dino Miranda, U.S.
1996	Bonga Perkins, U.S.
1995	Rusty Keaulana, U.S.
1994	Rusty Keaulana, U.S.
1993	Rusty Keaulana, U.S.
1992	Joey Hawkins, U.S.
1991	Martin McMillan, Australia
1990	Nat Young, Australia
1989	Nat Young, Australia
1988	Nat Young, Australia
1987	Stuart Entwistle, Australia
1986	Nat Young, Australia

Motocross—All-time Results

250cc Supercross

Year	Champion	Hometown
2003	Ricky Carmichael	Havana, Florida
2002	Ricky Carmichael	Havana, Florida
2001	Ricky Carmichael	Havana, Florida
2000	Jeremy McGrath	Menifee, California
1999	Jeremy McGrath	Menifee, California
1998	Jeremy McGrath	Menifee, California
1997	Jeff Emig	Riverside, California
1996	Jeremy McGrath	Menifee, California
1995	Jeremy McGrath	Murrieta, California
1994	Jeremy McGrath	Murrieta, California
1993	Jeremy McGrath	Murrieta, California
1992	Jeff Stanton	Sherwood, Michigan
1991	Jean-Michel Bayle	Manosque, France
1990	Jeff Stanton	Sherwood, Michigan
1989	Jeff Stanton	Sherwood, Michigan
1988	Rick Johnson	El Cajon, California
1987	Jeff Ward	Mission Viejo, California
1986	Rick Johnson	El Cajon, California
1985	Jeff Ward	Mission Viejo, California
1984	Johnny O'Mara	Simi Valley, California
1983	David Bailey	Axton, Virginia
1982	Donnie Hansen	Canyon Country, California
1981	Mark Barnett	Bridgeview, Illinois
1980	Mike Bell	Lakewood, California
1979	Bob Hannah	Carson, Nevada
1978	Bob Hannah	Whittier, California
1977	Bob Hannah	Whittier, California
1976	Jim Weinert	Laguna Beach, California
1975	Jim Ellis	Cobalt, Connecticut
1974	Pierre Karsmakers	Netherlands

250cc Motocross

Year	Champion	Hometown
2003	Ricky Carmichael	Havana, Florida
2002	Ricky Carmichael	Havana, Florida
2001	Ricky Carmichael	Havana, Florida
2000	Ricky Carmichael	Havana, Florida
1999	Greg Albertyn	Johannesburg, South Africa
1998	Doug Henry	Oxford, Connecticut
1997	Jeff Emig	Riverside, California
1996	Jeff Emig	Riverside, California
1995	Jeremy McGrath	Murrieta, California
1994	Mike LaRocco	South Bend, Indiana
1993	Mike Kiedrowski	Acton, California
1992	Jeff Stanton	Sherwood, Michigan
1991	Jean-Michel Bayle	Manosque, France
1990	Jeff Stanton	Sherwood, Michigan
1989	Jeff Stanton	Sherwood, Michigan
1988	Jeff Ward	Mission Viejo, California
1987	Rick Johnson	El Cajon, California
1986	Rick Johnson	El Cajon, California
1985	Jeff Ward	Mission Viejo, California
1984	Rick Johnson	El Cajon, California
1983	David Bailey	Axton, Virginia
1982	Donnie Hansen	Canyon Country, California
1981	Kent Howerton	San Antonio, Texas
1980	Kent Howerton	San Antonio, Texas
1979	Bob Hannah	Carson City, Nevada
1978	Bob Hannah	Whittier, California
1977	Tony DiStefano	Morrisville, Pennsylvania
1976	Tony DiStefano	Morrisville, Pennsylvania
1975	Tony DiStefano	Morrisville, Pennsylvania
1974	Gary Jones	Hacienda Heights, California
1973	Gary Jones	Hacienda Heights, California
1972	Gary Jones	Hacienda Heights, California

125cc Motocross

Year	Champion	Hometown
2003	Grant Langston	Durban, South Africa
2002	James Stewart, Jr.	Haines City, Florida
2001	Michael Brown	Piney Flats, Tennessee
2000	Travis Pastrana	Annapolis, Maryland
1999	Ricky Carmichael	Havana, Florida
1998	Ricky Carmichael	Havana, Florida
1997	Ricky Carmichael	Havana, Florida
1996	Steve Lamson	Pollock Pines, California
1995	Steve Lamson	Pollock Pines, California
1994	Doug Henry	Oxford, Connecticut
1993	Doug Henry	Oxford, Connecticut
1992	Jeff Emig	Highland, California
1991	Mike Kiedrowski	Canyon Country, California
1990	Guy Cooper	Stillwater, Oklahoma
1989	Mike Kiedrowski	Canyon Country, California
1988	George Holland	Kerman, California
1987	Micky Dymond	Yorba Linda, California
1986	Micky Dymond	Yorba Linda, California
1985	Ron Lechien	El Cajon, California
1984	Jeff Ward	Mission Viejo, California
1983	Johnny O'Mara	Simi Valley, California
1982	Mark Barnett	Bridgeview, Illinois
1981	Mark Barnett	Bridgeview, Illinois
1980	Mark Barnett	Bridgeview, Illinois
1979	Broc Glover	El Cajon, California
1978	Broc Glover	El Cajon, California
1977	Broc Glover	El Cajon, California
1976	Bob Hannah	Whittier, California
1975	Marty Smith	San Diego, California
1974	Marty Smith	San Diego, California

GOLF

Tiger Woods ruled the PGA Tour in 2003, even though it was the first year since 1998 he failed to win a major tournament. He finished the year with five victories in 18 events and was named PGA Tour Player of the Year for a record fifth-straight time.

Success in 2003 was not limited to Woods, however. Mike Weir became the second left-hander — and first Canadian — to win the Masters. Tour rookie Ben Curtis shocked the golf world by winning the British Open, and journeyman Shaun Micheel was the surprise winner of the PGA Championship.

The biggest story of the first half of 2004 was Phil Mickelson's triumph at the Masters. By winning his first major in 42 pro attempts, Mickelson was finally removed from the list of the best players who had never won a major.

The women's tour was dominated — again — by Annika Sorenstam. Her six wins in 2003 made her the fourth player in history with at least five victories in four consecutive seasons. Early in 2004, she won two of the first four events she entered.

The buzz continued about 14-year-old phenom Michelle Wie and her booming drives and poise on the course. In 2003, she became the youngest player to win the U.S. Women's Amateur Public Links title. In January 2004, she fired a 68 in the second round of the PGA Tour's Sony Open, missing the cut by one shot. It was the lowest score by a female golfer playing in a men's event. At the start of the 2004 season, the high schooler finished fourth in the Kraft Nabisco Championship, the LPGA's first major.

AL TIELEMANS/SPORTS ILLUSTRATED

Tiger Woods led the PGA Tour in victories (five) in 2003 for the fifth-straight season.

Shaun Micheel won the 2003 PGA Championship, his first Tour victory.

ROBERT BECK/SPORTS ILLUSTRATED

Trivia Challenge

If Ernie Els wins two more majors, he'll become the sixth PGA Tour golfer to win the career Grand Slam. Which events does he need to win?

The Masters and the PGA Championship. Els won the U.S. Open in 1994 and 1997 and the British Open in 2002.

Annika Sorenstam earned her sixth Player of the Year award in 2003. Only Kathy Whitworth has more (seven).

ROBERT BECK/SPORTS ILLUSTRATED

At the PGA Tour's 2004 Sony Open, 14-year-old Michelle Wie missed the cut by just one shot.

BRAD MANGIN

Did You Know?

When Arnold Palmer teed off at the 2004 Masters, it was his 50th consecutive — and final — appearance at the game's most prestigious tournament. Palmer won the event in 1958, 1960, 1962, and 1964.

All-time Champions—Men

The Masters

Year	Winner
2004	Phil Mickelson
2003	*Mike Weir
2002	Tiger Woods
2001	Tiger Woods
2000	Vijay Singh
1999	Jose Maria Olazabal
1998	Mark O'Meara
1997	Tiger Woods
1996	Nick Faldo
1995	Ben Crenshaw
1994	Jose Maria Olazabal
1993	Bernhard Langer
1992	Fred Couples
1991	Ian Woosnam
1990	*Nick Faldo
1989	*Nick Faldo
1988	Sandy Lyle
1987	*Larry Mize
1986	Jack Nicklaus
1985	Bernhard Langer
1984	Ben Crenshaw
1983	Seve Ballesteros
1982	*Craig Stadler
1981	Tom Watson
1980	Seve Ballesteros
1979 †	*Fuzzy Zoeller
1978	Gary Player
1977	Tom Watson
1976	Ray Floyd
1975	Jack Nicklaus
1974	Gary Player
1973	Tommy Aaron
1972	Jack Nicklaus
1971	Charles Coody
1970	*Billy Casper
1969	George Archer
1968	Bob Goalby
1967	Gay Brewer, Jr.
1966	*Jack Nicklaus
1965	Jack Nicklaus
1964	Arnold Palmer
1963	Jack Nicklaus
1962	Arnold Palmer
1961	Gary Player
1960	Arnold Palmer
1959	Art Wall, Jr.
1958	Arnold Palmer
1957	Doug Ford
1956	Jack Burke, Jr.
1955	Cary Middlecoff
1954	*Sam Snead
1953	Ben Hogan
1952	Sam Snead
1951	Ben Hogan
1950	Jimmy Demaret
1949	Sam Snead
1948	Claude Harmon
1947	Jimmy Demaret
1946	Herman Keiser
1943–45	No tournament
1942	*Byron Nelson
1941	Craig Wood
1940	Jimmy Demaret
1939	Ralph Guldahl
1938	Henry Picard
1937	Byron Nelson
1936	Horton Smith
1935	*Gene Sarazen
1934	Horton Smith

* Winner in playoff.
† Playoff cut from 18 holes to sudden death.
Note: Played at Augusta National Golf Club, Augusta, Georgia.

All-time Champions—Men (cont.)

U.S. Open

Year	Winner	Year	Winner	Year	Winner
2004	Retief Goosen	1970	Tony Jacklin	1931	*Billy Burke
2003	Jim Furyk	1969	Orville Moody	1930	Bobby Jones
2002	Tiger Woods	1968	Lee Trevino	1929	*Bobby Jones
2001	*Retief Goosen	1967	Jack Nicklaus	1928	*Johnny Farrell
2000	Tiger Woods	1966	*Billy Casper	1927	*Tommy Armour
1999	Payne Stewart	1965	*Gary Player	1926	Bobby Jones
1998	Lee Janzen	1964	Ken Venturi	1925	*Willie MacFarlane
1997	Ernie Els	1963	*Julius Boros	1924	Cyril Walker
1996	Steve Jones	1962	*Jack Nicklaus	1923	*Bobby Jones
1995	Corey Pavin	1961	Gene Littler	1922	Gene Sarazen
1994	*Ernie Els	1960	Arnold Palmer	1921	Jim Barnes
1993	Lee Janzen	1959	Billy Casper	1920	Edward Ray
1992	Tom Kite	1958	Tommy Bolt	1919	*Walter Hagen
1991	*Payne Stewart	1957	*Dick Mayer	1917–18	No tournament
1990	*Hale Irwin	1956	Cary Middlecoff	1916	Chick Evans
1989	Curtis Strange	1955	*Jack Fleck	1915	Jerry Travers
1988	*Curtis Strange	1954	Ed Furgol	1914	Walter Hagen
1987	Scott Simpson	1953	Ben Hogan	1913	*Francis Ouimet
1986	Ray Floyd	1952	Julius Boros	1912	John McDermott
1985	Andy North	1951	Ben Hogan	1911	*John McDermott
1984	*Fuzzy Zoeller	1950	*Ben Hogan	1910	*Alex Smith
1983	Larry Nelson	1949	Cary Middlecoff	1909	George Sargent
1982	Tom Watson	1948	Ben Hogan	1908	*Fred McLeod
1981	David Graham	1947	*Lew Worsham	1907	Alex Ross
1980	Jack Nicklaus	1946	*Lloyd Mangrum	1906	Alex Smith
1979	Hale Irwin	1942–45	No tournament	1905	Willie Anderson
1978	Andy North	1941	Craig Wood	1904	Willie Anderson
1977	Hubert Green	1940	*Lawson Little	1903	*Willie Anderson
1976	Jerry Pate	1939	*Byron Nelson	1902	Laurie Auchterlonie
1975	*Lou Graham	1938	Ralph Guldahl	1901	*Willie Anderson
1974	Hale Irwin	1937	Ralph Guldahl	1900	Harry Vardon
1973	Johnny Miller	1936	Tony Manero	1899	Willie Smith
1972	Jack Nicklaus	1935	Sam Parks, Jr.	1898	Fred Herd
1971	*Lee Trevino	1934	Olin Dutra	1897†	Joe Lloyd
		1933	Johnny Goodman	1896†	James Foulis
		1932	Gene Sarazen	1895†	Horace Rawlins

*Winner in playoff. The 1990 playoff went to one hole of sudden death after an 18-hole playoff. In the 1994 playoff, Montgomerie was eliminated after 18 playoff holes and Els beat Roberts on the 20th. †Before 1898, 36 holes; from 1898 on, 72 holes.

British Open

Year	Winner	Year	Winner	Year	Winner
2004	*Todd Hamilton	1985	Sandy Lyle	1966	Jack Nicklaus
2003	Ben Curtis	1984	Seve Ballesteros	1965	Peter Thomson
2002	*Ernie Els	1983	Tom Watson	1964	Tony Lema
2001	David Duval	1982	Tom Watson	1963	*Bob Charles
2000	Tiger Woods	1981	Bill Rogers	1962	Arnold Palmer
1999	*Paul Lawrie	1980	Tom Watson	1961	Arnold Palmer
1998	*Mark O'Meara	1979	Seve Ballesteros	1960	Kel Nagle
1997	Justin Leonard	1978	Jack Nicklaus	1959	Gary Player
1996	Tom Lehman	1977	Tom Watson	1958	*Peter Thomson
1995	*John Daly	1976	Johnny Miller	1957	Bobby Locke
1994	Nick Price	1975	*Tom Watson	1956	Peter Thomson
1993	Greg Norman	1974	Gary Player	1955	Peter Thomson
1992	Nick Faldo	1973	Tom Weiskopf	1954	Peter Thomson
1991	Ian Baker-Finch	1972	Lee Trevino	1953	Ben Hogan
1990	Nick Faldo	1971	Lee Trevino	1952	Bobby Locke
1989††	*Mark Calcavecchia	1970	*Jack Nicklaus	1951	Max Faulkner
1988	Seve Ballesteros	1969	Tony Jacklin	1950	Bobby Locke
1987	Nick Faldo	1968	Gary Player	1949	*Bobby Locke
1986	Greg Norman	1967	Robert DeVicenzo	1948	Henry Cotton

*Winner in playoff.
††Playoff cut from 18 holes to 4 holes.

All-time Champions—Men (cont.)

British Open (cont.)

Year	Winner
1947	Fred Daly
1946	Sam Snead
1940–45	No tournament
1939	Richard Burton
1938	Reginald A. Whitcombe
1937	Henry Cotton
1936	Alfred Padgham
1935	Alfred Perry
1934	Henry Cotton
1933	*Denny Shute
1932	Gene Sarazen
1931	Tommy Armour
1930	Bobby Jones
1929	Walter Hagen
1928	Walter Hagen
1927	Bobby Jones
1926	Bobby Jones
1925	Jim Barnes

Year	Winner
1924	Walter Hagen
1923	Arthur G. Havers
1922	Walter Hagen
1921	*Jock Hutchison
1920	George Duncan
1915–19	No tournament
1914	Harry Vardon
1913	John H. Taylor
1912	Ted Ray
1911	Harry Vardon
1910	James Braid
1909	John H. Taylor
1908	James Braid
1907	Arnaud Massy
1906	James Braid
1905	James Braid
1904	Jack White
1903	Harry Vardon
1902	Alexander Herd
1901	James Braid

Year	Winner
1900	John H. Taylor
1899	Harry Vardon
1898	Harry Vardon
1897	Harold Hilton
1896	*Harry Vardon
1895	John H. Taylor
1894	John H. Taylor
1893	William Auchterlonie
1892**	Harold Hilton
1891	Hugh Kirkaldy
1890	John Ball
1889	*Willie Park, Jr.
1888	Jack Burns
1887	Willie Park, Jr.
1886	David Brown
1885	Bob Martin
1884	Jack Simpson
1883	*Willie Fernie
1882	Robert Ferguson

* Winner in playoff.
**Championship extended from 36 to 72 holes.

Trivia Challenge

Who holds the PGA record for most wins in a calendar year?

Byron Nelson with 18 in 1945

Legends

Lee Trevino won five majors, including two back-to-back British Open titles (1971, 1972).

WALTER IOOSS JR./SPORTS ILLUSTRATED

Lee Trevino, b. December 1, 1939, Dallas, Texas. Trevino won 29 events on the PGA Tour and has 29 victories on the Champions Tour (players age 50 and older). He turned pro in 1960, and won his first major, the U.S. Open, in 1968. Over the next 18 years, he won five more majors: the U.S. Open again (1971), the British Open (1971, 1972), and the PGA Championship (1974, 1984). In his first full season on the Champions Tour (1990), Trevino won seven tournaments and was named Player of the Year and Rookie of the Year.

Sam Snead, b. May 27, 1912, Ashwood, Virginia; d. May 23, 2002, Hot Springs, Virginia. Nicknamed "The Slammer" for his powerful drives off the tee, Snead holds the PGA Tour record for official victories (82). He won the Masters three times (1949, 1952, 1954), the PGA Championship three times (1942, 1949, 1951), and the British Open once (1946). He won the Greater Greensboro Open a record eight times. When he won it in 1965, he became the oldest winner in PGA Tour history (52 years, 10 months).

Ben Hogan, b. May 13, 1912, Dublin, Texas; d. July 25, 1997, Fort Worth, Texas. Hogan was one of the first players inducted into the World Golf Hall of Fame. He had 68 PGA Tour wins, was undefeated in Ryder Cup play, was named Player of the Year four times, and won the money title five times. He excelled in major championships and was best known for his tireless work on the course and in practice. Hogan won his nine majors in seven years, becoming one of five golfers to win all four majors at least once. (Tiger Woods, Jack Nicklaus, Gene Sarazen, and Gary Player are the others.) In 1953, he won all three majors in which he played: the Masters, U.S. Open, and British Open.

All-time Champions—Men (cont.)

British Open (cont.)

Year	Winner
1881	Robert Ferguson
1880	Robert Ferguson
1879	Jamie Anderson
1878	Jamie Anderson
1877	Jamie Anderson
1876	#Bob Martin
1875	Willie Park
1874	Mungo Park
1873	Tom Kidd
1872	Tom Morris, Jr.
1871	No tournament
1870	Tom Morris, Jr.
1869	Tom Morris, Jr.
1868	Tom Morris, Jr.
1867	Tom Morris, Sr.
1866	Willie Park
1865	Andrew Strath
1864	Tom Morris, Sr.
1863	Willie Park
1862	Tom Morris, Sr.
1861‡	Tom Morris, Sr.
1860†	Willie Park

#Tied, but opponent refused playoff. ‡The second annual Open was open to amateurs and pros. †The first event was open only to pro golfers.

Today's Stars

Jim Furyk, b. May 12, 1970, West Chester, Pennsylvania. Furyk has been one of the PGA Tour's most consistent golfers over the past six years. At the start of the 2004 season, he had won at least one event in six consecutive seasons. (Only Tiger Woods has more: at least one win in eight straight seasons.) But Furyk didn't emerge as a star until 2003, when he won his first major, the U.S. Open. His 72-hole score of 272 tied him for the record for the tournament's lowest score. He also won the Buick Open and finished in the Top 10 in 15 of the 27 events he entered.

Jim Furyk became the 57th player to make the U.S. Open his first career major championship.

SIMON BRUTY/SPORTS ILLUSTRATED

Davis Love III, b. April 13, 1964, Charlotte, North Carolina. Love played the best season of his 18-year pro career in 2003. He won a career-high four times and earned more than $6 million in a single season for the first time. Among his four wins was the distinguished Players Championship, often called golf's "fifth major." Love has won 18 tournaments and played on the Ryder Cup team five times. In 1997, he won the PGA Championship, his only major title.

Vijay Singh, b. February 22, 1963, Lautoka, Fiji. Singh nearly unseated Tiger Woods atop the PGA Tour in 2003. He won four times and had 18 Top 10 finishes in 27 events, giving him the first money title of his career. His $7,573,907 in 2003 earnings was the second-highest single-season amount in Tour history. Singh won the 1998 PGA Championship and the 2000 Masters.

2003-04 MEN'S TIME LINE

January 19, 2003: A week after winning the season-opening Mercedes Championship by eight strokes, Ernie Els holes a 43-foot birdie putt on the second playoff hole to defeat Aaron Baddeley and win the Sony Open. The win makes Els the first player in 14 years to win the PGA Tour season's first two events.

February 16, 2003: In his first event after knee surgery the previous December, Tiger Woods wins the Buick Invitational by four strokes. He goes on to win two of his next three events, including a record fourth-straight win at the Bay Hill Invitational.

April 13, 2003: Mike Weir holds off Len Mattiace in a playoff and becomes the first Canadian to win the Masters.

June 15, 2003: Jim Furyk wins the U.S. Open. It is his first major championship in 32 pro attempts. His final-round 71 gives him a four-day total of 272, and in a tie with Jack Nicklaus, Tiger Woods, and Lee Janzen for the event's lowest four-day total.

July 20, 2003: PGA Tour rookie Ben Curtis wins the British Open, becoming the first player since 1913 to win the event in his first attempt. Curtis goes on to win the Tour's Rookie of the Year Award.

August 17, 2003: In the season's final major, Shaun Micheel wins the PGA Championship, becoming the fourth first-time major champion of the season. On the final hole, Micheel seals his two-stroke victory over Chad Campbell with an iron shot from the rough that lands two inches from the cup.

November 23, 2003: The U.S. and International Teams share the coveted President's Cup trophy. After regulation, the event is tied at 17–17. Tiger Woods and Ernie Els begin a sudden death playoff. Woods drills a 12-foot par putt on the third hole to extend the playoff. Both teams decide to end the tournament in a tie because it is too dark for play to continue.

December 8, 2003: Tiger Woods edges out money winner Vijay Singh to win his fifth-straight Player of the Year Award, which is voted on by PGA Tour players. It is the sixth time in seven full seasons that Woods has won the award.

April 11, 2004: Phil Mickelson wins the Masters, his first major in 42 pro attempts. Mickelson birdies the final hole to beat Ernie Els.

All-time Champions—Men (cont.)

PGA Championship

Year	Winner
2004	Vijay Singh
2003	Shaun Micheel
2002	Rich Beem
2001	David Toms
2000	*Tiger Woods
1999	Tiger Woods
1998	Vijay Singh
1997	Davis Love III
1996	*Mark Brooks
1995	*Steve Elkington
1994	Nick Price
1993	*Paul Azinger
1992	Nick Price
1991	John Daly
1990	Wayne Grady

Year	Winner
1989	Payne Stewart
1988	Jeff Sluman
1987	*Larry Nelson
1986	Bob Tway
1985	Hubert Green
1984	Lee Trevino
1983	Hal Sutton
1982	Raymond Floyd
1981	Larry Nelson
1980	Jack Nicklaus
1979	*David Graham
1978	*John Mahaffey
1977†	*Lanny Wadkins
1976	Dave Stockton
1975	Jack Nicklaus
1974	Lee Trevino
1973	Jack Nicklaus

Year	Winner
1972	Gary Player
1971	Jack Nicklaus
1970	Dave Stockton
1969	Ray Floyd
1968	Julius Boros
1967	*Don January
1966	Al Geiberger
1965	Dave Marr
1964	Bobby Nichols
1963	Jack Nicklaus
1962	Gary Player
1961	*Jerry Barber
1960	Jay Hebert
1959	Bob Rosburg
1958	Dow Finsterwald

*Winner in playoff.
†Playoff changed from 18 holes to sudden death.

Did You Know?

At the 2003 Tour Championship, Tiger Woods broke Byron Nelson's record for consecutive cuts made (114).

All-time Champions—Men (cont.)

PGA Championship (cont.)

Year	Winner
1957	Lionel Hebert
1956	Jack Burke
1955	Doug Ford
1954	Chick Harbert
1953	Walter Burkemo
1952	Jim Turnesa
1951	Sam Snead
1950	Chandler Harper
1949	Sam Snead
1948	Ben Hogan
1947	Jim Ferrier
1946	Ben Hogan
1945	Byron Nelson
1944	Bob Hamilton
1943	No tournament
1942	Sam Snead
1941	Vic Ghezzi
1940	Byron Nelson
1939	Henry Picard
1938	Paul Runyan
1937	Denny Shute
1936	Denny Shute
1935	Johnny Revolta
1934	Paul Runyan
1933	Gene Sarazen
1932	Olin Dutra
1931	Tom Creavy
1930	Tommy Armour
1929	Leo Diegel
1928	Leo Diegel
1927	Walter Hagen
1926	Walter Hagen
1925	Walter Hagen
1924	Walter Hagen
1923	Gene Sarazen
1922	Gene Sarazen
1921	Walter Hagen
1920	Jock Hutchison
1919	Jim Barnes
1917–18	No tournament
1916	Jim Barnes

All-time Champions—Women

LPGA Championship

Year	Winner
2004	Annika Sorenstam
2003	Annika Sorenstam
2002	Se Ri Pak
2001	Karrie Webb
2000	*Juli Inkster
1999	Juli Inkster
1998	Se Ri Pak
1997	*Chris Johnson
1996	Laura Davies
1995	Kelly Robbins
1994	Laura Davies
1993	Patty Sheehan
1992	Betsy King
1991	Meg Mallon
1990	Beth Daniel
1989	Nancy Lopez
1988	Sherri Turner
1987	Jane Geddes
1986	Pat Bradley
1985	Nancy Lopez
1984	Patty Sheehan
1983	Patty Sheehan
1982	Jan Stephenson
1981	Donna Caponi
1980	Sally Little
1979	Donna Caponi
1978	Nancy Lopez
1977	Chako Higuchi
1976	Betty Burfeindt
1975	Kathy Whitworth
1974	Sandra Haynie
1973	Mary Mills
1972	Kathy Ahern
1971	Kathy Whitworth
1970	*Shirley Englehorn
1969	Betsy Rawls
1968	*Sandra Post
1967	Kathy Whitworth
1966	Gloria Ehret
1965	Sandra Haynie
1964	Mary Mills
1963	Mickey Wright
1962	Judy Kimball
1961	Mickey Wright
1960	Mickey Wright
1959	Betsy Rawls
1958	Mickey Wright
1957	Louise Suggs
1956	*Marlene Hagge
1955	†Beverly Hanson

* Won in playoff. The 1956 and 1997 titles were decided in sudden death; 1968 and 1970 were 18-hole playoffs. †Won match-play final.

U.S. Women's Open

Year	Winner
2004	Meg Mallon
2003	*Hilary Lunke
2002	Juli Inkster
2001	Karrie Webb
2000	Karrie Webb
1999	Juli Inkster
1998	†Se Ri Pak
1997	Alison Nicholas
1996	Annika Sorenstam
1995	Annika Sorenstam
1994	Patty Sheehan
1993	Lauri Merten
1992	*Patty Sheehan
1991	Meg Mallon
1990	Betsy King
1989	Betsy King
1988	Liselotte Neumann
1987	*Laura Davies
1986	*Jane Geddes
1985	Kathy Baker
1984	Hollis Stacy
1983	Jan Stephenson
1982	Janet Anderson
1981	Pat Bradley
1980	Amy Alcott
1979	Jerilyn Britz
1978	Hollis Stacy
1977	Hollis Stacy
1976	*JoAnne Carner
1975	Sandra Palmer
1974	Sandra Haynie
1973	Susie Berning
1972	Susie Berning
1971	JoAnne Carner
1970	Donna Caponi
1969	Donna Caponi
1968	Susie Berning
1967	Catherine LaCoste
1966	Sandra Spuzich
1965	Carol Mann
1964	*Mickey Wright
1963	Mary Mills
1962	Murle Breer

* Winner in playoff. †Winner on second hole of sudden death after 18-hole playoff ended in a tie.

All-time Champions—Women (cont.)

U.S. Women's Open (cont.)

Year	Winner
1961	Mickey Wright
1960	Betsy Rawls
1959	Mickey Wright
1958	Mickey Wright
1957	Betsy Rawls
1956	*Kathy Cornelius
1955	Fay Crocker
1954	Babe Zaharias
1953	*Betsy Rawls
1952	Louise Suggs
1951	Betsy Rawls
1950	Babe Zaharias
1949	Louise Suggs
1948	Babe Zaharias
1947	Betty Jameson
1946	Patty Berg

* Winner in playoff.

Legends

Beth Daniel, b. October 14, 1956, Charleston, South Carolina. Daniel joined the LPGA Tour in 1979 and won 13 times in her first five seasons. But she won only once over the next five. In 1989, at age 33, Daniel re-emerged as one of the sport's best. She won four titles that year and placed in the Top 10 twenty times in 25 starts. Her seven wins the following season included the LPGA Championship, her first major. In 1999, she became the 16th player inducted into the LPGA Tour Hall of Fame. In 2003, Daniel won her 33rd career tournament, the BMO Financial Group Canadian Women's Open, making her the oldest winner in Tour history (46 years, 8 months, 29 days).

Before joining the LPGA in 1979, Beth Daniel won the U.S. Women's Amateur title in 1975 and 1977.

DARRON CARROLL/ICON SMI

Patty Berg, b. February 13, 1918, Minneapolis, Minnesota. Berg won 57 events as a pro and three as an amateur — all major titles. From 1948 through 1962, she won 44 pro titles. Overall, she won an LPGA-record 15 majors. At the 1959 U.S. Open, Berg became the first woman in U.S. Golf Association history to hit a hole in one. Nearly 32 years later, she scored another hole in one, at age 73. In 1967, Berg was one of the first six players inducted into the LPGA Tour Hall of Fame. She was a founding member of the LPGA and its first president.

Patty Sheehan, b. October 27, 1956, Middlebury, Vermont. A six-time major champion, Sheehan won at least one event on the LPGA Tour every year from 1981 (her rookie season) through 1996, except for 1987, when she finished second three times. She had her best season in 1990, when she won five times and finished second five times. Her best tournament by far was the U.S. Open. She won it in 1992 and 1994. From 1988 through 1997, her worst finish at the event was 17th. Her 35th and final LPGA Tour victory was the Nabisco Dinah Shore, in 1996, when it was a major championship.

Today's Stars

The 2004 Kraft Nabisco Championship was Grace Park's first victory at a major LPGA tournament.

DARREN CARROLL

Grace Park, b. March 6, 1979, Seoul, South Korea. Park had a breakout season in 2003, her fourth on the LPGA Tour. She had one victory, five second-place finishes, and placed in the Top 10 in 19 of 26 events. One of her second-place finishes came in a sudden-death playoff against Annika Sorenstam at the LPGA Championship. Park led the Tour in rounds in the 60s (46) and total birdies (403). Early in 2004, she had already placed in the Top 10 at four tournaments and notched her fifth career victory at the season's first major, the Kraft Nabisco Championship.

Michelle Wie, b. October 11, 1989, Honolulu, Hawaii. Still a high school student and just 14 years old, Wie gets more attention than any other female golfer on the planet. In March 2003, she finished in a tie for ninth at the LPGA Tour's first major of the season, the Kraft Nabisco Championship. A year later, she moved closer to claiming the title, finishing fourth. But the reigning U.S. Amateur Public Links champion hasn't just boomed her 300-yard drives off LPGA Tour tees. In January 2004, Wie shot a 68 in the PGA Tour's Sony Open, missing the cut by one shot.

Juli Inkster, b. June 24, 1960, Santa Cruz, California. Before joining the pro tour, Inkster dominated women's amateur golf. She won the U.S. Women's Amateur title from 1980 through 1982, becoming the first woman since Virginia Van Wie in 1934 to win the title three consecutive times. In 1983, she joined the LPGA Tour and won the Safeco Classic on her way to becoming Rookie of the Year. Inkster has won 30 Tour events, including the LPGA Championship (1999, 2000) and the U.S. Open (1999, 2002). Overall, she has won seven majors, sixth on the all-time list. In 2003, Inkster won twice in 21 starts and had nine Top 10 finishes.

All-time Champions—Women (cont.)

Nabisco Championship

Year	Winner
2004	Grace Park
2003	Patricia Meunier-Lebouc
2002	Annika Sorenstam
2001	Annika Sorenstam
2000	Karrie Webb
1999	Dottie Pepper
1998	Pat Hurst
1997	Betsy King
1996	Patti Sheehan
1995	Nanci Bowen
1994	Donna Andrews
1993	Helen Alfredsson
1992	*Dottie Mochrie
1991	Amy Alcott
1990	Betsy King
1989	Juli Inkster
1988	Amy Alcott
1987	*Betsy King
1986	Pat Bradley
1985	Alice Miller
1984	*Juli Inkster
1983	Amy Alcott
1982	Sally Little
1981	Nancy Lopez
1980	Donna Caponi
1979	Sandra Post
1978	*Sandra Post
1977	Kathy Whitworth
1976	Judy Rankin
1975	Sandra Palmer
1974	*Jo Ann Prentice
1973	Mickey Wright
1972	Jane Blalock

* Winner in sudden-death playoff. *Note:* Designated fourth major in 1983; played at Mission Hills Country Club, Rancho Mirage, California.

All-time Champions—Women (cont.)

du Maurier Classic

Year	Winner
2000	Meg Mallon
1999	Karrie Webb
1998	Brandie Burton
1997	Colleen Walker
1996	Laura Davies
1995	Jenny Lidback
1994	Martha Nause
1993	Brandie Burton
1992	Sherri Steinhauer
1991	Nancy Scranton
1990	Cathy Johnston
1989	Tammie Green
1988	Sally Little
1987	Jody Rosenthal
1986	*Pat Bradley
1985	Pat Bradley
1984	Juli Inkster
1983	Hollis Stacy
1982	Sandra Haynie
1981	Jan Stephenson
1980	Pat Bradley
1979	Amy Alcott
1978	JoAnne Carner
1977	Judy Rankin
1976	*Donna Caponi
1975	*JoAnne Carner
1974	Carole Jo Callison
1973	*Jocelyne Bourassa

* Winner in sudden-death playoff. *Note:* Designated third major in 1979; discontinued in 2001.

Women's British Open

Year	Winner
2004	Karen Stupples
2003	Annika Sorenstam
2002	Karrie Webb
2001	Se Ri Pak

Note: Designated fourth major in 2001.

Fast Fact: On October 20, 2003, Annika Sorenstam became the first international LPGA player inducted into the World Golf Hall of Fame.

2003-04 WOMEN'S TIME LINE

March 30, 2003: Patricia Meunier-Lebouc wins the Kraft Nabisco Championship, her first major, by defeating defending champ Annika Sorenstam by one stroke. Thirteen-year-old Michelle Wie, an amateur from Hawaii, finishes in a tie for ninth place.

June 8, 2003: Annika Sorenstam narrowly edges Grace Park in a sudden-death playoff to win the LPGA Championship. Sorenstam and Park are the only players in the field to finish the tournament under par.

July 7, 2003: Hilary Lunke becomes the 14th LPGA player to make the U.S. Open her first career victory. She defeats Angela Stanford and Kelly Robbins in an 18-hole playoff.

August 3, 2003: Annika Sorenstam wins the Women's British Open by one stroke over Se Ri Pak. Sorenstam becomes only the sixth player to complete the LPGA's career Grand Slam.

September 14, 2003: The European squad wins eight of the 12 singles matches on the final day of the Solheim Cup team competition to defeat the U.S. by seven points. It is the largest margin of victory since the event began, in 1990 and only the third victory for Europe.

November 24, 2003: Lorena Ochoa wins the LPGA Tour's Rookie of the Year Award by a landslide. The 22-year-old made the cut in 23 of 24 events and placed in the Top 10 eight times.

March 28, 2004: Grace Park wins the Kraft Nabisco Championship over Aree Song for her first career major. Fourteen-year-old Michelle Wie finishes fourth.

MOTOR SPORTS

The 2004 Daytona 500 was a return to glory for devoted NASCAR fans. For the first time in his career, Dale Earnhardt, Jr., won NASCAR's most important race. The win was celebrated by millions of fans who also idolized his father, the late Dale Earnhardt. "Little E" earned his victory on the same track on which his legendary father was killed in an accident during the final lap of the 2001 race.

The 2003 Winston Cup season can be summed up in one word: consistency. Matt Kenseth won the last NASCAR Winston Cup championship. Stockcar racing's top series switched its name to the Nextel Cup series for the 2004 season. Kenseth won only one race but was ranked first in Top 10 finishes (25) and tied for seventh in Top 5s (11). He started the season with a 20th-place finish at Daytona, but a fourth-place finish in the Bass Pro Shops MBNA 500 three weeks later helped him take over the points lead. He never lost it.

Because Kenseth earned the championship with just one victory while Ryan Newman won a series-leading eight times but finished sixth in the points standings, NASCAR introduced a new scoring system for 2004. Under the "Chase for the Championship," drivers ranked in the Top 10 and any other driver within 400 points of the leader will have their points reset for the last 10 races on the schedule. The leader will be given 5,050 points. Each subsequent driver will be

In 2003, Matt Kenseth won the last Winston Cup Championship.

BOB JORDAN/AP; WALTER ARCE/ASP INC. (INSET)

given five points fewer than the driver directly ahead of him. NASCAR predicted that tightening the points between the leaders would make the last 10 races of the season more important than ever.

In other racing, Buddy Rice won the 2004 Indianapolis 500, his first IRL IndyCar Series victory. His win gained additional national attention because one of the owners of his car was late-night talk show host David Letterman.

Scott Dixon won the 2003 IRL IndyCar Series championship. He tied Sam Hornish, Jr., and Gil de Ferran for most wins for the season (3). Just before the end of the season, de Ferran, the two-time CART champion and 2003 Indianapolis 500 champion, announced his retirement.

Paul Tracy dominated the 2003 CART season and won its championship. He won seven races and became the first driver in 32 years to win the first three races of a season.

Jimmie Johnson finished second in the 2003 Winston Cup standings.

RUSTY JARRETT/GETTY IMAGES

Indy Racing League (IRL)

All-time Indianapolis 500 Winners

TONY GUTIERREZ/AP

Gil de Ferran

Year	Driver	Miles Per Hour (M.P.H.)
2004	Buddy Rice (450*)	138.518
2003	Gil de Ferran	156.291
2002	Helio Castroneves	166.499
2001	Helio Castroneves	141.574
2000	Juan Montoya	167.607
1999	Kenny Brack	153.176
1998	Eddie Cheever, Jr.	145.155
1997	Arie Luyendyk	145.827
1996	Buddy Lazier	147.956
1995	Jacques Villeneuve	153.616
1994	Al Unser, Jr.	160.872
1993	Emerson Fittipaldi	157.207
1992	Al Unser, Jr.	134.477
1991	Rick Mears	176.457
1990	Arie Luyendyk	185.981
1989	Emerson Fittipaldi	167.581
1988	Rick Mears	144.809
1987	Al Unser	162.175
1986	Bobby Rahal	170.722
1985	Danny Sullivan	152.982
1984	Rick Mears	163.612
1983	Tom Sneva	162.117
1982	Gordon Johncock	162.029
1981	Bobby Unser	139.084
1980	Johnny Rutherford	142.862
1979	Rick Mears	158.899

Year	Driver	M.P.H.
1978	Al Unser	161.363
1977	A.J. Foyt, Jr.	161.331
1976	Johnny Rutherford (255*)	148.725
1975	Bobby Unser (435*)	149.213
1974	Johnny Rutherford	158.589
1973	Gordon Johncock (332.5*)	159.036
1972	Mark Donohue	162.962
1971	Al Unser	157.735
1970	Al Unser	155.749
1969	Mario Andretti	156.867
1968	Bobby Unser	152.882
1967	A.J. Foyt, Jr.	151.207
1966	Graham Hill	144.317
1965	Jim Clark	150.686
1964	A.J. Foyt, Jr.	147.350
1963	Parnelli Jones	143.137
1962	Rodger Ward	140.293
1961	A.J. Foyt, Jr.	139.130
1960	Jim Rathmann	138.767
1959	Rodger Ward	135.857
1958	Jimmy Bryan	133.791
1957	Sam Hanks	135.601
1956	Pat Flaherty	128.490
1955	Bob Sweikert	128.213
1954	Bill Vukovich	130.840
1953	Bill Vukovich	128.740
1952	Troy Ruttman	128.922
1951	Lee Wallard	126.244
1950	Johnnie Parsons (345*)	124.00
1949	Bill Holland	121.327
1948	Mauri Rose	119.814
1947	Mauri Rose	116.338
1946	George Robson	114.820
1942-45	No races held during World War II	
1941	Floyd Davis/Mauri Rose	115.117
1940	Wilbur Shaw	114.277

Note: Miles per hour (M.P.H.) denotes average race speed. *Miles completed before race was called because of rain.

Indy Racing League (cont.)

All-time Indianapolis 500 Winners

Year	Driver	Miles Per Hour (M.P.H.)
1939	Wilbur Shaw	115.035
1938	Floyd Roberts	117.200
1937	Wilbur Shaw	113.580
1936	Louis Meyer	109.069
1935	Kelly Petillo	106.240
1934	Bill Cummings	104.863
1933	Louis Meyer	104.162
1932	Fred Fame	104.144
1931	Louis Schneider	96.629
1930	Billy Arnold	100.448
1929	Ray Keech	97.585
1928	Louis Meyer	99.482
1927	George Souders	97.545
1926	Frank Lockhart (400*)	95.904

*Miles completed before race was called because of rain.

Year	Driver	M.P.H.
1925	Peter DePaolo	101.127
1924	L.L. Corum / Joe Boyer	98.234
1923	Tommy Milton	90.954
1922	Jimmy Murphy	94.484
1921	Tommy Milton	89.621
1920	Gaston Chevrolet	88.618
1919	Howdy Wilcox	88.050
1917-18	No races held during World War I	
1916	Dario Resta (scheduled for 300 miles)	84.001
1915	Ralph DePalma	89.840
1914	Rene Thomas	82.474
1913	Jules Goux	75.933
1912	Joe Dawson	78.719
1911	Ray Harroun	74.602

STEVE HELBER/AP

Scott Dixon

All-time IRL Champions

Year	Driver
2003	Scott Dixon
2002	Sam Hornish, Jr.
2001	Sam Hornish, Jr.
2000	Buddy Lazier
1999	Greg Ray
1998	Kenny Brack
1996-97*	Tony Stewart
1996 (Series' first year)	Buzz Calkins and Scott Sharp (co-champions)

All-time IRL Rookies of the Year

Year	Driver
2003	Dan Wheldon
2002	Laurent Redon
2001	Felipe Giaffone
2000	Airton Dare
1999	Scott Harrington
1998	Robby Unser
1996-97*	Jim Guthrie
1996 (Series' first year)	N/A

*This season started in 1996 and ended in 1997.

Championship Auto Racing Teams (CART)

All-time CART Championship Series Champions

MARCIO JOSE SANCHEZ/AP

Year	Driver
2003	Paul Tracy
2002	Cristiano da Matta
2001	Gil de Ferran
2000	Gil de Ferran
1999	Juan Montoya
1998	Alex Zanardi
1997	Alex Zanardi
1996	Jimmy Vasser
1995	Jacques Villeneuve
1994	Al Unser, Jr.
1993	Nigel Mansell
1992	Bobby Rahal
1991	Michael Andretti
1990	Al Unser, Jr.
1989	Emerson Fittipaldi
1988	Danny Sullivan
1987	Bobby Rahal
1986	Bobby Rahal

Year	Driver
1985	Al Unser
1984	Mario Andretti
1983	Al Unser
1982	Rick Mears
1981	Rick Mears
1980	Johnny Rutherford
1979	Rick Mears

Fast Fact: Three women have competed in the Indianapolis 500: Janet Guthrie (1977-79), Lyn St. James (1992-97, 2000), and Sarah Fisher (2000-04).

Today's Stars

Helio Castroneves, b. May 10, 1975, Sao Paulo, Brazil. Castroneves won the Indianapolis 500 in 2001 in just his second IRL IndyCar Series start. The following year, he became the fifth driver to win the Indy 500 twice in a row and the first in the race's history to win it in each of his first two starts. In 2003, Castroneves had nine Top 5 finishes and added two more IRL wins, increasing his career total to five. He placed third overall in the point standings.

Matt Kenseth, b. March 10, 1972, Cambridge, Wisconsin. Kenseth earned just one victory in 2003 but still won his first Winston Cup title. He had 25 Top 10 finishes and 11 Top 5s. At the start of the 2004 season, Kenseth had eight career victories, including a Cup-leading five wins in 2002. He won the 2000 Rookie of the Year title over Dale Earnhardt, Jr., and was the first rookie to win the Coca-Cola 600. At age 19, he became the youngest driver to win an ARTGO Challenge Series race.

Jimmie Johnson, b. September 17, 1975, El Cajon, California. Johnson made a strong showing as a NASCAR rookie in 2002. He had 21 Top 10 finishes and tied the rookie record for wins (3). He placed fifth in the Winston Cup Series standings and was second behind Ryan Newman in the voting for Rookie of the Year. In 2003, he finished second to Matt Kenseth in the standings. Johnson earned three wins, 14 Top 5 finishes, and 20 Top 10s. Four months into the 2004 season, he was in first place in the standings with three wins and ten Top 5 finishes in 15 races.

Helio Castroneves won the Indy 500 in 2001 and 2002.

ROBERT LABERGE/GETTY IMAGES; MARY BUTKUS/AP (INSET)

Trivia Challenge

What was the closest margin of victory in the Indianapolis 500?

Al Unser, Jr., defeated Scott Goodyear by .043 of a second in 1992.

Did You Know?

NASCAR's Nextel Cup Series tracks are as long as 2.66 miles (Talladega Superspeedway) and as short as 0.526 of a mile (Martinsville Speedway). The three Nextel Cup tracks shorter than one mile around are called short tracks.

2003-04 TIME LINE

May 25, 2003: Gil de Ferran wins his first Indianapolis 500. Second place goes to de Ferran's teammate, Helio Castroneves, who was attempting to win his third-straight Indy 500.

August 25, 2003: Two-time CART champion and Indy 500 champion Gil de Ferran announces his retirement following the 2003 season. Penske Racing announces that two-time IRL champion Sam Hornish, Jr., formerly of Panther Racing, will drive for Penske in 2004 and replace de Ferran on the team.

September 21, 2003: Scott Dixon ties Helio Castroneves for the IRL points lead when he finishes second and Castroneves finishes sixth at the Toyota Indy 400.

October 12, 2003: Dixon clinches the IRL IndyCar Series championship when he finishes second in the season-ending Chevy 500 and Castroneves finishes 13th.

November 9, 2003: Matt Kenseth clinches his first Winston Cup championship with a fourth-place finish in the Pop Secret 400.

January 20, 2004: NASCAR announces changes in the scoring system for the Nextel Cup series. Drivers ranked in the Top 10 and any other driver within 400 points of the leader will have his points reset for the last 10 races of the season.

February 15, 2004: Dale Earnhardt, Jr., wins his first Daytona 500.

April 18, 2004: Rusty Wallace's winless streak is snapped at 105 when he wins the Advance Auto Parts 500.

May 30, 2004: Buddy Rice wins the rain-shortened 88th Indianapolis 500, his first IRL IndyCar Series victory.

June 30, 2004: Al Unser, Jr., a two-time Indy 500 winner, announces his retirement after a 22-year career.

Did You Know?

A white flag waved by the starter means that the lead driver has begun his final lap of the race.

National Association for Stock Car Automobile Racing (NASCAR)

All-time Winston Cup Champions

Year	Driver	Year	Driver	Year	Driver
2003	Matt Kenseth	1989	Rusty Wallace	1975	Richard Petty
2002	Tony Stewart	1988	Bill Elliott	1974	Richard Petty
2001	Jeff Gordon	1987	Dale Earnhardt	1973	Benny Parsons
2000	Bobby Labonte	1986	Dale Earnhardt	1972	Richard Petty
1999	Dale Jarrett	1985	Darrell Waltrip	1971	Richard Petty
1998	Jeff Gordon	1984	Terry Labonte	1970	Bobby Isaac
1997	Jeff Gordon	1983	Bobby Allison	1969	David Pearson
1996	Terry Labonte	1982	Darrell Waltrip	1968	David Pearson
1995	Jeff Gordon	1981	Darrell Waltrip	1967	Richard Petty
1994	Dale Earnhardt	1980	Dale Earnhardt	1966	David Pearson
1993	Dale Earnhardt	1979	Richard Petty	1965	Ned Jarrett
1992	Alan Kulwicki	1978	Cale Yarborough	1964	Richard Petty
1991	Dale Earnhardt	1977	Cale Yarborough	1963	Joe Weatherly
1990	Dale Earnhardt	1976	Cale Yarborough	1962	Joe Weatherly

National Association for Stock Car Automobile Racing (NASCAR)

All-time Winston Cup Champions (cont.)

Year	Driver
1961	Ned Jarrett
1960	Rex White
1959	Lee Petty
1958	Lee Petty
1957	Buck Baker
1956	Buck Baker
1955	Tim Flock
1954	Lee Petty
1953	Herb Thomas
1952	Tim Flock
1951	Herb Thomas
1950	Bill Rexford
1949	Red Byron

All-time Winston Cup Wins Leaders

1. Richard Petty (200)
2. David Pearson (105)
3. Bobby Allison (84)
(tie) Darrell Waltrip (84)
5. Cale Yarborough (83)
6. Dale Earnhardt (76)
7. Jeff Gordon (67)
8. Lee Petty (55)
(tie) Rusty Wallace (55)
10. Ned Jarrett (50)
(tie) Junior Johnson (50)
12. Herb Thomas (48)
13. Buck Baker (46)
14. Bill Elliott (44)
15. Tim Flock (40)
16. Bobby Isaac (37)
17. Mark Martin (34)
18. Fireball Roberts (32)
19. Dale Jarrett (31)
20. Rex White (28)
(tie) Fred Lorenzen (28)

All-time Winston Cup Rookies of the Year

Year	Driver
2003	Jamie McMurray
2002	Ryan Newman
2001	Kevin Harvick
2000	Matt Kenseth
1999	Tony Stewart
1998	Kenny Irwin
1997	Mike Skinner
1996	Johnny Benson
1995	Ricky Craven
1994	Jeff Burton
1993	Jeff Gordon
1992	Jimmy Hensley
1991	Bobby Hamilton
1990	Rob Moroso
1989	Dick Trickle
1988	Ken Bouchard
1987	Davey Allison
1986	Alan Kulwicki
1985	Ken Schrader
1984	Rusty Wallace
1983	Sterling Marlin
1982	Geoffrey Bodine
1981	Ron Bouchard
1980	Jody Ridley
1979	Dale Earnhardt
1978	Ronnie Thomas
1977	Ricky Rudd
1976	Skip Manning
1975	Bruce Hill
1974	Earl Ross
1973	Lennie Pond
1972	Larry Smith
1971	Walter Ballard
1970	Bill Dennis
1969	Dick Brooks
1968	Pete Hamilton
1967	Donnie Allison
1966	James Hylton
1965	Sam McQuagg
1964	Doug Cooper
1963	Billy Wade
1962	Tom Cox
1961	Woodie Wilson
1960	David Pearson
1959	Richard Petty
1958	Shorty Rollins

All-time Daytona 500 Champions

Year	Driver	M.P.H.
2004	Dale Earnhardt, Jr.	156.345
2003	Michael Waltrip	133.870
2002	Ward Burton	142.971
2001	Michael Waltrip	161.783
2000	Dale Jarrett	155.669
1999	Jeff Gordon	161.551
1998	Dale Earnhardt	172.712
1997	Jeff Gordon	148.295
1996	Dale Jarrett	154.308
1995	Sterling Marlin	141.710
1994	Sterling Marlin	156.931
1993	Dale Jarrett	154.972
1992	Davey Allison	168.256
1991	Ernie Irvan	148.148
1990	Derrike Cope	165.761
1989	Darrell Waltrip	148.466
1988	Bobby Allison	137.531
1987	Bill Elliott	176.263
1986	Geoffrey Bodine	148.124
1985	Bill Elliott	172.265
1984	Cale Yarborough	150.994
1983	Cale Yarborough	155.979
1982	Bobby Allison	153.991
1981	Richard Petty	169.651
1980	Buddy Baker	177.602
1979	Richard Petty	143.977
1978	Bobby Allison	159.730
1977	Cale Yarborough	153.218
1976	David Pearson	152.181
1975	Benny Parsons	153.649
1974	Richard Petty	140.894
1973	Richard Petty	157.205
1972	A.J. Foyt, Jr.	161.550
1971	Richard Petty	144.462
1970	Pete Hamilton	149.601
1969	Lee Roy Yarbrough	157.950
1968	Cale Yarborough	143.251
1967	Mario Andretti	146.926
1966	Richard Petty	160.627
1965	Fred Lorenzen	141.539
1964	Richard Petty	154.334
1963	Tiny Lund	151.566
1962	Fireball Roberts	152.529
1961	Marvin Panch	149.601
1960	Junior Johnson	124.740
1959	Lee Petty	135.521

CHRIS SANFORD/GETTY IMAGES

All-time Brickyard 400 Winners

Year	Driver	M.P.H.
2003	Kevin Harvick	134.554
2002	Bill Elliott	125.033
2001	Jeff Gordon	130.790
2000	Bobby Labonte	155.912
1999	Dale Jarrett	148.194
1998	Jeff Gordon	126.772
1997	Ricky Rudd	130.814
1996	Dale Jarrett	139.508
1995	Dale Earnhardt	155.206
1994	Jeff Gordon	131.977

NASCAR (cont.)

All-time Coca-Cola 600 Winners

Year	Driver	M.P.H.	Year	Driver	M.P.H.	Year	Driver	M.P.H.
2004	Jimmie Johnson	142.763	1989	Darrell Waltrip	144.077	1974	David Pearson	135.720
2003	Jimmie Johnson	126.198	1988	Darrell Waltrip	124.460	1973	Buddy Baker	134.890
2002	Mark Martin	137.729	1987	Kyle Petty	131.483	1972	Buddy Baker	142.255
2001	Jeff Burton	138.107	1986	Dale Earnhardt	140.406	1971	Bobby Allison	140.442
2000	Matt Kenseth	142.640	1985	Darrell Waltrip	141.807	1970	Donnie Allison	129.680
1999	Jeff Burton	151.367	1984	Bobby Allison	129.233	1969	Lee Roy Yarbrough	134.361
1998	Jeff Gordon	136.424	1983	Neil Bonnett	140.707	1968	Buddy Baker	104.207
1997	Jeff Gordon	136.745	1982	Neil Bonnett	130.058	1967	Jim Paschal	135.832
1996	Dale Jarrett	147.581	1981	Bobby Allison	129.326	1966	Marvin Panch	135.042
1995	Bobby Labonte	151.952	1980	Benny Parsons	119.265	1965	Fred Lorenzen	121.772
1994	Jeff Gordon	139.445	1979	Darrell Waltrip	136.674	1964	Jim Paschal	125.772
1993	Dale Earnhardt	145.504	1978	Darrell Waltrip	138.355	1963	Fred Lorenzen	132.418
1992	Dale Earnhardt	132.980	1977	Richard Petty	137.676	1962	Nelson Stacy	125.552
1991	Davey Allison	138.951	1976	David Pearson	137.352	1961	David Pearson	111.633
1990	Rusty Wallace	137.650	1975	Richard Petty	145.327	1960	Joe Lee Johnson	107.735

All-time Talladega 500* Winners

Year	Driver	M.P.H.	Year	Driver	M.P.H.	Year	Driver	M.P.H.
2004	Jeff Gordon	129.396	1991	Dale Earnhardt	147.383	1978	Lennie Pond	174.700
2003	Dale Earnhardt, Jr.	144.625	1990	Dale Earnhardt	174.430	1977	Donnie Allison	162.524
2002	Dale Earnhardt, Jr.	159.022	1989	Terry Labonte	157.354	1976	Dave Marcis	157.547
2001	Bobby Hamilton	184.003	1988	Ken Schrader	154.505	1975	Buddy Baker	130.892
2000	Jeff Gordon	161.157	1987	Bill Elliott	171.293	1974	Richard Petty	148.637
1999	Dale Earnhardt	163.395	1986	Bobby Hillin	151.552	1973	Dick Brooks	145.454
1998	Bobby Labonte	163.439	1985	Cale Yarborough	148.772	1972	James Hylton	148.728
1997	Terry Labonte	156.601	1984	Dale Earnhardt	155.485	1971	Bobby Allison	145.945
1996	Jeff Gordon	133.387	1983	Dale Earnhardt	170.611	1970	Pete Hamilton	158.517
1995	Sterling Marlin	173.188	1982	Darrell Waltrip	168.157	1969	Richard Brickhouse	153.778
1994	Jimmy Spencer	163.217	1981	Ron Bouchard	156.737			
1993	Dale Earnhardt	153.858	1980	Neil Bonnett	166.894			
1992	Ernie Irvan	176.309	1979	Darrell Waltrip	161.229			

Trivia Challenge

Which set of brothers has won the most NASCAR races?

Bobby Allison (84 victories) and Donnie Allison (10).

All-time Southern 500 Winners

Year	Driver	M.P.H.
2003	Terry Labonte	120.744
2002	Jeff Gordon	118.617
2001	Ward Burton	122.773
2000	Bobby Labonte	108.273
1999	Jeff Burton	107.816
1998	Jeff Gordon	139.031
1997	Jeff Gordon	121.149
1996	Jeff Gordon	135.757
1995	Jeff Gordon	121.231
1994	Bill Elliott	127.952
1993	Mark Martin	137.932
1992	Darrell Waltrip	129.114
1991	Harry Gant	133.508
1990	Dale Earnhardt	123.141
1989	Dale Earnhardt	135.462
1988	Bill Elliott	128.297
1987	Dale Earnhardt	115.520
1986	Tim Richmond	121.068
1985	Bill Elliott	121.254

BILL LIVINGSTON/WIREIMAGE.COM

*From 1969 through 1988, the race was known as the Talladega 500. From 1989 through 2001, it was known as the Die Hard 500. In 2001, it was again called the Talladega 500. Since 2002, the race has been called the Aaron's 499.

All-time Southern 500 Winners (cont.)

Year	Driver	M.P.H.	Year	Driver	M.P.H.	Year	Driver	M.P.H.
1984	Harry Gant	128.270	1968	Cale Yarborough	126.132	1952	Fonty Flock	74.510
1983	Bobby Allison	123.343	1967	Richard Petty	130.423	1951	Herb Thomas	76.900
1982	Cale Yarborough	115.224	1966	Darel Dieringer	114.830	1950	Johnny Mantz	76.260
1981	Neil Bonnett	126.410	1965	Ned Jarrett	115.924			
1980	Terry Labonte	115.210	1964	Buck Baker	117.757			
1979	David Pearson	126.259	1963	Fireball Roberts	129.784			
1978	Cale Yarborough	116.828	1962	Larry Frank	117.965			
1977	David Pearson	106.797	1961	Nelson Stacy	117.787			
1976	David Pearson	120.534	1960	Buck Baker	105.901			
1975	Bobby Allison	116.825	1959	Jim Reed	111.840			
1974	Cale Yarborough	111.075	1958	Fireball Roberts	102.590			
1973	Cale Yarborough	134.033	1957	Speedy Thompson	100.094			
1972	Bobby Allison	128.124	1956	Curtis Turner	95.067			
1971	Bobby Allison	131.398	1955	Herb Thomas	93.281			
1970	Buddy Baker	128.817	1954	Herb Thomas	94.930			
1969	Lee Roy Yarbrough	105.612	1953	Buck Baker	92.780			

Fast Fact: In 2004, NASCAR's top series changed its name from the Winston Cup Championship to the Nextel Cup Championship when Winston's 33-year reign as a NASCAR sponsor ended.

Legends

Bobby Allison is one of only four drivers to win the Daytona 500 three times.

ERIC SCHWEIKARDT

Bobby Allison, b. December 3, 1937, Hueytown, Alabama. Allison is a three-time winner of the Daytona 500 (1978, 1982, 1988) and is tied with Darrell Waltrip for third on the all-time NASCAR Cup Series victory list (84). He won his only Cup championship in 1983 but was a four-time runner-up during the modern era (since 1972). Allison was named one of NASCAR's 50 Greatest Drivers and inducted into the International Motorsports Hall of Fame in 1993.

Al Unser, b. May 29, 1939, Albuquerque, New Mexico. Unser is one of only three men to win the Indianapolis 500 four times (1970, 1971, 1978, 1987). His fourth win came five days before he turned 48, making him Indy's oldest winner. Unser won the CART championship series twice (1983, 1985) and ranks fourth on the all-time list for CART victories (39). Six men in Unser's family have started the Indy 500. In 1983, he became the first driver to race against his son (Al, Jr.) in the race.

Darrell Waltrip, b. February 5, 1947, Owensboro, Kentucky. Waltrip won NASCAR's Winston Cup Series three times (1981, 1982, 1985), tied for the third-most all-time. Over his 29-year career (1972-00), he won 84 races (tied for third-most all-time) and nearly $20 million. Waltrip holds the modern-era record for most wins from the pole in a season (eight, in 1981). He won the Coca-Cola 600 five times, more than any other driver. Waltrip was NASCAR's Most Popular Driver in 1989 and 1990 and the National Motorsports Press Association Driver of the Year in 1977, 1981, and 1982.

TENNIS

The big story of 2003 and early 2004 was the unbeatable Belgians — Justine Henin-Hardenne and Kim Clijsters. The two 20-somethings finished 2003 ranked Number 1 and Number 2 in the world, respectively. They faced each other in the finals of two Grand Slam events in 2003, the French Open and the U.S. Open. Henin-Hardenne won both matches. The 2004 season started out the same way, with Henin-Hardenne beating Clijsters in their Australian Open final.

U.S. players Serena Williams and her older sister Venus had dominated the women's tour, but they slogged through an injury-riddled 2003.

Serena began the season ranked Number 1 but finished at Number 3. She won the Australian Open and Wimbledon in 2003 but lost to Henin-Hardenne in the semi-finals of the French Open and pulled out of the U.S. Open because of a strained quadriceps muscle in her left knee. She also missed the Australian Open in 2004 while recovering from knee surgery.

MANNY MILLAN/SPORTS ILLUSTRATED

Andy Roddick won his first Grand Slam victory, the U.S. Open, in 2003.

Venus lost to her sister in the Australian Open and Wimbledon finals in 2003 and was defeated in the fourth round of the French Open. A strained abdominal muscle forced her to withdraw from the U.S. Open. She finished 2003 ranked Number 11.

On the men's side, 21-year-old Andy Roddick of the U.S. won his first Grand Slam title when he defeated Juan Carlos Ferrero of Spain at the U. S. Open in 2003. Roddick finished the year as the youngest American ever ranked Number 1 in the world.

Pete Sampras, one of the greatest men's players in tennis history, retired in 2003 with an emotional ceremony at the U.S. Open. Sampras, 32, won a record 14 Grand Slam championships, including five U.S. Open titles. But Andre Agassi finished 2003 ranked Number 4 in the world, becoming the oldest men's player (33) to finish in the Top 5 since 1987, when Jimmy Connors, then 35, was ranked fourth.

Grand Slam Tournaments: All-Time Men's Champions

Australian Championships

Year	Winner
2004	Roger Federer
2003	Andre Agassi
2002	Thomas Johansson
2001	Andre Agassi
2000	Andre Agassi
1999	Yevgeny Kafelnikov
1998	Petr Korda
1997	Pete Sampras
1996	Boris Becker
1995	Andre Agassi
1994	Pete Sampras
1993	Jim Courier
1992	Jim Courier
1991	Boris Becker
1990	Ivan Lendl
1989	Ivan Lendl
1988	Mats Wilander
1987	Stefan Edberg
1986	no tournament
1985	Stefan Edberg
1984	Mats Wilander
1983	Mats Wilander
1982	Johan Kriek
1981	Johan Kriek
1980	Brian Teacher
1979	Guillermo Vilas
1978	Guillermo Vilas
1977 (Dec.)	Vitas Gerulaitis
1977 (Jan.)	Roscoe Tanner
1976	Mark Edmondson
1975	John Newcombe
1974	Jimmy Connors
1973	John Newcombe
1972	Ken Rosewall
1971	Ken Rosewall
1970	Arthur Ashe
*1969	Rod Laver

* Became Open (amateur and professional) in 1969.

Note: Traditionally, the Australian Open was held in January. In 1977, it was moved to December, so there were two tournaments that year. It returned to January in 1987.

Grand Slam Tournaments: All-Time Men's Champions (cont.)

Australian Championships (cont.)

Year	Winner
1968	Bill Bowrey
1967	Roy Emerson
1966	Roy Emerson
1965	Roy Emerson
1964	Roy Emerson
1963	Roy Emerson
1962	Rod Laver
1961	Roy Emerson
1960	Rod Laver
1959	Alex Olmedo
1958	Ashley Cooper
1957	Ashley Cooper
1956	Lew Hoad
1955	Ken Rosewall
1954	Mervyn Rose
1953	Ken Rosewall
1952	Ken McGregor
1951	Richard Savitt
1950	Frank Sedgman
1949	Frank Sedgman
1948	Adrian Quist
1947	Dinny Pails
1946	John Bromwich
1941-45	no tournament
1940	Adrian Quist
1939	John Bromwich
1938	Don Budge
1937	Vivian B. McGrath
1936	Adrian Quist
1935	Jack Crawford
1934	Fred Perry
1933	Jack Crawford
1932	Jack Crawford
1931	Jack Crawford
1930	Gar Moon
1929	John C. Gregory
1928	Jean Borotra
1927	Gerald Patterson
1926	John Hawkes
1925	James Anderson
1924	James Anderson
1923	Pat O'Hara Wood
1922	James Anderson
1921	Rhys H. Gemmell
1920	Pat O'Hara Wood
1919	A.R.F. Kingscote
1916-18	no tournament
1915	Francis G. Lowe
1914	Arthur Wood
1913	E. F. Parker
1912	J. Cecil Parke
1911	Norman Brookes
1910	Rodney Heath
1909	Tony Wilding
1908	Fred Alexander
1907	Horace M. Rice
1906	Tony Wilding
1905	Rodney Heath

French Championships

Year	Winner
2004	Gaston Gaudio
2003	Juan Carlos Ferrero
2002	Albert Costa
2001	Gustavo Kuerten
2000	Gustavo Kuerten
1999	Andre Agassi
1998	Carlos Moya
1997	Gustavo Kuerten
1996	Yevgeny Kafelnikov
1995	Thomas Muster
1994	Sergi Bruguera
1993	Sergi Bruguera
1992	Jim Courier
1991	Jim Courier
1990	Andres Gomez
1989	Michael Chang
1988	Mats Wilander
1987	Ivan Lendl
1986	Ivan Lendl
1985	Mats Wilander
1984	Ivan Lendl
1983	Yannick Noah
1982	Mats Wilander
1981	Bjorn Borg
1980	Bjorn Borg
1979	Bjorn Borg
1978	Bjorn Borg
1977	Guillermo Vilas
1976	Adriano Panatta
1975	Bjorn Borg
1974	Bjorn Borg
1973	Ilie Nastase
1972	Andres Gimeno
1971	Jan Kodes
1970	Jan Kodes
1969	Rod Laver
*1968	Ken Rosewall
1967	Roy Emerson
1966	Tony Roche
1965	Fred Stolle
1964	Manuel Santana
1963	Roy Emerson
1962	Rod Laver
1961	Manuel Santana
1960	Nicola Pietrangeli
1959	Nicola Pietrangeli
1958	Mervyn Rose
1957	Sven Davidson
1956	Lew Hoad
1955	Tony Trabert
1954	Tony Trabert
1953	Ken Rosewall
1952	Jaroslav Drobny
1951	Jaroslav Drobny
1950	Budge Patty
1949	Frank Parker
1948	Frank Parker
1947	Joseph Asboth
1946	Marcel Bernard
1940-45	no tournament
1939	Don McNeill
1938	Don Budge
1937	Henner Henkel
1936	Gottfried von Cramm
1935	Fred Perry
1934	Gottfried von Cramm
1933	Jack Crawford
1932	Henri Cochet
1931	Jean Borotra
1930	Henri Cochet
1929	Rene Lacoste
1928	Henri Cochet
1927	Rene Lacoste
1926	Henri Cochet
†1925	Rene Lacoste

Wimbledon Championships

Year	Winner
2004	Roger Federer
2003	Roger Federer
2002	Lleyton Hewitt
2001	Goran Ivanisevic
2000	Pete Sampras
1999	Pete Sampras
1998	Pete Sampras
1997	Pete Sampras
1996	Richard Krajicek
1995	Pete Sampras
1994	Pete Sampras
1993	Pete Sampras
1992	Andre Agassi
1991	Michael Stich
1990	Stefan Edberg
1989	Boris Becker
1988	Stefan Edberg
1987	Pat Cash
1986	Boris Becker
1985	Boris Becker
1984	John McEnroe
1983	John McEnroe
1982	Jimmy Connors
1981	John McEnroe
1980	Bjorn Borg
1979	Bjorn Borg
1978	Bjorn Borg
1977	Bjorn Borg
1976	Bjorn Borg
1975	Arthur Ashe
1974	Jimmy Connors
1973	Jan Kodes
1972	Stan Smith
1971	John Newcombe
1970	John Newcombe
1969	Rod Laver
*1968	Rod Laver
1967	John Newcombe
1966	Manuel Santana
1965	Roy Emerson
1964	Roy Emerson
1963	Chuck McKinley
1962	Rod Laver
1961	Rod Laver
1960	Neale Fraser
1959	Alex Olmedo
1958	Ashley Cooper
1957	Lew Hoad
1956	Lew Hoad
1955	Tony Trabert
1954	Jaroslav Drobny
1953	Vic Seixas
1952	Frank Sedgman
1951	Dick Savitt
1950	Budge Patty
1949	Fred Schroeder, Jr.
1948	Bob Falkenburg
1947	Jack Kramer
1946	Yvon Petra
1940-45	no tournament
1939	Bobby Riggs
1938	Don Budge
1937	Don Budge
1936	Fred Perry
1935	Fred Perry
1934	Fred Perry
1933	Jack Crawford
1932	Ellsworth Vines

*Became Open (amateur and professional) in 1968.
† 1925 was the first year in which players from all countries were allowed to compete.

Today's Stars

Roger Federer started 2004 by winning three of five tournaments.

Roger Federer, b. August 8, 1981, Basel, Switzerland. Federer began 2004 with a bang, winning the Australian Open by defeating Marat Safin of Russia in the men's final. He won his first singles Grand Slam championship in 2003 by defeating Mark Philippoussis of Australia at Wimbledon. Federer finished 2003 ranked Number 2 in the world, the highest ranking of his six-year career. He also led the ATP in earnings, with $4,000,680.

Andre Agassi, b. April 29, 1970, Las Vegas, Nevada. Agassi finished 2003 ranked Number 4 in the world, the 14th Top 10 ranking of his 18-year career. His victory at the Australian Open was his eighth Grand Slam singles championship. In May 2003, he climbed to the Number 1 ranking to become the oldest player (33 years 13 days) to hold the top spot. Agassi is married to the legendary Steffi Graf, who won 22 women's singles Grand Slam titles before retiring in 1999.

Carlos Moya, b. August 27, 1976, Palma de Mallorca, Spain. At the start of 2004, Moya had won 14 championships and been ranked in the Top 10 four times since turning pro in 1995. In 1998, he won his first Grand Slam title, defeating fellow Spaniard Alex Corretja in the men's final of the French Open. In 1999, Moya ascended to the Number 1 world ranking and held the spot for two weeks. It was the first time a player from Spain had been ranked Number 1 since 1973.

Grand Slam Tournaments: All-Time Men's Champions (cont.)

Wimbledon Championships (cont.)

Year	Winner
1931	Sidney B. Wood, Jr.
1930	Bill Tilden
1929	Henri Cochet
1928	Rene Lacoste
1927	Henri Cochet
1926	Jean Borotra
1925	Rene Lacoste
1924	Jean Borotra
1923	Bill Johnston
1922	Gerald L. Patterson
1921	Bill Tilden
1920	Bill Tilden
1919	Gerald L. Patterson
1915-18	no tournament
1914	Norman E. Brookes
1913	Anthony F. Wilding
1912	Anthony F. Wilding
1911	Anthony F. Wilding
1910	Anthony F. Wilding
1909	Arthur W. Gore
1908	Arthur W. Gore
1907	Norman E. Brookes
1906	H. Laurie Doherty
1905	H. Laurie Doherty
1904	H. Laurie Doherty
1903	H. Laurie Doherty
1902	H. Laurie Doherty
1901	Arthur W. Gore
1900	Reggie F. Doherty
1899	Reggie F. Doherty
1898	Reggie F. Doherty
1897	Reggie F. Doherty
1896	Harold S. Mahoney
1895	Wilfred Baddeley
1894	Joshua Pim
1893	Joshua Pim
1892	Wilfred Baddeley
1891	Wilfred Baddeley
1890	William J. Hamilton
1889	William Renshaw
1888	Ernest Renshaw
1887	Herbert F. Lawford
1886	William Renshaw
1885	William Renshaw
1884	William Renshaw
1883	William Renshaw
1882	William Renshaw
1881	William Renshaw
1880	John T. Harley
1879	John T. Harley
1878	P. Frank Hadow
1877	Spencer W. Gore

United States Championships

Year	Winner
2003	Andy Roddick
2002	Pete Sampras
2001	Lleyton Hewitt
2000	Marat Safin
1999	Andre Agassi
1998	Patrick Rafter
1997	Patrick Rafter
1996	Pete Sampras
1995	Pete Sampras
1994	Andre Agassi
1993	Pete Sampras
1992	Stefan Edberg

Grand Slam Tournaments: All-Time Men's Champions (cont.)

United States Championships (cont.)

Year	Winner
1991	Stefan Edberg
1990	Pete Sampras
1989	Boris Becker
1988	Mats Wilander
1987	Ivan Lendl
1986	Ivan Lendl
1985	Ivan Lendl
1984	John McEnroe
1983	Jimmy Connors
1982	Jimmy Connors
1981	John McEnroe
1980	John McEnroe
1979	John McEnroe
1978	Jimmy Connors
1977	Guillermo Vilas
1976	Jimmy Connors
1975	Manuel Orantes
1974	Jimmy Connors
1973	John Newcombe
1972	Ilie Nastase
1971	Stan Smith
1970	Ken Rosewall
**1969	Stan Smith
1969	Rod Laver
*1968	Arthur Ashe
**1968	Arthur Ashe
1967	John Newcombe
1966	Fred Stolle
1965	Manuel Santana
1964	Roy Emerson
1963	Rafael Osuna
1962	Rod Laver
1961	Roy Emerson
1960	Neale Fraser
1959	Neale Fraser
1958	Ashley Cooper
1957	Mal Anderson
1956	Ken Rosewall
1955	Tony Trabert
1954	Vic Seixas
1953	Tony Trabert
1952	Frank Sedgman
1951	Frank Sedgman
1950	Arthur Larsen
1949	Pancho Gonzales
1948	Pancho Gonzales
1947	Jack Kramer
1946	Jack Kramer
1945	Frank Parker
1944	Frank Parker
1943	Joseph R. Hunt
1942	Fred R. Schroeder, Jr.
1941	Bobby Riggs
1940	Don McNeill
1939	Bobby Riggs
1938	Don Budge
1937	Don Budge
1936	Fred Perry
1935	Wilmer L. Allison
1934	Fred Perry
1933	Fred Perry
1932	Ellsworth Vines
1931	Ellsworth Vines

*Became Open (amateur and professional) in 1968.
**Separate amateur event held.

2003-04 MEN'S TIME LINE

January 26, 2003: Andre Agassi wins the Australian Open for the fourth time with a straight-set victory over Rainer Schuettler of Germany, 6–2, 6–2, 6–1.

March 9, 2003: Lleyton Hewitt of Australia defeats countryman Mark Philippoussis in a three-set final at the Franklin Templeton Tennis Classic, in Scottsdale, Arizona. The win is the first of two singles titles Hewitt won in 2003.

March 30, 2003: Andre Agassi of the U.S. wins the NASDAQ-100 Open for a tournament-record sixth time. He breaks the record of five, which was held by his wife, Steffi Graf.

April 27, 2003: Carlos Moya of Spain wins his 13th ATP title, at the Open Seat Godo, in Barcelona, Spain. It is the first ATP title he has won on home soil.

June 8, 2003: Juan Carlos Ferrero of Spain defeats Martin Verkerk of the Netherlands to win his first Grand Slam title, the French Open. Ferrero had lost in the men's final of the French Open the year before.

July 6, 2003: Roger Federer of Switzerland defeats Mark Philippoussis of Australia to win Wimbledon. He does not face a break point in the match and commits only nine unforced errors.

July 27, 2003: Andy Roddick of the U.S. wins his third title in five tournaments, the RCA Championships, in Indianapolis, Indiana.

September 7, 2003: Andy Roddick wins his first Grand Slam title, defeating Juan Carlos Ferrero in the U.S. Open. In the final, Roddick fires 23 aces and converts two of five break points.

November 16, 2003: Roger Federer wins the Tennis Masters Cup title in Houston, Texas, and finishes the year ranked Number 2. Andy Roddick is eliminated in the semi-finals of the tournament but finishes the year ranked Number 1.

February 1, 2004: Roger Federer clinches his second Grand Slam title, defeating Marat Safin of Russia in three sets at the Australian Open.

Grand Slam Tournaments: All-Time Men's Champions (cont.)

United States Championships (cont.)

Year	Winner
1930	John H. Doeg
1929	Bill Tilden
1928	Henri Cochet
1927	Rene Lacoste
1926	Rene Lacoste
1925	Bill Tilden
1924	Bill Tilden
1923	Bill Tilden
1922	Bill Tilden
1921	Bill Tilden
1920	Bill Tilden
1919	Bill Johnston
1918	R.L. Murray
1917	R.L. Murray
1916	Richard N. Williams
1915	Bill Johnston
1914	Richard N. Williams
1913	Maurice E. McLoughlin
1912	Maurice E. McLoughlin
1911	William A. Larned
1910	William A. Larned
1909	William A. Larned
1908	William A. Larned
1907	William A. Larned
1906	William J. Clothier
1905	Beals C. Wright
1904	Holcombe Ward
1903	H. Laurie Doherty
1902	William A. Larned
1901	William A. Larned
1900	Malcolm D. Whitman
1899	Malcolm D. Whitman
1898	Malcolm D. Whitman
1897	Robert D. Wrenn
1896	Robert D. Wrenn
1895	Frederick H. Hovey
1894	Robert D. Wrenn
1893	Robert D. Wrenn
1892	Oliver S. Campbell
1891	Oliver S. Campbell
1890	Oliver S. Campbell
1889	H. W. Slocum, Jr.
1888	H. W. Slocum, Jr.
1887	Richard D. Sears
1886	Richard D. Sears
1885	Richard D. Sears
1884	Richard D. Sears
1883	Richard D. Sears
1882	Richard D. Sears
1881	Richard D. Sears

Did You Know?

Andy Roddick of the U.S. holds the record for the fastest serve in tennis. He blasted a 153-mile-per-hour ace in London, England, in June 2004.

Legends

Pete Sampras, b. August 12, 1971, Washington, D.C. Sampras finished each year from 1993 through 1998 ranked Number 1 in the world. He is the all-time leader in men's Grand Slam singles titles (14). His powerful serve and brilliant serve-and-volley game made him arguably the best tennis player of all time. Sampras will be remembered most for his classy behavior. He rarely threw a temper tantrum or criticized a line judge. He was the perfect sport in victory and defeat. Sampras played his last match on September 8, 2002, and went out a winner by defeating longtime rival Andre Agassi for his fifth U.S. Open title.

Pete Sampras had a 14-4 record in Grand Slam finals in his 14-year career.

PHILIPPE MILLEREAU/DPPI/ICON SMI

Bjorn Borg, b. June 6, 1956, Sodertalje, Sweden. Borg won the French Open six times (1974-75, 1978-81) and Wimbledon five times (1976-80). He retired in 1983 with 57 singles championships. He was inducted into the International Tennis Hall of Fame in 1987. A baseliner with powerful ground strokes, Borg tried a comeback in 1991 but never made it past the first round of a tournament. He retired for good in 1993.

John McEnroe, b. February 16, 1959, Wiesbaden, Germany. The left-hander was known for his competitive fire and explosive temper. Mac was ranked in the Top 10 for 10 years of his 14-year career. His best season was 1984, when he won 13 of 15 singles championships. He won Wimbledon three times (1981, 1983-84) and the U.S. Open four times (1979-81, 1984).

Grand Slam Tournaments: All-Time Women's Champions

Australian Championships

Year	Winner
2004	Justine Henin-Hardenne
2003	Serena Williams
2002	Jennifer Capriati
2001	Jennifer Capriati
2000	Lindsay Davenport
1999	Martina Hingis
1998	Martina Hingis
1997	Martina Hingis
1996	Monica Seles
1995	Mary Pierce
1994	Steffi Graf
1993	Monica Seles
1992	Monica Seles
1991	Monica Seles
1990	Steffi Graf
1989	Steffi Graf
1988	Steffi Graf
1987 (Jan.)	Hana Mandlikova
1985 (Dec.)	Martina Navratilova
1984	Chris Evert Lloyd
1983	Martina Navratilova
1982	Chris Evert Lloyd
1981	Martina Navratilova
1980	Hana Mandlikova
1979	Barbara Jordan
1978	Chris O'Neil
1977 (Dec.)	Evonne Goolagong Cawley
1977 (Jan.)	Kerry Melville Reid
1976	Evonne Goolagong Cawley
1975	Evonne Goolagong
1974	Evonne Goolagong
1973	Margaret Smith Court
1972	Virginia Wade
1971	Margaret Smith Court
1970	Margaret Smith Court
* 1969	Margaret Smith Court
1968	Billie Jean King
1967	Nancy Richey
1966	Margaret Smith
1965	Margaret Smith
1964	Margaret Smith
1963	Margaret Smith
1962	Margaret Smith
1961	Margaret Smith
1960	Margaret Smith
1959	Mary Carter-Reitano
1958	Angela Mortimer
1957	Shirley Fry
1956	Mary Carter
1955	Beryl Penrose
1954	Thelma Long
1953	Maureen Connolly
1952	Thelma Long
1951	Nancye Wynne Bolton
1950	Louise Brough
1949	Doris Hart
1948	Nancye Wynne Bolton
1947	Nancye Wynne Bolton
1946	Nancye Wynne Bolton
1941-45	no tournament
1940	Nancye Wynne Bolton
1939	Emily Westacott
1938	Dorothy Bundy
1937	Nancye Wynne Bolton
1936	Joan Hartigan
1935	Dorothy Round
1934	Joan Hartigan
1933	Joan Hartigan
1932	Coral Buttsworth
1931	Coral Buttsworth
1930	Daphne Akhurst
1929	Daphne Akhurst
1928	Daphne Akhurst
1927	Esna Boyd
1926	Daphne Akhurst
1925	Daphne Akhurst
1924	Sylvia Lance
1923	Margaret Molesworth
1922	Margaret Molesworth

French Championships

Year	Winner
2004	Anastasia Myskina
2003	Justine Henin-Hardenne
2002	Serena Williams
2001	Jennifer Capriati
2000	Mary Pierce
1999	Steffi Graf
1998	Arantxa Sánchez-Vicario
1997	Iva Majoli
1996	Steffi Graf
1995	Steffi Graf
1994	Arantxa Sánchez-Vicario
1993	Steffi Graf
1992	Monica Seles
1991	Monica Seles
1990	Monica Seles
1989	Arantxa Sánchez-Vicario
1988	Steffi Graf
1987	Steffi Graf
1986	Chris Evert Lloyd
1985	Chris Evert Lloyd
1984	Martina Navratilova
1983	Chris Evert Lloyd
1982	Martina Navratilova
1981	Hana Mandlikova
1980	Chris Evert Lloyd
1979	Chris Evert Lloyd
1978	Virginia Ruzici
1977	Mima Jausovec
1976	Sue Barker
1975	Chris Evert
1974	Chris Evert
1973	Margaret Smith Court
1972	Billie Jean King
1971	Evonne Goolagong
1970	Margaret Smith Court
1969	Margaret Smith Court
** 1968	Nancy Richey
1967	Francoise Durr
1966	Ann Jones
1965	Lesley Turner
1964	Margaret Smith
1963	Lesley Turner
1962	Margaret Smith
1961	Ann Haydon
1960	Darlene Hard
1959	Christine Truman
1958	Zsuzsi Kormoczy
1957	Shirley Bloomer
1956	Althea Gibson
1955	Angela Mortimer
1954	Maureen Connolly
1953	Maureen Connolly
1952	Doris Hart
1951	Shirley Fry
1950	Doris Hart
1949	Margaret Osborne duPont
1948	Nelly Landry
1947	Patricia Todd
1946	Margaret Osborne
1940-45	no tournament
1939	Simone Mathieu
1938	Simone Mathieu
1937	Hilde Sperling
1936	Hilde Sperling
1935	Hilde Sperling
1934	Margaret Scriven
1933	Margaret Scriven
1932	Helen Wills Moody
1931	Cilly Aussem
1930	Helen Wills Moody
1929	Helen Wills
1928	Helen Wills
1927	Kea Bouman
1926	Suzanne Lenglen
† 1925	Suzanne Lenglen

Wimbledon Championships

Year	Winner
2004	Maria Sharapova
2003	Serena Williams
2002	Serena Williams
2001	Venus Williams
2000	Venus Williams
1999	Lindsay Davenport
1998	Jana Novotna
1997	Martina Hingis
1996	Steffi Graf
1995	Steffi Graf
1994	Conchita Martinez
1993	Steffi Graf
1992	Steffi Graf
1991	Steffi Graf
1990	Martina Navratilova
1989	Steffi Graf
1988	Steffi Graf
1987	Martina Navratilova
1986	Martina Navratilova
1985	Martina Navratilova
1984	Martina Navratilova
1983	Martina Navratilova
1982	Martina Navratilova
1981	Chris Evert Lloyd
1980	Evonne Goolagong Cawley
1979	Martina Navratilova
1978	Martina Navratilova
1977	Virginia Wade
1976	Chris Evert
1975	Billie Jean King
1974	Chris Evert
1973	Billie Jean King
1972	Billie Jean King
1971	Evonne Goolagong
1970	Margaret Smith Court
1969	Ann Haydon Jones
** 1968	Billie Jean King
1967	Billie Jean King

* Became Open (amateur and professional) in 1969.
** Became Open (amateur and professional) in 1968.
† 1925 was the first year in which players from all countries were allowed to compete.

Today's Stars

Justine Henin-Hardenne won two Grand Slam titles and six other tournaments in 2003.

SIMON BRUTY/SPORTS ILLUSTRATED

Justine Henin-Hardenne, b. June 1, 1982, Liege, Belgium. Henin-Hardenne began 2004 ranked Number 1. She won the French Open and U.S. Open in 2003 and kept up the pace by winning the Australian Open in 2004. Henin-Hardenne turned pro at age 17. At the start of 2004, she had won 14 WTA Tour singles titles.

Amelie Mauresmo, b. July 5, 1979, St. Germains en Laye, France. Despite fighting through various injuries in 2003, Mauresmo reached the quarterfinals of two Grand Slam events (French Open, U.S. Open) and finished the year with the Number 4 world ranking. At the start of 2004, she had won 10 WTA singles titles.

Serena Williams, b. September 26, 1981, Saginaw, Michigan. Williams has dominated women's tennis for the past two years. She began 2004 with 23 career singles titles and the Number 3 ranking. Williams's most impressive season was 2002, when she won three Grand Slam tournaments (French Open, U.S. Open, Wimbledon). She continued her winning ways by earning the Australian Open crown in 2003. Her four straight Grand Slam victories were dubbed the "Serena Slam." Williams was ranked Number 1 for 57 straight weeks from July 2002 through August 2003.

Fast Fact: Steffi Graf of Germany is the only player, male or female, to win each of the four Grand Slam singles titles at least four times.

Grand Slam Tournaments: All-Time Women's Champions (cont.)

Wimbledon Championships (cont.)

Year	Winner
1966	Billie Jean King
1965	Margaret Smith
1964	Maria Bueno
1963	Margaret Smith
1962	Karen Hantze Susman
1961	Angela Mortimer
1960	Maria Bueno
1959	Maria Bueno
1958	Althea Gibson
1957	Althea Gibson
1956	Shirley Fry
1955	Louise Brough
1954	Maureen Connolly
1953	Maureen Connolly
1952	Maureen Connolly
1951	Doris Hart
1950	Louise Brough
1949	Louise Brough
1948	Louise Brough
1947	Margaret Osborne
1946	Pauline Betz
1940-45	no tournament
1939	Alice Marble
1938	Helen Wills Moody
1937	Dorothy Round
1936	Helen Jacobs
1935	Helen Wills Moody
1934	Dorothy Round
1933	Helen Wills Moody
1932	Helen Wills Moody
1931	Cilly Aussem
1930	Helen Wills Moody
1929	Helen Wills
1928	Helen Wills
1927	Helen Wills
1926	Kathleen McKane Godfree
1925	Suzanne Lenglen
1924	Kathleen McKane
1923	Suzanne Lenglen
1922	Suzanne Lenglen
1921	Suzanne Lenglen
1920	Suzanne Lenglen
1919	Suzanne Lenglen
1915-18	no tournament
1914	Dorothea Lambert Chambers
1913	Dorothea Lambert Chambers
1912	Ethel Larcombe
1911	Dorothea Lambert Chambers
1910	Dorothea Lambert Chambers
1909	Dora Boothby
1908	Charlotte Cooper Sterry
1907	May Sutton
1906	Dorothea Douglass
1905	May Sutton
1904	Dorothea Douglass
1903	Dorothea Douglass
1902	Muriel Robb
1901	Charlotte Cooper Sterry
1900	Blanche Bingley Hillyard
1899	Blanche Bingley Hillyard

Grand Slam Tournaments: All-Time Women's Champions (cont.)

Wimbledon Championships (cont.)

Year	Winner
1898	Charlotte Cooper
1897	Blanche Bingley Hillyard
1896	Charlotte Cooper
1895	Charlotte Cooper
1894	Blanche Bingley Hillyard
1893	Charlotte Dod
1892	Charlotte Dod
1891	Charlotte Dod
1890	Lena Rice
1889	Blanche Bingley Hillyard
1888	Charlotte Dod
1887	Charlotte Dod
1886	Blanche Bingley
1885	Maud Watson
1884	Maud Watson

United States Championships

Year	Winner
2003	Justine Henin-Hardenne
2002	Serena Williams
2001	Venus Williams
2000	Venus Williams
1999	Serena Williams
1998	Lindsay Davenport
1997	Martina Hingis
1996	Steffi Graf
1995	Steffi Graf
1994	Arantxa Sánchez-Vicario
1993	Steffi Graf
1992	Monica Seles
1991	Monica Seles
1990	Gabriela Sabatini
1989	Steffi Graf
1988	Steffi Graf
1987	Martina Navratilova
1986	Martina Navratilova
1985	Hana Mandlikova
1984	Martina Navratilova
1983	Martina Navratilova
1982	Chris Evert Lloyd
1981	Tracy Austin
1980	Chris Evert Lloyd
1979	Tracy Austin
1978	Chris Evert
1977	Chris Evert
1976	Chris Evert
1975	Chris Evert
1974	Billie Jean King
1973	Margaret Smith Court
1972	Billie Jean King
1971	Billie Jean King
1970	Margaret Smith Court
1969	Margaret Smith Court
*1968	Virginia Wade
1967	Billie Jean King
1966	Maria Bueno
1965	Margaret Smith
1964	Maria Bueno
1963	Maria Bueno
1962	Margaret Smith
1961	Darlene Hard
1960	Darlene Hard
1959	Maria Bueno
1958	Althea Gibson
1957	Althea Gibson
1956	Shirley Fry
1955	Doris Hart
1954	Doris Hart
1953	Maureen Connolly
1952	Maureen Connolly
1951	Maureen Connolly
1950	Margaret Osborne duPont
1949	Margaret Osborne duPont
1948	Margaret Osborne duPont
1947	Louise Brough
1946	Pauline Betz
1945	Sarah Palfrey Cooke
1944	Pauline Betz
1943	Pauline Betz
1942	Pauline Betz
1941	Sarah Palfrey Cooke
1940	Alice Marble
1939	Alice Marble
1938	Alice Marble
1937	Anita Lizane
1936	Alice Marble
1935	Helen Jacobs
1934	Helen Jacobs
1933	Helen Jacobs

*Became Open (amateur and professional) in 1968.

2003-04 WOMEN'S TIME LINE

January 25, 2003: Serena Williams defeats her sister Venus, 7–6 (7–4), 3–6, 6–4, to win the Australian Open. Her fourth-straight Grand Slam victory in two years completes the "Serena Slam."

June 7, 2003: Justine Henin-Hardenne of Belgium wins her first Grand Slam singles championship, at the French Open, with a 6–0, 6–4 victory over fellow Belgian Kim Clijsters.

July 5, 2003: Serena Williams wins her second-straight Wimbledon title, defeating her sister Venus, 4–6, 6–4, 6–2.

July 6, 2003: Martina Navratilova ties Billy Jean King's record for most Wimbledon championships (20) by winning the mixed-doubles title with partner Leander Paes. The 46-year-old Navratilova becomes the oldest champion in Wimbledon history.

July 8, 2003: Serena Williams completes a full year as the world's Number 1-ranked player.

September 9, 2003: Justine Henin-Hardenne defeats Kim Clijsters, 7–5, 6–1, to win the women's singles championship at the U.S. Open. It is the first time two players from Belgium compete in a U.S. Open final.

September 28, 2003: Althea Gibson dies at age 76. Gibson was the first African American to compete at the U.S. Open (1950) and Wimbledon (1951).

January 31, 2004: Justine Henin-Hardenne wins her third Grand Slam singles title by defeating Kim Clijsters at the Australian Open.

April 18, 2004: Venus Williams wins the Family Circle Cup title, her first tournament victory in 14 months.

Grand Slam Tournaments: All-Time Women's Champions (cont.)

United States Championships (cont.)

Year	Winner
1932	Helen Jacobs
1931	Helen Wills Moody
1930	Betty Nuthall
1929	Helen Wills
1928	Helen Wills
1927	Helen Wills
1926	Molla Bjurstedt Mallory
1925	Helen Wills
1924	Helen Wills
1923	Helen Wills
1922	Molla Bjurstedt Mallory
1921	Molla Bjurstedt Mallory
1920	Molla Bjurstedt Mallory
1919	Hazel Hotchkiss Wightman
1918	Molla Bjurstedt
1917	Molla Bjurstedt
1916	Molla Bjurstedt
1915	Molla Bjurstedt
1914	Mary K. Browne
1913	Mary K. Browne
1912	Mary K. Browne
1911	Hazel Hotchkiss
1910	Hazel Hotchkiss
1909	Hazel Hotchkiss
1908	Maud Barger-Wallach
1907	Evelyn Sears
1906	Helen Homans
1905	Elisabeth Moore
1904	May Sutton
1903	Elisabeth Moore
**1902	Marion Jones
1901	Elisabeth Moore
1900	Myrtle McAteer
1899	Marion Jones
1898	Juliette Atkinson
1897	Juliette Atkinson
1896	Elisabeth Moore
1895	Juliette Atkinson
1894	Helen Hellwig
1893	Aline Terry
1892	Mabel Cahill
1891	Mabel Cahill
1890	Ellen C. Roosevelt
1889	Bertha L. Townsend
1888	Bertha L. Townsend
1887	Ellen Hansell

**Five-set final abolished.

Legends

Chris Evert, b. December 21, 1954, Fort Lauderdale, Florida. Evert was the queen of the baseline. Her powerful forehand and backhand rarely missed. She retired in 1989 after a 17-year career, with a record 157 singles championships. Her win-loss ratio of 1,309-to-146 is the highest winning percentage (90 percent) in pro tennis history. Evert won 18 Grand Slam titles and was ranked Number 1 in 1975-77 and 1980-81.

WALTER IOOSS JR./SPORTS ILLUSTRATED

Chris Evert won at least one Grand Slam title per year for 13 years (1974-86).

Evonne Goolagong Cawley, b. July 31, 1951, Griffith, New South Wales, Australia. Cawley is the only Aborigine (native Australian) to become an international tennis star. She won the singles championships at Wimbledon (1971, 1980), the French Open (1971), and the Australian Open (1974-77). Cawley's nickname was "Sunshine Supergirl" because of her friendly and gracious manner. She was inducted into the International Tennis Hall of Fame in 1988.

Maureen Connolly, b. September 17, 1934, San Diego, California; d. June 21, 1969, Dallas, Texas. Nicknamed Little Mo, the tiny right-hander (5' 4", 120 pounds) had fast and furious baseline strokes. In 1953, she became the first women's player to complete the Grand Slam by winning all four major tournaments in one year. Connolly's career was cut short in 1954 after only four years as a pro. She severely injured her leg when she was hit by a truck while riding a horse. She was inducted into the International Tennis Hall of Fame in 1968 and died of cancer a year later, at age 34.

Fast Fact: Serena Williams is one of only five women to hold all four Grand Slam women's singles titles at the same time. The others: Maureen Connolly, Margaret Smith Court, Martina Navratilova, and Steffi Graf.

CLIVE BRUNSKILL/GETTY IMAGES

Steffi Graf retired in 1999 with 22 Grand Slam singles titles.

All-Time Grand Slam Singles Champions

MEN

Player	Aus.	French	Wim.	U.S.	Total
Pete Sampras	2	0	7	5	14
Roy Emerson	6	2	2	2	12
Bjorn Borg	0	6	5	0	11
Rod Laver	3	2	4	2	11
Bill Tilden	†	0	3	7	10
Jimmy Connors	1	0	2	5	8
Ivan Lendl	2	3	0	3	8
Fred Perry	1	1	3	3	8
Ken Rosewall	4	2	0	2	8
*Andre Agassi	4	1	1	2	8
Henri Cochet	†	4	2	1	7
Rene Lacoste	†	3	2	2	7
Bill Larned	†	†	0	7	7
John McEnroe	0	0	3	4	7
John Newcombe	2	0	3	2	7
Willie Renshaw	†	†	7	†	7
Dick Sears	†	†	0	7	7

*Active player. †Did not compete.

WOMEN

Player	Aus.	French	Wim.	U.S.	Total
Margaret Smith Court	11	5	3	5	24
Steffi Graf	4	6	7	5	22
Helen Wills Moody	†	4	8	7	19
Chris Evert	2	7	3	6	18
Martina Navratilova	3	2	9	4	18
Billie Jean King	1	1	6	4	12
Maureen Connolly	1	2	3	3	9
*Monica Seles	4	3	0	2	9
Suzanne Lenglen	†	#2	6	0	8
Molla Bjurstedt Mallory	†	†	0	8	8
Maria Bueno	0	0	3	4	7
Evonne Goolagong	4	1	2	0	7
Dorothea L. Chambers	†	†	7	0	7
Nancye Wynne Bolton	6	0	0	0	6
Louise Brough	1	0	4	1	6
Margaret Osborne duPont	†	2	1	3	6
Doris Hart	1	2	1	2	6
Blanche Bingley Hillyard	†	†	6	†	6

*Active player. †Did not compete.

#Suzanne Lenglen also won four singles titles at the French Championships before 1925, when the tournament was first opened to players from all nations.

Did You Know?

In 1956, Althea Gibson of the United States became the first African American to win a Wimbledon championship. She won the doubles title with Angela Buxton of England. She also won the French Open singles title that year.

Trivia Challenge

Tennis returned to the Summer Olympics in 1988, in Seoul, South Korea. When was the last time tennis was an Olympic medal sport?

In 1924, at the Summer Olympics in Paris, France

SWIMMING

By dominating men's swimming in 2003, 18-year-old Michael Phelps of the U.S. set the stage for a showdown with sensation Ian Thorpe of Australia at the 2004 Summer Olympics, in Athens, Greece.

From April through August 2003, Phelps set eight world records, more than anyone since 1972, when Mark Spitz of the U.S. set nine world marks. Phelps already held four world records (100-meter butterfly, 200-meter butterfly, 200-meter individual medley (IM), 400-meter individual medley). He did the bulk of his gold mining at the 2003 world championships, in Barcelona, Spain: He won three gold medals, broke five world records, and beat Thorpe by two body lengths in the 200 IM. It was their first head-to-head meeting in a world or Olympic race.

Aaron Peirsol of the U.S. also continued to be a strong international contender. The 20-year-old won gold medals in the 100-meter and 200-meter backstroke at the 2003 worlds. He is the world-record holder in the 200 back.

On the women's side, 20-year-old Kaitlin Sandeno of the U.S. won six medals at the U.S. summer nationals, including gold medals in the 200-meter fly and the 200-meter and 400-meter IM. In March 2004, the USC junior broke the U.S. record in the 400 IM on her way to the gold medal at the NCAA championships. She also won the 200 IM gold.

UCLA senior Natalie Coughlin won the 100-meter backstroke and the 100-meter fly and placed third in the 200-meter back at the NCAA's. It was the third year in a row she medaled at the championships. She was also named NCAA Swimmer of the Year for the third-straight time.

Internationally, Sachiko Yamada of Japan came on strong. In December 2003, she won a gold medal in the 400-meter free and a silver medal in the 200 free at the U.S. Open Swimming Championships. In February 2004, she won gold medals in the 400, 800, and 1,500 free at the U.S. spring nationals.

From April through August 2003, 18-year-old Michael Phelps set eight world records.

HAMISH BLAIR/GETTY IMAGES

2003-04 Major Competitions—Men

U.S. National Championships (Spring)

ORLANDO, FLORIDA, FEBRUARY 10–14, 2004

Event	Swimmer, Team	Time
50-meter freestyle	Roland Schoeman, University of Arizona	22.12
100-meter freestyle	Michael Phelps, North Baltimore	49.05
200-meter freestyle	Michael Phelps, North Baltimore	1:46.47
400-meter freestyle	Chad Carvin, Mission Viejo	3:48.92
800-meter freestyle	Larsen Jensen, Mission Viejo	7:53.29
1,500-meter freestyle	David Davies, Great Britain	15:02.63
100-meter backstroke	Randall Bal, unattached	54.78
200-meter backstroke	Michael Phelps, North Baltimore	1:55.30
100-meter breaststroke	Vladislav Polyakov, Coral Springs	1:01.98
200-meter breaststroke	Vladislav Polyakov, Coral Springs	2:14.36
100-meter butterfly	Michael Phelps, North Baltimore	51.84
200-meter butterfly	Thomas Malchow, Club Wolverine	1:57.06
200-meter individual medley	Michael Phelps, North Baltimore	1:56.80
400-meter individual medley	Kevin Clements, North Baltimore	4:18.91
400-meter medley relay	Irvine Novaquatics	3:43.53
400-meter freestyle relay	Irvine Novaquatics	3:19.74
800-meter freestyle relay	The Danish Swimming Federation	7:26.72

U.S. National Championships (Summer)

COLLEGE PARK, MARYLAND, AUGUST 5–9, 2003

Event	Swimmer, Team	Time
50-meter freestyle	Neil Walker, Circle C Swimming	22.59
100-meter freestyle	Michael Phelps, North Baltimore	49.19
200-meter freestyle	Michael Phelps, North Baltimore	1:45.99 (A)
400-meter freestyle	Michael Phelps, North Baltimore	3:46.73 (A)
800-meter freestyle	Larsen Jensen, Mission Viejo	7:57.35
1,500-meter freestyle	Larsen Jensen, Mission Viejo	15:11.81
100-meter backstroke	Randall Bal, Stanford Swim	54.63
200-meter backstroke	Michael Phelps, North Baltimore	1:56.10
100-meter breaststroke	Ed Moses, Curl-Burke SC	1:01.11
200-meter breaststroke	Gary Marshall, Stanford Swim	2:13.28
100-meter butterfly	Eugene Botes, Big Cat Aquatics	53.20
200-meter butterfly	Brian Johns, Canada	1:59.29
200-meter individual medley	Michael Phelps, North Baltimore	1:55.94 (WR)
400-meter individual medley	Brian Johns, Canada	4:17.04
400-meter medley relay	Circle C Swimming	3:42.61
400-meter freestyle relay	Circle C Swimming	3:21.25
800-meter freestyle relay	Mission Viejo	7:24.43

2003-04 Major Competitions—Women

U.S. National Championships (Spring)

ORLANDO, FLORIDA, FEBRUARY 10–14, 2004

Event	Swimmer, Team	Time
50-meter freestyle	Michelle Engelsman, unattached	25.17
100-meter freestyle	Lindsay Benko, Trojan SC	55.43
200-meter freestyle	Lindsay Benko, Trojan SC	1:58.62
400-meter freestyle	Sachiko Yamada, Japan	4:09.37
800-meter freestyle	Sachiko Yamada, Japan	8:25.62
1,500-meter freestyle	Sachiko Yamada, Japan	16:06.13
100-meter backstroke	Haley Cope, unattached	1:01.92
200-meter backstroke	Pamela Hanson, Tennessee Aquatics	2:13.56
100-meter breaststroke	Amanda Beard, Tucson Ford	1:08.28
200-meter breaststroke	Amanda Beard, Tucson Ford	2:24.97
100-meter butterfly	Martina Moravcova, Southern Methodist	58.76
200-meter butterfly	Noelle Bassi, Berkeley Aquatic	2:10.96
200-meter individual medley	Amanda Beard, Tucson Ford	2:13.11
400-meter individual medley	Katie Hoff, North Baltimore	4:42.32
400-meter medley relay	Irvine Novaquatics	4:09.25
400-meter freestyle relay	Canada	3:45.38
800-meter freestyle relay	The Danish Swimming Federation	8:13.56

KEY (A)=American Record; (WR)=World Record

Trivia Challenge

Who was the first woman to swim the 100-meter backstroke in under one minute?

Natalie Coughlin of the U.S., in 2002 (59:58)

U.S. National Championships (Summer)

COLLEGE PARK, MARYLAND, AUGUST 5–9, 2003

Event	Swimmer, Team	Time
50-meter freestyle	Malia Metella, France	25.18
100-meter freestyle	Sarah Wanezek, Texas Aquatics	55.73
200-meter freestyle	Brittany Reimer, Canada	2:00.62
400-meter freestyle	Kalyn Keller, Trojan SC	4:10.68
800-meter freestyle	Kalyn Keller, Trojan SC	8:31.54
1,500-meter freestyle	Kalyn Keller, Trojan SC	16:08.64
100-meter backstroke	Lauren Rogers, Terrapins ST	1:02.50
200-meter backstroke	Jennifer Fratesi, Canada	2:12.47
100-meter breaststroke	Megan Quann, So. Sound Titan	1:08.80
200-meter breaststroke	Caroline Bruce, Wichita SC	2:27.88
100-meter butterfly	Emily Goetsch, North Baltimore	59.87
200-meter butterfly	Kaitlin Sandeno, Trojan SC	2:08.78
200-meter individual medley	Kaitlin Sandeno, Trojan SC	2:12.97
400-meter individual medley	Kaitlin Sandeno, Trojan SC	4:40.82
400-meter medley relay	Novaquatics	4:12.11
400-meter freestyle relay	Texas Aquatics	3:44.97
800-meter freestyle relay	Trojan Swim Club	8:10.79

2003-04 TIME LINE

June 28, 2003: Aaron Peirsol of the U.S. beats countryman Michael Phelps by 2.12 seconds in the 200-meter backstroke at a Grand Prix Series meet. One day later, Peirsol takes gold in the 100-meter back, defeating Randall Bal of the U.S.

July 22, 2003: Aaron Peirsol and his sister Hayley become the first siblings to win medals at the same swimming world championships. Hayley is second in the 1,500-meter freestyle. Thirty minutes later, Aaron wins the 100-meter backstroke.

July 27, 2003: Michael Phelps breaks his fifth world record at the same FINA world championships when he wins the 400-meter individual medley (IM) on the final day of competition. Mark Spitz of the U.S. broke seven world records at the 1972 Summer Olympics.

August 9, 2003: Continuing his domination in the pool, Michael Phelps becomes the first person to win five events at a national championship when he earns five gold medals at the U.S. summer nationals. He sets three U.S. records and one world record at the meet.

January 31, 2004: Three-time U.S. Olympian Jenny Thompson makes it four-for-four at the FINA Swimming World Cup. The 31-year-old wins the gold in the 100-meter freestyle and 50-meter butterfly after winning gold in the 100-meter fly and 50-meter free the night before.

February 14, 2004: Amanda Beard of the U.S. and Sachiko Yamada of Japan win three gold medals apiece as the 2004 spring nationals end, in Orlando, Florida. Beard wins the 100-meter and 200-meter breaststroke and 200-meter IM. Yamada wins the 400-meter, 800-meter, and 1,500-meter freestyle. Michael Phelps wins gold in all five events he competes in (200-meter IM, 200-meter back, 100-meter and 200-meter free, and 100-meter fly).

March 20, 2004: Organizers of the 2004 Summer Olympics announce that because of construction delays, there isn't enough time to build a roof over the swimming venue. It will be the first time since 1992 that Olympic swimming events will be held outdoors.

August 14, 2004: The swimming competition begins at the 2004 Summer Olympics, in Athens, Greece.

World and American Records—Men

Freestyle

Event	Time	Record Holder	Date	Site
50 meters	21.64	Alexander Popov, Russia (WR)	6-16-00	Moscow, Russia
	21.76	Gary Hall, Jr. (A)	8-15-00	Indianapolis, Indiana
100 meters	47.84	Pieter van den Hoogenband, Netherlands (WR)	9-19-00	Sydney, Australia
	48.17	Jason Lezak (A)	7-10-04	Long Beach, California
200 meters	1:44.06	Ian Thorpe, Australia (WR)	7-25-01	Fukuoka, Japan
	1:45.32	Michael Phelps (A)	8-16-04	Athens, Greece
400 meters	3:40.08	Ian Thorpe, Australia (WR)	7-30-02	Manchester, England
	3:44.11	Klete Keller (A)	8-14-04	Athens, Greece
800 meters	7:39.16	Ian Thorpe, Australia (WR)	7-24-01	Fukuoka, Japan
	7:48.09	Larsen Jensen (A)	7-25-03	Barcelona, Spain
1,500 meters	14:34.56	Grant Hackett, Australia (WR)	7-29-01	Fukuoka, Japan
	14:45.29	Larsen Jensen (A)	8-21-04	Athens, Greece

Backstroke

Event	Time	Record Holder	Date	Site
50 meters	24.80	Thomas Rupprath, Germany (WR)	7-27-03	Barcelona, Spain
	24.99	Lenny Krayzelburg (A)	8-28-99	Sydney, Australia
100 meters	53.45	Aaron Peirsol (WR, A)	8-21-04	Athens, Greece
200 meters	1:54.75	Aaron Peirsol (WR, A)	7-12-04	Long Beach, California

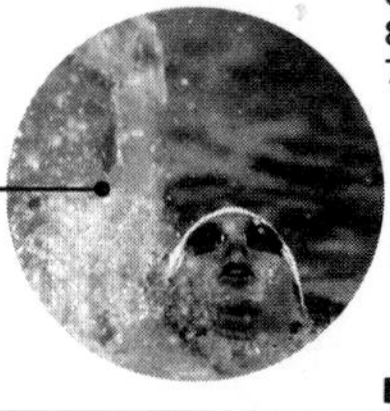

Aaron Peirsol, United States

VICTOR FRAILE/REUTERS

Breaststroke

Event	Time	Record Holder	Date	Site
50 meters	27.18	Oleg Lisogor, Ukraine (WR)	8-2-02	Berlin, Germany
	27.39	Ed Moses (A)	3-31-01	Austin, Texas
100 meters	59.30	Brendan Hansen (WR, A)	7-8-04	Long Beach, California
200 meters	2:09.04	Brendan Hansen (WR, A)	7-11-04	Long Beach, California

Butterfly

Event	Time	Record Holder	Date	Site
50 meters	23.30	Ian Crocker (WR, A)	2-29-04	Austin, Texas
100 meters	50.76	Ian Crocker (WR, A)	7-13-04	Long Beach, California
200 meters	1:53.93	Michael Phelps (WR, A)	7-22-03	Barcelona, Spain

Individual Medley

Event	Time	Record Holder	Date	Site
200 meters	1:55.94	Michael Phelps (WR, A)	8-9-03	College Park, Maryland
400 meters	4:08.26	Michael Phelps (WR, A)	8-14-04	Athens, Greece

Relays

Event	Time	Record Holder	Date	Site
400-meter medley	3:30.68	United States (WR, A) (Aaron Peirsol, Brendan Hansen, Ian Crocker, Jason Lezak)	8-21-04	Athens, Greece
400-meter freestyle	3:13.17	South Africa (WR) (Lyndon Ferns, Ryk Neethling, Roland Schoeman, Darian Townsend)	8-15-04	Athens, Greece
	3:13.86	United States (A) (Anthony Ervin, Neil Walker, Jason Lezak, Gary Hall, Jr.)	9-16-00	Sydney, Australia
800-meter freestyle	7:04.66	Australia (WR) (Grant Hackett, Michael Klim, Bill Kirby, Ian Thorpe)	7-27-01	Fukuoka, Japan
	7:07.33	United States (A) (Michael Phelps, Ryan Lochte, Peter Vanderkaay, Klete Keller)	8-17-04	Athens, Greece

KEY (A)=American Record; (WR)=World Record

Did You Know?

At the 2003 worlds, Aaron and Hayley Peirsol became the first siblings to win medals at the same swimming world championships. Aaron won a gold medal and Hayley won a silver medal.

World and American Records—Women

Freestyle

Event	Time	Record Holder	Date	Site
50 meters	24.13	Inge de Bruijn, Netherlands (WR)	9-22-00	Sydney, Australia
	24.63	Dara Torres (A)	9-23-00	Sydney, Australia
100 meters	53.52	Jodie Henry, Australia (WR)	8-18-04	Athens, Greece
	53.99	Natalie Coughlin (A)	8-29-02	Yokohama, Japan
200 meters	1:56.64	Franziska van Almsick, Germany (WR)	8-3-02	Berlin, Germany
	1:57.41	Lindsay Benko (A)	7-24-03	Barcelona, Spain
400 meters	4:03.85	Janet Evans (WR, A)	9-22-88	Seoul, South Korea
800 meters	8:16.22	Janet Evans (WR, A)	8-20-89	Tokyo, Japan
1,500 meters	14:45.29	Janet Evans (WR, A)	8-21-04	Athens, Greece

AL BELLO/GETTY IMAGES

Natalie Coughlin, United States

Backstroke

Event	Time	Record Holder	Date	Site
50 meters	28.25	Sandra Volker, Germany (WR)	6-17-00	Berlin, Germany
	28.49	Natalie Coughlin (A)	7-23-01	Fukuoka, Japan
100 meters	53.45	Aaron Peirsol (WR, A)	8-21-04	Athens, Greece
200 meters	2:06.62	Krisztina Egerszegi, Hungary (WR)	8-25-91	Athens, Greece
	2:08.53	Natalie Coughlin (A)	8-16-02	Fort Lauderdale, Florida

Breaststroke

Event	Time	Record Holder	Date	Site
50 meters	30.57	Zoe Baker, Great Britain (WR)	7-30-02	Manchester, England
	31.34	Megan Quann (A)	8-11-00	Indianapolis, Indiana
100 meters	1:06.37	Leisel Jones, Australia (WR)	7-21-03	Barcelona, Spain
	1:07.05	Megan Quann (A)	9-18-00	Sydney, Australia
200 meters	2:22.44	Amanda Beard (WR, A)	7-12-04	Long Beach, California

Butterfly

Event	Time	Record Holder	Date	Site
50 meters	25.57	Anna-Karin Kammerling, Sweden (WR)	7-30-02	Berlin, Germany
	26.00	Jenny Thompson (A)	7-26-03	Barcelona, Spain
100 meters	56.61	Inge de Bruijn, Netherlands (WR)	9-17-00	Sydney, Australia
	57.58	Dara Torres (A)	8-9-00	Indianapolis, Indiana
200 meters	2:05.78	Otylia Jedrejczak, Poland (WR)	8-4-02	Berlin, Germany
	2:05.88	Misty Hyman (A)	9-20-00	Sydney, Australia

Individual Medley

Event	Time	Record Holder	Date	Site
200 meters	2:09.72	Yanyan Wu, China (WR)	10-17-97	Shanghai, China
	2:11.70	Amanda Beard (A)	8-17-04	Athens, Greece
400 meters	4:33.59	Yana Klochkova, Ukraine (WR)	9-16-00	Sydney, Australia
	4:34.95	Kaitlin Sandeno (A)	8-14-04	Athens, Greece

Relays

Event	Time	Record Holder	Date	Site
400-meter medley	3:57.32	Australia (WR) (Giann Rooney, Liesel Jones, Petria Thomas, Jodie Henry)	8-21-04	Athens, Greece
	3:58.30	United States (A) (B.J. Bedford, Megan Quann, Jenny Thompson, Dara Torres)	9-23-00	Sydney, Australia
400-meter freestyle	3:35.94	Australia (WR) (Jodie Henry, Lisbeth Lenton, Alice Mills, Petria Thomas)	8-14-04	Athens, Greece
	3:36.39	United States (A) (Natalie Coughlin, Kara Lynn Joyce, Jenny Thompson, Amanda Weir)	8-14-04	Athens, Greece
800-meter freestyle	7:55.47	East Germany (WR) (Manuela Stellmach, Astrid Strauss, Anke Mohring, Heike Friedrich)	8-18-87	Strasbourg, France
	7:55.70	United States (A) (Lindsay Benko, Rachel Komisarz, Rhi Jeffrey, Diana Munz)	7-24-03	Barcelona, Spain

Legends

Matt Biondi won a total of 11 medals at three Olympics (1984, 1988, 1992).

RUSSEL McPHEDRAN/AP

Matt Biondi, b. October 8, 1965, Palo Alto, California. Biondi won seven medals (five gold, one silver, one bronze) at the 1988 Games. He became America's most decorated swimmer since Mark Spitz, who won seven medals at the 1972 Games. Two of Biondi's golds came in the 50-meter and 100-meter freestyle events. He won the other three in the 400-meter free, 400-meter medley, and 800-meter free relays. He was second in the 100-meter butterfly and third in the 200-meter free. Biondi returned to the Olympics in 1992, winning two gold medals (400-meter free and 400-meter medley relays) and a silver (50-meter free).

Mary T. Meagher, b. October 27, 1964, Louisville, Kentucky. Meagher was nicknamed "Madame Butterfly" because she held the world records in the 100-meter and 200-meter butterfly events for almost 20 years. She set her first world record — in the 200-meter fly — in 1979, as a 14-year-old. The U.S. did not compete in the 1980 Summer Olympics, but her qualifying times in both fly events at the U.S. Olympic trials were faster than those of the Olympic gold medalists. At the 1984 Games, she won gold medals in the 100-meter fly, 200-meter fly, and 400-meter medley relay. At the 1988 Games, Meagher earned a bronze in the 200-meter fly.

Michael Gross, b. June 17, 1964, Frankfurt, West Germany. The 6' 6" Gross was called "The Albatross" because his massive wingspan covered almost an entire swimming lane. He set his first world record — in the 200-meter freestyle — in 1983, at age 19. Over the next three years, he broke that record four more times and set six other world records. Gross competed in the Summer Olympics in 1984 and 1988. He had the most success in 1984, when he won gold medals in the 200-meter free and 100-meter butterfly and a silver in the 200-meter fly.

World Championship Results—Men

50-meter freestyle

1973-82	Event not held	
1986	Tom Jager, United States	22.49
1991	Tom Jager, United States	22.16
1994	Alexander Popov, Russia	22.17
1998	Bill Pilczuk, United States	22.29
2001	Anthony Ervin, United States	22.09
2003	Alexander Popov, Russia	21.92

100-meter freestyle

1973	Jim Montgomery, United States	51.70
1975	Andy Coan, United States	51.25
1978	David McCagg, United States	50.24
1982	Jorg Woithe, East Germany	50.18
1986	Matt Biondi, United States	48.94
1991	Matt Biondi, United States	49.18
1994	Alexander Popov, Russia	49.12
1998	Alexander Popov, Russia	48.93
2001	Anthony Ervin, United States	48.33
2003	Alexander Popov, Russia	48.42

200-meter freestyle

1973	Jim Montgomery, United States	1:53.02
1975	Tim Shaw, United States	1:51.04
1978	Billy Forrester, United States	1:51.02
1982	Michael Gross, West Germany	1:49.84
1986	Michael Gross, West Germany	1:47.92
1991	Giorgio Lamberti, Italy	1:47.27
1994	Antti Kasvio, Finland	1:47.32
1998	Michael Klim, Australia	1:47.41
2001	Ian Thorpe, Australia	1:44.06
2003	Ian Thorpe, Australia	1:45.14

400-meter freestyle

1973	Rick DeMont, United States	3:58.18
1975	Tim Shaw, United States	3:54.88
1978	Vladimir Salnikov, U.S.S.R.	3:51.94
1982	Vladimir Salnikov, U.S.S.R.	3:51.30
1986	Rainer Henkel, West Germany	3:50.05
1991	Joerg Hoffman, Germany	3:48.04
1994	Kieran Perkins, Australia	3:43.80
1998	Ian Thorpe, Australia	3:46.29
2001	Ian Thorpe, Australia	3:40.17
2003	Ian Thorpe, Australia	3:42.58

1,500-meter freestyle

1973	Stephen Holland, Australia	15:31.85
1975	Tim Shaw, United States	15:28.92
1978	Vladimir Salnikov, U.S.S.R.	15:03.99
1982	Vladimir Salnikov, U.S.S.R.	15:01.77
1986	Rainer Henkel, West Germany	15:05.31
1991	Joerg Hoffman, Germany	14:50.36
1994	Kieran Perkins, Australia	14:50.52
1998	Grant Hackett, Australia	14:51.70
2001	Grant Hackett, Australia	14:34.56
2003	Grant Hackett, Australia	14:43.14

World Championship Results—Men (cont.)

50-meter backstroke

1973-98	Event not held	
2001	Randall Bal, United States	25.34
2003	Thomas Rupprath, Germany	24.80

100-meter backstroke

1973	Roland Matthes, East Germany	57.47
1975	Roland Matthes, East Germany	58.15
1978	Bob Jackson, United States	56.36
1982	Dirk Richter, East Germany	55.95
1986	Igor Polianski, U.S.S.R.	55.58
1991	Jeff Rouse, United States	55.23
1994	Martin Zubero, Spain	55.17
1998	Lenny Krayzelburg, United States	55.00
2001	Matt Welsh, Australia	54.31
2003	Aaron Peirsol, United States	53.61

200-meter backstroke

1973	Roland Matthes, East Germany	2:01.87
1975	Zoltan Varraszto, Hungary	2:05.05
1978	Jesse Vassallo, United States	2:02.16
1982	Rick Carey, United States	2:00.82
1986	Igor Polianski, U.S.S.R.	1:58.78
1991	Martin Zubero, Spain	1:59.52
1994	Vladimir Selkov, Russia	1:57.42
1998	Lenny Krayzelburg, United States	1:58.84
2001	Aaron Peirsol, United States	1:57.13
2003	Aaron Peirsol, United States	1:55.92

50-meter breaststroke

1973-98	Event not held	
2001	Oleg Lisogor, Ukraine	27.52
2003	James Gibson, Great Britain	27.56

100-meter breaststroke

1973	John Hencken, United States	1:04.02
1975	David Wilkie, Great Britain	1:04.26
1978	Walter Kusch, West Germany	1:03.56
1982	Steve Lundquist, United States	1:02.75
1986	Victor Davis, Canada	1:02.71
1991	Norbert Rozsa, Hungary	1:01.45
1994	Norbert Rozsa, Hungary	1:01.24
1998	Frederik Deburghgraeve, Belgium	1:01.34
2001	Roman Sloudnov, Russia	1:00.16
2003	Kosuke Kitajima, Japan	59.78

200-meter breaststroke

1973	David Wilkie, Great Britain	2:19.28
1975	David Wilkie, Great Britain	2:18.23
1978	Nick Nevid, United States	2:18.37
1982	Victor Davis, Canada	2:14.77
1986	Jozsef Szabo, Hungary	2:14.27
1991	Mike Barrowman, United States	2:11.23
1994	Norbert Rozsa, Hungary	2:12.81
1998	Kurt Grote, United States	2:13.40
2001	Brendan Hansen, United States	2:10.69
2003	Kosuke Kitajima, Japan	2:09.42

50-meter butterfly

1973-98	Event not held	
2001	Geoff Huegill, Australia	23.50
2003	Matt Welsh, Australia	23.43

100-meter butterfly

1973	Bruce Robertson, Canada	55.69
1975	Greg Jagenburg, United States	55.63
1978	Joe Bottom, United States	54.30
1982	Matt Gribble, United States	53.88
1986	Pablo Morales, United States	53.54
1991	Anthony Nesty, Suriname	53.29
1994	Rafal Szukala, Poland	53.51
1998	Michael Klim, Australia	52.25
2001	Lars Frolander, Sweden	52.10
2003	Ian Crocker, United States	50.98

200-meter butterfly

1973	Robin Backhaus, United States	2:03.32
1975	Bill Forrester, United States	2:01.95
1978	Mike Bruner, United States	1:59.38
1982	Michael Gross, West Germany	1:58.85
1986	Michael Gross, West Germany	1:56.53
1991	Melvin Stewart, United States	1:55.69
1994	Denis Pankratov, Russia	1:56.54
1998	Denys Sylantyev, Ukraine	1:56.61
2001	Michael Phelps, United States	1:54.58
2003	Michael Phelps, United States	1:54.35

200-meter individual medley

1973	Gunnar Larsson, Sweden	2:08.36
1975	Andras Hargitay, Hungary	2:07.72
1978	Graham Smith, Canada	2:03.65
1982	Aleksandr Sidorenko, U.S.S.R.	2:03.30
1986	Tamás Darnyi, Hungary	2:01.57
1991	Tamás Darnyi, Hungary	1:59.36
1994	Jani Sievin, Finland	1:58.16
1998	Marcel Wouda, Netherlands	2:01.18
2001	Massimiliano Rosolino, Italy	1:59.71
2003	Michael Phelps, United States	1:56.04

400-meter individual medley

1973	Andras Hargitay, Hungary	4:31.11
1975	Andras Hargitay, Hungary	4:32.57
1978	Jesse Vassallo, United States	4:20.05
1982	Ricardo Prado, Brazil	4:19.78
1986	Tamás Darnyi, Hungary	4:18.98
1991	Tamás Darnyi, Hungary	4:12.36
1994	Tom Dolan, United States	4:12.30
1998	Tom Dolan, United States	4:14.95
2001	Alessio Boggiatto, Italy	4:13.15
2003	Michael Phelps, United States	4:09.09

400-meter medley relay

1973	United States (Mike Stamm, John Hencken, Joe Bottom, Jim Montgomery)	3:49.49
1975	United States (John Murphy, Rick Colella, Greg Jagenburg, Andy Coan)	3:49.00
1978	United States (Robert Jackson, Nick Nevid, Joe Bottom, David McCagg)	3:44.63
1982	United States (Rick Carey, Steve Lundquist, Matt Gribble, Rowdy Gaines)	3:40.84
1986	United States (Dan Veatch, David Lundberg, Pablo Morales, Matt Biondi)	3:41.25
1991	United States (Jeff Rouse, Eric Wunderlich, Mark Henderson, Matt Biondi)	3:39.66
1994	United States (Jeff Rouse, Eric Wunderlich, Mark Henderson, Gary Hall, Jr.)	3:37.74

World Championship Results—Men (cont.)

1998	Australia (Matt Welsh, Phil Rogers, Michael Klim, Chris Fydler)	3:37.98
2001	Australia (Matt Welsh, Ian Thorpe, Geoff Huegill, Regan Harrison)	3:35.35
2003	United States (Aaron Peirsol, Brendan Hansen, Ian Crocker, Jason Lezak)	3:31.54

400-meter freestyle relay

1973	United States (Mel Nash, Joe Bottom, Jim Montgomery, John Murphy)	3:27.18
1975	United States (Bruce Furniss, Jim Montgomery, Andy Coan, John Murphy)	3:24.85
1978	United States (Jack Babashoff, Rowdy Gaines, Jim Montgomery, David McCagg)	3:19.74
1982	United States (Chris Cavanaugh, Robin Leamy, David McCagg, Rowdy Gaines)	3:19.26
1986	United States (Tom Jager, Mike Heath, Paul Wallace, Matt Biondi)	3:19.59
1991	United States (Tom Jager, Brent Lang, Doug Gjertsen, Matt Biondi)	3:17.15
1994	United States (Jon Olsen, Josh Davis, Ugur Taner, Gary Hall)	3:16.90
1998	United States (Scott Tucker, Jon Olsen, Neil Walker, Gary Hall)	3:16.69
2001	Australia (Michael Klim, Ian Thorpe, Todd Pearson, Ashley Callus)	3:14.10
2003	Russia (Andrei Kapralov, Ivan Usov, Denis Pimankov, Alexander Popov)	3:14.06

800-meter freestyle relay

1973	United States (Kurt Krumpholz, Robin Backhaus, Rick Klatt, Jim Montgomery)	7:33.22
1975	West Germany (Klaus Steinbach, Werner Lampe, Hans Joachim Geisler, Peter Nocke)	7:39.44
1978	United States (Bruce Furniss, Billy Forrester, Bobby Hackett, Rowdy Gaines)	7:20.82
1982	United States (Rich Saeger, Jeff Float, Kyle Miller, Rowdy Gaines)	7:21.09
1986	East Germany (Lars Hinneburg, Thomas Flemming, Dirk Richter, Sven Lodziewski)	7:15.91
1991	Germany (Peter Sitt, Steffen Zesner, Stefan Pfeiffer, Michael Gross)	7:13.50
1994	Sweden (Christer Waller, Tommy Werner, Lars Frolander, Anders Holmertz)	7:17.74
1998	Australia (Daniel Kowalski, Grant Hackett, Ian Thorpe, Michael Klim)	7:12.48
2001	Australia (Michael Klim, Ian Thorpe, William Kirby, Grant Hackett)	7:04.66
2003	Australia (Grant Hackett, Craig Stevens, Nicholas Sprenger, Ian Thorpe)	7:08.58

Today's Stars

Inge de Bruijn holds the world records in the 50-meter freestyle and 100-meter butterfly.

NICK WILSON/GETTY IMAGES

Inge de Bruijn, b. August 24, 1973, Barendrecht, Netherlands. De Bruijn won gold medals in the 50-meter and 100-meter freestyle, and won the 100-meter butterfly in world-record time (56.61 seconds) at the 2000 Summer Olympics. She also helped the Netherlands win a silver medal in the 4x100-meter free relay. At the 2001 world championships, she won the 50-meter free, 100-meter free, and 50-meter fly. De Bruijn took home two gold medals (50-meter free, 50-meter fly) from the 2003 worlds.

Alexander Popov, b. November 16, 1971, Sverdlovsk, Russia. Popov won gold in the 50-meter and 100-meter freestyle at the 1992 and 1996 Summer Olympics. A few weeks after the 1996 Games, he was stabbed on a street in Moscow, Russia, and needed three hours of surgery to repair wounds to his lungs and kidneys. He was back in the pool in 1997 at the European championships and won the 100-meter free at the 1998 world championships. Popov won the silver medal in the 100-meter free at the 2000 Summer Olympics, then went into a slump. He returned to form in 2003, winning three gold medals at the world championships (50-meter free, 100-meter free, and 400-meter free relay).

Aaron Peirsol, b. July 23, 1983, Irvine California. Peirsol won a silver medal in the 200-meter backstroke at the 2000 Summer Olympics and has been improving ever since. His gold medal in the 200-meter back at the 2001 world championships earned him the event's Number 1 ranking for the year. At the 2002 Pan Pacific Games, Peirsol won gold medals in the 100-meter back, 200-meter back, and 400-meter medley relay, in which the U.S. set the world record. At the 2003 worlds, he won gold in the 100-meter and 200-meter back, and helped the U.S. win the gold in the 400-meter medley relay. (The team broke its own world record.)

World Championship Results—Women

50-meter freestyle

1973-82	Event not held	
1986	Tamara Costache, Romania	25.28
1991	Zhuang Yong, China	25.47
1994	Le Jingyi, China	24.51
1998	Amy Van Dyken, United States	25.15
2001	Inge de Bruijn, Netherlands	24.47
2003	Inge de Bruijn, Netherlands	24.47

100-meter freestyle

1973	Kornelia Ender, East Germany	57.54
1975	Kornelia Ender, East Germany	56.50
1978	Barbara Krause, East Germany	55.68
1982	Birgit Meineke, East Germany	55.79
1986	Kristin Otto, East Germany	55.05
1991	Nicole Haislett, United States	55.17
1994	Le Jingyi, China	54.01
1998	Jenny Thompson, United States	54.95
2001	Inge de Bruijn, Netherlands	54.18
2003	Hanna-Maria Seppala, Finland	54.37

200-meter freestyle

1973	Keena Rothhammer, United States	2:04.99
1975	Shirley Babashoff, United States	2:02.50
1978	Cynthia Woodhead, United States	1:58.53
1982	Annemarie Verstappen, Netherlands	1:59.53
1986	Heike Friedrich, East Germany	1:58.26
1991	Hayley Lewis, Australia	2:00.48
1994	Franziska Van Almsick, Germany	1:56.78
1998	Claudia Poll, Costa Rica	1:58.90
2001	Giaan Rooney, Australia	1:58.57
2003	Alena Popchanka, Belarus	1:58.32

400-meter freestyle

1973	Heather Greenwood, United States	4:20.28
1975	Shirley Babashoff, United States	4:16.87
1978	Tracey Wickham, Australia	4:06.28
1982	Carmela Schmidt, East Germany	4:08.98
1986	Heike Friedrich, East Germany	4:07.45
1991	Janet Evans, United States	4:08.63
1994	Yang Aihua, China	4:09.64
1998	Chen Yan, China	4:06.72
2001	Yana Klochkova, Ukraine	4:07.30
2003	Hannah Stockbauer, Germany	4:06.75

800-meter freestyle

1973	Novella Calligaris, Italy	8:52.97
1975	Jenny Turrall, Australia	8:44.75
1978	Tracey Wickham, Australia	8:24.94
1982	Kim Linehan, United States	8:27.48
1986	Astrid Strauss, East Germany	8:28.24
1991	Janet Evans, United States	8:24.05
1994	Janet Evans, United States	8:29.85
1998	Brooke Bennett, United States	8:28.71
2001	Hannah Stockbauer, Germany	8:24.66
2003	Hannah Stockbauer, Germany	8:23.66

1,500-meter freestyle

1973-98	Event not held	
2001	Hannah Stockbauer, Germany	16:01.02
2003	Hannah Stockbauer, Germany	16:00.18

50-meter backstroke

1973-98	Event not held	
2001	Haley Cope, United States	28.51
2003	Nina Zhivanevskaya, Spain	28.48

100-meter backstroke

1973	Ulrike Richter, East Germany	1:05.42
1975	Ulrike Richter, East Germany	1:03.30
1978	Linda Jezek, United States	1:02.55
1982	Kristin Otto, East Germany	1:01.30
1986	Betsy Mitchell, United States	1:01.74
1991	Krisztina Egerszegi, Hungary	1:01.78
1994	He Cihong, China	1:00.57
1998	Lea Maurer, United States	1:01.16
2001	Natalie Coughlin, United States	1:00.37
2003	Antje Buschschulte, Germany	1:00.50

200-meter backstroke

1973	Melissa Belote, United States	2:20.52
1975	Birgit Treiber, East Germany	2:15.46
1978	Linda Jezek, United States	2:11.93
1982	Cornelia Sirch, East Germany	2:09.91
1986	Cornelia Sirch, East Germany	2:11.37
1991	Krisztina Egerszegi, Hungary	2:09.15
1994	He Cihong, China	2:07.40
1998	Roxanna Maracineanu, France	2:11.26
2001	Diana Mocanu, Romania	2:09.94
2003	Katy Sexton, Great Britain	2:08.74

50-meter breaststroke

1973-98	Event not held	
2001	Xuejuan Luo, China	30.84
2003	Xuejuan Luo, China	30.67

100-meter breaststroke

1973	Renate Vogel, East Germany	1:13.74
1975	Hannalore Anke, East Germany	1:12.72
1978	Julia Bogdanova, U.S.S.R.	1:10.31
1982	Ute Geweniger, East Germany	1:09.14
1986	Sylvia Gerasch, East Germany	1:08.11
1991	Linley Frame, Australia	1:08.81
1994	Samantha Riley, Australia	1:07.96
1998	Kristy Kowal, United States	1:08.42
2001	Xuejuan Luo, China	1:07.18
2003	Xuejuan Luo, China	1:06.80

200-meter breaststroke

1973	Renate Vogel, East Germany	2:40.01
1975	Hannalore Anke, East Germany	2:37.25
1978	Lina Kachushite, U.S.S.R.	2:31.42
1982	Svetlana Varganova, U.S.S.R.	2:28.82
1986	Silke Hoerner, East Germany	2:27.40
1991	Elena Volkova, U.S.S.R.	2:29.53
1994	Samantha Riley, Australia	2:26.87
1998	Agnes Kovacs, Hungary	2:25.45
2001	Agnes Kovacs, Hungary	2:24.90
2003	Amanda Beard, United States	2:22.99

50-meter butterfly

1973-98	Event not held	
2001	Inge de Bruijn, Netherlands	25.90
2003	Inge de Bruijn, Netherlands	25.84

100-meter butterfly

1973	Kornelia Ender, East Germany	1:02.53
1975	Kornelia Ender, East Germany	1:01.24
1978	Joan Pennington, United States	1:00.20
1982	Mary T. Meagher, United States	59.41
1986	Kornelia Gressler, East Germany	59.51
1991	Qian Hong, China	59.68
1994	Liu Limin, China	58.98

World Championship Results—Women (cont.)

1998	Jenny Thompson, United States	58.46
2001	Petria Thomas, Australia	58.27
2003	Jenny Thompson, United States	57.96

200-meter butterfly

1973	Rosemarie Kother, East Germany	2:13.76
1975	Rosemarie Kother, East Germany	2:13.82
1978	Tracy Caulkins, United States	2:09.87
1982	Ines Geissler, East Germany	2:08.66
1986	Mary T. Meagher, United States	2:08.41
1991	Summer Sanders, United States	2:09.24
1994	Liu Limin, China	2:07.25
1998	Susie O'Neill, Australia	2:07.93
2001	Petria Thomas, Australia	2:06.73
2003	Otylia Jedrzejczak, Poland	2:07.56

200-meter individual medley

1973	Andrea Huebner, East Germany	2:20.51
1975	Kathy Heddy, United States	2:19.80
1978	Tracy Caulkins, United States	2:14.07
1982	Petra Schneider, East Germany	2:11.79
1986	Kristin Otto, East Germany	2:15.56
1991	Li Lin, China	2:13.40
1994	Lu Bin, China	2:12.34
1998	Wu Yanyan, China	2:10.88
2001	Martha Bowen, United States	2:11.93
2003	Yana Klochkova, Ukraine	2:10.75

400-meter individual medley

1973	Gudrun Wegner, East Germany	4:57.71
1975	Ulrike Tauber, East Germany	4:52.76
1978	Tracy Caulkins, United States	4:40.83
1982	Petra Schneider, East Germany	4:36.10
1986	Kathleen Nord, East Germany	4:43.75
1991	Li Lin, China	4:41.45
1994	Dai Guohong, China	4:39.14
1998	Chen Yan, China	4:36.66
2001	Yana Klochkova, Ukraine	4:36.98
2003	Yana Klochkova, Ukraine	4:36.74

400-meter medley relay

1973	East Germany (Ulrike Richter, Renate Vogel, Rosemarie Kother, Kornelia Ender)	4:16.84
1975	East Germany (Ulrike Richter, Hannelore Anke, Rosemarie Kother, Kornelia Ender)	4:14.74
1978	United States (Linda Jezek, Tracy Caulkins, Joan Pennington, Cynthia Woodhead)	4:08.21
1982	East Germany (Kristin Otto, Ute Gewinger, Ines Geissler, Birgit Meineke)	4:05.80
1986	East Germany (Kathrin Zimmermann, Sylvia Gerasch, Kornelia Gressler, Kristin Otto)	4:04.82
1991	United States (Janie Wagstaff, Tracey McFarlane, Crissy Ahmann-Leighton, Nicole Haislett)	4:06.51
1994	China (He Cihong, Dai Guohong, Liu Limin, Lu Bin)	4:01.67
1998	United States (Kristy Kowal, Lea Maurer, Jenny Thompson, Amy Van Dyken)	4:01.93
2001	Australia (Dyana Calub, Sarah Ryan, Petria Thomas, Leisel Jones)	4:01.50
2003	China (Shu Zhan, Xuejuan Luo, Yafei Zhou, Yu Yang)	3:59.89

400-meter freestyle relay

1973	East Germany (Kornelia Ender, Andrea Eife, Andrea Huebner, Sylvia Eichner)	3:52.45
1975	East Germany (Kornelia Ender, Barbara Krause, Claudia Hempel, Ute Bruckner)	3:49.37
1978	United States (Tracy Caulkins, Stephanie Elkins, Jill Sterkel, Cynthia Woodhead)	3:43.43
1982	East Germany (Birgit Meineke, Susanne Link, Kristin Otto, Caren Metschuk)	3:43.97
1986	East Germany (Kristin Otto, Manuela Stellmach, Sabine Schulze, Heike Friedrich)	3:40.57
1991	United States (Nicole Haislett, Julie Cooper, Whitney Hedgepeth, Jenny Thompson)	3:43.26
1994	China (Le Jingyi, Ying Shan, Le Ying, Lu Bin)	3:37.91
1998	United States (Catherine Fox, Lindsey Farella, Melanie Valerio, B.J. Bedford)	3:42.11
2001	Germany (Petra Dallman, Antje Buschschulter, Katrin Meissner, Sandra Volker)	3:39.58
2003	United States (Natalie Coughlin, Lindsay Benko, Rhi Jeffrey, Jenny Thompson)	3:38.09

800-meter freestyle relay

1973-82	Event not held	
1986	East Germany (Manuela Stellmach, Astrid Strauss, Nadja Bergknecht, Heike Friedrich)	7:59.33
1991	Germany (Kerstin Kielgass, Manuela Stellmach, Dagmar Hase, Stephanie Ortwig)	8:02.56
1994	China (Le Ying, Yang Alhua, Zhou Guabin, Lu Bin)	7:57.96
1998	Germany (Silvia Szalai, Antje Buschschulte, Janina Goetz, Franziska Van Almsick)	8:01.46
2001	Great Britain (Nicola Jackson, Janine Belton, Karen Legg, Karen Pickering)/United States (Natalie Coughlin, Cristina Teuscher, Julie Hardt, Diana Munz)*	7:56.53
2003	United States (Lindsay Benko, Rachel Komisarz, Rhi Jeffrey, Diana Munz)	7:55.70

Fast Fact: At the 1972 Summer Olympics, U.S. swimmer Mark Spitz won seven gold medals, all in world-record time. In two Olympic appearances (1968, 1972), he won a total of 11 medals (nine gold, one silver, and one bronze).

*Because of timing malfunctions and an overturned disqualification of the U.S., gold medals were awarded to Great Britain and the U.S.

TRACK AND FIELD

The 2003-04 track-and-field season will be remembered more for two big-name athletes involved with drug-related scandals off the track than for their remarkable performances on it. At the 2003 World Outdoor Championships, in Paris, France, U.S. sprinter Kelli White convincingly won the 100-meter and 200-meter races. Less than a week later, she tested positive for a banned stimulant. On May 19, White was suspended from competition for two years. She was stripped of all medals earned since 2000 and cannot compete at the 2004 Olympics. In October 2003, it was also revealed that, in June, middle-distance runner Regina Jacobs of the U.S., the world indoor record holder in the 1,500 meters, had tested positive for the steroid THG.

Despite the scandals, some good news emerged. In September 2003, Paul Tergat of Kenya set the men's marathon world record by winning the Berlin (Germany) Marathon in 2:04.55. Olympic gold medalist Marion Jones of the U.S. took off all of 2003 to have a baby and was back in action in 2004. The sprinter ran the first race of her return in February, at the Millrose Games, in New York City. She blazed to victory in the 60-meter dash in 7.21 seconds.

At the World Indoor Track

Marion Jones won the first race she entered after a year off, at the 2004 Millrose Games, in New York City.

SIMON BRUTY/SPORTS ILLUSTRATED

and Field Championships, in March, Gail Devers of the U.S. won the women's 60 meters in 7.08 seconds. It was her third career indoor title in the event. Allen Johnson of the U.S. won the 60-meter hurdles in 7.36 seconds, tying the U.S. record and winning his third indoor world gold medal in the event.

The National Track and Field Hall of Fame opened on January 24, 2004, in New York City. The Hall is home to such memorabilia as one of the golden spikes sprinter Michael Johnson of the U.S. wore at the Summer Olympics in 1996 and the aerodynamic bodysuit Marion Jones wore at the 2000 Games.

Fast Fact: High jumper Dick Fosbury of the U.S. changed the way athletes go over the bar. Until 1968, most high jumpers went over the bar face first. But Fosbury discovered he could go higher by going over the bar with his back to it. He won the gold medal at the 1968 Olympics using the "Fosbury Flop," which most jumpers use today.

MICHAEL DALDER/REUTERS

Paul Tergat of Kenya broke the world record in the men's marathon in 2003.

2003 USA Outdoor Track and Field Championships

JUNE 19–22, 2003, PALO ALTO, CALIFORNIA

Men's 100 Meters

Athlete	Team	Mark
Bernard Williams	Nike	10.11
Tim Montgomery	Nike	10.15
Jon Drummond	Nike	10.18

Women's 100 Meters

Athlete	Team	Mark
Torri Edwards	adidas	11.13
Gail Devers	Nike	11.16
Inger Miller	Nike	11.17

Men's 200 Meters

Athlete	Team	Mark
Darvis Patton	adidas	20.15
John Capel	adidas	20.17
Joshua Johnson	Nike	20.22

Women's 200 Meters

Athlete	Team	Mark
Torri Edwards	adidas	22.45
Allyson Felix	unattached	22.59
LaTasha Jenkins	Nike	22.65

Men's 400 Meters

Athlete	Team	Mark
Tyree Washington	Nike	44.33
Calvin Harrison	Nike	44.62
Jerome Young	adidas	44.79

Women's 400 Meters

Athlete	Team	Mark
Sanya Richards	Texas	51.01
Demetria Washington	Nike	51.54
De'Hashia Trotter	Tennessee	51.78

Men's 800 Meters

Athlete	Team	Mark
David Krummenacker	adidas	1:45.53
Khadevis Robinson	Nike	1:46.21
Jonathon Johnson	Texas Tech	1:46.76

Women's 800 Meters

Athlete	Team	Mark
Jearl Miles-Clark	Team New Balance	1:58.84
Nicole Teter	Nike	1:59.91
Jennifer Toomey	Nike	2:00.12

Men's 1,500 Meters

Athlete	Team	Mark
Jason Lunn	Nike	3:44.00
Bryan Berryhill	adidas	3:44.30
Grant Robison	Stanford	3:44.83

Women's 1,500 Meters

Athlete	Team	Mark
Regina Jacobs	Nike	4:01.63
Suzy Favor Hamilton	Nike	4:03.70
Tiffany McWilliams	Mississippi State	4:10.85

Men's 5,000 Meters

Athlete	Team	Mark
Tim Broe	adidas	13:35.23
Adam Goucher	Nike	13:35.67
Jorge Torres	Reebok	13:36.42

Women's 5,000 Meters

Athlete	Team	Mark
Marla Runyan	Nike	15:16.18
Shalane Flanagan	North Carolina	15:20.54
Shayne Culpepper	adidas	15:23.59

Men's 10,000 Meters

Athlete	Team	Mark
Alan Culpepper	adidas	27:55.36
Meb Keflezighi	Nike	27:57.59
Daniel Browne	Nike	28:03.48

2003 USA Outdoor Track and Field Championships (cont.)

Women's 10,000 Meters

Athlete	Team	Mark
Deena Drossin	Asics	31:28.97
Elva Dryer	Nike	31:35.74
Katie McGregor	adidas	31:54.78

Men's 110-Meter Hurdles

Athlete	Team	Mark
Allen Johnson	Nike	13.37
Terrence Trammell	Mizuno	13.38
Larry Wade	Nike	13.43

Women's 100-Meter Hurdles

Athlete	Team	Mark
Gail Devers	Nike	12.61
Miesha McKelvy-Jones	Nike	12.62
Jenny Adams	Nike	12.68

Men's 400-Meter Hurdles

Athlete	Team	Mark
Eric Thomas	Nike	48.76
Bershawn Jackson	unattached	49.01
Joey Woody	adidas	49.22

Women's 400-Meter Hurdles

Athlete	Team	Mark
Raasin McIntosh	Texas	54.62
Joanna Hayes	Nike	54.76
Sandra Glover	Nike	55.12

Men's 3,000-Meter Steeplechase

Athlete	Team	Mark
Steve Slattery	Nike	8:23.58
Daniel Lincoln	Nike	8:24.10
Robert Gary	adidas	8:24.82

Women's 3,000-Meter Steeplechase

Athlete	Team	Mark
Briana Shook	Toledo	9:44.71
Kathryn Andersen	Brigham Young	9:47.17
Lisa Nye	Nike	9:49.14

Men's 20,000-Meter Race Walk

Athlete	Team	Mark
Kevin Eastler	U.S. Air Force	1:23:52.20
Tim Seaman	NYAC	1:24:47.37
John Nunn	U.S. Army	1:25:15.89

Women's 20,000-Meter Race Walk

Athlete	Team	Mark
Michelle Rohl	Moving Comfort	1:34:31.06
Joanne Dow	adidas	1:34:57.79
Teresa Vaill	Walk USA	1:36:38.38

Men's High Jump

Athlete	Team	Mark
Jamie Nieto	unattached	2.30
Matt Hemingway	unattached	2.27
Terrance Woods	unattached	2.27

Women's High Jump

Athlete	Team	Mark
Amy Acuff	Asics	1.95
Gwen Wentland	Nike	1.92
Tisha Waller	Nike	1.92

Men's Pole Vault

Athlete	Team	Mark
Timothy Mack	Nike	5.70
Jeff Hartwig	Nike	5.70
Derek Miles	Nike	5.70

Women's Pole Vault

Athlete	Team	Mark
Stacy Dragila	Nike	4.50
Jillian Schwartz	Nike	4.40
Kellie Suttle	Nike	4.35
Melissa Mueller	Nike	4.35
Tracy O'Hara	unattached	4.35
Mary Sauer	Asics	4.35
Becky Holliday	unattached	4.35

Men's Long Jump

Athlete	Team	Mark
Savante Stringfellow	Nike	8.22
Melvin Lister	unattached	7.82
Erick Walder	unattached	7.74

Women's Long Jump

Athlete	Team	Mark
Rose Richmond	Indiana	6.56
Monique Freeman	unattached	6.39
Pamela Simpson	U.S. Army	6.34

Men's Triple Jump

Athlete	Team	Mark
Kenta Bell	Nike	17.59
Walter Davis	Nike	17.55
Aarik Wilson	Indiana	16.65

Women's Triple Jump

Athlete	Team	Mark
Yuliana Perez	unattached	14.23
Teresa Bundy	Nike	13.79
Monica Cabbler	unattached	13.46

Men's Shot Put

Athlete	Team	Mark
Adam Nelson	Nike	20.61
Christian Cantwell	Nike	20.57
Dan Taylor	Ohio State	20.29

Women's Shot Put

Athlete	Team	Mark
Kristin Heaston	unattached	18.33
Seilala Sua	Nike	17.69
Adriane Blewitt	unattached	17.47

2003 USA Outdoor Track and Field Championships (cont.)

Men's Discus

Athlete	Team	Mark
Doug Reynolds	unattached	62.71
Joshua Ralston	Texas A&M	62.66
Nick Petrucci	Team HIPP	62.09

Women's Discus

Athlete	Team	Mark
Seilala Sua	Nike	60.01
Gina LoMonaco	unattached	59.26
Roberta Collins	unattached	58.66

Men's Hammer Throw

Athlete	Team	Mark
John McEwen	NYAC	72.96
Patrick McGrath	unattached	72.12
Thomas Freeman	unattached	70.08

Women's Hammer Throw

Athlete	Team	Mark
Dawn Ellerbe	NYAC	66.76
Jukina Dickerson	Florida	65.58
Erin Gilreath	Florida	64.83

Women's Javelin

Athlete	Team	Mark
Erica Wheeler	unattached	56.85
Kim Kreiner	Nike	56.39
Denise O'Connell	unattached	53.38

Men's Javelin

Athlete	Team	Mark
Joshua Johnson	unattached	76.16
Justin St. Clair	unattached	74.02
Ozie Oscar Duncan	unattached	72.67

Decathlon

Athlete	Team	Points
Tom Pappas	Nike	8,784
Bryan Clay	unattached	8,482
Paul Terek	World's Greatest Athlete Decathlete Club	8,275

Heptathlon

Athlete	Team	Points
Shelia Burrell	Nike	6,159
Kim Schiemenz	unattached	6,003
Tiffany Lott-Hogan	unattached	5,843

Legends

Wilma Rudolph, sprinter, b. June 23, 1940, St. Bethlehem, Tennessee; d. November 12, 1994, Nashville, Tennessee. Rudolph was the first U.S. woman to win three gold medals in one Olympics. In 1960, she won gold in the 100 meters and 200 meters, and anchored the 4x100-meter relay team. Rudolph's rise to world-class sprinter was remarkable. As a child, she had polio, which caused her to lose the use of her left leg. She wore a leg brace from age 6 to 12 until therapy finally healed her leg. She began sprinting in eighth grade.

Wilma Rudolph won a bronze medal at the 1956 Summer Olympics and three gold medals at the 1960 Games.

JERRY COOKE

Edwin Moses, hurdler, b. August 31, 1955, Dayton, Ohio. Moses set a track-and-field winning streak that may never be equaled: 107 straight finals victories in the 400-meter hurdles from September 1977 through May 1987. His wins included gold medals at Summer Olympics in 1976 and 1984. In the last race of his career, he won the bronze medal at the 1988 Games. He was inducted into the National Track and Field Hall of Fame in 1994.

Al Oerter, discus thrower, b. September 13, 1936, Astoria, New York. Oerter is the first track-and-field athlete to win the same event at four different Olympics. He won gold in the discus throw in 1956, 1960, 1964, and 1968. In 1962, he became the first athlete to throw the discus over 200 feet (200 feet 5½ inches). Oerter retired in 1969 but tried to qualify for his fifth Olympic team at the 1980 trials. He placed fourth and was named an alternate on the team, but the U.S. did not attend those Games.

2003 World Outdoor Track and Field Championships

AUGUST 23–31, 2003, PARIS, FRANCE

Women's 100 Meters

Athlete	Country	Mark
Torri Edwards	United States	10.93
Zhanna Block	Ukraine	10.99
Chandra Sturrup	Bahamas	11.02

Men's 100 Meters

Athlete	Country	Mark
Kim Collins	St. Kitts/Nevis	10.07
Darrel Brown	Trinidad	10.08
Darren Campbell	Great Britain	10.08

Women's 200 Meters

Athlete	Country	Mark
Anastasiya Kapachinskaya	Russia	22.38
Torri Edwards	United States	22.47
Muriel Hurtis	France	22.59

Men's 200 Meters

Athlete	Country	Mark
John Capel	United States	20.30
Darvis Patton	United States	20.31
Shingo Suetsugu	Japan	20.38

Women's 400 Meters

Athlete	Country	Mark
Ana Guevara	Mexico	48.89
Lorraine Fenton	Jamaica	49.43
Amy Mbacke Thiam	Senegal	49.95

Men's 400 Meters

Athlete	Country	Mark
Jerome Young	United States	44.50
Tyree Washington	United States	44.77
Marc Raquil	France	44.79

Women's 800 Meters

Athlete	Country	Mark
Maria Mutola	Mozambique	1:59.89
Kelly Holmes	Great Britain	2:00.18
Natalya Khrushchelyova	Russia	2:00.29

Men's 800 Meters

Athlete	Country	Mark
Djabir Said-Guerni	Algeria	1:44.81
Yuriy Borzakovskiy	Russia	1:44.84
Mbulaeni Mulaudzi	South Africa	1:44.90

Women's 1,500 Meters

Athlete	Country	Mark
Tatyana Tomashova	Russia	3:58.52
Sureyya Ayhan	Turkey	3:59.04
Hayley Tullett	Great Britain	3:59.95

Men's 1,500 Meters

Athlete	Country	Mark
Hicham El Guerrouj	Morocco	3:31.77
Mehdi Baala	France	3:32.31
Ivan Heshko	Ukraine	3:33.17

Women's 5,000 Meters

Athlete	Country	Mark
Tirunesh Dibaba	Ethiopia	14:51.72
Marta Dominguez	Spain	14:52.26
Edith Masai	Kenya	14:52.30

Men's 5,000 Meters

Athlete	Country	Mark
Eliud Kipchoge	Kenya	12:52.79
Hicham El Guerrouj	Morocco	12:52.83
Kenenisa Bekele	Ethiopia	12:53.12

Women's 10,000 Meters

Athlete	Country	Mark
Berhane Adere	Ethiopia	30:04.18
Werknesh Kidane	Ethiopia	30:07.15
Yingjie Sun	China	30:07.20

Men's 10,000 Meters

Athlete	Country	Mark
Kenenisa Bekele	Ethiopia	26:49.57
Haile Gebrselassie	Ethiopia	26:50.77
Sileshi Sihine	Ethiopia	27:01.44

Men's 3,000-Meter Steeplechase

Athlete	Country	Mark
Saif Saaeed Shaheen	Qatar	8:04.39
Ezekiel Kemboi	Kenya	8:05.11
Eliseo Martin	Spain	8:09.09

Women's 100-Meter Hurdles

Athlete	Country	Mark
Perdita Felicien	Canada	12.53
Brigitte Foster	Jamaica	12.57
Miesha McKelvy	United States	12.67

Men's 110-Meter Hurdles

Athlete	Country	Mark
Allen Johnson	United States	13.12
Terrence Trammell	United States	13.20
Xiang Liu	China	13.23

Women's 400-Meter Hurdles

Athlete	Country	Mark
Jana Pittman	Australia	53.22
Sandra Glover	United States	53.65
Yuliya Pechonkina	Russia	53.71

Men's 400-Meter Hurdles

Athlete	Country	Mark
Felix Sanchez	Dominican Republic	47.25
Joey Woody	United States	48.18
Periklis Iakovakis	Greece	48.24

Women's 20-Kilometer Race Walk

Athlete	Country	Mark
Yelena Nikolayeva	Russia	1:26.52
Gillian O'Sullivan	Ireland	1:27.34
Valentina Tsybulskaya	Belarus	1:28.10

2003 World Outdoor Track and Field Championships (cont.)

Men's 20-Kilometer Race Walk

Athlete	Country	Mark
Jefferson Perez	Ecuador	1:17.21
Francisco Javier Fernandez	Spain	1:18.00
Roman Rasskazov	Russia	1:18.07

Men's 50-Kilometer Race Walk

Athlete	Country	Mark
Robert Korzeniowski	Poland	3:36.03
German Skurygin	Russia	3:36.42
Andreas Erm	Germany	3:37.46

Women's High Jump

Athlete	Country	Mark
Hestrie Cloete	South Africa	2.06
Marina Kuptsova	Russia	2.00
Kajsa Bergqvist	Sweden	2.00

Men's High Jump

Athlete	Country	Mark
Jacques Freitag	South Africa	2.35
Stefan Holm	Sweden	2.32
Mark Boswell	Canada	2.32

Women's Pole Vault

Athlete	Country	Mark
Svetlana Feofanova	Russia	4.75
Annika Becker	Germany	4.70
Yelena Isinbayeva	Russia	4.65

Svetlana Feofanova, Russia

EZRA SHAW/GETTY IMAGES

Men's Pole Vault

Athlete	Country	Mark
Giuseppe Gibilisco	Italy	5.90
Okkert Brits	South Africa	5.85
Patrik Kristiansson	Sweden	5.85

Women's Long Jump

Athlete	Country	Mark
Eunice Barber	France	6.99
Tatyana Kotova	Russia	6.74
Anju Bobby George	India	6.70

Men's Long Jump

Athlete	Country	Mark
Dwight Phillips	United States	8.32
James Beckford	Jamaica	8.28
Yago Lamela	Spain	8.22

Women's Triple Jump

Athlete	Country	Mark
Tatyana Lebedeva	Russia	15.18
Etone Francoise Mbango	Cameroon	15.05
Magdelin Martinez	Italy	14.90

Men's Triple Jump

Athlete	Country	Mark
Christian Olsson	Sweden	17.72
Yoandri Betanzos	Cuba	17.28
Leevan Sands	Bahamas	17.26

Women's Shot Put

Athlete	Country	Mark
Svetlana Krivelyova	Russia	20.63
Nadezhda Ostapchuk	Belarus	20.12
Vita Pavlysh	Ukraine	20.08

Men's Shot Put

Athlete	Country	Mark
Andrei Mikhnevich	Belarus	21.69
Adam Nelson	United States	21.26
Yuriy Bilonog	Ukraine	21.10

Women's Discus

Athlete	Country	Mark
Irina Yatchenko	Belarus	67.32
Anastasia Kelesidou	Greece	67.14
Ekaterini Voggoli	Greece	66.73

Men's Discus

Athlete	Country	Mark
Virgilijus Alekna	Lithuania	69.69
Robert Fazekas	Hungary	69.01
Vasiliy Kaptyukh	Belarus	66.51

Women's Javelin

Athlete	Country	Mark
Mirela Manjani	Greece	66.52
Tatyana Shikolenko	Russia	63.28
Steffi Nerius	Germany	62.70

Men's Javelin

Athlete	Country	Mark
Sergey Makarov	Russia	85.44
Andrus Varnik	Estonia	85.17
Boris Henry	Germany	84.74

Women's Hammer

Athlete	Country	Mark
Yipsi Moreno	Cuba	73.33
Olga Kuzekova	Russia	71.71
Manuela Montebrun	France	70.92

Men's Hammer

Athlete	Country	Mark
Ivan Tikhon	Belarus	83.05
Adrian Annus	Hungary	80.36
Koji Murofushi	Japan	80.12

Women's 4x100-Meter Relay

Athlete	Country	Mark
Patricia Girard, Muriel Hurtis, Sylviane Felix, Christine Arron	France	41.78
Angela Williams, Chryste Gaines, Inger Miller, Torri Edwards	United States	41.83
Olga Fyodorova, Yuliya Tabakova, Marina Kislova, Larisa Kruglova	Russia	42.66

2003 World Outdoor Track and Field Championships (cont.)

Men's 4x100-Meter Relay

Athlete	Country	Mark
John Capel, Bernard Williams, Darvis Patton, Joshua Johnson	United States	38.06
Vicente de Lima, Luciano Edson Ribeiro, Andre Domingos, Claudio Roberto Souza	Brazil	38.26
Timothy Beck, Troy Douglas, Patrick van Balkom, Caimin Douglas	Netherlands	38.87

Women's 4x400-Meter Relay

Athlete	Country	Mark
Me'Lisa Barber Demetria Washington, Jearl Miles Clark, Sanya Richards	United States	3:22.63
Olesya Zykina, Yuliya Pechonkina, Anastasiya Kapachinskaya, Natalya Nazarova	Russia	3:22.91
Sandie Richards, Allison Beckford, Ronetta Smith, Lorraine Fenton	Jamaica	3:22.92

Did You Know?

The U.S. topped the medal charts at the world outdoor championships in 2003: 10 gold medals, eight silver, and two bronze. It was the U.S.'s best medal count at the outdoor worlds since 1993.

Men's 4x400-Meter Relay

Athlete	Country	Mark
Calvin Harrison, Tyree Washington, Derrick Brew, Jerome Young	United States	2:58.88
Leslie Djhone, Naman Keita, Stephane Diagana, Marc Raquil	France	2:58.96
Brandon Simpson, Danny McFarlane, Davian Clarke, Michael Blackwood	Jamaica	2:59.60

Heptathlon

Athlete	Country	Points
Carolina Kluft	Sweden	7,001
Eunice Barber	France	6,755
Natalya Sazanovich	Belarus	6,524

Decathlon

Athlete	Country	Points
Tom Pappas	United States	8,750
Roman Sebrle	Czech Republic	8,634
Dmitry Karpov	Kazakstan	8,374

Women's Marathon

Athlete	Country	Mark
Catherine Ndereba	Kenya	2:23:55
Mizuki Noguchi	Japan	2:24:14
Masako Chiba	Japan	2:25:09

Men's Marathon

Athlete	Country	Mark
Jaouad Gharib	Morocco	2:08:31
Julio Rey	Spain	2:08:38
Stefano Baldini	Italy	2:09:14

2003–04 Marathons

Chicago Marathon

OCTOBER 12, 2003

Men	Country	Time
Evans Rutto	Kenya	2:05:50
Paul Koech	Kenya	2:07:07
Daniel Njenga	Kenya	2:07:41

Women	Country	Time
Svetlana Zakharova	Russia	2:23:07
Constantina Tomescu-Dita	Romania	2:23:35
Jelena Prokopcuka	Latvia	2:24:53

New York Marathon

NOVEMBER 2, 2003

Men	Country	Time
Martin Lel	Kenya	2:10:30
Rodgers Rop	Kenya	2:11:11
Christopher Cheboiboch	Kenya	2:11:23

Women	Country	Time
Margaret Okayo	Kenya	2:22:31
Catherine Ndereba	Kenya	2:23:03
Lornah Kiplagat	Netherlands	2:23:43

London Marathon

APRIL 18, 2004

Men	Country	Time
Evans Rutto	Kenya	2:06:18
Sammy Korir	Kenya	2:06:48
Jaouad Gharib	Morocco	2:07:02

Women	Country	Time
Margaret Okayo	Kenya	2:22:35
Ludmila Petrova	Russia	2:26:02
Constantina Tomescu-Dita	Romania	2:26:52

Boston Marathon

APRIL 19, 2004

Men	Country	Time
Timothy Cherigat	Kenya	2:10:37
Robert Cheboror	Kenya	2:11:49
Martin Lel	Kenya	2:13:38

Women	Country	Time
Catherine Ndereba	Kenya	2:24:27
Elfenesh Alemu	Ethiopia	2:24:43
Olivera Jevtic	Serbia and Montenegro	2:27:34

World Records—Men

Event	Mark	Record Holder	Date	Site
100 Meters	9.78	Tim Montgomery, United States	9-14-02	Paris, France
200 Meters	19.32	Michael Johnson, United States	8-1-96	Atlanta, Georgia
400 Meters	43.18	Michael Johnson, United States	8-26-99	Seville, Spain
800 Meters	1:41.11	Wilson Kipketer, Denmark	8-24-97	Cologne, Germany
1,000 Meters	2:11.96	Noah Ngeny, Kenya	9-5-99	Rieti, Italy
1,500 Meters	3:26.00	Hicham El Guerrouj, Morocco	7-14-98	Rome, Italy
Mile	3:43.13	Hicham El Guerrouj, Morocco	7-7-99	Rome, Italy
2,000 Meters	4:44.79	Hicham El Guerrouj, Morocco	9-7-99	Berlin, Germany
3,000 Meters	7:20.67	Daniel Komen, Kenya	9-1-96	Rieti, Italy
Steeplechase	7:55.28	Brahim Boulami, Morocco	8-24-01	Brussels, Belgium
5,000 Meters	12:37.36	Kenenisa Bekele, Ethiopia	5-31-04	Hengelo, Netherlands
10,000 Meters	26:20.31	Kenenisa Bekele, Ethiopia	6-8-04	Ostrava, Czech Republic
20,000 Meters	56:55.6	Arturo Barrios, Mexico	3-30-91	La Flache, France
Hour	21,101 meters	Arturo Barrios, Mexico	3-30-91	La Flache, France
25,000 Meters	1:13:55.8	Toshihiko Seko, Japan	3-22-81	Christchurch, New Zealand
30,000 Meters	1:29:18.8	Toshihiko Seko, Japan	3-22-81	Christchurch, New Zealand
Marathon	2:04:55	Paul Tergat, Kenya	9-28-03	Berlin, Germany
110-Meter Hurdles	12.91	Colin Jackson, Great Britain	8-20-93	Stuttgart, Germany
400-Meter Hurdles	46.78	Kevin Young, United States	8-6-92	Barcelona, Spain
20-Kilometer Walk	1:17:22	Javier Fernandez, Spain	4-28-02	Turku, Finland
30-Kilometer Walk	2:01:44.1	Maurizio Damilano, Italy	10-3-92	Cuneo, Italy
50-Kilometer Walk	3:40:57.9	Thierry Toutain, France	9-29-96	Héricourt, France
4x100-Meter Relay	37.40*	United States (Mike Marsh, Leroy Burrell, Dennis Mitchell, Carl Lewis)	8-8-92	Barcelona, Spain
		United States (Jon Drummond, Andre Cason, Dennis Mitchell, Leroy Burrell)	8-21-93	Stuttgart, Germany
4x200-Meter Relay	1:18.68	Santa Monica TC (Mike Marsh, Leroy Burrell, Floyd Heard, Carl Lewis)	4-17-94	Walnut, California

*Shared record

Hicham El Guerrouj, Morocco

PHIL COLE/GETTY IMAGES

Today's Stars

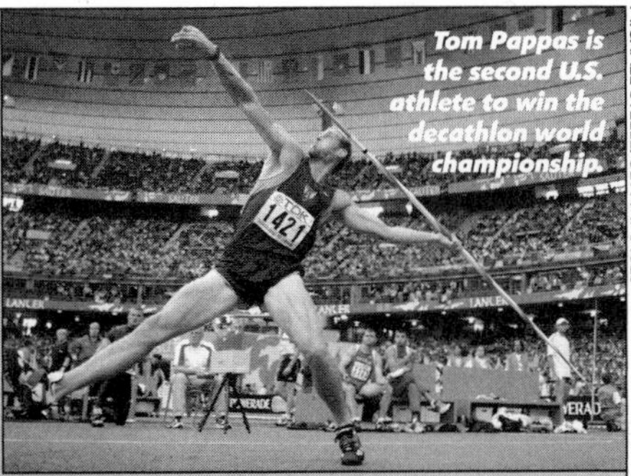

Tom Pappas is the second U.S. athlete to win the decathlon world championship.

MICHAEL STEELE/GETTY IMAGES

Tom Pappas, decathlete, b. September 6, 1976, Azalea, Oregon. Pappas can do it all. In 2003, he became the second American to win the gold medal in the 10-event decathlon at the world outdoor championships. Pappas also won the gold medal in the seven-event heptathlon at the world indoor championships in 2003. He finished fifth in the Olympic decathlon in 2000.

Maria Mutola, middle-distance runner, b. October 27, 1972, Maputo, Mozambique, Africa. Mutola is the master of the 800 meters. She won the race at the world outdoor championships in 2003 and the world indoor championships in 2004. She also won the 800 at the Summer Games in 2000. She was the first athlete from Mozambique to win an Olympic gold medal.

Tyree Washington, sprinter, b. August 28, 1974, Riverside, California. The 400-meter specialist had a stellar season in 2003. He won the event 10 times in a row. His streak ended at the world outdoor championships, where he won the silver medal. He was also the 2003 U.S. outdoor champion and the 2004 world indoor champion. Washington was a member of the U.S. 4x400-meter relay team that holds the world record (2:54.20, set in 1998).

World Records—Men (cont.)

Event	Mark	Record Holder	Date	Site
4x400-Meter Relay	2:54.20	United States (Jerome Young, Antonio Pettigrew, Tyree Washington, Michael Johnson)	7-22-98	New York, New York
4x800-Meter Relay	7:03.89	Great Britain (Peter Elliott, Garry Cook, Steve Cram, Sebastian Coe)	8-30-82	London, England
4x1,500-Meter Relay	14:38.8	West Germany (Thomas Wessinghage, Harald Hudak, Michael Lederer, Karl Fleschen)	8-17-77	Cologne, Germany
High Jump	8 ft 1/2 in	Javier Sotomayor, Cuba	7-27-93	Salamanca, Spain
Pole Vault	20 ft 1 3/4 in	Sergei Bubka, Ukraine	7-31-94	Sestriere, Italy
Long Jump	29 ft 4 1/2 in	Mike Powell, United States	8-30-91	Tokyo, Japan
Triple Jump	60 ft 1/4 in	Jonathan Edwards, Great Britain	8-7-95	Goteborg, Sweden
Shot Put	75 ft 10 1/4 in	Randy Barnes, United States	5-20-90	Westwood, California
Discus Throw	243 ft	Jurgen Schult, East Germany	6-6-86	Neubrandenburg, Germany
Hammer Throw	284 ft 7 in	Yuri Syedikh, U.S.S.R.	8-30-86	Stuttgart, Germany
Javelin Throw	323 ft 1 in	Jan Zelezny, Czech Republic	5-25-96	Jena, Germany
Decathlon	9,026 pts	Roman Sebrle, Czech Republic	5-27-01	Gotzis, Austria

KEN REGAN/CAMERA 5

Javier Sotomayor, Cuba

World Records—Women

Event	Mark	Record Holder	Date	Site
100 Meters	10.49	Florence Griffith Joyner, United States	7-16-88	Indianapolis, Indiana
200 Meters	21.34	Florence Griffith Joyner, United States	9-29-88	Seoul, Korea
400 Meters	47.60	Marita Koch, East Germany	10-6-85	Canberra, Australia
800 Meters	1:53.28	Jarmila Kratochvílová, Czechoslovakia	7-26-83	Munich, Germany
1,000 Meters	2:28.98	Svetlana Masterkova, Russia	8-23-96	Brussels, Belgium
1,500 Meters	3:50.46	Qu Yunxia, China	9-11-93	Beijing, China
Mile	4:12.56	Svetlana Masterkova, Russia	8-14-96	Zurich, Switzerland
2,000 Meters	5:25.36	Sonia O'Sullivan, Ireland	7-8-94	Edinburgh, Scotland
3,000 Meters	8:06.11	Wang Junxia, China	9-13-93	Beijing, China
Steeplechase	9:01.59	Gulnara Samitova, Russia	7-4-04	Iraklion, Greece
5,000 Meters	14:24.68	Elvan Abeylegesse, Turkey	6-11-04	Bergen, Norway
10,000 Meters	29:31.78	Wang Junxia, China	9-8-93	Beijing, China
Hour	18,340 meters	Tegla Loroupe, Kenya	8-8-98	Borgholzhausen, Germany
20,000 Meters	1:05:26.6	Tegla Loroupe, Kenya	9-3-00	Borgholzhausen, Germany
25,000 Meters	1:27:05.9	Tegla Loroupe, Kenya	9-21-02	Mengerskirchen, Germany

STU FORSTER/GETTY IMAGES

Tegla Loroupe, Kenya

Fast Fact: At the Summer Olympics, men compete in the 10-event decathlon (100 meters, long jump, shot put, high jump, 400 meters, 110-meter hurdles, discus throw, pole vault, javelin, and 1,500 meters). Women compete in the seven-event heptathlon (100-meter hurdles, shot put, high jump, 200 meters, long jump, javelin throw, 800 meters).

World Records—Women (cont.)

Event	Mark	Record Holder	Date	Site
30,000 Meters	1:45:50.0	Tegla Loroupe, Kenya	6-6-03	Warstein, Germany
Marathon	2:15:25	Paula Radclifffe, Great Britain	4-13-03	London, England
100-Meter Hurdles	12.21	Yordanka Donkova, Bulgaria	8-20-88	Stara Zgora, Bulgaria
400-Meter Hurdles	52.34	Yuliya Pechenkina, Russia	8-8-03	Tula, Russia
5-kilometer Walk	20:02.60	Gillian O'Sullivan, Ireland	7-13-02	Dublin, Ireland
10-kilometer Walk	41:56.23	Nadezhda Ryashkina, Russia	7-24-90	Seattle, Washington
4x100-Meter Relay	41.37	East Germany (Silke Gladisch, Sabine Reiger, Ingrid Auerswald, Marlies Gohr)	10-6-85	Canberra, Australia
4x200-Meter Relay	1:27.46	United States (LaTasha Jenkins, LaTasha Colander-Richardson, Nanceen Perry, Marion Jones)	4-29-00	Philadelphia, Pennsylvania
4x400-Meter Relay	3:15.17	U.S.S.R. (Tatyana Ledovskaya, Olga Nazarova, Maria Pinigina, Olga Bryzgina)	10-1-88	Seoul, Korea
4x800-Meter Relay	7:50.17	U.S.S.R. (Nadezhda Olizarenko, Lyubov Gurina, Lyudmila Borisova, Irina Podyalovskaya)	8-5-84	Moscow, Russia
High Jump	6 ft 10 1/4 in	Stefka Kostadinova, Bulgaria	8-30-87	Rome, Italy
Pole Vault	16 ft 1 1/4 in	Yelena Isinbayeva, Russia	8-24-04	Athens, Greece
Long Jump	24 ft 8 1/4 in	Galina Chistyakova, U.S.S.R.	6-11-88	Leningrad, Russia
Triple Jump	50 ft 10 1/4 in	Inessa Kravets, Ukraine	8-10-95	Goteborg, Sweden
Shot Put	74 ft 3 in	Natalya Lisovskaya, U.S.S.R.	6-7-87	Moscow, Russia
Discus Throw	252 ft	Gabriele Reinsch, East Germany	7-9-88	Neubrandenburg, Germany
Hammer Throw	247 ft 3 in	Mihaela Melinte, Romania	8-29-99	Rudlingen, Switzerland
Javelin Throw	234 ft 8 in	Osleidys Menéndez, Cuba	7-1-01	Réthymno, Greece
Heptathlon	7,291 pts	Jackie Joyner-Kersee, United States	9-23-88/9-24-88	Seoul, Korea

Did You Know?

Women were not allowed to run in the marathon until the 1984 Summer Olympics. The 26.2-mile event was thought to be too grueling for them.

Trivia Challenge

Which of the following is not an Olympic event: Hammer throw, 3,000-meter steeplechase, or 60-meter dash?

60-meter dash

2003-04 TIME LINE

August 31, 2003: On the final day of the world outdoor championships, the U.S. wins three relay gold medals (men's 4x100 meters, men's 4x400 meters, women's 4x400 meters).

September 28, 2003: Paul Tergat of Kenya runs the Berlin (Germany) Marathon and sets the men's world record: 2:04:55.

February 6, 2004: Sprinter Marion Jones of the U.S. wins the 60-meter dash at the Millrose Games, in New York City. The race is the first Jones runs since having a baby in 2003.

March 6, 2004: Tatyana Lebedeva of Russia sets an indoor world record in the triple jump (15.36 meters) at the World Indoor Championships, in Budapest, Hungary.

March 7, 2004: Roman Sebrle of the Czech Republic upsets Tom Pappas of the U.S. to win the heptathlon at the world indoor championships.

March 13, 2004: Kimberly Smith of Providence College wins the 3,000-meter race at the NCAA Indoor Championships. Her time of 8:49.18 sets the collegiate record in the event.

March 20, 2004: Kenenisa Bekele of Ethiopia wins the short-course race (4 kilometers) at the 2004 World Cross Country Championships. The next day, he wins the long-course race (12 kilometers). It is the third time the 21-year-old wins both races at the event.

SUMMER OLYMPICS

From August 13–29, 2004, the XXVIII Summer Olympics were held in Athens, Greece.

More than 11,000 athletes from 202 countries competed in 28 sports. The United States led the medal haul, with 103. Russia was second (92) and China was third (63).

The story of the Games was U.S. swimmer Michael Phelps. He won eight medals, tying gymnast Aleksandr Dityatin of Russia, who won eight in 1980. Gymnast Paul Hamm won the first Olympic individual all-around gold medal by a U.S. man and Carly Patterson won the second by a U.S. woman. In team sports, the U.S. women's softball and basketball teams went undefeated to earn gold. The U.S. men's hoops team settled for bronze.

The next Summer Games will be held in Beijing, China, in 2008.

LAURENT REBOURS/AP

The 2004 Summer Olympics returned to Athens, Greece, the birthplace of the Games.

2004 Sport-by-Sport Results

ARCHERY
WOMEN
- Individual

GOLD – Sung Hyun Park, South Korea
SILVER – Sung Jin Lee, South Korea
BRONZE – Alison Williamson, Great Britain

- Team

GOLD – South Korea
SILVER – China
BRONZE – Taiwan

MEN
- Individual

GOLD – Marco Galiazzo, Italy
SILVER – Hiroshi Yamamoto, Japan
BRONZE – Tim Cuddihy, Australia

- Team

GOLD – South Korea
SILVER – Taiwan
BRONZE – Ukraine

BADMINTON
WOMEN
- Singles

GOLD – Ning Zhang, China
SILVER – Mia Audina, Netherlands
BRONZE – Mi Zhou, China

- Doubles

GOLD – China
SILVER – China
BRONZE – South Korea

MEN
- Singles

GOLD – Taufik Hidayat, Indonesia
SILVER – Seung Mo Shon, South Korea
BRONZE – Soni Dwi Kuncoro, Indonesia

- Doubles

GOLD – South Korea
SILVER – South Korea
BRONZE – Indonesia

- Mixed Doubles

GOLD – China
SILVER – Great Britain
BRONZE – Denmark

BASEBALL
GOLD – Cuba
SILVER – Australia
BRONZE – Japan

BASKETBALL
WOMEN

GOLD – USA
SILVER – Australia
BRONZE – Russia

MEN

GOLD – Argentina
SILVER – Italy
BRONZE – USA

Misty May (left) and Kerri Walsh, United States

JOHN BIEVER/SPORTS ILLUSTRATED

BEACH VOLLEYBALL
WOMEN

GOLD – Misty May and Kerri Walsh, USA
SILVER – Shelda Bede and Adriana Behar, Brazil
BRONZE – Holly McPeak and Elaine Youngs, USA

MEN

GOLD – Ricardo Alex Santos and Emanuel Rego, Brazil
SILVER – Javier Bosma and Pablo Herrera, Spain
BRONZE – Patrick Heuscher and Stefan Kobel, Switzerland

BOXING
- Light Flyweight

GOLD – Yan Bhartelemy Varela, Cuba
SILVER – Atagun Yalcinkaya, Turkey
BRONZE – Shimming Zou, China; and Sergey Kazakov, Russia

2004 Sport-by-Sport Results (cont.)

▪ Flyweight
GOLD – Yuriorkis Gamboa Toledano, Cuba
SILVER – Jerome Thomas, France
BRONZE – Fuad Aslanov, Azerbaijan; and Rustamhodza Rahimov, Germany

▪ Bantamweight
GOLD – Guillermo Rigondeaux Ortiz, Cuba
SILVER – Worapoj Petchkoom, Thailand
BRONZE – Bahodirjon Sooltonov, Uzbekistan; and Aghasi Mammadov, Azerbaijan

▪ Featherweight
GOLD – Alexei Tichtchenko, Russia
SILVER – Song Guk Kim, North Korea
BRONZE – Seok Hwan Jo, South Korea; and Vitali Tajbert, Germany

▪ Lightweight
GOLD – Mario Cesar Kindelan Mesa, Cuba
SILVER – Amir Khan, Great Britain
BRONZE – Murat Khrachev, Russia; and Serik Yeleuov, Kazakhstan

▪ Light Welterweight
GOLD – Manus Boonjumnong, Thailand
SILVER – Yudel Johnson Cedeno, Cuba
BRONZE – Boris Georgiev, Bulgaria; and Ionut Gheorghe, Romania

▪ Welterweight
GOLD – Bakhtiyar Artayev, Kazakhstan
SILVER – Lorenzo Aragon Armenteros, Cuba
BRONZE – Oleg Saitov, Russia; and Jung Joo Kim, South Korea

▪ Middleweight
GOLD – Gaydarbek Gaydarbekov, Russia
SILVER – Gennadiy Golovkin, Kazakhstan
BRONZE – Suriya Prasathinphimai, Thailand; and Andre Dirrell, USA

Andre Ward, United States

AL TIELEMANS/SPORTS ILLUSTRATED

▪ Light Heavyweight
GOLD – Andre Ward, USA
SILVER – Magomed Aripgadjiev, Belarus
BRONZE – Utkirbek Haydarov, Uzbekistan; and Ahmed Ismail, Egypt

▪ Heavyweight
GOLD – Odlanier Solis Fonte, Cuba
SILVER – Viktar Zuyev, Belarus
BRONZE – Mohamed Elsayed, Egypt; and Naser Al Shami, Syria

▪ Super Heavyweight
GOLD – Alexander Povetkin, Russia
SILVER – Mohamed Aly, Egypt
BRONZE – Roberto Cammarelle, Italy; and Michel Lopez Nunez, Cuba

CANOE/KAYAK SLALOM RACING

WOMEN

▪ K1 Kayak Single
GOLD – Elena Kaliska, Slovakia
SILVER – Rebecca Giddens, USA
BRONZE – Helen Reeves, Great Britain

MEN

▪ K1 Kayak Single
GOLD – Benoit Peschier, France
SILVER – Campbell Walsh, Great Britain
BRONZE – Fabien Lefevre, France

▪ C1 Canoe Single
GOLD – Tony Estanguet, France
SILVER – Michal Martikan, Slovakia
BRONZE – Stefan Pfannmoeller, Germany

▪ C2 Canoe Double
GOLD – Slovakia
SILVER – Germany
BRONZE – Czech Republic

CANOE/KAYAK FLATWATER RACING

WOMEN

▪ K1 500 meters
GOLD – Natasa Janics, Hungary
SILVER – Josefa Idem, Italy
BRONZE – Caroline Brunet, Canada

▪ K2 500 meters
GOLD – Hungary
SILVER – Germany
BRONZE – Poland

▪ K4 500 meters
GOLD – Germany
SILVER – Hungary
BRONZE – Ukraine

MEN

▪ K1 500 meters
GOLD – Adam van Koeverden, Canada
SILVER – Nathan Baggaley, Australia
BRONZE – Ian Wynne, Great Britain

▪ K1 1,000 meters
GOLD – Eirik Veraas Larsen, Norway
SILVER – Ben Fouhy, New Zealand
BRONZE – Adam van Koeverden, Canada

▪ K2 500 meters
GOLD – Germany
SILVER – Australia
BRONZE – Belarus

▪ K2 1,000 meters
GOLD – Sweden
SILVER – Italy
BRONZE – Norway

▪ K4 1,000 meters
GOLD – Hungary
SILVER – Germany
BRONZE – Slovakia

▪ C1 500 meters
GOLD – Andreas Dittmer, Germany
SILVER – David Cal, Spain
BRONZE – Maxim Opalev, Russia

▪ C1 1,000 meters
GOLD – David Cal, Spain
SILVER – Andreas Dittmer, Germany
BRONZE – Attila Vajda, Hungary

▪ C2 500 meters
GOLD – China
SILVER – Cuba
BRONZE – Russia

▪ C2 1,000 meters
GOLD – Germany
SILVER – Russia
BRONZE – Hungary

Fast Fact: In 1912, women were allowed to compete in swimming at the Olympics for the first time. Fanny Durack of Australia won the 100-meter freestyle event. The female competitors swam in long woolen swimsuits with skirts.

2004 Sport-by-Sport Results (cont.)

WOMEN

■ Road Race
GOLD – Sara Carrigan, Australia
SILVER – Judith Arndt, Germany
BRONZE – Olga Slyusareva, Russia

■ Individual Time Trial
GOLD – Leontien Zijlaard-van Moorsel, Netherlands
SILVER – Dede Demet-Barry, USA
BRONZE – Karin Thuerig, Switzerland

MEN

■ Road Race
GOLD – Paolo Bettini, Italy
SILVER – Sergio Paulinho, Portugal
BRONZE – Axel Merckx, Belgium

■ Individual Time Trial
GOLD – Tyler Hamilton, USA
SILVER – Viatcheslav Ekimov, Russia
BRONZE – Bobby Julich, USA

ERIC RISBERG/AP

Tyler Hamilton, United States

CYCLING (TRACK)

WOMEN

■ 500-meter Time Trial
GOLD – Anna Meares, Australia
SILVER – Yonghua Jiang, China
BRONZE – Natallia Tsylinskaya, Belarus

■ 3,000-meter Individual Pursuit
GOLD – Sarah Ulmer, New Zealand
SILVER – Katie Mactier, Australia
BRONZE – Leontien Zijlaard-van Moorsel, Netherlands

■ Sprint
GOLD – Lori-Ann Muenzer, Canada
SILVER – Tamilla Abassova, Russia
BRONZE – Anna Meares, Australia

■ Points Race
GOLD – Olga Slyusareva, Russia
SILVER – Belem Guerrero Mendez, Mexico
BRONZE – Erin Mirabella, USA

MEN

■ 1-kilometer Time Trial
GOLD – Chris Hoy, Great Britain
SILVER – Arnaud Tournant, France
BRONZE – Stefan Nimke, Germany

■ 4,000-meter Individual Pursuit
GOLD – Bradley Wiggins, Great Britain
SILVER – Brad McGee, Australia
BRONZE – Sergi Escobar, Spain

■ Team Sprint
GOLD – Germany
SILVER – Japan
BRONZE – France

■ 4,000-meter Team Pursuit
GOLD – Australia
SILVER – Great Britain
BRONZE – Spain

■ Points Race
GOLD – Mikhail Ignatyev, Russia
SILVER – Joan Llaneras, Spain
BRONZE – Guido Fulst, Germany

■ Sprint
GOLD – Ryan Bayley, Australia
SILVER – Theo Bos, Netherlands
BRONZE – Rene Wolff, Germany

■ Madison
GOLD – Australia
SILVER – Switzerland
BRONZE – Great Britain

■ Keirin
GOLD – Ryan Bayley, Australia
SILVER – Jose Escuredo, Spain
BRONZE – Shane Kelly, Australia

CYCLING (MOUNTAIN BIKE)

WOMEN
GOLD – Gunn-Rita Dahle, Norway
SILVER – Marie-Helene Premont, Canada
BRONZE – Sabine Spitz, Germany

MEN
GOLD – Julien Absalon, France
SILVER – Jose Antonio Hermida, Spain
BRONZE – Bart Brentjens, Netherlands

DIVING

DANIEL BEREHULAK/GETTY IMAGES FOR FINA

Chantelle Newbery, Australia

WOMEN

■ 3-meter Springboard
GOLD – Jingjing Guo, China
SILVER – Minxia Wu, China
BRONZE – Yulia Pakhalina, Russia

■ 10-meter Platform
GOLD – Chantelle Newbery, Australia
SILVER – Lishi Lao, China
BRONZE – Loudy Tourky, Australia

■ Synchronized 3-meter Springboard
GOLD – Minxia Wu and Jingjing Gao, China
SILVER – Vera Ilyina and Yulia Pakhalina, Russia
BRONZE – Irina Lashko and Chantelle Newbery, Australia

■ Synchronized 10-meter Platform
GOLD – Lishi Lao and Ting Li, China
SILVER – Natalia Goncharova and Yulia Koltunova, Russia
BRONZE – Blythe Hartley and Emilie Heymans, Canada

MEN

■ 3-meter Springboard
GOLD – Bo Peng, China
SILVER – Alexandre Despatie, Canada
BRONZE – Dmitri Sautin, Russia

■ 10-meter Platform
GOLD – Jia Hu, China
SILVER – Mathew Helm, Australia
BRONZE – Liang Tian, China

■ Synchronized 3-meter Springboard
GOLD – Nikolaos Siranidis and Thomas Bimis, Greece
SILVER – Andreas Wels and Tobias Schellenberg, Germany
BRONZE – Robert Newbery and Steven Barnett, Australia

2004 Sport-by-Sport Results (cont.)

■ Synchronized 10-meter Platform
GOLD – Liang Tian and Jinghui Yang, China
SILVER – Peter Waterfield and Leon Taylor, Great Britain
BRONZE – Mathew Helm and Robert Newbery, Australia

EQUESTRIAN

■ Individual Eventing
GOLD – Leslie Law, Great Britain
SILVER – Kimberly Severson, USA
BRONZE – Philippa Funnell, Great Britain

■ Team Eventing
GOLD – France
SILVER – Great Britain
BRONZE – USA

■ Individual Dressage
GOLD – Anky van Grunsven, Netherlands
SILVER – Ulla Salzgeber, Germany
BRONZE – Beatriz Ferrer-Salat, Spain

■ Team Dressage
GOLD – Germany
SILVER – Spain
BRONZE – USA

■ Individual Jumping
GOLD – Cian O'Connor, Ireland
SILVER – Rodrigo Pessoa, Brazil
BRONZE – Chris Kappler, USA

■ Team Jumping
GOLD – Germany
SILVER – USA
BRONZE – Sweden

LYNN JOHNSON/SPORTS ILLUSTRATED

Mariel Zagunis, United States

FENCING

WOMEN

■ Individual Sabre
GOLD – Mariel Zagunis, USA
SILVER – Xue Tan, China
BRONZE – Sada Jacobson, USA

■ Individual Épée
GOLD – Timea Nagy, Hungary
SILVER – Laura Flessel-Colovic, France
BRONZE – Maureen Nisima, France

■ Individual Foil
GOLD – Valentina Vezzali, Italy
SILVER – Giovanna Trillini, Italy
BRONZE – Sylwia Gruchala, Poland

■ Team Épée
GOLD – Russia
SILVER – Germany
BRONZE – France

MEN

■ Individual Sabre
GOLD – Aldo Montano, Italy
SILVER – Zsolt Nemcsik, Hungary
BRONZE – Vladislav Tretiak, Ukraine

■ Individual Épée
GOLD – Marcel Fischer, Switzerland
SILVER – Lei Wang, China
BRONZE – Pavel Kolobkov, Russia

■ Individual Foil
GOLD – Brice Guyart, France
SILVER – Salvatore Sanzo, Italy
BRONZE – Andrea Cassara, Italy

■ Team Sabre
GOLD – France
SILVER – Italy
BRONZE – Russia

■ Team Épée
GOLD – France
SILVER – Hungary
BRONZE – Germany

■ Team Foil
GOLD – Italy
SILVER – China
BRONZE – Russia

FIELD HOCKEY

WOMEN
GOLD – Germany
SILVER – Netherlands
BRONZE – Argentina

MEN
GOLD – Australia
SILVER – Netherlands
BRONZE – Germany

GYMNASTICS

WOMEN

■ Team
GOLD – Romania
SILVER – USA
BRONZE – Russia

■ Individual All-Around
GOLD – Carly Patterson, USA
SILVER – Svetlana Khorkina, Russia
BRONZE – Nan Zhang, China

■ Vault
GOLD – Monica Rosu, Romania
SILVER – Annia Hatch, USA
BRONZE – Anna Pavlova, Russia

■ Uneven Bars
GOLD – Emilie Lepennec, France
SILVER – Terin Humphrey, USA
BRONZE – Courtney Kupets, USA

■ Balance Beam
GOLD – Catalina Ponor, Romania
SILVER – Carly Patterson, USA
BRONZE – Alexandra Georgiana Eremia, Romania

■ Floor Exercise
GOLD – Catalina Ponor, Romania
SILVER – Nicoleta Daniela Sofronie, Romania
BRONZE – Patricia Moreno, Spain

■ Trampoline
GOLD – Anna Dogonadze, Germany
SILVER – Karen Cockburn, Canada
BRONZE – Shanshan Huang, China

BILL FRAKES/SPORTS ILLUSTRATED

Paul Hamm, United States

MEN

■ Team
GOLD – Japan
SILVER – USA
BRONZE – Romania

■ Individual All-Around
GOLD – Paul Hamm, USA
SILVER – Dae Eun Kim, South Korea
BRONZE – Tae Young Yang, South Korea

■ Floor Exercise
GOLD – Kyle Shewfelt, Canada
SILVER – Marian Dragulescu, Romania
BRONZE – Jordan Jovtchev, Bulgaria

■ Pommel Horse
GOLD – Haibin Teng, China
SILVER – Marius Daniel Urzica, Romania
BRONZE – Takehiro Kashima, Japan

2004 Sport-by-Sport Results (cont.)

■ Rings
GOLD – Dimosthenis Tampakos, Greece
SILVER – Jordan Jovtchev, Bulgaria
BRONZE – Yuri Chechi, Italy
■ Vault
GOLD – Gervasio Deferr, Spain
SILVER – Evgeni Sapronenko, Latvia
BRONZE – Marian Dragulescu, Romania
■ Parallel Bars
GOLD – Valeri Goncharov, Ukraine
SILVER – Hiroyuki Tomita, Japan
BRONZE – Xiaopeng Li, China
■ Horizontal Bar
GOLD – Igor Cassina, Italy
SILVER – Paul Hamm, USA
BRONZE – Isao Yoneda, Japan
■ Trampoline
GOLD – Yuri Nikitin, Ukraine
SILVER – Alexander Moskalenko, Russia
BRONZE – Henrik Stehlik, Germany

HANDBALL
WOMEN
GOLD – Denmark
SILVER – South Korea
BRONZE – Ukraine
MEN
GOLD – Croatia
SILVER – Germany
BRONZE – Russia

JUDO
WOMEN
■ 48 kg
GOLD – Ryoko Tani, Japan
SILVER – Frederique Jossinet, France
BRONZE – Julia Matijass, Germany; and Fen Gao, China
■ 52 kg
GOLD – Dongmei Xian, China
SILVER – Yuki Yokosawa, Japan
BRONZE – Amarilys Savon, Cuba; and Ilse Heylen, Belgium
■ 57 kg
GOLD – Yvonne Boenisch, Germany
SILVER – Sun Hui Kye, North Korea
BRONZE – Deborah Gravenstijn, Netherlands; and Yurisleidy Lupetey, Cuba
■ 63 kg
GOLD – Ayumi Tanimoto, Japan
SILVER – Claudia Heill, Austria
BRONZE – Urska Zolnir, Slovenia; and Driulys Gonzalez, Cuba
■ 70 kg
GOLD – Masae Ueno, Japan
SILVER – Edith Bosch, Netherlands
BRONZE – Annett Boehm, Germany; and Dongya Qin, China
■ 78 kg
GOLD – Noriko Anno, Japan
SILVER – Xia Liu, China
BRONZE – Lucia Morico, Italy; and Yurisel Laborde, Cuba
■ +78 kg
GOLD – Maki Tsukada, Japan
SILVER – Dayma Beltran, Cuba
BRONZE – Tea Donguzashvili, Russia; and Fuming Sun, China
MEN
■ 60 kg
GOLD – Tadahiro Nomura, Japan
SILVER – Nestor Khergiani, Georgia
BRONZE – Min Ho Choi, South Korea; and Khashbaatar Tsagaanbaatar, Mongolia
■ 66 kg
GOLD – Masato Uchishiba, Japan
SILVER – Jozef Krnac, Slovakia
BRONZE – Georgi Georgiev, Bulgaria; and Yordanis Arencibia, Cuba
■ 73 kg
GOLD – Won Hee Lee, South Korea
SILVER – Vitaliy Makarov, Russia
BRONZE – Leandro Guilheiro, Brazil; and James Pedro, USA

FRANCK FIFE/AFP/GETTY IMAGES

James Pedro (dark uniform), United States

■ 81 kg
GOLD – Ilias Iliadis, Greece
SILVER – Roman Gontyuk, Ukraine
BRONZE – Dmitri Nossov, Russia; and Flavio Canto, Brazil
■ 90 kg
GOLD – Zurab Zviadauri, Georgia
SILVER – Hiroshi Izumi, Japan
BRONZE – Mark Huizinga, Netherlands; and Khasanbi Taov, Russia
■ 100 kg
GOLD – Ihar Makarau, Belarus
SILVER – Sung Ho Jang, South Korea
BRONZE – Ariel Zeevi, Israel; and Michael Jurack, Germany
■ +100 kg
GOLD – Keiji Suzuki, Japan
SILVER – Tamerlan Tmenov, Russia
BRONZE – Indrek Pertelson, Estonia; and Dennis van Der Geest, Netherlands

MODERN PENTATHLON
WOMEN
GOLD – Zsuzsanna Voros, Hungary
SILVER – Jelena Rublevska, Latvia
BRONZE – Georgina Harland, Great Britain
MEN
GOLD – Andrey Moiseev, Russia
SILVER – Andrejus Zadneprovskis, Lithuania
BRONZE – Libor Capalini, Czech Republic

Trivia Challenge

Which athlete has won the most medals (lifetime) at the Summer Olympics?

Gymnast Larysa Latynina of the Soviet Union won a total of 18 medals at the 1956, 1960, and 1964 Summer Games.

2004 Sport-by-Sport Results (cont.)

RHYTHMIC GYMNASTICS

Team
GOLD – Russia
SILVER – Italy
BRONZE – Bulgaria

Individual All-Around
GOLD – Alina Kabaeva, Russia
SILVER – Irina Tchachina, Russia
BRONZE – Anna Bessonova, Ukraine

ROWING

WOMEN

Single Sculls
GOLD – Katrin Rutschow-Stomporowski, Germany
SILVER – Ekaterina Karsten-Khodotovitch, Belarus
BRONZE – Rumyana Neykova, Bulgaria

Double Sculls
GOLD – New Zealand
SILVER – Germany
BRONZE – Great Britain

Lightweight Double Sculls
GOLD – Romania
SILVER – Germany
BRONZE – Netherlands

Quadruple Sculls
GOLD – Germany
SILVER – Great Britain
BRONZE – Australia

Pair
GOLD – Romania
SILVER – Great Britain
BRONZE – Belarus

Eight
GOLD – Romania
SILVER – USA
BRONZE – Netherlands

MEN

Single Sculls
GOLD – Olaf Tufte, Norway
SILVER – Jueri Jaanson, Estonia
BRONZE – Ivo Yanakiev, Bulgaria

Double Sculls
GOLD – France
SILVER – Slovenia
BRONZE – Italy

Lightweight Double Sculls
GOLD – Poland
SILVER – France
BRONZE – Greece

Quadruple Sculls
GOLD – Russia
SILVER – Czech Republic
BRONZE – Ukraine

Pair
GOLD – Australia
SILVER – Croatia
BRONZE – South Africa

Four
GOLD – Great Britain
SILVER – Canada
BRONZE – Italy

Lightweight Four
GOLD – Denmark
SILVER – Australia
BRONZE – Italy

Eight, United States

ANDY CLARK/GETTY IMAGES

Eight
GOLD – USA
SILVER – Netherlands
BRONZE – Australia

SAILING

WOMEN

Keelboat: Yngling Class
GOLD – Great Britain
SILVER – Ukraine
BRONZE – Denmark

Double-handed Dinghy: 470 Class
GOLD – Greece
SILVER – Spain
BRONZE – Sweden

Single-handed Dinghy: Europe Class
GOLD – Siren Sundby, Norway
SILVER – Lenka Smidova, Czech Republic
BRONZE – Signe Livbjerg, Denmark

Windsurfing
GOLD – Faustine Merret, France
SILVER – Jian Yin, China
BRONZE – Alessandra Sensini, Italy

MEN

Double-handed Dinghy: 470 Class
GOLD – USA
SILVER – Great Britain
BRONZE – Japan

Single-handed Dinghy: Finn Class
GOLD – Ben Ainslie, Great Britain
SILVER – Rafael Trujillo, Spain
BRONZE – Mateusz Kusznierewicz, Poland

Keelboat: Star Class
GOLD – Brazil
SILVER – Canada
BRONZE – France

Open Single-handed Dinghy: Laser Class
GOLD – Robert Scheidt, Brazil
SILVER – Andreas Geritzer, Austria
BRONZE – Vasilij Zbogar, Slovenia

Open Double-handed Dinghy: 49er Class
GOLD – Spain
SILVER – Ukraine
BRONZE – Great Britain

Open Multihull: Tornado Class
GOLD – Austria
SILVER – USA
BRONZE – Argentina

Windsurfing
GOLD – Gal Fridman, Israel
SILVER – Nikolaos Kaklamanakis, Greece
BRONZE – Nick Dempsey, Great Britain

2004 Sport-by-Sport Results (cont.)

SHOOTING

WOMEN

10-meter Air Pistol
GOLD – Olena Kostevych, Ukraine
SILVER – Jasna Sekaric, Serbia-Montenegro
BRONZE – Maria Grozdeva, Bulgaria

10-meter Air Rifle
GOLD – Li Du, China
SILVER – Lioubov Galkina, Russia
BRONZE – Katerina Kurkova, Czech Republic

25-meter Pistol
GOLD – Maria Grozdeva, Bulgaria
SILVER – Lenka Hykova, Czech Republic
BRONZE – Irada Ashumova, Azerbaijan

50-meter Rifle 3 Position
GOLD – Lioubov Galkina, Russia
SILVER – Valentina Turisini, Italy
BRONZE – Chengyi Wang, China

Trap
GOLD – Suzanne Balogh, Australia
SILVER – Maria Quintanal, Spain
BRONZE – Bo Na Lee, South Korea

Kim Rhode, United States

DOUGLAS C. PIZAC/AP

Double Trap
GOLD – Kim Rhode, USA
SILVER – Bo Na Lee, South Korea
BRONZE – E Gao, China

Skeet
GOLD – Diana Igaly, Hungary
SILVER – Ning Wei, China
BRONZE – Zemfira Meftakhetdinova, Azerbaijan

MEN

10-meter Air Pistol
GOLD – Yifu Wang, China
SILVER – Mikhail Nestruev, Russia
BRONZE – Vladimir Isakov, Russia

10-meter Air Rifle
GOLD – Qinan Zhu, China
SILVER – Jie Li, China
BRONZE – Jozef Gonci, Slovakia

10-meter Running Target
GOLD – Manfred Kurzer, Germany
SILVER – Alexander Blinov, Russia
BRONZE – Dimitri Lykin, Russia

25-meter Rapid-fire Pistol
GOLD – Ralf Schumann, Germany
SILVER – Sergei Poliakov, Russia
BRONZE – Sergei Alifirenko, Russia

50-meter Pistol
GOLD – Mikhail Nestruev, Russia
SILVER – Jong Oh Jin, South Korea
BRONZE – Jong Su Kim, North Korea

50-meter Rifle 3 Position
GOLD – Zhanbo Jia, China
SILVER – Michael Anti, USA
BRONZE – Christian Planer, Austria

50-meter Rifle Prone
GOLD – Matthew Emmons, USA
SILVER – Christian Lusch, Germany
BRONZE – Sergei Martinov, Belarus

Trap
GOLD – Alexei Alipov, Russia
SILVER – Giovanni Pellielo, Italy
BRONZE – Adam Vella, Australia

Double Trap
GOLD – Ahmed Almaktoum, United Arab Emirates
SILVER – Rajyavardhan S. Rathore, India
BRONZE – Zheng Wang, China

Skeet
GOLD – Andrea Benelli, Italy
SILVER – Marko Kemppainen, Finland
BRONZE – Juan Miguel Rodriguez, Cuba

SOCCER

WOMEN
GOLD – USA
SILVER – Brazil
BRONZE – Germany

MEN
GOLD – Argentina
SILVER – Paraguay
BRONZE – Italy

SOFTBALL

GOLD – USA
SILVER – Australia
BRONZE – Japan

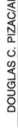

Jenny Finch, United States

JOHN W. McDONOUGH/SPORTS ILLUSTRATED

SWIMMING

WOMEN

50-meter Freestyle
GOLD – Inge de Bruijn, Netherlands
SILVER – Malia Metella, France
BRONZE – Lisbeth Lenton, Australia

100-meter Freestyle
GOLD – Jodie Henry, Australia
SILVER – Inge de Bruijn, Netherlands
BRONZE – Natalie Coughlin, USA

200-meter Freestyle
GOLD – Camelia Potec, Romania
SILVER – Federica Pellegrini, Italy
BRONZE – Solenne Figues, France

400-meter Freestyle
GOLD – Laure Manaudou, France
SILVER – Otylia Jedrzejczak, Poland
BRONZE – Kaitlin Sandeno, USA

800-meter Freestyle
GOLD – Ai Shibata, Japan
SILVER – Laure Manaudou, France
BRONZE – Diana Munz, USA

100-meter Backstroke
GOLD – Natalie Coughlin, USA
SILVER – Kirsty Coventry, Zimbabwe
BRONZE – Laure Manaudou, France

200-meter Backstroke
GOLD – Kirsty Coventry, Zimbabwe
SILVER – Stanislava Komarova, Russia
BRONZE – Reiko Nakamura, Japan and Antje Buschschulte, Germany

2004 Sport-by-Sport Results (cont.)

■ 100-meter Breaststroke
GOLD – Xuejuan Luo, China
SILVER – Brooke Hanson, Australia
BRONZE – Leisel Jones, Australia

■ 200-meter Breaststroke
GOLD – Amanda Beard, USA
SILVER – Leisel Jones, Australia
BRONZE – Anne Poleska, Germany

■ 100-meter Butterfly
GOLD – Petria Thomas, Australia
SILVER – Otylia Jedrzejczak, Poland
BRONZE – Inge de Bruijn, Netherlands

■ 200-meter Butterfly
GOLD – Otylia Jedrzejczak, Poland
SILVER – Petria Thomas, Australia
BRONZE – Yuko Nakanishi, Japan

■ 200-meter Individual Medley
GOLD – Yana Klochkova, Ukraine
SILVER – Amanda Beard, USA
BRONZE – Kirsty Coventry, Zimbabwe

■ 400-meter Individual Medley
GOLD – Yana Klochkova, Ukraine
SILVER – Kaitlin Sandeno, USA
BRONZE – Georgina Bardach, Argentina

■ 400-meter Medley Relay
GOLD – Australia
SILVER – USA
BRONZE – Germany

■ 400-meter Freestyle Relay
GOLD – Australia
SILVER – USA
BRONZE – Netherlands

■ 800-meter Freestyle Relay
GOLD – USA
SILVER – China
BRONZE – Germany

Yana Klochkova, Ukraine

HEINZ KLUETMEIER/SPORTS ILLUSTRATED

MEN

■ 50-meter Freestyle
GOLD – Gary Hall, Jr., USA
SILVER – Duje Draganja, Croatia
BRONZE – Roland Mark Schoeman, South Africa

■ 100-meter Freestyle
GOLD – Pieter van den Hoogenband, Netherlands
SILVER – Roland Mark Schoeman, South Africa
BRONZE – Ian Thorpe, Australia

■ 200-meter Freestyle
GOLD – Ian Thorpe, Australia
SILVER – Pieter van den Hoogenband, Netherlands
BRONZE – Michael Phelps, USA

■ 400-meter Freestyle
GOLD – Ian Thorpe, Australia
SILVER – Grant Hackett, Australia
BRONZE – Klete Keller, USA

■ 1,500-meter Freestyle
GOLD – Grant Hackett, Australia
SILVER – Larsen Jensen, USA
BRONZE – David Davies, Great Britain

■ 100-meter Backstroke
GOLD – Aaron Peirsol, USA
SILVER – Markus Rogan, Austria
BRONZE – Tomomi Morita, Japan

■ 200-meter Backstroke
GOLD – Aaron Peirsol, USA
SILVER – Marcus Rogan, Austria
BRONZE – Razvan Florea, Romania

■ 100-meter Breaststroke
GOLD – Kosuke Kitajima, Japan
SILVER – Brendan Hansen, USA
BRONZE – Hugues Duboscq, France

■ 200-meter Breaststroke
GOLD – Kosuke Kitajima, Japan
SILVER – Daniel Gyurta, Hungary
BRONZE – Brendan Hansen, USA

■ 100-meter Butterfly
GOLD – Michael Phelps, USA
SILVER – Ian Crocker, USA
BRONZE – Andriy Serdinov, Ukraine

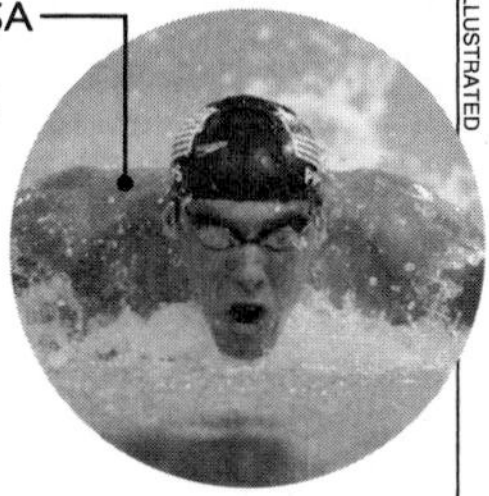

Michael Phelps, United States

SIMON BRUTY/SPORTS ILLUSTRATED

■ 200-meter Butterfly
GOLD – Michael Phelps, USA
SILVER – Takashi Yamamoto, Japan
BRONZE – Stephen Parry, Great Britain

■ 200-meter Individual Medley
GOLD – Michael Phelps, USA
SILVER – Ryan Lochte, USA
BRONZE – George Bovell, Trinidad and Tobago

■ 400-meter Individual Medley
GOLD – Michael Phelps, USA
SILVER – Erik Vendt, USA
BRONZE – Laszlo Cseh, Hungary

■ 400-meter Medley Relay
GOLD – USA
SILVER – Germany
BRONZE – Japan

■ 400-meter Freestyle Relay
GOLD – South Africa
SILVER – Netherlands
BRONZE – USA

■ 800-meter Freestyle Relay
GOLD – USA
SILVER – Australia
BRONZE – Italy

SYNCHRONIZED SWIMMING

■ Duet
GOLD – Russia
SILVER – Japan
BRONZE – USA

■ Team
GOLD – Russia
SILVER – Japan
BRONZE – USA

Did You Know?

In 2004, Olympic swimming events were held outdoors for the first time since 1992. Temperatures were in the 90s, but eight world records were broken.

2004 Sport-by-Sport Results (cont.)

TABLE TENNIS

WOMEN

Singles
GOLD – Yining Zhang, China
SILVER – Hyang Mi Kim, North Korea
BRONZE – Kyung Ah Kim, South Korea

Doubles
GOLD – China
SILVER – South Korea
BRONZE – China

MEN

Singles
GOLD – Seung Min Ryu, South Korea
SILVER – Hao Wang, China
BRONZE – Liqin Wang, China

Doubles
GOLD – China
SILVER – Hong Kong
BRONZE – Denmark

TAEKWONDO

WOMEN

Under 49 kg
GOLD – Shih Hsin Chen, Taiwan
SILVER – Yanelis Yuliet Labrada Diaz, Cuba
BRONZE – Yaowapa Boorapolchai, Thailand

Under 57 kg
GOLD – Ji Won Jang, South Korea
SILVER – Nia Abdallah, USA
BRONZE – Iridia Salazar Blanco, Mexico

Under 67 kg
GOLD – Wei Luo, China
SILVER – Elisavet Mystakidou, Greece
BRONZE – Kyung Sun Hwang, South Korea

Over 67 kg
GOLD – Zhong Chen, China
SILVER – Myriam Baverel, France
BRONZE – Adriana Carmona, Venezuela

MEN

Under 58 kg
GOLD – Mu Yen Chu, Taiwan
SILVER – Oscar Francisco Salazar Blanco, Mexico
BRONZE – Tamer Bayoumi, Egypt

Under 68 kg
GOLD – Hadi Saei Bonehkohal, Iran
SILVER – Chih Hsiung Huang, Taiwan
BRONZE – Myeong Seob Song, South Korea

Under 80 kg
GOLD – Steven Lopez, USA
SILVER – Bahri Tanrikulu, Turkey
BRONZE – Yossef Karami, Iran

Over 80 kg
GOLD – Dae Sung Moon, South Korea
SILVER – Alexandros Nikolaidis, Greece
BRONZE – Pascal Gentil, France

Did You Know?

At the first modern Olympics, in 1896, fencing competitors wore white uniforms, and the tip of the weapons was dipped in ink. When a fencer scored a hit, his weapon left an ink spot on the opponent's uniform. White uniforms are still worn today, but hits are scored electronically.

TENNIS

WOMEN

Singles
GOLD – Justine Henin-Hardenne, Belgium
SILVER – Amélie Mauresmo, France
BRONZE – Alicia Molik, Australia

Doubles
GOLD – China
SILVER – Spain
BRONZE – Argentina

Justine Henin-Hardenne, Belgium

CLIVE BRUNSKILL/GETTY IMAGES

MEN

Singles
GOLD – Nicolas Massu, Chile
SILVER – Mardy Fish, USA
BRONZE – Fernando Gonzalez, Chile

Doubles
GOLD – Chile
SILVER – Germany
BRONZE – Croatia

TRACK AND FIELD

WOMEN

100 meters
GOLD – Yuliya Nesterenko, Belarus
SILVER – Lauryn Williams, USA
BRONZE – Veronica Campbell, Jamaica

200 meters
GOLD – Veronica Campbell, Jamaica
SILVER – Allyson Felix, USA
BRONZE – Debbie Ferguson, Bahamas

400 meters
GOLD – Tonique Williams-Darling, Bahamas
SILVER – Ana Guevara, Mexico
BRONZE – Natalya Antyukh, Russia

800 meters
GOLD – Kelly Holmes, Great Britain
SILVER – Hasna Benhassi, Morocco
BRONZE – Jolanda Ceplak, Slovenia

1,500 meters
GOLD – Kelly Holmes, Great Britain
SILVER – Tatyana Tomashova, Russia
BRONZE – Maria Cioncan, Romania

5,000 meters
GOLD – Meseret Defar, Ethiopia
SILVER – Isabella Ochichi, Kenya
BRONZE – Tirunesh Dibaba, Ethiopia

10,000 meters
GOLD – Huina Xing, China
SILVER – Ejegayehu Dibaba, Ethiopia
BRONZE – Derartu Tulu, Ethiopia

2004 Sport-by-Sport Results (cont.)

■ 20-kilometer Walk
GOLD – Athanasia Tsoumeleka, Greece
SILVER – Olimpiada Ivanova, Russia
BRONZE – Jane Saville, Australia

■ 100-meter Hurdles
GOLD – Joanna Hayes, USA
SILVER – Olena Krasovska, Ukraine
BRONZE – Melissa Morrison, USA

■ 400-meter Hurdles
GOLD – Fani Halkia, Greece
SILVER – Ionela Tirlea-Manolache, Romania
BRONZE – Tetiana Tereshchuk-Antipova, Ukraine

■ High Jump
GOLD – Yelena Slesarenko, Russia
SILVER – Hestrie Cloete, South Africa
BRONZE – Viktoriya Styopina, Ukraine

■ Pole Vault
GOLD – Yelena Isinbayeva, Russia
SILVER – Svetlana Feofanova, Russia
BRONZE – Anna Rogowska, Poland

■ Long Jump
GOLD – Tatyana Lebedeva, Russia
SILVER – Irina Simagina, Russia
BRONZE – Tatyana Kotova, Russia

■ Triple Jump
GOLD – Francoise Mbango Etone, Cameroon
SILVER – Hrysopiyi Devetzi, Greece
BRONZE – Tatyana Lebedeva, Russia

■ Shot Put
GOLD – Yumileidi Cumba, Cuba
SILVER – Nadine Kleinert, Germany
BRONZE – Svetlana Krivelyova, Russia

■ Discus Throw
GOLD – Natalya Sadova, Russia
SILVER – Anastasia Kelesidou, Greece
BRONZE – Irina Yatchenko, Belarus

■ Javelin Throw
GOLD – Osleidys Menendez, Cuba
SILVER – Steffi Nerius, Germany
BRONZE – Mirela Manjani, Greece

■ Hammer Throw
GOLD – Olga Kuzenkova, Russia
SILVER – Yipsi Moreno, Cuba
BRONZE – Yunaika Crawford, Cuba

■ 4x100-meter Relay
GOLD – Jamaica
SILVER – Russia
BRONZE – France

■ 4x400-meter Relay
GOLD – USA
SILVER – Russia
BRONZE – Jamaica

Justin Gatlin, United States

SIMON BRUTY/SPORTS ILLUSTRATED

■ Heptathlon
GOLD – Carolina Kluft, Sweden
SILVER – Austra Skujyte, Lithuania
BRONZE – Kelly Sotherton, Great Britain

■ Marathon
GOLD – Mizuki Noguchi, Japan
SILVER – Catherine Ndereba, Kenya
BRONZE – Deena Kastor, USA

MEN

■ 100 meters
GOLD – Justin Gatlin, USA
SILVER – Francis Obikwelu, Portugal
BRONZE – Maurice Greene, USA

■ 200 meters
GOLD – Shawn Crawford, USA
SILVER – Bernard Williams, USA
BRONZE – Justin Gatlin, USA

■ 400 meters
GOLD – Jeremy Wariner, USA
SILVER – Otis Harris, USA
BRONZE – Derrick Brew, USA

■ 800 meters
GOLD – Yuriy Borzakovskiy, Russia
SILVER – Mbulaeni Mulaudzi, South Africa
BRONZE – Wilson Kipketer, Denmark

■ 1,500 meters
GOLD – Hicham El Guerrouj, Morocco
SILVER – Bernard Lagat, Kenya
BRONZE – Rui Silva, Portugal

Hicham El Guerrouj, Morocco

BILL FRAKES/SPORTS ILLUSTRATED

■ 3,000-meter Steeplechase
GOLD – Ezekiel Kemboi, Kenya
SILVER – Brimin Kipruto, Kenya
BRONZE – Paul Kipsiele Koech, Kenya

■ 5,000 meters
GOLD – Hicham El Guerrouj, Morocco
SILVER – Kenenisa Bekele, Ethiopia
BRONZE – Eliud Kipchoge, Kenya

■ 10,000 meters
GOLD – Kenenisa Bekele, Ethiopia
SILVER – Sileshi Sihine, Ethiopia
BRONZE – Zersenay Tadesse, Eritrea

■ 20-kilometer Walk
GOLD – Ivano Brugnetti, Italy
SILVER – Francisco Javier Fernández, Spain
BRONZE – Nathan Deakes, Australia

■ 50-kilometer Walk
GOLD – Robert Korzeniowski, Poland
SILVER – Denis Nizhegorodov, Russia
BRONZE – Aleksey Voyevodin, Russia

■ 110-meter Hurdles
GOLD – Xiang Liu, China
SILVER – Terrence Trammell, USA
BRONZE – Anier Garcia, Cuba

■ 400-meter Hurdles
GOLD – Felix Sanchez, Dominican Republic
SILVER – Danny McFarlane, Jamaica
BRONZE – Naman Keita, France

■ High Jump
GOLD – Stefan Holm, Sweden
SILVER – Matt Hemingway, USA
BRONZE – Jaroslav Baba, Czech Republic

■ Pole Vault
GOLD – Timothy Mack, USA
SILVER – Toby Stevenson, USA
BRONZE – Giuseppe Gibilisco, Italy

2004 Sport-by-Sport Results (cont.)

■ Long Jump
GOLD – Dwight Phillips, USA
SILVER – John Moffitt, USA
BRONZE – Joan Lino Martinez, Spain

■ Triple Jump
GOLD – Christian Olsson, Sweden
SILVER – Marian Oprea, Romania
BRONZE – Danila Burkenya, Russia

■ Shot Put
GOLD – Yuriy Bilonog, Ukraine
SILVER – Adam Nelson, USA
BRONZE – Joachim Olsen, Denmark

■ Discus Throw
GOLD – Virgilijus Alekna, Lithuania
SILVER – Zoltan Kovago, Hungary
BRONZE – Aleksander Tammert, Estonia

■ Javelin Throw
GOLD – Andreas Thorkildsen, Norway
SILVER – Vadims Vasilevskis, Latvia
BRONZE – Sergey Makarov, Russia

■ Hammer Throw
GOLD – Koji Murofushi, Japan
SILVER – Ivan Tikhon, Belarus
BRONZE – Esref Apak, Turkey

■ 4x100-meter Relay
GOLD – Great Britain
SILVER – USA
BRONZE – Nigeria

■ 4x400-meter Relay
GOLD – USA
SILVER – Australia
BRONZE – Nigeria

■ Decathlon
GOLD – Roman Sebrle, Czech Republic
SILVER – Bryan Clay, USA
BRONZE – Dmitriy Karpov, Kazakhstan

■ Marathon
GOLD – Stefano Baldini, Italy
SILVER – Mebrahtom Keflezighi, USA
BRONZE – Vanderlei Lima, Brazil

TRIATHLON

WOMEN
GOLD – Kate Allen, Austria
SILVER – Loretta Harrop, Australia
BRONZE – Susan Williams, USA

MEN
GOLD – Hamish Carter, New Zealand
SILVER – Bevan Docherty, New Zealand
BRONZE – Sven Riederer, Switzerland

Hamish Carter, New Zealand

REUTERS/MIKE HUTCHINGS

VOLLEYBALL

WOMEN
GOLD – China
SILVER – Russia
BRONZE – Cuba

MEN
GOLD – Brazil
SILVER – Italy
BRONZE – Russia

Brenda Villa, United States

STUART FRANKLIN/GETTY IMAGES

WATER POLO

WOMEN
GOLD – Italy
SILVER – Greece
BRONZE – USA

MEN
GOLD – Hungary
SILVER – Serbia-Montenegro
BRONZE – Russia

WEIGHTLIFTING

WOMEN

■ 48 kg
GOLD – Nurcan Taylan, Turkey
SILVER – Zhuo Li, China
BRONZE – Aree Wiratthaworn, Thailand

■ 53 kg
GOLD – Udomporn Polsak, Thailand
SILVER – Raema Lisa Rumbewas, Indonesia
BRONZE – Mabel Mosquera, Colombia

■ 58 kg
GOLD – Yanqing Chen, China
SILVER – Song Hui Ri, North Korea
BRONZE – Wandee Kameaim, Thailand

■ 63 kg
GOLD – Nataliya Skakun, Ukraine
SILVER – Hanna Batsiushka, Belarus
BRONZE – Tatsiana Stukalava, Belarus

■ 69 kg
GOLD – Chunhong Liu, China
SILVER – Eszter Krutzler, Hungary
BRONZE – Zarema Kasaeva, Russia

■ 75 kg
GOLD – Pawina Thongsuk, Thailand
SILVER – Natalia Zabolotnaia, Russia
BRONZE – Valentina Popova, Russia

■ +75 kg
GOLD – Tang Gonghong, China
SILVER – Mi Ran Jang, South Korea
BRONZE – Agata Wrobel, Poland

MEN

■ 56 kg
GOLD – Halil Mutlu, Turkey
SILVER – Meijin Wu, China
BRONZE – Sedat Artuc, Turkey

■ 62 kg
GOLD – Zhiyong Shi, China
SILVER – Maosheng Le, China
BRONZE – Israel Jose Rubio, Venezuela

2004 Sport-by-Sport Results (cont.)

■ 69 kg
GOLD – Guozheng Zhang, China
SILVER – Bae Young Lee, South Korea
BRONZE – Nikolay Pechalov, Croatia

■ 77 kg
GOLD – Taner Sagir, Turkey
SILVER – Sergey Filimonov, Kazakhstan
BRONZE – Oleg Perepetchenov, Russia

■ 85 kg
GOLD – George Asanidze, Georgia
SILVER – Andrei Rybakou, Belarus
BRONZE – Pyrros Dimas, Greece

■ 94 kg
GOLD – Milen Dobrev, Bulgaria
SILVER – Khadjimourad Akkaev, Russia
BRONZE – Eduard Tjukin, Russia

■ 105 kg
GOLD – Dmitry Berestov, Russia
SILVER – Igor Razoronov, Ukraine
BRONZE – Gleb Pisarevskiy, Russia

■ +105 kg
GOLD – Hossein Reza Zadeh, Iran
SILVER – Viktors Scerbatihs, Latvia
BRONZE – Velichko Cholakov, Bulgaria

Hossein Reza Zadeh, Iran

BOB MARTIN/SPORTS ILLUSTRATED

WRESTLING (FREESTYLE)

WOMEN

■ 48 kg
GOLD – Irini Merleni, Ukraine
SILVER – Chiharu Icho, Japan
BRONZE – Patricia Miranda, USA

■ 55 kg
GOLD – Saori Yoshida, Japan
SILVER – Tonya Verbeek, Canada
BRONZE – Anna Gomis, France

■ 63 kg
GOLD – Kaori Icho, Japan
SILVER – Sara McMann, USA
BRONZE – Lise Legrand, France

■ 72 kg
GOLD – Xu Wang, China
SILVER – Gouzel Maniourova, Russia
BRONZE – Kyoko Hamaguchi, Japan

MEN

■ 55 kg
GOLD – Mavlet Batirov, Russia
SILVER – Stephen Abas, USA
BRONZE – Chikara Tanabe, Japan

■ 60 kg
GOLD – Yandro Miguel Quintana, Cuba
SILVER – Masuod Jokar, Iran
BRONZE – Kenji Inoue, Japan

■ 66 kg
GOLD – Elbrus Tedeyev, Ukraine
SILVER – Jamill Kelly, USA
BRONZE – Makhach Murtazaliev, Russia

■ 74 kg
GOLD – Buvaysa Saytiev, Russia
SILVER – Gennadiy Laliyev, Kazakhstan
BRONZE – Ivan Fundora, Cuba

■ 84 kg
GOLD – Cael Sanderson, USA
SILVER – Eui Jae Moon, South Korea
BRONZE – Sazhid Sazhidov, Russia

■ 96 kg
GOLD – Khadjimourat Gatsalov, Russia
SILVER – Magomed Ibragimov, Uzbekistan
BRONZE – Alireza Heidari, Iran

■ 120 kg
GOLD – Artur Taymazov, Uzbekistan
SILVER – Alireza Rezaei, Iran
BRONZE – Aydin Polatci, Turkey

WRESTLING (GRECO-ROMAN)

MEN

■ 55 kg
GOLD – Istvan Majoros, Hungary
SILVER – Gueidar Mamedaliev, Russia
BRONZE – Artiom Kiouregkian, Greece

■ 60 kg
GOLD – Ji Hyun Jung, South Korea
SILVER – Roberto Monzon, Cuba
BRONZE – Armen Nazarian, Bulgaria

■ 66 kg
GOLD – Farid Mansurov, Azerbaijan
SILVER – Seref Eroglu, Turkey
BRONZE – Mkkhitar Manukyan, Kazakhstan

■ 74 kg
GOLD – Alexandr Dokturishivili, Uzbekistan
SILVER – Marko Yli-Hannuksela, Finland
BRONZE – Varteres Samourgachev, Russia

■ 84 kg
GOLD – Alexei Michine, Russia
SILVER – Ara Abrahamian, Sweden
BRONZE – Viachaslau Makaranka, Belarus

■ 96 kg
GOLD – Karam Ibrahim, Egypt
SILVER – Ramaz Nozadze, Georgia
BRONZE – Mehmet Ozal, Turkey

■ 120 kg
GOLD – Khasan Baroev, Russia
SILVER – Georgiy Tsurtsumia, Kazakhstan
BRONZE – Rulon Gardner, USA

Fast Fact: In the ancient Olympic Games, athletes threw the javelin for accuracy. Today, the athlete who throws it the farthest gets the gold.

Trivia Challenge

Who is the youngest athlete to win a gold medal in the modern Olympics (since 1896)?

Marjorie Gestring of the U.S. won the springboard diving competition at the 1936 Summer Olympics. She was 13 years, 268 days old.

WINTER OLYMPICS

On June 19, 1999, Turin, Italy, was selected to host the XX Winter Olympics in 2006. Five other cities had bid for the Games: Helsinki, Finland; Klagenfurt, Austria; Poprad-Tatry, Slovakia; Sion, Switzerland; and Zakopane, Poland.

The XX Olympics will be held from February 10-26, 2006. More than 2,500 athletes from 80 countries will compete in seven sports. Figure skating, ice hockey, alpine skiing, snowboarding, and short-track speed skating will be among the most popular events. Figure skater Sasha Cohen, short-track speed skater Apolo Ohno, and alpine skier Bode Miller are among the U.S. athletes who are expected to compete.

JOHN BIEVER

The opening ceremony at the Winter Games in 2002, in Salt Lake City, Utah

Did You Know?

In 2002, bobsledder Vonetta Flowers of the U.S. became the first African-American athlete to win a gold medal at the Winter Olympics.

All-time Winter Olympic Medal Winners

NATIONS—OVERALL

Nation	GOLD	SILVER	BRONZE	TOTAL
NORWAY	94	93	73	260
SOVIET UNION (1956-88)	78	56	59	193
UNITED STATES	70	70	51	191
AUSTRIA	41	57	65	163
GERMANY	54	51	37	142
FINLAND	41	51	49	141
EAST GERMANY (1956-88)	39	37	35	111
SWEDEN	36	28	38	102
SWITZERLAND	32	33	36	101
CANADA	30	28	37	95

Today's Stars

Bode Miller, alpine skier, b. October 12, 1977, Easton, New Hampshire. Miller is known for his all-out style. He was the World Cup giant slalom champion in 2003-04, the first U.S. man to win the title since Phil Mahre won it in 1982-83. Miller finished fourth overall in the Cup standings. He was second overall in the Cup standings in 2002-03 and won gold medals in the combined (downhill and slalom) and giant slalom events at the World Alpine Championships, in 2003. Miller's surge to the top of men's skiing came in 2002 at the Winter Olympics, where he won silver medals in the combined and giant slalom.

Ross Powers, snowboarder, b. February 10, 1979, Londonderry, Vermont. Powers is now one of snowboarding's elder statesmen. He was nine when he competed in his first U.S. Open Snowboarding Championship. He has won the championship twice and finished second once. Powers won the Halfpipe gold medal at the Olympics in 2002 and the bronze in 1998. (Snowboarding became an official Olympic medal sport in 1998.) He has won two Winter X Games gold medals (Slopestyle and Halfpipe).

Sasha Cohen, figure skater, b. October 26, 1984, Westwood, California. Cohen is known for her graceful skating as well as her dazzling jumps and spins. For the past two years, she has been the dominant female skater in the world. Cohen won four elite competitions between October and November 2003. At the start of 2004, she finished second at the U.S. and world championships. She trains with Robin Wagner, who coached Sarah Hughes of the U.S. to the Olympic gold medal in 2002.

CARL YARBROUGH

Bode Miller won two silver medals at the Olympics in 2002.

Trivia Challenge

True or False. In 1980, the U.S. hockey team defeated the U.S.S.R. for the Olympic gold medal.

False. The U.S. defeated the U.S.S.R. in the semi-final game, 4–3. They went on to win the gold medal by defeating Finland, 4–2.

WINTER OLYMPICS

Past Winter Olympic Hosts

				COMPETITORS MEN	WOMEN	NATIONS
XIX	2002	SALT LAKE CITY, UTAH	February 8-24	1,513	886	77
XVIII	1998	NAGANO, JAPAN	February 7-22	1,488	814	72
XVII	1994	LILLEHAMMER, NORWAY	February 12-27	1,217	522	67
XVI	1992	ALBERTVILLE, FRANCE	February 8-23	1,313	488	64
XV	1988	CALGARY, ALBERTA, CANADA	February 13-28	1,110	313	57
XIV	1984	SARAJEVO, YUGOSLAVIA	February 8-19	1,100	274	49
XIII	1980	LAKE PLACID, NEW YORK	February 13-24	839	233	37
XII	1976	INNSBRUCK, AUSTRIA	February 4-15	892	231	37
XI	1972	SAPPORO, JAPAN	February 3-13	800	206	35
X	1968	GRENOBLE, FRANCE	February 6-18	947	211	37
IX	1964	INNSBRUCK, AUSTRIA	January 29-February 9	891	200	36
VIII	1960	SQUAW VALLEY, CALIFORNIA	February 18-28	522	143	30
VII	1956	CORTINA d'AMPEZZO, ITALY	January 26-February 5	688	132	32
VI	1952	OSLO, NORWAY	February 14-25	585	109	30
V	1948	ST. MORITZ, SWITZERLAND	January 30-February 8	592	77	28
--	1944	CORTINA d'AMPEZZO, ITALY	Canceled because of World War II			
--	1940	GARMISCH-PARTENKIRCHEN, GERMANY	Canceled because of World War II			
IV	1936	GARMISCH-PARTENKIRCHEN, GERMANY	February 6-16	588	80	28
III	1932	LAKE PLACID, NEW YORK	February 4-13	231	21	17
II	1928	ST. MORITZ, SWITZERLAND	February 11-19	438	26	25
I	1924	CHAMONIX, FRANCE	January 25-February 4	245	13	16

AL BELLO/GETTY IMAGES

Bjorn Daehlie

Fast Fact: In 1988, figure skater Katarina Witt of Germany became the first woman in 52 years to win the women's singles event at two straight Olympics (1984, 1988).

All-time Winter Olympic Medal Winners

INDIVIDUALS—OVERALL—MEN

ATHLETE, Nation	SPORT	GOLD	SILVER	BRONZE	TOTAL
BJORN DAEHLIE, Norway	Nordic Skiing	8	4	0	**12**
SIXTEN JERNBERG, Sweden	Nordic Skiing	4	3	2	**9**
Seven tied with 7.					

All-time Winter Olympic Medal Winners (cont.)

INDIVIDUALS—OVERALL—WOMEN

ATHLETE, Nation	SPORT	GOLD	SILVER	BRONZE	TOTAL
RAISA SMETANINA, U.S.S.R./United Team	Nordic Skiing	4	5	1	**10**
LYUBOV EGOROVA, United Team/Russia	Nordic Skiing	6	3	0	**9**
LARISSA LAZUTINA, United Team/Russia	Nordic Skiing	5	3	1	**9**
STEFANIA BELMONDO, Italy	Nordic Skiing	2	3	4	**9**
Four tied with 8.					

INDIVIDUALS—GOLD

MEN		WOMEN	
BJORN DAEHLIE, Norway	**8**	**LYUBOV EGOROVA,** United Team/Russia	**6**
OLE EINAR BJOERNDALEN, Norway	**5**	**LYDIA SKOBILKOVA,** U.S.S.R.	**6**
ERIC HEIDEN, United States	**5**	**BONNIE BLAIR,** United States	**5**
A. CLAS THUNBERG, Finland	**5**	**LARISSA LAZUTINA,** United Team/Russia	**5**
Nine tied with 4.		*Four tied with 4.*	

Legends

Johann Olav Koss won a total of five Olympic medals in 1992 and 1994

SIMON BRUTY/GETTY IMAGES

Johann Olav Koss, speed skater, b. October 29, 1968, Oslo, Norway. Koss dominated men's long-track speed skating at the Olympics in 1994. He won gold medals in the 1,500 meters, 5,000 meters, and 10,000 meters in world-record time. Koss also won gold in the 1,500 meters and silver in the 10,000 meters at the Games in 1992. He retired from skating after the 1994 Games and helped raise money for children in countries at war.

Alberto Tomba, alpine skier, b. December 19, 1966, Lazzaro di Savenna, Italy. Tomba won the slalom and giant slalom events at the Olympics in 1988. Four years later, he became the first alpine skier to win the same event in back-to-back Olympics when he won the giant slalom at the 1992 Games. He also won a silver medal in the slalom. At the 1994 Olympics, Tomba's strong second run in the slalom moved him from 12th place to second, earning him the silver medal.

Jayne Torvill and Christopher Dean, ice dancers, b. October 7, 1957, Nottingham, England (Torvill) and July 27, 1958, Nottingham, England (Dean). Torvill and Dean's program at the Olympics in 1984 is considered the greatest ice-dancing performance in history. Skating to the music of Maurice Ravel's "Bolero," their elegant style earned perfect scores (6.0) for artistic impression from all nine judges. Torvill and Dean also won the ice-dancing world championship four years in a row (1981-84) and a bronze medal at the Games in 1994.

SPORTS DIRECTORY

BASEBALL

Major League Baseball
245 Park Avenue
New York, NY 10167
(212) 931-7800

Anaheim Angels
Angel Stadium of Anaheim
2000 Gene Autry Way
Anaheim, CA 92806
(714) 940-2000

Arizona Diamondbacks
Bank One Ballpark
401 East Jefferson Street
Phoenix, AZ 85004
(602) 462-6500

Atlanta Braves
Turner Field
755 Hank Aaron Drive
Atlanta, GA 30315
(404) 522-7630

Baltimore Orioles
Oriole Park at Camden Yards
333 W. Camden Street
Baltimore, MD 21201
(410) 685-9800

Boston Red Sox
Fenway Park
4 Yawkey Way
Boston, MA 02215
(617) 267-9440

Chicago Cubs
Wrigley Field
1060 West Addison
Chicago, IL 60613
(773) 404-2827

Chicago White Sox
U.S. Cellular Field
333 West 35th Street
Chicago, IL 60616
(312) 674-1000

Cincinnati Reds
Great American Ball Park
100 Main Street
Cincinnati, OH 45202
(513) 765-7000

Cleveland Indians
Jacobs Field
2401 Ontario Street
Cleveland, OH 44115
(216) 420-4200

Colorado Rockies
Coors Field
2001 Blake Street
Denver, CO 80205
(303) 292-0200

Detroit Tigers
Comerica Park
2100 Woodward Avenue
Detroit, MI 48201
(313) 471-2000

Florida Marlins
Pro Player Stadium
2267 Dan Marino Boulevard
Miami, FL 33056
(305) 626-7400

Houston Astros
Minute Maid Park
501 Crawford Street
Houston, TX 77002
(713) 259-8000

Kansas City Royals
Kauffman Stadium
One Royal Way
Kansas City, MO 64129
(816) 921-8000

Los Angeles Dodgers
Dodger Stadium
1000 Elysian Park Avenue
Los Angeles, CA 90012
(323) 224-1500

Milwaukee Brewers
Miller Park
One Brewers Way
Milwaukee, WI 53214
(414) 902-4400

Minnesota Twins
Metrodome
34 Kirby Puckett Place
Minneapolis, MN 55415
(612) 375-1366

Montreal Expos
Olympic Stadium
4549 Pierre-de-Coubertin Avenue
Montreal, Quebec H1V 3N7 Canada
(514) 253-3434

New York Mets
Shea Stadium
123-01 Roosevelt Avenue
Flushing, NY 11368
(718) 507-6387

New York Yankees
Yankee Stadium
161st Street and River Avenue
Bronx, NY 10451
(718) 293-4300

Oakland Athletics
Network Associates Coliseum
7000 Coliseum Way
Oakland, CA 94621
(510) 638-4900

Philadelphia Phillies
Citizens Bank Park
One Citizens Bank Way
Philadelphia, PA 19148
(215) 463-6000

Pittsburgh Pirates
PNC Park
115 Federal Street
Pittsburgh, PA 15212
(412) 323-5000

San Diego Padres
PETCO Park
100 Park Boulevard
San Diego, CA 92101
(619) 881-6500

San Francisco Giants
SBC Park
24 Willie Mays Plaza
San Francisco, CA 94107
(415) 972-2000

Seattle Mariners
Safeco Field
P.O. Box 4100
Seattle, WA 98194
(206) 346-4001

St. Louis Cardinals
Busch Stadium
250 Stadium Plaza
St. Louis, MO 63102
(314) 421-3060

Tampa Bay Devil Rays
Tropicana Field
One Tropicana Drive
St. Petersburg, FL 33705
(727) 825-3137

Texas Rangers
The Ballpark in Arlington
1000 Ballpark Way
Arlington, TX 76011
(817) 273-5222

Toronto Blue Jays
SkyDome
1 Blue Jays Way
Suite 3200
Toronto, Ontario M5V 1J1
Canada
(416) 341-1000

PRO FOOTBALL

National Football League
280 Park Avenue
New York, NY 10017
(212) 450-2000

Arizona Cardinals
8701 South Hardy Drive
Tempe, AZ 85284
(602) 379-0101

Atlanta Falcons
4400 Falcon Parkway
Flowery Branch, GA 30542
(770) 965-3115

Baltimore Ravens
11001 Owings Mills Boulevard
Owings Mills, MD 21117
(410) 654-6200

Buffalo Bills
One Bills Drive
Orchard Park, NY 14127
(716) 648-1800

Carolina Panthers
Bank of America Stadium
800 South Mint Street
Charlotte, NC 28202
(704) 358-7000

Chicago Bears
1000 Football Drive
Lake Forest, IL 60045
(847) 295-6600

Cincinnati Bengals
One Paul Brown Stadium
Cincinnati, OH 45202
(513) 621-3550

Cleveland Browns
76 Lou Groza Boulevard
Berea, OH 44017
(440) 891-5000

Dallas Cowboys
One Cowboys Parkway
Irving, TX 75063
(972) 556-9900

Denver Broncos
13655 Broncos Parkway
Englewood, CO 80112
(303) 649-9000

Detroit Lions
222 Republic Drive
Allen Park, MI 48101
(313) 216-4000

Green Bay Packers
1265 Lombardi Avenue
Green Bay, WI 54304
(920) 496-5700

Houston Texans
Reliant Stadium
Two Reliant Park
Houston, TX 77054
(832) 667-2000

Indianapolis Colts
P.O. Box 535000
Indianapolis, IN 46253
(317) 297-2658

Jacksonville Jaguars
One ALLTEL Stadium Place
Jacksonville, FL 32202
(904) 633-6000

Kansas City Chiefs
One Arrowhead Drive
Kansas City, MO 64129
(816) 920-9300

Miami Dolphins
7500 S.W. 30th Street
Davie, FL 33314
(954) 452-7000

Minnesota Vikings
9520 Viking Drive
Eden Prairie, MN 55344
(952) 828-6500

New England Patriots
Gillette Stadium
One Patriot Place
Foxboro, MA 02035
(508) 543-8200

New Orleans Saints
5800 Airline Highway
Metairie, LA 70003
(504) 733-0255

New York Giants
Giants Stadium
East Rutherford, NJ 07073
(201) 935-8111

New York Jets
1000 Fulton Avenue
Hempstead, NY 11550
(516) 560-8100

Oakland Raiders
1220 Harbor Bay Parkway
Alameda, CA 94502
(510) 864-5000

Philadelphia Eagles
NovaCare Complex
One NovaCare Way
Philadelphia, PA 19145
(215) 463-2500

Pittsburgh Steelers
3400 South Water Street
Pittsburgh, PA 15203
(412) 432-7800

SPORTS DIRECTORY

San Diego Chargers
Qualcomm Stadium
4020 Murphy Canyon Road
San Diego, CA 92123
(858) 874-4500

San Francisco 49ers
4949 Centennial Boulevard
Santa Clara, CA 95054
(408) 562-4949

Seattle Seahawks
11220 N.E. 53rd Street
Kirkland, WA 98033
(425) 827-9777

St. Louis Rams
1 Rams Way
St. Louis, MO 63045
(314) 982-7267

Tampa Bay Buccaneers
One Buccaneer Place
Tampa, FL 33607
(813) 870-2700

Tennessee Titans
460 Great Circle Road
Nashville, TN 37228
(615) 565-4000

Washington Redskins
21300 Redskins Park Drive
Ashburn, VA 20147
(703) 726-7000

OTHER LEAGUES

Canadian Football League
50 Wellington Street East
3rd floor
Toronto, Ontario M5E 1C8
Canada
(416) 322-9650

NFL Europe
280 Park Avenue
New York, NY 10017
(212) 450-2000

PRO BASKETBALL

National Basketball Association
645 Fifth Avenue
New York, NY 10022
(212) 407-8000

Atlanta Hawks
One CNN Center
Atlanta, GA 30303
(404) 827-3800

Boston Celtics
151 Merrimac Street
Boston, MA 02114
(617) 854-8000

Charlotte Bobcats
100 Hive Drive
Charlotte, NC 28217
(704) 357-0252

Chicago Bulls
1901 W. Madison Street
Chicago, IL 60612
(312) 455-4000

Cleveland Cavaliers
1 Center Court
Cleveland, OH 44115
(216) 420-2000

Dallas Mavericks
2500 Victory Avenue
Dallas, TX 75219
(214) 665-4600

Denver Nuggets
1000 Chopper Circle
Denver, CO 80204
(303) 405-1100

Detroit Pistons
Three Championship Drive
Auburn Hills, MI 48326
(248) 377-0100

Golden State Warriors
1011 Broadway
Oakland, CA 94607
(510) 986-2200

Houston Rockets
1510 Polk Street
Houston, TX 77002
(713) 758-7200

Indiana Pacers
125 South Pennsylvania Street
Indianapolis, IN 46204
(317) 917-2500

Los Angeles Clippers
1111 South Figueroa Street
Suite 1100
Los Angeles, CA 90015
(213) 742-7500

Los Angeles Lakers
555 North Nash Street
El Segundo, CA 90245
(310) 426-6000

Memphis Grizzlies
175 Toyota Plaza
Suite 150
Memphis, TN 38103
(901) 205-1234

Miami Heat
601 Biscayne Boulevard
Miami, FL 33132
(786) 777-4328

Milwaukee Bucks
1001 North Fourth Street
Milwaukee, WI 53203
(414) 227-0500

Minnesota Timberwolves
600 First Avenue North
Minneapolis, MN 55403
(612) 673-1600

New Jersey Nets
390 Murray Hill Parkway
East Rutherford, NJ 07073
(201) 935-8888

New Orleans Hornets
1501 Girod Street
New Orleans, LA 70113
(504) 301-4000

New York Knicks
Two Pennsylvania Plaza
New York, NY 10121
(212) 465-5867

Orlando Magic
8701 Maitland Summit Boulevard
Orlando, FL 32810
(407) 916-2400

Philadelphia 76ers
3601 South Broad Street
Philadelphia, PA 19148
(215) 339-7600

Phoenix Suns
201 East Jefferson Street
Phoenix, AZ 85004
(602) 379-7900

Portland Trail Blazers
One Center Court
Suite 200
Portland, OR 97227
(503) 234-9291

Sacramento Kings
One Sports Parkway
Sacramento, CA 95834
(916) 928-0000

San Antonio Spurs
One SBC Center
San Antonio, TX 78219
(210) 444-5000

Seattle SuperSonics
351 Elliott Avenue West
Suite 500
Seattle, WA 98119
(206) 281-5800

Toronto Raptors
40 Bay Street, Suite 400
Toronto, Ontario M5J 2X2
Canada
(416) 815-5600

Utah Jazz
301 West South Temple
Salt Lake City, UT 84101
(801) 325-2500

Washington Wizards
601 F Street, NW
Washington, D.C. 20004
(202) 661-5000

WOMEN'S NATIONAL BASKETBALL ASSOCIATION

WNBA
645 Fifth Avenue
New York, NY 10022
(212) 688-9622

Charlotte Sting
129 W. Trade Street
Suite 700
Charlotte, NC 28202
(704) 357-0252

Connecticut Sun
1 Mohegan Sun Boulevard
Uncasville, CT 06382
(860) 862-4000

Detroit Shock
Three Championship Drive
Auburn Hills, MI 48326
(248) 377-0100

Houston Comets
Two Greenway Plaza
Suite 400
Houston, TX 77046
(713) 627-9622

Indiana Fever
125 S. Pennsylvania Street
Indianapolis, IN 46204
(317) 917-2500

Los Angeles Sparks
HealthSouth Training Center
2151 East Grand Avenue
Suite 100
El Segundo, CA 90245
(310) 341-1000

Minnesota Lynx
600 First Avenue North
Minneapolis, MN 55403
(612) 673-1600

New York Liberty
Two Pennsylvania Plaza
New York, NY 10121
(212) 564-9622

Phoenix Mercury
201 East Jefferson Street
Phoenix, AZ 85004
(602) 514-8333

Sacramento Monarchs
One Sports Parkway
Sacramento, CA 95834
(916) 928-0000

San Antonio Silver Stars
One SBC Center
San Antonio, TX 78219
(210) 444-5050

Seattle Storm
351 Elliott Avenue West
Suite 500
Seattle, WA 98119
(206) 281-5800

Washington Mystics
MCI Center
601 F Street, NW
Washington, D.C. 20004
(202) 661-5000

HOCKEY

National Hockey League
1251 Avenue of the Americas
47th floor
New York, NY 10020
(212) 789-2000

Mighty Ducks of Anaheim
Arrowhead Pond of Anaheim
2695 Katella Avenue
Anaheim, CA 92806
(714) 940-2900

Atlanta Thrashers
One CNN Center
12th floor, South Tower
Atlanta, GA 30303
(404) 827-5300

Boston Bruins
FleetCenter
One FleetCenter
Suite 250
Boston, MA 02114-1303
(617) 624-1900

Buffalo Sabres
HSBC Arena
One Seymour H. Knox III
Plaza
Buffalo, NY 14203
(716) 855-4100

Calgary Flames
Pengrowth Saddledome
P.O. Box 1540
Station M
Calgary, Alberta T2P 3B9
Canada
(403) 777-4636

Carolina Hurricanes
RBC Center
1400 Edwards Mill Road
Raleigh, NC 27607
(919) 467-7825

Chicago Blackhawks
United Center
1901 W. Madison Street
Chicago, IL 60612
(312) 455-7000

Colorado Avalanche
Pepsi Center
1000 Chopper Circle
Denver, CO 80204
(303) 405-1100

SPORTS DIRECTORY

Columbus Blue Jackets
Nationwide Arena
200 West Nationwide Boulevard
Columbus, OH 43215
(614) 246-4625

Dallas Stars
Dr. Pepper StarCenter
2601 Avenue of the Stars
Frisco, TX 75034
(214) 387-5500

Detroit Red Wings
Joe Louis Arena
600 Civic Center Drive
Detroit, MI 48226
(313) 396-7544

Edmonton Oilers
Skyreach Centre
11230-110th Street
Edmonton, Alberta T5G 3H7
Canada
(780) 414-4000

Florida Panthers
Office Depot Center
One Panther Parkway
Sunrise, FL 33323
(954) 835-7000

Los Angeles Kings
HealthSouth Training Center
555 N. Nash Street
El Segundo, CA 90245
(310) 535-4500

Minnesota Wild
317 Washington Street
St. Paul, MN 55102
(651) 602-6000

Montreal Canadiens
Bell Centre
1260 de la Gauchetière West
Montreal, Quebec H3B 5E8
Canada
(514) 932-2582

Nashville Predators
Gaylord Entertainment Center
501 Broadway
Nashville, TN 37203
(615) 770-2300

New Jersey Devils
Continental Airlines Arena
P.O. Box 504
East Rutherford, NJ 07073
(201) 935-6050

New York Islanders
1535 Old Country Road
Plainview, NY 11803
(516) 501-6700

New York Rangers
Madison Square Garden
Two Pennsylvania Plaza
14th floor
New York, NY 10121
(212) 465-6486

Ottawa Senators
Corel Centre
1000 Palladium Drive
Ottawa, Ontario K2V 1A5
Canada
(613) 599-0250

Philadelphia Flyers
Wachovia Center
3601 South Broad Street
Philadelphia, PA 19148
(215) 465-4500

Phoenix Coyotes
ALLTEL Ice Den
9375 East Bell Road
Scottsdale, AZ 85260
(480) 473-5600

Pittsburgh Penguins
Mellon Arena
66 Mario Lemieux Place
Pittsburgh, PA 15219
(412) 642-1300

San Jose Sharks
HP Pavilion at San Jose
525 West Santa Clara Street
San Jose, CA 95113
(408) 287-7070

St. Louis Blues
Savvis Center
1401 Clark Avenue
St. Louis, MO 63103
(314) 622-2500

Tampa Bay Lightning
St. Pete Times Forum
401 Channelside Drive
Tampa, FL 33602
(813) 301-6500

Toronto Maple Leafs
Air Canada Centre
40 Bay Street
Suite 400
Toronto, Ontario M5J 2X2
Canada
(416) 815-5700

Vancouver Canucks
General Motors Place
800 Griffiths Way
Vancouver, British Columbia
V6B 6G1
Canada
(604) 899-4600

Washington Capitals
401 Ninth Street, NW
Suite 750
Washington, D.C. 20004
(202) 266-2200

COLLEGE SPORTS

National Collegiate Athletic Association (NCAA)
700 W. Washington Street
P.O. Box 6222
Indianapolis, IN 46206-6222
(317) 917-6222

Atlantic Coast Conference
P.O. Drawer ACC
Greensboro, NC 27417-6724
(336) 854-8787

Big East Conference
222 Richmond Street
Suite 110
Providence, RI 02903
(401) 272-9108

Big Ten Conference
1500 West Higgins Road
Park Ridge, IL 60068-6300
(847) 696-1010

Big 12 Conference
2201 Stemmons Freeway
28th floor
Dallas, TX 75207
(214) 742-1212

Big West Conference
2 Corporate Park
Irvine, CA 92606
(949) 261-2525

Conference USA
35 East Wacker Drive
Suite 650
Chicago, IL 60601
(312) 553-0483

Ivy League
228 Alexander Street
Princeton, NJ 08544
(609) 258-6426

Mid-American Conference
24 Public Square
15th floor
Cleveland, OH 44113
(216) 566-4622

Pacific-10 Conference
800 S. Broadway
Suite 400
Walnut Creek, CA 94596
(925) 932-4411

Southeastern Conference
2201 Richard Arrington Boulevard North
Birmingham, AL 35203
(205) 458-3000

Western Athletic Conference
9250 East Costilla Avenue
Suite 300
Englewood, CO 80112
(303) 799-9221

MISCELLANEOUS SPORTS

Association of Tennis Professionals Tour (ATP)
201 ATP Boulevard
Ponte Vedra Beach, FL 32082
(904) 285-8000

Championship Auto Racing Teams (CART)
5350 Lakeview Parkway South Drive
Indianapolis, IN 46268
(317) 715-4100

Indy Racing League
4565 West 16th Street
Indianapolis, IN 46222
(317) 484-6526

Ladies Professional Golf Association (LPGA)
100 International Golf Drive
Daytona Beach, FL 32124
(386) 274-6200

Major League Soccer
110 East 42nd Street
10th floor
New York, NY 10017
(212) 450-1200

National Association for Stock Car Auto Racing (NASCAR)
1801 W. International Speedway Boulevard
Daytona Beach, FL 32114-1243
(386) 253-0611

PGA Tour
112 PGA Tour Boulevard
Ponte Vedra Beach, FL 32082
(904) 285-3700

United Soccer Leagues
14497 North Dale Mabry Highway
Suite 201
Tampa, FL 33618
(813) 963-3909

United States Olympic Committee
One Olympic Plaza
Colorado Springs, CO 80909
(719) 866-4500

USA Basketball
5465 Mark Dabling Boulevard
Colorado Springs, CO 80918
(719) 590-4800

USA Cycling
One Olympic Plaza
Colorado Springs, CO 80909
(719) 866-4581

USA Hockey
1775 Bob Johnson Drive
Colorado Springs, CO 80906
(719) 576-8724

USA Track & Field
1 RCA Dome
Suite 140
Indianapolis, IN 46225
(317) 261-0500

U.S. Bobsled and Skeleton Federation
P.O. Box 828
Lake Placid, NY 12946
(518) 523-1842

U.S. Figure Skating Association
20 First Street
Colorado Springs, CO 80906
(719) 635-5200

U.S. Luge Association
35 Church Street
Lake Placid, NY 12946
(518) 523-2071

U.S. Ski and Snowboard Association
P.O. Box 100
Park City, UT 84060
(435) 649-9090

U.S. Soccer Federation
1801 South Prairie Avenue
Chicago, IL 60616
(312) 808-1300

U.S. Speedskating
P.O. Box 450639
Westlake, OH 44145
(440) 899-0128

U.S. Swimming, Inc.
One Olympic Plaza
Colorado Springs, CO 80909
(719) 866-4578

USA Water Polo, Inc.
1631 Mesa Avenue
Suite A-1
Colorado Springs, CO 80906
(719) 634-0699

Women's United Soccer Association
6205 Peachtree Dunwoody Road
Atlanta, GA 30328
(678) 645-0800

WTA Tour (Women's Tennis)
One Progress Plaza
Suite 1500
St. Petersburg, FL 33701
(727) 895-5000